Terrorism in Context

Terrorism in Context

Edited by
Martha Crenshaw

The Pennsylvania State University Press
University Park, Pennsylvania

Library of Congress Cataloging-in-Publication Data

Terrorism in context / edited by Martha Crenshaw.
    p.   cm.
    Includes bibliographical references and index.
    ISBN 0-271-01014-2. — ISBN 0-271-01015-0 (pbk.)
    1. Terrorism—Congresses.   2. Terrorism—History—Congresses.
    I. Crenshaw, Martha.
    HV6431.T4665   1995
    363.3'2—dc20   93-13785
                                                      CIP

Published by The Pennsylvania State University Press,
University Park, PA 16802-1003

It is the policy of The Pennsylvania State University Press to use acid-free paper
for the first printing of all clothbound books. Publications on uncoated stock
satisfy the minimum requirements of American National Standard for Information Sciences—Permanence of Paper for Printed Library Materials, ANSI
Z39.48–1984.

Contents

List of Contributors

Martha Crenshaw, Wesleyan University
Richard Gillespie, University of Portsmouth
Jerrold D. Green, University of Arizona
Ian S. Lustick, University of Pennsylvania
Peter H. Merkl, University of California, Santa Barbara
Martin A. Miller, Duke University
David Scott Palmer, Boston University
Philip Pomper, Wesleyan University
Donatella della Porta, Università degli Studi di Firenze
Francisco José Llera Ramo, Universidad del País Vasco
Goldie Shabad, The Ohio State University
Charles Townshend, University of Keele
Paul Wallace, University of Missouri
Michel Wieviorka, Ecole des Hautes Etudes en Sciences Sociales

Preface

The purpose of the project that led to this volume was to advance the analysis of political terrorism by commissioning a series of comparative case studies written by specialists from different disciplines (history, political science, and sociology) on a variety of past and present campaigns of oppositional terrorism, which, as these studies show, is often closely connected to state repression. The guiding premise behind this collection of case studies is that terrorism as a general phenomenon cannot adequately be explained without situating it in its particular political, social, and economic contexts, and that scholars most knowledgeable about those specific contexts can best analyze the role of terrorism in them. Systematic and comparative case studies are an essential foundation for general theoretical explanations of terrorism.

No assemblage of case studies of terrorism could hope to be fully comprehensive, given the large number of examples from which to choose. An editor can aspire only to include some of the most important cases—significant because of their political consequences, because they represent an important type of case, or because the problem they present is intrinsically interesting. It is also important to avoid an exclusive concern with current events and with the developed West and to extend the scope of the analysis to the past and to the non-Western world.

The introduction to this volume outlines an approach to analyzing terrorism in disparate historical contexts and deals in a preliminary way with the controversial issue of defining the concept. It is an essay that sets the stage for the individual case studies that follow, but does not pretend to review the expansive literature on terrorism or to summarize the major schools of thought.

Historical analysis begins in Part I with two classic cases of past terrorism, marking the beginning of revolutionary terrorism in Europe. Martin A. Miller examines the trends leading to anarchist terrorism in

Western Europe and the United States in the 1880s and 1890s. Philip Pomper analyzes Russian revolutionary terrorism from the 1860s to the Bolshevik Revolution.

Much oppositional terrorism in the nineteenth and early twentieth centuries was directed toward the overthrow of the major autocracies and imperial regimes of Europe—Russia, Germany, Austria-Hungary, Italy, and Spain—but after 1870 anarchist terrorism also targeted constitutional governments, particularly the French Third Republic. Although it can be argued that the evolution of terrorism exhibits such profound discontinuities that one cannot locate historical origins at all, the historians who wrote these case studies believe that the roots of much contemporary terrorism lie in this period of rapid and tumultuous change. Through the experiences of Russian revolutionaries and European anarchists, terrorism came to be an integral part of a Western revolutionary tradition that was imitated around the world. In particular, Miller argues that anarchist terrorism represents a transitional phase between premodern and modern political violence. What was at issue for nineteenth-century revolutionaries was the struggle for social and political justice, the transformation of politics and society from within, in keeping with the legacy of the French Revolution. Anarchists, who originated the concept of "propaganda of the deed," sought to abolish social and political institutions entirely, seeing all centralized structures as inherently repressive and unjust. They prized spontaneity and disdained organization, relying instead on the symbolic properties of terrorism. Revolutionaries in Russia, despite their many ideological divisions, sought instead to establish a new political order through the mobilization of the masses. The idea of the conspiratorial revolutionary underground leading the masses in the Jacobin or Blanquist tradition was an important step in the evolution of terrorism.

Left-wing terrorists in Italy and in Germany in the 1970s and 1980s also presented themselves as social revolutionaries. It came as a shock in the 1970s—an era promised to herald the end of ideology and the beginning of postindustrialism and postmaterialism, not to speak of postmodernism—that liberal democracies in Italy and Germany should face left extremist organizations that challenged the legitimacy of the state on grounds of fundamental structural injustice. Cycles of mass protest in what seemed to be stable, prosperous, and cohesive societies unexpectedly created a favorable climate for terrorism. Small groups were able to exploit conflicts that they did not produce but that they judged to be the inevitable result of the inequities inherent in capitalism and liberalism and the signal that the time for revolution was ripe. They confused the capacity for protest with the potential for revolution, overestimated the extent of social disequilibrium, and underestimated the resilience of liberal democracy. Nevertheless, their actions shook both society and government.

Donatella della Porta and Peter H. Merkl, respectively, consider the Italian and German records. For Italians terrorism was the most important political phenomena of the 1970s, and the regime saw it as a serious and even potentially mortal challenge. As late as the 1990s, and even from prison, the German Red Army Faction (RAF) through its successor groups could attract widespread publicity and challenge the government's commitment to democratic principles. Terrorism was an urban phenomenon, as it had been a century earlier, and many of those who identified themselves as revolutionaries were students and intellectuals. Furthermore, the Red Brigades and the Red Army Faction, like their anarchist predecessors, resorted to terrorism as a primary method. They possessed little capacity or inclination for organizing mass action. In both contemporary instances, however, the power of ideology appeared to be weaker than it was among the early revolutionaries and anarchists (although in both earlier and later cases faith in the efficacy of terrorism and willingness to assume its risks, more than ideological differences, distinguished terrorists from other radicals). Both governments responded to terrorism with significant restrictions of civil liberties. A tendency to confuse protest and terrorism also shaped the public reaction, just as in the late nineteenth century governments and societies identified anarchism with terrorism.

In explaining these processes of motivation and commitment, Donatella della Porta stresses social and psychological factors, particularly the interaction between individual, group, and social environment. In Italy the state eventually found that encouraging "repentance" was successful in bringing terrorism to an end. Terrorism attracted less popular support in Germany than it did in Italy, its adherents were fewer, and the magnitude of terrorist violence was lower. However, terrorism continued to trouble Germany even after reunification and the revelation that the RAF was linked to the East German secret police. Peter H. Merkl emphasizes that German terrorism was not a continuous phenomenon and that the response of state and society was more remarkable than the group and its actions. The government's overreaction contributed to the persistence of sporadic terrorism.

Inspired by the success of the Cuban Revolution, left-wing terrorism developed in Latin America in the late 1960s and 1970s, with far more destructive consequences than in Europe. Although ultimately unsuccessful, it served as a model for aspiring revolutionaries in Western Europe, the United States, and Canada. One of the most notable cases in the 1970s was Argentina, analyzed here by Richard Gillespie. Two decades later Peru was preoccupied with the terrorism of another revolutionary organization, Sendero Luminoso (SL), or Shining Path. David Scott Palmer traces the growth of Sendero from 1980 to the 1990s.

In Argentina several thousand people joined the violent opposition, and tens of thousands more provided active support. The Argentine "urban guerrillas," unlike their European counterparts, hoped to make terrorism the accompaniment to a rural insurgency that would overthrow the Peronist regime, which they had initially welcomed but came to regard as repressive and unrepresentative. The opposition engaged in open military combat with the armed forces and even "liberated" areas of the countryside. But terrorism and other forms of armed resistance from the Montoneros and the Ejércitos Revolucionares del Pueblo (ERP)—lumped together as "urban guerrilla warfare"—provoked a terrible and massive counterreaction from the Right and from the military, culminating in a military takeover and the launching of a "dirty war" against opponents of the regime that resulted in thousands of "disappearances." Although the "urban guerrillas" never developed the mass base they sought, the whole of Argentine society was caught up in the conflict between the government and the Left.

The violence of SL is deeply ideological rather than ethnic, according to Palmer, despite the group's attempts to recruit support among the Indian population. Peru's economic crisis was an important historical precondition for the emergence of Sendero Luminoso as a major social and political force. By the 1990s what began as a small radical university-based organization posed such a threat to Peru's stability that the democratically elected government of Alberto Fujimori declared a state of martial law. The goal of Sendero Luminoso is a fundamental redistribution of Peru's resources to benefit a peasant class that would remain under SL's control. Terrorism is a carefully planned part of a long-term strategy of attrition meant to reduce the government's authority and to bring about a rural revolution along Maoist lines. The campaign has been characterized by a remarkable combination of tactical flexibility and ideological rigidity under the charismatic leadership of Abimael Guzmán, who was captured in 1992. The government has responded to terrorism with a repressive military strategy that only plays into Sendero Luminoso's hands, but in Palmer's view Sendero is still unlikely to win the popular support that would guarantee victory, largely because of its repressive treatment of the peasantry, who are the main victims of the conflict.

The third part of this volume concerns conflicts driven by the ambitions of minorities in divided societies. In such contexts communities that perceive themselves as possessing distinct and separate ethnic or religious identities are enclosed within the confines of a state that they struggle to influence, if not control. The issue, then, is the now painfully familiar one of who will live and rule in what territory with what borders. In circumstances of ethnic conflict, terrorism is intended to assert or defend the identity of a minority that appears to be threatened by the dominance of the larger community, which usually responds with terrorism of its own. What is at stake in secessionist or irredentist drives is control of territory. Terrorism reflects both integrative and disintegrative forces because it strengthens the solidarity of the minority and reinforces the hostility of the majority. It can easily escalate into civil war and communal conflict. Conflicts of this type are extremely difficult to resolve; they seem to end rarely in reasoned compromise, more often in explosions of anger and passion or bitter resignation due to weariness, if they end at all. This form of terrorism is thus extraordinarily persistent, as illustrated in the three cases included in this volume.

The Irish Republican Army, the subject of Charles Townshend's chapter, traces its history at least to the nineteenth century. The early IRA is a formative case comparable to Russian and anarchist terrorism, and the post-1970 incarnation of the organization, which resurfaced in the context of a Catholic civil rights protest movement, remains active more than twenty years later. Resistance to the British presence in Northern Ireland, expressed in terrorism as well as other violent and nonviolent strategies, is rooted in nationalism, religion, and hostility to military occupation, merged with radicalism motivated by republican ideologies, which were initially linked to revolutionary conspiracies on the European continent. The French Revolution was an initial source of inspiration for Ireland, just as it was for the continental secret societies that were the forerunners of European terrorism. However, what is at stake for the IRA of today is the end of the Protestant domination of Northern Ireland and the unity of all of Catholic Ireland, not the revolutionary transformation of society and politics. For the British government and for the Protestants of Northern Ireland, the conflict involves a simple question of majority rule within existing borders. The conflict takes on a "paramilitary" character, as Townshend describes it, because the IRA is seen as the legitimate army of the Catholics of Northern Ireland and indeed of the mythical and true Ireland, which was betrayed by the compromise that established a separate Northern Ireland in 1921. Extrication from British rule is the primary justification for terrorism. According to Townshend, the extraordinary persistence of terrorism owes as much to political culture as to strategic reasoning. Reliance on "physical force" is perceived as a moral duty, not a choice.

Basque terrorism in Spain resembles Irish nationalist terrorism in its challenge to the legitimacy of the state. The Euzkadi ta Askatasuna (Basque Homeland and Freedom, or ETA) seeks an independent Basque state, incorporating provinces of both Spain and France. Like the IRA, ETA exploits cultural divisions and may be part of a "latent civil war," as Charles Townshend characterizes the conflict in Northern Ireland. The organization, despite internal factionalism, has persisted and even flourished through periods of major political change, including a transition to democracy that it managed to jeopardize but not to destroy. Support for ETA among Basques is weaker than support for the IRA among Catholics in Northern Ireland, perhaps because Basques are not an economically deprived class.

A central question for coauthors Goldie Shabad and Francisco José Llera Ramo is why Basque terrorism did not end when the conditions that first motivated it changed. Why did the liberalization and expanded Basque autonomy that came with democracy fail to dissuade ETA from violence? Shabad and Llera ask if the concessions made to Basque autonomy could be interpreted as a reward for terrorism, thus encouraging intransigence. Like Townshend, they point to a culture of violence that developed during the repressive years of Franco's reign and remains sufficiently strong to structure Basque perceptions of the role of the state and especially the security forces. Shabad and Llera also emphasize the political context for terrorism, including the complexities of center-periphery relations in Spain as they shape regional demands for autonomy.

India, the world's largest democracy, faces grave challenges from violent separatist movements in the Punjab, Kashmir, and Assam. At issue is whether India should become a Hindu state or persist in the drive to become genuinely multiethnic and secular, as intended by the founders of state, who had wanted to resolve the Hindu-Muslim conflict that led to partition between India and Pakistan. Paul Wallace analyzes the Sikh resort to terrorism in the Punjab and the government response. In his view, the conflict is fueled by a fear of loss of religious and ethnic identity in a society dominated by the outlook of a Hindu majority and supporting a government perceived as unresponsive and coercive; it is not the result of material deprivation or overt discrimination. Sikhs play a prominent role in the social, economic, and political life of India. Wallace considers not only violence directed against the state but also the state's role as a causal agent in violence and the degree to which reliance on military coercion can shift a democratic state toward authoritarianism. He argues that a government faced with the danger of separatism should not abandon the political process in favor of military repression, and that the assertion of a political-religious identity can be accommodative as well as irredentist. The government's ineptitude and political opportunism on all sides played an important role in pushing Sikh militants to violence.

The fourth part of the volume considers the relation between terrorism, nationalism, and the state. In each of the three cases analyzed here—the Algerian war, the Arab-Israeli conflict, and the revolution in Iran—terrorism is linked to the establishment of nation-states. It can be regarded as part of a successful nationalist struggle to form or consolidate a state. The case of Algeria demonstrates the role of terrorism in a war for national independence from colonial rule. Terrorism organized by nationalist forces and by groups opposed to independence was an integral part of the protracted and costly struggle over the future of French dominance in Algeria. What was at stake for Algerians was the choice between national independence or continued subordination to a minority regime that persistently denied any semblance of equality to the vast non-European majority. The issue for the settlers and French military who fought in vain to keep Algeria French was the maintenance of privilege as well as attachment to the land. The French of the metropole, who were the ultimate arbiters, were reluctant to relinquish the idea of France as a colonial state. Terrorism, as well as the military response to terrorism, contributed to the erosion of the public's commitment to that objective. To the victors and the emulators of the victors, nationalist terrorism in Algeria may have appeared "successful" because Algeria won her independence. To others, notably including Albert Camus, it was a political and personal tragedy. He compared the FLN unfavorably to the Russian revolutionaries of the nineteenth century, whom he regarded as virtuous terrorists, self-sacrificing and discriminating. Violence in Algeria in the 1990s is a result of the failure of the FLN to establish and consolidate political legitimacy. Ironically, the government's repressive response to the terrorism of Islamic militant groups is reminiscent of the French response to the FLN. The revolution has come full circle.

Terrorism in the context of the Israeli-Palestinian conflict shared some of the features of terrorism in Algeria. At stake was the future of two communities that sought to inhabit and control the same land. Each asserted an inalienable and historically justifiable right to the same territory. Zionist violence against the British in the 1940s is often cited as an example of "successful" terrorism, teaching the lesson that violence pays. The Algerian revolution inspired Palestinian resistance to Israel after 1967. However, according to Ian S. Lustick, the function of terrorism was as much to mobilize a constituency as to defeat the adversary.

He maintains that terrorism was initially more "solipsistic" than other-directed. As such, it reflected the political cultures that supported the fundamental identities of each party to the conflict. The solipsistic character of terrorism impeded conflict resolution, and only when violence was directed toward altering the strategic calculations of the adversary was compromise possible.

Religion is a factor in Middle Eastern as in Irish terrorism, and its significance became especially acute after the Iranian revolution. Both the resistance to the shah in the 1970s and the secular opposition to the Khomeini regime in the 1980s employed terrorism. But it was the victorious Islamic government's support for terrorism against both domestic and foreign opponents, in apparent furtherance of the goal of spreading Islamic revolution throughout the Middle East, that attracted attention in the West. The fear of a tidal wave of Islamic "fundamentalism" quickly took root, especially when pro-Iranian groups began to target Americans in Lebanon. However, according to Jerrold D. Green, Western audiences may have misunderstood the significance of terrorism because they perceived it as an aberration, rather than a central part of Iranian politics for decades. Western observers probably exaggerate the force of religion as a motivation for terrorism. That terrorism should be part of the Islamic regime's drive to consolidate the revolution and to spread it throughout the region should not have been surprising. Terrorism was not the result of irrational fanaticism but of political calculation. It was learned behavior, not the result of primordial forces. The Iranian government is capable of controlling terrorism when it proves counterproductive.

This collection concludes with an essay by sociologist Michel Wieviorka, who draws out and then knits together same of the common themes of the book and outlines their implications for further research on terrorism.

Acknowledgments

This collection is the product of a research project funded by the Ford Foundation, whose generous support extended to sponsoring a conference at Wesleyan in 1989 at which these ideas were initially presented and discussed. This project would not have been possible without the financial support of the Ford Foundation during 1987–89 and the helpfulness and encouragement of Gary Sick. The Harry Frank Guggenheim Foundation also assisted with the 1989 meeting. We are indebted as well to Wesleyan University, and past presidents Colin G. Campbell and William M. Chace. Many people commented on all or portions of this manuscript, and the participants at the 1989 conference were a source of lively stimulation. We are grateful to all of them. The invited discussants at the conference receive special thanks: on Russia, Deborah Hardy and Norman Naimark; on anarchism, Marie Fleming; on Ireland, J. Bowyer Bell and John Finn; on Spain, Juan L. Linz; on Italy, Robin Erica Wagner-Pacifici and Leonard Weinberg; on Germany, Jo Groebel and Donald Schoonmaker; on Algeria, John Talbott and Ian S. Lustick; on the Arab-Israeli conflict, Ann Mosely Lesch and Ehud Sprinzak; on Iran, Gary Sick and Barry Rubin; on India, Atul Kohli and Richard Cronin; on Peru, Cynthia McClintock and Gustavo Gorriti; and on Argentina, Maria Moyano and Juan Corradi.

It is also a pleasure to acknowledge the support of Sanford G. Thatcher at Penn State Press and the expert assistance of Keith Monley in copyediting the manuscript. At Wesleyan, Janet DeMicco helped immeasurably. So, too, did Jane Tozer, Iris Shimony, and Mark Kiefer.

Introduction

1

Thoughts on Relating Terrorism to Historical Contexts

Martha Crenshaw

Both the phenomenon of terrorism and our conceptions of it depend on historical context—political, social, and economic—and on how the groups and individuals who participate in or respond to the actions we call terrorism relate to the world in which they act.[1] Questions about this interaction can be organized around three themes: the historical context

1. This essay does not purport to be a review of the extensive literature on terrorism. For general bibliographies, see Amos Lakos, *International Terrorism: A Bibliography* (Boulder: Westview Press, 1986); idem, *Terrorism, 1980–1990: A Bibliography* (Boulder: Westview Press, 1991); Edward F. Mickolus with Peter A. Flemming, *Terrorism, 1980–1987: A Selectively Annotated Bibliography* (Westport, Conn.: Greenwood Press, 1988); and Alex P. Schmid and Albert J. Jongman et al., *Political Terrorism: A New Guide*

of the concept of terrorism; the causal relationship between terrorism and its political, social, and economic environment; and the impact of terrorism on this setting.

The case studies in this volume all wrestle with the difficulties of clearly defining the concept of terrorism as a basis for theoretical explanation. Attempts to specify the unique qualities of terrorism and to establish the boundaries between terrorism and other forms of political violence invariably provoke dispute. Suffice it to say initially that terrorism is a conspiratorial style of violence calculated to alter the attitudes and behavior of multiple audiences. It targets the few in a way that claims the attention of the many. Thus a lack of proportion between resources deployed and effects created, between the material power of actors and the fear their actions generate, is typical. Among systematic and organized modes of civil or international violence, terrorism is distinguished by its high symbolic and expressive value. The discrepancy between the secrecy of planning and the visibility of results gives it even more shock value.

Even if the problem of definition could be conclusively settled, this subject—relating terrorism to social, political, and economic environment—is not an easy one to address. Evidence of the connections between the occurrence of terrorism and its setting is hard to acquire, not only because the decisions behind terrorism are secret but also because the active participants in terrorism usually number so few. Terrorism is not mass or collective violence but rather the direct activity of small groups, however authentically popular these groups may be: even if supported by a larger organization or political party, the number of active militants who engage in terrorism is small. These few may be isolated from the broader society; on the other hand, they may act as an extremist offshoot of a larger social movement, profiting from the patronage of a significant segment of the population, however resistant to measurement such silent support may be. Moreover, governments and their agents can practice terrorism, whether to suppress domestic dissent or to further international purposes, such as the export of revolution in the case of Iran. Such use is usually carefully concealed in order to avoid public attribution of responsibility.

Furthermore, although we argue here that links between violence and historical conditions do exist, we wish to avoid deterministic explanations. No analyst would claim that specified sets of conditions invariably produce terrorism. The authors of these case studies recognize that the

---

to *Actors, Authors, Concepts, Data Bases, Theories, and Literature* (New Brunswick, N.J.: Transaction Books, 1988).

causal chain that leads to the commission of acts of terrorism is complex. It can be pictured as a narrowing funnel, a last stage of which is the decision to commit an act of terrorism. A general theory based on conditions is impossible because the final decision depends on the judgments individual political actors make about these conditions. There is nothing automatic about the choice of terrorism. Like any political decision, the decision to use terrorism is influenced by psychological considerations and internal bargaining, as well as by reasoned or strategic reactions to opportunities and constraints, perceived in light of the organization's goals. It is possible, however, to integrate macro and micro levels of analysis in order to discover which elements in what situations encourage oppositions or states to turn to terrorist tactics, the former to resist authority or establish a new regime and the latter to crush real or anticipated resistance or consolidate the state's power. Both causes and consequences of terrorism can only be understood in terms of interactions among political actors, primarily governments and oppositions, at specific points in history. It is thus well to remember that with the passage of time and the benefit of hindsight, we may be tempted to ascribe a calculated rationality to past actions that is ultimately misleading.

Even though we argue that there is a connection to be studied and that analyzing it can produce explanations without resorting to sweeping cross-national generalizations, another potential obstacle to useful analysis affects the nature of the comparisons that can be made. It is reasonable to ask whether a comparative study of the relation between terrorism and context is possible without a control group. Rather than look at a dozen cases where terrorism developed, perhaps we should look at similar backgrounds and compare those cases where terrorism emerged with those where it did not. Several responses to this anticipated criticism come to mind. In the first place, the task of finding an appropriate control group is extremely difficult, since we cannot experiment by creating identical conditions in different times and places. Nor do we have a general theory of terrorism to guide our comparison. However, these case studies do consider comparable groups within the same society, such as the different reactions in Basque and Catalan regions to the prospect of autonomy from the Spanish state. Within the same context, oppositions debate the use of terrorism and draw different conclusions. Such differences reveal how idiosyncratic responses to circumstances can be. A primary purpose of this set of case studies is to look for patterns, but meanwhile we realize that the presence of the same dependent variable or result does not necessarily mean that the explanation is the same in each case. Although in an ideal scientific world an episode of "terrorism" would be identical in each circumstance, historical reality cannot be tested under laboratory conditions, especially when that reality involves violence. Terrorism is an ambiguous variable not easily measured or quantified, in part because there are multiple forms of terrorism, and they are easily confused with other styles of violence.

A further aspect of the approach to terrorism adopted in this volume is that it does not focus exclusively on the causes of violence to the neglect of consequences. The scope of the analysis extends to outcomes as well as motivations. It is critically important to assess the effects of terrorism on society and on the political process, as well as the responses to terrorism by society and by political structures. Our lack of knowledge in this area is due in part to the complexity of the issue. But it also seems that realistic appraisals of the impact of terrorism are often lost in a tide of sensationalistic exaggerations. Furthermore, terrorism shapes interactions among political actors over long periods of time through a dynamic process in which violence alters the conditions under which it initially occurs. Many consequences are unintended, but it is rare that terrorism (or, more frequently, the government's reaction to oppositional terrorism) does not alter political institutions, values, and behavior as well as the functioning of society. These case studies relate terrorism to the management of social and political change. They consider its effects on state structures in terms of both stability and democracy. The cases include both democracies and authoritarian regimes, developed and developing states.

Yet another issue in the study of civil violence is the contention that research assumes that oppositions are exclusively initiators, whereas governments are responders or defenders, who merely react to terrorist challenges. In this volume, we assume that responsibility for violence in political conflict can be and often is shared. The process of violence is interactive. Whereas governments do respond to resistance from society (or at least justify their actions as defensive), a political opposition may not have been "terrorist" until the government initiated confrontation. By acting in anticipation of resistance, governments can provoke violence. The state's use of force against nonviolent protest can be an important precipitant for oppositional terrorism. For example, the death of a demonstrator at the hands of the West German police was a catalyst for the activation of the Red Army Faction in the 1970s. Governments may also encourage extremist factions through political manipulations designed to undercut more powerful mainstream opposition parties, as the Indian government did in the Punjab.

In examining both the causes and the consequences of terrorism, a central question is the relation between terrorism and political legitimacy, particularly in democratic states or those on the road to democracy. We must ask, for example, why terrorism occurs in participatory democracies and why it survives or even thrives on transitions from authoritarian to democratic rule, as it has apparently done in Spain and Peru. It poses a particular danger to the stability of multiethnic democracies, such as India. Finding an effective democratic response to terrorism is a policy problem that is central to the politics, both international and domestic, of our time. Thus we consider the issue of which responses to terrorism are most effective both in suppressing terrorism and in maintaining democracy.

CONCEPTS AND SUBJECTIVE CONTEXTS

The context for terrorism does not consist entirely of objective historical factors. Equally important to understanding terrorism is its symbolic, or perceptual, context, based on what could be termed subjective conditions. These factors are contingent upon our understanding of terrorism as a political issue—the self-presentation of those who use terrorism and the construction governments and publics place on it. It is clear from surveying the literature on terrorism, as well as the public debate, that what one calls things matters. There are few neutral terms in politics, because political language affects the perceptions of protagonists and audiences, and such effect acquires a greater urgency in the drama of terrorism. Similarly, the meanings of terms change to fit a changing context. Concepts follow politics.

The task of definition, which necessarily involves transforming "terrorism" into a useful analytical term rather than a polemical tool, must be considered in light of the relation between language and politics. One of the goals of analysis is to establish a referential context for terrorism and to explicate the grounds on which the concept is contested. Critics of the term may charge that these grounds are ideological rather than intellectual and that terrorism has been appropriated by conservative thinkers who wish to condemn the proponents of revolutionary change. This criticism is not surprising, since concepts are part of the belief systems of political actors and they are given meaning through political use. Reluctance to define the term because of the risk of partisan bias is apparent in some of these case studies. Ian S. Lustick, for example, hesitates to restrict the term at all and analyzes terrorism in the context of the Arab-Israeli conflict by including all historical phenomena that have been called terrorism by either side. Scholars who deal with the subject of terrorism try constantly to resolve this contradiction between the need to develop a bounded concept on which theoretical explanation can be built and the desire to avoid the appearance of taking sides in the political conflict that motivates the activity or the label of terrorism. They are aware that political sympathies affect interpretations of actions as legitimate or illegitimate and that the term "terrorist" is often meant to imply "illegitimate."

Conceptions of terrorism affect not only scholarship but government policy and popular reactions. In modern societies, political conceptions are communicated and even originated by the news media, an institution that serves not only as a channel for transmitting information about terrorism but also as a magnifying glass. It simplifies the problem of terrorism by focusing the attention of the public on the newsworthy aspects of the phenomenon, which tend to be its extraordinary or shocking characteristics, rather than on any banal or mundane qualities it may possess. Thus, terrorism is described as the dramatic, outrageous, and objectionable. At the same time, many oppositions that use terrorism are fully aware of the opportunities for publicity inherent in their environment and exploit their own newsworthiness with varying degrees of deftness. Although the image of terrorism is often a critical component of its effectiveness as a method of political communication, not all terrorists entertain friendly relations with the news media. They often object to the image conveyed by the press. Moreover, states as well as many extremists of the right typically seek to avoid publicity when they are involved in terrorism.

It is understandable, given the negative connotation of the term today, that contemporary governments and oppositions reject the label "terrorist." As these propositions about the changing nature of concepts and their dependence on political practice imply, such a pejorative understanding has not always been the case. Russian revolutionaries and anarchists of the nineteenth century not only accepted the label as a compliment but claimed it as a badge of honor. In the years since the era of revolutions in the nineteenth century, the meaning of the term has changed to convey opprobrium rather than admiration (although not in all circumstances; the Secret Army Organization during the Algerian War did not shrink from the label). The reasons for this interpretive shift reside in changes in the phenomenon of terrorism itself and in its historical contexts.

It is thus necessary to recognize that an important aspect of terrorism is its social construction, which is relative to time and place, thus to historical context. It is not a neutral descriptive term. Even scholarly definitions of terrorism are subjective because they must take into account ordinary language uses of the term, which contain value judgments. Because of this we are led to ask who calls what terrorism, why, and when. Since "terrorism" is a political label, it is an organizing concept that both describes the phenomenon as it exists and offers a moral judgment. A label is a useful shorthand, combining descriptive, evocative, and symbolic elements, but its meanings are inherently flexible and ambiguous. They may even be contradictory.

When people choose to call the actions of others "terrorist" or to label others as "terrorists," this choice often has a prescriptive policy relevance as well as a moral connotation. As a way of framing consciousness, the choice of terminology has a particular relevance to assessing the legitimacy of political authority. Political language affects the perceptions of audiences and their expectations about how the problem thus evoked will be treated. That is, by defining and identifying a problem, labels may also indicate a preferred solution. It is well to remember, however, that the users of political language are not entirely free to shape it; once concepts are constructed and endowed with meaning, they take on a certain autonomy, especially when they are adopted by the news media, disseminated to the public, and integrated into a general context of norms and values. A term cannot be used to refer to phenomena that are completely foreign to its original connotation. Changes in political language can only follow the contours of changes in the social and political environment, especially ideological shifts, but scholars can attempt to shape these contours through the judicious use of language.

That terms like terrorism should be contested is a normal part of the political process. Political language evolves through challenges. Critics of policies that labels serve to legitimize are quick to question the usefulness and appropriateness of the labels. Politics involves competition to define terms, as actors attempt to impose their own interpretations of history. In contemporary politics, calling adversaries "terrorists" is a way of depicting them as fanatic and irrational so as to foreclose the possibility of compromise, draw attention to the real or imagined threat to security, and promote solidarity among the threatened. Using the term terrorism can imply not only that an adversary employs a particular strategy or style of violence but also that the "true nature" of the opponent is thereby revealed. By defining the PLO as a terrorist organization, for example, Israeli policy makers precluded recognition or negotiations. Furthermore, the government was bound by its own label; dealing with the PLO appeared as a major concession. This example also reminds us of the international dimensions of political labeling. The United States and Israel tend to share common conceptions of terrorism, but when talking to the PLO became a matter of American political interest, these conceptions diverged. In 1988 the United States accepted the PLO's formal renunciation of "terrorism" (although the two sides did not agree on a precise definition), but to Israel the group remained a "terrorist organization."

Thus, conceptions of terrorism affect the ways in which governments define their interests, and interests also determine reliance on labels or their abandonment when politically convenient. The label can, however, blind governments to the distinction between violent and nonviolent dissent. It can also influence the selection of targets for state repression. For example, because the Argentine military conceived of terrorism as the symptom of a disease to be eradicated, the whole of society was seen as contaminated, and thus society itself became the target of terrorism from above. The government determined not only to destroy organized opposition but to cleanse society of the tendencies that had motivated resistance. In Italy, the term "terrorism" was not used until midway through the Red Brigade's campaign of violence, although their activities remained essentially the same. In Northern Ireland, the official criminalization of the IRA was part of an effort to deny special status; such criminalization led to prison hunger strikes. West Germany pursued a similar policy. Labeling minorities as terrorist may intensify communal conflict, as it has in India. Labeling revolutionary movements terrorist risks minimizing their importance. The Peruvian government may have delayed responding to Sendero Luminoso, because it was initially dismissed as a mere "terrorist organization," implying the absence of popular support or military power. Possibly reintegration of "repentant" terrorists was easier in Italy because left-wing militants were considered misguided youth, not professional revolutionaries.

The 1980s concept of "state-sponsored" terrorism, which attracted many Western governments, is derived in large part from attempts to explain Iran's behavior after the Islamic revolution. The seizure of the American diplomatic hostages in Tehran marked the origin of the term's growing currency. Although the types of activities that fall under the rubric of state-sponsored terrorism are scarcely new—for example, the Russian government was suspected of supporting the Serbian nationalists who assassinated Archduke Franz Ferdinand of Austria-Hungary in 1914—the concept became popular in the 1980s. It simplified the problem of how to combat terrorism by making it an act of international aggression, even an act of war. The real ambiguity surrounding the causes of terrorism, which makes devising an appropriate remedy so hard, could be ignored by assuming that hostile states were the real cause.

In fact, state sponsorship is frequently connected to the idea of "surrogate warfare," perhaps because policy makers, especially in the United States during the Reagan era, were not satisfied that the label of terrorism alone conveyed a sufficient sense of danger or prescribed an appropriate response. Of course, in the United States the metaphor is prevalent; every policy campaign, whether directed against drugs, wasteful energy consumption, smoking, or other social ills, merits the status of a war. Still, calling actions terrorism may dictate a military, not political, response and justify exceptional measures. The crisis becomes an emergency. Terrorism becomes the sort of aggression that is dangerous to appease.

Oppositions who use terrorism also attempt to provide frames of reference and comparisons that place them in a morally advantageous light (for example, appealing to the analogy of resistance to fascism in the 1930s and 1940s). Both sides try to situate terrorism in a broader conceptual context. What is curious is that oppositions also seem to wish to appropriate the metaphor of warfare to describe terrorism, although for reasons that appear incompatible with those we are ascribing to governments.

An underground organization using terrorism probably defines terrorism as warfare in order to acquire political recognition and status, which in turn can confer legitimacy, which is exactly what governments resist. To be engaged in warfare is a justification for terrorism as well as a claim to powerful status. The smaller and the more extreme the group becomes, it seems, the more likely it is to call itself an "army" (such as the Red Army Faction, the Japanese Red Army, or the Red Brigades); but one would not want to overlook the Irish Republican Army, which uses the term to remind us of its heritage. Most underground groups borrow the symbols and trappings of military discipline and procedure. Yet acts of terrorism do not typically resemble acts of warfare. "Hard" or well-defended targets of military or defensive value to the enemy are rarely the targets of terrorism; to the contrary, terrorists seem to prefer noncombatants. When military units engage in actions that we might refer to as terrorism, they are called "unconventional" or "special" operations. A military self-conception can even be self-defeating. According to Richard Gillespie, when the Montoneros of Argentina began describing themselves as an armed force, they were compelled to recognize that they were inferior to government security forces. As a terrorist organization without military pretensions, they seemed powerful.

Nevertheless, in criticizing this metaphor for its political implications, we recognize that it forces us to ask what terrorism is. Where should terrorism be situated in the continuum between peace and war? What analogies and historical comparisons are relevant? What does terrorism tell us about the changing nature of military force in the contemporary world? Should it be seen in the context of warfare in some cases, protest in others? Is it a sign that modern warfare is steadily becoming less "conventional," that is, politicized?

Defining terrorism becomes particularly troublesome when it occurs against a background of extensive violence. We cannot assume that terrorism is discontinuous with collective political violence. Even the best scholarly intentions may not suffice to distinguish terrorism from protest, guerrilla warfare, urban guerrilla warfare, subversion, criminal violence, paramilitarism, communal violence, or banditry. For example, which elements in the broad spectrum of violence in Ireland since the eighteenth century should rightly be called terrorism? Which revolutionary or counterrevolutionary practices during the eight years of the Algerian war constituted terrorism? In Argentina, terrorism developed as oppositional violence but became an even more important part of the government response. The proliferation of sometimes confusing terms (paramilitarism, urban guerrilla warfare, militarism, national liberation, armed struggle, or gang warfare) is indicative of the dilemma of distinguishing terrorism in particular from political violence in general. Since the word has a readily available negative meaning and distinctions seem inconsistent, it is easy to attribute terrorism to one's enemies and anything else to one's friends. The problem of definition is thus exacerbated when actors do not use terrorism exclusively but combine it with other modes of political action, which is frequently the case.

One reason for the power of terrorism as a political label, and hence for its controversialism, is not only its usefulness but its symbolic appeal. Terrorism has acquired a political value that can outlast short-term strategic failures. It persists despite negative outcomes. Terrorism projects images, communicates messages, and creates myths that transcend historical circumstances and motivate future generations. These myths may of course be deceptive or contradictory. As Philip Pomper points out, a case in point is the appeal of Nechaevism, with its paradoxical combination of ruthlessness and heroism, to Russian revolutionaries. It may be true of much terrorism (especially the more discriminating forms) that audiences react with both admiration for its daring and revulsion at its cruelty. It is easy for terrorism to become the cutting edge of a movement and to define an ideology. Undeniably it possesses an aura of perversely tragic glamour.

CAUSES OF TERRORISM

In linking terrorism to historical setting, it is logical to start by asking how social, political, or economic conditions contribute to its emergence.

Several factors may be relevant to the motivations behind terrorism: for example, the socialization of the individuals who become "terrorists"; the quality of terrorism as both responsive and sustained behavior; its representativeness and continuity with nonviolent forms of political action; its purpose, which is to produce social change; and the availability of opportunities.

Consider first the question of the individual's passage into terrorism. Included among those who join organizations that practice terrorism and who become active participants in planning or implementing terrorist actions are entrepreneurial types who create independent organizations (often splinters from larger social movements) as well as those who are recruited into long-standing organizations such as Spain's ETA (Euzkadi ta Askatasuna) or the IRA. The latter type of organization provides a convenient and accessible structure for participation, with specialized roles, hierarchies, and social support functions. Consequently, the incentives for participation should be different in these two circumstances.

Joining a radical organization may not be completely voluntary, since chance or coercion may intervene, but we should still ask what direct or indirect experiences might have motivated someone to take this step, as Donatella della Porta does in her chapter on left-wing terrorism in Italy. Disappointments and frustrations with nonviolent action are frequently cited as motivations in both democratic and authoritarian environments. Some case studies in this volume refer to psychic wounds inflicted on people at an impressionable age, to instances where demands for change were summarily rejected by governments and idealistic ambitions were crushed. Another influence may be solidarity with groups that move collectively to terrorism, this solidarity sometimes taking the form of membership in a rebellious counterculture (often springing from a student or university environment) or in the radicalized factions of a traditional or religious culture, as in Iran or India. The attractions of extremist violence for people with little to lose, free time, high energy levels, and a longing for excitement may be the factors that link the demographic characteristics of a society, or levels of unemployment, to terrorism. (These considerations cannot in themselves, however, explain specifically why terrorism, rather than paramilitary street fighting or some other form of group violence, would result.)

Government actions may trigger personal decisions to resort to terrorism. Radicals' perceptions of the role of the state seem to be deeply affected by the past. The burden of history in Germany, Italy, and Spain shapes the attitudes of oppositions toward governments. German and Italian left-wing terrorists identified with the resistance to fascism during the Second World War. The memory of the Holocaust led some

Israeli Jews to reject any appearance of passivity and to struggle to overcome a self-image of the Jew as helpless victim. Personal rather than vicarious or remembered experiences in refugee camps (as in the case of the Palestinians) or in prisons or detention centers (Palestinians and the IRA) are also instigating factors. In these cases, what directs the individual toward participation may not only be the grimness of the experience but the contact with the resistance organization, for whom the government has provided an excellent location for recruiting and indoctrination. In effect, the government creates an opportunity.

Another general factor that may act as a stimulus or as a facilitator is exposure to ideologies that justify violence or to evidence that violence works. These ideologies owe much to the experience of national liberation movements in the postwar world, but in Europe the French Revolution had already proved that violence was both morally right and politically efficacious. Today, awareness of the availability of terrorism as an option—whether it be assassinations of heads of state or hijackings—is inescapable. The visibility of terrorism enhances its contagiousness.

Nevertheless, any analysis of socialization, or of the relation between the individual and the environment, confronts the problem that the people who respond to these environmental stimuli are few in number and that uniformities among them remain hard to find. Furthermore, this line of argument may not explain state terrorism, because most of the experiences noted here are appropriate to oppositions, not to government bureaucracies or even to right-wing terrorism.

We are thus encouraged to go beyond the backgrounds and experiences of individuals to look at different types of causal links between terrorism and historical context. We know, for example, that terrorism is made possible by the support of a circle of people that extends beyond those militants who actively participate. The existence of social support networks may need less explanation in divided societies where terrorism is inspired by the nationalism or communal solidarity of minorities or by their need to confirm an ethnic and religious identity. In authoritarian regimes, such as Argentina under military rule or tsarist Russia, popular support for violent opposition is also understandable. What is harder to explain is support for ideological terrorism in the advanced industrial democracies. The term "sympathizer" became a symbol of disloyalty in Germany, although popular support for movements of the radical Left was actually more pervasive in Italy. Supporters who remain "legal" when an opposition movement moves underground constitute an important link with the wider society. The extent of support can be estimated through public opinion polls showing approval of the goals behind terrorism or through the number of votes for political parties linked to violent undergrounds, such as Herri Batasuna in Spain, Sinn Fein in Northern Ireland, or Akali Dal in India. Social support is equally important to state terrorism. Governments could not resort to terrorist practices without the consent or approval of important elements of the political and social elite. How this acceptance of violence is secured and maintained is a critical question.

The development of terrorism is also related to context because it is systematic, deliberate, and sustained over time; it is not spontaneous or purely expressive, as some other forms of civil violence (riots, for example) may be. Engaging in terrorism usually requires a sustained commitment, which the individual must be able to justify in terms of society's (or some part of society's) values and aspirations. In this volume we note that many individual terrorists need to feel virtuous or altruistic. Because terrorism is explicitly justified, by those who use it, in terms of widely held social values (and this holds for left extremist groups as well as nationalists), it differs fundamentally from family or criminal violence. It makes an explicit claim to political relevance. Emotions may influence commitments, but they are controlled and channeled through collective decision-making processes that give motivations an ideological cast. Actors who use terrorism excuse or even manipulate what they recognize to be its unacceptability as a political or military method by referring to shared values. They may see themselves acting as representatives of groups within society, defending and preserving an identity, or preventing the assimilation of a religious or ethnic community into an alien society that would dilute its values and traditions. These feelings extend to xenophobia in some cases, such as Iran and possibly Peru. Even in Italy and West Germany terrorism was justified as a rejection of foreign "imperialist" influence. Alternatively, users of terrorism may think of themselves as bringing about a better society for all, thus acting in the interest of a collective good, not as a selfish contender for power in a narrow political arena.

These general ideals and goals may not be unique to the individuals and groups who use terrorism, and they may not be clear or well understood, but they do reflect perceptions of what constituencies want. Because the actors who use terrorism seek to influence critical audiences, they respond to what they perceive the dispositions of these audiences to be. Terrorists may of course misperceive their circumstances and exaggerate the extent to which the "people" (often conceived of in highly abstract terms) are prepared to offer sympathy or condone violence. Radical groups who use terrorism try to adapt their behavior to conditions in order to change those conditions, however imperfect their impressions may be.

One implication of this argument is that studies of terrorism should take into account the possibilities of *representativeness* and *continuity*. In divided societies, we can see that the existence of a long-standing conflict of interest, the persistence of real grievances based on long-standing patterns of discrimination and inequality, the deep loyalty to community values and to the symbols and myths developed over centuries, and the government's contested legitimacy may produce an environment in which groups using terrorism, such as the IRA or the PLO, are genuinely representative of a popular base. We would not say that the IRA represents all Catholics, but we would admit that it represents the aspirations of some Catholics. The PLO claim to represent Palestinian opinion is less equivocal. The resort to force in such circumstances is not only expected, it may also be considered a point of honor. If terrorism seems to be the only effective means of armed struggle, then resistance and terrorism become synonymous. The constituency for terrorism will almost certainly understand and possibly admire terrorism even if hostile to it as a method, in part because the users of terrorism can claim to be representative. Loyalty works both ways. In such circumstances, continuity and representativeness may be linked.

In other societies, however, the representativeness and continuity of terrorism may be questionable. Its users (for example, in Italy and West Germany) do not typically belong to the class they claim to represent, and in fact workers eventually rejected the middle-class students who aspired to act in their name. Western radical organizations were not composed of those members of society who were excluded from economic prosperity, political influence, or access to power. In fact, radicals from privileged backgrounds in present-day western Europe and the United States, as in Russia a century earlier, often appeared to feel guilty precisely because they did not share the miseries of the dispossessed. On the other hand, terrorism has been continuous with protest, which evolved from nonviolent to violent demonstrations and then to terrorism. In Italy, for example, large numbers of people participated in the protest movements in the 1970s, which created an atmosphere of pervasive and anarchic violence. The continuity between terrorism and protest was short-lived, however, because protest subsided as terrorism escalated. Links to social movements may thus be more fragile than connections to ethnic communities.

The efficiency of governments is another variable in explaining whether radical oppositions are isolated from social support networks. Because of government pressure, going underground may place such strains on social relations that only organizations with support systems based on communal loyalty can survive. Perhaps in nonindustrial countries where government control over territory and penetration of society are weak, extremist organizations enjoy not only greater autonomy but also greater freedom to maintain contacts outside the underground. But in settings where government authority is stronger, radicals isolate themselves when they choose illegality (which sometimes precedes their resort to terrorism, as it did in West Germany). Then the solidarity they initially felt for the masses may give way to loyalty to the group, as happened in Italy.

In either situation, one active link between organization and environment is the recruitment process. The need to replenish cadres requires adjustment to the changing attitudes of the sectors of the population that are most likely to feel sympathetic and prepared to accept the risk of engaging in violent opposition. Goals and targets shift accordingly.

The idea of the continuity or discontinuity of terrorism, in terms of its association with other forms of political action commonly practiced in a society, raises another question about context. If we are to pronounce terrorism discontinuous, we have to define normal political practice and identify the point at which the break or discontinuity occurs. We must define standards of acceptable political behavior in different domestic as well as foreign contexts. What should we conclude if all collective action were violent? In Iran, for example, it appears that terrorism became increasingly continuous with domestic practice but discontinuous with the norms of foreign policy. Possibly terrorism was less incompatible with regional standards than with international expectations. It is possible, however, that the aggressive rhetoric of Khomeini's regime as much as its deeds made the violence it sponsored appear especially outrageous.

Another important question that these case studies address is the relation between the emergence of terrorism and the existence of opportunities for effective collective action, whether nonviolent protest or mass revolution. Several authors mention the absence of mediating institutions in democracies, especially opposition parties, as a factor in the growth of terrorism. In India, for example, popular demands are not effectively articulated or transmitted to the governing authorities. The kidnapping of Aldo Moro in 1978 was in part a response to the "historic compromise," the Communist party's entry into Italy's governing coalition. The Red Brigades saw what some might think of as a broadening of the government as a betrayal of the Left, which no longer had an effective voice against the system. However, in Spain, violence increased after the advent of democracy and the inauguration of a socialist government. So terrorism is not simply a reaction to lack of electoral opportunity. Nor does it necessarily signal frustration over the impossibility of revolution. In Russia and in Algeria, terrorism accompanied mass revolutionary violence. The two alternatives were not mutually exclusive. In some cases, as the context for political action becomes more violent, terrorism increases because the users of terrorism are encouraged by what they see as a prospect of quick victory. The FLN (Front de Libération Nationale, Algeria) apparently thought that a final push of urban terrorism in 1956 would compel the French to negotiate. The anticipation of success, not the failure of alternatives, motivated terrorism. Thus, terrorism is not necessarily a substitute for collective action, whether peaceful or violent.

A further point to consider is the *purposefulness* of terrorism as a style of violence. We note that terrorism is intended to affect the attitudes of popular audiences by altering their dispositions toward the government and its challengers. It is also calculated to affect the government's decision making, as are other strategies of violence such as deterrence or compellence. However, in contrast to terrorism, these strategies are principally meant to influence leaders, not publics; and thus they do not possess terrorism's quality of resonance. Nor do they, like terrorism, depend centrally on the commission of acts of violence in order to convey a message; if a threat is implemented, for example, deterrence has failed. Furthermore, the audiences for terrorism are multiple. They include sympathizers, in which case terrorism is meant to elicit excitement or enthusiasm, strengthen solidarity, or redeem the past; antagonists, whom terrorism is intended to shock, intimidate, or coerce; and "neutrals," especially foreign publics whose attention and interest are sought.

Terrorism is thus generated in anticipation of a public reaction and becomes part of an interactive process. Terrorism's constituencies are particularly important to its changing dynamics. ETA, for example, must surely react to public protest against terrorism. The IRA is sensitive to the probability that indiscriminate anticivilian terrorism alienates its constituency and even learns from its mistakes. Members of the FLN disagreed over the wisdom of using terrorism in metropolitan France, because some leaders hoped to enlist the support of the French public. The Russian revolutionary parties were encouraged by evidence of liberalism among the Russian public (when Vera Zasulich was acquitted by a jury, for example). In turn, governments, especially democracies, try to mobilize public opinion against terrorism.

The studies in this volume do not claim that terrorism is uniquely purposive, although in analyzing decisions to use terrorism as attempts to respond to and change conditions, we assume at least a limited rationality. Terrorism can, however, develop a momentum that diverts it from its original purpose, whether that purpose is to stimulate the imaginations of potential supporters or to terrify adversaries. But our argument that terrorism is linked to context is strengthened by the observation that such a self-perpetuating dynamic is often precipitated by specific events and external circumstances that provoke emotions of despair, rage, or vengeance. These precipitating events are usually the actions of elites in power. Violence on the part of the government can justify the pursuit of vengeance and confirm the radical critique of authority as relentlessly oppressive. Terrorism can then merge into a cycle of revenge and retaliation, which neither side fully controls. In this respect, then, it may come to resemble communal violence.

CONTEXT AND CONSEQUENCES

These case studies consider the effects as well as the causes of terrorism. They analyze the impact of terrorism on conditions—on government institutions, political processes, relations between state and society, underlying social conflicts, and social norms and values. What sorts of changes does terrorism produce, assuming that analysis can identify and isolate its effects?

An initial set of questions is based on the proposition that the key to the effectiveness of terrorism in producing social and political change may lie in the attitudes and behavior of critical audiences. Which audiences are critical to outcomes? On what factors do their reactions depend? What determines the receptivity or sensitivity to terrorism of different audiences? How volatile are popular reactions to terrorism? Which audiences most influence government responses?

Audiences react to two aspects of the issue: the case brought to their attention by terrorism and the particular method of terrorism, that is, the style of violence. The two reactions are distinctive attributes of an overall cognitive and emotional response. Not everyone who supports a cause will approve of any method of achieving it, but sympathy for ideological objectives will make approval of the method more likely. However, people who disapprove of the cause will almost certainly reject the method. Audiences are more likely to approve discriminate tactics than indiscriminate tactics, but only if the victim can be blamed. Moral judgments about responsibility for conditions and the appropriateness of violent responses influence popular reactions.

We are thus encouraged to look closely at the predispositions of popular audiences in order to understand their reactions. These attitudes, based on cultural imprinting as well as personal experience and values, are formed gradually over long periods of time. We cannot understand the responses of the Iranian public to anti-American terrorism without knowing the legacy of the reign of the shah and the inherent plausibility of conspiratorial explanations for political events. Nor can we comprehend the fear of disorder and extremism in West Germany or the uncontested nature of the state's legitimacy without knowledge of Germany's past. Past experiences, in effect, suggest the broader issues with which the public will associate terrorism.

Nevertheless, analysis of the process of terrorism must go beyond understanding the preconceptions of audiences. Regardless of attitudes at the outset of a campaign of terrorism, repetition may numb populations or exhaust their patience and almost certainly bore the media; as people become accustomed to high levels of civil violence or as the novelty of terrorism wears off, they may cease to be impressed or frightened. Another possibility is that the escalation of terrorism will produce a public backlash. Furthermore, in provoking government repression, oppositional terrorism may attract sympathy for its cause but simultaneously increase the costs of opposing the government. Clearly, choices of strategies (assassinations versus bombings, for example) will influence public attitudes.

The multiple audiences for terrorism may diverge significantly from one another in terms of their sensitivities and predispositions. Variability and complexity in the groups receiving the message of terrorism have increased with the growing network of mass communications media. Because terrorism produces a set of simultaneous reactions, which may contradict or reinforce one another, its consequences are difficult to control, both for the initiator of terrorism and the government or institution seeking to prevent it. No matter how discriminating the individual act of terrorism, its effects are imprecise (the Sikh bodyguards who assassinated Indira Gandhi, for example, surely did not foresee the wave of indiscriminate Hindu violence against Sikhs that swept through India). The initiator of terrorism cannot determine who receives the message, and unintended audiences may misinterpret the meaning. If Palestinian hijackings and airport attacks were meant to restore the morale or honor of the Palestinian community, they did so at the price of deepening American and Israeli hostility and resistance to compromise. Internally directed terrorism (meant to arouse a community or build morale in the organization) may be the most difficult for external audiences to comprehend. This suggests that the effects of terrorism are more predictable when the audiences for terrorism are limited and homogeneous and that it may succeed with one audience while failing with another.

Perhaps the difficulty of controlling a strategy for provocation (a strategy for which the terrorist style may be better designed than other forms of violence) is due to the problem of multiple audiences. The audience for such a strategy may be internal as much as external; provocation of government violence could be an attempt to broaden a base of popular support by increasing the number of people who are engaged in the conflict. Provocation could also be an attempt to legitimate an ideology by demonstrating that claims against the government are credible. The RAF in West Germany, for example, sought to show that the federal republic was actually a thinly disguised replica of the Nazi regime. But government repression may frighten would-be supporters of terrorists' goals into passivity; the costs of resistance may become too high. The oppositional groups who use terrorism extensively can rarely protect the populations they put at risk from government persecution or communal vengeance. Indiscriminate repression or vengeance equalizes risk, but it is not clear whether a coerceive reaction to terrorism increases support for the government or for the opposition. Public attitudes with regard to these issues are difficult to discover; whether people act out of loyalty or fear, or a combination of the two, is hard to know. In Peru, for example, rural populations in Ayacucho province are exposed to pressure from both government and Sendero Luminoso.

An important question is whether it is necessary for violence to hurt the enemy (to "terrorize," intimidate, or cause visible distress) in order to excite friends and supporters. Is the generation of positive feelings about oneself dependent on inflicting harm on the other? Must terrorism have a victim in order to elicit the approval of constituencies? If so, why is inflicting harm on others necessary to asserting one's own identity, overcoming victim status, or organizing popular support? Terrorism may be more satisfactory than other styles of violence as compensation for inferiority not only because it is low-cost but because it is a dramatic symbol of hostility and a provocative stimulant to counteraction.

At the same time, the cases analyzed in this volume suggest that terrorism can be meant to educate, arouse, and stir an ethnic group or a social class not only to act against an enemy but also to compete for power within a community. Thus employed, terrorism can fragment the collectivity it is intended to unite. The rivalries within ETA, exacerbated by terrorism, are an excellent example. Disagreement over the wisdom of using or sponsoring terrorism also seemed to divide the Iranian government in the post-Khomeini era.

Furthermore, we must question the permanence of the social and political changes that appear to be the results of terrorism. Changes in public opinion are not necessarily barometers of change in the political system. Drastic and sudden reactions to terrorism may also be ephemeral. Furthermore, in several of the countries considered here terrorism has not ended, and we remain uncertain of its long-term effects.

We know little about the links between terrorism and major political change. In Russia, terrorism was part of the chain of events that led to revolution in 1917, but we do not know whether it was necessary to the success of the Bolsheviks. In Iran, terrorism against the shah was associated with a successful revolution, but Jerrold D. Green argues that it was actually counterproductive. In both Russia and Iran, when the revolutionaries who had used terrorism against the old regime turned against the new regime, they were ruthlessly suppressed. So whereas terrorism was part of a process of fundamental change, the users of terrorism did not directly benefit. Similarly, in Argentina, terrorism brought not revolution but a ruthless military repression. In the two colonial contexts considered here, Algeria and the Palestine Mandate, terrorism played a role in successful nationalist challenges to foreign rule. In Algeria, after independence the resistance organization that used terrorism came to power (not without brief internal struggles for dominance), but in Israel, members of Lehi and the Irgun waited for thirty years. Terrorism is linked to change in the constitutional status of Northern Ireland, which lost its autonomy when the Stormont government was revoked after the IRA was reconstituted in the early 1970s. In this case, one might argue that liberalization of the regime was a result of both Protestant and IRA terrorism and of Catholic civil rights protests.

The political changes in Northern Ireland might suggest, perhaps paradoxically, that terrorism can work as protest, leading to reform of underlying conditions (greater equality or regional autonomy, for example). In India, Spain, and Northern Ireland, governments have responded to nationalist terrorism by increasing coercive powers in attempts to destroy the infrastructure of the terrorist organizations but also by pursuing reforms intended to remedy the grievances that underlie public support for or tolerance of violent extremism. Are governments responding to terrorism or to collective action that seems to be a more spontaneous expression of popular opinion? We should also ask how reforms have affected the internal stability and cohesiveness of violent oppositions. Have reforms, for example, benefited moderates or extremists? Why have reforms in Spain, India, and Ireland, even the transition to democracy in Spain, not yet ended terrorism? The context seems to have been transformed, but terrorism has not.

In other circumstances democracies as well as authoritarian regimes respond to terrorism with repression rather than reforms. An early example was the response to anarchist terrorism in the nineteenth century. Such a choice might be a deliberate policy of counterterrorism or the result of constraints on the ability to implement reforms. The agricultural reforms that might alleviate rural discontent are expensive. For example, both because of the cost (for a country already in dire economic straits) and because of the state of insecurity in areas dominated by Sendero Luminoso, the economic reforms that might make a political difference are problematic for the Peruvian government. In divided societies, opposition from the majority may pose obstacles to making concessions to minority demands.

The western European democracies confronting terrorism saw a growth in power of state security institutions. West German and Italian governments also upgraded intelligence-gathering and surveillance functions, bringing the government into a more intrusive role vis-à-vis society. In West Germany, Spain, Italy, and the United Kingdom, antiterrorist legislation restricted civil liberties. The normative context for political action might also have changed as radical ideologies that appeared to support terrorism were discredited in the eyes of the public.

In this analysis, we are also concerned about the long-range consequences of state terrorism, both to suppress domestic opposition (as in Iran and Argentina) or to further foreign policy goals (Iran, and possibly Israel). For Iran, terrorism has so far failed to spread Islamic revolutions through the Middle East. On the international level, it has resulted in isolation, even ostracism. Yet terrorism abroad may have helped consolidate the revolution at home. In Argentina, the military dictatorship crushed the resistance of the ERP (Ejército Revolucionario del Pueblo) and the Montoneros, but at a price that made it hard for the military to establish its legitimacy. When the military regime was eventually replaced by a democracy, the issue of punishment for those responsible for the terrorism of the state became a traumatic and divisive issue.

An important question for many of these case studies is how governments can control terrorism while maintaining democratic freedoms. There appears to be no single easy answer. Democracies struggle with terrorism from the Left and from the Right, as well as from nationalist or separatist interests. They must balance a perceived need to control the direct consequences of terrorism, by maintaining order and security, with the realization that any coercive response to terrorism reduces democratic freedoms. Is it possible to deal successfully with terrorism without resorting to coercion? Are reforms alone ever sufficient to prevent or to halt terrorism? Can repression and reform be combined?

Ending terrorism may require a change in the motivations of the individuals involved. How do conditions change so as to decrease incentives for terrorism? What might cause individuals to abandon the initial commitment that bound them to a terrorist role? When do people who use terrorism cease to believe in their own justifications? Under what circumstances can the individuals who have participated in terrorism be reintegrated into society? Environments may be more or less hospitable to exit and reentry. The reabsorption potential of a society may depend on public attitudes (for example, sympathy for the cause, if not the method) or public policies (such as the Italian policy of rewarding "repentance"). In divided societies, where terrorism is likely to be continuous with nonviolent collective action, reintegration may be simpler. Yet in Spain, offers of negotiations and of amnesty appear only to have provoked factional violence. In Italy, the Catholic church played an important role as an institutional mediator for reintegration. Successful adaptation may thus depend on many factors: a social environment that does not provide justifications for terrorism but permits reintegration, appropriate government policies that reward exit, and institutions that facilitate the process.

CONCLUSIONS

The case studies that follow address these questions about the relation of historical settings to the causes and effects of terrorism as well as to our understanding of the phenomenon. This is not to say, of course, that their emphases are the same or that their answers are identical. The types of factors that have been suggested in this introductory essay can be combined in different ways to explain the origins and the outcomes of terrorism in individual cases. The causes and effects of terrorism are comprehensible only in terms of political conflicts in specific historical time periods. There are commonalities among instances of terrorism, but each case is unique. Terrorism remains unpredictable in part because its multiple contexts are dynamic. Governments and challengers respond differently to similar circumstances. Original conditions change as a result of terrorism. Even the meaning of the term changes as politics and society change. Thus, these chapters explain terrorism as part of broader processes of political and social change. Proceeding from the nineteenth century to the present, they show how terrorism has evolved in different historical, geographical, and cultural contexts. Taken together, they provide useful histories of the most important and interesting cases of terrorism as well as interpretations and analyses of the relation between terrorism and its setting.

Part I

The European Origins of Revolutionary Terrorism

2

The Intellectual Origins of Modern Terrorism in Europe

Martin A. Miller

A new and somewhat hideous race of martyrs is now born.
Their martyrdom consists in consenting to inflict suffering on
others; they become the slaves of their own domination. For man
to become god, the victim must abase himself to the point of
becoming the executioner....
Therefore, the history of contemporary nihilism is nothing but
a prolonged endeavor to give order by human forces alone and
simply by force, to a history no longer endowed with order.
—Albert Camus, *The Rebel*

THE RISE OF POLITICAL VIOLENCE

To paraphrase Marx and Engels, "a specter was haunting Europe" at the
end of the nineteenth century—the specter of terrorism. All the powers
of old Europe had entered into a holy alliance to exorcise this specter.
Long before Europe learned about the Red Army Faction, the Red
Brigades, and the Baader-Meinhof group, terrorism was striking fear
into the hearts of the Continent's most powerful leaders. Efforts to break
the success of a series of spectacular assassinations seemed to have been
in vain. In a remarkably revealing diary entry written by Friedrich von
Holstein in August 1884, the anxieties of the ruling elite over terrorist

acts is clearly enunciated: "The Crown Princess is terrified of attempts on her life. She recently discussed with somebody in great detail the further security measures which might be taken. She demanded a considerable increase in the police estimates and the formation of a large and efficient secret police."[1]

There had been good reason for such concern, and the situation would soon become even more disconcerting. In 1878 alone, two attacks were made on the life of the German emperor, one on the king of Spain, and one on the king of Italy. In 1881, Alexander II of Russia was blown to death by a bomb in an assassination conspiracy carefully planned by a revolutionary organization, the People's Will. President Carnot of France was killed in 1894, an event followed by the assassinations of the premier of Spain (1897), the empress of Austria (1898), the king of Italy (1900), and the president of the United States (1901). This is in addition to a still larger number of *attentats* against lower-level officials in Europe. Moreover, these acts were a prelude to the even higher degrees of political violence that broke out in Russia in the first decade of the twentieth century, which included the assassination of the minister of education (1901); the minister of the interior (1902); the governor-general of Finland (1904); another interior minister (1904); the governor-general of Moscow, who was also the tsar's uncle (1905); and, in a climax of terror, the prime minister, Peter Stolypin, arguably the most politically significant figure in the country aside from the tsar (1911). Most of these attacks were the work of a faction of the Russian Socialist Revolutionary Party, which in the words of a recent student of the subject, not only surpassed the People's Will Party in terms of destroying officials of the Romanov autocracy but also "achieved a clear preeminence in the field of political murder."[2]

Terrorism during the nineteenth century, however significant and influential it was at the time, was also important because it provided the historical link between its premodern antecedents and its contemporary manifestations in the late twentieth century. To state the argument even more forcefully, groups like the Red Brigades and Baader-Meinhof are

1. Unpublished archival document cited in Andrew Carlson, *Anarchism in Germany* (Metuchen, N.J.: Scarecrow Press, 1972), 1:274.
2. Franklin Ford, *Political Murder* (Cambridge: Harvard University Press, 1986), 243. See, in addition to the chapter by Philip Pomper in this volume, Manfred Hildermeier, "The Terrorist Strategies of the Social-Revolutionary Party in Russia, 1900–1914," in *Social Protest, Violence, and Terror in Nineteenth- and Twentieth-Century Europe*, ed. Wolfgang J. Mommsen and Gerhard Hirschfeld (New York: St. Martin's Press, 1982), 80–87; Hélène Carrère d'Encausse, *The Russian Syndrome* (New York: Holmes and Meier, 1992), 216–81; and Anna Geifman *Thou Shalt Kill: Revolutionary Terrorism in Russia* (Princeton: Princeton University Press, 1993).

the products of an evolutionary development of terrorist organizations that coalesced into their modern structure in the course of the nineteenth century. Although the term "terrorism" appears to have originated in Robespierre's revolutionary France during the 1790s,[3] the phenomenon of coercive force used by individuals or groups to intimidate society or to threaten the lives of political authorities has existed and been discussed for many centuries. Two separate currents in the premodern period created the original foundation for contemporary terrorism. One was the secular conceptualization of tyrannicide, or regicide, which can be traced back to Aristotle on a theoretical level and, on a more concrete level, to Plutarch's analysis of the conspiracy involved in Caesar's assassination. The other was religious militancy, professed by Islamic, Judaic, and early Christian groups dedicated to violence and murder "for higher causes," groups that in many ways bear remarkable resemblance to modern terrorist organizations.[4]

The necessity of killing the unjust ruler is a notion that lies at the heart of the modern justification of terrorism and that can be found in political treatises throughout the centuries. For Aristotle and the Greeks, a tyrannical ruler was considered a pathological departure from the desirable forms of governing authority. Aristotle described the ways in which such rulers, by their abuse of power and attacks on their subjects, create conspiracies that eventually destroy them. Cicero was even more direct when he stated that "it is a virtue to kill" tyrants, and that they "should be erased from human society. For, just as certain parts of our bodies are amputated if they begin to appear bloodless and lifeless, and to infect the other members, so these cruel and ravenous beasts in human form should be cut off from what may be called mankind."[5]

John of Salisbury (1225–74), who served Thomas à Becket and later

3. Alex P. Schmidt, *Political Terrorism* (Amsterdam, 1983; New Brunswick, N.J.: Transaction Press, 1986), 65–67. This is the most comprehensive bibliography on the subject of terrorism. Often overlooked, however, is the use of the term in classical Rome. See Tacitus, *The Annals of Imperial Rome* (Baltimore: Penguin, 1959), especially "The Reign of Terror," ch. 8, 193–221.

4. See the suggestive research in David C. Rapoport, "Fear and Trembling: Terrorism in Three Religious Traditions," *American Political Science Review* 78 (1984): 658–77. See also Rapoport, *Assassination and Terrorism* (Toronto: Canadian Broadcasting Corporation, 1971), 9–12.

5. Marcus Tullius Cicero, *Brutus, on the Nature of the Gods, on Divination, on Duties*, ed. Richard McKeon (Chicago: University of Chicago Press, 1950), 571. See Aristotle's illuminating discussion of political revolutions in *The Basic Works of Aristotle*, ed. Richard McKeon (New York: Random House, 1941), 1232–64, which contains book V of his *Politics*. See esp. 1256 and 1261 on attempting assassination.

the Bishop of Chartres after being exiled from England, wrote in his treatise *Policraticus* that a tyrant "oppressed the people by rulership based upon force." By ruling in this manner, "it is plain that it is the grace of God which is being assailed." Therefore, he concludes, "it is just for public tyrants to be killed and the people thus set free for the service of God." Edward Saxby, in opposition to Cromwell, published his book *Killing No Murder* in 1657, in which he expressed the sense of fear and intimidation that embodies modern terrorism: "[The tyrant's] bed, his table, is not secure; and he stands in need of other guards to defend him against his own. Death and destruction pursue him wheresoever he goes; they follow him everywhere, like his fellow travelers, and at last they will come upon him like armed men. . . . He shall flee from the Iron weapon, and a bow of steel shall strike him through, because he hath oppressed and foresaken the poor, because he hath violently taken away a house which he builded not."[6]

These discussions of tyrannicide were not exercises in mere theory. Long before Louis XVI was executed by decree of the revolutionary government of France in 1791, many heads of state and oligarchic leaders of the aristocracy with pretensions to power had suffered similar fates.[7] Nevertheless, because the French Revolution inaugurated the secular rule of popular sovereignty as the new form of state legitimacy in Europe, it is often assumed that the regicide of Louis XVI differed in motive from the regicides and other acts of political violence carried out earlier during the Wars of Religion. This turns out not to be true. The fusion of religious and secular components is far more characteristic of the rise of modern terrorism than the neatly posited boundary lines separating any secular trend from the religious motivations of the past.

One further key point demarcating the rise of modern terrorism was a change in targets and technology more than in tactics and intent. Before the nineteenth century, acts of tyrannicide (or regicide) most frequently involved attacks on a specific abuser of or perceived threat to authority, from Thomas More (executed "from above" by King Henry VIII) to Jean Paul Marat (assassinated "from below" in a gesture of anti-Jacobinism by Charlotte Corday). Beginning with Italy's Carbonari, however, the objects of attack expanded to include individuals *associated* with the unjust

6. John Dickenson, ed., *The Statesman's Book of John of Salisbury* (New York: Knopf, 1927), 335, 370. William Allen [Edward Saxby], *Killing No Murder*, as reproduced in Olivier Lutaud, *Des révolutions d'Angleterre à la révolution française* (La Haye: M. Nijhoff, 1973), 400.

7. Charles I's execution in 1649 during the Cromwellian wars is the most well-known of these premodern regicides, but the list is a long one. See the chart "Major Political Murders and Executions in the Age of the Wars of Religion," in Ford, *Political Murder*, 147–50.

authority. The weaponry of terrorism also changed, becoming more deadly and intimidating, as advances in chemical technology made dynamite the weapon of choice over the suddenly obsolete dagger. Still, the expansion of the field of objects for assassination to include officials serving the tyrant was of greater importance. It was this shift that created the *limited terrorism* of the nineteenth century. Saxby's chilling description (cited above) of the relentless pursuit of oppressive rulers was not applicable to virtually anyone directly connected with the government. A century later, the further expansion of the acts of intimidation and violence to include members of society would establish the *terrorism without boundaries* of our time.

The boundary lines were irrevocably shifted during the upheavals of the French Revolution. Edmund Burke expressed the shock of millions of his contemporaries (as did Catherine the Great for the crowned heads of Europe in her letters to Jacob Grimm) at the possible consequences of this shattering of boundaries. For them, not only were ill-trained mobs seeking power, but the use of violence now appeared to spread to the citizenry as a whole, which was mobilized collectively against a legitimate regime as never before in European history. In reality, the whole definition of legitimacy was being recast in France, and the revolution was creating a new identity of "citizen" as well as a new ruling ideology of popular sovereignty. All of this was to have a direct impact on the rise of terrorism. Instead of dealing with an unjust ruler, future advocates of political violence would turn against the state itself, which embodied these new popular and national aspirations.

Perhaps most important, discrete objects of violence now were transformed into indiscriminate subjects of violence. First, the target was no longer solely the unjust ruler (as in the tyrannicide era) but a widened spectrum of individuals and groups associated explicitly or symbolically with that ruler. Second, the new indiscriminate violence was used both by the state against society (Robespierre's Terror) and by society against the state (the anti-Jacobin "conspiracies"). Thus political violence became the province of virtually undifferentiated subjects who were simultaneously its potential victims, replacing the discrete objects of the past, and its perpetrators.

In addition, during the French revolutionary era, explanations of tyrannicide and political violence moved irrevocably from a religious to a secular context. Earlier arguments made over the centuries on behalf of killing the abusive ruler had been justified frequently by reference to religious values. This was certainly true of John of Salisbury and Edward Saxby in their impassioned explanations of the circumstances in which killing a ruler was either acceptable or necessary. All that disappears once we move into the post-1789 period, when arguments are made by Robespierre, St. Just, and so many other ideologues of revolution entirely in terms of the rights of man and on behalf of a new, just, secular polity on earth, not in heaven. For these reasons, tyrannicide became "an antiquated idea" during the revolutionary era in France.[8]

The institutional origins of modern terrorism can be located in the structure of the Carbonari secret organizations, which began to operate during the Napoleonic era. To be sure, Filippo Buonarroti and François-Noël or Gracchus Babeuf collaborated against the French regime in 1795 in their Conspiracy of Equals circle.[9] Similarly, Auguste Blanqui (1805–81) developed in the following decades much of the formative strategy and tactics of insurrectionary barricade struggles and seizure of power.[10] However, they were not engaged in terrorist campaigns. The lines separating revolutionary and terrorist activities have not always been clear, and at times the two have intersected. The careers of Buonarroti, Babeuf, and Blanqui, however, belong in the former category, in contrast to the nationalistic Carbonari who clearly were engaged in terrorist campaigns to achieve their goals.[11]

The first Carbonari group was founded as early as 1807 in Naples with the intention of opposing Napoleonic rule in southern Italy. Many Carbonari leaders had already had experience in the secret societies of the Freemasons and other "fraternal" organizations, but they became highly politicized as a result of their hostility to the imperial regime of Joachim Murat (1808–15), Bonaparte's brother-in-law. After the collapse of the Napoleonic empire, the Carbonari grew in strength as they turned their energies against the Bourbon monarch, Ferdinand I, who had been

8. On this period, particularly in connection with the rise of a new terrorist mentality during the French Revolution, see Oscar Jaszi and John D. Lewis, *Against the Tyrant* (New York: Free Press, 1957), 108–10; Michael Phillip Carter, "The French Revolution: 'Jacobin Terror,' " in *The Morality of Terrorism: Religious and Secular Justifications*, ed. David C. Rapoport and Yonah Alexander (New York: Columbia University Press, 1989), 133–51; and Simon Schama, *Citizens* (New York: Knopf, 1989), 726–92.

9. Buonarroti's *History of Babeuf's Conspiracy for Equality* (London: Hetherton, 1836), although clearly partisan, remains a revolutionary classic. Robespierre is defended as the authentic revolutionary, and the descriptions of violence are portrayed as, e.g., "the horrible butchery" of the aristocracy, the Dantonists, etc. See 248–49. On Buonarroti's widespread and enduring influence on nationalist unity and revolutionary organizations in Europe, see James Billington, *Fire in the Minds of Men* (New York: Basic Books, 1980), esp. 87–93, 114–18, 173–78.

10. See Max Nomad, "August Blanqui," in *Apostles of Revolution* (New York: Collier, 1961), 21–82.

11. For an alternative interpretation, see Zeev Ivianski, "The Terrorist Revolution: Roots of Modern Terrorism," in *Inside Terrorist Organizations*, ed. David C. Rapoport (New York: Columbia University Press, 1988), 129–49.

"restored" to the throne in the Kingdom of Naples by the Congress of Vienna settlements. Dedicated to an alternative governing structure, the Carbonari groups multiplied northward with increasing popular support into other Italian principalities. Their emphasis was on a constitutional republic as the basis for a united Italy. The Carbonari succeeded sufficiently to spawn similar "national liberation" organizations from Greece to France during the Restoration era, which ultimately laid the groundwork for the massive revolutionary upheavals in 1848.

One of the unique characteristics of the hierarchically organized Carbonari secret societies was the combination of this revolutionary modernism with a powerful attachment to the traditionalism of religious rituals. The name itself was taken from a legend about a charcoal burner who renounced civilization in favor of a pastoral existence in the forest. Many of the elaborate rites, which embodied mystical as well as political symbols, concerned the uses of charcoal substances.

More to the point, initiates into the Carbonari groups had to receive a crown of thorns and a cross. The cross served symbolically "to crucify the tyrant who persecutes us." The crown of thorns should "pierce his head." Also, new members received a cord, which was to lead the tyrant to the gallows, and leaves, conceptualized as "nails to pierce his hands and feet." In addition, other symbolic items presented to the initiates were explained in clear terms of tyrannicidal violence: "The pick-axe will penetrate his breast and shed the impure blood that flows in his veins. The axe will separate his head from his body. . . . The pole will serve to put the scull of the tyrant upon. The furnace will burn his body. . . . The fountain will purify us from the vile blood we have shed."[12]

Contemporary documentary accounts of the Carbonari movement's activities show that the members were dedicated to "dethroning tyrants and destroying monarchy, and erecting upon their ruins an independent republic." These accounts also reveal the Carbonari's deep involvement with terrorist tactics. Governments were to be overthrown by rebellion and by assassination, in "imitation of Brutus." The dagger was the most commonly used weapon of attack on ruling authorities, but members were encouraged to "provide themselves even with poisoned weapons and with ammunition in order to be ready at the first opportunity." The victims of Carbonari justice and those named as "enemies of freedom" included not only royal government and army officials, magistrates, and police chiefs, but also members of the church who continued to remain

---

12. [Bartoldi], *Memoirs of the Secret Societies of the South of Italy* (London: Murray, 1821), 32–33. See also R. John Rath, "The Carbonari: Their Origins, Initiation Rites and Aims," *American Historical Review* 69, no. 21 (1964): 353–70.

loyal to the monarchical regime. In what is clearly one of the earliest uses of the word in the modern context, the term "terror" is actually mentioned in a Carbonari memoir to describe these various acts of rebellion.[13]

As the decades wore on, the contradictions of the Restoration era grew more glaring. Increasing numbers of revolutionary socialists and nationalists stood unalterably opposed to the archaic conservative regimes imposed on Europe by the Congress of Vienna in 1815. At the same time, the social-class chasm between the bourgeoisie and the proletariat widened, even as they both reached for positions of political and economic power largely denied to them by the restored monarchies. In 1848, the successors of the Carbonari—from Mazzini's Young Italy organizations to the Communist League—could be constrained no longer, as revolutionary upheavals broke out all across the European continent.

Early in 1849, a year after Marx and Engels had published the *Communist Manifesto* and at a point when the antimonarchical forces of revolt could still claim successes, Karl Heinzen (1809–80), a German radical democrat and publicist, penned an essay that has justifiably been called the first example of "a full-fledged doctrine of modern terrorism."[14] Heinzen had been expelled from the University of Bonn in 1829 for a speech he gave that was critical of the absence of academic freedom. He served in the Prussian army and spent eight years as a tax official in the Prussian civil service until his resignation in 1844. That year Heinzen published a pamphlet, *The Prussian Bureaucracy*, in which he attacked the entire civil service system. Summoned to court for this publication, Heinzen chose to flee the country. Traveling in Europe, mainly in Switzerland, Heinzen met Karl Marx, Ludwig Feuerbach, and Arnold Ruge, but he found them insufficiently radical. Heinzen's political ideas,

13. [Bartoldi], *Memoirs of the Secret Societies*, esp. 174–93. The term "terror" appears on 177, and "assassination" on 154. Also, revolts are encouraged with the aim of "destroying monarchy and especially the holy authority of the Pope" (181). There were estimates of 24,000 to 30,000 Carbonari members in Italy around 1820, all armed with daggers and muskets.

14. Walter Laqueur, *The Age of Terrorism* (Boston: Little, Brown, 1987), 28. Heinzen was anticipated in Russia by Pavel Pestel, one of the Decembrist conspirators in 1825, who formulated the concept of a *garde perdue*, which would be responsible for murdering the imperial family. Pestel's plan was a combination of traditional regicidal theory and more-contemporary revolutionary tactics rooted in the French experience in the 1790s. Although the *garde* was never realized, Pestel's ideas were well known to later generations of Russian revolutionaries. See Natan I. Eidelman, *Conspiracy Against the Tsar: Portrait of the Decembrists* (Moscow: Progress Publishers, 1985), on Pestel and the Decembrist movement. For a more detailed discussion of Pestel's radical ideas, see M. V. Nechkina, *Dvizhenie dekabristov* (Moscow: Akademia nauk, 1955), 2:58–88.

which emerged more coherently during the revolution of 1848–49, focused on the necessity for a "temporary republican dictatorship" to defeat the forces of reaction in Europe.[15] He also advocated French military aid to destroy the Prussian government, which he expressed along with many of his other political proposals in a short-lived journal, *Die Opposition*.

It was in his controversial and provocative 1849 essay "Murder," however, that Heinzen systematically formulated his doctrine on terrorism. He begins by positing his agreement with one of the "fundamental principles of humanity and justice, that any voluntary killing of another human being is a crime against humanity, that no one under any pretext whatsoever has the right to destroy another's life and that anyone who does kill another or has him killed is quite simply a murderer."[16]

He then goes on to show the many and varied ways in which human lives are brought to an end by the rulers of governments every day, from death-penalty executions to the manner in which "they organize obliteration on a grand scale and call it war." Heinzen continues his argument by stating, "If to kill is always a crime, then it is forbidden equally to all; if it is not a crime, then it is permitted equally to all." Murder, judging from its frequent occurrence in the past and the present, "is still a necessity, an unavoidable instrument in the achievement of historical ends." Thus, employing violence in order to achieve justice becomes essentially a tactical weapon of self-defense in an amoral world. If our enemies "can justify murder, even going so far as to claim a special privilege in the matter, then necessity compels us to challenge this privilege," Heinzen says.

From an examination of the uses of political violence by ruling parties in history, Heinzen comes to the conclusion that it is not the absolute value in the act itself that is condemned (as it should be), but rather that the acts are relativized in value depending on who is judging the intent. A regime decides which acts of killing are approved and rewardable (as in war) and which are illegal and punishable (assassination). Victims and heroes of murder, therefore, are created by circumstances. "Once killing

15. Carl Wittke, *Against the Current: The Life of Karl Heinzen* (Chicago: University of Chicago Press, 1945), 68. It should also be noted that with Heinzen, we move into an entirely secular explanatory system. Mazzini was the last major revolutionary who publicly admitted to a belief in God.

16. Originally published as "Der Mord" in *Die Evolution* (January–March, 1849), a selection in English translation may be found in Walter Laqueur and Yonah Alexander, eds., *Terrorism Reader* (New York: Meridian, 1987), 53–64, from which all quotes that follow are taken. See also the discussion in Carlson, *Anarchism in Germany* 1:19–22 and Wittke, *Against the Current*, 73–75.

has been accepted, the moral stance is seen to have no foundation, the legal is seen to be ineffectual, and the political is alone of any significance." Moreover, since murder has been condoned for centuries in this way, Heinzen rhetorically asks whether it is "not only a historical but also a physical necessity." If it is, it is difficult to demonstrate that "the blood of aristocrats is less suitable than the blood of democrats."

Having justified the existence of political violence, Heinzen then moves on to discuss the actual tactics of terrorism. "Even if we have to blow up half a continent or spill a sea of blood in order to finish off the barbarian party, we should have no scruples about doing it." Repressive governments have perfected the weapons of murder to an extraordinary degree; therefore, "we must answer blood with blood, murder with murder, destruction with destruction." Specifically, Heinzen mentions the need for opponents of absolutism to devote themselves to overcoming the state's superiority in organization, training, and numbers, as well as to the means of destruction. Fighters for freedom, consequently, must invent "new methods of killing" to neutralize the advantages of the army and the police. To counteract their extensive munitions factories and technological expertise in weaponry, Heinzen goes on to say, radical democrats need to learn how to prepare "substances whose destructive powers physics and chemistry have brought to light," such that maximum damage can be accomplished. He speculates on the need for concealed explosives and a powerful projectile or a "missile which one man can throw into a group of a few hundred, killing them all." Eventually, "a dozen democratic partisans would be able to do more damage than an entire battery of barbarian artillery." Heinzen also understood the importance of terrorist intimidation: "The revolutionaries must try to bring about a situation where the barbarians are afraid for their lives every hour of the day or night. They must think that every drink of water, every mouthful of food, every bed, every bush, every paving stone . . . may be a killer. For them as for us, may fear be the herald and murder the executor."

The quantum leap into the modern age of terrorist theory made by Heinzen in his essay "Murder" was matched in deed by the daring attempt on the life of Napoléon III by Felice Orsini nine years later. Although there had been earlier assassination attempts on European rulers,[17] Orsini's was the first to be carried out for explicitly political

---

17. One account cites eight attempts made on the life of Louis-Philippe during the 1830s. See Marius Boisson, *Les attentats anarchistes sous la troisième république* (Paris: Editions de France, 1931), 66 n. 1. Ford, *Political Murder*, 216–17, discusses other early nineteenth-century *attentats*.

reasons as part of a secret and transnational conspiracy in the context of simultaneously creating an atmosphere of intimidation and fear in the general society.

Orsini's influence was evident to his contemporaries who stood at one attitudinal pole or the other. Most Parisians were shocked; newspapers reflected social opinion that saw Orsini as a "wild beast" with his "laboratory of crime" (or bomb factory, in today's language).[18] Alexander Herzen, Russia's incomparable radical publicist, had a different picture. For him, Orsini was a man "of wild strength and terrific energy" who had made "a great name in history" for himself by his effort to murder the tyrannical emperor of France.[19]

Herzen's romanticized portrait of Orsini is only slightly exaggerated. Orsini was indeed a charismatic adventurer who was willing to risk his life for the higher cause of Italian independence. During his early years, when much of Italy was controlled by various Hapsburg regimes, Orsini committed himself to the revolutionary nationalist opposition. Influenced by the twin traditions of Buonarrotian theory and Carbonari deeds, Orsini became a leading Mazzinian during the 1840s. In the midst of the revolutionary events of 1848–49, Orsini's home district in the Romagne elected him a delegate to the assembly proclaimed by the Republic of Rome after Pope Pius IX was forced to flee the Vatican. Orsini's hostility toward Louis-Napoléon coalesced in the summer of 1849 when French soldiers were sent to occupy the Vatican and to restore Pius IX to power. From his perspective, this and the crushing of the republic were unnecessary acts of violence and of tyranny against the Italian people.

Orsini spent the next decade wandering in Europe in radical circles and involving himself in revolutionary activities against the Hapsburg and French regimes in Italy. Once, in 1854, he was arrested by the Austrian authorities after a failed insurrection, but he escaped from jail with outside aid. He published a popular account of his capture and escape in 1856, and the next year became something of a radical celebrity in England, where he went on several lecture tours and also published his memoirs.[20]

The climax of his search for vengeance against France was formulated and justified in the ancient manner of tyrannicide but carried out in the

18. Michael St. John Packe, *Orsini: The Story of a Conspirator* (Boston: Little, Brown, 1957), 265.

19. Alexander Herzen, *My Past and Thoughts* (Berkeley and Los Angeles: University of California Press, 1982), 371–74.

20. See Felice Orsini, *The Austrian Dungeons of Italy* (London: Routledge, 1856), and *Memoirs and Adventures of Felice Orsini, Written by Himself* (Edinburgh: T. Constable, 1857).

modern mode of terrorism. Orsini constructed an elaborately planned conspiracy, with international links stretching from Naples to London. There were two Italian accomplices at the scene who represented the primary level of the plan, but Orsini had established a complex secondary level that included a metal-weapons expert, a retired attorney known for his anarchist sympathies, and a French physician with radical political views, all of whom were in England. The bombs were obtained from a factory in Birmingham and were then smuggled to Belgium before being delivered to Orsini. In the course of events, one of Orsini's collaborators took into his apartment, apparently for purposes of seduction, a woman who turned out to be a spy for the authorities.

Nevertheless, on the evening of 14 January 1858, in front of the elegant opera building in Paris, Orsini managed to put his plan into action. As Emperor Napoléon III and the Empress Eugénie arrived in their carriage for the performance, three bombs were thrown in less than a minute, creating a frightening and spectacular explosion. The emperor and his wife escaped with only a few minor cuts from the bomb fragments, but there were 156 casualties lying wounded in the street. Of these, 28 were mounted police and another 31 were police agents assigned to security that evening. Eight people died from the blasts, including two innocent victims—a visiting American businessman and a thirteen-year-old boy. These deaths, more than anything else about the affair, outraged and shocked ordinary French citizens. The public outcry in the press over these victims contributed to the sentence of capital punishment that Orsini received at his trial. It was there that he proclaimed he had "resolved to kill Napoleon III for Italy's sake and that of a European-wide revolution . . . I acted as Brutus did. [The Emperor] killed my country; I decided to kill him." Although Orsini wrote, in a letter to the emperor two days before he died, that "assassination in whatever guise does not enter into my principles . . . and was never my system" in his struggle to free his "beloved Italians" from foreign occupation, his act was the moment in which modern terrorism became an operational reality and a permanent characteristic of Western society.[21]

The question for the future was not, as many statesmen believed, how to root out the phenomenon of terrorism, but rather the degree to which

21. The best account of the Orsini affair remains Packe, *Orsini*, esp. 216–81, in which the material quoted above can be found. Orsini's letter is on 278. See also the briefer and more recent description in Ford, *Political Murder*, 216–23. Orsini's pivotal role in the evolution of modern terrorism has been noted in recent Russian scholarship. See V. V. Vitiuk, and S. A. Efirov, *"Levyi" terrorizm na Zapade: Istoriia i sovremennost* (Moscow: Nauka, 1987), 16–17.

it would succeed in infecting and disrupting the functions of state and society. Judging from the years following Orsini's bold effort, the answer seemed to be that the frequency of terrorist acts was on an upward trajectory, rapidly escalating with no remedy in sight. Each new *attentat* appeared to bring down the existing walls of ethical tolerance and emotional security in ever widening sectors of society. Government officials promised, after each arrest, that the danger was under control, but the successors of Heinzen and Orsini continually found new destructive tactics to strike fear into the hearts of both statesmen and citizens.

Germany soon became the locus for both anarchists and terrorists, who sometimes had concerns in common and sometimes not. On 14 July 1861, a law student from Leibzig, Oscar Becker, tried unsuccessfully to kill Wilhelm I at Baden-Baden. At his trial, Becker stated that his motive was a desire to punish the Prussian ruler for not unifying Germany. He also admitted that he was directly inspired by Orsini's attempt to assassinate Napoléon III three years earlier. On 7 May 1866, Bismarck was wounded by shots fired by a student from Würtemberg, Ferdinand Blind, who was also influenced by Orsini.[22]

These acts, however, were pale by comparison with the two attacks in 1878 on the life of Emperor Wilhelm. These attacks alarmed not only German but also European society as a whole and ultimately led to legislation in Germany designed to limit the activities of all opposition movements. The first was the attempt made on 11 May by Emil Hoedel. Hoedel, who came from an impoverished and illegitimate background, had been involved with the German workers' movement for some time. He had, in addition, been a member of the Social Democratic party but was expelled because of his "ultraradical views" and because he had been charged with embezzling party subscription funds. His political ideas, however, owe more to anarchism than to Marxism. Hoedel was one of the first individuals willing to employ tactics of political violence who emerged from the ideological warfare of the 1860s and early 1870s between Bakunin and Marx over control of the International. Many rank-and-file radicals found themselves unable to make clear ideological choices and did not seem troubled about wandering from one camp to the other, as Hoedel did. In his case, there is substantial evidence to indicate that the assassination attempt was planned by Emil Werner, a Leibzig anarchist who was in turn the leader of the German section of the Jura

---

22. These and other assassination attempts at this time are discussed in Carlson, *Anarchism in Germany* 1:132–33. In Russia, Dmitry Karakozov unsuccessfully attempted to assassinate Alexander II in April 1866, but the event seems to have had little impact in Europe.

Federation in Switzerland, one of the strongest organizations in the anarchist movement. Moreover, Hoedel had certainly read a number of Bakunin's pamphlets and had discussed the new tactic of "propaganda by deed" with Werner and August Reinsdorf, both of whom were leading anarchists in Germany.[23]

Three weeks after Hoedel's attempt, before the newspapers had moved the Hoedel affair off their pages, Dr. Carl Nobiling shot himself after failing to kill the emperor in broad daylight on a Sunday afternoon, 2 June, in a fashionable Berlin neighborhood. Nobiling came from a well-to-do family, had earned a doctorate in political economy, and was a familiar and frequent patron of the Café National on Unter den Linden, where the emperor's carriage passed that day. Although Germans had tried to dismiss Hoedel as a deranged member of the lower orders, they were stunned that a representative of the cultured elite could be guilty of the attempted murder of the emperor. The act "turned Berlin into a city that was garrisoned as though it were in a state of siege." A massive police dragnet over the next few months led to the arrest and trial of 563 people, all but forty-two of whom were convicted of *lèse-majesté*, that is, either insulting the emperor or expressing approval of the assassination attempt.

A European-wide investigation began immediately after Nobiling's capture. The police, as the archival evidence shows, found out that Nobiling had attended Social Democratic party meetings and that he was known as a "Petroleur," a term that originally referred to Parisians who burned monuments during the last days of the Paris Commune of 1871 and that now indicated a specialist in explosives. Indeed, Nobiling's socialism included a belief in the use of dynamite to usher in the new era of liberty. He was also an anarchist in that he believed the state was the true enemy of the people and that private property had to be abolished and replaced by communal associations. During a search of his apartment, the police found not only weapons (two shotguns, two revolvers, and ammunition for all the weapons) but also evidence establishing a connection between Nobiling and the German section of the avowedly anarchist Jura Federation. Furthermore, Nobiling was discussed by Paul Brousse, one of Europe's most influential anarchist journalists, in a letter to Emil Werner before the attempt on Wilhelm. Brousse also praised Nobiling's courage in an article in his newspaper after the assassination attempt.[24]

23. For a thorough analysis of the Hoedel affair, see Carlson, *Anarchism in Germany* 1:115–37.

24. For details of the Nobiling case, see Carlson, *Anarchism in Germany* 1:139–71. Carlson is convinced that Emil Werner and the German section of the anarchist Jura Federation were behind both the Hoedel and the Nobiling attempts, but his evidence is not

Although the police did not turn up evidence revealing a widespread anarchist-terrorist conspiracy, the fact that Nobiling stated he was driven to complete the task started by Hoedel (and that both admitted the influence of Orsini) was sufficient for Chancellor Bismarck to take action. He had already prepared antisocialist legislation but was thus far unable to have the bills passed by the German Reichstag. In the heated atmosphere following the Hoedel and Nobiling attacks, Bismarck dissolved the Reichstag and called for new elections. A more conservative constituency was voted in, and the Socialist Law was passed on 19 October. Designed to halt the spread of socialism in Germany, the law contained provisions prohibiting the publication of socialist books and periodicals, gave the government the authority to close down any organization with socialist, anarchist, or communist orientations, and limited public agitators' freedom to speak on socialist topics. The law's impact was immediate and sweeping, as radical meetings were disbanded, party newspapers were confiscated, and many arrests were made. It was, as one historian of this period has called it, "the beginning of a white terror which inflicted severe blows" on German radicalism.[25] Any socialist, as far as the police and the courts were concerned, was a potential terrorist and thus a threat to the stability of the government.

ANARCHISM AND TERRORISM

The political theory of anarchism and the political action of terrorism have long been associated in the public mind. Despite the fact that many anarchists since Peter Kropotkin's time and numerous scholars of the anarchist movement have vigorously denied any justification of violence in the service of the social revolution, writers and journalists frequently continue to define anarchism in terms of societal chaos, class violence, and the literal destruction of the state.

The association may be controversial and debatable, but it is neither accidental nor absurd. The problem clearly emerged a century ago. In

---

conclusive and thus does not eliminate the dispute over this problem in the scholarly literature.

25. Peter Gay, *The Dilemma of Democratic Socialism* (New York: Collier, 1962), 40. European governments, for all their intelligence networks, rarely made distinctions between Marxist socialists, anarchists, and terrorists prior to World War I. The police files in the British, French, and German archives usually have dossiers on radical opposition activities in which antithetical groups are placed together under all-inclusive and stereotyped categories such as "nihilists."

1878, in addition to the two attempts made on the life of the German emperor, there were similar acts elsewhere. Alfonso XII of Spain and King Umberto of Italy were both the objects of assassination attempts (in October and November, respectively) that year. Europeans also learned of the fatal stabbing of the head of the tsarist national police (Third Section) by S. M. Kravchinsky and about the Russian radical, Vera Zasulich, who fired on the governor of St. Petersburg in an effort to protest his brutal treatment of political prisoners awaiting trial. Even more astonishing than the realization that the first act of modern terrorism by a woman had occurred was the later news that she was acquitted by a jury because of the humane motive behind her violent act. As events were soon to show, this was only the beginning of a wave of assassinations in Russia that climaxed in 1881 with the murder of the emperor.[26]

Since it was no longer possible to explain away these events as the pathological behavior of a few disturbed and isolated individuals, reports and commentators needed a theory to understand what began to be regarded as a rapidly spreading and potentially fatal danger to society. The explanatory theory was provided that very year by the anarchists. In a series of annual congresses held by the Jura Federation during the late 1870s, the notion of "propaganda by the deed" emerged. Although there is some dispute over who actually coined the term, there is little doubt that it was brought to public attention initially through the articles of Paul Brousse in 1877.[27] Influenced by the spontaneous popular outburst of the Paris Commune as well as by Bakunin's commitment to the revolutionary passion of the oppressed peasant masses, the concept was most directly shaped against the background of the Hoedel and Nobiling assassination attempts and the "Benevento uprising." In the spring of 1877, the anarchists Errico Malatesta and Carlo Cafiero led a band of peasants in the Italian village of Letino near Benevento to proclaim the abolition of the reign of Victor Emmanuel while they burned the property tax records of the area. The revolt was halted by the authorities shortly after, however, and Malatesta was imprisoned. Of

26. On the events in Russia, see Deborah Hardy, *Land and Freedom: The Origins of Russian Terrorism, 1876–1879* (New York: Greenwood Press, 1987), and S. S. Volk, *Narodnaia Volia* (Moscow: Nauka, 1966).

27. Paul Brousse, "La propagande par le fait," *Bulletin de la Fédération Jurassienne*, 5 August 1877, 1. See also his companion piece, "Hoedel, Nobiling, et la propagande par le fait," *L'Avant-garde*, 15 June 1878, 1. On Brousse, see David Stafford, *From Anarchism to Reformism: A Study of the Political Activities of Paul Brousse, 1870–90* (London: Wiedenfeld and Nicolson, 1970), 256–59. Orsini's influence is quite visible in the latter article, where he is twice mentioned explicitly. The term "propaganda by the deed" had also been used by Carlo Cafiero and by Errico Malatesta at the 1876 Berne anarchist congress.

equal significance was the strong anarchist movement, inspired in part by Bakunin, that developed in Spain in these years, in which political violence played an important role. The Jura anarchists were encouraged by these trends, which led to a flood of articles in the anarchist press calling for direct action, acts of insurrection, and confrontations with the authorities of the state at every opportunity.[28]

At this critical moment in the formation of a terrorist *mentalité* in European society, Johann Most (1846–1906) entered the scene with a radical analysis that permanently altered the situation. After surviving a childhood that was, by his own admission, "a nightmare," Most during the late 1860s transformed his impoverished and aimless existence into a dedicated commitment to socialism.[29] He developed a reputation as a fiery orator and agitator at local meetings in Zurich and Vienna, and this reputation led to arrests and periods of imprisonment. After an involvement with the German Marxist party under the leadership of August Bebel and Wilhelm Liebknecht, Most gradually began to develop a fascination with both anarchist theory and the recent assassination attempts on the life of the German emperor. His sympathetic portrayal of these and other later acts of "propaganda by the deed" not only led to his difficulties with the police but was the main cause of his eventual expulsion from the German Social Democratic party.[30] At the end of 1878, after being released from a prison term, he left Germany and went to London, where he established a new journal, *Freiheit*, with the support of a number of fellow anarchist and communist exiles.

Most's articles in *Freiheit*, thousands of copies of which were smuggled into Germany, emphasized the futility of the parliamentary path to radical change advocated by the German Social Democratic party, and declared openly that the "social question" could only be resolved by the path of violent revolution. His speeches as well as his articles focused on the efficacy of terrorism. He argued for the creation of anarchist cells and "armed workers organizations ready to repel, rifle in hand, any

28. See Max Nettlau, *Histoire de l'anarchie* (Paris: Editions du Cercle, 1971), 165–97; Marianne Enckell, *La Fédération jurassienne* (Paris: La Cité, 1971); and Walter L. Bernecker, "The Strategies of 'Direct Action' and Violence in Spanish Anarchism," in *Social Protest, Violence, and Terror*, ed. Mommsen and Hirschfeld, 88–111.

29. Emma Goldman, "Johann Most," *American Mercury* 8 (1926): 160–61. Goldman's attitudes toward Most went from uncritical devotion to savage criticism. Her article, therefore, cannot be read as an objective account but remains a valuable source of information. For a bibliography on Most, see Carlson, *Anarchism in Germany* 1:197–98.

30. Nomad, *Apostles of Revolution*, 269, sees this expulsion as the "great tragedy" of Most's political career, a crucial turning point in his drift toward an increasing reliance on violence.

encroachments upon the rights of the workers."[31] Kings, priests, or capitalists should all have been killed so long as they remained defenders of the old order. After the assassination of Alexander II of Russia, Most wrote, "May the day not be far off when a similar occurrence will free us from tyranny."[32]

Most continued his terrorist journalism in America, where he arrived in 1882. With even freer publishing conditions than he had had in London, Most printed some of the most extreme pro-terrorist articles in his paper, *Freiheit*, that have been published anywhere. For him, there was no longer an explicit area of battle against tyrannical rulers in which civilian society played no role. Most broke down the barriers entirely. There was no sacred space, no area that was "off-limits." Revolutionary terrorists could pursue their prey anywhere on the face of the earth. The terrorist, like the proletariat, had no fatherland.

Among Most's many points of "advice for terrorists," one finds mention of the importance of killing individuals of significance because of the greater impact: "The more highly placed [is] the one shot or blown up, and the more perfectly executed the attempt, the greater the propagandistic effect." To avoid surveillance and to get closer to the object of attack, it is desirable to "appear elegant and distinguished" in order to "deal the decisive blow, or set in motion some engine of hell concealed beforehand in some good hiding place." In order to raise funds to purchase weapons, Most considers it important that "he who wishes to undertake some action in the interests of the proletariat against its enemies" recognize the need for "confiscations." In other words, stealing from the "privileged robbers" of the government and the ruling classes to "finance operations" is not only acceptable but morally necessary. Moreover, it is "a duty," for the sake of the cause, to destroy anyone who intervenes to stop these operations.[33]

Most calls his doctrine "anarchist vengeance." Through these acts of violence, "we provoke"; "we stoke the fire of revolution and incite people to revolt in any way we can." These acts are "the call to arms" for the masses to rise and bring about "the natural lava flow of the social revolution." "Action is propaganda," Most writes, and by killing, the world learns. To ensure that this part of the process is maximized, Most urges his followers to place posters where the killing has been occurring, "setting out the reasons for the action in such a way as to draw from them the best possible benefit." On the issue of weapons, Most is equally

31. Ibid., 278.
32. Quoted from *Freiheit*, in Carlson, *Anarchism in Germany* 1:213.
33. [Johann Most], "Die beste Deckung ist der Hieb," *Freiheit*, 13 September 1884, 1.

clear. It is pointless and self-defeating to argue over which weapon is most effective. All weapons are useful, but only if one knows how to operate them. Too many revolutionaries "have paid with their lives" for having attempted to use a weapon "without first having made himself into a marksman."[34] To rectify this situation, Most published details on "revolutionary chemistry," which included instructions on explosive devices, flammable liquid compounds, poison bullets and daggers, as well as on the best places to hide and use them. Most proclaimed that the time for atonement for the crimes committed against society had arrived. Dynamite should be used to destroy homes, businesses, churches, factories, and the offices of the state. "Murder the murderers!" he wrote. "Rescue mankind through blood, iron, poison and dynamite."[35]

At the 1881 anarchist congress, which met in London, additional support for revolutionary terrorism was approved. Kropotkin, Malatesta, and the majority of the delegates went on record to register their agreement with tactics considered beyond the law by all existing governments. These included the application of chemistry to construct bombs for what were termed "offensive and defensive purposes."[36] Meanwhile, the use of bombs began to intensify, and the zone of war expanded significantly. For the police, it was as though Most and anarchists were directing an invisible army of warriors who were following their instructions with frightening precision. In Germany, anarchist cells across the country were uncovered. Searches revealed that the members of these small secret groups had copies of *Freiheit* as well as boxes of weapons that included everything from dynamite to poison-tipped daggers. Reports of murders in which anarchists were implicated appeared in Austrian newspapers with alarming frequency. In 1884, for example, a Viennese banker and his eleven-year-old son were hacked to death with an axe in front of his other son. Two anarchists, H. Stellmacher and A. Kammerer were apprehended, tried, and executed. A year later, in Switzerland, an anarchist plot to blow up the Federal Palace in Bern was

34. Ibid.

35. Quoted from *Freiheit*, in Carlson, *Anarchism in Germany* 1:254. Most also republished Karl Heinzen's essay "Murder" in his paper, which precipitated his arrest at the time of the McKinley assassination. See Wittke, *Against the Current*, 75 n. 8.

36. James Joll, *The Anarchists* (Cambridge: Harvard University Press, 1980), 111. See also Martin A. Miller, *Kropotkin* (Chicago: University of Chicago Press, 1976), 138–39. Not all anarchists supported propaganda by the deed. Brousse, whose article was responsible for introducing the formulation to the anarchist movement, gradually moved toward reformism. Andrea Costa began building the base for an alternative anarchist party that would compete in the constitutional arena of parliamentary politics. Kropotkin, who had his doubts even in 1881, at the time of the assassination of Alexander II, in later years spoke against political violence as an effective tactic.

discovered just in time to avert disaster. In addition, August Reinsdorf and Julius Lieske, both professed anarchists, were executed in 1885 after being convicted in connection with the Niederwald conspiracy against the German emperor.[37]

Terrorist attacks appeared to reach a crescendo during the 1890s, particularly in Paris. Although Charles Gallo threw a bottle of vitriol and fired several revolver shots from the gallery down into the crowded floor of the Paris stock exchange in 1886, this was to be only a prelude to the "decade of the bomb" that followed. At his trial, Gallo shouted the battle cry "Long live anarchy!" which would soon become uncomfortably familiar to European society. On 11 July 1892, François-Claudius Ravachol (Koeningstein) was executed by the French government after being convicted of a series of bizarre murders and damaging bombings in Paris. A self-proclaimed anarchist from the streets of lower-class St.-Etienne, Ravachol became a radical legend after he too shouted, "Long live anarchy!" upon hearing the death sentence in the courtroom.[38] In 1893, August Vaillant set off a bomb in the Paris Chamber of Deputies on behalf of the anarchist cause, proving that institutions of the government were no longer immune from the threat of terrorism. Jean Pauwels accidentally blew himself up at the Madeline Church in the heart of Paris while transporting a bomb on 15 March 1894. Emile Henry, long known to the police as an anarchist militant, placed a bomb in the crowded Café Terminus near the St.-Lazare railway station a week after Vaillant was executed. Twenty people were injured, of whom one later died. At his trial, Henry tried to explain to the court, the press, and the public at large the social conditions that he believed lay behind the rise of anarchist terrorism as well as the motives for his own deed.

> I was convinced that the existing organization was bad; I wanted to struggle against it so as to hasten its disappearance. I brought to the struggle a profound hatred, intensified every day by the revolting spectacle of society where all is base, all is cowardly, where everything is a barrier to the development of human passions, to the generous tendencies of the heart, to the free flight of thought. . . . I wanted to show the bourgeoisie that their pleasures would no longer be complete, that their insolent triumphs would be disturbed, that their golden calf would tremble violently on its pedestal, until the final shock would cast it down in mud and blood.

37. These events are discussed in Carlson, *Anarchism in Germany* 1:256–310.
38. Jean Maitron, *Ravachol et les anarchistes* (Paris: Julliard, 1964), 73.

. . . [Anarchists] do not spare bourgeois women and children, because the wives and children of those they love are not spared either. Are not those children innocent victims who, in the slums, die slowly of anaemia because bread is scarce at home; or those women who grow pale in your workshops and wear themselves out to earn forty sous a day, and yet are lucky when poverty does not turn them into prostitutes; those old people whom you have turned into machines for production all their lives, and whom you cast on to the garbage dump and the workhouse when their strength is exhausted? At least have the courage of your crimes, gentlemen of the bourgeoisie, and agree that our reprisals are fully legitimate!

He ended his speech with a solemn and (given the atmosphere of the time) intimidating threat:

You have hung men in Chicago, cut off their heads in Germany, strangled them in Jerez, shot them in Barcelona, guillotined them in Montbrison and Paris, but what you will never destroy is anarchism. Its roots are too deep; it is born at the heart of a corrupt society which is falling to pieces; it is a violent reaction against the established order. It represents egalitarian and libertarian aspirations which are battering down existing authority; it is everywhere, which makes it impossible to capture. It will end by killing you.[39]

By the close of the decade, the violent acts of propaganda by the deed were extended to the highest level of political power. Chiefs of state, or their nearest available representatives, were struck down at the rate of nearly one per year. In 1894, President Sadi Carnot of France was stabbed to death in Lyon by an Italian worker, Santo Caserio. In 1897, Premier Antonio Canovas of Spain was assassinated. A year later, Luigi Lucheni murdered Elizabeth, the empress of Austria. After several unsuccessful attempts, King Humbert of Italy was killed in 1900 by Gaetano Bresci, a thirty-year-old Italian immigrant to the United States. He joined an anarchist organization in Paterson, New Jersey, where he received his assassination instructions. In 1901, as if to show that no country was beyond the reach of terrorism, President William McKinley

39. Part of Henry's speech is translated in Joll, *The Anarchists*, 118–19. For a more comprehensive account of Emile Henry, see Jean Maitron, *Le Mouvement anarchiste en France* (Paris: François Maspéro, 1975), 238–47.

was murdered by Leon Czolgosz, who, though condemned as an anarchist, may have acted on his own impulses. Regardless, there is little doubt that he was influenced by the culture of political violence that had become so prevalent and permanent in all Western societies.

The emergence of terrorism came later to America than it did to Europe, but events well before the McKinley assassination had set the process in motion. The transformation of the American economy into an industrial capitalist system employing masses of impoverished European immigrants accelerated after the resolution of the Civil War. During the early 1880s, radical political groups were forming, some with appealing and sophisticated ideological explanations for the distress of this new proletariat. The anarchists were particularly prominent as they joined forces with the leaders of the strikes and other forms of labor violence erupting across the American urban landscape at this time. Radical publications urging the arming of the proletariat appeared from New York to San Francisco. Johann Most, following his arrival in 1882 from London, plunged into this ferment of protest in the pages of his paper, *Freiheit*. He intensified his calls for the use of bombs and the need for propagandists of the deed to "murder the murderers." Dynamite came to be viewed as the solution to "the social question" by increasing numbers of American immigrant workers who were influenced by Most's articles and pamphlets. A veritable "cult of dynamite" existed in this subculture, as reflected in the following verses published in the Chicago anarchist journal *The Alarm:*

> The slave hath no other weapon
> But the dagger, or dynamite,
> Is justified in using both,
> To snap the chain that binds him tight,
>
> At last a toast to science,
> To dynamite, the force.
> The force in our own hands;
> The world gets better day by day.
>
> Dynamite today, dynamite tonight,
> Most tells us how, he shows where,
> He says all in *Freiheit*
> And [in] his good little book on warfare.[40]

40. Reproduced in Paul Avrich, *The Haymarket Tragedy* (Princeton: Princeton University Press, 1984), 167–68. See 160–77 for a discussion of the "cult of dynamite" in America. The reference in the verse is to Most's *Revolutionary War Science*, published in New York in 1885. The complete title was: *A Little Handbook of Instruction in the Use and Preparation of Nitroglycerine, Dynamite, Gun-Cotton, Fulminating Mercury, Bombs, Fuses, Poisons, etc., etc.*

Anarchist activity in Chicago was particularly strong. It has been estimated that at least three thousand anarchist militants were at work in Chicago in the early 1880s, the majority of whom were of either German or Czech origin. The city had five major anarchist newspapers (three in German, one in Czech, and *The Alarm* in English), with a combined circulation of thirty thousand.[41] Many of these publications were calling for a violent clash with the state: "If we do not soon bestir ourselves for a bloody revolution, we cannot leave anything to our children but poverty and slavery. Therefore, prepare yourselves! In all quietness, prepare yourselves for the Revolution!"[42]

Labor violence finally erupted in a deadly clash with the Chicago police. After the managers of the McCormick Harvester Works hired several hundred armed Pinkerton agents to enforce a lockout of the workers, a meeting was called at Haymarket Square on 4 May 1886. As the meeting was nearing its end, someone threw a bomb toward the two hundred police who surrounded the square. The police shot into the crowd of demonstrators, some of whom were armed and fired back. Seven police officers died from wounds caused either by the explosion or by the gunfire. Moreover, at least twenty demonstrators may have been killed from the police fusillade; the estimates vary. The result of the Haymarket Affair was a massive repression of the anarchist movement in Chicago. After a hysterical political trial in which the ideology of anarchism was the actual defendant, four anarchists were convicted of responsibility for the bombing deaths and were hanged.[43] There was no evidence at the trial establishing the identity of the person(s) who actually threw the bomb.

Far from silencing the appeals of anarchism or terrorism, the Haymarket Affair was followed by other deeds of violence. Among the most sensational was the unsuccessful attempt made in 1892 on the life of Henry Clay Frick by the anarchist Alexander Berkman. Berkman was acting to avenge the deaths of striking workers shot by Pinkerton guards who had been hired by Frick during the Homestead steel strike that year. Together with Emma Goldman, Berkman preached anarchist doctrines throughout the period prior to World War I in public lectures as well as in his writings, which included his periodical, *Blast* (1916–17).[44] Goldman's *Mother Earth* was one of the most widely read anarchist

41. George Woodcock, *Anarchism* (Cleveland: World Publishing Co., 1962), 462.
42. *Die Arbeiter Zeitung*, 18 March 1886, quoted in ibid., 463.
43. See the recent analysis by Avrich, *The Haymarket Tragedy*, esp. 181–214.
44. For Berkman's account, see Alexander Berkman, *Prison Memoirs of an Anarchist* (New York: Schocken, 1970), 1–43. See also the version in Emma Goldman, *Living My Life* (New York: Dover, 1970), 1:83–107. Frick was the chairman of the Carnegie Corporation board, which owned the Homestead (Pennsylvania) works.

publications in America. The reaction of the American government to these publications and acts of violence was severe, particularly after the assassination of President McKinley by Czolgosz. For example, a law passed in 1903 banned the entry into the United States of anyone seeking immigration "who disbelieves or is opposed to all organized governments."[45] The equating of anarchists with European immigrant terrorists was now complete, both at the government level and in the public mind. Berkman and Goldman would later be deported to Russia as a consequence of specific legislation enacted against anarchists.

As the violence continued to expand in America, Europe, and Russia, the anarchists themselves tried to understand the phenomenon from their own ideological perspective. Kropotkin was never comfortable with violence, as his discussions on the subject of terrorism clearly show. On the one hand, he celebrated the assassination of Alexander II in 1881 as a "heroic act" and apologized for the assassin of the Empress Elizabeth, describing him as a man "driven mad by horrible conditions." On the other hand, he spoke against mass violence and the genocide of the bourgeoisie. Any revolution, he wrote, that triumphed by terror was unacceptable. In letters to friends, he expressed his fears that deeds of terror might become the only kind of propaganda in the future.[46]

Elisée Reclus, Kropotkin's French comrade, was less equivocal on the problem of terror. He refused to condemn any antistate acts of violence, which he regarded as the result of "horrible forces, the consequences of inevitable passions, the explosion of a rudimentary justice." Reclus wrote of Ravachol uncritically: "I know of few men who surpass him in nobleness." Moreover, he interpreted the word "violent" to mean "strong" in this social context. Force was being used by anarchists in order for justice to be served. "It goes without saying," Reclus wrote, "that I regard every revolt against oppression as a just and good act."[47]

45. *An Act to Regulate the Immigration of Aliens into the United States*, 57th Cong., 2d sess., ch. 1012 (1903), 122.

46. The evidence for these views is in P. A. Kropotkin, *Selected Writings on Anarchism and Revolution*, edited, with an introduction, by Martin A. Miller (Cambridge: MIT Press, 1970), 21–24.

47. Reclus's views on terrorism are discussed and quoted in Marie Fleming, "Propaganda by the Deed: Terrorism and Anarchist Theory in Late Nineteenth Century Europe," in *Terrorism in Europe*, ed. Yonah Alexander and Kenneth A. Meyers (New York: St. Martins Press, 1982), esp. 23–25. See also idem, *The Anarchist Way to Socialism: Elisée Reclus and Nineteenth Century European Anarchism* (London, 1979), 204–19. In a similar vein, the anarchist art critic Félix Fénéon wrote, "The anarchist acts of terrorism have done a lot more for propaganda than twenty years of pamphlets by Reclus or Kropotkin." Fénéon was probably the person responsible for the bombing of the fashionable Foyot Hotel in Paris on 4 April 1894. See Joan U. Halperin, *Félix Fénéon: Aesthete and Anarchist in Fin-de-siecle Paris* (New Haven: Yale University Press, 1988), 274, 276, 373 n. 1.

The discourse on violence among the theoreticians of anarchism continued with the contributions of Errico Malatesta. Anarchists, Malatesta explained, are opposed to violence. They are in fact dedicated to "the removal of violence from human relations." However, because the obstacle to this goal is primarily the coercive power of the state, violence is justifiable "when it is necessary to defend oneself and others from violence. It is where necessity ceases that crime begins." Thus, the violence of the victims and slaves against the forces of the capitalist state "is always morally justifiable." Although this argument had been made by Johann Most and Elisée Reclus before him, Malatesta added the problem of the legal system to the discussion. Laws, he argued, are never either divinely ordained, as the world's religions professed, or an organic part of the natural order, as the natural-law theorists maintained. The law is made by governments and supported by armies of bureaucracies. If laws were not imposed on society, these coercive institutions would be unnecessary. Thus, when laws oppress the society, the only recourse people have is to oppose those individuals and institutions of the state responsible for enforcing the unjust legal system.

Conflict, violence, and ultimately, insurrection are inevitable in such antagonistic circumstances. Revolution, for Malatesta, "must be violent because a transitional, revolutionary violence is the only way to put an end to the far greater, and permanent, violence which keeps the majority of mankind in servitude." Malatesta repeatedly distinguished between bourgeois violence—the gratuitous, destructive acts committed against the society, which he condemned—and "anarchist violence," which he approvingly understood as acts of resistance against and liberation from the brutality of the state.[48]

Mention should also be made of Emma Goldman's essay "The Psychology of Political Violence," published in 1911. In her attempt to analyze the motives behind the wave of terrorism during the 1890s, Goldman equated propaganda by the deed with the elemental forces of nature. "To the earnest student," she wrote, "it must be apparent that the accumulated forces in our social and economic life, culminating in a political act of violence, are similar to the terrors of the atmosphere, manifested in storm and lightning." Extending her comparison, Goldman described the intensification of pain from which ordinary people suffer every day as it "accumulates in the human soul, the burning, surging passion that makes the storm inevitable."[49]

48. For these quoted passages and other comments by Malatesta on the problems of violence and terror, see Vernon Richards, ed., *Errico Malatesta: His Life and Ideas* (London: Freedom Press, 1965), 53–71.

49. All passages quoted in this paragraph and the next can be found in Emma Goldman, "The Psychology of Political Violence," in *Red Emma Speaks: Selected Writings and*

To demonstrate her point, she provided extensive quotations from the trial speeches of Vaillant, Czolgosz and Caserio, which succeed in eliciting from the reader compassion and empathy with their plight rather than outrage for their crimes. From these speeches, Goldman concluded, first, that anarchism and political violence could not be associated as synonymous, since there were clear examples of other political parties that had been "goaded into violence during the last fifty years: the Mazzinians in Italy, the Fenians in Ireland and the Terrorists in Russia," none of whom were anarchists. Moreover, most anarchists eschewed violence, as Malatesta made clear. Second, to blame anarchists like herself for the acts of terrorism in society was a means of diverting attention from the root causes of the violence. The anarchists were interpreters of the violence, not its instigators. Anarchism, Goldman stated, was a political philosophy expressing the dreams of exploited masses seeking to rebel against the inhumane conditions imposed on them by the political, economic, and social institutions of authority. The guilt for the political homicides committed by Vaillant, Czolgosz, Caserio, and numerous others lies in "the social conditions that drive human beings to despair." In addition, those who were caught and convicted believed they were acting on behalf of millions of others. Goldman quotes Vaillant at his trial: "Make no mistake: the explosion of my bomb is not only the cry of the rebel Vaillant, but the cry of an entire class which vindicates its rights, and which will soon add acts to words." It was the demand to abolish a society "in which every day we see suicides caused by poverty, and prostitution flaring at every street corner, a society whose principal monuments are barracks and prisons."

Whether ambivalent or not, the major figures in the international anarchist movement felt compelled to justify the deeds of political violence and to interpret them as the outbreak of open warfare between state and society. They were less clear about their own influence in the rise of terrorism, in part because of their ideological commitments. Anarchism was, after all, a doctrine uncompromisingly convinced of the spontaneous, undirected, uncontrolled rebellion by the people to establish voluntary institutions in a future, egalitarian, stateless society. It would have been the height of ideological contradiction to have admitted that an intellectual elite was responsible for these individual or mass acts of social protest. Nevertheless, many anarchist leaders may have been compelled to celebrate terrorism (as Reclus did) or to "rationalize" it with reservations (as Kropotkin did), precisely because of their ideology.[50]

Speeches by Emma Goldman, ed. Alix K. Shulman (New York: Vintage Books, 1972), 210, 211, 213, 220–21, 224.

50. Marie Fleming, in "Propaganda by the Deed," concludes that anarchist "theory was

In any event, in the years immediately prior to the First World War, Europe witnessed both the last major theorist of violence and the spawning of a new social movement that played a role in reducing the level of terrorism. The theorist was Georges Sorel (1847–1922), who synthesized a number of contradictory intellectual formations into a new doctrine of revolutionary political violence. Unlike many of his radical predecessors, Sorel spent decades laboring like an ordinary bourgeois in the existing system before turning against it. Trained in engineering and mathematics, he worked for twenty years in the French Department of Public Works. After promotion to the rank of chief engineer and receiving the award of Chevalier of the Legion of Honor, Sorel retired from his post in 1892. He lived off a small inheritance left by his mother, read voraciously, and began publishing a series of articles in socialist journals in the late 1890s.

What is particularly interesting about Sorel is that he permitted himself to wander beyond the traditional intellectual boundaries of his time. The influences on his thought, therefore, come from sources as diverse and opposed as Marx and Henri Bergson. With the publication of his masterwork, *Reflections on Violence* (1906), Sorel brought these currents together, along with his deep reading in ancient Greek history and modern sociology. This extraordinarily influential book was not only repeatedly republished in French, but was translated into English, German, Italian, Russian, and Japanese.[51]

Much of Sorel's vocabulary appears to be Marxist, but his discourse is actually a critique of the foundations of the Enlightenment tradition on which Marx shaped his own thinking. Sorel rejected the basic propositions of this rationalist paradigm by asserting his belief in the forces of spontaneity, chaos, and conflict. In his view, a person was not a creature of reason who seeks to live life through the achievement of purposeful goals. On the contrary, Sorel saw human society as a seething cauldron of ungovernable forces. He was therefore as critical of bourgeois authority as he was of socialist "utopians," all of whom were dominated by the imposed and artificial "laws" of history leading to illusions of perfectability in the future. Sorel is one of the few radicals who was critical of the French Revolution, which he saw as the epitome of the process of

---

at the mercy of [terrorist] practice and compelled by its own internal logic to respond favorably to the violence committed in its name" (26).

51. For biographical details on Sorel and a searching analysis of his work, see Isaiah Berlin, "Georges Sorel," in *Against the Current: Essays in the History of Ideas* (New York: Penguin, 1982), 296–332, and Irving L. Horowitz, *Radicalism and the Revolt Against Reason* (London and Amsterdam: Feffer and Simons, 1968).

reducing human existence to rigid rules, despotic power, and overly planned authoritarian institutions.

Sorel emphasized the heroic role of the proletarian class, which alone could achieve emancipation from the immoral values and oppressive nature of the contemporary bourgeois order. "To live," he wrote, "was to resist." Resistance, in turn, would lead to renewal. To accomplish this renewal, Sorel formulated his notions of permanent class war as the setting for modern society, of proletarian violence as the mechanism of resistance, and of the general strike as the means to achieve liberation. He stood opposed, however, to "the civilized socialism of our professors" as a corruption of the proletariat's unconscious and natural drive toward freedom.[52]

Moreover, he believed that the working class could succeed only if it rejected utopian ideological doctrines and relied instead on its unquestioned faith in myths. In using the term "myth," Sorel had in mind "a body of images capable of evoking instinctively all the sentiments which correspond to the different manifestations of the war undertaken by socialism against modern society." The movement that, according to Sorel, best embodied this principle in daily action was syndicalism, because it concentrated "on the drama of the general strike." Strikes in general, more than any other act, were able to evoke the sentiments of resistance from the workers, to mobilize them with a "maximum of intensity appealing to their painful memories of particular conflicts." Socialism, in this way, achieved a level of reality among a wide sector of the proletariat that "language [i.e., ideology] cannot give us with perfect clarity."[53] The general strike, which resulted from the accumulation of individual strikes, became possible once the power of the myth had spread. Resistance, in Sorel's words, was transformed into "an undivided whole."

Sorel's analysis of the problem of violence was more sophisticated than those which preceded him. To be sure, he incorporated the earlier moral positions of terror as a weapon of self-defense used by desperate and frustrated victims of a corrupt and violent political order. However, he went further by defining social myths as the dynamic power motivating the behavior of the masses. Myths create social solidarity because they are rooted (as ideology is not) in both the unconscious dimension of the human personality and in the rituals and ceremonial aspects of ordinary life. Whereas intellectuals may perceive reality through abstract categories of analysis, workers grasp reality intuitively and in images. For this

52. Georges Sorel, *Reflections on Violence* (New York: Collier-Macmillan, 1969), 98.
53. Ibid., 127–28.

reason, myths bind the members of society together in a common bond and also inspire action by galvanizing the energy of resistance among the oppressed working classes.

The function of violence for Sorel is also different from that function as understood by earlier theorists. Violence is the weapon of the proletariat and is used to bring down the bourgeois world of power, money, and immortality. Its purpose is not aggressive homicidal vengeance, random killing, or purposeless self-sacrifice. Violence is, pure and simple, the supreme act of resistance, whose aim is moral regeneration in collective action through the strike. Sorel distinguished between "middle-class force," which he considered acts of sheer destruction against the lives and property of society's victims, and "proletarian violence," in which those victims, seeking to be free, resist the coercive authority of their masters and assert their moral and voluntary power to take control of their own lives.[54]

THE CULTURE OF POLITICAL VIOLENCE

As the years following the publication of *Reflections on Violence* were to show, Sorel was quite prophetic. His vision of mass proletarian violence, asserted through the increasing use of labor strikes, was transformed into reality with the growth of unions and workers' organizations in Europe and America. At the same time, with the important exception of Russia, where assassinations of public officials were renewed with unparalleled frequency and success,[55] propaganda by the deed went into decline. The interconnection of these two currents was not merely coincidental. Political violence did not come to an end; it was transformed into labor violence on the eve of the Great War. As proclaimed by Arnold Roller in his 1903 pamphlet, *Direct Action*, "economic and social violence against economic tyrants follows in the footsteps of political violence."[56]

The development of workers' organizations from spontaneously gener-

54. Ibid., 177–78. A similar distinction between what might be called just and unjust violence was made earlier by Malatesta. See page 51.

55. See Boris Savinkov, *Memoirs of a Terrorist* (New York: A. and C. Boni, 1931). For a succinct listing of the major *attentats* in Russia between 1901 and 1911, see Ford, *Political Murder*, 242–43. The most comprehensive study of this period is Geifman, *Thou Shalt Kill*. See also Vitiuk, and Efirov, *"Levyi" terrorizm*, 64–91.

56. Quoted in Ulrich Linse, " 'Propaganda by Deed' and 'Direct Action': Two Concepts of Anarchist Violence," in *Social Protest, Violence, and Terror*, ed. Mommsen and Hirschfeld, 216.

ated, ad hoc groups into organized bodies of class-conscious proletarians seeking specific economic demands took place over several decades. With the rapid growth of industrialization across the European continent, the working class swelled to unparalleled levels.[57] With this growth came new forms of opposition and new channels for the expression of discontent by the proletariat.[58] Already by the 1890s, as the Marxist parties were establishing the Second International, a syndicalist federation of labor organizations was being organized in France under Jules Guesde. This federation was able to include anarchists as well, as evidenced by the election of Ferdinand Pelloutier to the post of general secretary in 1895. Also that year, at the annual congress at Limoges, a general labor confederation was created. Similar trade unions sprang up elsewhere in Europe. In this way, as socialist party memberships became increasingly involved in parliamentary oppositions and proletarian strike activities expanded, the workers' movement gradually overwhelmed the terrorist acts of the propagandists of the deed. Although the last act of terrorism during this "era of the bomb"—the assassination of the Austrian archduke in Sarajevo, which triggered the start of World War I—would not occur until 1914, this form of political violence was by that time a rarity rather than the frequent occurrence it had been earlier.

Another factor that contributed to the decline of acts of political violence inspired by the notion of propaganda by the deed was the powerful effort made by the governments of Europe to combat these attacks. Beginning with the savage repression in 1871 that brought an end to the Paris Commune, European authorities instituted systematic programs on a variety of levels designed to eliminate the constant threat of assassination attempts. Police forces trained specialized agents to infiltrate anarchist groups, acting sometimes quietly as double agents and at other times more brazenly as agents provocateurs. There was harsh retaliation in Germany; Bismarck waged a determined campaign to eliminate the entire socialist opposition during the 1880s. In addition, governments made international agreements to wipe out all "anarchists, nihilists, and potential assassins." The Rome Conference of 1898 prescribed the death penalty for anyone convicted of an assassination attempt carried out against a head of state. The St. Petersburg Protocol of 1904 reflected further international cooperation by the governments of Europe to stop acts of terrorism, most of which were identified as

57. See the interpretation in Arno Mayer, *The Persistence of the Old Regime* (New York: Pantheon, 1981), 17–78, which emphasizes the enormous resistance of traditional structures and attitudes to the emergence of the institutions of the proletariat.

58. For a discussion of this phenomenon, see Eric Hobsbawn, *The Age of Empire, 1875–1914* (New York: Pantheon, 1987), 122–41.

anarchist.[59] It should be noted that the refusal of both England and Switzerland to join in this endeavor weakened the enforcement of these agreements.

The war years brought into the world a violence that surpassed anything the most extreme theorists of terrorism could ever have imagined. Once the war was finally concluded and Western society began the long process of reconstruction, some observers believed that the terrorism of the past decades—as preached by Most and as practiced by Ravachol—was a thing of the past. Politicians looked ahead to a world under the guidance of the League of Nations, and European intellectuals and writers were far more concerned with problems of alienation and ennui in the postwar years than they were with matters of political violence.

From the vantage point of the late twentieth century, however, the years between the world wars appear but an interlude in the evolution of terrorism, a deceptive calm before the emergence of an even more ferocious period of political violence reaching further around the globe and deeper into the lives of ordinary civilians. One of the most insidious aspects of this new wave of violence was its role as a functional part of the postwar opposition political organizations, most of which were dedicated to extreme nationalist ideologies. Some of these groups developed into political parties that took control of their countries, as was the case with the fascist movements in Germany, Italy, and Spain. Their leaders, once in power, introduced state terrorism on an unprecedented scale. In the Soviet Union, Stalinism also created a vast bureaucracy rooted in appeals to nationalism as much as to communism, and this bureaucracy categorized and then eliminated numerous "enemies of the state." Other groups, having nothing in common with either fascism or communism, remained in the opposition underground. The Sinn Fein party in Ireland, for example, waged a nationalist war of violence against British rule between 1919 and 1921, and this war continues to erupt in spasms of terrorism and counterterrorism into our own time.

In the formation and development of modern terrorism, certain patterns can be discerned that can be useful in understanding the nature of modern terrorism as a whole. One generalization that should be put to rest is the nineteenth-century theory that anarchism was the cause of terrorism. Whether one wishes to accept or reject Emma Goldman's arguments in this regard, it is clear that forms of terrorism existed long before there was an anarchist movement and continue to function long after the most popular era of anarchism has receded. Much of the history

59. See Linse, " 'Propaganda by Deed,' " 205–6.

of terrorism in Russia had far less to do with anarchism than it had with groups (like the People's Will and the Socialist Revolutionary Party's Battle Organization) dedicated to forms of socialism that certainly included plans for governmental authority. To be sure, there have always been antistatist motives inherent in terrorist acts, and the major anarchist theorists during the 1880s and 1890s supported the tactic of "propaganda by the deed." Nevertheless, this is a far cry from demonstrating a causal connection between anarchism and terrorism. It is more accurate to see the two currents as fusing at a historical moment, then separating.

There is, however, a connection between terrorism and anarchism that is frequently overlooked in the literature. One of terrorism's chief concerns, which it shares with anarchism, is the problem of political legitimacy. Terrorists historically have not only challenged but also rejected the moral and legal foundations of the modern state. Terrorism evolved, as described in this chapter, from attacks limited to specific objects (tyrants and heads of state considered unjust) to unlimited warfare against sectors of the governing order in which the line between society and the state was completely obliterated. Behind this expanding zone of battle was the desire to annihilate the implicit social contract that had traditionally defined and bound together Western societies. Former distinctions between tyrants and the oppressed were no longer operative. The entire relation between citizens and authorities became politicized. Although everyone might not have been guilty, no one was innocent. For the modern terrorist, the writer William Burroughs's phrase "to breathe is to collaborate" is a metaphorical article of faith.

Terrorism has always functioned most effectively in specific contexts. In the period I have examined, Europe (and, although regional factors may differ, America also) underwent a profound transformation. This is not the place to elaborate on these changes, but recall that nineteenth-century Europe was shaken by the decline and ultimate collapse of the empires of royal authority, the consolidation of the power of new nation-states, the destruction of the dominance of the old values of Europe's aristocratic and religious elites, combined with the emergence of a vast new underclass of uprooted urban laborers seeking answers to immense social problems from a newly entrenched and largely unresponsive bourgeoisie. At the same time, the validity of the eighteenth-century Enlightenment's idea of progress could no longer be assumed. Citizens of the new nation-states doubted that governments would be able to create a social order in which humanity's reason would be applied in such a way as finally to realize the age-old dreams of equality and justice for all. With the fall of the hegemony of the moral and social boundaries set up by the established regimes, in this era of rapid change, terrorists seized the opportunity to act violently in order to hasten the process of destruction or accomplish a specific goal presumably associated with the effort to bring about a new order. This will to destroy is a highly visible and urgent theme in the writings and actions of the terrorists I have examined.

Another important theme in the development of terrorism prior to World War I, which lies at the basis of its mood of violence, is the psychological problem of rage. The literature on the psychological and psychiatric aspects of terrorism has only begun to investigate the motivations for political violence and is still far from any conclusive findings.[60] It is obvious that although the population of a whole society can experience many of the same exogenous forces (wars, depressions, famines, tyrannies, etc.), only a small number actually become revolutionaries or terrorists in any historical time period. We must therefore concern ourselves with either endogenous forces or the particular impact that exogenous forces have on certain individuals because of their individual personalities, upbringing, and experiences. Also, if we are unwilling to categorize all terrorists as having psychopathic personality structures, we are left with a complex challenge in seeking to fathom the motivation for their violent acts.

Although this inquiry would require a separate study, I can at least emphasize here the importance of rage in the terrorist's mentality and hope that future studies will provide deeper insight into its significance. Rage is undeniably present in all of the terrorists I have examined. As opposed to anger, which is quite specific in terms of what provokes the feelings and who or what the subject is, rage is generalized, unfocused, and often of unknown etiology. One is angry at a parent, a child, or an object of authority (a teacher, an officer), but rage is expressed at abstractions (the bourgeois class, the church, the "system") or unconscious forces (fearful memories of past events, paranoid delusions). Rage does not always lead to violence but can when it is focused on certain concepts and under certain circumstances. Hannah Arendt has noted that "rage and violence turn irrational only when they are directed

60. For a good recent review of this literature, see Martha Crenshaw, "The Psychology of Political Terrorism," in *Political Psychology: Contemporary Problems and Issues*, ed. Margaret G. Hermann (San Francisco: Jossey-Bass, 1986), 379–413. For a clinical study that is meant to have broader application, see Franco Ferracuti and Francesco Bruno, "Psychiatric Aspects of Terrorism in Italy," in *The Mad, the Bad, and the Different*, ed. Israel L. Barak-Glantz and Ronald C. Huff (Lexington, Mass.: D. C. Heath, 1981), 199–213. See also Kent Layne Oots and Thomas C. Wiegele, "Terrorist and Victim: Psychiatric and Physiological Approaches from a Social Science Perspective," *Terrorism: An International Journal* 8, no. 1 (1985): 1–32, which contains a recent bibliography on this subject.

against substitutes." In other words, passive rage may be converted into active terrorism when individuals and groups become convinced that a ruler is responsible for the ills of society. The ruler is converted into a symbolic explanation of and a psychological substitute for the far more complicated and pluralistic sources of actual social, economic, and political distress. This conversion mechanism is often combined with the urge to achieve "justice" by destroying the deception and lies of the existing regime. Terrorists are driven "to tear the mask of hypocrisy from the face of the enemy, to unmask him and the devious machinations and manipulations that permit him to rule without using [explicitly] violent means, that is, to provoke action even at the risk of annihilation so that the truth may come out." This urge in turn produces "brotherhoods," circles and political organizations dedicated to the violent means of bringing about this disrobing of the enemy. It creates what Arendt calls "the community of violence"[61] and what I would call the culture of political violence.

At the end of the nineteenth century, this social rage was conceptualized as revenge. Orsini, Heinzen, and Most, as well as the terrorists of the 1880s and 1890s who bombed civilian targets with impunity in the name of anarchism, frequently justified their deeds as acts of vengeance. This was done in the name of an individual or an entire society. In the case of Ravachol, the bombings to which he confessed all had an avenging purpose: he struck successively against the apartment building of the judge who tried and sentenced a group of anarchists from the Clichy district of Paris; against the Lobau barracks in Paris, where the troops were stationed who had fired on unarmed demonstrators during a strike in Fourmies; and against the building of the attorney who was the prosecutor during the trial of the Clichy anarchists. Emile Henry placed his bombs to avenge the state's execution of August Vaillant, and Gaetano Bresci claimed he murdered King Humbert to save the Italian people from further oppression. One of the most popular socialist newspapers of the time, *La Question Sociale*, editorially proclaimed upon hearing of the execution of the anarchist Reinsdorf and another comrade, "We salute these two martyrs of the Revolution, certain that their deaths will be avenged with glory."[62] Emily Henry, in his trial speech

61. Hannah Arendt, *On Violence* (New York: Harcourt, Brace, 1970), 63–69.
62. *La Question Sociale* (Paris), no. 2, 19 February–10 March 1885, 60. There is no better example of this desire for social vengeance than the career of the Russian radical Sergei Nechaev. Nechaev not only was responsible for the murder of a member of his own Moscow circle in 1869 but also was the principal author of "The Catechism of a Revolutionary," one of the most chilling documents of planned mass terror ever written. Nechaev called his group and his newspaper "The People's Avenger." His journalistic contributions

quoted above, stated he "brought to the struggle a profound hatred" of the bourgeoisie. The modern reformulation of this fusion of social rage and revenge has been eloquently expressed by Albert Camus in *The Rebel* and by Frantz Fanon in *The Wretched of the Earth*.

Why is this rage to kill with a radical purpose held up as the explanatory justification? In a sense, terrorists are the expression of that part of Western culture that has moved beyond the paradigm of progress that has dominated our thinking since the eighteenth-century Enlightenment. We have long assumed, according to this theory, that the dilemmas of inequality and injustice could be solved either through the appropriate application of reason in governmental reform or through the evolution of a larger process of societal amelioration that was unfolding in a deterministic, lawful manner in history. It matters little whether one follows the classic texts of the conservative Edmund Burke or the liberal Jeremy Bentham for the former view, rather than the "conservative" G.W.F. Hegel or the "radical" Karl Marx as examples of the latter. The point is that terrorists in the post-Holocaust era have ceased to function within the framework of this central tenet of progress. They have chosen instead to kill not only because of the need to destroy a state leader who can be blamed for the continuation of economic poverty and political oppression, but also, and far more important, because they believe that secular evil can be overcome by destroying the value system of progress itself, which frequently includes the whole political and economic structure of our social order. The threatening or murderous deed thus becomes a Nietzschean or Sorelian assertion of will, to inspire meaning and purpose into a world that appears devoid of this raison d'être. It is also perceived as a renewal of one's individual significance in the context of a transcendent group devoted to violence as a means to realize fantasies of social improvement. So long as the government is seen as a callous oppressor and the society as an indifferent collaborator, terrorism can be justifed as a defense against these "modes of annihilation." Terrorism and nihilism therefore become the mechanisms of rebirth, acceptance, and progress. Terrorism, in other words, is "progress as nihilism" in the search for a new and better social order where existing "bourgeois" ethical standards, rooted in the idea of progress, are completely rejected.[63]

---

are filled with his boundless rage. See Philip Pomper, *Sergei Nechaev* (New Brunswick, N.J.: Rutgers University Press, 1979), esp. 90–94, for the "Catechism."

63. See the interesting argument on this subject in Harry Redner, *In the Beginning Was the Deed* (Berkeley and Los Angeles: University of California Press, 1982), esp. 178–79. I am also taking the discussion in Carl Becker's *Heavenly City of the Eighteenth Century Philosophers* (New Haven: Yale University Press, 1959) to its next and final

The major lesson to be learned from the origins of modern terrorism is that we are no longer dealing with isolated, "deranged" individuals or maniacal groups whose violent deeds, once understood and contained, can be eliminated by the organs of the state. As warfare has expanded from the specific battlefields of the premodern era to the global theater of today's nuclear strike range, within which anyone anywhere can become an incinerated or maimed victim, so too has terrorism enlarged its zone of battle. We are all possible hostages to threats and intimidations, and potential victims of violent attacks. In other words, we all live physically in the community of violence, and we all share the behavior and values of the culture of violence. Terror is a factor in our everyday thinking and planning—we fear bombs and hijackings during plane flights, where we are so utterly vulnerable; we consider avoiding certain neighborhoods or buildings; we may think twice about becoming involved in relations that carry implied risks.

In this sense, terrorism has succeeded to a large degree, not in attaining the specific objectives of any group or individual, but in making the threat of political violence a central concern in our lives. We must also realize that the agencies of government to which we entrust our security and which devote themselves to the eradiction of terrorism may, as the anarchists have frequently argued, be more a part of the problem itself than we wish to acknowledge. Last, it should be clear that terrorism has become a permanent part of modern Western society over the course of the last two centuries. It lies dormant at times but is not absent. When certain conditions combine, the dormant dimension is transformed into a highly active and very threatening form of violence, with which we are only beginning to learn to cope.

---

stage, when the concept of progress through the application of human reason and the belief in moral perfectability is exhausted and replaced by the motivation of modern terrorism.

3

Russian Revolutionary Terrorism

Philip Pomper

The century-long Russian revolutionary movement is a virtual laboratory for the study of a great many varieties of revolutionary expression, including terrorism. During the course of their long struggle with tsarism, Russian revolutionaries turned to terrorism repeatedly. In the nineteenth century, Russian terrorism, though often spectacular, was conducted on a relatively modest scale. Terrorist groups initially emerged from nonterrorist student movements; the scientistic nihilism of the 1850s and 1860s yielded isolated student terrorists whose bravado did not compensate for the frailty of their organizations. The lurid character of the nihilist conspiracies provoked a reaction within the student movement against the methods of the conspirators and toward more cautious tactics. Like nihilism, however, the populist movement that succeeded it also produced its terrorist phase. The "preparationist" populism of the late 1860s and early 1870s yielded Land and Freedom, the People's Will, and the mystique of the virtuous terrorist.[1]

The relative newness of terrorism in Russian political life, the use of dynamite bombs, and the resourcefulness with which the terrorists mined railways and streets and even penetrated the Winter Palace gave Russian terrorists an international reputation. The show trials of the period 1878–81 and pleas from such well-known figures as Leo Tolstoy to spare the lives of the revolutionaries only enhanced the terrorists' mystique. The mystique endured and so did terrorism in a variety of forms during the 1880s and 1890s, despite the growing appeal of social democracy, whose leaders initially opposed terrorism. Terrorism reached unprecedented heights in 1905–7, but it merged with a larger wave of uncoordinated violence, which ill fit the centralized and meticulously planned feats of either the Executive Committee of Narodnaia Volia (the People's Will) or the Combat Organization of the Socialist Revolutionary (SR) Party. In 1909 the SR Party's terrorist campaigns ended in scandal and removed from terrorism the mystique of the virtuous assassin. Although SR-sponsored terrorism continued, it did so with slight results. The movement had lost its inspiration and appeal.

In its early stages the growth of terror was intimately connected with the development of a student radical underground.[2] When study circles no longer satisfied them, and after propaganda and agitation failed to yield expected results, self-selected segments of the broader nihilist and populist student movements turned to terror. The strikingly amoral character of the Nechaev conspiracy in 1870–71 temporarily halted the drift toward terrorism among populists, but a decade later the People's Will gave terror a glittering reputation among young revolutionaries.[3]

1. During the mid to late 1870s the number of terrorist acts was small compared to the peak period, 1905–7. The most careful quantitative study of the terrorists of the 1870s shows only 131 terrorist acts for 1875–81, when terrorism reached its height during the "heroic" period of populism. See Stephen M. Young, "The Role of the Radical Fraternity in the Turn to Political Terror Within Russian Revolutionary Populism: A Statistical Analysis and Group Biography of Activists Within the Populist Movement of the 1870s" (Ph.D. diss., University of Chicago, 1980), 58, table 14.

2. For two good studies of the development of the radical subculture, see Daniel Brower, *Training the Nihilists: Education and Radicalism in Tsarist Russia* (Ithaca, N.Y.: Cornell University Press, 1975), and Abbott Gleason, *Young Russia: The Genesis of Russian Radicalism in the 1860s* (New York: Viking, 1980).

3. For Nechaev and his impact, see Philip Pomper, *Sergei Nechaev* (New Brunswick, N.J.: Rutgers University Press, 1979). For the decade of the seventies and the exploits of the People's Will, see B. S. Itenberg, *Dvizhenie revoliutsionnogo narodnichestva:*

Terrorism sustained its appeal during the reigns of Alexander III and Nicholas II.[4] Not just repression after the assassination of Alexander II but also dramatic social changes created a different context for terrorist operations. Between the mid-1890s and 1905 the formation of a broad, massive revolutionary front including urban workers, students, both urban and rural *obshchestvo* (the educated public, particularly organized professional groups), and the peasants dramatically changed the character of revolutionary violence. Between 1905 and 1907, SRs, anarchists, and Bolsheviks practiced terrorism on such a wide scale that it passed over into something akin to guerrilla action.[5] After a brief hiatus in roughly 1908–12, the revolutionary movement revived and finally achieved the mass violence of civil war after 1917.

Its intelligentsia inspiration and the Russian state's ambivalent commitment to modernization gave the Russian revolutionary movement a cyclical character. The process received its initial impulse in the late eighteenth century, when Catherine the Great, a sponsor of enlightenment and progress, pulled back from her original commitment and punished the most radical members of the intelligentsia. The characteristic dual threat to the rulers already existed: an internal threat in the form of massive, elemental rebellions of the underclasses that had

---

Narodnicheskie kruzhki i "khozhdenie v narod" v 70-kh godakh XIX veka (Moscow: Izdatel'stvo "Nauka," 1965); M. G. Sedov, *Geroicheskii period revoliutsionnogo narodnichestva* (Moscow: Izdatel'stvo "Mysl'," 1966); P. S. Tkachenko, *Revoliutsionnaia narodnicheskaia organizatsiia "Zemlia i Volia" (1876–1879 gg.)* (Moscow: Gosudarstvennoe izdatel'stvo vysshaia shkola, 1961); Deborah Hardy, *Land and Freedom: The Origins of Russian Terrorism, 1876–1879* (Westport, Conn.: Greenwood Press, 1987); S. S. Volk, *Narodnaia Volia, 1879–1882* (Leningrad: Izdatel'stvo "Nauka," 1966); Adam Ulam, *In the Name of the People* (New York: Viking, 1977); and the most distinguished single study, Franco Venturi, *Roots of Revolution: A History of the Populist and Socialist Movements in Nineteenth-Century Russia* (New York: Knopf, 1960).

4. Two studies of terrorism during the 1880s and early 1890s appeared in quick succession, but Naimark's is a far more thorough treatment. See Norman M. Naimark, *Terrorists and Social Democrats: The Russian Revolutionary Movement Under Alexander III* (Cambridge: Harvard University Press, 1983), and Derek Offord, *The Russian Revolutionary Movement in the 1880s* (Cambridge: Cambridge University Press, 1986). A doctoral dissertation treating a similar topic over a more extended time period is David A. Newell's "The Russian Marxist Response to Terrorism: 1878–1917" (Stanford University, 1981).

5. For the SRs, see Oliver Radkey, *The Agrarian Foes of Bolshevism* (New York: Columbia University Press, 1958); Jacques Baynac, *Les Socialistes-Révolutionnaires de mars 1881 à mars 1917* (Paris: Editions Robert Laffont, 1979); Manfred Hildermeier, *Die Sozialrevolutionäre Partei Russlands: Agrarsozialismus und Modernisierung im Zarenreich (1900–1914)* (Cologne: Bohlau Verlag, 1978); and Maureen Perrie, *Agrarian Policy of the Russian Socialist-Revolutionary Party* (London: Cambridge University Press, 1976). A basic study on which all of the others heavily rely is A. I. Spiridovich, *Histoire du terrorisme russe, 1886–1917* (Paris: Payot, 1930).

occurred repeatedly in seventeenth- and eighteenth-century Russia, and the external danger posed by the rapid development of western Europe. In the eyes of the rulers, an intelligentsia committed to serving the people rather than the state only exacerbated the internal threat. Under Catherine the interaction between an intelligentsia seeking social justice and a state trying to modernize and sustain its position within a system of competing states had already begun to take shape. Throughout the modern period the state exhibited its characteristic alternations of thaw and freeze, reform and reaction, ambivalent or vacillating rulers followed by "iron" ones.

The rulers shifted back and forth, aiding or abetting one side or the other in the constant struggles between bureaucrats bent on reform and traditionalists backed by gendarmes. These alternations and struggles within the state structure continuously interacted with the development of a revolutionary movement inspired by intelligentsia theoreticians.[6]

The Russian revolutionaries completed two cycles—the nihilist and the populist—between roughly 1855 and 1884. Although Marxism appeared in the mid-1880s, it obviously did not end in the same way that the earlier doctrines had. In any case, leading Marxists took whatever they found useful in revolutionary struggle from nihilism and populism—including terrorist tactics. The Bolshevik brand of Marxism, in particular, borrowed a page from the terrorists. At the beginning of the nihilist and populist cycles of the movement, a handful of *teoretiki* (theoreticians) frustrated by the Russian government's false promises and partial reforms and inspired by a vision of radical change would propagate a dominant school of thought. After a phase of self-education, their followers would pass over to proselytizing activities, ordinarily among the people closest to them, such as fellow students, friends, or family members. The most committed among them would then try to make contact with the *narod* (literally, the people), the oppressed and humiliated victims of the regime, whom Alexander Herzen had identified as the bearers of a native strain of socialism. The pilgrims sometimes had mainly philanthropic ends in view, but increasingly, they aimed at propagandizing the *narod*, at raising the peasants' indigenous socialist values to a higher level of consciousness. At first they spread their propaganda in an urban environment, mainly in cities with important educational institutions, after which the young revolutionaries might then try to spread their ideas in the countryside, perhaps as teachers. The most impatient and active members of the movement passed quickly

6. Philip Pomper, *The Russian Revolutionary Intelligentsia* (New York: T. Y. Crowell, 1970), ch. 1.

into agitational activities and sought the quickest path to mass up-heaval—and this tended to lead them to terrorism.

During each cycle of the Russian revolutionary movement a new intellectual trend incubated while the dominant one ran its course. Although closely related to the dominant ideology of the preceding cycle, the new doctrine would present a longer view of things and attract more "mature," scientifically oriented followers. In time, the long-term view would be replaced by a more militant one; and during the last phase of the cycle, science would once again be subordinated to action, an evolutionary perspective would give way to apocalyptic visions, patience would yield to extremism, and a heroic vanguard would assume social responsibility for the fate of the revolution. Thus, nihilism's elitist, scientistic, and utilitarian orientation gave way to Sergei Nechaev's and Michael Bakunin's anti-intellectualism and romantic devotion to violence. The Nechaev-Bakunin episode was followed by Peter Lavrov's variety of elitism, in which the "critically thinking minority" assumed responsibility for spreading its "scientific" vision, first to the intelligentsia and then to the *narod*. Within a short time, however, the impatient mood returned and with it a resurgence of Bakuninism and terrorism. The turn to terror at the end of the 1870s inspired a former Bakuninist, George Plekhanov, to rethink his position and convert to Marxism, which had been popular among the Lavrovists in the 1870s. Plekhanov and his disciples, however, took Marxism in a doctrinaire direction. Although Marxists at first borrowed freely from the legacy of nihilism and populism, they became antipopulist in their rhetoric and exaggerated the differences between themselves and the even more eclectic populists.

Marxism presented a new "scientific" and long-term view of change but proved to be no less vulnerable to the impatience of the revolutionary intelligentsia than previous doctrines. From the very outset, social democracy had to establish a modus vivendi with terrorism. The sectari-anism that later distinguished leading Russian Marxists did not dominate the movement during the 1880s or even for part of the decade of the 1890s. Many Marxists found a place for terror in their tactical repertoire in the later phases of the movement as well.

The Russian revolutionary movement thus presents not only a cyclical but a dialectical character. Within each cycle of the movement are found struggles between factions. The expectations raised by a theoretical outlook, combined with the militancy and impatience of those attracted to the movement, guaranteed frustration and provoked cries for more decisive action. This impatience affected Marxists no less than populists, even though the former presumably believed in the inevitability of the victory of the proletariat. Revolutionaries might have believed that history had ordained victory, but they decided for themselves precisely how they would comply with history's benign laws. The revolutionary subculture had its own dialectic of the cautious versus the more impatient and adventurous. Propaganda and agitation failed to yield desired results. The political police, called the Third Section during the reigns of Nicholas I and Alexander II and, beginning in the 1880s, Sections for the Preservation of Public Safety and Order—commonly known as the Okhrana—sent hundreds of young revolutionaries into dungeons, prisons, and Siberian exile, where physical and mental breakdown and suicide were not uncommon. After these depredations, the most impatient and committed revolutionaries found it easier to justify terror. Often inspired by motives of revenge for the casualties of the movement, they also found abundant political reasons for engaging in terror. Not infrequently, behind the dialectic of factions and theoretical justifications one finds personalities, whose motivations and styles of leadership led to internecine struggle and to extreme tactics.

THE NIHILIST CYCLE

An atmosphere of extremism in 1861–63 yielded the first serious polarization of the reform era. The relatively permissive climate of the late 1850s had provided the basis for a flourishing student movement, which rapidly evolved into something akin to our counterculture of roughly a century later. The Russian students, however, took a far different path. In their studied and systematic attempt to negate the values of the dominant culture and live according to "scientifically" derived values, the students and their ideological leaders created what some contemporary sociologists label a "contraculture."[7] The student contraculture of nihilism outraged the more conservative and moderate elements of educated society by its extravagances. These included outlandish dress, short hair for women, blue spectacles, and curt speech. Firebrands like Peter Zaichnevskii raised alarm to a new level by publishing the bloodthirsty pamphlet, *Young Russia* (1862). A series of suspicious fires in St. Petersburg in the spring of 1862, the rhetoric of violence in revolutionary pamphlets, and the Polish rebellion of 1863 prepared the way for the first serious reaction during the reign of Alexander II. Public opinion,

7. For a discussion of contraculture and counterculture, see J. M. Yinger, "Contraculture and Subculture," in *The Sociology of Subcultures*, ed. David O. Arnold (Berkeley: Glendessary Press, 1970), ch. 11, and idem, *Countercultures* (New York: Free Press, 1982), ch. 2.

increasingly guided by a chauvinistic press, turned against the students. The more radical students simply intensified their efforts to realize the way of life outlined in the writings of the *vlastiteli dum* (leading ideologues) and to pursue revolution. Experiments in communal living and popular pedagogy were transmuted into revolutionary conspiracies. In April 1866, Dmitrii Karakozov's attempt on the life of the tsar yielded "White Terror" and the beginning of a long, bitter war between tsarist gendarmes and revolutionaries.[8]

Karakozov's attempt to assassinate Alexander II can be taken as the *terminus a quo* of the terrorism of the sixties. He emerged from the radical student groups that formed in the aftermath of the repression of 1862–63, among whose casualties were Nicholas Chernyshevskii and Dmitrii Pisarev, the two most prominent ideologues of nihilism. Chernyshevskii's novel, *What Is to Be Done?* (published in 1863 during his imprisonment), and his martyrdom inspired the more radical students to form communes like the one described in his novel. Those who entered such arrangements, like those who formed the student subculture in general, tended to be well-educated members of the privileged strata who were trying to renounce their gentry status.[9] A number of the communes (often specializing in bookbinding or sewing) treated Chernyshevskii as a cult figure. The commune formed by Nicholas Ishutin feverishly pursued typical goals of the radicals of the period— propaganda and agitation among students, similar activities among the *narod*—all the while pursuing the rational communal life prescribed by Chernyshevskii. Several members of the commune planned to liberate their mentor from Siberian exile but failed to realize their goal. Instead, they formed a conspiracy to take vengeance for Chernyshevskii and for their disappointed hopes. By the mid-1860s, the long duel between terrorists and tsars had begun. The student-terrorist became the central actor in the drama.

The pattern of reform and reaction exhibited by the tsarist regime is a familiar one in modern Russian and Soviet political culture. On the one hand, the regime had to modernize in order to maintain its status as a

8. For the events leading up to and including Karakozov's attempt, see Venturi, *Roots of Revolution*, chs. 8–14.

9. All careful studies of the student movement of the 1860s establish the predominance of male children of the gentry. They were pursuing an elite track, generally enrollment in a classical gymnasium as preparation for a university or institute. The data suggest that there is no significant difference in the social profile of those who joined the elite by entering state institutions and those who joined the revolutionary movement and at times became terrorists. For example, see Brower, *Training the Nihilists*, and Vladimir C. Nahirny, *The Russian Intelligentsia, from Torment to Silence* (New Brunswick, N.J.: Transaction Books, 1983).

great power; on the other hand, it had to keep in check rising expectations and demands. The emphasis on enlightenment in the reign of Alexander II, for example, heightened the status of students, yet the radical subculture created by the students alarmed the public and called forth the wrath of the government. Alexander II's reformism and the rhetoric of enlightenment encouraged students to see themselves as the leading edge of progress, yet when they acted on their radical convictions, they discovered their relative isolation and impotence. The incomplete character of the reforms (from either a liberal or socialist perspective) created a continuing tension. Liberal public opinion vacillated between sympathy for the young radicals and revulsion at their excesses. Moreover, the relative somnolence of the Russian peasants, the first hope of Russian revolutionaries, inclined the revolutionaries toward terrorism. The first wave of extremism reflected the radicals' frustrated hope that the peasants would rebel in 1863, during the first phase of the exploitative land settlement connected with the emancipation. In fact, peasant rebellions began to die down. The same happened again in 1870. Nechaev based his conspiracy of 1869–70 on the prediction of massive peasant discontent that would presumably erupt in 1870, when the former serfs faced redemption payments connected with the next phase of the land settlement. Thus, in the period of nihilism, radical conspiracies and terrorism issued from rising expectations, frustration, government repression, and the refusal of some elements of the radical subculture to acquiesce in defeat.

The first prominent terrorists of the 1860s, Karakozov and Nechaev, though quite different in character, resemble each other in the murkiness of their motives and their proclivities for martyrdom. The nihilist subculture fed on literary images of heroic behavior, especially Chernyshevskii's fictional portrait of a supreme hero, Rakhmetov; the antinihilists presented antithetical images of moral disease and debauchery. The real-life terrorists of the 1860s seemed more like Dostoevsky's sickly transgressors than the healthy rational egoists portrayed by the nihilist ideologues. Not unexpectedly, the subculture tended to filter out unwanted information about conspirators and terrorists. The selective perception of the revolutionary movement turned pathological figures like Karakozov into heroic avengers and sufferers for the people. Older émigrés who had dedicated their lives to the liberation of the peasants played into the hands of self-styled avengers by justifying tsaricide and fostering a cult of Karakozov. Even Alexander Herzen, the most balanced and moderate of the "romantic exiles," published legends about Karakozov's fortitude under torture. Rumors in the underground connected Chernyshevskii with the assassination attempt and inspired a

Chernyshevskii-Karakozov cult. There were other revolutionary martyrs during this period—poets, publicists, army officers involved in the Polish rebellion of 1863—but none of them captivated the imagination of the radical subculture the way Chernyshevskii and Karakozov did.

Karakozov's strange story, obscured by questionable testimony, reveals how a somewhat unbalanced representative of the student underground selected himself to commit tsaricide. The stenographic account of Karakozov's interrogation contains the following self-characterization: "I was at first a student and then became a sick person—nothing more."[10] Karakozov's attempted assassination of the tsar provoked the government's "White Terror," which only further radicalized the student movement.

Nechaevism

A new leader found his voice at the angry student *skhodki* (generally, meetings; in this case, unauthorized student meetings for purposes of protest) of 1867–68. Nechaev, the next major figure in the history of Russian terrorism, quite consciously aimed both to achieve heroic stature and to create an effective organization—to succeed where Karakozov had failed. Nechaev's desperate effort to rally the surviving forces of the radical underground in 1869–70 also failed, but it did surpass previous conspiracies in its historical impact. Moreover, Nechaev's relationship with Bakunin prefigures, at least in its general features, Lenin's with Stalin. The Nechaev-Bakunin episode showed with striking clarity that certain kinds of symbiotic relations in revolutionary subcultures might yield disastrous results.

Effectively combining his own variety of charisma with astute psychological manipulation, fraud, intimidation, and blackmail, Nechaev acquired sufficient standing among revolutionary students to rule a frail network of conspiratorial cells. Approximately two-thirds of those involved in the Nechaev affair either were students or else had been enrolled in institutions of higher education shortly before their connection with Nechaev. Only 64 of 152 arrested conspirators were brought to trial, and 51, 80 percent of those tried, were between nineteen and twenty-five years old in 1869. The median age of all of those implicated in the conspiracy was twenty-two. Slightly more than 50 percent of those whose social background could be established were from the gentry estate, 10 percent were from well-to-do merchant families, 5 percent from the lower urban mercantile stratum, 12 percent from the clergy, and

10. M. M. Klevenskii, ed., *Pokushenie Karakozova* (Moscow, 1928), 16.

8 percent were the offspring of nongentry bureaucrats. The remaining 13 percent for whom social origins could be established were distributed among nongentry military, lower professional strata, and peasants.[11] Careful studies of revolutionaries during the 1870s show that youth and enrollment in higher education were the significant variables predicting revolutionism and that social estate entered into the picture in relation to these variables. Thus, the privileged social strata with easier access to higher education played a disproportionate role in the early stages of the revolutionary movement, and in the turn to terror as well. Although several women played prominent roles in the conspiracy, all but a handful of those involved were male. The conjunction of a leader who came from a poor, urban background (from the industrial city of Ivanovo-Voznesensk, a center of textile manufacture known as the Russian Manchester) and followers who came from privileged and relatively well-off families gave the Nechaev conspiracy much of its character.

Despite his own youth—he, too, was twenty-two in 1869—Nechaev knew how to manipulate young "repentant noblemen" by playing on their feelings of guilt. He exploited his own humble background, invented heroic sufferings at the hands of tsarist agents and a miraculous escape. Later, with the help of Bakunin and Nicholas Ogarev, Nechaev established his mystique as a man of the people with unbendable revolutionary will, courage, and cunning. Using to full benefit the psychological advantage of the plebian over the privileged in the revolutionary subculture, he also projected the qualities of a leader and man of action. His perpetual motion, from one conspiratorial nest to another, from Russia to Europe, and his decisiveness and willpower impressed his followers, many of whom had done little besides attending student protest meetings and discussion circles. Although radical students had been primed for the appearance of a revolutionary superman by the literature of the nihilist movement, few, until Nechaev set them into motion, had actually contemplated engaging in the kind of activity demanded by Nechaev and Bakunin's "Catechism of a Revolutionary."

The most dramatic episode in Nechaev's career, the murder of his fellow conspirator, Ivanov, in 1869, and the publication in the *Government Herald* of "The Catechism of a Revolutionary" along with the stenographic record of the trial of Nechaev's followers in 1871 (the first show trial under tsarist auspices) not only inspired Dostoevsky to write *The Possessed*, it also temporarily changed the direction of the revolutionary movement. Nechaevism became a negative lesson for the next radical generation—a reminder that the most committed revolutionaries

11. Pomper, *Sergei Nechaev*, 124.

might lack a sense of limits, that they might use means incompatible with their ends, that they might unleash "violence against brothers" and wound their own cause.

Nonetheless, despite the lurid revelations of 1871, an extremist element in the student subculture still found Nechaevism attractive. Young radicals packed the courtroom at the trial of the Nechaevists and openly expressed support for the defendants; eloquent speeches by lawyers for the defense and some of the self-justifications of the accused aroused sympathy; and the court's relative leniency shocked both Alexander II and his gendarmes.[12] The "unreliability" of the reformed court system and the sympathy of educated society for just retribution would be confirmed in 1878 with the acquittal of Vera Zasulich for her attempt on the life of the governor-general of St. Petersburg.[13] In 1871, however, the trial of the Nechaevists heightened educated society's suspicions about nihilists and strengthened the countertrends in the radical subculture: the return to an emphasis on scientific knowledge, critical thought, and self-education inspired by Peter Lavrov; and the preference for peaceful propaganda of the Chaikovskii Circle and its affiliates.

The rejection of Nechaevist methods is not so surprising in a revolutionary subculture inspired by the Russian intelligentsia's fundamental aim during the 1860s and 1870s: fusion of the scientific study of society and the pursuit of social justice. Yet, time and again, leaders like Nechaev reappeared. They placed action before knowledge, resorted to unscrupulous methods to generate a movement instead of patiently preparing social forces, and saw science mainly as a means to an end. Science became not so much a supreme guide to action as an instrument in the service of immediate political goals. The discipline of the organization overshadowed the discipline of science. The preeminently political types came to despise the very intelligentsia that had inspired them, even while continuing to justify their actions in "scientific" terms.

The impatient politicos came from a variety of backgrounds and operated in quite different contexts, but they all shared a number of characteristics: they obsessively pursued revolution at times when others withdrew from the fray; they were willing to use means rejected by most of their fellow revolutionaries as illegitimate; they violated not only the regime's norms but those of the revolutionary subculture that had nourished them; and they often merged personal ambitions and vendettas

12. Ibid., 119–23.
13. For Zasulich's career, see Wolfgang Geierhos, *Vera Zasulic und die russische revolutionare Bewegung* (Munich: Oldenbourg, 1977) and Jay Bergman, *Vera Zasulich: A Biography* (Stanford: Stanford University Press, 1983).

with revolutionism. It was difficult to distinguish their personal drive for power and revenge from their ideological commitments. The revenge motive is well advertised in the title of Nechaev's organization, the People's Revenge. Granting their total commitment to revolution, leaders like Nechaev would not play by the established rules of the game. They would convert any organization to which they belonged into personal instruments. Nechaev's current reputation within the Russian intelligentsia reveals that they have learned the lessons of twentieth-century politics well. They see Nechaev as a forerunner of figures like Hitler, Stalin, and Pol Pot, as well as an inspiration to contemporary terrorists, such as the Red Brigades.[14] Although a small-scale phenomenon, Nechaevism proved to be paradigmatic for large-scale political movements in the twentieth century.

Like armies during wartime, revolutionary organizations tend to promote those who are willing to advance under fire and those who seem to be most vigilant and resourceful when enemy encirclement threatens the unit. Revolutionary leaders do not have the luxury of choosing exclusively high-minded types for the tasks ahead of the organization. Trotsky justified hired guns succinctly: "During a war the most unimpeachable officer prefers the soldier who can carry out a daring mission, even if he had been a gangster earlier. . . . If you want to make an accusation of unscrupulousness as to means, then it shouldn't be directed against the officer, but against the war, or the regime that generated the war."[15] The revolutionary "army" recruited widely and attracted a great variety of people with different motives. Vengeful power seekers coexisted with self-sacrificing young idealists whose guilt before the *narod* impelled them above all toward martyrdom. Both self-sacrifice and ruthlessness often coexisted in one and the same individual, and the former tended to justify the latter in the eyes of comrades.

Even more important, in the conditions of the revolutionary underground, paranoid signals could not be distinguished from the rhetoric of vigilance and combativeness. Aberrant types could easily advance themselves. Even when detected by some, they could still convince others that their commitment and usefulness to the cause justified their excesses. Thus, however gross his crimes, Nechaev still enjoyed a mystique among some segments of both the old and the new generations of revolutionaries. His plebian background and ultimate martyrdom in

14. One of the current regime's most prominent spokesmen in the medium of drama, Mikhail Shatrov, placed Nechaev at the center of his recent play, *Diktatura sovesti* (Dictatorship of conscience).

15. Leon Trotsky, *Trotsky's Notebooks, 1933–35: Writings on Lenin, Dialectics, and Evolutionism*, trans. Philip Pomper (New York: Columbia University Press, 1986), 30.

the Peter and Paul Fortress gave him special appeal. He was rediscovered and rehabilitated first by the People's Will and later by the Bolsheviks.

Revolutionary fighters like Nechaev in the Russian revolutionary subculture had a particular psychological advantage vis-à-vis the émigrés, those who directed the movement from afar through their journals but who no longer experienced the threat of arrest, imprisonment, and Siberian exile. The guilty consciences of older *teoretiki* made them fair game for young extremists with real or imaginary (in Nechaev's case) battle wounds. To be sure, émigré leaders resorted to a variety of unsavory tactics in order to retain their positions. Now and again they promoted the Nechaev type as a valuable sort of hired gun. The Bakunin-Nechaev relation thus resembled the Lenin-Stalin one in many ways, despite considerable differences in the characters, psychologies, and abilities of the individuals in the two pairs. Both the fondness of some *teoretiki* (especially those of gentry origin) for tough, plebian "heroes" and the psychological leverage of the soldiers in the trenches over the generals in the chateaus played a role in the rise of the terrorists in the revolutionary movement. Thus, by 1870 one can see some of the characteristic weaknesses in the Russian revolutionary subculture that would permit the most brutal, aberrant sorts occasionally to rise to positions of leadership. Nechaev's career illustrated with utter clarity the process by which an intelligentsia movement could be seized by extreme elements whose modus operandi would lead to the destruction of the intelligentsia itself.

THE POPULIST CYCLE

Only roughly five years elapsed between the trial of the Nechaevists in 1871 and the gradual reemergence of terrorism under the auspices of Land and Freedom in 1876. By 1875 the remarkable "going to the people" of the preceding year had been crushed by massive arrests. Self-education, propaganda, and agitation, conducted at the expense of enormous self-sacrifice, had yielded little. The idealistic youths inspired by the writings of nihilists, ethical sociologists of the *narodnik* school (populists, extolling the socialist proclivities of the Russian peasant), anarchists, and Social Democrats were, on the whole, initially opposed to terrorism. Methods of recruitment into the circles that served as seedbeds for conspiracies of the mid to late 1870s had been designed to filter out potential Nechaevs. However, the seedbeds of revolution remained. The social background of the revolutionary circles still resembled that of the 1860s, with some important differences. Women of the gentry estate played a prominent role, at least partly because of the regime's handling of the plight of women seeking access to higher education. Ambitious and idealistic young women often enrolled in foreign schools, particularly in Switzerland, where they also became exposed to the ideas of Bakunin and Peter Lavrov and to the First International. In short, they received an education in revolutionism.[16] The government, alarmed at reports of their behavior, called them home in 1873. A significant number of the women who returned from Zurich in 1874 played important roles in the revolutionary movement of the 1870s. Prominent among them was Vera Figner, who later headed the Executive Committee of the People's Will.[17]

The participation of women seeking higher education strengthened the Lavrovist emphasis on knowledge during the period of reaction against Nechaevism in the early 1870s. However, Lavrov's "preparationism" proved to be an ephemeral phase in the movement. Bakuninist passion and the desire to plunge into revolutionary activity won out. The odd symbiosis of anarchism, populism, and organizational centralization reminiscent of the Bakunin-Nechaev episode quickly reasserted itself. Even the puritanism of the Chaikovskii Circle and the general preference of revolutionary groups for nonhierarchical forms of organization (in keeping with the fundamentally anarchistic spirit of the movement) failed, in the end, to prevent the drift toward extremes—Bakuninism, Jacobinism, and terror.

Two fundamental conditions impelled the revolutionaries toward centralized methods of organization and terrorism: the failure of the masses of people to respond to their propaganda and agitation, and the depredations of the tsarist police. Rather than abandon their theories about the *narod* and their revolutionary project, the most committed revolutionaries blamed themselves for inadequate tactics. Aside from developing new

16. See J. M. Meijer, *Knowledge and Revolution: The Russian Colony in Zurich* (Assen: Van Gorcum, 1955) and Richard Stites, *The Women's Liberation Movement in Russia: Feminism, Nihilism, and Bolshevism, 1860–1930* (Princeton: Princeton University Press, 1978), ch. 5.

17. The return of the women from Zurich at least partly accounts for the increase in the percentage of women involved in revolutionary activity in general (more than 21 percent of the movement) and terrorist activity in particular (slightly more 15 percent during the era of Land and Freedom and the People's Will), according to the best estimates. See Young, "The Role of the Radical Fraternity in the Turn to Political Terror," 24–25, 50. Stites, using less refined data, states that participation of women in the revolutionary movement increased from 3 percent in the 1860s to 12.5 percent in the 1870s. See Stites, *The Women's Liberation Movement in Russia*, 148–49.

methods of propaganda, agitation, and organization, they also (fatefully) decided to deal with the obstacle that had caused their comrades in the cause so much grief: the tsarist regime. The use of the word *istreblenie* (annihilation) with reference to the "obstacle" presented by the regime's gendarmes and symbols nicely expressed the attitude of the post-1875 terrorists.

The terrorism of the mid-1870s began somewhat haphazardly in individual acts of self-defense and retribution, mainly in the Ukraine. In 1876, Land and Freedom, the largest and most potent revolutionary organization to emerge after the debacles of the mid-1870s, legitimated the acts of self-defense that individual revolutionaries had already begun to use against police. Even more important, it provided for "disorganization" in its program. (Although Nechaev had defiantly embraced the word "terrorist," it was not acceptable to Land and Freedom in 1876.) Promoting an active form of self-defense (infiltration of the tsarist security organs, violent measures against spies and gendarmes, liberation of arrested revolutionaries), the advocates of disorganization planned direct action against the regime. Before the revolution, the disorganizers would undertake the annihilation of obnoxious officials; and at the moment of revolution, some planned to strike decisively against the regime's central symbol, the Winter Palace and its royal occupants. Moreover, despite the limited role assigned to terror by the formulators of the program of Land and Freedom, its importance grew until it became the focus of the organization's activity and also its public image. As had occurred with Nechaev's People's Revenge, leaders with a terrorist bent created special units, organizations that operated independently and secretly.

The motives for turning to violence during the era of Land and Freedom (1876–79) can be discerned in the character of terrorist acts as well as in the justifications put forward for them. Betrayal of comrades was seen as a particularly heinous act. Thus, traitors and police spies were handled brutally. Physical mistreatment and affronts to the dignity of imprisoned comrades also provoked rage. An insult in the form of a blow from a person in authority might lead to suicide, hunger strikes, and sometimes violent retribution by avengers. Such was the case with Vera Zasulich's shooting of F. F. Trepov, the governor-general of St. Petersburg, in his office in 1878. Trepov had A. S. Eme'lianov, a member of Land and Freedom, flogged for refusing to remove his hat during an inspection in the prison yard.

Zasulich is a particularly interesting figure, for she had been involved in the Nechaev affair but later in her revolutionary career became a Social Democrat and worked with Lenin on *Iskra* (The Spark). In an interview with the historian M. N. Pokrovskii she said that she "knew Lenin well . . . he is a person of the Nechaev type, unscrupulous about means in the service of revolution."[18] As someone who participated in the terrorist phases of two cycles of the revolutionary movement, Zasulich was peculiarly sensitive to extremism—and ultimately repudiated it. In 1878, however, she gave terror a good name. The regime's brutality went on trial in 1877–78, not just in Zasulich's case but in other show trials.[19] The revolutionaries and their liberal defenders used the strategy of turning the tables, of putting the regime on trial by using the prisoners' dock as a pulpit for impeaching the tsarist regime. Zasulich's acquittal and the celebrity of her case gave terrorism a considerable boost. In May 1878, shortly after Zasulich's trial, I. S. Turgenev wrote a prose poem entitled "The Threshold," portraying the virtuous woman terrorist. Whatever its value for conveying the morality and psychology of those who crossed the threshold of commitment to terrorism, Turgenev's "poem" probably captured something of the attitude of the liberal public.

I see a huge building. The front door is wide open; behind the door—deep gloom. A girl stands before a high threshold . . . a Russian girl. The impenetrable gloom chills the air; and together with an icy breath, a solemn, hollow voice issues from the depths of the building.

—O you, who wish to cross this threshold, do you know what awaits you?

—I know, the girl answers.

—Cold, hunger, hatred, ridicule, contempt, humiliation, imprisonment, disease, and death itself.

—I know.

—Total alienation, loneliness.

—I know, I'm ready. I'll endure all sufferings, all blows.

—Not only from enemies—but from kin, from friends?

—Yes, from them, too.

—Very well. Are you ready to sacrifice yourself?

—Yes.

—To be a nameless victim? You will perish and no one—no one will even know whose memory to honor!

18. Quoted in Trotsky, *Trotsky's Notebooks, 1933–35*, 29.

19. For a history of the trials during the 1870s and good statistical data on the magnitude of the movement, arrests, and sentences, see: N. A. Troitskii, *Tsarskie sudy protiv revolutionnoi rossii, politicheskie protsessy 1871–1880 gg.* (Saratov: Izdatel'stvo Saratovskogo universiteta, 1976).

—I need neither thanks nor pity. I don't need to have a name.
—Are you prepared to commit crimes?
The girl bowed her head . . .
—I am even prepared to commit crimes.
The voice did not, immediately continue its questioning.
—Do you know—it said at last—that you might lose faith in your present beliefs, you might realize that you deceived yourself and sacrificed your young life in vain?
—I know this, too. And yet I want to enter.
—Enter!
The girl strode across the threshold—and a heavy curtain closed behind her.
—Fool!—hissed someone.
—Saint!—came from somewhere, in reply.[20]

In 1878 the advocates of terror received considerable moral support for their cause, and this, along with the national mood following another exposure of Russia's relative inferiority, its diplomatic humiliation after the Russo-Turkish war of 1877–78, created a favorable climate for escalation of the conflict between the old regime and the revolutionaries. The period 1878–82 is called the crisis of the autocracy by the dean of Soviet historians of this period.[21] The word "crisis" best describes the perceptions of contemporaries during and after the terrorist campaign, which achieved its immediate aim, the assassination of Alexander II, in March 1881. The atmosphere of crisis led the regime to take extraordinary measures to defend itself against terrorism and inspired false hopes in the terrorists of the People's Will that they could achieve their minimum program—a constitutional regime. In Soviet historiography this span of time also embraces "the heroic period" of revolutionary populism. A prominent Western student of the crisis of 1878–82 assigns to the terrorism of this period the blame of precipitating the brutality of the last two reigns, the emergence of a police state, and the general escalation of conflict, with the well-known outcome.[22] Without passing judgment on this last interpretation, it is possible to say with certainty that 1878–82 was the turning point in the history of Russian terrorism. The heroes and heroines of the People's Will established terrorism as a

20. I. S. Turgenev, *Sobranie sochinenii v desiati tomakh* (Moscow: Gosudarstvennoe izdatel'stvo khudozhestvennoi literatury, 1962), 10:24–25. Translated by the author.

21. P. A. Zaionchkovskii, *Krizis samoderzhavie na rubezhe 1870–1880-kh gg.* (Moscow: Izdatel'stvo Moskovskogo universiteta, 1964).

22. Richard Pipes, *Russia Under the Old Regime* (New York: Scribner's, 1974), 298–318. See also Ulam, *In the Name of the People*, 366, 393–94.

noble activity in the eyes of later generations. They created the image of the virtuous assassin.

The terrorist era of 1878–82 also had a major impact on the history of the Russian revolutionary movement from a technical point of view. First, Land and Freedom and then the People's Will achieved a high level of professionalism in their techniques of underground organization. There was a significant division of labor, and not all members became involved in terrorist activity as such.[23] For example, the party managed to plant one of its members, N. V. Kletochnikov, in the offices of the political police, where he had access to information on spies and agents provocateurs. There were technical specialists, such as the dynamite expert N. I. Kibalchich, and expert smugglers, such as A. I. Zundelevich, who arranged the transport of people and printed matter across the borders of the empire. Their professionalism inspired many revolutionaries who did not engage in terror themselves but sought out *narodovol'tsy* as the best instructors in conspiratorial technique. Vladimir Il'ich Ul'ianov (Lenin) is a notable case. It is thus impossible to isolate the history of Russian terrorism from the broader history of the revolutionary movement, including that of social democracy. Both the methods and spectacular activities of terrorist organizations affected the larger movement continuously.

Finally, the Russian movement of the late 1870s yields fascinating material for students of the sociology and psychology of terrorism.[24] It is

23. Assessing the magnitude of the fraction engaging in terror depends on the criteria used for defining party membership and an act of terror. Young finds that 40.3 percent of the membership of Land and Freedom engaged in terrorist activity. On the other hand, he claims that a majority of the People's Will (60.4 percent) engaged in terrorist acts. Young created a scale of terrorist actions with expropriations lowest on the scale, followed by rescue attempts, armed resistance to arrest, killing of spies, then tsarist officials, and finally attempts to assassinate the tsar. See Young, "The Role of the Radical Fraternity in the Turn to Political Terror," 34, 39, 57. This contrasts with the lower figure of 10 percent for the People's Will given in Volk, *Narodnaia Volia, 1879–1882*, 234.

24. So far as sociology is concerned, the figures reveal, once again, that education and age remained the most important variables for predicting revolutionary behavior and its extreme expression, terrorism. See B. N. Mironov and Z. V. Stepanov, *Istorik i Matematika* (Leningrad: Izdatel'stvo "Nauka," 1975), 124–42. A large percentage (30 according to Mironov) of the revolutionaries still came from the gentry. Other studies roughly confirm this figure. People of gentry background became the ideological leaders of terrorism. Lev Tikhomirov and Nikolai Morozov, the main ideologues of terrorism, were both gentry. As in the 1860s, the clerical estate and the urban mercantile strata played significant roles because of the importance of literacy for membership in the revolutionary subculture. Higher education was a significant variable for predicting terrorist activity as well as revolutionary activity in general. Most revolutionary terrorists were young at the time of their participation in terrorist acts. They were generally in their early twenties when they joined the movement (like the Nechaevists) and in their mid-twenties when they engaged

a laboratory for studying conversion to terrorism. The proponents of increasing organizational centralism, secrecy, and terror not only had to overcome their comrades' aversion to any tactic that resembled Nechaevism, they also had to fight against the perception that they were diverting energy from the main tasks of the revolutionary movement—propaganda and agitation among social groups that would fuse into a mass, popular movement and overthrow the regime from below. A typical struggle between Jacobins and anti-Jacobins, terrorists and anti-terrorists, led to the decisive victory of the Jacobins and terrorists. Such moments were repeated in the history of other revolutionary organizations, both populist and Marxist. Assuming that some leaders may have had a personal affinity for paramilitary actions and violence, it is far more interesting to investigate why those who strongly opposed Jacobin methods and terrorism acquiesced in them and then pursued them with grim devotion. The latter group apparently made up the majority of the terrorist movement of the late 1870s and gave it its character.

The study of individual biographies and quantitative analysis yields the following: the commitment to the life of a professional revolutionary is the most important single condition for the emergence of systematic terrorism; the close ties formed in the process of apprenticeship, commitment, shared sacrifices, satisfying organizational work—in short, socialization in a kind of "radical fraternity"—created the emotional basis for acceptance of escalation to increasingly radical tactics.[25] Individuals who had shown no penchant for terror (indeed, who had seemed predisposed against it and had fought it earlier), in accepting terror, showed firmness of commitment, organizational discipline, and, above all, support for their comrades in the movement who had already sacrificed themselves. The conversion of many original *Chaikovtsy* (the advocates of peaceful propaganda who had reacted so strongly against Nechaevism) and *derevenshchiki* (the "villagers" who had opposed the "city" faction and the turn to terrorism) after 1879 is quite revealing. Even more telling is the conversion to terrorism of Peter Lavrov, formerly the foremost propo-

---

in their first terrorist activity. See Young, "The Role of the Radical Fraternity in the Turn to Political Terror," ch. 2, especially tables.

25. According to Young, "Not background or developmental factors, not a terrorist profile or type within the activist movement, but simply involvement in the radical fraternity dictated the course of an individual's revolutionary career. Sharing in this community's collective sense of frustration and rage, of desire for revenge as well as a search for viable, new tactical avenues of revolution, individuals of widely divergent persuasion and personality chose to pursue the same tactical path: political terrorism" ("The Role of the Radical Fraternity in the Turn to Political Terror," 44–45).

nent of "preparationism," that is, of the relatively long-term study and spread of scientific ideas, both in the ranks of revolutionaries and the *narod* in the 1870s. Thus, the escalation of terror led to an odd symbiosis of dignified *teoretiki* of the older generation, dutiful, self-effacing, virtuous assassins like the Russian woman depicted by Turgenev in "The Threshold," and the usual handful of those who had a penchant for becoming a law unto themselves.

The most dramatic moment in the institutionalization of terror occurred in 1878–79. Land and Freedom, an organization that had explicitly subordinated terror to other activities and was reluctant to channel scarce human and material resources into terrorism, split over the new, more rigorous and alarmingly Nechaevist mode of organization proposed by Alexander Mikhailov and over the place of terrorism in the party's program. In the winter of 1878–79 increased terrorism, police raids, the capture of leading disorganizers, Alexander Solov'ev's attempt on the life of Alexander II in April 1879, and even more severe administrative measures had created an atmosphere of crisis. Executions of the captured terrorists in the spring and summer of 1879 added to the escalation of violence. At a conference held in Voronezh in June 1879, the orthodox *narodniki* tried to restrain the growing emphasis on "political" rather than social aims, but the ablest organizers in the party and some of the leading younger theoreticians moved into the camp of the disorganizers. G. V. Plekhanov, the outstanding theoretical mind among the *narodniki*, headed an ephemeral splinter group, the Black Repartition, while Andrei Zheliabov, who emerged from the Voronezh conference as a leading proponent of terror, became the central figure of the People's Will.

THE ERA OF NARODNAIA VOLIA, 1879–1894

Terrorism in 1879 became associated with the politicos in the broader *narodnik* movement, those who concentrated their efforts on producing an immediate change in the structure of the state. A liberal constitutional regime, they believed, would permit them to spread socialist propaganda and achieve their real goal—a federation organized according to socialist principles. The urban-based *politiki* of the People's Will assumed dominance over the *derevenshchiki* (the villagers) in the movement. A recent study suggests that after conversion of the People's Will, *narodniki*, in justifying their decision, tended to exaggerate their own failures among the peasants and the government's repressive measures against them.[26]

26. Hardy, *Land and Freedom*, 132–59.

This in turn suggests that the internal dynamics of the revolutionary subculture rather than a combination of peasant inertia and government repression played the major role in the turn toward terror. The subgroup within the movement that projected the most heroic image won converts with its program and rhetoric. This may seem odd in view of the fact that the terrorists of the People's Will inserted a liberal, constitutional phase in their program—a seeming retreat from the preferred direct path to socialism. However, by going on the attack, they made themselves the apparently more dynamic and optimistic group within the broader *narodnik* movement. By shifting the center of activity to an urban environment, they lightened all of their tasks, whether organizational or propagandistic, and made life more bearable for themselves. Life with the *narod* in rural isolation was burdensome, even for self-sacrificing *derevenshchiki*. Not only the need to assert the vitality of the movement but also the need for affiliation with like-minded people and for a richer cultural milieu apparently played a significant role in the choice of an urban setting. One should add, too, that an urban milieu made detection of revolutionary activity more difficult.

The justifications offered for the turn to terror and for the decision to launch a campaign to assassinate the tsar suggest how difficult it was for most *narodniki* to reconcile themselves to the new tactic. The program of the Executive Committee of the People's Will, first published in the organization's journal on 1 January 1880, summarized the targets and goals of political assassination: Terror would be used against the most harmful members of the regime; it would be used to dispose of spies; it would be invoked in retaliation for the government's most heinous acts. Terrorist successes would show the *narod* that the government was not invincible, raise morale, and instill revolutionary fervor.[27] Thus, terror would presumably be only the catalyst for a wider struggle.

In retrospect, many of the arguments adduced in favor of terrorism by the *narodovol'tsy* in 1879 seem like rationalizations for a tactic based on a longing for heroism—a desire to strike a blow at the highest authority, to perform a *podvig* (heroic deed). Not all of the terrorists were averse to facing the issue directly. Nikolai Morozov, who thought of himself and his comrades as latter-day William Tells and Charlotte Cordays, passionately promoted the philosophy of the heroic deed. However, the majority of the *narodniki* resisted efforts to deny or downplay the central role of the people and the democratic process of revolution. Although the Jacobins rose to prominence in 1879, Lev Tikhomirov, the

27. S. S. Volk, ed., *Revolutionnoe narodnichestvo* (Moscow: Izdatel'stvo "Nauka," 1965), 2:173.

most influential Jacobin and de facto theoretical leader of the People's Will, had to blunt any tactical formulations suggesting a seizure of power, a coup d'état in the name of the people. Jacobinism offended Sof'ia Perovskaia and Andrei Zheliabov, leading terrorists who had only reluctantly accepted terrorism and tried to keep propaganda and agitational activities at the forefront. They reasoned that by assassinating the tsar and crippling the regime, they would hasten a democratic process of self-determination. Through terror they would force concessions culminating in the convocation of a constituent assembly. Like the Social Democrats after them, mainstream adherents of the People's Will believed in the need for a liberal phase of development in preparation for socialism. Hence, they attracted the sympathies of left liberals. Few *narodovol'tsy* agreed with Peter Tkachev, a Jacobin with Blanquist leanings who believed that a socialist revolution had to be made for the people—and as quickly as possible.[28]

Despite the great costs of terrorism, already evident in 1878–79, the *politiki* dominated the *narodnik* movement beginning in 1879 and continued to exercise a decisive influence during the 1880s and 1890s, long after the Executive Committee of the People's Will had been destroyed. Clearly, the appeal of terrorism had little to do with real political achievements, for the assassination of Alexander II yielded a long period of emergency rule and heightened repression. Once the worst part of the regime's crisis of confidence had passed, Alexander III mocked "senseless dreams" of constitution. Not only the feverish dreams of the Jacobins among the *narodovol'tsy* for a seizure of power but hopes for secondary goals quickly faded. However, the mystique of the People's Will lived on. The revolutionary momentum generated by the terrorist activity of 1878–82 sustained the party even though Vera Figner, the last major figure of the executive committee still at large in Russia, was arrested in February 1883.

The heightened attraction of terrorism now more clearly issued from the *podvig* itself, the annihilation of a targeted official, rather than from the attainment of a change in conditions furthering the stated goal of social revolution. Once the People's Will assassinated Alexander II, it assured itself a powerful and enduring mystique and a continuing stream of recruits.[29] The leading figures of the executive committee became

28. Hardy, *Land and Freedom*, 138–44, and *Petr Tkachev, the Critic as Jacobin* (Seattle: University of Washington Press, 1977), 276–302.

29. The total number of persons convicted for connections with Narodnaia Volia between 1881 and 1894 reached the impressive figure of 5,851, of which 27 were executed and 342 either imprisoned or exiled to a labor camp. The remaining 5,482 received less severe sentences. However, these thousands did not launch successful campaigns of terror like

revolutionary celebrities and martyrs after their trial and execution. Although Lavrov had more than a decade earlier called for sober organizational work instead of fanaticism and martyrdom, he now added his support to the People's Will. Shortly before his death in 1883, Karl Marx too gave his blessing to the heroes and heroines of the People's Will, who had shaken one of the pillars of reaction in Europe; and Engels wrote favorably of the valiant struggle of the tsar's heroic opponents.

The People's Will retained its position as Russia's leading revolutionary party long after the assassination of Alexander II, the destruction of the executive committee, and the importation of social democracy. Despite its failure to achieve any of the political and social changes sought in its program, the People's Will still was the only revolutionary party to have wounded the tsarist regime. However, the People's Will showed the schismatic tendencies typical of extremist groups. A split between the *teoretiki* and veterans of the older generation and the "young" *narodovol'tsy* with new tactical ideas emerged by 1884.[30] Based in St. Petersburg and organized with the assistance of the double agent Degaev, the young opposed the post-1881 Jacobins. They sought to reconnect the movement with the villages and factories and to diminish central control. The efforts of the émigrés to retain centralized control failed. When the police arrested German Lopatin, the executive committee's agent, in October 1884, he carried an uncoded list of party members and addresses. This veteran conspirator of almost legendary skill delivered into the hands of the police several hundred members, many of them just recruited into new organizations. The decimation of the People's Will in October–November 1884 led to a change in the party's character and location. The focus of terrorism shifted, once again, to the southern part of the Russian Empire.[31]

After 1884 it became increasingly difficult to sustain the illusion of a united party led by a powerful executive committee. For a time, Lev Tikhomirov of the old executive committee, in Paris, played the role of leading *teoretik*, but one could not speak of a coordinated and centralized party. The parallel existence of a Social Democratic emigration, led by Plekhanov, and growing affiliates in Russia complicated matters. Not only did Narodnaia Volia have to fight internal schisms, it also had to face the challenge of Marxism's growing popularity. However, even after the collapse of 1884, social democracy could not seriously challenge the

those of the original executive committee. For the figures, see Naimark, *Terrorists and Social Democrats*, 42.

30. Naimark, *Terrorists and Social Democrats*, ch. 2; and Offord, *The Russian Revolutionary Movement in the 1880s*, 59–60.

31. Naimark, *Terrorists and Social Democrats*, ch. 4.

mystique of Narodnaia Volia. Those attracted to social democracy by Plekhanov's brilliant polemics nonetheless collaborated with *narodovol'-tsy*. The émigré *teoretiki* trying to enforce party orthodoxies could not counteract the impulse toward collaboration and joint activity among revolutionary groups in this period or, indeed, in later periods of revolutionary ferment.

Defections occurred from the ranks of terrorism, but its appeal remained strong. During the late 1880s, Narodnaia Volia's leading *teoretik*, Tikhomirov, underwent a personal crisis, which led to his break not only with terrorism but with revolutionism. Tikhomirov defected decisively in 1888, definitively ending the sway of the old executive committee over the new recruits still attracted by its mystique. On the other hand, Peter Lavrov, who had at first only reluctantly affiliated himself with Narodnaia Volia, now became a zealous advocate. In keeping with his sense of *partiinost'* (a spirit of loyalty and self-subordination to the leading revolutionary party), Lavrov believed that one had to support the revolutionary party in the special forms it might take at any given historical moment. History had not provided Russia with any better vehicle for prosecuting the cause of socialism. The ecumenical Lavrov had continually adapted himself to what he perceived to be the leading edge of the movement, but in his later years he showed a stubborn, sectarian loyalty to Narodnaia Volia. His rationale for allying himself with Narodnaia Volia reveals, once again, that important figures in the history of Russian terrorism were motivated not by any special penchant for terrorism but by a need to sustain the movement's momentum and to keep alive the organizational nucleus of a revolutionary party.

The terrorist wing of the revolutionary movement had acquired so powerful a mystique that Lavrov could not imagine a nonterrorist group succeeding it as a party nucleus. Moreover, ecumenism aside, Lavrov still asserted Russia's special historical path of development, which had yielded the *narodnik* perspective and Narodnaia Volia. In this respect, his thinking in the mid 1880s harmonized with that of the continuing stream of recruits to Narodnaia Volia. Thus, Lavrov remained a mainstay of the *narodovol'tsy* current as coeditor of *Vestnik Narodnoi Voli* (The messenger of the People's Will) until it ceased publication in 1886, and called for a revival of the old executive committee at the Paris Congress of the Second International in 1889. Like the other *teoretiki*, in emigration he became more sectarian than the home-based *praktiki*. His split with Plekhanov and the Social Democratic Group for the Liberation of Labor did not accurately reflect the trends within Russia.[32]

32. See Philip Pomper, *Peter Lavrov and the Russian Revolutionary Movement* (Chicago: University of Chicago Press, 1972), 208–19.

Although supported by Lavrov and other émigrés more stably committed than Tikhomirov, Russian terrorism did not depend on them for its inspiration. The southern-based terrorists expressed the bitterness and revolutionary zeal of groups with special grievances. The anti-Semitism and pogroms following the assassination of Alexander II and increasing persecution of Jews in the Russian Empire magnified the participation of Jews in the terrorist movement.[33] Although they had played prominent roles in the heroic phase of Narodnaia Volia, only after 1884 did Jewish and other minority figures assume clear dominance in leadership roles. The Bogoraz-Orzhikh (V. G. Bogoraz and B. D. Orzhikh) groups in the South reflected the growing prominence of Jews as terrorists. Their somewhat feverish activity and hopes in 1885 were not matched by any significant results in the form of political assassinations. The government successfully liquidated the southern *narodovol'tsy* in 1886–87 before they could carry out their plans to assassinate the minister of the interior, Tolstoi. However, several revolutionaries who began their careers in the groups of southern *narodovol'tsy* in the mid-1880s later played prominent roles in the creation of the Socialist Revolutionary Party, the twentieth-century resurrection of Narodnaia Volia.[34]

The scene of major action shifted northward again in March 1887, when the government foiled a plot to assassinate Alexander III. Fomented by a group of students at St. Petersburg University, the conspiracy is notable mainly because it involved Alexander Ul'ianov, Lenin's brother, and Bronislaw Pilsudksi, brother of Josef Pilsudski, the future dictator of Poland. Alexander Ul'ianov followed a well-trodden path when he moved from student corporate activities and protests to membership in a terrorist group. Moreover, he exhibited a mixture of social democratic and terrorist notions typical of a significant segment of the revolutionary movement. Like many of the revolutionaries of the 1880s (and of the 1870s as well) he did not find it difficult to accept Marx's authority in economics and simultaneously approve the reasoning behind the commitment to terror.[35]

33. For a recent article on the participation of Jews in Russian terrorism and their motivations, see Zeev Ivianski, "Fathers and Sons: A Study of Jewish Involvement in the Revolutionary Movement and Terrorism in Tsarist Russia," *Terrorism and Political Violence* 1 (April 1989): 137–55.
34. Naimark, *Terrorists and Social Democrats*, 110.
35. Ibid., 143–46. Recent studies of the Shevyrev conspiracy and Ul'ianov's participation, such as Offord and Naimark, accept the standard, idealized version of Ul'ianov's personality and behavior. Under close scrutiny, Alexander Ul'ianov had a suicidal bent. His father's death precipitated a psychological crisis and probably led to his decision to engage in terror—and its likely consequences. Furthermore, he needlessly involved his sister Anna and made her an unwitting accomplice. See E. V. Wolfenstein, *The Revolutionary Personality: Lenin, Trotsky, Gandhi* (Princeton: Princeton University Press, 1967),

The foiling of the plot to assassinate Alexander III did not put an end to the efforts of *narodovol'tsy* to repeat the achievement of the original executive committee, but after Tikhomirov's defection in 1888 the myth of the old party suffered irreparable damage. The failure of the Dembo-Ginsburg conspiracy, which aimed to assassinate Alexander III on 1 March 1889, and the loss of several veteran conspirators significantly lowered the morale of the movement. The provincialization of terrorist conspiracy under the leadership of the Nechaev-like Sabunaev did not save it from the depredations of the Okhrana. Thus, after Lopatin's arrest in 1884, Narodnaia Volia suffered a series of failures and defeats: the arrests of leaders who tried to keep alive the centralized, unified party; the foiling of plots to assassinate Alexander III; increasing defections to social democratic and liberal alternatives or even, in isolated cases, to monarchism, as with Tikhomirov; and finally, the famine of 1891–92, marked by the "dark" behavior of the peasants and an even greater blow to the morale of *narodniki* in general. All of this hastened the end of the era of Narodnaia Volia but by no means signaled an end to the appeal of terror or the disappearance of faith in agrarian revolution.

It is not easy to summarize the position of terrorism among revolutionary groups with differing theories of historical progress. Quite clearly, doctrinal differences counted, but in practice the lines between revolutionary groupings wavered. Most revolutionaries sought ways to sustain the vitality of the movement and to achieve their immediate goal, the replacement of Russia's autocratic system by a liberal, constitutional regime. The reactionary character of the regime during the last two reigns kept a stream of recruits flowing into radical parties. Liberals, Marxists, and *narodovol'tsy* all sought to bring down the autocracy, even though they differed about what would follow. In given circumstances, liberals (later, Kadets) and Marxists (Social Democrats) found it politically expedient to support terrorism. Russian revolutionaries, still thwarted in their efforts at propaganda and agitation, continued to treat terrorism as a necessary weapon against autocracy. However, during the mid-1890s the dramatic growth of labor unrest gave the social democratic movement the impetus it needed to outstrip, at least temporarily, the heirs of Narodnaia Volia. For roughly a decade, until the peasant rebellions of 1902 in the Ukraine and their aftermath, the terrorists of the agrarian wing of the revolutionary movement were eclipsed. Furthermore, the continuous growth of mass unrest in the form of student movements, large-scale agrarian disturbances, strikes in the Russian

---

43–44, and Philip Pomper, *Lenin, Trotsky, and Stalin: The Intelligentsia and Power* (New York: Columbia University Press, 1990), ch. 2.

Empire's industrial centers, and the exacerbation of the grievances of the nationalities in the empire created a far different context for terrorism in the twentieth century.

THE SOCIALIST REVOLUTIONARY PARTY

The SR Party revived the terrorist tradition of Narodnaia Volia in the period 1901–2, but some of the party's pioneering figures rejected its urban orientation and resurrected the notion that socialism might be achieved immediately in the countryside. Revolutionary circles in the Black-Earth zone and Volga (mainly Voronezh, Tambov, and Saratov provinces) stubbornly clung to the *narodnik* belief in the combustibility of the village. The agrarian disturbances in Poltava, Khar'kov, and Saratov in 1902 confirmed their faith. One of the leaders of the Saratov group, Victor Chernov, emigrated, became the SR Party's premier theoretician, and, like earlier *narodnik* theorists, made agrarian socialism the revolution's primary goal. The changing conditions in the villages during the modernization drive under Ministers of Finance I. A. Vyshnegradskii and Sergei Witte had indeed incubated peasant revolutionaries there, as well as in urban centers. Not only did villagers have more contact with the cities through a stratum of workers who maintained ties with the countryside, they themselves were becoming more literate and more open to propaganda. Despite police crackdowns, the mass bases and infrastructure for revolutionary activity expanded. The intelligentsia "third element" working in zemstvos, students rusticated after the student rebellions of 1899–1901, *narodniki* who were veterans from the era of the going to the people and who returned from exile in the mid 1890s, and émigré journalists now found mass constituencies responsive to their propaganda. Terror, too, met with greater success. However, as with earlier phases of the movement, urban centers provided the vast majority of recruits to the revolutionary parties, and the major terrorist campaigns were urban based.[36]

Although numerically few compared to the total perpetrated by less centralized groups, the assassinations organized by the SR Party's combat organization were spectacular because of the high rank of the victims. The repression of the student rebellions of 1899–1901 provided

36. The most thorough study and analysis of the structure and location of SR branches and affiliates is Hildermeier, *Die Sozialrevolutionäre Partei Russlands: Agrarsozialismus und Modernisierung im Zarenreich (1900–1914)*.

terrorist organizations with numerous recruits. One expelled student, P. V. Karpovich, catalyzed the turn to terror by assassinating the minister of education, N. P. Bogolepov, in February 1901. Like Zasulich in 1978, Karpovich acted on his own. Not until April 1902 did SR-sponsored terror achieve its first success, the assassination of D. S. Sipiagin, minister of internal affairs. Next came unsuccessful attempts to remove other "pillars" of the old regime and oppressors of the people, among them, K. P. Pobedonostsev, procurator of the holy synod, and E. P. Obolenskii, governor of Khar'kov, whose brutal suppression of the rebellion in his province in April 1902 had earned him the Order of St. Vladimir. The award was presented by the new minister of internal affairs, V. K. von Plehve, who did not fare as well as Obolenskii. Von Plehve was killed by the SR Combat Organization under the leadership of E. F. Azev in July 1904.

The chief targets of the combat organization were governors, ministers, and police officials who were seen as the main props of the regime and had earned reputations for harshness in suppressing rebellions, whether student or peasant, for sponsoring anti-Semitism, and for other affronts to the revolutionary cause and to human dignity. The rhetoric of the SR publications and the memoirs of participants reveal that revenge was a central motive of the assassinations campaign. As in the mid-1880s, Jews (most notably, G. A. Gershuni, M. R. Gots, and Azev) played a central role in all aspects of terrorism—theoretical, organizational, and technical. Also, in keeping with the trend already noticeable in the mid-1870s, substantial numbers of women became actively involved in revolutionary activities—including terrorism.[37] However, until 1905–6 the revolutionary organizations still drew mainly on the young and the educated, and the leaders of the party continued to be drawn from the ranks of the intelligentsia.[38]

37. According to Maureen Perrie, women constituted 15 percent of the SR Party before 1917 ("The Social Composition and Structure of the Socialist-Revolutionary Party Before 1917," *Soviet Studies* 24, no. 2 [1972]: 235). However, within the combat organization itself during the period 1902–10, there was a relatively high number of women, approximately one-third of the members according to a source cited in James H. Billington, *Fire in the Minds of Men* (New York: Basic Books, 1980), 494. It is notable, too, that a higher percentage of the Jewish contingent (25.4 percent) were women than was true of Great Russians (13.3 percent), for example (Perrie, "The Social Composition and Structure of the Socialist-Revolutionary Party Before 1917," 237). Other students of terrorism suggest higher figures for women terrorists in the Russian movement as a whole. Walter Laqueur writes that "almost a quarter" of Russian terrorists were women, but does not elaborate (*The Age of Terrorism* [Boston: Little, Brown, 1987], 79).

38. Studies of the social composition of the SR Party for the peak years 1905–7 yield the following: Of those engaged in terrorist activity, roughly half (90 of 179) called themselves

Under Gershuni's leadership, the combat organization gained virtual autonomy from the Central Committee of the SR Party and became a law unto itself, a squad of avengers. This arrangement played into the hands of Azev, one of the most puzzling figures in the history of the revolutionary movement. Azev, all the while in the pay of the Okhrana, skillfully maneuvered between the SR Combat Organization and the tsarist security network. One hypothesis asserts that he permitted the assassination of von Plehve because he sought revenge for the Kishinev pogrom of April 1903, which he blamed on von Plehve.[39] After Gershuni's arrest in July 1906, Azev became the main organizer of terror and, as member of both the SR Central Committee and the SR Combat Organization, the leading *praktik* in the SR Party operating in Russia. Only the émigré sponsor of terror, M. R. Gots, had similar status. Within Russia, Boris Savinkov rose to a position second only to Azev in the combat organization, which achieved its most notable successes during the period July 1904–February 1905.

The appearance of personalities like Azev and Savinkov alongside figures like I. P. Kaliaev and Dora Brilliant, whom Camus called *assassins purs*, brings home once again the heterogeneity of the recruits of terrorism. Kaliaev assassinated Grand Duke Sergei Alexandrovich in February 1905, only after showing a degree of humanity not commonly found among contemporary terrorists. Although within killing distance of the grand duke's carriage, he did not throw his bomb earlier, when he knew it would endanger the lives of the grand duke's wife and children. Assassins like Kaliaev embodied the ethic of self-sacrifice for the cause. They scrupulously narrowed their sights to the targeted evil, shrank from violence that would take innocent lives, and on principle gave up their lives in payment for the lives they took. They often showed little sense of politics and resented the reluctance with which the SRs supported terror.

---

workers. As noted by Perrie, about 70 percent of the "worker" terrorists who operated in the heavily Jewish area of the Russian Empire, the "pale of settlement," were probably more literate and had powerful motives of revenge because of anti-Semitism. Furthermore, the "workers" were more likely to be artisans, employees of small workshops, rather than factory workers. Those who declared themselves peasants accounted for only about one-ninth (20 of 179) of the SRs engaged in terrorist actions, considerably less than those who called themselves intellectuals (37). The median age of SR terrorists in 1906–7 was 22.1 years, quite similar to earlier generations of terrorists. See Maureen Perrie, "Political and Economic Terror in the Tactics of the Russian Socialist-Revolutionary Party before 1914," in *Social Protest, Violence, and Terror in Nineteenth- and Twentieth-Century Europe*, ed. Wolfgang J. Mommsen and Gerhard Hirschfeld (New York: St. Martin's Press, 1982), 67–68.

39. Boris Nicolaevsky, *Aseff, the Spy*, trans. George Reavey (Garden City, N.Y.: Doubleday, Doran and Company, 1934), 68–69.

Like Narodnaia Volia, the SR Party did not condone terror in states where parliamentary regimes permitted political opposition. Yet Kaliaev felt kinship with Italian and French terrorists and could not accept the party's point of view. However meticulous he himself might be about killing innocents during acts of terror, Kaliaev would not condemn terrorists like Ravachol, who did take innocent lives.[40] The zealots of the combat organization found it difficult to observe party discipline, to weigh priorities and resources, and to forgo opportunities for terror against appropriate targets. Savinkov saw the combat organization as a sort of military brotherhood, which claimed his absolute loyalty and devotion, a loyalty far more intense than anything he felt for the party as a whole. Indeed, the party's scruples and efforts to rein in terror created perpetual tension between him and them. The tendency of the SR leaders to call a halt to terror campaigns when they felt the political situation in Russia no longer warranted it, and Azev's game with the Okhrana, which made him stall and call off terror at times, created a difficult situation for the zealots.

After February 1905 new Okhrana infiltration crippled the efforts of the combat organization.[41] Their successes had been spectacular in nature but few in number. In October 1905 the October Manifesto further complicated matters. The SR Party's theorists could not easily justify terrorism after a parliamentary regime had been won, but the terrorists wanted to sustain their campaign. The central committee voted to suspend operations but to preserve the combat organization and hold it in readiness in the event of counterrevolution. In November 1905 the central committee reoriented the party toward the larger social and economic tasks that presumably lay open after the October Manifesto and its promise of a parliament. However, at its First Congress in December 1905–January 1906 the party reversed itself and reactivated the combat organization. The regime had shown its will to fight back. It had dissolved both the St. Petersburg Soviet and the Moscow Soviet, the latter in armed struggle. The relative strength of the tsarist forces and weakness of the revolutionaries convinced the SRs that they still needed the weapon of terror. Once again, Azev took command, seconded by

40. Boris Savinkov, *Souvenirs d'un terroriste* (Paris: Editions champ libre, 1982), 80.

41. At this time, the Okhrana recruited Nikolai Tatarov, a long-time SR, as agent provocateur. Tatarov became an agent and then member of the central committee. With Tatarov working for them, the Okhrana had the luxury of two highly placed agents in the SRs, and this naturally worked to the discomfiture of Azev. See Nicolaevsky, *Azeff, the Spy*, 111–27. For a systematic study of Okhrana infiltration of the SRs, see Nurit Schleifman, *Undercover Agents in the Russian Revolutionary Movement: The SR Party, 1902–14* (New York: St. Martin's Press, 1988), ch. 1.

Savinkov and Moiseenko, but the provisional character of the SR commitment to terror and Azev's double-dealing kept the successes of the
combat organization to a minimum.[42]

In 1905–6 massive strikes, peasant actions against landlords and local
authorities, the appearance of soviets and peasant unions, and the
recruitment of tens of thousands into Socialist Revolutionary and Social
Democratic organizations created both opportunities and dilemmas for
the revolutionary parties. Varying reactions to the peaks and troughs of
the revolution of 1905 led not only to the revival of the combat organization but to the splitting off of the Popular Socialists on the right and the
Maximalists on the left. The government's efforts to split the broad
revolutionary front by a combination of concessions and use of force
eventually led to the isolation of the more radical elements, some of
which engaged in actions not easily distinguished from banditry or pure
anarchism. In 1906, contrary to the official SR program, the Maximalists
called for the immediate institution of socialism in both industry and
agriculture. Advocates of "agrarian terror" since 1904, the Maximalists
sponsored a wide array of violent actions (arson, theft, murder) against
the landowners and the regime that protected them, and had little
inclination for painstakingly prepared assassination campaigns.[43] At first,
the Maximalists actually benefited from the party's repudiation of them,
in view of the crippling of the combat organization by Azev's betrayals.
They financed their independence by the successful expropriation of
several hundred thousand rubles from the Moscow Society of Mutual
Credit in the spring of 1906.[44] It should be noted, however, that the style
of terrorist activity engaged in by the Maximalists (bombings, holdups,
shootings, arson) merged with the swelling wave of decentralized, open
violence of 1905–7 and should be distinguished from the traditionally
centralized terrorist campaigns typical of Russian terrorism since the
advent of Narodnaia Volia. Little distinguished the Maximalists from the
anarchists, whose heavily Jewish personnel made cities with large Jewish
populations the scene of intense violence. The pogroms of 1905 played
more than a small role in precipitating the terrorist epidemic of 1906–7.[45]

42. The SRs decided to abandon terror once again after the opening of the Duma in May
1906. The combat organization managed only a partially successful attempt on the governor-
general of Moscow, Dubasov, a few days before the opening of the Duma. Dubasov was
disabled but not killed by the attack.

43. M. I. Sokolov, a leader of the Maximalists, had advocated agrarian terror as early
as 1904. See Maureen Perrie, *Agrarian Policy of the Russian Socialist-Revolutionary
Party*, 94–97.

44. Ibid., 156.

45. For the anarchists, see Paul Avrich, *The Russian Anarchists* (New York: W. W.
Norton, 1978), esp. ch. 2.

However, the sensational successes of the Maximalists made them a focus of Okhrana activity and led to their quick demise, partly with Azev's collusion. In mid-1907, within a few months after the arrest of Sokolov, their most dynamic and effective leader, the SR Maximalists became defunct.[46]

Terror achieved an epidemic form in the context of a mass movement and massive recruitment into all of the revolutionary parties. The heroic deeds of 1902–5, the successful early phases of the revolution of 1905, followed by pogroms and delayed but ultimately forceful repression of both urban and rural movements by the military might of the regime, brought the most militant elements together. Party affiliation and ideological prescriptions could not prevent sympathy for terror or even participation in it. The image of the morally justified revolutionary avenger gripped not only the combat organization but revolutionaries of all stripes. Both aggressive self-defense and efforts to keep the revolution alive by violence inspired militants to ignore usual party lines and collaborate in armed struggle during the latter part of 1905. By the end of 1905 the regime had crushed the mass movement in the major cities. After the failure of the uprising of the Moscow Soviet during December 1905, efforts at partisan actions merged almost imperceptibly with the wave of terrorism of 1906–7.[47]

Although violence increased massively during 1906–7, the increasing awkwardness of Azev's position and the Okhrana's changing character led to the crippling of centrally organized political terror.[48] Azev frus-

46. For a brief summary of the Maximalist movement, see Spiridovich, *Histoire du terrorisme russe, 1886–1917*, ch. 14.

47. Some figures presented in a recent article by Anna Geifman ("The Kadets and Terrorism, 1905–7," *Jahrbücher für Geshchichte Osteuropas* 36 [1988]: 250–51) suggest the extent of the violence in this period. From October 1905 through April 1906, 288 employees of the Ministry of the Interior were killed and 383 wounded. At the end of October 1906 the toll of all government officials killed or wounded had reached 3,611. By the end of 1907 the figure was approximately 4,500 officials killed or wounded. During 1905–7 terrorists killed 2,180 private citizens and wounded 2,530. The total casualties, killed and wounded, official and private for 1905–7, therefore exceeded 9,000. Another estimate presented in the Duma in 1907 showed 6,580 killed by terrorists, and this suggests a far greater casualty total than 9,000. See ibid., 250 n. 18. Estimates of those killed by terrorists vary widely, with Trotsky presenting figures of 233, 768, and 1,231 for 1905, 1906, and 1907, respectively, without presenting a source (*Stalin* [New York: Grosset and Dunlap, 1941], 95).

48. This can be appreciated by comparing the casualties cited above for the overall campaign of terror and SR-sponsored terror. In 1902 there were two acts of terror; in 1903, three; in 1904, one. There were fifty-one such acts for 1905; seventy-eight for 1906; and sixty-two for 1907. As noted above, these were by far the peak years for terror in the Russian Empire. After this, terror dropped off precipitately. In 1908–11 there were eight acts in all. Thus, in the period of 1902–11, there were 205 acts of SR-sponsored terror, with

trated the SR Combat Organization's campaign to assassinate Peter Stolypin, tsarist Russia's first prime minister under the new parliamentary arrangement. After dissolving the First Duma, Stolypin became a target, but not only for the combat organization. The Maximalists conducted their own campaign and succeeded in destroying Stolypin's villa in August 1906, with heavy loss of life—but not Stolypin's.[49] In the bizarre aftermath, Azev, trying to save his own position with the Okhrana, convinced the Central Committee of the SR Party to disclaim responsibility for the bombing of the villa and to condemn the Maximalists' attempt. The upshot of all of the maneuvering and failure to achieve any spectacular results was the resignation of Azev and Savinkov from their leading positions in the combat organization, which was reconstituted with less autonomy under the leadership of Leon Zilberberg at the SR Soviet in October 1906.

Not just Russian revolutionary terrorism but the movement as a whole was powerfully affected by the interaction of the revolutionaries and the regime's political police, an interaction that one prominent student of revolutionism has called "the symbiosis of extremes."[50] As noted above, the Third Section, the old internal security agency organized by Nicholas I, had been abolished in 1880 and was soon replaced by the Okhrana. The regime rapidly professionalized its security forces during the crisis precipitated by the People's Will and increasingly relied on agents provocateurs, a reliance suggested by the emergency measures established in France under Napoléon III. The Russian security agencies not only infiltrated the revolutionary parties at the highest levels, they also competed with the revolutionaries in organizing workers. The labor organizations of S. V. Zubatov and G. A. Gapon played central roles in

---

all but fourteen occurring in 1905–7. Moreover, the targets were often impressive, among them two ministers; thirty-three governors, governors-general, and vice-governors; sixteen mayors, section chiefs of the Okhrana, chiefs of police, procurators, assistants to procurators, and section chiefs of detectives; twenty-four prison chiefs and supervisors of exile labor camps and jails; twenty-six police officers and district police officers and their assistants; seven generals and admirals; fifteen colonels; eight barristers; and twenty-six spies and agents provocateurs. Furthermore, most of the targets were killed or wounded. See Perrie, "Political and Economic Terror," 67; K. V. Gusev, *Partiia eserov, ot melkoburzhuaznogo revoliutsionizma k kontr-revoliutsii* (Moscow: Izdatel'stvo "Mysl'," 1975), 75; and Radkey, *The Agrarian Foes of Bolshevism*, 69.

49. The regime responded to this sensational act of terror, in which twenty-seven people were killed and Stolypin's two children wounded, with field courts-martial and swift "justice." They executed 1,144 by April 1907 by this method and more than two thousand additional persons by ordinary courts-martial in 1905–8. By August 1907 the police had arrested or exiled approximately fifteen thousand SRs. See Schleifman, *Undercover Agents in the Russian Revolutionary Movement*, 65.

50. The phrase is James Billington's from *Fire in the Minds of Men*, 469.

the workers' movement before and during 1905. The regime clearly lost control over the police agencies charged with the suppression of movements threatening its existence. Both the massive character of the revolutionary movement and the hypertrophy of the police network reflected the complex and, ultimately, doomed effort of the regime to modernize and rebuild its might yet simultaneously maintain control over the forces unleashed by economic and social change. In 1912, on the eve of World War I, the Okhrana had a large permanent staff, although there is disagreement about its size. Estimates range widely. One places the permanent staff at fifty thousand and paid agents at twenty-six thousand.[51] Bizarre figures like Azev, Zinaida Zhuchenko (who participated in the Moscow uprising of December 1905 and infiltrated the SR Moscow Regional Committee), Solomon Ryss (an SR Maximalist double agent), and Dmitrii Bogrov (a former anarchist and self-declared SR who killed Stolypin while in the employ of the police) embodied the "symbiosis" of the police and the revolutionaries, just as Gapon epitomized the confusion of identity of those who began as agents of the regime, switched over to the revolutionaries, and then faltered and once again collaborated with the Okhrana.[52] Although Azev escaped the revenge of his SR colleagues and died a natural death in 1918, Gapon's double-dealing was discovered, and he was assassinated by the SRs in April 1906.

The decentralization of terror in 1906, with the formation of several SR combat groups, complicated matters for the Okhrana, as well as for Azev and Savinkov. "Flying detachments," particularly of the northern organization, distinguished themselves.[53] The year 1907 began with a series of three assassinations organized by Zilberberg and Albert Trauberg ("Karl"), both resourceful and dynamic leaders. Although the Okhrana captured Zilberberg and Trauberg in 1907, they discovered that they were paying too high a price without Azev. The survivors of Zilberberg's group began to plot the assassination of Nicholas II, this time with Azev's knowledge. Fully informed, Prime Minister Stolypin used the intelligence on the SR plot both to foil it in April 1907 and to attack the SRs, who were participating in the Second Duma. Stolypin's strategy for dissolution of the Second Duma depended on the work of the Okhrana's agents provocateurs, who provided documents revealing Socialist Revolutionary and Social Democratic conspiracies to kill the

51. Laqueur, *The Age of Terrorism*, 134. The figures relied on by Laqueur are challenged by Schleifman, who believes that the number of salaried secret agents "hardly exceeded a few thousand." See Schleifman, *Undercover Agents in the Russian Revolutionary Movement*, 48.

52. For a brief survey of Gapon's career, see Nicolaevsky, *Azeff, the Spy*, 137–48.

53. Spiridovich, *Histoire du terrorisme russe, 1886–1917*, ch. 13.

tsar and to foment mutiny in the armed forces. At no point did the Okhrana's methods developed in the struggle against terror have greater political consequences. With a new electoral law under Stolypin's "coup d'état" of June 1907 and a more compliant Third Duma, the regime bought itself a few years of relative stability.

Stolypin's actions only spurred SR determination. After the dissolution of the Second Duma, the SRs decided to go ahead with a concerted effort to assassinate Nicholas II, this time by reconstituting the old combat organization. Gershuni and Azev took charge once again. With Azev at the helm, the spectacular deeds planned for 1907, including blowing up the State Council, did not materialize. By February 1908 with Azev's help the Okhrana had thwarted the last major SR campaign, but the assassination of the tsar remained a possibility. Azev now remained the unchallenged chief of terror, for Gershuni had died in 1907. Azev did not always play the Okhrana's game. But for a quirk of fate, Nicholas II might have been assassinated with Azev's complicity while on board the cruiser Riurik on 7 October 1908. However, before the end of 1908 Vladimir Burtsev, a Paris-based revolutionary who, with help of repentant Okhrana agents, became the movement's chief unmasker of agents provocateurs, provided the SRs with sufficient information to convict Azev. The SRs formally accused him in January 1909. The Azev scandal affected not only the revolutionaries but the government, which was forced to try A. A. Lopukhin, Azev's former employer, who had betrayed him to Burtsev. The Okhrana's intrigues with Azev yielded, on the one hand, the crushing of the revolutionary movement and, on the other, a revelation of the methods to which the regime had stooped in order to combat terror. According to Boris Nicolaevsky, after the revelations of 1908–9 "the terror as a method of fighting became politically and psychologically impossible."[54] The prerevolutionary era of the virtuous terrorist who killed and died in the name of the people thus came to an end with the Azev scandal.

The violent actions, including carefully planned "expropriations" engaged in by the revolutionary parties beginning in 1905, had revealed that the ideological line dividing anarchists from Social Revolutionaries and Social Democrats (particularly Bolsheviks) did not prevent consider-

---

54. Nicolaevsky, *Aseff, the Spy*, 287. For an interesting study of the impact of the revelation that Azev was an agent provocatuer, see Schleifman, *Undercover Agents in the Russian Revolutionary Movement*, chs. 2–4. According to Schleifman, "The dam that burst in the wake of the affair and its aftermath did more damage to the party than the storm that struck it during the exposure itself. From this point of view, the Azef affair is perhaps better likened to a cluster bomb which goes off in phases, each phase deadlier than the last" (119).

able crossing over into common activities. However, by 1909–10 terrorism had brought the major revolutionary parties to the lowest point in their history as mass parties. The use of force and fraud to acquire funds needed to support party activities and to gain advantages in factional struggle discredited Lenin and, alongside other problems, led to the virtual disintegration of his faction. The discovery of Azev's double-dealing in 1908 virtually destroyed the sustaining myth of Russian terrorism, what one historian calls their theodicy of violence.[55] So long as the SRs believed in the purity of their motives and the heroic character of their actions, they could live with the existence of secret, autonomous, costly terrorist operations. Once tainted, however, the combat organization could not easily justify its existence. For all practical purposes, the centralized organization of terror ceased to exist in prerevolutionary Russia after the Azev scandal. The discovery of the machinations of Okhrana agents behind the most glorious acts of heroic terrorism brought the era of Russian revolutionary terrorism to an inglorious end.

To be sure, postrevolutionary politics provided an epilogue to the history of Russian revolutionary terrorism. The left SRs who had allied themselves with the Bolsheviks after the October Revolution turned terror against the new rulers of Russia after the peace treaty of Brest-Litovsk was signed by the Central Powers and Russia in March 1918. Maria Spiridonova declared on 24 June 1918 that it was time to revive terror against the agents of German imperialism.[56] The left SRs directed their wrath first against the German ambassador, Count Wilhelm von Mirbach, whom they assassinated on 6 July 1918. After splitting from the party during the summer of 1918, a terrorist wing led by Boris Kamkov and Irina Kakhovskaia went underground. On 1 August 1918 Kakhovskaia's and Boris Donskoi's group in the Ukraine assassinated General Hermann von Eichorn in Kiev. In the summer of 1918 left SR terrorists assassinated such major high-ranking Bolsheviks as V. Volodarskii and M. S. Uritskii. On 5 September 1919 they exploded a bomb in the building that housed the Moscow Committee of the Communist Party, leaving twelve dead, including the party secretary, V. M. Zagorskii, and thirty wounded, most notably Nikolai Bukharin.[57] However, the Communist regime under Lenin showed a fierce will to retain

55. Manfred Hildermeier, "Terrorist Strategies in Russia, 1900–14," in Social Protest, Violence and Terror, ed. Mommsen and Hirschfeld, 86. The most recent and also most thorough study of this period is Anna Geifman, Thou Shalt Kill: Revolutionary Terror in Russia, 1894–1917 (Princeton, N.J.: Princeton University Press, 1993).

56. Isaac Steinberg, Spiridonova (Freeport: Books for Libraries Press, 1971), 209.

57. Gusev, Partiia eserov, 308, and Leonard Schapiro, The Origin of the Communist Autocracy (New York: Praeger, 1965), 126.

exclusive power and consolidated its control during 1918–22. The show trial of twenty-four SR leaders that took place in Moscow during the summer of 1922 is a historical coda to the story of Russian revolutionary terrorism. The Communist regime put an end to the heirs of the People's Will and subjected the peasants, the first love of Russian revolutionaries, to forms of state terror previously unknown in modern history.

SUMMARY AND CONCLUSIONS

The following conclusions can be drawn about the appearance and role of terror during the cycles of the revolutionary movement in Russia:

1. Before the appearance of Narodnaia Volia, isolated efforts to assassinate Alexander II created ambivalence about terror. Karakozov became a heroic martyr figure, but Nechaev's murder of a "traitor" inspired revulsion. Nechaevism probably delayed the onset of systematic terror and affected the moral tenor of the movement. The heroic (self-sacrificing) deed, often an individual act of revenge against a harsh official or a symbolic blow against the regime's center, the tsar, became the major goal of Russian terrorism during the era of Narodnaia Volia, despite attempts to rationalize terror and give it concrete political and social aims. Although aberrant (suicidal, paranoid) individuals joined terrorist groups, they were exceptional. Membership in a terrorist organization signified commitment to the movement, to the "radical fraternity," and acceptance of tactics that, for whatever reason, at a given moment seemed to be the only way to sustain the vitality and momentum of the revolutionary movement. Narodnaia Volia's assassination of Alexander II was sufficiently spectacular to sustain revolutionary morale despite the executive committee's failure to force a change in the regime.

2. After the destruction of the executive committee, terrorist actions were widely planned during the 1880s and 1890s, but with no striking successes. Rather, the mystique of Narodnaia Volia insured continued recruitment, the perpetuation of the conspiratorial tradition, and the continuation of the heroic duel with high authorities. No firm line separated narodovol'tsy from Social Democrats in practice in Russia during much of this period, but the heroic image of Narodnaia Volia overshadowed social democracy until the mid-1890s.

3. In 1902 the SRs revived the tradition of Narodnaia Volia and achieved striking successes between 1902 and 1905. The massive violence of the period 1905–7 included the tradition of centrally organized terror, but terror was no longer conducted solely by the lonely heroic student or

the professionally exacting small organization subordinated (although perhaps autonomous in its sphere) by a broader party guided by intelligentsia *teoretiki*. The widespread violence of the period verged on guerrilla warfare. The most militant revolutionaries, including Lenin, thought of themselves as conducting partisan actions and paid greater attention to the military requirements of the insurrection. However, they did not have the goals that one might expect of genuine guerrilla leaders. For the most part urban-based, they aimed for social revolution, a mass uprising against the regime, rather than the consolidation of their small bands into larger units to liberate zones by means of military operations and to create their own government in such zones.[58] On the regime's side, despite numerous casualties at all levels of its administration, it still commanded sufficient security forces, military strength, and political will to deal with centrally organized terror against the royal family, ministers, and governors and with the less meticulously organized acts of violence by increasingly nonintelligentsia affiliates of the SR Party, Maximalists, anarchists, and Bolsheviks.

4. Receptivity to terror as a weapon did not necessarily signify lack of political acumen or a quixotic and self-destructive mentality. Rather, it sometimes signified militancy and a will to power particularly suited to the political context in which Russian revolutionaries found themselves. To be sure, one might question (as some Socialist Revolutionaries and Social Democrats did) the expenditure of party resources on centralized terrorist ventures, easily infiltrated by the Okhrana and only infrequently yielding spectacular results. It is difficult to measure the efficacy of terrorism as such for the revolution. It has been argued that the regime's response to terror destroyed any chances for reform. In this view, terror caused a hardening of the regime, the hypertrophy of the police apparatus, and a narrowing of alternatives. However, the courage of the terrorists, their ability to attract both sympathy and admiration, kept the tradition powerful and probably enhanced the popularity of both Narodnaia Volia and its heir, the SR Party. Each in its day convinced the left wing of the liberal parties of the efficacy of terror in bringing about a change of regime. The SRs inspired some of the Bolsheviks to follow suit during 1905–7. Furthermore, the SRs, a party associated with terror as well as with agrarian socialism, won considerably more votes than any other party in the elections to the Constituent Assembly in November 1917.

5. The striking failures of SR leadership and organization played into

58. See Laqueur's distinction between guerrilla and terrorist movements in *The Age of Terrorism*, 5.

the hands of tsarist agents before 1917 and into Lenin's during and after 1917. Even granting this, had Lenin played by the political rules of the game long understood by socialist parties in Russia and still in force in 1917, an SR-led government might have been legally established in 1918. But given Lenin's will to power and the inability of SR leaders to create a party capable of rule, the SR Party could exploit neither its popularity nor the legal advantage won in Russia's first free elections. Despite the last, desperate actions of the left SRs, the SRs fell, as did the other parties, to Lenin's Bolsheviks. Although formally eschewing individual terror, Lenin had shown considerable flexibility in his approach to terror and was not at all reluctant to establish and sustain postrevolutionary state terror. Stalin, who knew the revolutionary tradition well and whose fear of a revival of revolutionary terrorism affected his behavior in the mid-1930s, far outdid his mentor in exercising state terror on a vast scale.

Part II

Modern Revolutionary Terrorism

4

Left-Wing Terrorism in Italy

Donatella della Porta

It is probably not far from the truth to say that terrorism is, for Italians, the single most important political phenomenon in their memory of the 1970s. In the same period, similar political violence emerged in other Western democracies. However, only in Italy did it reach such intensity and persistence as to be considered a serious challenge to the regime. A

The information used in this chapter was collected by the author in the framework of a wider research program on political violence and terrorism led by the Carlo Cattaneo Institute of Bologna since 1981. This study is part of my Ph.D. dissertation at the European University Institute. A revised version of the dissertation is in Donatella della Porta, *Il terrorismo di sinistra* (Bologna: Il Mulino, 1990). I wish to thank Martha Crenshaw, Robin Wagner-Pacifici, and Leonard Weinberg for their helpful comments.

few figures, referring to the years between 1969 and 1982, help to recall the climate of that period: 4,362 events of political violence; 6,153 unclaimed bombings against property; 2,712 attacks for which terrorist groups claimed responsibility, 324 of which were against people, with 768 injured and 351 killed; 657 denominations used by dozens of underground organizations;[1] and thousands of militants involved in the "armed struggle." Moreover, terrorism is usually considered to have been a constant presence during all of the 1970s and part of the 1980s.

What is now called terrorism took very different forms. It is worth noting, for instance, that the term "terrorism" started to be used by media and public opinion only in the second half of the 1970s. The political violence of the first half of the decade was instead called by different names: extremism, subversivism, *squadrismo*, and *stragismo*. The slaughters perpetrated by neofascist groups—seventeen people killed on 12 December 1969 by a bomb in the Bank of Agriculture in Milan, six killed on a train in July 1970, eight killed during a union meeting in Brescia, and twelve killed on a train near Bologna in 1974—had been, indeed, the most brutal forms of political violence when it came mainly from the radical Right.[2] In the same years, leftist groups also started to turn to violence, but it was largely unorganized. Left-wing terrorism was almost unknown to the larger public at least until 1976. It was only in the second half of the 1970s that left-wing terrorism started to attract the attention of the media and public opinion.[3]

Many analysts tried to understand the reasons for such a long and widespread wave of political violence. Most of them explained terrorism

1. See Donatella della Porta and Maurizio Rossi, *Cifre crudeli: Bilancio dei terrorismi italiani* (Bologna: Cattaneo, 1984), 18–19, 44, and 60–61, and idem, "I terrorismi in Italia tra il 1969 e il 1982," in *Il sistema politico italiano*, ed. Gianfranco Pasquino (Bari: La Terza, 1985), 418–56.

2. On right-wing terrorism in Italy, see R. Minna, "Il terrorismo di destra," in *Terrorismi in Italia*, ed. Donatella della Porta (Bologna: Il Mulino, 1984), 21–73; F. Ferraresi, "La destra eversiva," in ibid., 227–93; and Enrico Pisetta, "Per una storia del terrorismo nero," *Il mulino* 32 (1983): 738–70.

3. Journalistic accounts include P. Agostini, *Mara Cagol: Una donna nelle prime Brigate rosse* (Padua: Marsilio, 1980); Giorgio Bocca, *Il terrorismo italiano, 1970–1978* (Milan: Rizzoli); idem, *Noi terroristi: 12 anni di lotta armata ricostruiti e discussi con i protagonisti* (Milan: Garzanti, 1985); Ido Faré and Franco Spirito, *Mara e le altre* (Milan: Feltrinelli, 1979); Luigi Manconi, *Vivere con il terrorismo* (Milan: Mondadosi, 1979); Giorgio Manzini, *Indagini su un brigatista rosso* (Turin: Einaudi, 1979); Roberto Mazzetti, *Genesi e sviluppo del terrorismo in Italia* (Rome: Armando, 1979); Gianpaolo Pansa, *Storie italiane di violenza e terrorismo* (Rome: La Terza, 1980); Vincenzo Tessandori, *BR, imputazione banda armata* (Milan: Garzanti, 1977); Alessandro Silj, *Mai pì senza fucile* (Florence: Vallecchi, 1977); Soccorso Rosso, *Le Br* (Milan: Feltrinelli, 1976); and idem, *Napoli, I Nap* (Milan: Feltrinelli, 1976).

in terms of some "Italian peculiarity" in economic, social, political, or cultural systems. My approach takes terrorist organizations as the main focus of research and uses sociological categories developed for the study of phenomena with which terrorism shares some characteristics. Terrorist groups are considered here as special forms of political organizations. Terrorism is defined as the activity of those clandestine organizations that, by a continued and almost exclusive use of illegal forms of action, aim to attain their political goals through profound transformations of state institutions. Terrorist groups are, nevertheless, distinctive. They can be seen as secret societies, persistent types of relations that bind participants in secret activities.[4] They are also high-risk institutions,[5] since participation creates high probabilities of deep disruption in everyday life. And they are greedy institutions, insofar as "they seek exclusive and undivided loyalties and they attempt to reduce the claims of competing roles and status positions on those they wish to encompass within their boundaries."[6]

This analysis of Italian left-wing terrorism is divided into three parts in order to deal with three different levels: society, group, and individual. In the first part, the preconditions for the rise of terrorism are sought in the social and political structure. In the second, the organizational dynamics of terrorist groups are taken into account. In the third part, the individual motivations are analyzed. These three analytical levels of the research on terrorism are synthesized in Figure 4.1. An explanation of terrorism should be able to identify the web of resources that underground organizations draw from their environment, which are in turn influenced by the outcomes of terrorist activities. Intersections between individuals and organizations can be conceptualized in terms of mobilization theory and militance theory. The first refers to the incentives that underground organizations offer to individuals. The second refers to the motivations behind an individual's decision to participate.

Empirical evidence is presented on the social origins and political backgrounds of terrorists as well as on the structures, actions, and ideologies of underground groups. Trial records and the daily press have been consulted to provide information on thirteen armed groups.[7] A

---

4. B. H. Erickson, "Secret Societies and Social Structures," *Social Forces* 60 (1981): 189.

5. See Doug McAdam, *Political Process and the Development of Black Insurgency, 1930–1970* (Chicago: University of Chicago Press, 1982).

6. Lewis Coser, *Greedy Institutions: Patterns of Undivided Commitment* (New York: Free Press, 1974), 4.

7. The data refer to the four most important organizations: the Red Brigades (Brigate Rosse, BR), the Proletarian Armed Groups (Nuclei Armati Proletari, NAP), Front Line (Prima Linea, PL), and the Communist Fighting Formations (Formazioni Comuniste Combattenti, FCC). The "minor" groups are the Armed Fighting Formations (Formazioni

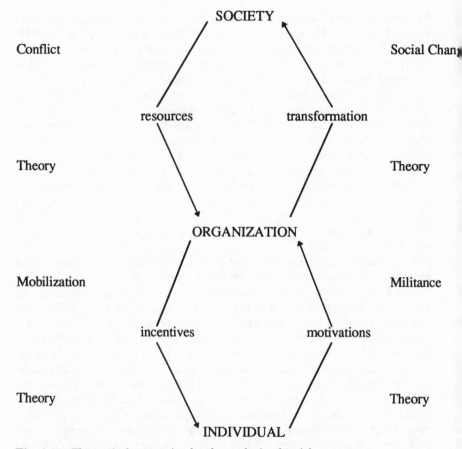

Fig. 4.1. Theoretical categories for the analysis of social movements

---

Armate Combattenti, FAC), the Communist Fighting Units (Unità Comuniste Combattenti, UCC), the Communist Attack Division (Reparti Comunisti d'Attacco, RCA), the Armed Proletarians for Communism (Proletari Armati per il Comunismo, PAC), the Red Guerrilla (Guerriglia Rossa, GR), later called the 28th of March Brigade (Brigata 28 Marzo), the Lo Muscio Brigade (Brigata Lo Muscio), the Revolutionary Communist Movement (Movimento Comunista Rivoluzionario, MCR), the For Communism (Per il Comunismo), and the Nuclei. On all these organizations, I collected qualitative information related to their ideologies and structures in the different phases of their histories. Also, using trial records as a source, I built two data sets for quantitative analysis. In one, almost twelve hundred attacks carried out by terrorist organizations between 1970 and 1983 are recorded, with information on the time, the place, the targets, the forms of action, and the outcomes of each event. In the second, information on personal registry office data, social origins, and political activities of more than one thousand members of underground organizations is recorded.

second source of information is a series of twenty-eight life histories, based on interviews with former left-wing terrorists.[8]

POLITICAL-OPPORTUNITY STRUCTURES AND THE ITALIAN TERRORIST CYCLE

The emergence and evolution of left-wing terrorism can be understood as the effect of an internally differentiated strategic adaptation within the social-movement sector to the different phases of protest cycles in relation to the available political-opportunity structure.[9] In order to explain terrorism, it is necessary to look at the interactions between protesters and authorities, as well as the interactions between the different organizations active during the protest.[10] What follows describes the evolution of the opportunity structure in the different stages of the protest and for the different actors involved in it.

A political-opportunity structure defines the potential for loss and gain in the use of disruptive repertoires available in the environment to new groups. In Sidney Tarrow's analysis, the variables that define the opportunity structure of a protest movement are the relative openness or closedness of its formal access to politics; the stability of the political system; and the presence of potential allies, that is, the availability and orientation of other political actors.[11] A protest cycle is a dynamic "made up of a series of individual and group decisions to take conflictual collective action on the part of both 'movement' and non-movement

8. These interviews, coordinated by the Carlo Cattaneo Institute of Bologna, were carried out during research on political violence in Italy.

9. Donatella della Porta and Sidney Tarrow, "Unwanted Children: Political Violence and the Cycle of Protest in Italy," *European Journal of Political Research* 14 (1986): 607–32. On the cycle of protest of the late 1960s in Italy, see Sidney Tarrow, *Disorder and Democracy* (New York: Oxford University Press, 1989).

10. On the relations between social movements and terrorism, see Albert Melucci, "Appunti su movimento, terrorismo e società italiana," *Il mulino* 27 (1978): 253–67; idem, "New Movements, Terrorism, and the Political System: Reflections on the Italian Case," *Socialist Review* 56 (1981): 97–136; and Michel Wieviorka, *Sociétés et terrorisme* (Paris: Fayard, 1988). For structural explanations of Italian terrorism, see Sabino Acquaviva, *Guerriglia e guerra rivoluzionaria in Italia* (Milan: Rizzoli, 1979); Luigi Bonanate, "Il teorema del terrorismo," *Il mulino* 27 (1978): 574–95; Franco Ferrarotti, *Alle radici della violenza* (Milan: Rizzoli, 1979); Nicole Tranfaglia, "La crisi italiana e il problema storico del terrorismo," in *Rapporto sul terrorismo*, ed. Mauro Galleni (Milan: Rizzoli, 1981), 477–544.

11. Sidney Tarrow, *Struggling to Reform* (Ithaca, N.Y.: Cornell University, Western Society Paper no. 15, 1983), 140–44.

actors and the responses to their actions by elites and others."[12] The cycle of protest occurs when protest events intensify in time and the protest spreads out to different social sectors and geographical areas. The rise of violent fringe groups is influenced by the characteristics of the political-opportunity structure in the different phases of protest.

The political-opportunity structure not only changes over time, it is also different for the different political and social actors involved in the protest cycle. More than one organization is active in any collective movement, and more than one collective movement acts in the same historical context. As Roberta Garner and Mayer Zald put it, multiple social movements cohabit in the same social-movement sector, which is defined as a network of conflictual and cooperative relations among the movement organizations in a society at a given moment.[13] The same opportunity structure has, therefore, different effects on the social-movement organizations. Various actors will be affected differently by the environment.

In Figure 4.2, data are shown on the evolution of two indicators of political violence that are not related to clandestine groups: left-wing violence (i.e., violence in the street) and left-wing bombings (i.e., unclaimed attacks against property).

The data can also be considered as indicators of protest activities. Two waves of protest developed in Italy during the 1970s. Their evolution coincided with that of the terrorist waves. The first clandestine organizations arose in the ascending phase of the protest cycle that had started in the late sixties and, for at least the first half of the decade, seemed to represent the more radical fringes of a peaceful mass movement. In the second half of the 1970s, Italian left-wing terrorism began to have an influence on the political system. The development of terrorist organizations coincided with the rapid radicalization of a second wave of protest. It is in this period that Italian terrorism reached a level of duration and intensity that made it unusual in comparison with other industrial democracies.

The Protest Cycle of the Late 1960s

Political violence emerged as one of the by-products of the protest cycle of the late 1960s. A study of the characteristics and the dynamics of that cycle describes the development of violent tactics. The most relevant conclusion is that "the curve of violence is by no means isomorphic with

12. Della Porta and Tarrow, "Unwanted Children," 610.
13. Roberta Garner and Mayer N. Zald, "The Political Economy of the Social Movement Sector" in *The Challenge of Social Control*, ed. Gerald Suttles and Mayer N. Zald (Norwood, N.J.: Ablex, 1985), 143–45.

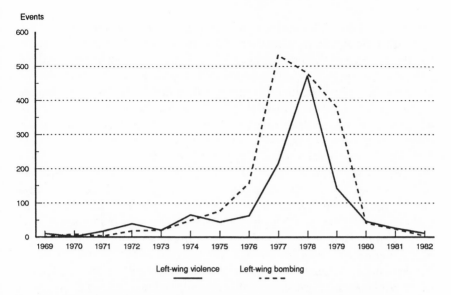

Source: Donatella della Porta and Maurizio Rossi, Cifre Crudeli (Bologna: Cattaneo, 1984), 60–65.

Fig. 4.2.   Evolution of political violence by year, from 1969 to 1982

the curve of protest as a whole: it rose later, was more likely to take small group forms than to involve masses of people, and was not an important aspect of the intense height of the cycle."[14] The first phases of the protest were indeed peaceful. Violence spread out occasionally, owing to clumsy police actions during mass public demonstrations or owing to clashes with right-wing organizers. In the early 1970s new themes appeared in the political arena, and the number of social actors and political organizations increased. A different kind of violence then emerged: small-group organized violence increased, while mass actions diminished in number and became less spontaneous.

Terrorism, therefore, developed at the end of the protest cycle. Its causes, however, lie in the development of collective action throughout the whole cycle and in those characteristics of Italian society that favored that evolution. Three peculiarities of the Italian case explain the high degree of violence.[15] The first is the high density of the social-movement

14. Della Porta and Tarrow, "Unwanted Children," 627.
15. On the student movements of the late 1960s in several countries, see Massimo Teodori, *Storia delle nuove sinistre in Europa (1956–1976)* (Bologna: Il Mulino, 1976); Ronald Fraser, ed., *1968: A Student Generation in Revolt: An International Oral History* (New York: Pantheon Books, 1988); and Gianni Statera, *Storia di una utopia* (Milan: Rizzoli, 1973).

sector in terms of the number of organizations, which is very likely related to the strong politicization of Italian society. The second factor is the persistence of the protest cycle, that is, the long period of sustained protest. This period, which has been described as a final point in the consolidation of the Italian democracy, introduced changes, such as the beginning of modern industrial relations, that were deep enough to explain the duration and intensity of the protest. A third characteristic is the escalation of conflict, produced by a repressive strategy that included the use of the radical Right by state institutions.

Demands for reforms were widespread in society. Many grievances had appeared after major changes had been introduced into the social and cultural spheres by the rapid economic boom of the 1960s. One of the main characteristics of the Italian cycle of protest was in fact the spread of the mobilization from the university to the most heterogeneous strata of the population: from the industrial workers to those groups traditionally less prone to collective action, such as white-collar workers, technicians, professionals, prisoners, soldiers, and the like. Their claims ranged from calls for modernization to the defense of corporate interests.

A second characteristic of the Italian protest cycle relates to the political culture of the social-movement sector. The *conventio ad excludendum* that had kept the Italian Communist Party (Partito Comunista Italiano, PCI) in the opposition had impeded the process of ideological deradicalization that the main left-wing parties had gone through in other Western countries. Moreover, in Italy the student movement was not rooted in youth countercultures but used the language of the two "adult" subcultures: the Catholic and the Communist. The generational conflict was expressed in a radicalization of old value systems, not the elaboration of a new one.

The extension of protest to many different social groups and the radicalization of political culture produced a third characteristic of the protest cycle: a density caused by the presence of a high number of different political organizations competing with each other for recruits and legitimacy. The decline of protest accentuated the conflict between political actors with institutional power and those who had been excluded. At the end of the first half of the 1970s, traditional political actors succeeded in assuming greater control of protest. Other organizations in turn reacted to their lack of institutional resources by an increasing use of the symbolic incentives connected with radicalization. As protest declined, the number of organizers became too large with regard to the demands of their organizations. Some gave up political activities, but others intensified their involvement in politics by becoming political "professionals" or radicalizing their voluntary participation.[16] Disappointed with the results of legal forms of action, extreme fringes of the movement constituted the main base for recruitment into clandestine organizations.

To understand the radicalization of protest, the characteristics of the political-opportunity structure must be taken into account. The first phase of the state response featured a merely repressive strategy by center-right governments. At least until 1974, use of neofascist violence was a substantial part of the institutional policy for dealing with collective action. The wider campaign of right-wing activities in the story of the Italian Republic took three forms: the *squadrismo* (i.e., violence undertaken by small, militarily organized groups, or squads) of the young militants of traditional right-wing organizations, the indiscriminate bombings of the neofascist terrorists, and more than one attempted coup d'état. In all these cases, right-wing violence, and the widespread opinion that it was tolerated and even helped by members of the government, provided a powerful justification for the use of more-radical forms of action by left-wing groups.

The refusal by a part of the ruling class to integrate the new demands—together with the wide range of the grievances voiced during the protest—yielded a protest cycle that was much more enduring than the corresponding wave of social movements in other Western countries. In Italy, in fact, protest started in the universities in 1967 and spread in the next years to the high school system, where it persisted at least for the entire first half of the 1970s. The most intense cycle of industrial strikes started in the autumn of 1969 and lasted until 1973. The skills necessary to organize a social movement, developed during these events, were also used for campaigns on housing problems or the cost of living.

The attitude of some institutional actors toward protest changed in the first years of the cycle. At the outset, both the Communist party (PCI) and the trade unions had channeled emerging demands. From 1974 on, however, the oil crisis and the government's austerity policy began to force the trade unions into a defensive position. Violent forms of action, which had been tolerated in the past as a means of strengthening collective identity, were criticized by the trade union leaders. At the same time, the trade unions became more centralized.[17] And as for the Communist party, between the end of 1973 and the beginning of 1974 the

16. Alessandro Pizzorno, "Terrorismo e quadro politico," *Mondo operaio* 31, 4, 5–18.
17. Marino Regini, *I dilemmi del sindacato* (Bologna: Il Mulino, 1981), 48–50.

strategy of unity of left-wing forces was supplanted by that of the historical compromise between Catholics and Communists. The social-movement organizations lost, therefore, their main allies.

It should be added, however, that the first wave of left-wing terrorism was almost over by 1976. A reform of the secret services, which had been responsible for the protection of the right-wing terrorists, was implemented. In 1974, two specialized institutions were created: the General Inspectorate for Action Against Terrorism (Ispettorato Generale per la Lotta contro il Terrorismo) and the Special Group of Judiciary Police (Nucleo Speciale di Polizia Giudiziaria) in Turin. In only two years their activity brought about the dissolution of the NAP and the arrest of most of the leaders of the BR. According to the interrogations of some BR members, in 1976 fewer than a dozen regular members of the organization were outside prison. No other underground left-wing group was active in that year.

The 77 Movement and the Second Wave of Terrorism

As mentioned above, the unusual features of the Italian case are mainly to be found in the evolution of the terrorist phenomenon in the second half of the 1970s. The second wave of terrorism coincided with the sudden rise and rapid disappearance of a new wave of protest, usually referred to by the media as the 77 Movement. Ambiguous in its ideology and violent in its forms, it ended in a few months, leaving behind a large number of semilegal organizations. Some of them disappeared once they had organized a few bombings; others became more and more organized and contributed to the steady flow of attacks against people between 1978 and 1980. Three features of this period are important: (1) the tumultuous emergence of a new and different phase of protest; (2) the imperviousness of the political system to this specific type of social movement; and (3) the existence of semilegal and clandestine organizations as a "supply" of skills and recruits for organized political violence.

The 77 Movement was initially extremely heterogeneous.[18] Although the precipitating factor was a university reform proposal, many different grievances, external both to the factory and to the educational system, dominated protest from the beginning: from housing problems to high

18. On the 77 Movement, see Pietro Bernocchi et al., *Movimento settantasette: Storia di una lotta* (Turin: Rosemberg e Sellier, 1979); F. Calvi, *Camerade P38* (Paris: Grasset, 1982); Goad Lerner, Luigi Manconi, and Marino Sinibaldi, *Uno strano movimento di strani studenti* (Milan: Feltrinelli, 1978); Mario Monicelli, *L'ultrasinistra in Italia* (Bari: La Terza, 1978); idem, *La follia veneta* (Rome: Editori Riuniti, 1981); and Corrado Stajano, *L'Italia nichilista: Il caso Donat Cattin, la rivolta, il potere* (Milan: Mondadori, 1982).

inflation rates, from the spread of heavy drugs to the lack of social infrastructures in the new periphery of the industrial cities, from youth unemployment to working conditions in the small factories of the underground economy.

These demands were not necessarily hostile to the democratic system. Even with all its contradictions, most of the heterogeneous set of demands expressed by the 77 Movement could have been met through institutionalized bargaining. The closed nature of the political system can, however, be explained in another way. This movement was, indeed, external to the "universe of the traditional political discourse," that is, to the traditional definition of what has to be considered political and of the functions that politics has to fulfill. The ideology of the movement paid little attention to problems of economic exploitation or political power but aimed instead at what the scholars of the new collective movements have defined as a search for identity.[19] Thus, the new demands did not find institutional actors available to represent them legitimately in the political system.

The victory of secular forces in the referendum on divorce and the gains of the PCI in the local elections of 1975, confirmed in the general elections of the following year, also had a negative effect on the surviving social-movement organizations. After the electoral victory of 1976, the strategy of the PCI was influenced by the desire to be seen as a reliable party and a possible partner in the national government. In July 1977, an agreement between the Christian Democratic Party (Democrazia Cristiana, DC) and the PCI led to the formation of the Andreotti government with the abstention (or nonopposition) of the Communist party. In March 1978, the PCI voted its "confidence" in the new government. The strategic changes in the PCI affected Andreotti's behavior toward the emerging youth movement: from an awkward attempt to co-opt the movement to the total rejection of all the demands represented in the protest. At the same time, the groups of the New Left suffered a serious electoral failure that undermined their potential for working as an institutional channel for the new collective demands.

Protest became more radical because of the untimeliness or inadequacy of political institutions in dealing with protest. The previous cycle of protest had been partially successful in terms of reform. In comparison with other industrialized countries that did not experience domestic terrorism, the historical weakness of the Italian bourgeoisie made the

19. In the rich scientific literature on new social movements, see, for instance, Alain Touraine, *La voix et le regard* (Paris: Seuil, 1978), and Alberto Melucci, *L'invenzione del presente* (Bologna: Il Mulino, 1983).

Italian political system eventually more permeable to protest.[20] The positive evolution of the confrontation between the political system and the collective actors was, however, soon blocked by economic crisis. In the meantime, some collective actors were slowly integrated into the bargaining process. During the second protest cycle, the political system was even more closed to demands concerning specific issues as well as to institutional recognition of new collective subjects. Only after a long time did local governments start to respond, even in a confused way, to the grievances voiced in the turmoil of 1977. Whereas in the previous phase the identity of the movement found institutional recognition, in the second cycle of the protest the conflict between institutional forces and emerging actors stopped short of the threshold of recognition.[21]

The emergence of a second wave of left-wing terrorism was influenced also by a degree of continuity with the previous protest cycle, in terms of both protest repertoires and movement organizations. Thus, violent forms of action were still widespread among the "survivors" of the first cycle. The duration of the cycle had favored an increase in the number of violent incidents and in the degree of violence used in physical confrontations with police and neofascists. During the marches, the "arms" carried by militants had changed gradually from stones to sticks, from sticks to crossbars, from crossbars to Molotovs, from Molotovs to pistols. The number of people killed during these marches had steadily increased. Specialized branches had been built inside some radical organizations to perform acts of violent protest.

The expansion of violence was fostered by the survival of groups founded in the first half of the 1970s. Many existing political networks participated in the sequence of events of 1977: "youth proletarian circles," *consultori* organized by the feminist movement, "rounds" against heroin sellers, committees for the "self-reduction" of electricity bills, and leftist "pirate" radio stations. These groups were mainly composed of very young militants but also included organizers (or political entrepreneurs) socialized into politics in the late 1960s. The presence of some leaders of the previous generation impeded radical change in the political culture. Moreover, these groups formed a reservoir for recruitment for the most radical organizations, which had already established some

20. Comparative analyses of the reactions of the Italian and French political systems to the protest of the late 1960s can be found in A. Gigliobianco and Michele Salvati, *Il maggio francese e l'autunno caldo italiano: La risposta di due borghesie* (Bologna: Il Mulino, 1980), and Sidney Tarrow, "I movimenti degli anni '60 in Italia e Francia e la transizione al capitalismo maturo," *Stato e mercato* 12 (1984): 339–62.

21. Luigi Manconi, "Movimenti e nuovi movimenti: Identita e negoziazione," *Quaderni piacentini* 22 (1983): 8, 75–113.

underground structures. These groups, together with the surviving BR, offered a supply of skills for the armed struggle.[22]

The Terrorism Crisis in the 1980s

The strategy chosen by the state influenced the evolution of the underground organizations. After 1976, antiterrorist policies were unsuccessful, despite the awareness of danger. Though official statistics on arrests of terrorists have never been published, my data indicate that fewer than 20 percent of militants were arrested before 1980. Judges and police started, however, to have important results after 1980, with 42 percent arrested in that year and 37.2 percent in the following years.

Why was the state response so weak? First, the state lacked specialized security institutions at least until 1979. Italian repressive institutions were traditionally poorly prepared and supported. Moreover, there was a chronic lack of coordination between the different institutions and within them. The two bodies formed in 1974 to fight terrorism had been dissolved in 1976, for reasons never explained. Some of their functions had later on been assumed by the Central Office for Special Investigations and Operations (Ufficio Centrale per le Investigazioni e le Operazioni Speciali, Ucigos). But when it was created in 1978, much of the knowledge acquired two years before had already been lost. The same can be said for a new Nucleo Speciale, established by the Carabinieri in the same year. Only in 1980 was the legal basis for a coordination of antiterrorism activities introduced into legislation that gave the Interior Ministry responsibility for coordinating and directing police forces in the areas of order and security.

The secret services had passed through a quite turbulent period. The old secret service was dissolved because it had protected right-wing terrorism. Only in 1977 were the new services organized, namely, the SISMI (Servizio Informazioni Sicurezza Militare) for external and military security and the SISDE (Servizio Informazioni Sicurezza Democratica) for internal security. However, a few years later the new services were accused of deviations from their institutional tasks when the names of their commanders in chief were found on the list of members of the Masonic lodge P2.[23]

22. Gianfranco Pasquino, "Sistema politico bloccato e insorgenza del terrorismo: Ipotesi e prime verifiche," in *La prova delle armi*, ed. Gianfranco Pasquino (Bologna: Il Mulino, 1984), 217.

23. About the "deviations" of the Italian intelligence services, see Giuseppe De Lutiis, *Storia dei servizi segreti* (Rome: Editori Riuniti, 1984); Paul Furlong, "Political Terrorism in Italy: Responses, Reactions, and Immobilism," in *Terrorism: A Challenge to the State*, ed. Juliet Lodge (Oxford: Martin Robertson, 1981), 11–56; Giorgio Galli, *Storia del partito armato* (Milan: Rizzoli, 1986); Robert Katz, *I giorni dell'ira: Il caso Moro senza censure*

Many so-called emergency laws were enacted in this period: judicial procedures were modified; limits for preventive detention were suspended; special prisons were established. Moreover, increased penalties for terrorist crimes were introduced by two other "emergency" laws, in 1978 and 1980, that defined the specific crimes of "kidnapping for terrorist or subversive aims," "association with aims of terrorism and subversion of democratic order," and "attack with terrorist or subversive aims." The "aggravating circumstance" for terrorist crimes brought about an augmentation of penalties of up to 50 percent of the normal ones, exclusion from extenuating circumstances and parole, and the extension of up to one-third of the maximum time in preventive custody.

The a posteriori judgment on the "antiterrorism" laws was that when weighed against the degeneration of the civil rights they produced, they did not compensate with any efficacy in combating terrorism.[24] The increase in penalties for terrorist crimes had little deterrent effect. The limitations of the individual rights of citizens and defendants seemed useless against terrorism and dangerous to the legitimacy of the state.[25]

In the same period, repression sharply increased against radical, but legal, organizations, with the result that people were pushed into the underground. Many of the new members of terrorist organizations were in fact members of radical groups who joined terrorist organizations in order to have logistical support while evading arrest. My data on the evolution of recruitment in left-wing terrorist organizations indicate, in fact, a big jump in 1979, when the judiciary and police institutions increased repression against the semilegal groups of the so-called *autonomia*, survivors of the 77 Movement.[26]

More effective were the provisions of the 1980 law that provided "compensation" for the members of underground organizations who cooperated with investigations. These measures went from immunity from punishment to the reduction of penalties of up to 50 percent. In the

---

(Rome: ADN Kronos, 1982); Sergio Flamigni, *La tela del ragno: Il delitto Moro* (Rome: Edizioni Associate, 1988); Stefano Rodotà, "La risposta dello stato al terrorismo: Gli apparati," in *La prova delle armi*, ed. Pasquino, 77–93; Luciano Violante, "Politica della sicurezza, relazioni internazionali e terrorismo," in ibid., 95–120.

24. Vittorio Grevi, "Sistema penale e leggi dell'emergenza: La risposta legislativa al terrorismo," in *La prova delle armi*, ed. Pasquino, 49.

25. For instance, Magistratura democratica, Osservazioni sul decreto legge 15 dicembre 1979, n. 625 concernente misure urgenti per la tutela dell'ordine democratico, in *Foro italico* V (1980).

26. On one of the most discussed trials against several leaders of the 77 Movement, see Giorgio Bocca, *Il caso 7 aprile: Toni Negri e la grande inquisizione* (Milan: Feltrinelli, 1980), and Giancarlo Scarpari, "Processo a mezzo stampa: Il 7 aprile," *Quale quistizia* 51 (1979): 225–92.

same direction, a new law provided that "compensations" had to be proportional to the "amount" of cooperation with its outcome. Merely belonging to an underground group, the aiding and abetting of nonpunishable members, and minor crimes related to arms and explosives were declared nonpunishable when the defendant abandoned the underground group. In the case of a full confession of one's own crimes, sentences from fifteen to twenty-one-years were substituted for life sentences. Other sentences were reduced by one-third and could not exceed fifteen years. In the case of cooperation that yielded evidence identifying one or more accomplices, a life sentence was commuted to imprisonment of between ten and twelve years, and other penalties were reduced by one-third. A further reduction of one-third was applied to those who offered an exceptional contribution by aiding in the dissolution of entire networks. Moreover, those who had already served half of their penalty could be paroled. In 1982, a new law expanded the number of cases in which the norms about collaboration could be applied.

These provisions were criticized as "anticonstitutional" because they introduced different treatments for the same crimes. In other words, the penalties depended on the degree of assistance provided to the authorities, not the seriousness of the crime. There was also the risk that fake confessions would be given in order to improve one's own position or take revenge against someone else. It was acknowledged, however, that the "compensations" hastened the crisis in terrorist organizations. According to data provided by the minister of justice, 389 members of the terrorist organizations took advantage of the 1980 and 1982 laws (78 as "major repented," 134 as repented, and 177 as dissociated) and abandoned terrorism.

Isolated in the social-movement sector, which had come to be critical of violent strategies, the underground organizations started now to look for alternative sources of support. During the 1970s, the left-wing underground organizations had refused the "help" of various foreign secret services and had spent very limited energies in developing a network of contacts with other underground groups active abroad. In the 1980s, both organizations formed out of the original BR tried to improve their international connections. In Europe there was a wave of terrorist bombings credited to the BR together with the German, French, and Belgian left-wing undergrounds. Moreover, in contrast to previous years, terrorist attacks in Italy were directed against "international" as well as domestic targets. The first action of this type was the kidnapping of General James Dozier, carried out by the Colonna Veneta of the BR. During the kidnapping, which lasted from 18 December 1981 to 28 January 1982 (when a special antiterrorist police squad liberated

Dozier), the BR had contacts with the Bulgarian secret services in an attempt to exchange information for weapons and money. The February 1984 assassination of the American diplomat Leamon Hunt can be explained as compensation by the BR for the material support they got from Palestinians. In 1986, the BR claimed responsibility for the assassination of the former mayor of Florence, Lando Conti, which they defined as an attack against the pro-Israeli policies of the minister for foreign affairs, Giovanni Spadolini.

ORGANIZATIONAL DYNAMICS OF THE UNDERGROUND

The Strategic Choice of Clandestinity

Clandestine organizations originated within legal groups, as shown in Figure 4.3. Underground organizations were built by individuals who shared not only previous experience of political involvement in legal organizations but also strong solidarity bonds deriving from interpersonal relations in the same small groups. For example, BR was founded in Milan by militants of one of the many leftist groups, the Metropolitan Political Collective (Collettivo Politico Metropolitano, CPM). Some of them came from "Marxist-Leninist" backgrounds, others from militancy in the more traditional Left. In all the towns in which PL was present, its founders had similar experiences in the Communist Committees for Worker Power (Comitati Comunisti per il Potere Operaio, CCPO), constituted by a merger of militants from PO and Continuous Struggle (Lotta Continua, LC), another among the main organizations of the New Left. From the same local section of LC (Sesto San Giovanni) came the members of the Communist Committees (Comitati Comunisti) that preceded the CCPO.

The NAP were constituted by a small group coming from LC. The FCC originated in Milan, during the summer of 1977, from a split in the *collettivi* that published the magazine *Rosso* (Red) founded a few years earlier by former militants of PO. From the same organization, *Rosso* (Collettivo Autonomo della Barona, Collettivo Stadera), the PAC arose during 1978 in Venice and Milan. From the CCPO came, in the same year, the UCC in Rome and Milan and the FAC in Rome and Turin. From other networks of people who had formerly been members of underground formations came the other groups I have analyzed in my research: from FCC, RCA in the spring of 1978 and GR in the beginning

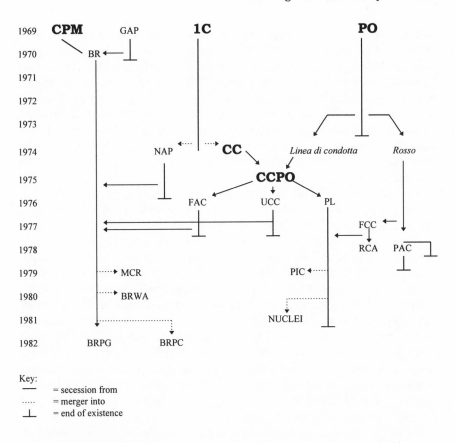

Key:

— = secession from
..... = merger into
⊥ = end of existence

Linea di condotta and *Rosso* are movement publications. The acronyms of legal groups are in boldface; the others are clandestine groups.

Fig. 4.3.   Political origins of left-wing underground organizations by year

of 1979; from the RCA, the Lo Muscio Brigade in 1980; from PL, For Communism in 1979 and Nuclei in 1981; from the BR and the FAC, MCR in 1979. Emotional bonds stemming from kinship and friendship linked the members of these networks.

Many interpretations of the rise of terrorist organizations stress ideological variables, such as those related to the "workerist" doctrine that emerged in the 1960s.[27] My findings show that armed groups grew

27. Angelo Ventura, "Il problema storico del terrorismo italiano," *Rivista storica italiana* 92 (1980): 125–51; idem, "Il problema delle origini del terrorismo di sinistra," in *Terrorismi in Italia*, ed. della Porta, 75–152; and Severino Galante, "Alle origini del partito armato," *Il mulino* 30 (1981): 444–87.

within legal political organizations that espoused ideologies that justified violence. For example, the CPM's magazine wrote of the necessity to convince "the fighting proletarian masses of the principle that there is no political power without military power."[28] PO and LC were often accused of exalting political violence and approving, in their newspapers, the first activities of the BR. Many members of the editorial staff of *Rosso* and *Senza Tregua* were prosecuted for "armed insurrection against the powers of the state" in proceedings in which judges emphasized the propaganda in favor of social and political violence contained in the two magazines.

Ideology seems, therefore, to have played an important role in pushing the militants of some organizations toward terrorism. Nevertheless, it did not determine the choice of armed struggle. The more general content of these ideologies—the definition of the enemy, the prefiguration of future society, and so on—was not unique to the groups from which terrorist organizations originated. On the contrary, these ideas were widespread in the leftist culture. Nor were specific recommendations related to strategies restricted to those groups that chose terrorist practices. If it is true that CPM and PO spoke of insurrection and LC wrote "all and now," it is also true that in the early 1970s the same slogans were adopted by other organizations that decided not to build a military structure. Individuals and groups that eventually criticized terrorism were former adherents to the same organizations. Needless to say, very few of the militants, not only of LC and PO but also *Rosso* and *Senza Tregua*, went underground.

Ideologies operate as facilitating factors, resources or constraints, in the formation of actors and in the definition of their strategies. No comprehensive explanation for the action of an organization can rely exclusively on political beliefs. Ideologies are also rationalizations for decisions to escalate violence. In Italy, violence was justified in terms of the prevailing social-movement culture, characterized by such ideological components as the mythology of the imminent revolution, the definition of democracy as a mask that hides exploitation, contempt for human life, the sovereignty of ideology over theory, the individual's sacrifice to the common goal, and calls for violent overthrow of state institutions.[29] Ideological principles that could have prepared the ground for terrorist ideologies were widespread in the movement's culture.

28. Quoted in Silj, *Mai più senza fucile*, 89. Translated by the author, as are all subsequent translations, unless otherwise noted.
29. See Noudo dalla Chiesa, "Del sessantotto e del terrorismo," *Il Mulino* 30 (1981): 53–93, and idem, "Le culture politiche: Il terrorismo di sinistra," in *Terrorismi in Italia*, ed. della Porta, 293–330.

Some elements of the leftist political culture were, therefore, conducive to underground organizations. Their emergence, however, required the radicalization of forms of action, which, in turn, produced a further radicalization in ideology. My findings on terrorist organizations show that they emerged in towns that experimented with the more violent modes of political expression. BR emerged in Milan, precisely where workers' and students' struggles expressed themselves in mass demonstrations, often confronted by police forces. In Milan, between the end of the 1960s and the beginning of the 1970s, some militants of the student movement were killed during police attacks or fights with right-wing militants. This climate favored the spread of slogans calling for vengeance. Again in Milan, many armed groups (PL, FCC, RCA, GR, Lo Muscio Brigade, PAC, just to name a few) formed in the second half of the 1970s, when the city saw the greatest number of violent incidents: from the proletarian expropriations that started in 1974 through the first physical attacks against factory managers made by organizations other than BR to the armed demonstration of 1976–77.

The two major terrorist groups spread later to Turin, where workers' and urban movements had taken the most dramatic forms: squattings that ended in physical fights with police, and "armed inrushes." Then, starting in 1976, a growing number of underground organizations arose in Rome: UCC, FAC, the BR's Roman column, and many small armed groups with only a very narrow range of action. This happened, once again, in the context of a radicalization of forms of action that occurred later than in the big northern industrial towns. There, too, violence increased when the police attempted to clear squatted houses, during physical fights with right-wing militants, and during the complex evolution of the 77 Movement. By contrast, attempts by armed organizations to build terrorist bases failed in those areas where violence was limited.

Some of the organizations that survived until the end of the cycle without finding a niche for institutionalization built compartmentalized branches, mainly defensive in the beginning, from which the underground groups developed. As will be shown in the next part of this chapter, the biographies of many of the founders of terrorist organizations reveal the role played by their participation in violent collective actions during the period of political socialization. Most of the promoters of armed formations had participated in semimilitary underground branches of legal organizations. Many of the PL's founders in Turin, Milan, and Florence belonged to *servizio d'ordine* of LC. Many of the first BR militants in Turin and Rome participated in the semilegal structures of PO and of the groups organized around the review *Linea di condotta* (Line of conduct). Other promoters of BR in Turin came from the first armed group active in Italy, the GAP. The FCC emerged from a split in the groups organized around *Rosso* and, more exactly, from the Communist Brigades (Brigate Comuniste), appointed for the armed defense of public demonstrations and illegal actions. Again, militants of LC or PO's *servizio d'ordine* participated in the foundation of UCC and FAC as well as in that of PL. Many of the younger promoters of FCC, PL, and other "minor" formations in Milan took part in proletarian expropriations and armed demonstrations in the second half of the 1970s. A certain number of the first Roman BR's militants had been prosecuted as members of one of the most violent groups of Workers Autonomy (Autonomia Operaia), the Collettivo di Via dei Volsci. Some NAP and PAC militants, ordinary delinquents who became involved in politics during their stays in prison, had experiences in illegal actions, even if for nonpolitical aims. Many of the small clandestine groups that arose after 1979 were founded by terrorists coming from the major armed organizations.

The last stage in the rise of a terrorist organization is the choice of clandestinity. The presence in the environment of ideological and strategic resources that foster the choice of extreme forms of action and the formation of networks composed of militants socialized into political violence is not a sufficient explanation for terrorism. Not all the organizations belonging to the social-movement sectors used the same tactics to fight for their aims. To understand the reasons why only a few groups chose to go underground, it is necessary to introduce the problematic subject of strategic choices in collective action.[30]

Terrorism originated in an escalation in the use of illegal activities that pushed some of the more involved groups to choose clandestinity in order to escape the detection of the authorities. The precipitating event in the definitive exit from legality was an action of repression by the state against some specific groups. Faced with these precipitating events, political leaders, after debating the different choices, split in order to experiment with different strategies. There was, therefore, no direct causal relation between precipitating event and final choice of strategy. This can be supported by looking at the different stages in the founding of the three main terrorist organizations: BR, PL, FCC.

The history of the foundation of the BR is one of continuous splits in a local group. The choice of clandestinity was gradual. In the beginning,

---

30. For a definition of the concept of strategic choice, see John Child, "Organization, Structure, Environment, and Performance: The Role of Strategic Choice," *Sociology* 6, no. 1 (1972): 1–22. For an analysis of strategic choices in social movements, see William A. Gamson, *The Strategy of Social Protest* (Homewood, Ill.: Dorsey Press, 1975).

BR adopted tactics that were illegal but not very different from those that were tolerated in the environment of the movements. The group first adopted the strategy of double militance: clandestinity of the organization but public activity of its members. This worked until May 1972, when the group suffered arrests and house searches, and at that point many militants decided to go underground. Not all members accepted this decision, and accordingly, some of them dropped out.

The rise of PL can also be analyzed in terms of gradual choices made by some subgroups within the CCPO. A strategy aimed at combining the use of illegal tactics with the preservation of legal structures emerged progressively: from the emergence of a splinter group from LC that supported the necessity of arming in 1973 to the building of a small armed group in Milan's periphery of Sesto San Giovanni, from the constitution of the Communist Committees in the same year to their merger with a nucleus of PO's militants in 1976.[31] The failure of this program is shown by the internal splits and the legal persecution of some militants that followed the first assassination they carried out. To deal with this crisis, the CCPO split at the end of 1976. While one group criticized illegal actions, the group constituting the military structure of the organization chose to become more and more compartmentalized and to use more violent forms of action. So, PL was founded.

The history of the groups gathered around the review *Rosso*, from which FCC arose, is similar to that of CCPO. In this case, too, some groups chose, through a series of decisions, to adopt increasingly more violent means of action. Emerging in Milan between the end of 1974 and the beginning of 1975, these groups used illegal methods: not only bombs or Molotovs against cars or houses, but also armed protest marches, proletarian expropriations, and robberies. The debate over the need for a stronger militarization of the organization arose in May 1977 after the assassination of a policeman during a demonstration. This contributed to the spread of fear of repression. A faction of the organization favored mass action, but the leaders of the military structure chose to arm themselves.

The strategic choice of clandestinity by a political organization is therefore a gradual process and is not without reversals. It reflects previously existing divisions in the leadership and is an instrument adopted by a faction to face a crisis. The decision to go underground

31. For the story of LC, see L. Bobbio, *Lotta continua: Storia di una organizzazione rivoluzionaria* (Rome: Savelli, 1979). On Potere Operaio, see Giovanni Palombarini, *Il 7 Aprile: Il processo e la sua storia* (Venice: L'Arsenalle, 1982). On the so-called *autonomia*, see Luciano Castellano, ed., *Autop: La storia e i documenti di Potere operaio* (Milan: Savelli, 1980).

minimizes some costs, even though benefits are also reduced. The presence of favorable environmental conditions and of networks of militants socialized to violent forms of collective action permit this choice. Inside the same protest cycle, different groups and organizations, all forming part of the same culture, produce different ideological elaborations and practices, often stressing diversity in order to improve their specific relevance inside their environment. The strategic choices of the movement's leaders are influenced by the "entrepreneurial" attempt to define a specific political identity. Accordingly, different tactics are tested by different organizations and by different factions of the same organization. Faced with favorable environmental conditions, some groups decide to test the effectiveness of a radicalization of their repertoires and modes of organization as a way of differentiating themselves from other organizations active in the same movement. During demobilization, some factions within the more radical organizations increase both their use of violent tactics and the compartmentalization of their organization. The emergence of underground formations is therefore the consequence of a process of polarization and division between moderate and radical factions of the same organization. The factions that go underground are those lacking other kinds of resources but possessing the skills necessary for a greater use of violence.

Aims of Underground Organizations

Many definitions of terrorism stress that terrorist organizations seek to terrorize the enemy. Yet undergrounds, like other political organizations, must also fulfill many different tasks, the most important of which is consensus building. A main aim is the recruitment of new members. The different features of underground groups—organizational structures, actions, and ideology—are adapted to this end.

Organizational Structures and Recruitment

Terrorist structures are basically unsuitable for attracting new members. Clandestinity and compartmentalization reduce the possibility of making contacts with potential recruits. Centralization also slows recruitment procedures by requiring hierarchical controls on the new members. Nevertheless, Italian terrorist groups did succeed in creating decentralized mass bodies that were open to nonmembers when a relatively large potential constituency rendered attempts to recruit less risky. When the environment was more hostile, the task of recruiting new people was left in the hands of a few isolated militants.

Italian terrorist organizations adopted two models: one decentralized, open, and flexible, the other rigidly compartmentalized. The choice between these models was influenced by environmental conditions. The first was preferred when a higher propensity to violence pushed for the maximization of recruitment opportunities, even at the price of a heightened risk of arrests. The second was preferred in hostile environments to minimize the risk of arrests, even at the cost of minimizing recruitment potential.

The first model was made possible by the nonclandestinity of militants and the presence of semiautonomous rank-and-file structures. Although clandestinity is fundamental to a terrorist organization, not all terrorist militants went underground. Organizations that emerged in periods favorable to armed struggle preferred the principle of "clandestinity in military action but not in proselytism" by which "the militants kept their legal identities and regular occupations, while only their participation in the group was secret."[32]

In practice this organizational model worked only partially: it required a complete lack of compartmentalization, and very often the participation of people in terrorist groups was well known inside the networks in which they tried to recruit. It was only the widespread acceptance of a high degree of political violence in the task environment that kept militants from being arrested.

The underground groups that emerged in the second half of the 1970s also included some organizational branches particularly suitable for recruitment. These bodies were open to people who did not share all the aims of the organizations but were nevertheless available for actions on a small scale at the local level. They were loosely structured: the Squadre Operaie Combattenti (Fighting Worker Squads) or the Ronde Proletarie di Combattimento (Fighting Proletarian Patrols) in the case of PL; the Squadre Armate Proletarie (Proletarian Armed Squads) for the FCC; the Squadre Comuniste dell'Esercito Proletario (Communist Squads of the Proletarian Army) of the RCA. Also, the BR had their Nuclei di Movimento Proletario di Resistenza Offensivo (Nuclei of the Proletarian Movement of Offensive Resistance), founded in Rome and Naples, where the organization had emerged in the second half of the 1970s, in an environment more favorable to armed struggle.

In most of the formal documents, the *squadre* are defined as rank-and-file structures with a small range of action. They were usually organized on a territorial level, reflecting the structure of the movements from

---

32. FCC, "Statuto" (mimeo), and Examination, Court of Turin, Investigating Magistrate's Bill of Indictment, Juridical Proceeding No. 321/80.

which they drew militants. Most of them would act inside single neighborhoods with the task of acquiring information on the targets of specific action, on the "military presence" in the area, and on the more important social problems. They were usually organized within already existing political groups, which they tried to influence and from which they drew recruits. One member of these *squadre*, or *ronde*, the "commander," was usually responsible for their activity to the *comando di zona* (zone command). Formally, the zone command had to decide the general aims of activity campaigns, whereas the *squadre* could choose only the specific targets and were usually dependent on the main organization for arms and money. Their militants, however, often did not consider themselves submissive to the organization's hierarchy. The degree of autonomy changed over time according to the environment and the strategic choices of the leadership. Thus, the *squadre* permitted different levels of involvement and helped to keep links to the social-movement militants.

The flexibility of this organizational model was effective for recruitment tasks. The relative autonomy of the *squadre* made it possible for them to recruit whole nuclei coming from homogeneous political backgrounds. But the decentralized and loosely compartmentalized structure showed its weaknesses when its potential constituency dramatically diminished. In fact, it required the sacrifice of security measures and so made the group more vulnerable to repressive responses. Notwithstanding some attempts to change their structures, most of the underground groups were easily defeated.

The compartmentalized model of organization was less effective in recruiting, because there was no structure that was open to external sympathizers. Only people able to pass a long screening process that evaluated military courage and fidelity to the organization were accepted. The rules on centralization and vertical hierarchy were strictly respected, and disagreement was not tolerated. Typical of this structure is the BR, whose military vocabulary was particularly striking. The body formally charged with the task of recruitment was the Fronte Operaio (Worker Front) or Fronte Massa (Mass Front). The function of the *fronte* was to organize activities in factories or other places where potential supporters might be found. According to *statuto*, in the structure of the *fronte* the BR militants of Fiat should have had the opportunity to meet those of Alfa Romeo and to decide together on propaganda actions. But, in practice, the functioning of the *fronte* was subordinated to the compartmentalized and hierarchical principles emphasized in the "columns" structure. The *fronti* were, therefore, dependent on the centralized hierarchy whose power was never affected.[33]

33. Giancarlo Caselli and Donatella della Porta, "La storia delle Brigate Rosse: Strutture, organizzative e strategie d'azione," in *Terrorismi in Italia*, ed. della Porta, 153–221.

The task of recruiting new members was, actually, accomplished by the "irregular" militants. From the group's beginning, members of the BR were divided into regular and irregular forces. The "regular" militants were clandestine, were engaged full-time, and lived underground, even when they were not sought by the police. The "irregular" militants limited their clandestinity to involvement with the organization. The irregular militants could keep their jobs and live with their families so they could contact sympathizers. Their task was, in fact, "to win popular support for the organization by building centers and articulations of revolutionary power." The scant attention given to recruitment was nevertheless illustrated by the subordinate role of the irregular forces. Only the regular militants, who constituted the "more conscious and generous cadres produced by the armed struggle," could, in fact, be part of the "vertical structure of command."[34] To go underground was the logical conclusion to a terrorist career and a path to promotion or upward mobility.

In the BR, the recruitment process was therefore conducted in long stages, with intense ideological indoctrination, carried out by regular militants. With the exception of periods when a larger potential constituency made recruitment easier, security was the priority. The need for internal cohesion discouraged the recruitment of groups of people coming from the dissolution of other illegal organizations. Even when environmental conditions were favorable, the legacy of an organizational model built to cope with a more threatening situation prevented many sympathizers from actually joining the BR. When the violent cycle of protest of the late 1970s was over, however, the compartmentalized structure helped the BR to survive state repression and to recruit new militants (to replace those arrested) from among the survivors of the other groups. The two types of organization produced different types of recruitment: a block-model recruitment, in the first case, and a differential model, in the second case. Both of them revealed, however, the unsuitability of clandestine structures for recruitment.

Repertoires of Action and Recruitment

Repertoires of action are a second tool organizations can manipulate in order to recruit.[35] A dilemma for the terrorist organizations is that they have to use the media to get the attention of the public, even that of

34. BR, "Alcune questioni per la discussione sull'organizzazione."
35. Charles Tilly, *From Mobilization to Revolution* (Reading, Mass.: Addison Wesley, 1978).

their sympathetic constituency. Yet tactics that catch the attention of the media are often useless in convincing people to become terrorists. Data on the targets and tactics of terrorist actions in Italy during the last decade show that the underground organizations often carefully selected their targets in order to get positive feedback from the militants of the social movements that were considered as the main reservoirs of new members. Yet the tactics they used alienated supporters.

In Table 4.1, the activities of various terrorist organizations have been distributed according to "function."[36]

Strong differences exist between the BR and other leftist groups. A very high percentage of BR actions concentrate on factories: 40 percent, as against 11 percent for the other terrorist groups. Also, actions against political targets are more numerous for the BR (24 percent) than for other groups (10 percent). The most tragic example of BR strategy was the kidnapping and assassination of the president of the Christian Democratic party, Aldo Moro.[37] By contrast, other groups concentrate (31 percent, against a very low 6 percent for the BR) on what can be defined as social propaganda: their targets were real estate agencies, supermarkets, small business, drug dealers, neuropsychiatrists, security guards, computer services, and advertising agencies.

Table 4.1.   Functions of terrorist actions

Function	Red Brigades		Other Leftist		Total	
	%	No.	%	No.	%	No.
Factory propaganda	40.4	262	11.2	67	26.4	329
Social propaganda	5.7	37	30.7	184	17.7	221
Political propaganda	23.9	155	9.7	58	17.1	213
War against state	17.1	111	17.4	104	17.2	215
Military defense	5.2	34	4.8	29	5.1	63
Financing	7.1	46	25.4	152	15.9	198
Other	0.5	3	0.8	5	0.6	8
Total[a]	52.0	648	48.0	599	100.0	1,247

[a]Since more than one option is possible for each event, the total is bigger than the number of cases. Percentages are calculated on the basis of options.

36. The function is a variable that not only indicates the kind of target struck but also traces the meaning of the action in the strategy of the group; its determination is based on statements of the organizations and declarations of their militants.

37. On the Moro kidnapping, see Giorgio Bocca, *Moro: Una tragedia italiana* (Milan: Bompiani, 1978); David Moss, "The Kidnapping and Murder of Aldo Moro," *Archive Européenne de Sociologie* 20 (1981): 265–95; and Robin Wagner-Pacifici, *The Moro Morality Play* (Chicago: University of Chicago Press, 1986).

These differences can be explained as strategic choices made on the basis of the availability of potential supporters. When the BR emerged in the beginning of the 1970s, the workers in the big factories were indeed the main reference point for the militants of the radical Left. In concentrating their actions on the big factories, the BR did not try to convince workers to join their organizations; instead, they hoped to draw new members from the more radical leftist groups with Marxist-Leninist ideologies. It is not by chance that the first actions of the BR were carried out in factories where organized groups had risen in opposition to trade unions and where violence was an accepted part of industrial conflict. Moreover, specific targets were often chosen in the departments where radical sympathizers worked.

The wish to acquire new supporters may also account for some initial violence against right-wing trade unionists. Violence against "Fascists" was the most "legitimated" in the leftist culture. The persons chosen were usually at a low level of the factory hierarchy because their "direct" responsibility for the "oppression" of workers was most visible. Extensive documentation detailing the "personal responsibility" of targets was handed out in the big factories, in order to convince sympathizers that the victims deserved punishment.

A different potential constituency forced the "latecomer" underground organizations to look in another direction for an audience. The targets chosen reflected the preferences of the militants of the 77 Movement, from which the terrorist groups of the late 1970s planned to recruit. Since the 77 Movement was a form of youth protest, based outside the big factories and organized in territorial structures,[38] the terrorist organizations took up the main themes of the youth movement in that period: housing problems, cost of living, unemployment and underemployment, and drugs. Power was considered a social, rather than a political, phenomenon. The favored targets were therefore agencies and agents exhibiting the "penetration" of social control.

Very small terrorist groups performed specialized activities, in terms of geographic concentration and functional sectors. Most of these groups were active only in one town, and sometimes only in one neighborhood. Their specialization was evident in the selection of targets, which reflected the different potential constituencies the terrorist groups aimed

38. See Donatella della Porta, "Le cause del terrorismo nelle società contemporanee," in *Terrorismo e violenza politica: Tre casi a confronto: Stati Uniti, Germania e Giappone*, ed. Donatella della Porta and Gianfranco Pasquino (Bologna: Il Mulino, 1983), 9–47, and Donatella della Porta, "Struttura della opportunità politiche, evoluzione dei movimenti collettivi e terrorismo di sinistra: Qualche riflessione sul caso Italiano," *Quaderni della Fondazione Feltrinelli* 32 (1986): 137–57.

to reach: the underproletariat, for the NAP; terrorists in prison, for RCA and Nuclei; movements active in housing problems, for MCR; and those active around the media, for GR.

The tactics of terrorist groups also reflected to some extent their choice, or need, to recruit in a specific task environment. The BR carried out more bloody forms of action: 28.9 percent of their actions were aimed at persons, whereas for the other leftist groups such action amounted to only 7.7 percent.[39] This preference, though related to their superior military skills, was nevertheless mainly a consequence of their recruitment preferences. The other terrorist groups aimed to recruit in an environment favorable to less destructive mass violence.

Ideology and Recruitment

Political organizations can orient ideology to recruitment. The literature on terrorist ideologies concentrates on the following elements: primacy of practice over theory, appeals to violence as a way of "waking up" the working class, romantic confidence in the voluntarism of small vanguards, and existential moralism that theorizes that heroic sacrifice is the only alternative to despair. The ideology of terrorist groups is often seen, in this case, as a governing factor in their strategic choices. Ideology is, however, also part of the strategic choices of the organization. The role of ideology in political movements has recently been analyzed in terms of frame alignment.[40] The ideology is, in fact, a tool for enlarging the potential supporters of an organization by adopting some symbols and values highly valued in certain groups. The choice of the frames the organization wants to align itself with is therefore related to the constituency in which it is looking for potential supporters.

A comparison of different terrorist groups' ideologies in Italy would therefore enable us to single out the constituencies they rely on for finding new members. The BR maintained, for instance, a Marxist-Leninist ideology. In their documents the working class is the revolutionary subject, the capitalist system is the enemy, the state is the guard dog of the bourgeoisie, and Christian Democracy is its party. The other terrorist groups instead adopted a relatively new ideological framework: social oppression is more a question of individual alienation than economic exploitation, and power controls the private lives of individuals and does not merely limit itself to political domination. The revolutionary role has

39. Della Porta and Rossi, "I terrorismi in Italia," 33–34.
40. See David A. Snow and Robert D. Benford, "Ideology, Frame Resonance, and Participant Mobilization," in *From Structure to Action*, ed. Klandermans, Hanspeter Kriesi, and Sidney Tarrow (Greenwich, Conn.: JAI Press, 1988), 197–217.

been taken over by the so-called *operaio sociale* (worker in the society) to which almost all urban youth can be assimilated. These two different ideological models promoted different strategies of action and modes of organization. Difference in ideology also reflected the different collective movements active in the periods in which these organizations arose. The Marxist-Leninist ideology of the BR had to attract the militants of Marxist-Leninist groups that were more violence-prone at that time. The purpose of the ideological statements of the other organizations was, instead, "ideological alignment" with the divided groups of the New Left. Their ideology was a tool for acquiring new recruits in an environment where, in that period, sympathizers with armed struggle were more numerous.

The attention paid by the underground organizations to adapting ideology to circumstances is shown in the way these political groups explained and justified changes in their strategies. The BR justified the initial choice of armed struggle in terms understandable to their potential constituency: the danger of a fascist coup. The fear of growing authoritarianism, widespread in the Italian Left, was emphasized by the BR in their justification of physical violence as a necessary defense. The BR presented a synthesis of armed struggle against fascists and armed struggle in the factories against the image of a fascist coup as a capitalist attempt to get back what the working class had conquered. To stand up to a strong working class and its own contradictions, the bourgeoisie had, according to the BR, "to make its power apparatuses more right-wing," thus attempting to obtain once again control of the factories by means of "the growing despotism against the working class, and the militarization of the state and of the class struggle, the intensification of repression as a strategic measure."[41]

When repression made direct intervention in the bigger factories more and more dangerous, the BR changed accordingly to focus on more "political" targets. This shift was explained as a consequence of the growing intervention of political institutions in the economic sphere. The state was described as an expression of the imperialism of the big corporations: the "Imperialist State of the Corporations," or SIM in the Italian acronym.[42]

The enemy was described in different terms at different times, according to the ideology of a changing potential constituency. In the second half of the 1970s the enemy was no longer fascism but social democracy.[43]

41. BR, "Brigate Rosse" (1971, mimeo, available—as are the BR documents in the notes that follow—at the Instituto Carlo Cattaneo in Bologna).
42. BR, "Risoluzione della direzione strategica" (1975, mimeo).
43. BR, "Risoluzione della direzione strategica" (1979, mimeo).

By attacking the Communist party and trade unions, the BR tried to win the sympathy of the young militants of the late 1970s protest groups, whom the traditional Left vigorously opposed.

The BR also changed their definition of social allies when violent groups with non-Marxist-Leninist ideologies emerged in the social-movement sector. At the end of the 1970s, manual workers in the social services, marginal people, and the unemployed were considered the closest allies of the working class.[44] The call for building a "Proletarian Movement of Offensive Resistance" incorporating marginal urban youth was also a way of appealing to those sectors of the population that had recently become involved in political violence.[45]

The Evolution of Underground Organizations

The evolution of political organizations can take two directions. The normal institutionalization process is characterized by deradicalization, routinization of participation, and acceptance by the system. The encapsulation-implosion process, which is more typical of clandestine groups, is characterized instead by radicalization, all-pervasive militance, and dramatic limitations on exchanges with the external environment. This second process makes terrorist groups less and less like political organizations and more and more like religious sects. This process occurs on three levels: organizational structure, strategy, and ideology.

Changes in the Structures of Organizations

The evolution of the organizational model has four characteristics: centralization, factionalism, compartmentalization, and structuration. Centralization was most visible in groups boasting larger memberships. Growing difficulties in being accepted by the task environment reduced the potential importance and autonomy of rank-and-file structures. The various *squadre* disappeared. The risks of being discovered also concentrated decision making in a small group of clandestine leaders.

Hypercentralization reduced tolerance for dissent in a period when strategic decisions for survival produced splits, and thus factionalism, inside the dominant coalition. Widespread discontent over the "militarization" of the organizations both reflected and stimulated the personal conflicts normally produced by small-group dynamics.

Factionalism was also increased by compartmentalization which be-

44. BR, "Risoluzione della direzione strategica" (1977, mimeo).
45. BR, "Risoluzione della direzione strategica" (1978, mimeo).

came more rigid when repression increased and social support shrank. To avoid infiltration by agents provocateurs, the organizations jettisoned those branches open to external sympathizers. Moreover, some rules of behavior that had existed on paper but not in practice were now enforced. Personal interactions of militants were checked; encounters with other members of the same groups were forbidden if they were not essential to the activities of the organization; the circulation of information was reduced. Barriers to entrance were raised, and exchanges at the boundaries of different organizations were dramatically reduced.

At the same time, in a peculiar process of structuration, some clandestine groups, to give the impression of growing organizational strength, increased the number of structures, specialized in a number of subfunctions. Their names became longer and longer, while their membership diminished, sometimes to one sole member.

Changes in Strategy

As clandestine groups evolved, their strategies also changed. Both tactics and targets were transformed. First, action became more violent. Indicators of this process can be found in the proportion of actions against people out of the total of terrorist activities, in the number of people injured and killed during terrorist events, and in the tactics most often used by the terrorist groups. All indicators show the existence of a long period in which terrorist organizations did not attack people, followed then by a rapid radicalization toward more violent methods. The number of actions against people came to surpass that of actions against property.

The data illustrated in Figure 4.4 refer to the numbers of terrorist episodes from 1970 to 1983. The two curves refer to the overall number of events and to the number of events that produced physical damage to human beings. In both cases the frequencies are by year.

Up to 1973, the number of events was limited, and only four were directed against people. Left-wing terrorism remained sporadic in the following two years: four attacks against people in 1974 and nine in 1975, with an average of fifty total events.

The turning point was 1976, which witnessed a sudden rise both in the total number of terrorist events and in the number directed against people; the latter rose to 16 while the number of actions against property climbed to 87. The biggest jump occurred in the following year, when actions against people more than doubled, reaching 36, as did the number of actions against property, which reached 165. Whereas in 1977 Italy had the highest frequencies of actions against property, in 1978 attacks

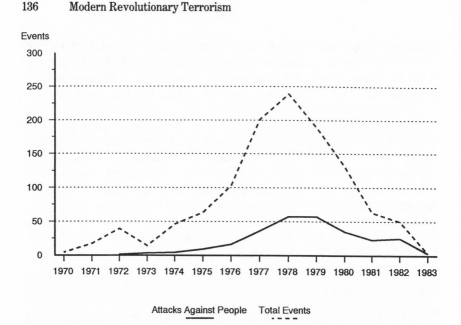

Fig. 4.4.   Evolution of left-wing terrorist events by year, from 1970 to 1983

on people reached their maximum level of 57. The same level was maintained in 1979, when the number of actions against property began to decrease (to 132). This decline was more clear-cut in 1980, when the number of episodes against people went down to 35 and that against property to 95. It continued to fall in the following two years, but the actions against property decreased faster, to 40 in 1981 and to 25 in 1982. The number of actions against people instead remained higher, with 23 in 1981 and 25 in 1982.

The number of people injured or killed during terrorist events dramatically increased. As shown in Table 4.2, after an initial phase in which the activities of the clandestine groups consisted mainly of car bombings or "symbolic" kidnappings, attacks against people and unplanned conflicts with police came to be the most widespread forms of action. Bombings against property diminished from 75 percent in the years between 1970 and 1973 to 15 percent between 1981 and 1982, with an average of 55 percent in the other years. Conversely, attacks on persons rose from zero before 1973 to 12 percent between 1974 and 1977, doubling to an average of 24 percent in the following years.

The evolution toward increasingly lethal acts was a consequence of the need to attract the attention of the media, which had become accustomed to earlier and less dramatic tactics. One result was the narrowing of the

Table 4.2.   Actions used by clandestine organizations

Action	Up to 1973 %	1974 to 1977 %	1978 to 1980 %	1981 to 1983 %	Total No.	Total %
Bombing	74.7	59.8	50.5	15.4	691	52.4
Breaking and entering	5.3	13.9	7.4	3.4	125	9.5
Kidnapping	5.3	1.9	1.1	6.8	29	2.2
Assault	0.0	12.0	23.4	26.5	236	17.9
Conflict with police	0.0	2.9	2.5	13.7	46	3.5
Robbery	14.7	9.5	14.9	34.2	191	14.5
Total[a]	5.7	39.2	46.2	14.5	1,318	100.0

[a]More than one form was sometimes used in the same event. Percentage and totals are based on the number of forms.

potential constituency, which by the end of the process was restricted to the militants of underground groups. The choice of more-violent forms of action could also have been a way of demonstrating military superiority in the competition among terrorist organizations for recruits from other illegal groups.

The radicalization of repertoires accompanied a displacement of organizational goals. Propaganda activities, those with political targets as well as those with social ones, both in the factory and outside it, were abandoned in favor of defending militants against state repression. Targets changed to include police; and actions were aimed at obstructing judicial activities, through attacks against judges, lawyers, and witnesses, and at inflicting physical "punishment" on former comrades who were considered traitors.

Changes in Ideology

The self-image that clandestine groups tried to project changed: from the "armed branch of the movement," or the "armed movement," it became the "army"; from brigade or squad it became party. With the passage of time, the interpretation of the armed struggle as a stimulus for a revolutionary process led by the working class was abandoned. The role of the organization became to refuse to accept the system. The clandestine organizations almost renounced presenting themselves as a "guide" or "example" for the revolutionary class and affirmed their role as the last expression of an existentialist struggle.

The image of the enemy also changed. The vision of the adversary became more immanent: power was no longer the "capitalist class" but something that permeated society, which thus explained the absence of potential allies. Outside the organization there was only evil. There were no longer distinctions between objective faults and subjective responsibilities, or structural predispositions and false consciousness. Consequently, justification for the strategy adopted was transformed. Giving up Machiavelli and Lenin for Sorel and Fanon, organizations no longer justified political crimes as a revolutionary need but exalted "war" as an instrument of liberation in itself.

Finally, even the structure of language changed. Terrorist documents relied less and less on terms and categories borrowed from Marxism-Leninism or other doctrines widespread in the social-movement sector. They composed a new vocabulary of terms and categories coined inside the terrorist groups and comprehensible only to their members. Thus, the need to justify increasingly violent action encouraged ideological elitism. Symbols were no longer those shared by the political culture of the radical Left. The creation of a special jargon understood only by the militants reduced to zero the possibility of propaganda messages being spread outside. One way of coping with the resulting isolation was to stress the boundaries between inside and outside, "good" and "bad."

INDIVIDUAL MOTIVATIONS IN UNDERGROUND ORGANIZATIONS

Individual Motivations for Joining Clandestine Organizations

Existing studies on the members of terrorist organizations are usually quite biased. Participation is connected with addictive personalities, foolishness, egocentric characteristics, or repeated frustration in building positive identities. I assume, however, that motivations for joining terrorist groups can be understood in the same terms as are used for other types of political participation.[46]

46. Donatella della Porta, "Recruitment Processes in Clandestine Political Organizations: Italian Left-wing Terrorism," in *From Structure to Action*, ed. Klandermans, Kriesi, and Tarrow, 155–69; idem, "I militanti delle organizzazioni clandestine de sinistra in Italia," *Rivista italiana di scienza politica* 17 (1987): 23–55; and idem, "Incentiva alla militanza nelle organizzazioni clandestine di sinistra," *Polis* 2 (1988): 233–58. On life histories of members of underground organizations, see also Claudio Novaro, "Reti di solidarietà e scelte terroristiche: un caso piemontese," *Polis* 2 (1988), and Diego Novelli and Nicole Tranfaglia, *Vite sospese* (Milan: Garzanti, 1988). On the characteristics of members of terrorist groups, see Leonard Weinberg, "The Violent Life," in *Political Violence in Contemporary Society*, ed. Peter H. Merkl (New York: Free Press, 1986), 145–67.

My qualitative data on Italian terrorists show that recruitment occurred in homogeneous groups, aggregated on the basis of multiple ties. Table 4.3 presents the number of personal ties that new recruits had with members of the underground groups they eventually joined. Some caution is needed in the analysis of this table. The existing personal ties are, in fact, more numerous than those traceable from judicial sources. The category "no ties" is, in fact, dropped, since it is very likely that personal ties existed even though they were not revealed by our source. A couple of observations are still worth making. First, in at least 843 responses out of 1,214, the decision to join an underground organization was taken by people who had at least one friend who was already involved. Second, in 74 percent of these cases, there was more than one friend, and in 42 percent, there were even more than seven.

Analysis and interviews confirm the important role played by solidarity in the decision to become a terrorist. Decisions to join underground organizations were taken by cliques of people connected to one another by simultaneous involvements in more than one activity. For example, cases frequently involved next-door neighbors who worked in the same division of a big factory, schoolmates who used to vacation together, or cousins who belonged to the same voluntary association. Moreover, affective ties were often very intense: in 298 cases, militants of underground organizations had at least one relative, usually husband or wife, brother or sister, who shared their commitment.

According to these data, therefore, social interactions, rather than individual characteristics, explain participation in underground groups. To understand personal motivations, it was necessary to look at the primary groups in which individuals participated in everyday life and, especially, at their positive affective ties with valued others. Recruitment

Table 4.3. Personal ties between terrorist organizations and new recruits

No. of Personal Ties	No. of Responses	% of Responses	% of Cases
1	220	26.1	28.6
2	123	14.6	16.0
3	40	4.7	5.2
4	64	7.6	8.3
Between 5 and 7	45	5.5	5.9
8 and more	351	41.6	45.6
Total responses[a]	843	100.0	109.6

Missing cases: 371.
Valid cases: 769.

[a]Some people were active in more than one clandestine organization.

was in part explained by structural proximity and affective interactions with members of a group.

Several explanations for the role of social networks in influencing individuals who join a terrorist organization can be found in life histories. The desire to conform was especially strong in peer groups that involved very young people. Very intense friendship ties strengthened the pressure to conform. The intensity of these relations explains the high propensity to honor the involvement with the group. Participation in high-risk organizations was, therefore, more likely when it reinforced preexisting solidarity relations. Social networks also worked as communication channels through which information passed and acquired meaning and relevance. The kind of cliques people frequented affected the kind of political messages that reached them and the ideological appeals that were translated into concrete actions. Personal networks also reduced the risks involved in recruiting because the recruiter could trust the recruit and vice versa. Networks therefore helped to maintain loyalty.

The relevance of personal contacts in recruitment in Italian terrorist organizations is confirmed by the relations that existed between recruits and recruiters. Table 4.4 shows that in as many as 88 percent of the cases in which the nature of the tie with the recruiter is known, she or he is not a stranger; in 44 percent, she or he is a personal friend; and in 20 percent, she or he is a relative.

These results are confirmed by the testimony of a Front Line militant. Speaking of recruitment he said, "[It] happened . . . through completely personal ties. In this way the comrades of the *squadre* contacted people whom they knew for a long time, who would have entertained the idea of joining the *squadre* or at least would not have been shocked or created

Table 4.4. Relations of terrorist recruits with their recruiters

Relation with Recruiter	No.	% of Responses	% of Cases
Unknown	42	11.6	12.3
Wife/husband	51	14.0	15.0
Other kin	22	6.1	6.4
Friend	159	43.8	46.6
Workmate	34	9.4	10.0
Political comrade	55	15.2	16.1
Total responses[a]	363	100.0	106.5

Missing cases: 799.
Valid cases: 341.

[a]Some people were active in more than one clandestine organization.

problems for the security of the comrades who made the contact."[47] The presence of reciprocal affective ties was essential in reducing the risks for a clandestine organization.

The presence of strong affective ties is therefore a powerful explanation of individual motivation. It is not, however, sufficient to predict who will and who will not join. Involvement in some kind of professional or family network can exert countervailing effects on individual willingness to join some political groups. Research on social-movement organizations has shown that in order for a personal relation to lead to recruitment, it has to involve two people who share not only friendship but interests, values, and membership in other voluntary associations. Research on Italian terrorism shows that in some cases preexisting political networks played important roles. The most common motivation to join was the wish to show solidarity with cliques of friends who shared a previous commitment to small political groups. Table 4.5 displays information on the legal organizations to which militants belonged before joining clandestine organizations.

The data refer only to those cases in which previous legal militancy could be traced. Nevertheless, it is striking to note that terrorists

Table 4.5. Legal political organizations to which terrorists belonged before joining underground groups

Legal Organization	No.	% of Responses	% of Cases
Italian Communist Party	17	2.1	2.8
Trade unions	40	4.9	6.5
New Left	232	28.5	37.7
of which:			
Lotta Continua	75	9.2	12.2
Potere Operaio	52	6.4	8.5
Autonomous collectives	518	63.6	84.2
of which:			
Comitati Comunisti	56	6.9	9.2
Senza Tregua	32	3.9	5.2
Rosso	42	5.2	6.8
Other	7	0.8	1.2
Total responses[a]	814	100.0	132.4

Missing cases: 525.
Valid cases: 615.

[a]Some people were active in more than one clandestine organization.

47. Quoted in Court of Turin, Public Prosecutor's Charge, Juridical Proceeding No. 321/80, 69.

had often exhibited a legal political commitment before joining the underground groups. It indicates that recruitment into terrorism involved "political" people, that is, people who already had a political identity.

The percentage of people coming from the traditional Left is very low: only 3 percent for the Communist party, a slightly higher 6.5 percent for trade unions. Hypotheses referring to the disillusionment felt by "hard" Communist militants when faced with the softening of their party do not fit reality. By contrast, 38 percent of terrorists had been involved in the New Left. In this group the percentage of people who had participated in the PO and LC was quite high. As mentioned earlier, these organizations have often been accused of providing the structures for the emerging terrorist formations, in particular by building semilegal bodies defined as "strategic articulations" of an organic terrorist project.[48] My data on the political careers of militants show that very few people shifted to terrorism directly from these two groups. Instead, the breakdown of these groups gave rise to a process of "autonomization" of *comitati di base* (rank-and-file committees) and *collettivi operai* (workers collectives) under the guardianship of the New Left.[49] It was in these small political nuclei, characterized by radical ideologies and violent tactics, that many future terrorists continued their political involvement.

The militants of the late 1960s movement who chose radicalization were few in number. The sharp increase in recruitment came about only when the entrepreneurial efforts of these people located a large potential base in another group of violence-prone political militants. Too young to have been involved in the New Left, the members of the "second generation" of terrorists started their political socialization in those groups that grew out of the crisis of the New Left. As many as 84 percent of terrorists had been active in the nuclei formed around the two magazines *Rosso* and *Senza Tregua*, in the Circoli del Proletariato Giovanile, or in the small Comitati di Quartiere active in the popular city neighborhoods.

These groups were very small. In my table, the item "Autonomous collectives" aggregates ninety-three subitems. In at least eighty-nine of them the size of the organization was small enough to allow for the assumption that strong personal bonds were developed among all the members. To sixty-five of these subitems I have been able to trace at least two future terrorists who had shared their previous political experience. Very often the choice of joining clandestine organizations

48. For this hypothesis, see, for instance, Ventura, "Il problema delle origini."
49. For this hypothesis, see also Palombarini, *Il 7 aprile*.

involved an even larger network of "political" companions: from forty-seven of these groups came at least three future terrorists, from thirty-five at least four; from eleven more than five. Decisions to join the armed struggle were, in all these cases, collective ones.

In-depth interviews and evaluations permit a better interpretation of these quantitative data. The testimony of former members reveals the great importance they attached to membership in the same small, legal political group in everyday life. Even where friendship networks external to the political milieu existed, their importance tended to diminish as political socialization developed. The amount of time spent in political activities increased the amount of contacts with political comrades. At the same time, the strengthening of friendship ties inside the group augmented the value of political involvement, encouraging people to dedicate more and more time to those activities. In this way, other ties lost the capacity to exert countervailing effects on the formation of the personality. As already suggested for other kinds of political socialization,[50] commitment engendered isolation from the outside world, which enforced the loyalty to the new group. Political friends became the most influential peer group.

To sum up, Italian clandestine organizations recruited members through dense networks of social relations, where political ties were strengthened by bonds based on friendship and kinship. These groups created loyalties and communication channels. Individual motivations can be traced to solidarity with groups of people with whom a political identity was shared. The understanding of personal motivation requires, however, a deeper analysis of the processes of political socialization that build collective identities.

Primary research supports the hypothesis that the formation of political collective identities is influenced by the political climate in which people have their first political experiences. The political climate in Italy influenced both the degree of importance of a political identity in personal life and the specific meaning of political activities. Personal participation in physical confrontations with police or adversaries favored the formation of militants with a high predisposition to the use of violence. The lack of medium-range success increased the need for symbolic substitutes, often found in radical ideologies that prescribed that social change could only be obtained through a long war against the enemy. Physical fights were considered the highest expression of a political commitment that had became the most important element in the building of their collective identities.

50. Kenneth Keniston, *Young Radicals: Notes on Committed Youth* (New York: Harcourt, Brace and World, 1968).

The life histories of Italian terrorists confirm that people recruited to clandestine organizations tended to use violence as a political means and that political identity was important to the formation of their personalities. Participation in violent collective actions is always recalled as an important experience in their political socialization. Many members of armed formations had belonged to the semimilitary structures of nonclandestine organizations. In the history of their political activity are episodes of squattings, confrontations with police or neofascists, use of Molotov cocktails to "defend" marches, and arrests. The use of violence by right-wing activists and police is cited as a justification for personal involvement in illegal and violent activities.

To conclude, people become involved in terrorist activities when they belong to dense political networks and are socialized to accept violence. Previous exposure to violence predisposes individuals to involvement in terrorism. Participation in violence produces a kind of militant for whom political commitment is identified with physical fights rather than with negotiation or compromise. For these people, the use of physical violence precedes, rather than follows, entrance into terrorist organizations. The threshold of clandestinity was often passed "involuntarily," sometimes even without awareness.

Persistence of Commitment in Left-Wing Underground Groups

What kept people inside terrorist organizations? Why did they maintain their commitment even after they were in jail? The risks and the costs of participation were, of course, high. Militance in underground groups implied intense involvement, in terms of both time and resources. Clandestinity imposed strong limitations on relations with the external environment and produced deep changes in everyday life. The constraints on communication with the external world exerted pressure for complete identification with the terrorist group. Moreover, participation in underground organizations created the risk of being arrested or even killed. The use of arms implied emotional costs as well, related to the possibility of wounding or killing other persons. How were these costs balanced to make participation in a terrorist group attractive?

Certainly material constraints made it more difficult to leave the terrorist organization. For those who went underground in order to avoid arrest, participation in a terrorist organization was rewarded by the logistical support they needed to stay clandestine. The risk of being arrested is recalled in many life histories as the main reason for going underground. As one of them stated, "I could not stay at home and be quiet, while waiting for them to come and take me."[51] Once underground, participation in terrorist organizations was the only means of finding what they needed to survive: money, lodging, papers. Even if poor in material resources, the underground organizations were able to provide militants with places to live, false identity documents, and money. Many militants of the small terrorist organizations joined the bigger ones in order to have better material support.

A second material constraint that forced a persistence of commitment was the risk of retaliation by the terrorist organization. For many years, however, this risk did not exist. They were in fact free to quit their organizations, provided that they did not steal arms or money and did not try to persuade others to desert. Only in the beginning of the 1980s did militants perceive the risk of retaliation as threatening. When some arrested cadres collaborated with the police, the terrorist organizations reacted by punishing the "traitors" or "suspected traitors." According to many interviews, this situation made it more difficult for some of the militants in prison to quit their organizations, and in many cases delayed their decision.

Material constraints are not, however, a powerful explanation for the persistence of commitment. People stayed in the underground even when they were not sought by the police, and even when they were under arrest and could improve their material conditions by collaborating with the judges. In order to understand the persistence of commitment, one must consider that the definition of costs and benefits is subjective. Recent studies on social movements stress individual perceptions.[52] Militance implies the building of a collective identity and influences the way in which militants evaluate the costs and benefits of participation.

There was, first, the grounding of the individual identity in a larger community and the definition of this community, which passed through identification with the peer group. The development of affective ties during frequent and exclusive interactions compensated for the limits on relations with the external world. In the beginning, the rules that restricted meetings with comrades from the same terrorist organization were often broken by the members. When a terrorist organization was founded, for instance, the militants knew each other, and their solidarity

51. Interview with G. G., 29. See note 8 above. Copies of the interviews are available at the Instituto Carlo Cattaneo in Bologna. Further references to the interviews will be cited in text.
52. Alessandro Pizzorno, "Scambio politico e identità collettiva nel conflitto di classe," in *Conflitti in Europa*, ed. Colin Crouch and Alessandro Pizzorno (Milan: Etas Libri, 1977), 407–33, and Albert O. Hirschman, *Shifting Involvements: Private Interests and Public Action* (Princeton: Princeton University Press, 1981).

was strengthened by living together. As one of them recalled, the founders of the BR shared the same apartment for years, long before going underground.[53] The foundation of the group was "a matter of friendship." Especially in the rank-and-file structures and in the small organizations, the militants "had always known each other."

The importance attached to participation in small, legal political groups has already been stressed. These group dynamics continued to operate after the formation of a terrorist group. The words used by the interviewees to characterize relations with their comrades testify to strong emotional bonds: "absolute human relations," "solidarity even in the small things," "relations free from any material interest," and "affective generosity." Moreover, the time spent with fellow comrades is recalled as a very happy one: "parties following some actions," "big component of conviviality," "merry brotherhood," and so on. Ties among comrades became more and more important when interactions with people external to the organization became "impossible to cultivate."

Moreover, the importance of solidarity with the other members of the underground groups was increased by sharing a common mission and risks, which compensated for renouncing other personal ties. These affective ties pushed the individuals to more-demanding forms of participation when a friend was in danger. The following passage from an interview describes this process of becoming responsible for others and the search for "equal punishment" as a symbol of loyalty: "A deep change and distortion [came into] my life because, by devoting myself totally to this kind of involvement spiritually related . . . to my friend who had to go underground, to this idea of our convulsed lives . . . I had these images of the necessity, the rightness, the beauty of that kind of sacrifice" (interview with Gu. M., 58–59).

Solidarity with close friends in prison was often recalled as an important reason for remaining in the terrorist organization. As a militant said, referring to her husband and herself, "I believe that if G. had not been in prison since 1977, L. and I would have not continued for such a long time. . . . The fact that Chicco was in prison was an important element for continuing, because he was a friend of ours" (interview with S. R., 68). Moreover, loyalty to friends who were in prison often motivated more-active participation. One of the interviewees explained that "it was when S. was arrested that I found the emotional energy that pushed me to carry out the first actions for the organizations" (interview with Gi. M., 15). Another militant said, "This kind of involvement with

53. Alberto Franceschini, Piervittorio Buffa, and Franco Giustolisi, *Mara, Renato e io: Storia dei fondatori della Brigate Rosse* (Milan: Mondadori, 1988).

my friends means that at the end of the game either we were all outside or we were all inside [prison], because if some of us are out and some of us are in, I don't give up my friends. . . . This meant I would decide to drown because, if my friends had drowned because of a belief that I shared, well if they are there and I can't help them, I prefer to be with them" (interview with Gu. M., 58–59).

However, frequent interactions among friends became dangerous for the security of the organizations. A more compartmentalized organizational structure then reduced contacts inside the group. At that point solidarity within the peer group was partially replaced by loyalty to the organization. The affective loads once discharged on the comrade-friend shifted to a more abstract community of those who practiced the armed struggle. Loyalty was strengthened by the reference to shared heroes: the comrades who had died during terrorist actions. The death of a fellow member created emotional strains and a desire for revenge in all those who believed in the armed struggle. This theme emerges, for instance, in the following testimony of a rank-and-file member: "When you are entangled in a vicious circle . . . it is very difficult to judge from the outside, because there were, for instance, episodes such as the deaths of Matteo and Barbara—they had such a strong emotional impact. . . . Then you are inside a spiral of revenge and retaliation because when you are in that game, you have to play" (interview with Gi. M., 35).

Another source of identification was comrades in prison. All the militants felt responsible for their destiny, whether they knew one another or not. As many interviews demonstrate, any desire to quit was felt as a "betrayal of those who were in prison." The militants in prison, in contrast, developed a "sense of responsibility" toward those on the outside who risked their lives to free them. The following passages describe this reciprocal emotional "blackmail." In the first, the feelings of those who were outside are described. As one of the leaders of PL put it, even in the beginning of the eighties, when the defeat of their organization was more than evident,

> we continued to fight above all for our comrades who were in prison. . . . Choices of death, of individual death, were based on this very thing: solidarity with those who were in prison. Because for all these people, it would have been much better if they had escaped abroad or surrendered. And instead they made this unbelievable choice. It is not by chance that the whole story finished in October 1982 in Florence [in prison] when we all met [for a trial], and so, all together we could decide that it is over, that we quit. We no longer have the problem of a reciprocal

blackmail, of a solidarity that . . . had become reciprocal blackmail between those who were inside and those who were outside. (Interview with S. R., 69)

This second passage describes, in the same period, the feelings of those who were in prison toward their comrades outside: "It was a situation in which we were all for declaring the dissolution of the organization, the end of the experience of the armed struggle. But at that point the comrades outside wrote a very radical document for 'continuing' the struggle, and we did not feel morally like avoiding their requests. So, all that happened many years later" (interview with N. S., 48).

The persistence of commitment also resulted from a need to maintain self-respect. To use Hirschman's concepts, a high initial investment reduced the likelihood of exit; the higher the costs already paid, the stronger the need for an adequate reward.[54] Since this was not achieved, a psychological mechanism pushed to "raise the bid" instead of quitting. Involvement, therefore, persisted because surrendering implied "losing" everything that had already been paid as a cost for entry. Even when the deep crisis of the organization increased the perceived costs of participation, as one rank-and-file member put it, "the idea of quitting the organization produced feelings of guilt—because, after having already paid such a price, to quit meant to admit that all that we had done had been useless" (interview with *Marco*, 2/63). The following passages from the life histories of two very young militants of PL in Turin also refer to the search for redemption. One said that he had been convinced that "the only chance for redemption I have, from a moral point of view, both for the violence I produced and the violence I suffered . . . is to go right to the end" (interview with Gu. M., 73–74). Another explained that his commitment to the terrorist organization increased after he had to go underground, in part as a result of "this ideological belief that I had to pursue the way I had undertaken in order to find—or, better, to try to find—a reason for my previous participation in a murder" (interview with Ga., 19).

Loyalty to the "revolutionary community" therefore allowed militants to ignore the price they had already paid. The possibility of defining political murder as "proletarian justice," or imprisonment as a step in the fight for freedom, helped militants to keep their own self-respect. Most of those who had come to criticize armed struggle expressed an overall positive judgment about their past—thus employing a psychological

54. Albert O. Hirschman, *Exit, Voice, and Loyalty: Responses to Decline in Firms, Organizations, and States* (Cambridge: Harvard University Press, 1970).

device to keep one's own sense of self-respect—because, as put by one of the interviewees, "it would be very sad if, at this point, I could only say, I was damn wrong, everything I did was wrong, look how stupid I was; but now that is over, and I can start again" (interview with M. S., 98).

Ideology also offered ways of reducing the psychological costs of participation in terrorist organizations. Research on political organizations has analyzed the role of ideology in reducing the information needed to act, simplifying the complexity of the real world, and providing the symbols on which to build a collective identity. The ideology of the terrorist organizations offered (1) a justification of political violence, including political murder; (2) an image of the external world that masked the failures of the armed struggle; and (3) a positive evaluation of the role of individual action.

The acceptance of political murder is one of the main "objective" costs of militance in an underground organization, and the ideology of the terrorist groups aimed to persuade the militants of its legitimacy. Political violence was justified as being in the tradition of the working-class movement, and the armed struggle was defined as the only form of political action in the present historical phase. In the life histories, militants acknowledged that references to the "fathers of socialist thought" were used to justify the choice of the armed struggle: "We were supported in this also by famous quotes from Marxist literature, where violence appeared as absolutely legitimate, as part of the history of the working class. Once it is decided that the historical conditions allow for that kind of organization, the rest is only a technical consequence" (interview with M. F., 21). The reference to important works of Communist theory was "a technique of identification, that is, it offered images with which people could easily identify themselves. . . . It was nothing but a way to make ourselves known, to speak a common language that probably none of us would have spoken on his own. It was a way to identify ourselves with the history and the tradition of the progressive movements of our century" (interview with N. S., 35–36).

Ideology also legitimated violence through a depersonalization of the victims, defined as nothing but parts of the capitalist system. "Tools of the system" and later "pigs" or "watch dogs" were the words used by underground groups to define their victims. The whole ideological system was founded on an absolute opposition "friend-enemy."[55] The victims were therefore considered not as human beings made of flesh and blood, but as symbols. As shown in the following long passages from two life

55. Luigi Manconi, "Il nemico assoluto: Antifascismo e contropotere nella fase aurorale del terrorismo di sinistra," Polis 2 (1988), 259–86.

histories, this ideology was deeply internalized. The first shows how the definition of the victims as "small wheels of a machine" led the militants to dismiss the idea that they had killed other human beings. Giving an account of her participation in a murder, a militant said:

> We lived the problem of death inside a big ideology. . . . I am one of those who killed the policeman Lo Russo in Turin. . . . Well, I lived that murder inside this logic of the function, because he was a warden, and he was well known as a "torturer," as we used to say, so I had all the justifications of the ideology. . . . For me it was a routine job. And this is the very aberration of the ideology; on one side, there are your friends, and on the other, there are your enemies; and the enemies are a category; they are functions; they are symbols. They are not human beings. And so they have to be dealt with as absolute enemies, so that you have a relation of absolute abstraction with death. (Interview with S. R., 62–63)

Within this ideology, political crimes were presented as acts of justice. The following meticulous description of the preparation for an attack illustrates the psychological devices that permitted militants to define the most brutal action as a "bureaucratic need":

> You make a political analysis, but then you need a victim. If you want to hit the Christian Democracy in a neighborhood, you need a target . . . then, you start to look for this victim . . . you read the newspapers, you infiltrate their meetings, and you try to find out. Then you have singled out your victim; he is physically there; he is the one to be blamed for everything. In that moment there is already the logic of a trial in which you have already decided that he is guilty; you only have to decide about his punishment. So you have a very "emphatic" sense of justice; you punish him not only for what he has done but also for all the rest. Then, you don't care anymore which responsibilities that person has; you give him them all . . . he is only a small part of the machine that is going to destroy all of us. (Interview with A. S., 45)

The ideology of the underground organizations was also characterized by a high degree of mystification of reality. Ambiguity was often singled out as a characteristic of the ideology of political organizations, especially of those poor in material resources. This ambiguity obscured the failure of the organization by defining its defeats as victories. The ideology of the Italian underground groups was, for instance, ambivalent because it did not give any indication about the preconditions for the different stages of the revolutionary process, which was instead considered a kind of historical necessity.

This was combined with a more-than-optimistic image of the success of the armed struggle. The documents of the groups were full of statements such as "the worse, the better," "the near victory of the working class," and "the forthcoming revolution." This image of reality was so deeply internalized by the militants as still to be present in their recollections, which contain a misplaced certainty that the armed struggle was widespread in the social movement: "Hundreds of people supported us," "We were deep rooted at Fiat and Pirelli," "We were in contact with the working class," "There was a very large legitimation for our actions," and "Our hypothesis was going to be accepted at a mass level." Moreover, the short-term outcomes of terrorist activities were defined as "victory of the working class." As one of the interviewees recalled, "A foreman whose car had been set on fire becomes much more submissive" (interview with N. S., 25). For a long period the militants had few doubts about the victory of their organization, the working class, and the revolution. Defeats were denied and described as indicators of the necessity to "shift to a new phase of the struggle."

The selection of sources of information was the device by which this unreal image of the external world was built. Clandestinity, in fact, drastically reduced external contacts; comrades from the same organization became the only source of information. The following quotation demonstrates that mystifications were the result of a continuous series of "small lies":

It was a sum of small lies. In fact, each of us . . . tried to give credit to the image of an underground organization that was deep-rooted in the society, that enjoyed more popularity, more support, more consensus. This did not happen through big lies but through the small lies we told each other. . . . "But do you know that . . . the concierge understood that I am a member of the Red Brigades, and not only does she not denounce me but rather, if she sees a policeman, she manages to warn me? Do you know that the people of that cafe understood who I am, and when I go there, the barman offers me a drink? Do you know that in that factory, when we wounded that foreman, they opened a bottle and toasted?" (Interview with E. F., 38)

The persistence of commitment was also brought about by the internalization of a value system that emphasized the heroic role of a small minority. The importance of militance was not justified by a precise image of a future society. Ideas about the aims of the revolution were, on the contrary, extremely vague. The role of individuals was, instead, described according to quasi-existentialist explanations. As in other political sects, a positive emphasis was put on ideals as a way of living outside of normal standards, courage as a duty of the true believer, sacrifice as shared suffering.

The prospect of an "adventurous life" is recalled in some interviews as a reward in itself, at least in the first phases of participation. The dangers involved in participation in a terrorist organization were considered "the expression of a dynamic and interesting life" and were opposed to the dullness of normal life. According to a militant, a group identity was built on this "diversity": "The group was made homogeneous by this peculiar attitude; it finds in this diversity its identity and its sublimation. These attitudes are therefore exalted and become its raison d'être. . . . The very fact of being a clandestine organization becomes gratifying in itself; because you are a 'fighter,' you have a very dynamic life; I mean your life is not boring and dull" (interview with M. C., 42).

Together with adventure, action became rewarding in itself. Militance in a terrorist group was exacting: a huge amount of time was required to fulfill organizational tasks. Most of the activities were not, however, related to the practical needs of organizational survival; they had instead a symbolic value. Activism was contrasted with the renunciation of the political struggle by those who had not joined the armed struggle. The emphasis on guns and military success reflected the importance accorded to action in the value system of the underground. The fascination with guns is acknowledged in many interviews with male militants: "The gun which gives you more strength" (interview with A. S., 33); or "The arms have a charm in themselves; it is a charm that makes you feel more macho. . . . Sometimes I showed them to women to try to seduce them" (interview with P. L., 79). This belief pushed militants to evaluate the effectiveness of armed struggle on the basis of its military achievements. "Satisfaction" and "gratification" came from military success. As a militant put it, "The very fact of seeing that thing burning and falling down—that made me happy" (interview with Av., 28). Or, as another militant acknowledged, "We had this tendency to find our gratification only at the military level; therefore we went and did what had to be done" (interview with A. B., 57).

Moreover, group mythology considered individual sacrifice to be a duty of a "freedom fighter," and this notion became more and more widespread as the organization declined. A rationale for militance in the underground organizations was found in the necessity of "keeping alive the revolutionary movement" by "opposing pacification." As phrased in one of the interviews, "From 1980 on, the only aim is to resist. . . . There is no longer the idea of an advancing revolution: 'Let's continue on, we are many, we are beautiful'; we are not beautiful; we are not many; we are only poor chaps who meet and say, 'O.K., let's try to do something while we wait; let's try to create again a revolutionary situation.' . . . If we want to synthesize that in a slogan, it was to resist at any price, without allowing them to reabsorb the movement and to impose social peace" (interview with M. C., 50).

Individual Exit from Terrorist Organizations

Militants began to perceive changes in the environment and in the characteristics of terrorist organizations as early as 1979. Most of the interviewees asserted that they started to feel isolated and to criticize the terrorist organizations they belonged to. "This organization . . . is lacerated because it cannot solve its problems, . . . is at an impasse. . . . All the people I knew were in prison; those with whom I had started were not there anymore; nobody was there; nothing was there" (interview with A. S., 54). The growing brutality of the terrorist crimes disgusted the same militants, especially some actions of retaliation, such as the assassination in prison of a very young member accused of being a traitor or the assassination of two private guards, with the sole aim of "denouncing" the suspected betrayal of another militant.

The temptation to take advantage of the new "repentance" laws grew stronger. "You cannot think that a person who, from the perspective of the building of Communist society, was ready to undergo long periods of imprisonment or even to die—when he/she realizes that . . . the political defeat is there, you cannot think . . . he/she can freely and easily agree to pay such a high price. . . . When the old ideological categories are abandoned, the indispensable need to start again to believe, to hope, to work for something new and different arises" (interview with I. R., 59–60).

The "repentance" law of 1980 exploited the discontent of some members in order to defeat the terrorist organizations. But it did not take into account group dynamics. Many of the militants who were in the process of quitting terrorism were in fact compelled to react to the "betrayal" of some of their fellow comrades by confirming their loyalty to the organization. Solidarity toward comrades also influenced the process of quitting underground organizations. Interviews expressed such sentiments as "You do not give up on the basis of an individual decision"; "You have to wait for the others"; "You have to wait for a process of collective consciousness-raising" so that "you do not damage the rapports with the other prisoners"; and "You reduce the burden coming from the acknowledgment of your mistakes." As one of the interviewees stated, "I felt like somebody who had to preserve at any cost that collective, I had to save those personal relations . . . because with them, it was a life lived together" (interview with S. R., 31–33 passim). One militant said, "Although there were many conflicts, on one side there was solidarity, friendship, and the necessity to make a common front in prison; on the other side, the lack of a possibility for a political exit from the organization" (interview with A. B., 120). These solidarity bonds were, therefore, often strengthened when the only choice was between a complete collaboration with the state—with a corresponding loss of political identity—and loyalty to friends-comrades. The climate of intimidation inside the special prisons also hampered these processes of quitting the terrorist organizations.

For most of the militants, only when they could not avoid recognizing defeat was it possible for a new orientation in the antiterrorism legislation to facilitate their leaving the organizations. Political and administrative actions came to recognize the importance of "reconciliation." The institution of the so-called *aree omogenee*—where, on the basis of their own requests, former terrorists could ask to spend their period of imprisonment together—created the possibility for this "political exit" from terrorism. In June 1986, a new law—Nuove proposte per la difesa dell'ordinamento constituzionale attraverso la dissociazione—reduced penalties for those who had abandoned the armed struggle without any collaboration or confession. A reformist prison policy created the preconditions for a reintegration of former terrorists into society, through professional training and, above all, through the use of alternatives to imprisonment, such as house arrest, controlled custody, and permission to work outside prisons. At different times and in different ways—but with only very few exceptions as far as left-wing terrorism is concerned—most of the former militants acknowledged the failure of their political project and expressed a new confidence in the democratic system.

CONCLUDING REMARKS

My explanation of the emergence and evolution of left-wing underground organizations in Italy is based on the use of three analytical levels: macro, meso, and micro. The assumption is that in order to understand the phenomenon, it is necessary to look not only at the environmental preconditions but also at individual perceptions of the external opportunities, and not only at individual propensities but also at historical preconditions for the emergence of those propensities. Moreover, I look at the terrorist organizations as structured groups, composed of different interests, influenced by their environment but capable of strategic choices in their attempts to reach organizational aims. In concluding, I pay more attention to the integration of these three levels of analysis in a global explanation.

First, some conclusions on the origins of the terrorist organizations can be presented in a formal model in which the preconditions present in the environment, the characteristics of the networks of mobilized individuals, and the strategic choices of collective actors are represented. My findings are summarized in the Figure 4.5.

For terrorism to emerge, certain resources, defined as interests, ideologies, and tactics, had to be present in the environment.

Collective interests that were not efficiently mediated. Clandestine political organizations claimed to be the representatives of collective interests present in society. They nevertheless did not represent specific interests that were different from those protesters acted on. The choice of tactics was not strictly related to the nature of the interests involved; it was instead a result of interaction between political groups and the state. The presence of mobilizable interests, not yet institutionally mediated, encouraged some organizations to increase their influence in the political marketplace through radicalization of actions.

Political culture that justified violence. The political formations that went underground had espoused ideologies allowing the use of physical violence as a means of political intervention. Nevertheless, the adoption of armed struggle was not an unavoidable result of ideology. The spread of a violent political culture was a necessary resource for the development of armed groups. The ideology of some organizations permitted them to choose terrorist practices, removing constraints against the use of illegal strategies. It offered, furthermore, an ex post facto justification for the adoption of armed action and military structures.

Use of violent tactics. The organizations that opted for clandestinity used extremely violent forms of action even before going underground. Organized violence developed gradually in the interactions of different actors in conflict. When efficient institutional mediation of interests was not forthcoming, the extension of mobilization produced radicalization. In this way, a legacy of violent tactics spread and was legitimated by different organizations.

Accordingly, these environmental preconditions gave rise to *political*

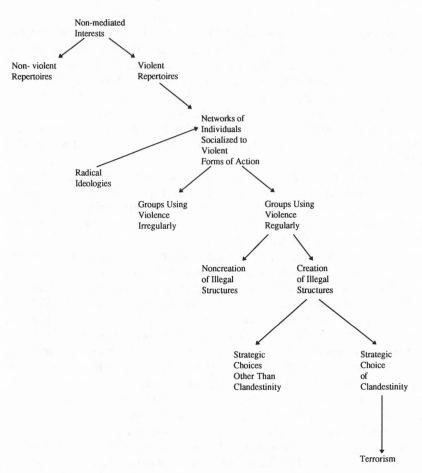

Fig. 4.5.   A model for the emergence of clandestine organizations

groups with semilegal structures. Clandestine organizations were founded by individuals who were tied to one another by a common militance in protest organizations. These organizations were not distinctive as far as interests, ideologies, or tactics were concerned. Their shared characteristic was, instead, the presence of semilegal structures. As the information on the previous political activities of the founders and on the histories of the main underground groups has shown, the groups that went underground were those with specific resources to spend on violent activities. In the case of armed formations solidarity networks were mainly composed of individuals who had previously used violent forms of political action. Their socialization gave them a conception of collective involvement related more to direct forms of action than to bargaining processes.

The building of an underground organization was, nevertheless, a political decision, taken by previously existing groups; it involved *a strategic choice by an organized group*. Groups using illegal strategies arose when interests were not effectively mediated by the institutional system, when the political culture predisposed them to violence, and when social movements used violent tactics. By experimenting with different strategies, some organizations found that the adoption of more and more violent tactics attracted recruits. To counter state repression, clandestinity offered the advantage of minimizing some costs, such as the risk of arrest, even at the price of minimizing the benefits available in the short run. The radicalization of tactics, ideology, and organizing formulas was thus an instrument to strengthen the identity of the group. Violent activism provided surrogate symbolic compensations for the lack of practical effectiveness. The choice of violent actions answered demands present in the movement during the phases of demobilization.

Furthermore, with regard to the evolution of the Italian terrorist groups, the same condition of clandestinity brought about a series of vicious circles in which each attempt to face problems at a certain level produced new difficulties at the next. The centralization and structuration of the organizational model met the task of protecting the militants and involving them deeper and deeper inside the organization. Its consequence was, nevertheless, their further isolation from the outside world and, with it, the loss of channels for information and recruitment. Also, an increasingly compartmentalized structure was aimed at protecting the group and strengthening personal involvement. One of its effects was, however, to fuel personal rivalries, producing new splits.

Given the impossibility of using the normal means of propaganda, terrorist organizations needed to use the media as an intermediary to spread their message. The logic of news selection adopted by the media forced them to use more and more violent tactics. Their actions thus became so bloody that they produced disapproval even in the social areas that were more prone to violent tactics. The purpose of woundings and assassinations became to demonstrate the efficacy of the organization and therefore to strengthen the integration of militants and to recruit inside the terrorist sector. But the escalation of tactics attracted police repression.

Under pressure from the police, contacts with the external world were reduced to demands for logistical support. The tactics terrorist organizations adopted for getting financial resources were those typical of common criminality, exposed them to increased risks of armed fights with police, and damaged the image of the organizations before the public. The urgency of finding money and arms for the survival of the growing number of militants forced into clandestinity brought about a dangerous dependence on secret services and organized crime. To deny the defeats, the clandestine groups developed cryptic ideologies of highly symbolic value for insiders but with no meaning for the external world. As the survival of the organizations came to depend on the outcome of military battles with the state, the uneven distribution of forces was decisive in the defeat of the terrorist group.

Therefore, the evolution of terrorist organizations cannot be fully understood without taking into account dynamics that are neither the direct effect of environmental changes nor the result of a rational organizational strategy. A critical role is played by intrinsic processes that are neither foreseen nor planned by the organization, nor vital to the equilibrium of the system. Generally speaking, the evolution of a political organization is influenced by internal tensions among the different aims it has to fulfill. In the special case of terrorist organizations, their decline seems to be connected to a series of unforeseen consequences following the choice of clandestinity. Some subsequent choices, those oriented toward the solution of the survival problem, produce unplanned results and reduce the range of action available. Each transformation requires new changes in the structure and functioning of clandestine organizations. But these changes have, in turn, perverse effects to which the terrorist leaders react by bringing about a further transformation. Not being able to overcome the crisis, they descend deeper and deeper into a downward spiral in which each successive turn reduces the strategic options available in the future.

The evolution faced by the Italian clandestine organizations is similar to that of other terrorist groups active in the same historical period in other industrial democracies, such as the Federal Republic of Germany, the United States, Japan, Canada, and Spain. Similar internal dynamics account for the decline of terrorist organizations in different historical contexts. The abandonment of social propaganda for a "private war" against the state leads to the decline. Caught between arrests and the loss of some initial sympathy, groups stop recruiting and focus on defending their internal cohesion. Most of the activities of the terrorist organizations aim at sustaining the commitment of those who are already members.

Underground groups are able to keep the commitment of most of their members even when the crisis in their organizations becomes evident. The persistence of commitment in terrorist organizations is explained by a very high level of identification with the organization. Through a gradual process of material and emotional involvement, this identification shifts from the small peer group to the community of the armed struggle. Moreover, commitment increases because of the motivational process that endeavors to adhere to a cause for which high costs have already been paid. Persistence of commitment is motivated by ego involvement in some choices that push for continuity in order to preserve self-respect, by fear of losing the support of the peer group, and by a sense of belonging dramatized by the exposure to shared risks. The same factors have been singled out in other analyses of clandestine organizations.[56]

Underground organizations are also highly isolated from external reality, making it extremely difficult for their militants to perceive defeat. By reducing the possibilities of communicating with the external world, the terrorist organization becomes, in fact, the only source of information. This facilitates the internalization by the militants of the organization's ideology. Justification for the use of violence is therefore found in a highly abstract and simplified image of the world, where the victims are presented as small wheels of a mechanism, a small elite of "freedom fighters" as being in charge of imposing the real justice, and the *enjeu* for the class conflict as a military one. At the same time, the lack of any reference to the preconditions and the progression of a revolutionary process makes the ideology extremely flexible and the organization less and less vulnerable to external defeats.

In Italy, this kind of dynamic delayed the process of quitting the underground organizations but could not, however, prevent it. After frequently lengthy processes of individual and collective reflections, almost all the militants of the left-wing terrorist groups decided to abandon their commitment to violent political action. The abandonment of this commitment, as well as the reintegration of those who had quit, was facilitated by particular laws that allowed former members to maintain a collective identity and solidarity bonds among one another outside the terrorist organization. These widespread "exits" from the terrorist groups indicate that the cycle of political violence in Italy is over. The remaining small nuclei, only sporadically active underground, represent a different, far less dangerous phenomenon.

---

56. Martha Crenshaw, "The Subjective Reality of the Terrorist: Ideological and Psychological Factors in Terrorism," in *Current Perspectives on International Terrorism*, ed. Robert O. Slater and Michael Stohl (London: Macmillan, 1988), 12–46.

5

West German Left-Wing Terrorism

Peter H. Merkl

> In the Federal Republic of the sixties, a democracy with far too
> few democrats, a protest generation—that had not yet fully
> become what it wanted to be—collided with an establishment and
> a police that even twenty years after 1945, still had not become
> what the Basic Law (constitution) intended it to be.
> —Klaus Jünschke, *Spätlese: Texte zu RAF und Knast*

"Baader-Meinhof"—the names that in the seventies inspired panic and
passionately divided the German Left (part of which was in the government), that trigger memories of student and youth rebellion against
establishment paranoia and repression—are still being invoked today, in
the nineties, and for dubious reasons. The principals of the original
Baader-Meinhof group have long since died or distanced themselves
pointedly from the quixotic quest that had long ago lost even its own
self-righteous sense of purpose. Some of its erstwhile followers were

The author would like to acknowledge the assistance and advice received from Elizabeth
Bomberg, Nitish Dutt, Jo Groebel, Klaus Wasmund, Donatella della Porta, Don Schoonmaker, and many others.

discovered after the fall of the Berlin Wall in East Germany, where the Communist State Security Service (Stasi) had given them new names, apartments, and jobs to help them hide from their violent past of many years ago. The successor RAF (Rote Armee Fraktion [Red Army Faction]) groups of the eighties had as little in common with Baader-Meinhof and company as do copycat murderers with a notorious *crime de passion*. They may name their groups after some of the flamboyant Baader-Meinhof principals, but they share neither their complex motives and hesitations nor their extraordinary impact on their contemporaries. It would be rather misleading, therefore, simply to swallow their claims of continuity and treat them as the natural outgrowth and sequel to the paroxysms of the sixties and seventies.

I have chosen, therefore, to break up the chronological sequence and to present the lesser-known story of West German terrorism in the eighties first. Social scientists have to be careful with chronological accounts that implicitly suggest, *post quem propter quem*, that the earlier events may be the ineluctable cause of the murders of another generation. To most readers, the Baader-Meinhof group of the seventies is an old story and, by now, deserves a rather different interpretative and reflective treatment involving the whole of West German society at the time. I attempt such an account following the description of the new terrorists of the eighties and early nineties, and of their curious jailhouse strikes and protests, which are the only things they seem to have in common with the Baader-Meinhof principals in their hour of defeat.

Equipped with large posters supporting the hunger strike of thirty-two imprisoned RAF terrorists and evidently with forged keys to the advertisement display frames of the municipal bus company, an unknown team blanketed Hamburg-Uhlenhorst with its poster campaign one March night in 1989. The posters quoted Federal Chancellor Helmut Kohl to the effect that "this state will not give in to the terrorists in custody as long as I am here," and added in red, "Then he's got to go." Other posters in metropolitan areas and ample press coverage dramatized the protest of the prisoners against their alleged "torture by isolation" since early February; the press insisted that, in fact, prisoners had been allowed visitors, correspondence, and daily contacts with other imprisoned terrorists. The controversy really revolved around the prisoners demand for *Zusammenlegung*, or consolidation of terrorist prisoners into two or three larger groups, and it preoccupied the major political parties and the *Länder* ministers of justice. The new Berlin mayor Walter Momper (SPD)[1] had appealed

---

1. The 1989–90 West Berlin government rested on a coalition of the Social Democrats (Sozialdemokratische Partei Deutschlands, or SPD) and the Alternative List (AL), which has long included elements of the Berlin "alternative scene" sympathetic to urban protests

to the *Bundestag* president, Rita Süssmuth (Christlich-Demokratische Union [Christian Democratic Union], or CDU), and to the *Präses* of the Protestant churches, Jürgen Schmude (SPD), to mediate the dispute. The ministers-president of *Länder* in which RAF terrorists were jailed were also brought into the act by North Rhine–Wesphalian minister-president Johannes Rau, who had been the SPD chancellor candidate against Kohl in the 1987 election. Both Süssmuth and Schmude indicated their willingness to play a role, whereas Federal Attorney General Kurt Rebmann—who had the authority to decide about the location and relocation of prisoners—and conservative justice officials expressed their doubts about any special procedures to be applied only to the terrorists, many of whom had been convicted of multiple murders. Demonstrations by so-called autonomous and alternative groups occurred, including the occupation of the south tower of the Cologne Cathedral and the defacing of a huge mural in Hamburg that commemorated the harbor's eight hundredth anniversary. The press fell into predictable camps: liberal newspapers (e.g., *Frankfurter Rundschau, Süddeutsche Zeitung*) advocated some sort of dialogue, while the conservative press (e.g., *Die Welt*) denounced a dialogue as "giving in to blackmail." There was even a public opinion poll (ZDF Barometer, 17 April 1989) that reported 81 percent of the respondents (even 55 percent of Greens supporters) opposing a *Zusammenlegung*.[2]

There could be little doubt that the RAF had once more captured the attention of the nation, even from jail. It had done so without violence to persons so far, even though there were acts of vandalism—for example, at a department store, a car dealership, and CDU headquarters in Hamburg. Conservative critics reminded the public of the long series of hunger strikes and of the prominent RAF prisoners' suicide of 1977 at Stammheim prison, Stuttgart, following the abortive hijacking of a Lufthansa jet to Mogadishu, Somalia, that was intended to spring them

---

such as the occupation of houses. Momper's office in fact was occupied by hunger-strike sympathizers pressing their demands. On the evolution of the West Berlin "scene," see Dieter Claessens and Karin de Ahna, "Das Milieu der Westberliner 'scene' und die Bewegung 2. Juni," in Wanda von Baeyer-Katte, Dieter Claessens, Hubert Feger, and Friedhelm Neidhardt, *Gruppenprozesse*, vol. 3 of *Analysen zum Terrorismus* (Opladen: Westdeutscher Verlag, 1982), 20–181, esp. 143–74, and Sebastian Scheerer, "Deutschland: Die ausgeburgerte Linke," in Henner Hess, Martin Moerings, Dieter Pass, Sebastian Scheerer, and Heinz Steinert, *Angriff auf das Herz des Staates* (Frankfurt: Suhrkamp, 1988), 1:257–92.

2. See *Frankfurter Rundschau*, 30 March 1989, 1; *Hannoversche Allgemeine*, 14 April 1989; *Süddeutsche Zeitung*, 30 March 1989, 1; and *Generalanzeiger Bonn*, 11 April 1989.

from prison. When the plane was stormed by a special counterterrorism squad flown in from Bonn, RAF leaders—Ulrike Meinhof had hanged herself earlier—Andreas Baader, Gudrun Ensslin, and Jan-Carl Raspe killed themselves at Stammheim, while the most prominent RAF kidnap victim, Hanns Martin Schleyer, was murdered. Among the hunger strikers of 1989, there were four who were involved in Schleyer's murder, some of whom (Brigitte Mohnhaupt and Christian Klar) once before, in December 1984, started a hunger strike demanding to be granted the status of political prisoners. Would there be hijackings and threats of violence again to spring the prisoners from jail, possibly after their consolidation? Would not consolidation from their scattered locations facilitate attempts at escape or at their liberation by *coup de main* from the outside? Would they raise the old demand for political-prisoner status again, or even claim the rights of military prisoners of war? Most of them refused to be in the company of the common criminals sentenced under the same statutes against homicide, bodily harm, kidnapping, and bank robbery. Although the hunger strike was soon called off, there was no indication that the "hard core"—about fifteen persons—of the RAF had given up the armed struggle. Nevertheless, there is considerable doubt about the cohesion and continuity of the organization that has suffered many defections and by now is said to be in its fifth or sixth "generation" of terrorists. Since 1972, after the first and original generation was captured, an ever-widening gulf, with few exceptions, began to open up between the goals of the original leadership and those of their successors; this makes disaggregating the phases and the groups, instead of treating them as one continuous phenomenon, reasonable. The context and the response of society and state to the RAF, furthermore, have long since become more remarkable than the group itself and its actions.

Why are the demands of imprisoned terrorists and the responses of the state important to this investigation? The fact that most West German terrorists are or have been in prison of course puts their conduct there in the limelight. But also germane is their continuing effort to maintain fighting morale among the imprisoned and those outside and to retain public attention for their cause by a series of hunger strikes, nine so far. Their strikes have revived German prison reform movements and strengthened prison support groups, which, in some cases, even supplied future RAF recruits. The reactions of a limited, sympathetic public and of the hostile or indifferent majority as well as of West German officialdom are no less noteworthy. As German terrorism researchers remind us, terrorists perceive their violent, paramilitary actions as a kind of warfare against enemies and antagonists, a private war against the state and "the system," with all the social psychological changes that this implies. "The state's reactions and measures, such as the conditions of imprisonment . . . are parts of this complex of relationships and conditions of terrorist action."[3] The curious gradations among circles of supporters, rivals, and alleged sympathizers and the efforts of the establishment to paint all its critics and political opponents as "terrorist sympathizers" also require further analysis. Finally, the revolutionary rationale of the RAF, as laid out in its own statements, needs to be measured against its actions and compared to commonsense explanations of their stated objectives.

THE DECADE OF THE EIGHTIES

As the eighties came to a turbulent end with the fall of the Communist regime in East Germany, a number of prominent fugitive RAF members resurfaced from hiding and, under the new state's witness law, revealed secrets of RAF actions in the seventies. The Stasi, it turned out, had given them new identities, jobs, and homes when they were trying to drop their violent careers, they said. West German authorities wondered out loud whether and to what extent the Stasi might have supported their destabilizing activities as terrorists in the West both before and after giving them shelter.

The recurrent resurgence of the names and deeds of RAF terrorists of the earlier period should suggest neither that the threat of German left-wing terrorism has dwindled down to the level of jailhouse revolts nor that there have not been profound changes that set off the hectic seventies from the somewhat more subdued eighties. The once hierarchically organized Baader-Meinhof group of military covert-action commandos has been replaced by several autonomous groups that are actually harder for the police to control than were their disciplined predecessors.[4] The abduction of Berlin CDU leader Peter Lorenz, early in 1975, was met with helpless indecision and with the freeing of six convicted terrorists, who were permitted to fly to Yemen and soon returned for further terrorist actions. Back in the "German Autumn" of 1977, also, and during the years leading up to it, a good dozen RAF terrorists seemed to have

3. See Herbert Jäger's conclusions and suggestions for further consideration in Herbert Jäger, Gerhard Schmidtchen, and Lieselotte Süllwold, *Lebenslaufanalysen*, vol. 2 of *Analysen zum Terrorismus* (Opladen: Westdeutscher Verlag, 1981), 235. Translated by the author, as are all subsequent translations, unless otherwise noted.
4. Federal Ministry of the Interior, *Verfassungsschutzbericht 1985* (Bonn, 1986).

the democratic state over a barrel and the public in such a desperate state of mind that only the most extreme and often constitutionally dubious means were capable of calming the exaggerated fears of the moment.

But in the ensuing years, while the government learned to tough it out during Schleyer's captivity and the Mogadishu hijacking, crisis staffs and the Federal Criminal Office (BKA) took on sweeping authority in the country and at times took liberties with the constitutional protections and rights of individual citizens in order to track down the terrorists. A rather small staff of investigators grew into an internal security apparatus involving thousands of employees and routine security measures that governed and noticeably distorted the everyday life of all prominent politicians, law-enforcement officials, and business leaders, and still were unable to stop the attempts on the lives of two campaigning politicians in 1990. For Germans knowledgeable about the details of the rampant Nazi police state and the propensity of some of their countrymen to feel—in the absence of any corroborating evidence whatsoever—that such measures were required to pursue and catch evildoers, this was a chilling reminder of a reckless past.[5] In the case of Schleyer, it turned out later, the no-holds-barred chase even caused the police to ignore early leads that would have led them to the kidnapped business leader and might have saved him. By today, many observers indeed wonder if this new security state has taken on a self-perpetuating life of its own, and its supporters have learned to use the terrorist threat for purposes of their own.

Nevertheless, more careful and unassailable police work in the early seventies did lead to the capture of the RAF leaders and to their self-destruction in Stammheim prison. Further arrests in subsequent years soon brought to an end the hectic seventies, which had begun with the violent rescue of the imprisoned Baader by a team that included Meinhof, Ensslin, and a few others.[6] The June 2d Movement had taken its name

5. For a careful review of questionable police conduct and dubious ordinances and laws, see Fritz Sack, "Die Reaktion von Gesellschaft, Politik und Staat auf die Studentenbewegung," in Fritz Sack and Heinz Steinert, *Protest und Reaktion*, vol. 4/2 of *Analysen zum Terrorismus* (Opladen: Westdeutscher Verlag, 1984), 160–208, and Uwe Berlitz and Horst Dreier, "Die legislative Auseinandersetzung mit dem Terrorismus," in ibid., 228–98; see esp. 295–99, where the de facto state of siege under the guise of normal conditions is compared to the uses of the emergency power in the Weimar Republic. See also the telling account of the effect of security measures on politicians, like Interior Minister Maihofer, by Günter Hofmann, "Bonn, 1987," in *Einschüsse: Besichtigung eines Frontverlaufs 10 Jahre nach dem deutschen Herbst*, ed. Michael Sontheimer and Otto Kallscheuer (Berlin: Rotbuch, 1987), 33–38.

6. Baader was in prison for setting fires, with Ensslin, in Frankfurt department stores in April 1968 and fled while awaiting the result of a judicial appeal.

from the date of the 1967 student demonstrations against a visit from the shah of Iran to Berlin, at which the police had killed a student in the ensuing police riot. With the end of the seventies, however, the June 2d Movement officially abandoned the "armed struggle," though the RAF did not. During the eighties, even though the RAF refused to give up the ghost, the organizational basis of West German left-wing terrorism changed. In particular, while the RAF proper seemed to be less visible, a fringe of auxiliary and sympathizer groups began to carry out terrorist actions on their own. The level of actual RAF activities dropped, except for isolated campaigns and periods; and it was more likely to attempt to capitalize on the issues and concerns of other movements, such as the Peace Movement, than to generate a consistent line of its own. One major exception, perhaps, was the Euroterrorist alliance of the RAF, the French Action Directe (AD), and the Belgian Communist Combatant Cells (CCC), which accounted for many attacks on NATO facilities and personnel and on businesses and people associated with the Western alliance. There was also an attempt at cooperation with the Italian Red Brigades. This relative internationalization, or Europeanization, of RAF activities makes it more difficult at times to attribute particular actions to one or the other of these movements, especially when the target was NATO and its member states. Consequently, RAF actions are not always set clearly in a setting of domestic causes, origins, and objectives; and incidents in one country may have a major impact on terrorist activities in another.

In spite of the programmatic RAF statements of Ulrike Meinhof and Horst Mahler in the early seventies, which routinely identified U.S. imperialism and NATO as "the heart of the imperialist-feudal system," RAF actions against such targets were rare amid the concentrated attacks on West German politicians, business figures, and law-enforcement personnel. The major exception was the attempt to assassinate the supreme commander of the NATO forces in Europe, General Alexander Haig, on his way from his home to NATO headquarters near Brussels in June 1979. A bomb hidden by the RAF in a bridge exploded seconds after the general's car had crossed it. A series of attacks against the U.S. presence in the Federal Republic followed. The widespread public concern over the stationing of cruise missiles and Pershing IIs, which in 1981 culminated in the Peace Movement, makes it difficult to know to what extent the RAF and its friends were only trying to capitalize on the well-known public preoccupation. In any case, RAF "sympathizer groups" firebombed U.S. military facilities in Frankfurt and Wiesbaden and attempted to torch the U.S. library in West Berlin and the Dow Chemical corporation in Düsseldorf. An organization called Black Block bombed two American military installations near Frankfurt and tried to destroy the railroad line to the Rhine-Main air base; others bombed the U.S. Consulate General in Frankfurt and American facilities in Kassel and Berlin, as well as some West German military targets.[7]

Anti-NATO activities were stepped up further in August 1981, when the RAF planted a car loaded with explosives at the U.S. Air Force headquarters at Ramstein, which injured twenty soldiers and secretaries. Two weeks later an ambush squad fired two antitank rockets at a car in which the U.S. Army commander in Europe, General Frederick Kroesen, and his wife were riding. One rocket hit the trunk of the car, but the general and his wife escaped unhurt. In Verona the following December, Red Brigade members kidnapped U.S. Army Brigadier General James Dozier and held him until he was freed by the Italian police, who had conducted a sweep involving three hundred arrests and the discovery of several of the terrorists' weapons caches. But there was no evidence of coordination with the anti-NATO campaign of the RAF or its auxiliaries who accounted for the bulk of terrorist activities in Germany.[8]

In the same year, rivals of the RAF also attracted attention. One was Guerrilla Diffusa, a congeries of anarchists, Maoists, the "autonomous Left," as well as gays and punk rockers, which also attracted urban squatters and ecological activists. Theirs has tended to be a low-level kind of terrorism of little clear direction. They resemble *autonomia* in Italy, which also supplies a breeding and recruiting ground for the Red Brigades.

The Revolutionary Cells (RZ), another rival organization dating back to the early seventies,[9] claimed credit for all the anti-U.S. bombings of 1982, mostly tying them to President Reagan's visit in Germany. They already had a long-standing reputation for bombing American-based multinational companies, whom they blamed for exploiting and dominating the Third World. In June 1981 their small cells (four to five members) bombed U.S. Army Fifth Corps headquarters in Frankfurt and U.S. officer clubs in Hanau, Gelnhausen, and Bamberg. They also bombed IBM and Data Control corporations in Düsseldorf. An attempt to blow

7. See the chronicle in *Terrorism: An International Journal* 6 (1981): 380–84.

8. According to David T. Schiller, "Germany's Other Terrorists," *Terrorism* 9 (1987), 57–65, by 1985, only a small fraction of some 350 terrorist acts and 500 acts of sabotage could be attributed to the RAF itself.

9. From its beginnings in 1973, the RZ differentiated itself by taking exception to the RAF theory that only the "revolutionary intelligentsia," or student elites, should guide the revolution. Instead, they stressed the need to keep each action *in contact with* the masses, a kind of Maoist "mass line." See *Revolutionärer Zorn* 1 (May 1975): 6, and 4 (January 1978): 17.

up the American Forces Network radio station in Berlin was foiled at the last minute.

In 1982 the RAF had been holding up banks when West German police succeeded in arresting Brigitte Mohnhaupt, Adelheid Schulz, and Christian Klar, their biggest triumph since the seizure of Baader, Meinhof, and Ensslin in 1972. Investigations had already yielded over a dozen RAF caches with weapons, documents, photos, and other supplies in Hamburg, Frankfurt, and elsewhere. The next year, 1983, was even worse for the RAF, as effective counterterrorist activity, as in Italy, curbed most activities. The RZ brought off some attacks on West German arms manufacturing and computer firms rather than American targets. Also, a bomb was placed inside a fire extinguisher in a U.S.-owned building in February, and an antimissile action in December involved breaking into the U.S. camp at Mutlangen, the first site selected for missile deployment, and attacking a Pershing missile there with sledgehammers.[10]

The following year must have been the time the first serious contacts occurred between the RAF and AD, following some RAF feelers toward the Basque ETA and the Red Brigades. There is some evidence that the AD's assassination of French defense official General René Audran in January 1985 may have involved RAF members who identified themselves with the late Elizabeth van Dyck, who had been a party to the 1977 RAF killings of Federal Prosecutor Siegfried Buback, Schleyer, and the banker Jürgen Ponto (she was killed in 1979). The third organization to cooperate in a western European urban guerrilla movement, the Belgian CCC, was a new group that became known only since the antimissile campaigns and appeared to be less coordinated with the AD and RAF than these two were with each other. It should also be mentioned that left-wing groups such as the Greek National Front and the Portuguese FP 25 carried out major actions a few days after General René Audran's assassination. FP 25 attacked NATO ships in Lisbon harbor and tried to bomb NATO barracks in Beja. The Greek group set off a bomb in a bar frequented by U.S. servicemen, injuring seventy-eight people.[11]

For the RAF itself, the year 1984 provided little relief from its doldrums. On the contrary, in July, RAF members were arrested in a Frankfurt apartment, and in December, Mohnhaupt and Klar announced

10. See U.S. Department of State, *Patterns of Global Terrorism* (1981), 17; (1982), 12–13 and 18; and (1983), 21, 26, and 54.

11. See Hans Josef Horchem, "Terrorism in West Germany," *Conflict Studies* 186 (1986): 1–21. The French police have recently arrested and brought to trial twenty AD terrorists in Lyon alone.

their hunger strike for political-prisoner status. A few days later, a Siemens warehouse in Frankfurt was firebombed, presumably by a sympathizer group, and then a man in the uniform of a U.S. marine parked a car bomb near the NATO officers' training school at Oberammergau. The timing device malfunctioned, however, and the explosives turned out to be of Belgian origin. The Belgian CCC indeed was quite active, with violent assaults on NATO-oriented companies, communication towers, and political parties, not to mention an attack on a NATO pipeline. The French AD could boast of similar violence in France, including bombing the Atlantic Institute for International Affairs in Paris.[12]

Early in 1985 the threesome issued a joint communiqué in which they threatened further coordinated actions as an "anti-imperialist front." The documents seized from the RAF in mid-1984 had laid out plans to resume its "armed struggle" by first bombing key NATO installations simultaneously, then demanding that imprisoned RAF members be "consolidated," and finally proceeding to execute "representatives of repression." Having more or less carried out the first two phases and coordinated their plans with AD, two RAF gunmen murdered a prominent West German arms manufacturer, Ernst Zimmermann, at his home near Munich. The AD claimed responsibility for this act. In April 1985 further attacks were carried out by the RAF "fringe"—in particular, a bombing of a building in Hamburg and of a NATO pipeline in southern Germany. Three RAF members in stolen army uniforms tried to get into an ammunitions depot near the Austrian border but fled when guards wanted to check their papers. In August of the same year, the RAF exploded a car bomb in a parking area at the U.S. air base in Frankfurt. They obtained access by using the identity card of an American GI they had killed execution-style. The bomb killed two and injured twenty more;[13] and the RAF and the AD claimed credit for this action, which showed the increasingly indiscriminate nature of RAF violence. In November of the same year, a car bomb in a parking lot next to a shopping center favored by the U.S. military claimed thirty-two victims. In a year of rising international terrorist violence, much of it directed against American companies and individuals, West German left-wing terrorists were outdone by few other countries.

The RZ had at first been preoccupied with an elaborate analysis of the present and future political situation and the place of left-wing terrorism

---

12. See "Patterns of Global Terrorism: 1984," in *Terrorism* 9 (1987): 409 and 425–26.

13. See U.S. Department of State, *Patterns of Global Terrorism* (1985), 21–22 and 33–41.

in it. They made a point of not supporting RAF activities, including the hunger strike in the winter of 1984–85. Once the strike was abandoned, however, and in spite of their shrinking membership,[14] they launched "punitive attacks" on corporations that had allegedly fought against striking British miners. At the end of April 1985 bombs were set at the Deutsche Bank in Düsseldorf and at a Cologne chemical concern. A month later a NATO pipeline near Frankfurt was bombed.

Nineteen eighty-six was a banner year for international terrorism, particularly with regard to the Middle East and such sponsors of actions and groups in the West as Iran, Syria, and Libya. The RAF has always maintained its autonomy, but some members once sought training in El Fatah camps, and there was some collusion between the RAF and the PFLP (Popular Front for the Liberation of Palestine) at the time of the foiled plane hijacking from Mallorca to Mogadishu (1977), from which the Palestinian perpetrators hoped to get a large ransom and the release of two PFLP members from Turkish prisons. In 1985 there were renewed contacts with a PFLP spokesman in East Berlin, Bassam Abu Sharif, which resulted in a press conference and PFLP endorsement of the RAF. In June of the same year, the RAF combined forces with the Arab Revolutionary Organization and a group called the Peace Conquerors to bomb the Frankfurt airport.

In spring of 1986, Middle Eastern terrorism overshadowed RAF activities; in West Berlin, the German-Arab Friendship Association building was bombed—seven injured—and another bomb was detonated at the La Belle discotheque, killing three (two U.S. soldiers) and wounding two hundred (seventy of them Americans). Both terrorist acts were carried out with Syrian assistance, and the perpetrators have since been tried in German courts.[15] The Reagan administration claimed that there existed "incontrovertible proof of Libyan complicity" and carried out the well-known air strikes of 15 April against Tripoli and Benghazi, hoping to settle a personal score with Muammar Khadafy, who had sponsored so

14. Their estimated membership declined in 1984–85 from about 200 to 80. The RAF at that time was believed to have a "commando" of about 15 and a "legitimate fringe" of 200, not counting 36 members in custody. See Horchem, "Terrorism in West Germany," 4–7. The AD also was said to have 15 to 20 hard-core members and 120 to 130 sympathizers. According to the official count of 1984, of 148 left-wing terrorist actions in the FRG, the RAF only accounted for 18, the RZ for 11 (including Red Zora, a women's terrorist group). Those attributed to miscellaneous groups and "weekend terrorists" numbered 116. See Federal Ministry of the Interior, *Verfassungsschutzbericht 1984* (Bonn, 1985).

15. A Syrian intelligence officer at the Syrian embassy in East Berlin evidently supplied the explosives to Farouk Salameh and Ahmed N. M. Hasi, the brother of Nezar Hindawi, who was convicted in Britain of attempting to plant, with the help of his pregnant girlfriend, a bomb on an El Al airliner.

many other terrorist operations and groups all over the world. U.S. Continental allies pointedly withheld all assistance, including permission for the aircraft to fly over their territory. Years later the East German Stasi files confirmed the claim of Libyan complicity. This dramatic action overshadowed most other terrorist activities of 1986, including those of West German groups whose attacks of record had been declining in numbers since 1984.[16]

The RAF nevertheless carried out a number of bombings in 1986, preceded by a notable retreat from the indiscriminate violence of the two previous years. At a secret conference of terrorist support groups in February, the RAF acknowledged its errors of the parking-lot bombings and the killing of an American soldier for his identity card. The next ten targets of bombs, therefore, were specifically warned or bombed at midnight to avoid unintended casualties. But in July of that year the RAF clearly intended to kill a Siemens executive, Karl-Heinz Beckurts— who was known for his involvement with nuclear weapons and the Strategic Defense Initiative (SDI)—with a remote-control ambush bomb. They also meant to gun down Gerold von Braunmühl, a second-echelon diplomat and specialist on East-West relations. They claimed he was a "covert diplomat of imperialist war strategy" and shot him with the same pistol that had murdered Schleyer almost exactly nine years earlier. Rather to the public embarrassment of the terrorists, von Braunmühl's five brothers responded by publishing an eloquent appeal to the RAF to begin a public dialogue relating such actions to stated RAF goals. The terrorists never answered the brothers' plea.[17]

No action so far—except the usual intimidation and terror—has resulted from an RAF hit list discovered late in 1986. On it were former chancellor Helmut Schmidt, Minister of Economic Cooperation and Development Jürgen Warnke, and Jürgen Moellemann, like von Braunmühl, an aide of Foreign Minister Hans-Dietrich Genscher at the time. The police eventually arrested Renaud Laigle, an AD member linked to the August 1986 RAF bombing of the U.S. Rhine-Main air base. A raid on the stock exchange in Frankfurt coincided with the hunger strike of

---

16. *Patterns of Global Terrorism* (1986), 5, 26–27, and 34–36. Cf. *Frankfurter Rundschau*, 2 February 1986, which reported that the Federal Ministry of the Interior claimed a 30 percent increase in politically motivated attacks by early 1986, many of them aimed at German businesses and industries involved in defense. See also the *Wall Street Journal* (Europe), 17 April 1984.

17. *Nürnberger Nachrichten*, 14 October 1987. For the text of the von Braunmühl brothers' letter, see *Taz*, 7 November 1986, or the reprint in Klaus Hartung et al., *Der blinde Fleck: Die Linke, die RAF und der Staat* (Frankfurt: Neue Kritik, 1987), 201–4. The brothers also contributed an amount to the prisoner support groups.

April 1989; at least six masked attackers stormed into the premises, beating employees and lobbing firebombs onto the main trading floor. Two people were injured, but the police captured three of the attackers. At about the same time, in the second week of April, the supporters of the hunger strike claimed responsibility for an arson attack on a branch of the West German General Electric Company (AEG).

The last years of the eighties were characterized more by the dramatic and recurrent antiterrorist warnings in the West German press than by stepped-up RAF activity. Already at the beginning of 1986 the head of the antiterror department of the BKA in Wiesbaden, Klaus-Herbert Becker, credited the RAF with having become ever more cunning and difficult to detect and indicated that, for whatever reason, the RAF had been back in the country for some time. Whether it was their language problems, more-intense antiterrorist surveillance abroad, or a fear of losing touch with the changing youth scene that brought them back, the RAF seemed to have left its usual hiding places abroad, perhaps the better to play its role in the Euroterrorist campaign.[18] A year and a half later the *Christian Science Monitor* had a feature announcing that the RAF had regrouped after a string of arrests and was planning a fresh wave of attacks.[19] In the fall of 1988, on the occasion of the large IMF–World Bank meeting in Berlin, an RAF gunman attempted to assassinate a senior Finance Ministry official in Bonn, Hans Tietkemeyer, for having "created misery for millions of people in the Third World."[20] The Berlin meeting, consequently, received thousands of police officers for additional protection. Neither the target nor his driver were hurt. The rearrangement of the entire German political landscape brought on by the collapse of the Berlin Wall and by German unification seemingly stunned German left-wing terrorists and drastically shrunk their small base of sympathizers, who may also have felt embarrassed at the revelations about the failings of Communist rule in East Germany— these ranged from Stasi repression and clandestine support for the RAF to the total failure of the economic utopia of communism. To keep up the appearance of the vitality of the movement under these circumstances, the RAF resorted to spectacular assassinations whose perpetrators were never caught. One was the killing of Alfred Herrhausen, the head of the Deutsche Bank, one of the three largest private banks in Germany, a

18. See *Die Welt*, 30 December 1985.

19. *Christian Science Monitor*, 10 August 1987. For other warnings in the press, usually from official sources, see *Süddeutsche Zeitung*, 20 March 1987; *Die Welt*, 14 August 1987 and 30 June 1988; *Frankfurter Allgemeine Zeitung*, 21 January 1989; and the *Wall Street Journal* (Europe), 17 April 1989.

20. *New York Times*, 21 September 1988.

short time after the wall fell. Herrhausen had been prominent in East-West financial dealings and in assessments of the crisis of the East German economy and its likely future after German unification. A second spectacular was the 1 April 1991 shooting of Detlev Rohwedder, the head of the Trust Agency (Treuhandanstalt) in charge of privatizing East German state-owned enterprises. Both assassinations were evidently meant to wreak vengeance for the failure of the Communist economy and its "takeover" by West German bankers and managers. Violence born of Communist impotence thus rounded out what can only be regarded as lean years for the RAF.

THE PREHISTORY OF GERMAN LEFT-WING TERROR

The earlier phases of left-wing terrorism in West Germany are well known and frequently described, even though there is still an amazing amount of controversy about them.[21] By now there is also a new retrospective literature by former adherents and observers, critically reflecting on the original terrorist enterprise and the public reaction to it. Briefly, a complex prehistory culminated in the escalation of the student protest movement in the late sixties. The RAF and other movements began to develop around 1968 and by mid-1970 entered a stage of hectic activities interrupted by the capture of the principals in 1972. Terrorist activities by no means ended with this capture but turned into a "free-the-guerrilla guerrilla movement" in a crescendo of attempts to spring the captives in the years from 1972 to 1977. The suicides in prison of Meinhof (1976), Baader, Ensslin, and Raspe (all three 18 October 1977) did set an end to this phase. A successor phase had already begun as early as 1973–74 with a second generation of RAF recruits, which, for example, included a Hamburg group (February Four) of new RAF members as well as a number of further groupings from various sources.

The prehistory, at least for serious students of left-wing terrorism, is both the most interesting and the most controversial part. The controversy particularly involves the relative importance of the pieces of the

21. The controversies particularly separate Left from Right, and radical democratic from conservative opinion. Essentially, the conservatives identify with the institutions, values, and policies under attack in the years 1966–69 and for that reason see no merit whatsoever—and plenty of unjust criticism—in the student movement's assault on the establishment.

puzzle that, among other early antecedents, link the early development to the Internationale Situationniste and its German branch, Subversive Aktion, in West Berlin, of which Rudi Dutschke was a member in 1964–65. Subversive Aktion was part of the first Berlin commune and engaged in a string of "surrealistic" confrontational happenings of minor significance throughout the sixties.[22] Although some observers credit the rich revolutionary doctrines and "actionist" temper of the situationists with supplying the activist spark to the Berlin comrades, the crucial connection more likely was the marriage of the early commune with the SDS (Socialist Student Association), once a student affiliate of the SPD but expelled in 1960. Unlike the milder conduct associated with the utopianism of the situationists, the parting of the ways between SPD and SDS had all the earmarks of the bitter political struggles that had accompanied the 1959 transformation of the rightward-moving SPD into a *Volkspartei* willing to drop the old Marxist left and to clasp to its bosom the economic, social, and foreign policies of the governing CDU/CSU (Christlich-Soziale Union [Christian Social Union]). The SDS was accused of unwillingness to abandon its contacts with the now outlawed KPD (Kommunistische Partei Deutschlands [Communist Party of Germany]) and to the Communist state party (SED [Sozialistische Einheitspartei Deutschlands]) of East Germany, in addition to being mired in hidebound Marxist theorizing at the very moment the parent party was moving toward pragmatic and more broadly based concerns.[23]

Similarly political in motivation was the decade-long (1958–68) campaign against the Emergency Laws, which, by 1966, was spearheaded by the APO (Außert parlamentarische Opposition [Extraparliamentary Opposition]), an antiauthoritarian coalition of student groups—including the SDS—trade unionists, and other socialist and liberal groups. There was also the precedent of the antinuclear war campaign and, most of all, the widely shared apprehension that the governing Christian Democrats were about to bring back the police state of the Third Reich. The Emergency Laws were supposed to fill a major gap in the constitution, and early drafts indeed manifested an authoritarian spirit more appropriate to the Bismarckian empire than to democratic post-1945 Germany.[24] The fear of a comeback of authoritarian government took on

22. See Scheerer, "Die ausgebürgerte Linke," 282–85. There was also a very active Munich branch from which Dieter Kunzelmann eventually went to Berlin.
23. Ibid., 213–28. Some of the criticism also involved SDS participation in the Campaign Against Atomic Death of those years, which had enjoyed the backing of Communist as well as non-Communist, trade-union, socialist, and religious supporters.
24. See Michael Schneider, *Demokratie in Gefahr? Der Konflikt um die Notstandsgesetze* (Bonn: Neue Gesellschaft, 1986), 9–80.

panic proportions when a compliant SPD joined the CDU/CSU in the grand coalition of 1966, thereby providing a constitution-amending majority for the actual passage of the controversial enactments. In the end, to be sure, the draft was modified and most of its harshest critics mollified, but there could be no mistaking the widespread identification of the government stance with its Nazi antecedents, especially with respect to constitutional freedoms and safeguards.[25]

Similar attitudes and perceptions on the part of student activists and communards toward the West Berlin and West German police characterized the subsequent confrontations between the student movement and the authorities. Some observers blame the survival of repressive pre-1945 police methods on the presence of many former Nazi police officials or judges reinstated in their old careers by postwar constitutional amendments (ART. 131) and amnesties under Adenauer. Others seek the cause of the survival of German authoritarianism in the excessive defensiveness of German officialdom, university professors who lashed out harshly against underground critics, and a media that tended toward the crudest simplification of the issues raised by the "disorderly, unkempt longhairs." The West Berlin setting aggravated the situation because the city had long felt under siege by the surrounding Communist territory and, since 1955, tens of thousands of additional students from West and East Germany had flooded university facilities to the breaking point. The new generation of the sixties, far from their elders' experiences of World War II and catastrophic defeat and destruction, created their own values, group life, even slang, ready to challenge the shibboleths of the founders of the postwar West German order, including the influence of the United States and the Western hegemony over the nations of the Third World or Latin America.

There is no need to go into the details of the genesis and evolution of the student rebellion,[26] which has been widely discussed in the literature. Suffice it to say that the rigidly authoritarian responses of police, city, and university authorities tempted the rebels into escalating the "violation of rules" and police instructions, and that the rebels' growing numbers made them believe that the authorities would, or could, never stop them. Their causes—domestic democratization, pacifism, and antiimperialism—appeared to them immensely superior to the old authoritarianism and the disreputable involvements of the establishment, such as

25. See the account by Claessens and de Ahna, "Das Milieu," 38–45 and 166–67, where other aspects of the antiauthoritarian movement are described as well.

26. One of the causes was a benevolent attempt by the Berlin city government to reform the Free University in the direction of greater accountability and efficiency. As in Paris and in Italy at about the same time, such efforts provoked a violent reaction.

in South Africa and the Vietnam War. The authorities for their part could hardly comprehend and, if they did, deeply resented the serious criticisms of their authoritarian democracy by the students and the Left. Mutual hatreds and stigmatizations characterized their escalating clashes, and there was a propensity on both sides for all-out battle. The authorities, of course, proved the stronger of the two, and their transgressions of German laws and morality were odious precisely because they were the authorities, duty-bound to obey the law themselves. There is no excuse in a *Rechtsstaat* (state of law) for chasing and clubbing demonstrators and, of course, even less for the killing of student demonstrator Benno Ohnesorg by the police after he had already been beaten into submission during the demonstration against the visit of the shah of Iran, 2 June 1967.[27]

The slaying of Ohnesorg not only triggered student demonstrations throughout the Federal Republic, with participants symbolically carrying coffins and denouncing the police excesses, but also captured the attention of responsible journalists and newspapers.[28] There was a parliamentary investigation by the Bundestag, and the West Berlin police president, Erich Duensing, had to resign. But the students' and other rebels' attitude toward the police, encouraged also by later clashes, remained impotent rage, frequently aggravated by the self-serving, hateful explanations of police conduct given by the press and by various Berlin establishment figures. It was very easy in this setting to feel that one had to defend oneself with lethal force against a lawless, violently repressive, and arbitrary authority that seemingly ignored its own legal and constitutional standards. It was also most plausible to perceive the established authorities as a crypto-fascist, or closet Nazi, force—in spite of democratic elections and majority support[29]—which would inevitably

27. The inexcusable conduct included the prominent participation of Iranian secret police with truncheons (*Jubelperser*) in the beating of student demonstrators. See the careful description of the entire scenario, including its replay in the justifications of the police actions by police authorities and by the politicians in office, by Sack and Steinert, *Protest und Reaktion*, 145–63. Similar procedural transgressions by the police have been common in West Berlin. These transgressions have been characterized by the police trapping demonstrators in closed-off alleys and inner courts of buildings and clubbing and striking them down, even when they have offered no resistance, before arrest and detention, if any.

28. The Springer press (*Bildzeitung, Die Welt*) earned the dislike of the student rebels by fanning the flames of stigmatization and misreporting the events of the clash.

29. The anti-Communist mind-set of the West Berlin public was not mollified by the death of Ohnesorg. A massive counterdemonstration organized by the Berlin Senate (city government), the trade unions, and the Springer press assembled some eighty thousand West Berliners in front of the Schöneberg Rathaus in February 1968—public employees

reveal its true nature upon a little provocation. As Rudi Dutschke put it, "If we were in Latin America, it's clear I would fight weapon in hand. [But here] we are fighting so none will ever need to take up arms."[30]

The use of police violence out of all proportion to a legitimate state interest removed much of the well-inculcated taboo against the oppositional use of similar violence in self-defense and lent legitimacy to the terrorist acts to come. Against the ugly pogrom mood among the West Berlin establishment, violence escalated quickly. In April 1968 a nearly fatal attempt was made on Rudi Dutschke's life (11 April), and two department-store fires were set in Frankfurt by Baader, Ensslin, and two others (3 and 4 April). The assassination of Martin Luther King (4 April) supplied a further signal that radicalized the students. A demonstration march to the Springer press resulted in the breaking of windows, street brawls with Springer workers, and the burning of newspaper trucks with Molotov cocktails supplied, as it later turned out, by an agent provocateur.[31]

The genie of violence was out of the bottle, untrammeled by bourgeois inhibitions, ready for attack on the hostile media and authorities, and all this with an exhilarating sense of freedom after years of repression and frustration. Perhaps their very success and its reverberations brought about their undoing—on 1 May 1968 the SDS assembled a demonstration of thirty thousand in Berlin; ten days later fifty thousand demonstrated in Bonn against the acceptance of the Emergency Laws; and in Paris *les événements* broke out. Soon sober reflection set in, the "manic phase" ended, and there was a renewed sense of impotence and frustration. The student movement began to disintegrate into many directions: Young Socialists, the newly founded Communists (DKP), Maoists, Trotskyists, trade-union activists, gay and feminist groups, child-care groups (*Kinderläden*), and rural communes.

As the mighty student movement died, following its most activist, even violent peak, it spun off small but intensely violent movements much as a dying hurricane might spawn tornadoes. The German literature on terrorism calls them the *Zerfallprodukt* (by-product of disinte-

---

were released from work—and physically threatened whoever looked like a long-haired student or like Dutschke himself.

30. Quoted by Claessens and de Ahna, "Das Milieu," 82. However, one of the later RAF principals, Holger Meins, was already showing a homemade movie to the comrades on how to make Molotov cocktails for an assault on the Springer press.

31. The agent, Peter Urbach, was in the pay of the Berlin Verfassungsschutz. See ibid., 85–87. This was only the first of a number of subsequent street battles and militant demonstrations. The parallel between the assassination of King and the attempt on Dutschke, who had also spoken out against the use of violence, was not lost on the students.

gration) of a brilliant social movement, and in a comparative context, I have called this the fire-sale theory of terrorism[32]—after the revolutionary fire burnt out, its high-sounding, though fire-damaged, values became the easy rationalizations of trigger-happy zealots. Some critics of the German terrorism literature have warned against the tunnel vision of both the terrorists themselves and the conservative enemies of the student movement, who insist that the student movement directly and logically led to terrorist excesses, when in fact it had many and varied consequences, including political apathy and depression, a rueful return to the major parties, a "long march through West German institutions," the citizen initiatives, the women's movement, and peace, ecological, and alternative movements—all of them rather nonviolent.[33] The same caveat of course, applies to the logic of condemnation: it should be possible at the same time to condemn the later terrorist violence, to approve of most of the police measures to apprehend the guilty, to support the constitutional right of APO and the student movement to demonstrate, and to condemn the public hate campaign and police lawlessness unleashed on them by the Berlin Senate and the media.

The immediate upshot of the clash between the student demonstrators and their nemesis were two distinct phases of transformation marked by the two martyr events. The first followed the killing of Ohnesorg on 2 June 1967, and the second began with the nearly fatal attempt on Dutschke on 11 April 1968, after the concentrated hate campaign of the Springer press against him and the SDS-led student movement.[34] The reaction of students and of many nonstudents from all walks of life featured attacks on Springer press establishments all over the Federal Republic and the biggest street battles since the Weimar Republic.[35] An estimated sixty thousand protesters participated, and the clashes re-

32. See Peter H. Merkl, *Political Violence and Terror: Motifs and Motivations* (Berkeley and Los Angeles: University of California Press 1986), 235–36, 336, and 340. See also Peter Waldmann, "Wann schlagen politische Protestbewegungen in Terrorismus um? Lehren aus der Erfahrung der 70er Jahre," in *Konsens und Konflikt: 35 Jahre Grundgesetz*, ed. Albrecht Randelzhofer and Werner Süss (Berlin: DeGruyter, 1986), 401–28.

33. Heinz Steinert, "Erinnerung an den linken Terrorismus," in Hess et al., *Angriff*, 1:18.

34. These events parallel others from the Weimar period, when the hate campaign of the conservative *Kreuzzeitung* and the entire conservative establishment against Foreign Minister Walter Rathenau (1922) and former Chancellor Matthias Erzberger (1921) triggered their assassination by the radical right-wing *Fehme*, as well as other violent deeds of a misguided patriotism. See Klaus Epstein, *Matthias Erzberger and the Dilemma of German Democracy* (Princeton: Princeton University Press, 1959).

35. Springer tabloids, newspapers, and other periodicals at the time accounted for 37 percent of West German newsprint. See Scheerer, "Die ausgebürgerte Linke," 262–79.

sulted in two fatalities and four hundred injured persons. Sympathizers in many foreign cities attacked German establishments, such as Porsche and Mercedes agencies in Rome. But this street violence, in spite of the appellations of "terror" given by the media and the establishment to justify their own actions, was obviously quite different from the terrorist activity yet to come. For one thing, the SDS-led movement increasingly fell apart in the absence of Dutschke and his persuasive mix of strategy and reflective analysis, as labor and student activists discovered they had less and less in common. A last major battle with Berlin police at the Tegeler Weg (4 November 1968) confirmed the disintegration of the movement, even though this time the rebels really fought the police with bricks and stones à la Paris, inflicting 130 injuries (receiving twenty of their own) and, at one time, turning a captured water cannon on their enemies. They proved that even in Germany, protesters could fight their official tormentors to a draw. Their clashes nevertheless also produced thousands of judicial investigations and threatened prosecutions of protesters on various charges until the amnesty of early 1970 broke the evil spell. The new Brandt administration induced thousands of the young rebels to join and work "inside the system" and, at least as an internal opposition, inside the new governing parties, the SPD and FDP.[36]

THE EMERGENCE OF TERRORISM

The real beginnings of German left-wing terrorism were outside the SDS-led movement that, a week before the attempted assassination of Dutschke, disavowed the department store fires set by Baader and Ensslin in Frankfurt. There were serious discussions of urban guerrilla warfare and clandestine action in the SDS and among the communards but no attempt to put theory into action.[37] None of the later RAF activists had played a major role in the SDS, although many participated in student demonstrations and in clashes with the police. Several of the

36. See ibid., 278–88. The influx of the rebels into the Young Socialists (SPD) and Young Democrats (FDP, or Freie Demokratische Partei) created its own dynamics of internal conflict. See Peter H. Merkl, "Factionalism: The Limits of the West German Party-State," in *Faction Politics: Political Parties and Factionalism in Comparative Perspective*, ed. Frank P. Belloni and Dennis C. Beller (Santa Barbara, Calif.: Clio Press, 1978), 250–54, and the German sources cited there.

37. SDS leaders such as Dutschke and Hans Jürgen Krahl considered an urban version of rural guerrilla warfare a realistic option. See Rudi Dutschke, *Geschichte ist machbar*, ed. Jürgen Miermeister (Berlin: Rotbuch, 1980), 9, for a quote from a talk given at the SDS conference of 1967.

residential communes were said to have been infiltrated by police agents provocateurs who supplied not just Molotov cocktails but time bombs and the rhetoric of violence to go with them.[38] These communes, especially Commune I and the Wieland commune, did later become seedbeds for RAF and June 2d recruits, but this was mostly under the influence of the spreading drug and dropout subculture, in particular the self-styled Hashish Rebels and other groups with names such as Black Front, Black Rats, Palestine Front TW (Tupamaros West Berlin), Commando Red Christmas, and Amnesty International TW. In 1969 and 1970 these "primitive anarchists" set off bombs against judges, prosecutors, jail directors, and others throughout Berlin, with varying results, and were caught up in projects to free comrades from jail until so many of their own were inside prison walls that their activities began to atrophy.

These politicized dropouts and Hashish Rebels represented a diffuse kind of terrorism based on spontaneity, cultural revolution, and drug-centered lifestyles—not incompatible with situationist philosophy—that would have resisted any attempt to subordinate them to a carefully considered political strategy.[39] There was indeed a great deal of naïve playfulness about these self-styled West Berlin (and Munich) Tupamaros, who also sought contact with the Vietcong, the PLO, and the real Tupamaros of Uruguay, none of it very seriously.[40] Rather more important was the *Knastcamp* (convict camp) of July 1969 in Ebrach, near Bamberg, a somewhat chaotic gathering that included some of the Berlin principals of the "scene" on their way south to lie low in Italy. But

38. See the account by RAF defector Bommi (Michael) Baumann, *Wie alles anfing* (Frankfurt: Sozialistische Verlagsauslieferung, 1977), 47–48. The communards had five representatives (sometimes dubbed the Polit-Clowns) in the Berlin SDS executive board in early 1967, and their presence led to tensions between the nonstudent communes and the student clientele. The communards were expelled from the SDS in April 1967, when the SDS sought to reaffirm its student government mandate with a grassroots vote (*Urabstimmung*), which was a resounding success in the face of a challenge by dubious university authorities. The tension between students and nonstudent elements continued, for example, between Baader, a school dropout, and Mahler, as well as Meinhof, who actually admired the uncouth Baader as a man of action.

39. See Claessens and de Ahna, "Das Milieu," 89–122. There were also revealing mutual criticisms between, for example, Communist militants and Hashish Rebels, who accused each other of being refugees from the authoritarian past or of frivolous politics.

40. See Scheerer, "Die ausgebürgerte Linke," 290–92. Among other uncoordinated targets, the Jewish Community House in Berlin was bombed by them on the thirty-first anniversary of Kristallnacht, the 1938 Nazi pogrom in which synagogues were burnt, thousands of Jews arrested, and Jewish shops and dwellings vandalized. There was a lot of spontaneous identification with the PLO among these "infantile anarchists," who often produced slogans calling themselves the Palestine group and invoking the name El Fatah to shock the Berlin establishment and not a few of their fellow groups.

this encampment set important precedents for organizing sympathizers around causes associated with imprisoned terrorists.

The RAF proper was founded in May 1970 by Ulrike Meinhof, the well-known editor of *Konkret*, a saucy Communist journal, and the voice of the antiauthoritarian movement, and by Horst Mahler, a prominent APO attorney of similar persuasion. This new group shared the theoretical vision developed by Dutschke and Krahl in the fall of 1967: a socialistically organized society for Germany and heavy emphasis on the Third World liberation movements, in particular in China, Latin America, and Algeria. The often-invoked "revolutionary will" and "foci," however, went far beyond the SDS model in integrating political anarchism into a socialist-anarchist fighting faith opposed both to the "new fascism" attributed to the Federal Republic and France in the years since 1967, and to the socialist critics of anarchist violence.[41] The RAF clearly intended to establish an intellectually respectable creed—against the primitivism of the Hashish Rebels and other "infantile anarchists"— while believing fervently that military-style action was more important than theorizing. They underlined their readiness for action with the freeing of Baader (whose sentence would have ended early in 1972) during a meeting under police guard with Meinhof.[42] Three armed women, one of them Ensslin, and a masked gunman carried it off and, along with Baader and Meinhof, got away in two cars, also driven by women. With this dramatic initiation, and considerable criticism from many old SDS adherents, the first-generation RAF was launched on its brief trajectory.

In the escalating phase of terrorist violence of 1970, the RAF— presumably the West German section of an international red army—was by no means the only, or most violent, group spun off by the disintegrating student movement of 1969. The rash of bombings and arson attacks of the Hashish Rebels and self-styled Tupamaros in the winter of 1969–70 against law-enforcement personnel, the KaDeWe department store, and

41. See ibid., 292–309, for details. Dutschke, of course, had already gone a considerable distance toward the "propaganda of the deed" with his situationist antecedents. Full elaboration of the theories of the "new fascism," the role of the Third World, and the primacy of action, as well as Meinhof and Mahler's reading of the socialist classics, can be found in Iring Fetscher and Günter Rohrmoser, *Ideologien und Strategien*, vol. 1 of *Analysen zum Terrorismus* (Opladen: Westdeutscher Verlag, 1981).

42. Meinhof had requested this meeting at a social science institute so they could discuss their collaboration on a book about wayward youth. For narrative details, see Stefan Aust, *Der Baader-Meinhof Komplex* (Hamburg: Hoffmann und Campe, 1985), 12–16 (English translation, *The Baader-Meinhof Group* [London: Bodley Head, 1987]). An institute employee was seriously injured, with a bullet stuck in his liver, but his assailant later claimed he had not at all meant to hit him.

other targets of 1970 signified a kind of transition from spontaneous to professional terrorist violence.[43] The violent activities of these groups also extended to Munich, where the old situationist and communard Fritz Teufel alone set half a dozen arson fires before his arrest in mid-July.[44] Nevertheless, arrests and defections quickly depleted the ranks of the non-RAF activists and even of the new RAF in the second half of 1970, to the point where terrorist activity in general began to decline. Horst Mahler and four RAF women, including two from the May action to free Baader, were arrested in October. Inmate support groups with names like Red Help and Black Help became a major presence in the terrorist-oriented public from about that mid-1970 and early 1971 on.[45] The terrorist inmates and their support groups swore to keep up the political struggle even from inside the prison walls. At the same time, a string of arson attacks in the spring of 1971 was accompanied by leaflets calling for "freedom for all prisoners."

The RAF also became involved in several unsuccessful attempts to free RAF prisoners. It systematically armed its members and supplied itself with the necessary funds and materials for terrorist action, including automobiles, by periodic bank robberies and related actions. Dramatic events abroad, such as Bloody Sunday in Northern Ireland or the Attica prison riot and its suppression in New York State, were curiously reflected in "commemorative" terrorist attacks or at least public statements. The non-RAF elements in 1971–72 sought to distance themselves pointedly from RAF elitism. They eventually chose the name June 2d Movement, a reference to the date of Ohnesorg's death. They claimed that because of their proletarian origins, they had grown up with violence and had little taste for the intellectualizing ways of the RAF. Their interest in freeing their own friends from prison was most easily advanced, they said, by kidnapping prominent figures in business and politics. Their activities, however, remained as diffuse as those of their antecedents, the Hashish Rebels and Tupamaro groups. To quote a former June 2d member, Gerald Klöpper: "The RAF, with its intellectual origins, saw itself globally as the extended arm of the anti-imperialist

43. There was also a series of threatening letters sent by the Palestine Front TW to Protestant churches, attacks of revenge against certain journalists, and a campaign to free the imprisoned Bommi Baumann, whom his supporters had made into an idol and leader, in jail, of the Hashish Rebels and Tupamaros West Berlin (TW).

44. See Claessens and de Ahna, "Das Milieu," 122–29.

45. By June of 1971, Black Help, which only started half a year earlier, was taking care of fifty-seven inmates, including ten Hashish Rebels. Such organizations also promised legal counseling and, at times of demonstrations or street confrontations, medical assistance for the injured. See ibid., 129–32.

liberation movement. We, however, did not need such derivative reasons. We wanted to free ourselves and did not require the bombing of the Vietnamese people as a reason for resistance. If you have to show up at 7:00 A.M. in your factory and put up day after day with the despotism of factory life (as old Marx called it), with repression and denial of your rights, then that is your reason."[46]

But the writer of these lines also mentions discussions about the role of the urban guerrilla and rejects a purely military approach to that role because the security apparatus of a modern state is always able on these grounds to outdo the terrorists, who tend to turn into mere "free-the-guerrilla guerrillas."[47]

For the RAF, the arrests of October 1970 were soon followed by others and by fatal shoot-outs with the police, as the security apparatus of the Federal Republic demonstrated its towering superiority. One activist (Astrid Proll) was caught in May 1971; another (Petra Schelm) was shot to death in Hamburg in the course of a major police sweep, Aktion Kobra, two months later. In October 1971, a police officer was killed by the RAF, and an armed RAF suspect was arrested, although her gun was not the murder weapon. At a Kaiserlautern Bank heist in December 1971, the RAF killed another police officer. In March 1972, an RAF man, wanted for arson and for inflicting bodily injury, was killed in Augsburg. Two more were arrested in Hamburg, and one of them injured a policeman so seriously that he died three weeks later.

In May 1972, RAF commandos, often named after RAF inmates or casualties, launched a series of bombings: The one at the U.S. Army headquarters in Frankfurt killed an American officer and injured thirteen people. A second bomb placed in the car of Federal Judge Wolfgang Buddenberg maimed his wife. A third bomb, this time with a five-minute warning, injured seventeen at the Springer building in Hamburg. A fourth bomb killed three American soldiers at the U.S. Army headquarters in Heidelberg. This RAF offensive, however, was quickly followed by disaster. In the first two weeks of June police arrested in rapid succession Baader and two other RAF notables, Holger Meins and Jan-

---

46. Gerald Klöpper, "Widerstand gegen die Staatsgewalt: Erfahrungen aus der Bewegung 2. Juni," in *Einschüsse*, ed. Sontheimer and Kallscheuer, 63. For a list of the June 2d Movement attacks, see Claessens and de Ahna, "Das Milieu," 161–63; see also Klöpper, "Widerstand gegen die Staatsgewalt," 58–77, esp. 62–65.

47. Klöpper, who in 1981 became a Berlin Senate candidate for the Alternative List/ Greens, also expressed his uneasiness about such RAF actions as the kidnapping and murder of Schleyer and the hijacking of the plane to Mogadishu, which actions he viewed from prison and described with the words, "Now the [Springer] *Bildzeitung* turned out to be right after all with its description of terrorism" (Klöpper, "Widerstand gegen die Staatsgewalt," 69).

Carl Raspe, in Frankfurt, Ensslin in Hamburg, and Meinhof in Hannover. By this time, the West German police were so jittery that during a nocturnal search for terrorist safehouses, a nervous policeman gunned down an innocent, unarmed (and stark naked) foreigner, Ian McLeod, in his bedroom in Stuttgart. But the core of the RAF was now safely under lock and key, or so it seemed.

Actually, it was merely another phase, with the center of the struggle moved to the prison scene. From 17 January to 12 February 1973, forty RAF prisoners went on a hunger strike to compel the authorities to "lift the prison isolation." Seven of their attorneys, moreover, for four days did their hungering demonstratively before the Federal High Court building in Karlsruhe. Most of the following May and June, eighty prisoners embarked on a second hunger strike, insisting on treatment equal to that of other inmates (but not on integration with them) and on free information. A court ordered that the solitary confinement of two RAF members be ended. In September 1974, forty RAF prisoners began another hunger strike, the longest yet and one enjoying widespread public sympathy in spite of new, unflattering revelations about RAF activities.[48] By this time, Astrid Proll, after three years of incarceration, had obtained a medical release and promptly dropped from sight. At the end of October 1974, members of a Committee Against Torture of Political Prisoners, including two prominent future terrorists,[49] occupied the Amnesty International center in Germany in order to compel its support, although there was no evidence of torture whatsoever. After fifty-four days of hunger strike, though sometimes force-fed, Holger Meins died; but the strike continued. From 17 December on, the strikers' demands changed to *Zusammenlegung* (consolidation) in one prison as well as an end to isolation. On 5 February 1975 the hunger strike ended with minor concessions.

In the meantime, the June 2d Movement had not been idle.[50] In November 1974 a commando attempted to kidnap court president Günter von Drenckmann, the highest Berlin judge, and shot him to death when he resisted his kidnappers. At the end of February 1975 another commando kidnapped Peter Lorenz, the Berlin CDU chief, in the midst of an election campaign. The authorities agreed to release five imprisoned terrorists and to fly them to Aden, South Yemen, accompanied by a

48. In June 1974, Berlin terrorists executed one of their own, Ulrich Schmückler, whom they accused of collaboration with the Constitutional Protection Office (Bundesamt für Verfassungsschutz). The case was never cleared up.

49. Susanne Albrecht and Karl-Heinz Dellwo.

50. The previous year, two of them broke out of jail, although one of them was recaptured eighteen months later.

clergyman and former Berlin mayor, Heinrich Albertz (who had been lord mayor on that fateful June 2d of 1967). Horst Mahler was also offered his freedom, but he declined. Unlike the disastrous precedent of the kidnapped Israeli Olympic athletes in 1972 (when the Bavarian state police had tried to trick the Palestinian kidnappers),[51] the Berlin authorities carried out their promises, which in turn led to a bitter public outcry over giving in to blackmail and encouraging such actions in the future.

The RAF indeed must have been greatly encouraged too, for on 24 April 1975 the RAF Commando Holger Meins seized the German embassy in Stockholm, took twelve hostages, and demanded the release of twenty-six political prisoners back home. But the Bonn government was adamant in its refusal, even after the terrorists killed two embassy officials. During the storm on the embassy, an RAF bomb went off prematurely, killing one terrorist and fatally wounding a second. Four were arrested. The purpose of the embassy seizure had been to free the RAF principals whose trial was to begin a month from then in Stammheim prison in Stuttgart. Baader, Ensslin, Meinhof, and Raspe were charged with murder and attempted murder, among other things.

To appreciate their attitudes toward these charges, one needs to recall a little anecdotal sidelight of the 1970 freeing of Andreas Baader. As related by Stefan Aust, Ulrike Meinhof apparently asked the two policemen guarding Baader whether they were married, and she seemed discomfitted when they both replied that they were and that they had children too. Meinhof, who at the time had small children herself, had evidently taken it for granted that *Bullen* (cops) were single and that their possible deaths would leave no bereaved widows or orphans. This sociopathic streak that dehumanizes all law-enforcement and military personnel as well as targeted politicians and bureaucrats, perceiving them as creatures that deserve to be killed, is also common to the sympathizer literature. There one is surprised to notice that authors often refuse to count terrorist victims of this description as "innocent victims."[52] The same pathological attitude also characterized the terrorist recruits from the Socialist Patients Collective of Heidelberg (SPK), a

51. The police had agreed to let them leave on a plane with their hostages but posted sharpshooters at the airport. Their shots evidently missed, and the PFLP massacred their hostages, only to be shot or captured in turn. The kidnapping was arranged with the help of the RZ and carried out by a PLO affiliate, Black September.

52. See, for example, the chronology in Sontheimer and Kallscheuer, *Einschüsse*, 171–81, where, after mentioning two policemen killed earlier by the RAF, only the 1972 death of a boat builder at the British Yacht Club, who was blown up by a terrorist bomb, rates the label "the first victim" who was not "involved."

psychiatric-group-therapy collective that decided to blame all its troubles on the outside world. "Destroy what destroys you," they said and turned all their self-hatred and anger on West German society and, of course, on the government. Considerable numbers of these SPK recruits played prominent roles in such enterprises as the murder of the alleged "traitor" Schmückler, the shooting of Drenckmann, and the raid on the Stockholm embassy.[53]

TOWARD THE GERMAN AUTUMN

With the trial, the German terrorist drama moved toward an inevitable climax, even though, or perhaps precisely because, the principal RAF members were in prison. Not only were there further killings of both RAF members and police and additional arrests also of June 2d members, such as Teufel in 1975, but that year ended with the raid of Ilyich Ramirez Sanchez, alias Carlos, and a commando of five on the OPEC conference in Vienna. The commando killed three persons, including two guards, and forced the conference to broadcast a declaration condemning Israel (which may not have been too difficult for the OPEC participants) and to spirit the six, including two German RAF terrorists, Hans Joachim Klein and Gabriele Kröcher-Tiedemann, to Algeria. The following May 1976, Ulrike Meinhof was found hanging from a pipe in her cell in Stammheim prison.[54] The same month, another German terrorist and an Israeli guard were blown up at Tel Aviv airport by a bomb in the former's suitcase.

In June 1976 the Bundestag passed the first antiterrorist laws and amendments, which, for example, proscribed the formation of and membership in a terrorist group and authorized surveillance of the correspondence between terrorist prisoners and their attorneys. The twenty-four imprisoned RAF members had, with the help of their attorneys, established such an effective information network for both inmates and

---

53. See Wanda von Baeyer-Katte, "Das sozialistische Patientenkollektiv im Heidelberg," in von Baeyer-Katte et al., *Gruppenprozesse*, 184–304.

54. The discouragement weighing on her may have been aggravated by the failure of Operation Leo, a plot to seize former Swedish Minister of the Interior Anna-Greta Leijon in order to spring the RAF prisoners. The plan involved a multinational team and failed disastrously. See Jacob Sundberg, "Operation Leo: Description and Analysis of a European Terrorist Operation," *Terrorism* 5 (1981): 197–232. The account by Aust, *Der Baader-Meinhof Komplex*, suggests that she was hounded into despair by her fellow inmates Ensslin and Baader.

outside supporters—circular letters appeared at regular intervals—that they remained in almost full control of RAF actions inside and outside of jail. This meant, among other things, that their hunger strikes were so well orchestrated that Baader, for example, was able to monitor everybody's weight loss and, therefore, any noncompliance with the discipline of the strike. The technology of information was easily accessed by this group, which had earlier shown its aptitude by modifying commercial radio sets to receive police and other security messages, to broadcast themselves, to interfere with police communications, and to detonate remote-control bombs. But an investigation of the content of the surviving jail communications also shows the deteriorating morale of the principal RAF terrorists, whose hopes for mobilizing massive revolutionary resistance outside had proved totally unrealistic.[55] This demoralization alone appears to be sufficient motive for committing suicide, even though the sympathetic Left until recently still liked to cast doubt on the RAF suicides in prison.

Outside the prison the situation began to build up to a climax. Later in June 1976, Palestinian terrorists abducted an Air France airliner to Entebbe, Uganda, and demanded the release in various Western countries of fifty-three prisoners, including Raspe and several other imprisoned RAF and June 2d members (including Teufel), but not the other RAF principals. An Israeli commando stormed the plane and freed its passengers; two died. More German terrorists were arrested: one in Athens; one in Vienna, who was sentenced to twelve years in prison; and a couple of June 2d members in Hamburg, who were sentenced to ten and eleven years. Another two terrorists were arrested in Stockholm and handed over to the Federal Republic. By April 1977 as many as one hundred terrorist prisoners were participating in the hunger strike, demanding *Zusammenlegung*, an end to isolation, and the minimal treatment accorded prisoners of war under the Geneva Convention.

The conflict inside and outside now went into high drama. On 7 April 1977 an RAF commando in Karlsruhe assassinated the federal prosecutor, Siegfried Buback, along with his driver and a guard. Like Walter Rathenau in 1922, he was shot from a motorcycle that pulled up next to him in traffic. At the end of April the court handed down the sentences against Baader, Ensslin, and Raspe: lifelong imprisonment for four murders and thirty-four attempted murders. West German law had abolished the death penalty after the war. Three other courts handed out

55. See Friedhelm Neidhart, "Soziale Bedingungen terroristischen Handelns: Das Beispiel der Baader-Meinhof-Gruppe (RAF)," in von Baeyer-Katte et al., *Gruppenprozesse*, 326–27 and 330–31.

seven more life sentences, including one to one of Buback's assassins who was seriously injured during capture. An additional terrorist received four years for belonging to a terrorist organization. In July the CEO of the Dresdner Bank, Jürgen Ponto, was killed after a distant member of his family—a young woman terrorist, as it turned out—gained admittance to his house for her hit team to kidnap him. In August three more terrorists were arrested, and an attempted rocket attack, with a self-made rocket launcher, on the Federal Prosecutor's Office was foiled. On 5 September, finally, another RAF commando kidnapped Hanns Martin Schleyer, the head of the German Employers Association, in Cologne, and killed his driver and three policemen. The kidnappers demanded the release of eleven imprisoned terrorists but were refused. Two more terrorists were captured, including another one of the Buback assassins. The Bundestag then passed the law permitting temporary solitary confinement for terrorists—the eleven targeted for exchange with Schleyer had actually been in solitary since his kidnapping—and momentarily blocking access of the terrorist attorneys to their clients (*Kontaktsperre*). One of the more prominent attorneys, Klaus Croissant, was arrested in Paris and extradited on charges of aiding and abetting criminal acts.

On 13 October 1977, four Palestinians hijacked a Lufthansa plane full of vacationers on their way back from Mallorca to Frankfurt, diverted it at first to Cyprus and then to Dubai, Bahrain, Aden, and eventually Mogadishu, Somalia. The hijackers repeated the demand of the Schleyer kidnappers and added the release of two Palestinians and a ransom of $15 million. On their way, they executed the captain of the plane to show their determination to do the same with the ninety-one German passengers and crew. The crisis staff of the Schmidt government still refused to give in, despite an ultimatum to kill all the hostages.[56] But a specially trained antiterrorist unit of the West German border police, GSG 9, was flown in secretly and on the night of 17 October stormed the plane, killing three of the hijackers and freeing the hostages. The next morning, Baader, Ensslin, and Raspe were found dead in their cells, Ensslin hanging from the window and the other two shot to death, and a fourth terrorist was found stabbed but alive; all were presumed to have attempted suicide, although how they managed to receive weapons and

56. Schleyer's son, Hanns Eberhard, actually raised the ransom and made a desperate attempt legally to compel the federal and state authorities involved to release the eleven terrorists in exchange for his father's life. See Aust, *Der Baader-Meinhof Komplex*, 543–52. The eleven prisoners were informed of the action because, among other reasons, they had to be asked whether they accepted the deal and what country they wanted to be flown to in case the operation succeeded.

communicate so well in spite of *Kontaktsperre* and solitary confinement has never been completely cleared up.

The principals had been told of the hijacking, and Baader had said that he had never approved of "such actions against uninvolved civilians" and that the ruthlessness of the second and third generations of terrorists was really the fault of the antiterrorist policy of the federal government in Bonn. Ensslin gave prison chaplains letters—which have since disappeared—that were to be transmitted to the Federal Chancellery "in case of an execution," an expression never clarified. Raspe probably heard the announcement of the freeing of the hostages in Mogadishu shortly after midnight on his transistor radio and used a secretly constructed electronic communication system to set the stage for the common suicide of the four. Baader had a smuggled-in pistol, hidden in a record player, and used the weapon to make it look like a murder, firing two shots from a standing position into the wall and mattress of his cell. He then killed himself with a shot in the back of his neck while squatting on the floor. Raspe also had a smuggled-in gun, which he put to his temple while sitting on the edge of the bed. Ensslin used a piece of loudspeaker cable in the cell to hang herself from the bars in the window, and the fourth terrorist stabbed herself four times with a table knife in the chest.[57] She later testified that she had heard muffled shots at about 5:00 A.M., but, apparently, no one else did. The politicians, naturally, were ready to believe that it was a series of suicides even before the coroner's examination began, and they blamed the smuggling in of guns on the terrorists' attorneys. By the same token, sympathizers of the terrorists made it an article of faith that it was murder, perhaps even by a jailhouse death squad.[58] A day after the death of Baader, Ensslin, and Raspe, Schleyer's bullet-riddled body was found in the trunk of a car in Mulhouse, Alsace.

The terrorist incidents of the German Autumn of 1977 still continued, just like a storm that cannot be expected to die down in an instant. A shoot-out in Amsterdam resulted in the capture of two German terrorists. Another RAF principal, Ingrid Schubert, hanged herself in Stadelheim prison in Munich. Toward the end of the year, a shoot-out with

57. See ibid., 541–52, 553, 560–65, and 575–77.

58. From the sympathizers' point of view, there were precedents for such executions of prisoners in detention: the killing of Rosa Luxemburg and Karl Liebknecht in 1919 in Berlin. But such an execution would have made more sense before the freeing of the hostages. See the discussion of evidence pro and con in ibid., 581–92, including the account of repeated lapses of security, such as occurred during a remodeling of the Stammheim jail cells, when all kinds of outside contacts could have smuggled in guns. Meanwhile, some of the terrorists sheltered by the Stasi until 1990 have testified that there were indeed elaborate group suicide plans if the hijacking were to fail.

Swiss customs officers bagged two more RAF members, who were subsequently sentenced to fifteen and eleven years; and there were further arrests, trials, and sentences early in 1970. One of these involved another attorney accused of helping with the information system of terrorist prisoners and of being involved in a terrorist group: two years in prison and a fine of DM 75,000. In March 1978 yet another terrorist hunger strike began. In the meantime, a Berlin court trial examined charges of participation in the Drenckmann assassination and the kidnapping of Lorenz against six terrorists, including Fritz Teufel and Gerald Klöpper. More terrorists were arrested in Paris, London, and Bulgaria and extradited to Germany. Yugoslavia also captured four but preferred to deport them to a country of their choice.[59] In September a terrorist suspect in the killings of Buback, Ponto, and Schleyer was recognized in Düsseldorf and shot to death by the police. Half a year later a second suspect in the same crime was killed in a police stakeout.

During this period of aftermath, RAF actions appeared to be limited to commandeering the DPA press agency in Frankfurt, where seven RAF men and four women forced the employees to publish a statement in defense of the RAF prisoners. But of course there were also further hunger strikes: a seventh one began in April 1979, involving seventy inmates, and once again demanded *Zusammenlegung*. An eighth hunger strike begun in February 1981 involved 120 prisoners, who demanded not only better conditions in jail but also "arming the resistance, organizing illegality, and supporting the armed resistance throughout Western Europe."[60] As an expression of their sentiment at this time, the strike was really not a serious bargaining instrument but a plaintive cry of existential frustration at a world that refused to behave their way. The whole decade had begun with high hopes and great promise for them but had turned into a scene as depressing as the inside of a prison cell.

INTERPRETING WITH THE BENEFIT OF HINDSIGHT

Many aspects of West German left-wing terrorism suggest that analysis of the phenomenon will resist a simplistic chronological-narrative ap-

---

59. They included Mohnhaupt and three other important RAF members. One of them, Rolf-Clemens Wagner, was arrested a year later during a bank robbery in which an innocent bystander was killed. The sentences in the Drenckmann-Lorenz trial included two fifteen-year terms and, for Teufel, one to five years.

60. See Sontheimer and Kallscheuer, *Einschüsse*, 180–81.

proach. To begin with, even the RAF—not to mention the June 2d Movement and RZ—lacked the kind of unity and identity that is suggested by an organizational history. Not only were there major tensions and conflicts at the very apex of the hierarchical organization from the beginning (and a considerable amount of outside manipulation by the agents provocateurs of the Federal Constitutional Protection Office),[61] but the unity of command between leadership and operatives from about 1973–74 on became more of a myth than a reality. The second, third, and succeeding generations increasingly formed their own largely autonomous groups and carried out independent actions that could be claimed to be in harmony with the goals of the original leadership only through great efforts at ex post facto interpretation by RAF members in prison and their friends outside. Current successor groups are united by the RAF myth only, without any remaining organizational nexus. If one can say the RAF once was one of several tornadoes spun off from the APO and the student movement, one can also consider today's successor groups each a little tornado spawned by the RAF and identified only with its name, just as RAF commandos liked to name themselves—in a deliberate effort at mythmaking—after fallen martyrs like Holger Meins or Elisabeth van Dyck. Serious analysts should not be taken in by such appearances without further evidence of a functioning organization.

Once the RAF had cut its swath through the political landscape, moreover, future recruits were likely to be attracted to it in a very different way, less by the original political and ideological rationale and more by the killings and violent action.[62] This is also evident from the increasingly cruder rationalizations for violent action. The moral uneasiness expressed, for example, by Mahler and later by Meinhof about some of the RAF actions involving physical harm to unintended victims—such as the bombing of the Springer building in Hamburg in which seventeen lowly assistant editors were injured—was only the beginning of a growing moral estrangement between the original thrust of the RAF and the killer mentality of later recruits. Meinhof's early words about clashes with the "pigs [police]" and "*natürlich wird geschos-*

---

61. It is also amazing how well the West German authorities, and even the East German authorities who were involved in the departure and return of the early RAF from the El Fatah camp in the Middle East, were informed about practically every aspect of the group's activities in the second half of 1970.

62. See the careful description of the stages of RAF history by Neidhardt, "Soziale Bedingungen terroristischen Handelns," 318–93, esp. 331–32. See also the *Spiegel* interview with Peter-Jürgen Boock and his statement that, from 1975, the RAF no longer engaged in critical reflection on its actions (*Der Spiegel*, 23 February 1981). Boock dropped out in 1979 but is still in prison, trying for a reduction of a double life sentence.

sen [of course we'll shoot]" already represented a kind of brave whistling in the dark that concealed her own doubts about the use of violence. Even the "man of action," Baader, had major scruples about hijacking innocents, such as the vacationers on the Lufthansa plane "Landshut," and threatening their lives in order to spring him and other RAF leaders from prison. Admittedly, he failed to protest and did not refuse to be ransomed,[63] but it is easy to contrast his earlier antihijacking stance with the fatuous post-Mogadishu declaration by one RAF successor group outside bewailing "the massacre [of the Palestinian hijackers by the GSG 9 commando] at Mogadishu and at Stammheim." One can imagine a real massacre of the eighty-six innocent passengers by the ruthless Palestinians who had already killed the plane's pilot, threatened to blow up the plane with everybody inside, and would very likely have begun killing the passengers one by one if their ultimatum again was not met. By itself such a violation of the scruples of the original RAF leaders seems a plausible reason for their suicidal despair.

The willful dilution of the moral thrust of the first RAF generation by later recruits becomes even clearer upon examination of the reflections of former RAF activists such as Klaus Jünschke, who, released after sixteen years imprisonment—originally a life sentence for participating in a bank heist in which a guard was killed—and passionate engagement with the prisoners' movement and prison reform, had some withering comments for the entire enterprise. Writing in the left-wing *Tageszeitung* (*Taz*) in 1986, he viewed the bombing of the Rhine-Main air base of August 1985 and the execution of a twenty-year-old American soldier for his identity card as signs "that the RAF no longer has a responsible leadership" and condemned "this degenerate crew that had the nerve . . . to boast of this cowardly murder and to present it as a new quality in the anti-imperialist struggle . . . in Western Europe." He was also concerned with the contribution that this ruthlessness of the terrorists had made to the buildup of right-wing politics and of the overwhelming internal security apparatus of today: "West German terrorism had . . . this unbelievable effect because it allowed itself from the very beginning to be used by interested parties. We thought with our political actions to overcome the exploitation and domination and, in reality, were only used to make the conditions that we wanted to change uglier yet."[64] In spite

63. Horst Mahler, on the earlier occasion of the Lorenz kidnapping and freeing of June 2d prisoners, had resolutely refused to be included in exchanging his freedom, along with others, for that of Lorenz.

64. Klaus Jünschke, *Spätlese: Texte zu RAF und Knast* (Frankfurt: Neue Kritik, 1988), 157. Jünschke had been estranged from the RAF since before the German Autumn of 1977 and finally made his exit public in 1981.

of his bitterness about the conditions of the RAF incarceration, he viewed the cause of the RAF against the West German state with skepticism and was critical of RAF unwillingness to discuss its goals and answer questions: "Despite all excesses and dubious deaths, things in the Federal Republic are done in a democratic, constitutional [*rechts-staatlich*] way. . . . The whole concept of the [RAF] war is based on a lie. . . . Today I think that it was a fundamental error from the very beginning to say that the situation can only be changed by violence, if at all."[65]

Jünschke is less troubled by the unplanned shoot-outs and unintended victims at various RAF actions than by the very principle of the RAF offensive, "that we decided deliberately and intentionally to kill people," as in the 1972 bombings of the U.S. headquarters in Frankfurt and Heidelberg or of the Springer building in Hamburg. At that moment, Jünschke writes, "we experienced how our sympathizers suddenly became afraid, and many of us did too. . . . The decision to kill had passed a borderline that was simply too much for us and our supporters. . . . What made us terrorists was that for the freedom and happiness of all people, we were ready to kill people, rather arbitrarily selected victims."[66]

By today, Jünschke feels, the "concept of the urban guerrilla has failed" and become counterproductive, not least because of the elitist contempt of the RAF for the feelings of ordinary people. The emphasis on unreflective military-style commando action of the RAF "attracts types with aggressive hang-ups, unstable juveniles who cannot tolerate critical thinking [about the true, long-range interest of our cause]. . . . You have become too much like the fascists you claim to be fighting." He called upon the RAF to give up the armed struggle and upon the state to resocialize and reintegrate them into West German society in the manner of the Italian *pentiti* legislation or the Tupamaro amnesty in Uruguay.[67]

The negative assessment of the RAF's military approach to the problems of West German democracy in the seventies was widely, if not universally, shared on the Left. However understandable the beginnings

65. Ibid., 146–48. Prominent members of the Greens party have proposed a public dialogue with the RAF. The public letter of the von Braunmühl brothers, in Jünschke's opinion, deserved a response from the RAF (ibid., 186).

66. Ibid., 162–63. Jünschke was also very unhappy with the RAF militants of 1977 in Hamburg and Frankfurt who "stifled the shock over the dead of Stammheim with the execution of Schleyer" (ibid., 169). A number of other RAF figures, such as Klöpper and Mahler, also opposed the assassinations of 1977 and the Mogadishu affair.

67. Ibid., 165–68 and 180–81. Many RAF members in prison and outside indeed have long dissociated themselves from it (ibid., 184–86 and 190).

may have been against the background of conservative governments in West Berlin and Bonn, the Vietnam War, and the intense APO and student protests of 1967–68, the political scene soon began to change fundamentally, and most of the rebellious Left followed the change. In Bonn, Willy Brandt took over, proclaiming "more democracy," inviting young leftists to join his reform administration, and launching a major new campaign of reconciliation with Communist Eastern Europe, the *Ostpolitik*. The Vietnam War eventually wound down too, and even the cold warriors of the West Berlin city government began, albeit reluctantly, to mend their ways. Once-rebellious students and leftists of most persuasions went "into the system" in large numbers, some for a "long" but nonviolent "march through German institutions," many to settle down with pragmatic undertakings of planning and reform. Only the terrorists—in increasing isolation from their erstwhile supporters and often criticized as "red fascists" or "left-wing fascists" by others on the left[68]—continued to march in the opposite direction as if they were following a different drummer. More likely they found the cloak-and-dagger play so stimulating they kept on hoping for a revolutionary uprising of the masses against all reasonable expectations.

Such a major lapse in the seasoned political judgment of someone like Ulrike Meinhof or Horst Mahler really cries out for an explanation. Their revolutionary quest in the face of changing mass public opinion is so quixotic and extraordinary that it is difficult to view it as a product of the evolving political environment of the seventies. Perhaps the only cogent explanation can come from analysis of the patterns of political socialization or individual life histories of RAF members. While they may not shed sufficient light on the political evolution of Meinhof, Baader, and Ensslin,[69] such analyses appear to explain reasonably well how the rank-and-file recruits of the RAF, once attracted, continued to act out the roles and labels they had taken on. It is hardly surprising that among typical attributes of the left-wing terrorists analyzed in this fashion are a great longing for a community with a cause and a tendency to become so dependent on this community as to lose the sense of outside reality.[70] Differentiated by their positions in terrorist organizations—and

68. Jürgen Habermas coined the phrase "red fascism," which is familiar also from the Italian terrorist debate and was probably used already in the Weimar Republic. See the critical comments of the well-known Daniel Cohn-Bendit, a Sponti radical, in *Einschüsse*, ed. Sontheimer and Kallscheuer, 153–70.

69. Various investigators, such as Jillian Becker in *Hitler's Children* (Philadelphia: J. B. Lippincott, 1977), have made an attempt to understand the RAF leaders, at times with psychohistorical methods, but hardly with satisfactory results.

70. See Klaus Wasmund, "The Political Socialization of West German Terrorists," in *Political Violence and Terror*, ed. Merkl, 203–25, and Jäger, Schmidtchen, and Süllwold, *Lebenslaufanalysen*.

there are considerable differences between the various West German groups[71]—each terrorist career is like a ticking time bomb that has to go through the full length of its programmed cycle unless captured and deactivated before it has exploded and burnt itself out.

Although the socioenvironmental conditions that set each career on its path may have been crucial then, this particular set of conditions—student rebellion, APO, SPK, prisoners' support group—only accounts for lighting the fuse in a likely personality. The fuse may keep on burning, even though the initial conditions have changed. Other socioenvironmental factors, however, may take over—such as the small-group dynamics of terrorist life in the underground, police persecution, and isolation from the nonterrorist public—and reinforce the heroic sense of battling the mighty state or the vast imperialist apparatus by bombing or assassinating its symbolic representatives and facilities. The heroics of a terrorist career, in fact, may actually be enhanced more by the realization that this is a hopeless, friendless quest against overwhelming odds than by realistic expectations of a revolutionary uprising of the masses. Surely the RAF theorists must soon have understood that such mass support was most unlikely to materialize and that overwhelming majorities of West Germans were horrified by the ideas and deeds of the RAF,[72] yet they persisted in their increasingly pointless and thoroughly unconstructive quest. They also failed to speak out when successor groups went far beyond their original intent and relative self-restraint.

POLITICAL OVERTONES OF TERROR RESEARCH

In the wake of the German Autumn of 1977, the Permanent Conference of *Land* Ministers of the Interior commissioned a group of scholars to

71. Neidhardt found, for example, that the "overcentralized RAF'" and the "undercentralized" June 2d Movement and RZ differed also in a wide range of other features. See his "Linker und rechter Terrorismus," in von Baeyer-Katte et al., *Gruppenprozesse*, 434–74.

72. By way of counterpoint, SPD deputy Antje Vollmer compiled a list of "missed opportunities" of the establishment to ease the return of RAF principals to conformity with the rules of West German society: (1) pardoning the department-store arsonists Baader, Ensslin, and Proll in 1969; (2) Nobel Prize winner Böll's proposal to grant Meinhof a pardon or free exile in late 1971; (3) the moment in the RAF trial at Stammheim in September 1975 when the accused were adjudged fit to stand trial by independent experts; and several more. See her interview in *Der blinde Fleck*, 188–90. Vollmer evidently does not share the conviction that the RAF crossed the Rubicon when the first intentional violence was inflicted on persons.

examine the phenomenon of German terrorism, so that the public could be enlightened as to the whys and wherefores of what had happened. Consequently, teams of social scientists were selected with an eye to representing partisan and other points of view, at least within the mainstream. In the first half of the eighties, then, five hefty volumes appeared on ideologies and strategies, terrorist life histories, group structure and dynamics, and reactions of state and society to terrorism, right and left. This series of volumes, entitled *Analyses of Terrorism*, raised considerable scholarly and political controversy and, after a few years, was followed by another two volumes by a team that had participated in the fourth volume of the *Analyses*, but only with misgivings. In their additional volumes, they stressed comparisons with left radical and terrorist movements in Italy, France, Spain, and the Netherlands in a more elaborate fashion than before.[73] These scholarly disagreements, not to mention their political overtones, are crucial to our understanding of German terrorism. In the last years, moreover, a second commission of experts has addressed the broader question of politically motivated violence in the streets and squares of the Federal Republic, and its results are also expected to shed more light on terrorism.

The issue at the heart of the dispute over the *Analyses*, and by implication over earlier public discussions of left-wing terror, are fundamental to the political confrontation between Right and Left inasmuch as they influence the choice of approach to the study of the political confrontation between right-wing and left-wing terrorism.[74] For the last twenty-five years the parties right of center, conservative media, and the law-enforcement establishment have insisted that left-wing terror is the natural outcome of student and other rebellions against authority, of intellectuals questioning authority and "flirting with Communism," and of left-wing governments, such as Willy Brandt's coalition of SPD and FDP, "coddling terrorists" and other lawbreakers. The intellectuals, including such prominent writers as Heinrich Böll and Hans Magnus Enzensberger, were accused of being the "intellectual trailblazers" (*Wegbereiter*) of terrorism, brainwashing students and others with their persuasive thinking. The entire Left, or at least the more oppositional elements in it, were lumped together in the Springer press and in statements of right-wing politicians as "terrorist sympathizers," or the *Sympathisantenszene*, a slogan that became a very effective political weapon of obfuscation at the height of the worst RAF violence.

73. See Hess et al., *Angriff auf das Herz des Staates*, 2 vols. The comparative parts are in volume 2.
74. The discussion of right-wing terrorism, curiously, has never considered the possibility that it too might reflect deep-seated discontents of society and the state.

Of course, if these perceptions are correct, voters should have elected only tough-minded CDU/CSU governments, which would not have given an inch to intellectual propaganda, not to mention to outright terrorist blackmail.[75] At the same time, the antiterrorist security apparatus—mostly the Constitutional Protection Office and the BKA—should have been built up at great expense and given a great expanded staff and every possible technological advantage over the sinister foe. Stringent antiterrorist legislation needed to be passed—for example, restricting the contacts between imprisoned terrorists and their attorneys or disbarring the latter for an excess of zeal in defending their clients. Aside from this recourse to the legislature, the right-wing approach to terrorism emphasized executive action, emergency privileges for crisis staffs and police, and ex post facto covers for excessive use of force or illegal operations, such as wiretaps. This "hour of the executive" also prevailed under Willy Brandt's SPD/FDP successors, who were in power in Bonn during the prime time of left-wing terror.

The left-wing perceptions of the rise of terrorism in the Federal Republic, by contrast, tend to link postwar governments and law enforcement to a quasi-continuation of the Third Reich using other means. Left-wing terrorism has been very much a German phenomenon and cannot be understood except as a product of the contradictions of postwar West German society and of the role of the state at the "heart" of which its violence has been aimed. The link to the Third Reich was perceived as present not only in the authoritarianism of the Emergency Laws but also in police and jail procedures and in German criminal law. It was regarded as indisputable in the close identification of the Bonn government with the interests of big business in Germany and abroad, with the United States, and with the "imperialist" oppression and exploitation visited by the governments of industrialized core countries upon marginal populations in their own countries and on the periphery of the less developed world. Left-wing writers also claimed that the ideological anti-Communism typical of antiterrorist policies was unique to the Federal Republic and that oppressive and marginalizing state policies literally produced or at least shaped left-wing terrorism. Their most persuasive proof of this has been the rhetoric of the Springer press and of right-wing politicians such as the late Franz Josef Strauss, which indeed often hewed to a propaganda of exclusionism and marginalization.[76]

75. Radical-right movements such as the new Republican party, the National Democrats (NDP), and the German People's Union (DVU) were quick to pick up on this new popularity of tough-minded law-and-order and antiterrorist issues, which may explain the great attraction of policemen and other law-enforcement personnel to these movements.
76. At some point this right-wing rhetoric also tends to link its exclusion of left-wing rebels, feminists, gays, and lesbians from the national community with the exclusion of or

How has this political division affected terrorism research? Aside from the more obvious charges of bias—that research sponsored by the right wing or by the government might just pillory a lot of people as "sympathizers"[77]—the question is first of all one of focus. The more conservative researchers tend to take a very narrow view of what they ought to examine, usually only the terrorist movements and their deeds, and this often in a way that suggests far more unity and cohesion among "the terrorist movement" and its alleged antecedents than empirical analysis would seem to warrant. According to their detractors, conservative approaches also like to descend to the microsocial, biographical, and psychological levels, which in the view of left-wing critics tends to reduce the great causes dear to the terrorists to the level of idées fixes, idiosyncratic personal maladjustments, or products of a broken home—to bellyaches rather than American imperialism in the Third World. From the perspective of German left-wing scholars, life history or psychological microanalysis is irrelevant and inappropriate. Even a systematic psychoanalytical account of the thirty-two RAF recruits that came from the psychiatric SPK of Heidelberg is really a blow below the ideological belt.

The approach preferred by German left-wing scholars instead emphasizes the role of general social conditions and of the state as the antagonist of left-wing critics who may turn violent if denied legitimate expressions of opinion and goaded into "armed resistance." The RAF and the June 2d Movement, according to this view, are incomprehensible without discussing the prior confrontations pitting the APO and students against the police. Understanding the terrorists also requires an examination of their charges that the West German establishment still embodied fascism and that it supported American imperialist depredations in the Third World, particularly in Vietnam, and aggression against Communist countries in eastern Europe. Like the extreme right-wing position, the left-wing one tends to go overboard in what it condemns. Discounting such ideological distortions on both sides, however, we may be able to collate complementary aspects of both approaches and arrive at a more complete view of the realities of West German terrorism.

---

discrimination against foreign workers, gypsy minorities, and others of questionable fit in the right-wing heaven.

77. See, for example, the critical review of the *Analyses* by Wolf-Dieter Narr, "Terror breitgewalzt," in *Leviathan* 17, no. 1 (1989): 15–45, esp. 15 and 18–19, where the author asks whether the subject of the analysis is to be the alleged "sympathizers and ideology suppliers." It should be noted also that German social scientists have become a great deal more suspicious of contract research than they used to be, including government-sponsored contract research.

THE SOCIAL-SCIENTIFIC PERSPECTIVE

The five volumes of the *Analyses* and the follow-up contain much that is illuminating for comparative terrorism research in spite of their patchiness, unevenness, and occasional bias. Iring Fetscher and Günter Rohrmoser's analysis of the writings of Mahler and Meinhof on the urban guerrilla against the background of classical socialist theory, for example, makes clear the extent to which, in particular, Ulrike Meinhof's "psychological-moralizing" approach was very far from the left-wing mainstream; hers was a romantic and naïve activism that dispensed with the working masses of industrialized countries and lived mostly on conspiratorial theories and the borrowed misery of former colonial situations far from her ken. Fetscher and Rohrmoser bring out, for example, the absence of a clear strategic concept underlying the attacks of spring 1972 on facilities of the U.S. Army, the German police and courts, and the Springer press.[78] The eventual withdrawal of the United States from Vietnam, logic would suggest, also should have posed a problem of strategic redirection to a movement that had relied so heavily on the Vietnam War for justification of its most extreme actions. In a manner of speaking, Meinhof's theories were led *ad absurdum* precisely by the crudeness of Baader and Ensslin, whom she had so unthinkingly admired in the early days of the RAF. Most of the RAF members hardly knew their Marx and Lenin before imprisonment gave them the opportunity to read them, and there is no reason to believe that any other German terrorist groups graduated from reading Marx, Engels, and Lenin to terrorist action.

The stress on action before theory—however some West German scholars and writers may object to such "psychological reductionism"—plainly suggests that the personal inclination toward terrorist action made theoretical justification rather irrelevant, and this among by and large highly intelligent and educated people: "I throw bombs at the establishment, therefore I am [a left-wing fighter]." Or, "Have semiautomatic gun, will travel." This appears to be a terrorism *sui generis* that has very little to do with what Marx and Lenin were concerned about, except for the use of their rhetoric as an afterthought.[79]

78. Fetscher and Rohrmoser, *Ideologien und Strategien*, 40–43 and 67–71. There is also a detailed description of the ideological disagreements within the RAF leadership. Mahler was far more indebted to mainstream Marxism and for that reason soon began to resist the wild flights of the actionist imagination. See also Aust, *Der Baader-Meinhof Komplex*, 261–62.

79. Both Leon Trotsky and Lenin specifically rejected terrorism because they believed the linkage between the oppressed masses and the would-be revolutionaries to be paramount. A terrorism on behalf of distant Third World peoples or unorganized consumers still requires specific and clear endorsement by the "beneficiaries" for its legitimation.

Fetscher particularly examined the RAF charge that the Federal Republic was a "fascist system" deeply involved with the international "fascist imperialism" of the United States and that its reactions to student unrest and RAF terror every day revealed a process of increasing "fascistization," this last charge bearing overtones of a self-fulfilling prophecy.[80] The fascism charge, of course, mirrored the flawed "theories of fascism" of the seventies, which, as in the Weimar Republic, tended to identify it with capitalism and even with the reformist socialism of the SPD rather than with the forces of racial imperialism that culminated in perpetrating the Holocaust and brutalizing other allegedly lesser breeds. According to the "theories of fascism," reformist socialism and advanced capitalism together produce a manipulative repertoire—fascism—that, with minor concessions to the workers and scapegoats such as the Jews and antagonistic foreign nations, is said to blind the masses to the capitalistic purpose of exploitation and domination. This RAF interpretation and old Weimar Communist theory may have made sense for a while to the small contemporary forces and intellectuals to the left of Willy Brandt's SPD. To the overwhelming majority of West Germans, however, it seemed not only absurd but unfair, a maligning of West German democracy by people who identified themselves with the repressive, pseudodemocratic dictatorships of the East. None of the scholars of the *Analyses*, of course, accept these "delusive systems based on projection," and many denounce them as outrageous.[81]

A balanced view should really be based on a realistic assessment of the Nazi movement and the Third Reich as well as of the ambiguities of German left-wing terrorism. While it is true that Nazi views and policies, except for early anticapitalistic tendencies, made no attempt to alter the basic mechanism of "organized capitalism" in Germany, they routinely violated private-property rights, intervened massively, and soon imposed the politico-economic system of a war economy. It makes little sense to characterize the Nazis as the protagonists of international capitalism,

---

Otherwise, it is merely a game of pretense among some of the privileged youth of the developed core countries.

80. Some of the accusations of police lawlessness, government overreaction, and prison stringency, however justified from the point of view of a reformist group committed to constitutional rights under the Basic Law, were also incongruous with the RAF leaders' views on the use of violence and the marked exemption of the GDR and other Communist dictatorships of the day from the accusations. It is not logical to demand adherence to one set of standards from the adversary and a totally different set from oneself and one's friends.

81. See Fetscher and Rohrmoser, *Ideologien und Strategien*, 185–203 and 294–95, and especially Ulrich Matz and Gerhard Schmidtchen, *Gewalt und Legitimität*, vol. 4/1 of *Analysen zum Terrorismus* (Opladen: Westdeutscher Verlag, 1983).

which they fought from the beginning.[82] Their "imperialism" was emphatically based on notions of national and racial superiority; witness the goals and conduct of the Second World War and the massive genocide practiced on Jews, Slavs, Gypsies, and others.

The alleged survivals of Nazi authoritarianism into the sixties and seventies in German society and law enforcement were mostly remainders of German traditional (pre-Nazi) authoritarianism in family life, education, and police procedures, especially in the minds of the older generation but also visible in the human relations, for example, of some young Communist groups that were no paragons of democracy and tolerance either. In addition to this lingering authoritarianism, the older generation also embraced anti-Communism and fear of the Soviet Union and clung to American protection for reasons so obvious at the time that only young Germans of the Left could deny them. The West Germans had barely escaped becoming part of the satellite empire of the Soviets and knew all too well what Communist rule had meant in East Germany from 1945 through the sixties. NATO and the United States were their security. Western capitalism was embraced—with the usual German interventionist modifications—because it brought overwhelming prosperity in contrast to life in East Germany. In this sense, indeed, a mind striving for rationalization could speak of the German masses having been "bought," but such logic is ridiculous.

Worse yet, there is a grave flaw in some of the interpretations that are based on occasional statements by RAF leaders, such as Meinhof, that have likened the American engagement in Vietnam or the RAF prisoners' fear of being murdered in jail to conduct and conditions at Auschwitz.[83] The analogy is a beguiling one if it denotes that the RAF wanted to stop the killing of Vietnamese and of RAF prisoners out of guilt feelings over the Holocaust. Unfortunately, this interpretation ignores the evolution of Meinhof's views toward a pronounced hostility toward Israel, the military training sought by the RAF in an El Fatah camp, and the numerous expressions of strident hostility toward Israel and the Israelis among all the left-wing terrorist groups, beginning with those of the self-styled West Berlin Tupamaro groups. There was a Palestine

---

82. The premise underlying identification of fascism with capitalism is that since the fascists refused to follow the revolutionary line of the Communists and the Communist belief that capitalism was the root of all social evils, the fascists must be the defenders of capitalism, and any trace of fascism must be identical with the triumph of capitalism.

83. See Scheerer, "Die ausgebürgerte Linke," 336. See also Peter Fritzsche, "Terrorism in the Federal Republic of Germany and Italy: Legacy of the '68 Movement or 'Burden of Fascism'?" *Terrorism and Political Violence* 1, no. 4 (1989): 466–81; Hoffman, "Bonn, 1987," 45–46; and Aust, *Der Baader-Meinhof Komplex*, 280.

faction in the RAF. RZ members helped the PFLP to kidnap and murder the Israeli athletes in 1972, and in a widely circulated statement afterward, the imprisoned Ulrike Meinhof praised this action of the PLO's Black September group as exemplary for the revolutionary strategy of the anti-imperialist struggle that "might give the West German Left its identity back." As she explained in a letter to the other RAF leaders, who emphatically accepted her reasoning, she wanted to express the common goals of RAF and Black September, namely, "the material annihilation of imperialistic rule . . . and in the material attack, the propagandist action: the act of liberation in the act of annihilation."[84] None of this sounds like the voice of the avengers of Auschwitz.

DATA ON INDIVIDUAL TERRORISTS

Quite illuminating and comparable to the findings and surveys in other countries are the results of the study of the life histories and individual case records of some 227 left-wing terrorists charged or sentenced by the end of 1978, most of them RAF and June 2d members. Unlike the terrorists of the German radical Right, the 227 had four times the number of parents in the higher occupational categories (independents, higher white-collar and executive and civil service status, and the professions) as the population average. Female left-wing terrorists were to an even higher degree the daughters of the German upper classes: five times the average. Workers and farmers were distinctly underrepresented among the 227, which may help to explain the terrorists' disdain for the working masses of their country.[85] Their ages were typically concentrated in the second postwar generation (born between 1941 and 1955), which also supplied most of the "1968ers" of the student movement, especially the birth cohorts of 1941–47. This generation appears to be politically different from that of the 1,537 "left-wing extremists" (not terrorists) sentenced for violations of the law between 1978 and 1983—mostly anarchists and "autonomous" alternativists involved in the

---

84. See Aust, *Der Baader-Meinhof Komplex*, 260–62. Black September derived its name from the massacre of twenty thousand Palestinians by King Hussein's Jordanian troops, which massacre it sought to avenge, in an extraordinary example of displacement, on the Israelis. Meinhof's editorials in *Konkret* before 1967, by contrast, were quite pro-Israeli.

85. See Matz and Schmidtchen, *Gewalt und Legitimität*, 21–22. Incidentally, the proportional representation of skilled workers is much closer to their share in the population than is that of unskilled or semiskilled laborers or that of farmers.

antimissile campaign of the early eighties and overwhelmingly (85.4 percent) born after 1955.[86]

About one-third of the left-wing terrorists of the seventies were women. Lieselotte Süllwold notes that women were at least as likely as men to have attained leading positions among the terrorists, came less often from broken homes, and otherwise closely resembled the socialization experience of male terrorists.[87] On the other hand, Margaret Mitscherlich-Nielsen and Edelgart Quensel associate female terrorists with patriarchal fathers who were at once tyrannical and childish and were indulged with secret contempt by the mothers. The daughters received confused messages, lacked self-esteem, and developed an intense need for external confirmation by a group or an influential person who might bring authenticity and identity. Disproportionate numbers of the female terrorists had graduated from a *Gymnasium* and had attended a university. A much larger percentage of both sexes than the average population of comparable age were unemployed or employed only partly or intermittently. There are strong signs of downward social mobility between the fathers and their terrorist offspring, and disproportionate numbers left the university without completing their course of studies.[88]

From this basis the life-history research proceeds to the more revealing but also slippery areas of how the family and school background of the terrorists may be different from that of young people of comparable age. No less than 69 percent of the men and 52 percent of the women reportedly had major clashes with parents, schools, or employers—33 percent with their parents, 18 percent with employers—of prior records of criminal or juvenile offenses, many of them repeated entries. Although

86. Federal Ministry of the Interior, *Verfassungsschutzbericht 1983* (Bonn, 1984), 27. The largest number among these cases (43.99 percent) were classified as students at the high school or university level.

87. The female percentage is far lower than the 60 percent suggested by Charles A. Russell, A. Bowman, and H. Miller in "Profile of a Terrorist," *Terrorism* 1 (1977): 17–34. For Süllwold's findings, see Jäger, Schmidtchen, and Süllwold, *Lebenslaufanalysen*, 106–10. Süllwold also reports a disproportionate number of lesbians among the women (5 or 7 percent), as well as of divorcees and of girlfriends of male terrorists. See also the discussion of other explanations there, 109.

88. Jäger, Schmidtchen, and Süllwold, *Lebenslaufanalysen*, 24–28. Among white-collar categories (30 percent of the total) and workers (19 percent), for example, the fathers occupied far higher status than their children. There were more than five times as many academic dropouts among the seventies' terrorists than in comparable age groups. Most of them also were Protestants or indicated no religious affiliation. See Susanne von Paczensky, ed., *Frauen und Terrorismus* (Reinbek: RoRoRo, 1978), 13–23. The RZ also had a women's branch, Rote Zora, which particularly addressed women's problems, especially those of Third World women, with terrorism.

there are no exact population averages or control groups with which to compare, the percentages are so large as to suggest in many cases a conflict-ridden youth aggravated by parental death, divorce, remarriage, and other misfortunes of modern societies. German social scientists sometimes refuse to accept such evidence, because it falls short of a theory of causation of terrorism,[89] but the parallels to such information about other violent movements, for example, the Weimar storm troopers of 1928–33, are striking.[90] Human behavior, of course, has never been subject to simple cause-and-effect relations. In spite of their socialization patterns, every German terrorist could just as well have turned away from terrorism, being a creature endowed with free will; and some did.

The researchers also tabulated many other relevant features about their 227 cases, including special skills, intelligence, drug consumption (Baader and Ensslin were notable examples), residence in alternative communes, previous participation in illegal or legal demonstrations, roles in terrorist groups, and preferred literature.[91]

INSIDE AND OUTSIDE THE TERRORIST ORGANIZATIONS

Some of the researchers asked why some terrorists had turned away from their engagement and when. About one fourth did, most while in jail—a major reason for keeping them separated from each other—and most among those were specialized in a relevant skill rather than in exercising leadership. Although only a few indicated why they quit the group, usually because of the means employed or because of both means and goals, disproportionate numbers of defectors attempted suicide (11 percent), and many appear to have been swayed by such factors as breaking off their education or job training, drastic mood swings, or the

89. See, for example, Narr, "Terror breitgewalzt," 21–23, who complains that this is just another example of psychological analysis that separates the psychogenesis of a politically violent career from the meaningful social context of violent action. He fails to explain, however, why all the other people exposed to the same "social context" have not resorted to terrorism.

90. See Peter H. Merkl, *Political Violence Under the Swastika: 581 Early Nazis* (Princeton: Princeton University Press, 1975), and idem, *The Making of a Stormtrooper* (Princeton: Princeton University Press, 1980; Boulder: Westview, 1987).

91. One interesting small finding concerned the noticeable differential in verbal intelligence between those born before 1950 and those born after that date, especially after 1955. This suggests that as time passed, an increasingly cruder clientele joined the terrorists (Jäger, Schmidtchen, and Süllwold, *Lebenslaufanalysen*, 40).

end of a significant personal relationship in their lives. They were generally less violent and somewhat less involved in the groups and had also exhibited better social integration in their personal backgrounds, suggesting, perhaps, the ego strength required for the turnaround. Karin de Ahna examined forty-seven defectors (Schmidtchen, 58) and found a heavy preponderance of them (thirty-one) had dropped out by 1974, many already by 1972 (nineteen), most of them after a year or less; these numbers remind one of the higher turnover rates found in Western Communist parties during the interwar and immediate postwar years. Most of the defectors (but not during the early years) belonged to the RAF. Getting arrested and being confined was the major triggering experience for defection (40 percent of the defectors). Sometimes, as in the case of Gerald Klöpper, dropping out was accompanied by critical statements about how the RAF, with the plane hijacking of 1977, had violated its own principles "never to act against the people."[92] Some of the more notable defections have encouraged the demand for an Italian-style *pentiti* bill promising reduced sentences or, most recently, the "state's witness" (*Kronzeugen*) law that offers reduced charges for cooperation with the prosecutor.

The researchers also addressed the problem posed by, on the one hand, the general absence of psychiatric symptoms and illnesses—Wanda von Baeyer-Katte speaks of "no real psychiatric patients"—and, on the other, the attitudes that distinguished the terrorists from the normal, everyday range of West German personalities. Symptomatic of those attitudes was the "monotonous" language of terrorist statements, their frequent reiteration of certain buzzwords such as "metropolis," "war of liberation," "imperialism," and choice pejoratives for police and establishment figures. Extremes of dogmatism and pathos, exaggerated emotions, and dramatic description prevail, and most important, there was a strongly extrapunitive attitude (the fault always lies with the other side, no matter how overwhelming one's own provocations) and a thinking in the starkest black-and-white terms that admitted of no gray areas and no moral doubts. Süllwold and others have related these views to the unresolved conflicts in values and perception—shades of the "dynamics of prejudice" literature—that the minds of the respondents sought to

92. See ibid., 40–61 and the tables on 62–77. See also Karin de Ahna, "Wege zum Ausstieg: Fördernde und Hemmende Bedingungen," in von Baeyer-Katte et al., *Gruppenprozesse*, 477–521. By definition, the decision to defect shows that the terrorists were not subject to any kind of internal group compulsion but had gone along of their own free will, which is not to say that it was easy to drop out after having developed a close identification with the terrorist cell.

resolve by gross simplifications (monoperceptosis), turning everything into a simple either-or dichotomy and taking one side only. Once an enemy had been declared and made into the absolute moral evil, the world became simple, and any means were justified for fighting this evil. Soon the "struggle" itself became the goal, and this in turn could satisfy deep personal needs. This struggle orientation made plausible the fixation of many terrorists[93]—and some of the antiterrorist operatives— on the image of a "war" between the terrorist-insurgents and the state, an image justifying military thinking and the killing of targeted persons as well as whoever else got in the way of military action.[94] In their vengeful reactions to their own casualties, of course, they acted more like close relatives than like soldiers in a war who expect to suffer some losses too. Even self-inflicted death, beginning with that of Holger Meins, was invariably termed a murder and became a clarion call for revenge. The courts and correctional institutions of the Federal Republic were regarded as military agencies of the "system's war" against the Third World and its terrorist "defenders." Hence the kidnapping and assassination of judges, including the accidental maiming of a judge's wife with an explosive meant for her husband, were accepted without another thought. This war image may also explain the labored hostility of RAF prisoners toward even the lowliest prison personnel and the contradictions between the prisoner negotiations for better treatment inside and the violent RAF actions outside.[95] Ensslin and Meinhof also put contacts with their children completely out of their minds, presumably because they interfered with their soldierly poses, Ensslin from the beginning and Meinhof from Christmas 1973. The war must go on.

The war image probably reached its ultimate internalization with the reversal of social reality for the patients of the Socialist Patients Collective (SPK) of Heidelberg, whose doctor convinced them to return in kind the warlike hostility they had allegedly received from West German

93. See Jäger, Schmidtchen, and Süllwold, *Lebenslaufanalysen*, 100–106, where the social role of drug use (as opposed to its pharmacological impact) and of idiosyncratic personality adaptations are discussed, with emphasis on the variety of personality types among the terrorists and on the fear and opportunism that characterized leader-follower relations in the RAF.

94. See Herbert Jäger and Lorenz Böllinger, "Studien zur Sozialisation von Terroristen," in Jäger, Schmidtchen, and Süllwold, *Lebenslaufanalysen*, 118–231, esp. 157–67. The friend-enemy dichotomy can be exemplified with many quotations, best of all from Holger Meins's last letter: "Fighting against the pigs [I am] a man struggling for the liberation of mankind, a revolutionary . . . this to me is serving the people—RAF'" (ibid., 159–60).

95. See Jünschke, *Spätlese*, 151, who now regrets his rigid rejection of any kind gesture by jail personnel. Most RAF prisoners continued to view themselves as soldiers and read "psychoterror" and brainwashing into most prison regulations.

society. Their paranoia and depression were evidently relieved when they joined the RAF, with whom they had been living cheek by jowl anyway at their quarters in Heidelberg. Their reversal of social reality— "destroy that which is destroying you"—does present a close analogy to the worldview of many RAF activists and also for some of the Communist and Trotskyist groups that supplied much of the recruitment pool for the various terrorist organizations.[96] It must have been easy for their "antipsychiatric" guru, Wolfgang Huber, to convince the patients of the validity of blaming the powers that be for their own malaise.

THE POLITICAL CONTEXT

The distinction between the inside and the outside of West German left-wing terrorism brings us back to the need to bear in mind the political context and the shadings of public opinion about that context. As Stefan Aust characterized the spring of 1972, "This was not the time for reason. The newspapers were stirring up more fear of the Baader-Meinhof group daily, whipping up emotions, and thus giving the members of the group, who regularly studied the reports of their activities in the press, a sense of their own importance."[97] And it was not merely the press that discovered the diminutive band of terrorists to be an inexhaustible source of reader, or public, interest. The conservative Christian Democrats, who in 1969 had just been ousted after twenty years in power, immediately learned to use the terrorists to attack the victorious Social Democrats as "siblings of terrorism" and many left-wing intellectuals as "sympathizers" with terrorism. Worse yet, prominent right-wing SPD leaders fulminated in similar terms against left-wing critics in their own party,[98] further fueling the vast overestimation of the terrorist challenge by the West German public, among whom the names of the principal

96. See Aust, *Der Baader-Meinhof Komplex*, 163–70, and von Baeyer-Katte, "Das sozialistische Patientenkollektiv," 190–207, 248–60, and 283–304. See also Franz Wördemann, *Terrorismus: Motive, Täter, Strategien* (Munich: Piper, 1977), esp. parts 1, 5–7, and 271–74.
97. Aust, *Baader-Meinhof Group*, 191.
98. Minister President Heinz Kühn of North Rhine–Westphalia, for example, said, "You can't have a Meinhof as a teacher or a Baader as a policeman," in justification of the passage of the prohibition against radicals in the public service (*Radikalenerlass*).

terrorists soon became household words.[99] The governing coalition of SPD and FDP, for its part, clearly felt that it had to prove its dedication to the antiterrorist campaign by building up the police apparatus and by a show of toughness and quick successes. Finding themselves under attack by both the conservative Right and the dominant middle-of-the-road part of the SPD/FDP government, left-wing intellectuals also rose to the challenge by defending some of the terrorist statements and actions even when the latter were quite out of character with their own views. The intellectual Left and those who called the Left "terrorist sympathizers" thus carried on a battle in which the real terrorists and their few remaining supporters played merely a shadowy role, providing a make-believe target for the shadowboxing of the conservative Right just as the specter of fascism continued to exercise the great minds of the Left, who on occasion even adopted the issues of prison reform highlighted by the RAF.

In the meantime, the RAF progressively used up its real sympathizers. At first the RAF fugitives were sheltered and assisted mostly by Meinhof's old personal friends, who, without intending any political endorsement, also loaned them vehicles and keys to safe hiding places. There were also political contacts, old leftists, and trade unionists ever ready to shelter political fugitives and help them get on, perhaps from old guilt feelings about not having done enough to shelter Jews and political refugees under the Nazis. "A sympathizer," RAF member Gerhard Müller said, "that is one to whom you can say, Look at the evil state here, fascism, torture, murder, etc.—give me your passport, okay?"[100] But political contacts became more judgmental, especially after the bombings of 1972, and all of these helpers were appalled at the rudeness, ingratitude, and arrogance of their clandestine "guests," who often abused them with names denoting hypocrisy and cowardice and treated their property with the disdain reserved for the privileged classes.

Once the principals were in jail, their notoriety and especially the hunger strikes helped them to raise a veritable army of real sympathiz-

99. According to a much-quoted 1971 Allensbach poll—still cited by Meinhof at the RAF trial years later—82 percent of West German adults had heard of the Baader-Meinhof group; one-fourth of the adult respondents under thirty admitted to "certain sympathies with it"; and in Protestant northern Germany, one of ten adults (5 percent in the whole country) expressed a willingness to shelter a hunted RAF terrorist for a night. This was after the death of Petra Schelm but before the bombing campaign to come. See Aust, *Der Baader-Meinhof Komplex*, 173–74.

100. *Der Spiegel*, 3 October 1977, 30. Keys, identity papers, and later the arrangement of car and apartment rentals were commonly performed by the kinds of helpers—not necessarily in political sympathy—described here.

ers. Many very young people joined the new Committees Against Isolation and Torture and extreme left-wing groups willing to stage demonstrations and propaganda campaigns in big cities, claiming, for example, that Holger Meins had been murdered and calling for revenge in messages spray painted on the walls of houses and churches.[101] An estimated two thousand mourners appeared at Meins's funeral at an obscure Hamburg cemetery. The police had sought to arrest forty RAF suspects in the years 1970–72, but by 1974 they were looking for three hundred. The BKA, by this time, already spoke of ten thousand sympathizers or more, possibly inflating the figures to suit the mood of the new Schmidt/ Genscher administration. By the end of the German Autumn in 1977–78, the president of the Hamburg Constitutional Protection Office thought there were about 1,500 terrorist sympathizers in West Berlin and another 2,500 in West German cities.[102]

By 1983 the Federal Constitutional Protection Report already preferred not to give estimates and to speak not of a "sympathizer scene" but of an RAF *Umfeld* (environment), defined as "groups that have the function of intensive propaganda campaigns for the goals of the RAF, the support of imprisoned RAF members and helpers and their demands, the maintenance of the flow of information with underground and imprisoned RAF members, and the execution of orders of those in the underground." The narrowly defined RAF *Umfeld* became known as the Anti-imperialists or *Anti-impis*, who have been involved, along with "autonomous" groups in the "antiwar campaign" of the eighties, in a campaign to transmute the "rocket pacificism" of the German Peace Movement into a struggle against U.S. imperialism.[103] Since this campaign was predicated on the acceptance of the RAF's anti-imperialist theory by the autonomous groups and other allied groups, however, the RAF *Umfeld* made little headway. They were somewhat more successful in winning at least temporary allies for the campaign for "consolidation of RAF prisoners with those from the anti-imperialist resistance," that is, from other left-wing extremist groups. The desired improvements in

101. The revenge turned out to be the assassination of von Drenckmann, which was cheered by the RAF prisoners and these same sympathizers outside. Left-wing intellectuals such as Böll and Dutschke expressed shock over this killing and promptly found themselves denounced for hypocrisy by the RAF leaders.

102. See Hans-Dieter Schwind, ed., *Ursachen des Terrorismus in der Bundesrepublik* (Berlin: DeGruyter 1978), 5–19.

103. Ibid., 95. In 1983, when this was just one group and one campaign among many on the extreme Left, its members also participated in violent protests against the NATO missiles in Hamburg and Bremerhaven. The numerous autonomous groups, often clad in black, and especially the anti-NATO groups among them, continued to be a target for RAF recruitment in spite of their commitment to "unarmed resistance."

the prison circumstances, the supporters of this campaign have admitted, are to facilitate the continuation of the struggle of the RAF from prison. Ever ready to don the mantle of constitutional freedoms they do not themselves believe in, they claim that the judicial prosecution of RAF suspects—and of RAF *Umfeld* members on charges of helping or campaigning for the RAF—implies a Nazi-like criminalization of legitimate protest and constitutes "political justice."

6

Political Violence in Argentina: Guerrillas, Terrorists, and *Carapintadas*

Richard Gillespie

Los ferros pesan,
pero no piensan.
—Carlos Olmedo

During the 1970s the whole of Argentine society was afflicted by political violence. Initially the insurgent groups that sought to adapt Guevarist principles of guerilla warfare to the conditions of their highly urbanized country were quite selective in their choice of targets, but the violent response from the Right proved far less discriminate. At no stage did the majority of Argentines become embroiled in the conflict, causing it to assume the true proportions of civil war, but nobody's life was untouched by the bloodshed or by the pervasive culture of fear.

The urban guerrilla strategy attracted more recruits in Argentina than

The author thanks María Moyano and Juan Corradi, discussants at the Wesleyan conference

in any other Latin American country: several thousand intervened in armed operations and tens of thousands actively supported them.[1] Most Argentines, however, were affected as victims or prospective victims of the right-wing response to insurgency. Operating increasingly through the state, the impact of the Right's violence was extremely diffuse, for under attack were not only the guerrillas but the society that had bred them. And of course, the state's capacity to destroy was much greater than that of the insurgents. For several years in the late 1970s, the agents of right-wing violence were in power, and most Argentines were obliged to adopt strategies for personal survival. The press exercised self-censorship; the judiciary was impotent; the church collaborated.[2] Families and individuals turned in on themselves, allowing fear to constrain their behavior, their conversation, and even their thoughts.

The years that introduced the word *desaparecido* to the political lexicon at times approximated—grotesquely—the apocalyptic vision of the American satirist who once depicted a future in which kidnapping had become the dominant form of social intercourse. In the early 1970s political abductions had occurred on average once every eighteen days; by mid-1976 the average was over five a day.[3] At least 9,000 victims never reappeared and must be considered among the post-1976 military junta's 10,000–30,000 victims.[4] The level of repressive violence under

"Terrorism in Context," for their perceptive and stimulating comments, and Roberto Baschetti for copies of several of the documents cited in this chapter.

1. Elsewhere I have put the number of armed Montoneros in their peak year of 1975 at over 5,000 (if one includes both integrated guerrillas and the more marginal *milicianos*), and I have cited various occasions when pro-Montonero rallies attracted crowds of 100,000 (Richard Gillespie, *Soldiers of Perón: Argentina's Montoneros* [Oxford: Oxford University Press, 1982], ch. 4 and 178). Several estimates of the Montoneros' peak armed strength have been higher: Christopher Roper suggested 7,000 (*The Guardian* [London], 26 March 1979), as did *The Economist* (London), 26 January 1980, in a special survey on Argentina, whereas Robert Cox, former editor of the *Buenos Aires Herald*, put it at over 10,000. Most estimates give the ERP (Ejército Revolucionario del Pueblo, or People's Revolutionary Army) only a fraction of the Montoneros' numbers; Peter Waldmann, however, puts both organizations at 3,000–4,000: see his "Anomía social y violencia," in *Argentina, hoy*, ed. Alain Rouquié, (Mexico City: Siglo XXI, 1982), 212. An apparent military intelligence report entitled "Informe especial: Actividades OPM 'Montoneros,' año 1976," gives the following Montonero totals for September 1976: integrated members 991 (391 *oficiales* plus 600 *aspirantes*); *milicianos* 2,700; sympathizers and collaborators 5,500; total 9,191. By this time the Montoneros were clearly in decline.

2. Andrew Graham-Yooll, *The Press in Argentina 1973–8* (London: Writers and Scholars Educational Trust, 1979), and Emilio F. Mignone, *Iglesia y dictadura* (Buenos Aires: Ediciones del Pensamiento Nacional, 1986).

3. Juan C. Marín, *Los hechos armados: Un ejercicio posible* (Buenos Aires: CICSO, 1984), 81.

4. CONADEP (Comisión Nacional Sobre la Desaparición de Personas), *Nunca más* (Buenos Aires: EUDEBA, 1984), 16.

military rule was out of all proportion to guerrilla violence, which claimed almost 700 victims according to regime figures; it represented an escalation in comparison with the state-sponsored violence of the Argentine Anti-Communist Alliance, the Triple A death squad set up under the preceding Peronist government, which had claimed approximately 2,000 victims since 1973.[5]

It is not only the scale but also the multifaceted nature of Argentina's violence that has attracted international interest. To shed light on the imbroglio, it is necessary to begin by clarifying the types of violence that were involved in the conflict. The need for this is reinforced by the fact that perceptions within Argentina often differed from external perceptions of the violence, which were greatly influenced by Western European experiences.

The insurgent forces included dozens of tiny groups that attempted to initiate guerrilla warfare in the late 1960s. Among them, five grew to become the most significant organizations of the early 1970s, these being the People's Revolutionary Army (ERP), the Montoneros, the Peronist Armed Forces (FAP), the Revolutionary Armed Forces (FAR), and the Armed Forces of Liberation (FAL). The picture became further simplified around 1973, when some guerrillas decided that changed circumstances counseled the termination of their armed struggle. With the military relinquishing office, free elections being held, and Perón returning to Argentina, some Peronists, chiefly associated with the FAP, responded to new opportunities for open political activity. Meanwhile, those who held on to a perspective of armed struggle became polarized around the leading Peronist guerrilla organization, the Montoneros, and the Marxist ERP.

Influenced by Guevarism, the Montoneros initially saw themselves as a "politico-military organization," whereas under the influence of the Chinese and Vietnamese models, the originally Trotskyist ERP envisaged itself as the embryo of a people's army under the direction of the Workers' Revolutionary Party (PRT), although in practice the membership of the PRT-ERP remained undifferentiated. Cuban and Asian influences were combined in both cases, although the nationalistic Montoneros never made international acknowledgments in public. As they grew, the Montoneros became more interested in Mao's writings on warfare and set about constructing a Montonero army directed by a Montonero party, and the ERP's admiration for Cuba was reflected in its decision to launch a rural *foco* in the province of Tucumán in 1974.

5. República Argentina, Poder Ejecutivo Nacional, *Terrorism in Argentina* (Buenos Aires, 1980), 314; *La Nación* (Buenos Aires), international edition, 12 May 1980; and Ignacio González Janzen, *La Triple A* (Buenos Aires: Contrapunto, 1986), 19.

The propensity to view these organizations as "terrorist" was always greater outside Argentina than within. Certainly the organizations did not conceive of themselves as "terrorist." They associated terrorism with former anarchists of the "propaganda by the deed" school, contemporary neofascist groups and the extreme left-wing European groups that resorted to violence after the collapse of the 1960s student movements. Their differences with these groups were not just ideological but concerned methods. While others sought to effect change through their own initiatives, even where the initiatives were designed to detonate a social explosion, the Argentine insurgents saw themselves as forming part of a popular movement and developing therein a people's war strategy in the belief that the movement could not triumph without its own armed forces. Only when the attempt to involve the masses in their strategy was clearly foundering, in the mid-1970s, did the Montoneros confront the state in a more conventional military fashion that involved substituting themselves for the masses far more consciously, yet even then their refusal to target innocent civilians set them apart from modern European terrorists. The Argentines' use of violence became less discriminate, but they never viewed the bombing of crowded public places as productive.

Nor did the Argentine public generally regard the insurgents as "terrorists." In the context of mounting popular opposition to a discredited and repressive military regime established by General Onganía in 1966, there was considerable reluctance to condemn the rebels, especially since many of their early deeds involved only symbolic violence, aimed against property rather than people. Public perceptions changed somewhat as the violent campaigns were stepped up, but the ERP's ill-fated adventure in Tucumán at least helped reinforce their "guerrilla" image. For some observers the Montoneros' resort to less discriminate violence after 1974 was at least "understood" in view of the activity of the Triple A death squad established by right-wing Peronists in 1973. For some, the violence of the Triple A and the "dirty war" initiated by the armed forces in 1975 (first in Tucumán and then nationally) made greater guerrilla violence, including attacks on civilian political opponents, seem more legitimate.

Analytically, a distinction between terrorist, referring to terror-inspiring methods and agents, and urban guerrilla warfare, "a form of unconventional war waged in urban and suburban areas for political objectives" and seen within the broader perspective of a people's war,[6] is essential for any understanding of the guerrilla movements of Argentina and Uruguay. However, in practice, the distinction was at times blurred,

6. Paul Wilkinson, *Terrorism and the Liberal State* (London: Macmillan, 1977), 60.

above all in the case of the Montoneros. Their founders included former activists of Catholic nationalist organizations, such as Tacuara, which, although only sporadically violent, were noted for unprovoked attacks on Communists and Jews. The impunity with which such groups operated in the 1960s was a mark of their good relations with the security services, a relationship that may have been crucial to the success of the first publicized act of the Montoneros: the kidnapping and assassination in 1970 of former president Pedro Eugenio Aramburu, a man despised by Peronists for his role in the 1955 coup against Perón and its aftermath and believed by the Onganía regime to be plotting its downfall.[7]

Further complicating the picture is the fact that at least one of the groups that joined the Montoneros during their early years had no "guerrilla" credentials whatsoever. The National Revolutionary Army (ENR) had been a handful of Peronists who had arrogated to themselves the mission of "crushing traitors" within their movement and who fulfilled it by assassinating trade-union leaders Augusto T. Vandor and José Alonso in 1969–70. The elimination of perceived traitors within Peronism became a more important part of the guerrilla repertoire in the period 1974–76, although a more selective use of violence characterized the final Montonero campaign of 1978–79.

The ERP and Montoneros' urban guerrilla strategy did not rule out some of the activities associated with European terrorist groups, such as bank raids and kidnappings of business leaders, especially those representing foreign corporations. However, the proceeds from such activities were put to a much more ambitious use by the Argentines—the building of an army capable of eventually defeating their country's standing army—instead of being used simply to finance and escalate a campaign of terror. The guerrillas became more "militaristic" as their vision of fomenting a people's war faded, and they were drawn increasingly into the reactive violence of vengeance killings as the conflict developed. Nonetheless, the objects of their violence were well-defined political enemies, and about 70 percent of their victims were men under arms.[8] The eventual wearing of uniforms by both the ERP and the Montoneros in their guerrilla operations symbolically reinforces the view that their violence essentially belonged to the domain of warfare, though to a strategically disastrous urban-guerrilla variant of it. In the case of their attacks on foreign businessmen, they may perhaps be regarded as

7. Eugenio Méndez, *Aramburu: El crimen imperfecto* (Buenos Aires: Sudamericana-Planeta, 1987); Próspero Germán Fernández Alvariño, *Z.-Argentina: El crimen del siglo* (Buenos Aires: published by the author, 1973); and Gillespie, *Soldiers of Perón*, 89–95.

8. República Argentina, *Terrorism*, 314.

having employed terrorist *tactics*, or as having entered a penumbra separating urban guerrilla warfare from terrorism, but these attacks were subordinate to an overall politico-military strategy. The violence of the Right fell more easily into the category of terrorism, and increasingly into that of state terrorism. During the half century preceding the 1970s, violent right-wing groups in Argentina had served periodically as "shock troops" whose purpose was to break strikes and disrupt associational activity that was deemed subversive. Since the Liga Patriótica Argentina in 1919, such groups had been effective because of support from or at least tacit connivance within the state. In the 1970s, however, the far Right went much further in their dominance within the state itself. The Triple A was established, ironically, in the Social Welfare Ministry headed by José López Rega, Perón's private secretary, and before long it had enlisted the top officers of the Federal Police as well as some individual army officers. Its violence was directed mainly against the Peronist Left, chiefly the noncombatant activists who were the most vulnerable.[9] The death squad's purpose was to discourage people from trying to develop a left-wing alternative to the Peronist government, by increasing the risks of involvement to a frightening level.

Following the military coup of 1976, the Triple A was absorbed into an infrastructure of state terror whose victims came from almost all sectors of Argentine society. Some of the military officers responsible for the new "task forces" that made thousands of people "disappear" acknowledged that they were carrying out a campaign of terrorism but claimed that it was the only way of tackling deeply rooted subversion.[10] Abroad, most developed countries initially turned a blind eye to the junta's methods or claimed that the "excesses" were the work of uncontrolled elements. Only gradually, as foreign nationals joined the list of victims and as the scale of the state's violence became known, did the condemnation increase. The Organization of American States, which sent an investigating team to Argentina, implicitly accused the junta of state terrorism in 1979,[11] a charge that had little effect on the British government, which only "discovered" the junta's human rights violations after the Falklands had been seized.

The fact that there were radically differing perceptions of the political

9. The most complete listing of victims appeared in *El Auténtico* (Buenos Aires), 26 November 1975, 5.

10. For example, General Ramón Camps, cited in John Simpson and Jana Bennett, *The Disappeared* (London: Sphere, 1986), 348.

11. Organization of American States, *Report on the Situation of Human Rights in Argentina* (Washington, D.C., 1980).

violence in Argentina underlines the crucial importance of studying its domestic context in order to understand the phenomenon.

THE CONTEXT

The environment in which various groups decided to wage an "armed struggle" is important not only because it helps explain why people resorted to violence but also because of its influence on public perceptions of the violence and thus the degree of popular "legitimacy" accorded to the "armed struggle." Only when taken in context can many violent activities usefully be characterized as terrorist or otherwise. This is generally the case when the victim is a civilian yet is an active participant in bitter social or political struggles.

Argentina's history has been marked by considerable violence since the country emerged as an independent state early in the nineteenth century. Conflict between unitarians and federalists was prevalent in the early decades of nationhood, and in the twentieth century military interventionism and popular rebellion have contributed to political instability. However, explanations of the 1970s violence that rely heavily on the country's political culture are unconvincing, since there are other Latin American countries—such as Mexico—that have distinctly stronger traditions of political violence yet failed to generate a significant guerrilla or terrorist movement in that decade,[12] in part because they possessed a more effective political system.

Since the Second World War, Argentina had experienced extreme political polarization, which still greatly affected political outlooks and behavior in the 1970s,[13] militating against the democratic spirit of compromise. The perception of Argentina as a "dependent" country encouraged nationalists to see problems in terms of a crude imperialism-versus-nation dichotomy; and for some of them, the rise of popular nationalism in the twentieth century led to further reductionism, with the nation identified with the people and imperialism with the oligarchy.

The military overthrow of Perón in 1955 produced much greater polarization not only because force was used to remove the first Argentine government to be elected on the basis of universal suffrage but also because the ensuing Aramburu government was vindictively and

12. Claudia Hilb and Daniel Lutzky, *La nueva izquierda argentina: 1960–1980* (Buenos Aires: Centro Editor de América Latina, 1984), 91.

13. Ibid., 27, and María Matilde Ollier, *El fenómeno insurreccional y la cultura política (1969–1973)* (Buenos Aires: Centro Editor de América Latina, 1986), 30–31.

violently anti-Peronist. It sought to completely eliminate Peronism from Argentina, even to the extent of outlawing public reference to Perón and removing Eva Perón's mortal remains from the country. When the Peronists attempted a halfhearted and badly coordinated civilian-military uprising themselves in 1956, Aramburu authorized the execution of twenty-seven rebels after their surrender, thereby showing his contempt for half the population. Between 1955 and 1973, Argentina's major popular movement, Peronism, either was prevented by proscriptions from participating in the political system or, when allowed to win elections (as in 1962), saw the results nullified by the military.

Besides profound political polarization, there was broad disillusionment with political democracy. Representative democracy had been introduced only in the twentieth century and had been subverted repeatedly by military interventions since 1930. Moreover, its quality under the early Perón governments of 1946–55 upset part of Argentina because of Peronism's less liberal facets. The fact that democracy never became consolidated engendered a broad cynicism that affected attitudes toward political parties, as did the corruption associated with previous Radical and Peronist governments. By the late 1960s there existed among the middle classes considerable skepticism concerning constitutional-party political activity, as well as an awareness that the post-1966 military regime headed by Onganía was not going to allow a return to even this limited type of activity—at least, not unless obliged to do so by popular pressure.

Sociologically, most of the violence of the 1970s was the product of a middle class that had become deeply fragmented. A modernization process that had begun in the 1950s had not succeeded in preventing precipitous national economic decline but had affected the cultural climate. Traditional institutions such as schools, the family, and the church were losing their effectiveness as socializing agencies. The middle class had lost much of its cohesion, and intransigence grew among its competing fragments. While the established sectors of the middle classes still tended to look to traditional values and institutional supports (ultimately the military), the young generation was swept by new cultural influences. Argentina's youth turned in great numbers against an older generation they blamed for their declining career prospects and the lack of effective political participation. Thus, there was an important element of children rebelling against parents in the rise of the guerrilla units, most of whose recruits were in their twenties; for them, "violence became the predominant communication strategy."[14]

14. Juan Corradi, *The Fitful Republic: Economy, Society, and Politics in Argentina* (Boulder: Westview Press, 1985), chs. 7 and 8.

The appeal of violent forms of radical action was enhanced by the apparent effectiveness of armed struggle (and more generally of voluntarism) in Cuba, a country altogether different from Argentina yet a country that had experienced a student revolution and was linked to Argentina through the presence of Che Guevara in the revolution and through the subsequent efforts of revolutionary Peronist, John William Cooke, to implant *foquismo* at home. Guevara's most influential contribution lay arguably in helping to export the myth and mystique of the *guerrillero heroico*, which encouraged many young Latin Americans to risk their lives in the name of a superior morality.

In contrast with this new Latin American revolutionary current inspired by Cuba, the traditional Argentine Left held little attraction for young people. The Communist party's working-class following, which had been substantial in the 1930s, had been lost since the rise of Peronism, and the Socialist party had embarked upon a course of terminal fragmentation in the 1950s. The traditional Left collectively had made the mistake of equating Peronism with fascism and as a result became isolated from the mass movement. Peronism's continuing hold over the working class after 1955 produced great frustration for the classical Left, whose youth groups responded by turning to armed struggle or by reconsidering the merits of Peronism, or both.

For many young Argentines from conservative backgrounds, the turn to violence was facilitated by the new mood that had taken hold of dissident circles within the Roman Catholic church. During the late 1960s, liberation theology was popularized by the magazine *Cristianismo y Revolución*, and radical Catholicism also acquired an organizational base through the founding of the Third World Priests Movement and in Catholic associations established for school and university students and young workers. Although they rarely advocated the initiation of armed struggle, the radical priests who sometimes worked with these groups at least conveyed the message that popular violence from below was a legitimate response to prolonged repressive violence from above, and they also urged fellow Catholics to side with the poor. Almost as influential was the example of Camilo Torres in Colombia, who had abandoned the priesthood in order to join a guerrilla movement, in which he died in 1966. Both the *foquista* triumphalism of the 1960s and the presentation of Torres and Guevara as martyrs—whether Christian or not—encouraged young Catholics to consider a resort to arms. Some of them, such as the former Tacuara people who were to become Montoneros, had exhibited violent tendencies already yet derived from the new Catholicism a readiness to revise their existing hostility toward Peronism and a greater moral legitimation of political violence. The Comando

Camilo Torres, which they established in 1967, claimed to stand for Peronism, socialism, and armed struggle.

Other founders of urban guerrilla organizations belonged to a more secular tradition of activism. Several of those who founded the FAP were old enough to have experienced the failure of the Resistencia Peronista of 1956–59, which had been characterized by a high level of improvised violence carried out by uncoordinated Peronist commandos and trade unionists.[15] The limitations of resistance and of the sporadic attacks undertaken by Peronist Youth groups in the early 1960s showed the need for strategy and organization if an armed struggle was to be sustained and waged more effectively.

The resistance experience also contributed to the emergence of the Marxist guerrilla. The Trotskyist Palabra Obrera had come under the spell of *foquismo* after encountering frustration in labor resistance activity; it went on to join the more combative wing of the PRT, which launched the ERP in the late 1960s. Far more numerous here, though, were the founders who came from a university background. Several ERP founders, including the central leadership, had studied at universities of the less developed Argentine interior, and there was a particularly crucial group that had studied economics together at the University of Tucumán.[16] Impressed by revolutionary advances in Cuba and Southeast Asia, their plans for armed struggle in Argentina seemed vindicated by the failure of mass struggles to prevent sugar mill closures during the 1960s and by the repression used by state forces when faced with peaceful protests. Some members of the provincial sugar workers' union helped create the ERP, but its membership was overwhelmingly middle class. There were also a few well-publicized cases of industrial militants who turned to armed struggle in response to the corrupt nature of the trade-union leadership, but proportionally they remained a tiny minority.

The turning point in the initiation of armed struggle was provided by the army's seizure of power in 1966 and the establishment of the Onganía dictatorship. Many of the urban-guerrilla founders had begun to discuss the feasibility of armed struggle by that year, and some had participated in violent actions; moreover, there had already been a couple of unsuccessful rural guerrilla ventures by the Uturuncos in 1959–60 and the People's Guerrilla Army (EGP) in 1963–64. Within the PRT the advocates of Guevarism were already starting to dilute the party's erstwhile

15. Daniel James, *Resistance and Integration: Peronism and the Argentine Working Class, 1946–1976* (Cambridge: Cambridge University Press, 1988), part 2.

16. Richard Gillespie, "Armed Struggle in Argentina," *New Scholar* 8, nos. 1 and 2 (1982): 400–404.

Trotskyist identity. For many of these pioneers, the Onganía coup and resultant military regime provided the conditions for successful guerrilla activity rather than the motives for taking up arms.

Nonetheless, the change of regime was crucial to the process of generating mass support for violent opposition. Onganía's coup represented a break with tradition in that the new military authorities showed no readiness to return power to civilians; their proclamation of an "Argentine Revolution" indicated a determination to suppress political liberties and civil rights for a lengthy period, until the social and economic structure of the country had been profoundly restructured. Although earlier military interventions had mainly hit the working class, Onganía's also represented a blow to many sectors of the middle class. Students in particular suffered as a result of the regime's suppression of the liberal universities' traditional autonomy. They were violently repressed when they attempted to protest; the student movement very quickly acquired its own martyrs. Police repression, declining career prospects, and cultural censorship all played their parts in radicalizing students, graduates, and not a few middle-class parents.

The intelligentsia—in the broader sense of the term—was not alone in its rebellion against military rule. The late 1960s saw the rise of a new combative trade unionism associated with the Confederación General del Trabajo de los Argentinos (CGTA), a militant labor confederation led by the Catholic radical Raimundo Ongaro. Many workers readily responded to the CGTA's calls for mass mobilizations, because recent attempts by Vandor and other labor leaders to obtain concessions through collaboration with the regime had proved fruitless. By 1969 the student leaders were coordinating their activities with the CGTA, and the axis of a broad protest movement was formed. Opposition also had an important provincial dimension, in part because the Onganía regime's economic policies were producing a shift of income from the interior toward Buenos Aires. The provinces of the interior felt neglected, if not exploited, by Buenos Aires, and their disaffection found expression in a series of cases of massive civil defiance in various towns and cities between 1969 and 1972. Though they were all put down, they nonetheless crucially undermined the military regime, leading civil and military elites alike to search for a political solution that would restore public order.

The Cordobazo, a popular insurrection in the city of Córdoba in May 1969, bore the marks of a provincial as well as a social protest in which workers, students, and other middle-class sectors were involved.[17] Initial

---

17. On the Cordobazo, see Beba Balvé, Miguel Murmis, and Juan C. Marin, *Lucha de calles, lucha de clases* (Buenos Aires: Ediciones de la Rosa Blindada, 1973), and Francisco J. Delich, *Crisis y protesta social: Córdoba 1969–1973* (Buenos Aires: Siglo XXI Argentina, 1975).

police attempts to repress the demonstrations led to the erection of barricades, the burning of vehicles, and the establishment of a "no-go area" in the city, protected by snipers. Although suppressed after two days, when troops were sent in, the Cordobazo, with its death toll of fourteen, weakened the position of Onganía, who was replaced a year later. The insurrectional potential it showed encouraged more people to take direct action, including engagement in violent forms of protest.

This largely unplanned and disorganized social violence helped generate an environment in which political violence of a more planned and organized nature also enjoyed a certain legitimacy. Opinion surveys found over 45 percent of the population refusing to condemn guerrilla actions at this time.[18] However, the guerrillas themselves often exaggerated the extent to which events such as the Cordobazo legitimized their own armed struggle. They applauded the uprising but pointed out its limitations: spontaneity could not be relied on to put permanent pressure on the military regime. Some went further than this and claimed a kind of popular mandate for their armed struggle; the Montoneros claimed that "the people" had learned a lesson from the Cordobazo and that the guerrillas were now responding to this advance in the consciousness of the masses.[19] Earlier the PRT had claimed that the Tucumán workers had gone through a similar learning experience when their protests against sugar mill closures had been violently repressed.[20] The facts are that the guerrilla pioneers had opted for armed struggle *before* the Cordobazo and that very different "lessons" could be drawn from this episode.[21] For example, some militants decided that the building of a revolutionary party or a strengthening of "combative" trade unions would give victory to the people. Nonetheless, the limitations of the Cordobazo did provide the pioneers with an argument that assisted recruitment to the guerrilla units.

The groundswell of disaffection with the regime created serious divisions within the military, and these gave rise to governmental crises from 1970 on.[22] As the generals began to see the need for a retreat to barracks to defuse the social unrest, the regime became unsustainable; it was a regime based on bayonets, but it could not use them, constrained as it was by its own loss of unity and authority and the need to involve the political parties in a solution to the problem of social unrest.

18. Ollier, *El fenómeno*, 101.
19. Ibid., 33, and *El Peronista* (Buenos Aires), 28 May 1974, 26–29.
20. Oscar R. Anzorena, *Tiempo de violencia y utopía* (Buenos Aires: Editorial Contrapunto, 1988), 133.
21. Ollier, *El fenómeno*, 39–42.
22. Alejandro A. Lanusse, *Mi testimonio* (Buenos Aires: Lasserre, 1977).

Meanwhile, the sight of the military retreating contributed to the perception that guerrilla violence was effective, even though the real causes of the regime's crisis were more complex.

Once the urban guerrillas had become established, by 1970, their degree of legitimacy was related not only to the illegitimacy of the regime but to the attitude toward them adopted by the leaders of the main popular movement. The Peronist leadership did not simply fail to condemn guerrilla attacks, it went so far as to send messages of congratulation. From exile Perón himself sent such letters to both the FAP and the Montoneros;[23] his representatives in Argentina, Héctor Cámpora (the future president) and Juan Manuel Abal Medina (brother of the first Montonero leader), addressed Peronist Youth rallies and echoed the crowds' slogans in support of the Montoneros and FAR. The guerrillas were regarded by Perón as a means of breaking a post-1966 stalemate between a regime "unable to stabilize itself but with sufficient material power to survive, and a mass movement powerful enough to submit it to constant harassment but not to overthrow it."[24]

Besides Perón's endorsement of violence, what lent legitimacy to several of the guerrilla groups was his designation of the collectively named Peronist Armed Organizations (OAP) as the "special formations" of the Peronist movement. This was particularly crucial for the success of the Montoneros and FAR, whose founders were very recent converts to Peronism, having been anti-Peronist right-wing nationalists or Guevarists previously. Perón's sponsorship was crucial to these guerrillas because it provided a political bridge to a worker-based mass movement for activists who belonged overwhelmingly to the middle class (and even upper middle class in the case of several of the original Montoneros).

This context helps explain why the armed struggle in Argentina was not generally perceived as terrorist in this period. Just as important was the nature of the violence. With few exceptions, the victims were people who had been involved in repression or who were deemed by many Peronists to be "traitors" to their movement for having defied Perón's instructions. More significantly, most of the violence was not against human targets but property, especially that of wealthy "oligarchs" and foreign corporations. The guerrillas' selectiveness in relation to targets was seen in messages they sent to the police, appealing to them not to stand in their way, since they too were part of "the people" or working

23. Roberto Baschetti, ed., *Documentos de la resistencia peronista, 1955–1970* (Buenos Aires: Puntosur, 1988), 439–40; *Cristianismo y Revolución*, September 1970; and *La Causa Peronista*, 3 September 1974.

24. John William Cooke, *Apuntes para la militancia* (Buenos Aires: Schapire, 1973), 29. Translated by the author, as are all subsequent translations.

class (the emphasis differing according to the populist or Marxist orientation of the guerrilla force).[25]

The selectiveness of early guerrilla violence, which has been analyzed in more detail elsewhere,[26] stemmed from the fact that the insurgents were not attempting to achieve their political objectives purely through the force of their own firepower. Their ambition to develop into people's armies ensured that in the early phase of warfare the careful cultivation of popular sympathy and support was paramount. Thus, the early guerrilla actions were predominantly acts of "armed propaganda": the hijacking of food-delivery vans for distribution in shanty towns, the bombing of buildings and monuments to mark Peronist and Guevarist anniversaries, the destruction of elite country clubs and the premises of foreign multinationals, brief commando-style occupations of small towns near to Buenos Aires and Córdoba, and so on.

However, even in this early phase there were some actions that were closer to the domain of terrorism than to urban guerrilla warfare, the targets being civilians. Trade-union leaders Vandor and Alonso were assassinated; there were several Montonero attacks on enemies within the Peronist movement; and a number of foreign business executives were kidnapped and a few killed (although the level of business abductions was far lower than in 1973–75). Yet even these acts of violence were not universally condemned. Vandor had incurred the wrath of Perón for becoming too independent, and he had been directly involved in violence against militant trade unionists.[27] The fact that labor leaders were generally accompanied by bodyguards—as were many business executives after the guerrilla threat became apparent—may to some extent have modified public perceptions of the civilian identity of the victim. However, it is important to note that the killings of the collaborationist union leaders were condemned by their more militant union rivals, including the CGTA, notwithstanding its subscription to the idea that "violence from below" was a legitimate response to "violence from above" and the assistance it gave to imprisoned guerrillas. It is also significant that these killings were condemned by some of the guerrilla organizations themselves, especially the FAP, which made a pertinent point: "If the workers' movement is not strong enough to get rid of its own parasites, it will not be strong enough to make a revolution."[28]

Evidently, even during the early phases of guerrilla warfare, some

25. Anzorena, *Tiempo de violencia*, 351.
26. Gillespie, *Soldiers of Perón*, ch. 3, and James Kohl and John Litt, *Urban Guerrilla Warfare in Latin America* (Cambridge: MIT Press, 1974), 311–38.
27. Rodolfo Walsh, *¿Quién mató a Rosendo?* (Buenos Aires: Ediciones de la Flor, 1987).
28. FAP, "Con las armas en la mano," *Cristianismo y Revolución*, April 1971, 77–80.

acts of violence were repudiated by the social groups whose support the guerrillas were seeking to cultivate. Yet the incidents most likely to cause outrage were greatly outnumbered by the kind of Robin Hood actions and spectacular stunts that had already endowed the Tupamaros in neighboring Uruguay with something of a romantic image. And sympathy for the guerrillas was rekindled periodically by illegal repressive actions on the part of the state, especially the massacre of sixteen guerrillas at Trelew in August 1972 as a reprisal for a major prison breakout by guerrillas held at Rawson in the south of Argentina, which succeeded only insofar as an advance party composed of six guerrilla commanders escaped.[29]

In this early pre-1973 phase, the guerrilla organizations were quite small and possessed no more than one thousand fully integrated members among them. However, they were able to compensate for their fragmentation by occasionally cooperating among themselves for major operations. Practical liaison and cooperation under the umbrella of the Organizaciones Armadas Peronistas (OAP) eventually led most of the Peronist groups to merge with the Montoneros. Moreover, in the Montonero case, at least, the guerrillas enjoyed visible and active popular support. Although they lacked the Peronist pedigree of the FAP (which was promoting the creation of Peronismo de Base: rank-and-file groups of militant, mainly working-class Peronists), the Montoneros in some ways were the most pragmatic guerrilla force. When Perón called for the unification of the diverse Peronist Youth groups in the early 1970s, the Montoneros immediately seized the opportunity to become centrally involved in this process through winning over the leading youth activist Rodolfo Galimberti; and they were also the first "special formation" to adapt tactically when Perón announced his readiness to take advantage of the possibility of an electoral end to the military regime. Because of their greater flexibility, the Montoneros were receiving much of the acclamation at Peronist Youth gatherings and Peronist election rallies during the final year of the military regime.

MOTIVATION

Unfortunately, very little illumination of individual motivation is provided by the existing literature on political violence in Argentina, and

29. Marín, Los hechos armados, 117, and Tomás Eloy Martínez, La pasión según Trelew (Buenos Aires: Granica, 1973).

the difficulties involved in procuring useful information from interviews with those who participated, a decade or two after they turned to violence, are self-evident.[30]

The fact that ideology in itself offers no real explanation why people turn to political violence is demonstrated particularly well by the Argentine case. Among those attracted by guerrilla warfare, there was both considerable ideological diversity and evolution. Some of the Montonero founders evolved from right-wing anti-Peronist nationalism to radical pro-Peronist nationalism; the ERP founders underwent a transition from Trotskyism to Guevarism; and the FAR shifted from Guevarist purism to tactical Peronism. Some continuity in guerrilla ideology was provided by Argentine nationalism in that some guerrillas evolved from a reactionary to a radical form of nationalism, often under the influence of liberation theology or in their search for a mass base. Nonetheless, the remarkable degree of flux indicates a lack of ideological certainty. The same is suggested by the experience of the Tacuara Revolutionary Nationalist Movement (MNRT), a left-wing splinter from Tacuara that in 1964 staged what is often regarded as Argentina's first urban guerrilla operation. Although the group was broken up immediately afterward, the leading survivors eventually found their way into at least three different guerrilla organizations: chiefly the FAP (Jorge Caffatti and others) but also the Montoneros (José Luis Nell) and ERP ("Joe" Baxter).

It is remarkable that Argentina, the country within Latin America where urban guerrilla organizations have had the greatest impact on political life and that has a large, abundantly talented intelligentsia, failed to produce an important guerrilla ideologist. In the case of the Montoneros, the original group had few university students and probably no graduates. The founders were intellectually mediocre, and those who survived went on to dominate the organization throughout its lifetime and increasingly discouraged internal criticism and debate. However, the ERP provides a contrast: its general staff was overwhelmingly composed of graduates, including the commander in chief, Mario Roberto Santucho.

One of the main reasons the guerrilla movements lacked firm ideological moorings was that *foquismo*, with its emphasis on immediate action, to some extent displaced a broader ideological definition. To quote one of the early pioneers, *foquismo* served as a kind of "super-ideology" that attracted groups emanating from the Left, Right, and Center on the

---

30. Nonetheless, some fascinating material will be available once the doctoral research findings of María Moyano have been published. See "Armed Struggle in Argentina, 1969–1979" (Ph.D. diss., Yale University, 1990).

basis of a method and an image.[31] What was originally put forward as a politico-military strategy became for its adherents the main issue separating revolutionaries from nonrevolutionaries; one became a revolutionary only through armed struggle. The political and ideological differences between guerrilla organizations did not fade completely; the political gulf separating the Montoneros and ERP was never bridged, despite increased practical cooperation between them in 1975–76. However, *foquismo* did serve to bring together groups of radically different ideological origins, and about half a dozen of them were involved eventually in organizational mergers. The process of unification seen in 1972–74 contrasts starkly with the general pattern of the Left's development in Argentina, and indeed in Latin America, which is generally one of splits and disintegration. On top of *foquismo*, what drew revolutionary groups together in Argentina in the early 1970s was the solidity and semi-insurrectional nature of mass support for Peronism, which facilitated unification on a Montonero-Peronist basis. Subsequently, Perón's death in 1974 and the rightward shift of the Peronist government under his widow, Isabel, created conditions for greater Montonero-ERP cooperation.

The appeal of *foquismo*, which overwhelmingly attracted people in their late teens and twenties, lay in the immediacy of its promised impact.[32] There was no need to wait until "objective conditions" for revolution or a "revolutionary consciousness" among the masses matured; small groups of revolutionaries could contribute to the development of these conditions by initiating an armed struggle. The thesis was particularly appealing in view of the perennial weakness of the Argentine Left and in view of Peronist control of the labor movement. The working class had demonstrated militancy on many recent occasions and thus seemed to possess real revolutionary potential, yet it appeared to the *foquistas* to be held back by a lack of politico-military organization and by the dead hand of, a trade-union bureaucracy that often sought to collaborate with the government of the day. Violent action was seen as a means of transforming this situation: by demonstrating the vulnerability of the state, it would encourage people to collaborate with or join the guerrillas.

Certainly, in terms of publicity, *foquismo* did achieve an immediate impact, which was interpreted as progress by its adherents. Of course,

31. Personal interview with Amanda Peralta, a founding member of the FAP, Warwick, 27 May 1986.
32. Envar El Kadri and Jorge Rulli, *Diálogos en el exilio* (Buenos Aires: Foro Sur, 1984), 40–41.

its high profile attracted repression as well as media attention, but early guerrilla losses proved no great deterrent to violent activity. The cult of the *guerrillero heroico* drawn from the Cuban revolution was embraced by the Argentine Guevarists and derived fresh impetus from the radical Catholic ideas of the mid-1960s. The promise of martyrdom for those who "fell" was particularly important for the Catholic militants, several of whom were regular church attenders right up to the moment of going underground (the Montoneros would establish a "chaplaincy" later, when they started to build the "Montonero Army"). If the prospect of martyrdom promised a certain immortality to all guerrillas, in the case of the Catholics death also held out the promise of expiation. It would seem that the early Montoneros, who were more marked by Catholic influence than their successors, were not completely convinced by their own arguments in favor of the secular legitimacy of violence, which usually included references to Perón's dictum "Violence in the hands of the people is not violence; it is justice." It has been claimed that on the occasion of one early Montonero killing, the group agreed in advance that the assassin would have to take his own life immediately after the act, and so it was.[33]

In the case of the Montoneros, many recruits joined in groups rather than as individuals, and group solidarity remained a central attraction of the organization and a source of cohesion. By no means were all members primarily attracted by the prospect of violent action; often they had found true comradeship in an existing social group, usually based on Catholic lay organizations, educational institutions, or clubs; and they sought to hold on to this valued *compañerismo* when other members of the group proposed an approach to the Montoneros.[34] Argentina's youth was living through particularly rebellious times, yet it was difficult for most young people to leave home until relatively late in life, when they achieved economic independence. Many therefore looked to groups of friends and associates to provide what was sometimes lacking in family life, and some finally achieved independence from their families when their groups entered the Montoneros. Ironically, their "liberation" came through accepting a new dependence.

Individual recruits were attracted to the Montoneros through branches of the Peronist Youth in 1973–74 and of the Authentic Party, a Montonero front, in 1975. These base-level groups were seen by the Montoneros as the key constituents of their "mass front," where legal activity in

33. Méndez, *Aramburu*, 123.
34. So far as I know, María Moyano is the first person to have emphasized the importance of group, as opposed to individual, incorporations into the Montoneros.

collaboration with the guerrilla organization proved possible until the end of 1975.[35] The most promising "mass front" activists would be given documents to read, and subsequently there would be discussions. Suitability for further integration would be indicated by total political agreement and by acceptance of armed struggle as the principal form of struggle. At the "ideological" level—to cite a guerrilla document—recruits would need to become practically involved in violence; they would need to accept progressively the "socialization" of their incomes and property; and they would need to bring in their partners. The suitable recruit would be of good character (dishonesty, robbery, usury, and human exploitation were supposedly disqualifications for entry into the organization), would act in solidarity with neighbors and workmates, and would "modify or criticize any individualist deviation in himself or in any other comrade."[36] To the extent that a recruit met these requirements, she or he would pass successively from simply being a militant of the mass-front group to become a *miliciano*, then an *aspirante*, and then finally an *oficial montonero*. The Montonero organization insisted on recruits leaving home and living together in small groups whose dependence on the guerrilla apparatus increased the more they became integrated. There was a process of moving from semi- to full clandestinity, during which contact with Argentine society decreased and the group (as part of the broader organization) became the predominant social reality for members, whose value system thus developed in growing isolation from that of society.

Guerrilla motivations changed over time. The writings of participants shed little light on how the experience of violence affected them personally. However, it would seem reasonable to suppose that for most participants the practice of violence became easier after the first few occasions. The daunting initiation test for many would-be Montoneros was to disarm a policeman by approaching him unarmed and sticking a finger in his back: a military rather than ideological or political test.[37] Thereafter the readiness to use violence increased, not just through habituation, but because companions and relatives were being killed by the enemy. In time, vengeance killings became a central component of

35. This discussion of Montonero recruitment policy is based on several cyclostyled guerrilla documents of the mid-1970s: "Síntesis de la reunión de la UBCL—'El Miliciano Logístico' "; "Síntesis de la reunión de UBCL: Formación de las unidades de aspirantes"; and "Aportes y propuestas para el desarrollo de la organización popular en el frente territorial."

36. "Síntesis . . . 'El Miliciano Logístico,' " 8.

37. Ollier, *El fenómeno*, 91.

the guerrilla repertoire, with both massacres of captured guerrillas and the operation of the Triple A death squads acting as important stimuli.

Organizationally, the fragmented structure of the Argentine guerrilla movement of the early 1970s may have encouraged escalation through competition. However, though this was a tendency, there were also repeated guerrilla attempts to collaborate and unite with one another. Several organizations believed that revolutionary success demanded the gradual integration of their forces into a single vanguard; all saw the need for at least logistical cooperation if the early guerrilla groups were to survive and to acquire the capacity to deliver major blows. When hunted by the authorities in late 1970, the early Montoneros were saved from extinction by the FAP, which lent them accommodation and money; there were several joint guerrilla operations by the Peronist organizations in 1971–72; the Montoneros, FAR, and ERP collaborated to stage the major guerrilla breakout from Rawson prison in August 1972 that preceded the Trelew Massacre; and in 1975–76, with the ERP in decline, there were arms exchanges between the ERP and Montoneros, the latter lent the former at least U.S. $500,000, and the Montoneros sent "observers" to spend a few months at rural ERP camps in Tucumán.[38]

It is important to note that in the Argentine case, once the armed struggle had been initiated, there was a major political opportunity to abandon violence while claiming to have contributed to a victory. The end of the military regime and the return of Perón from exile in 1973 were achievements that were widely valued, especially by Peronists. Both the core of the FAP and a minority of the Montoneros (the so-called *Leal* [loyal] tendency) used this opportunity to put an end to their violence, arguing that it had served its purpose and that very different types of activity were now desirable and possible.[39] The Montoneros adopted an intermediate position of suspending their armed struggle in order to make tactical use of the new political opportunities to mobilize mass support during the next sixteen months, but they carried out several covert operations during this phase. Never abandoning their strategic view that mass activity should be subordinate to armed struggle, they openly resumed hostilities in September 1974, following Perón's death and his replacement as president by his third wife, Isabel Martínez. Meanwhile, the ERP, minus the breakaway ERP 22 de Agosto faction but together with the Comando Nacional offshoot from the FAP,

38. Montoneros, "Informe sobre las relaciones con el PRT-ERP" (Cyclostyled document, [1976?]).

39. Nonetheless, several former FAP members were slain by the death squads or were forced by death threats to leave Argentina.

made hardly any strategic concessions to the change of the regime, despite Guevara's warnings against waging armed struggles against elected governments.[40]

The political amnesty of 1973, under which eight hundred political prisoners were released, gave guerrillas the opportunity to renounce violence and clandestinity.[41] Why more did not do so is fairly clear. First, the new political situation was quite fragile; given Perón's physical decline and the depth of the country's economic problems, some activists saw the new political period as no more than a brief interlude before the unreformed military would take over once more. Second, armed struggle was considered by the guerrillas to have played a major part in the downfall of the previous regime, so they had few doubts about its effectiveness. Third, the guerrillas must have been heartened in 1972–73 to see open manifestations of support for them at demonstrations and rallies, especially among young people; this was another sign to them that their strategy was being vindicated.

During the final phases of armed struggle, when violence persisted in spite of mounting indications of its counterproductiveness, organizational dynamics were exerting a major influence. Both the Montoneros and the Argentine army developed an infrastructure that tended to perpetuate violence well after it had ceased serving its original purpose. Vengeance remained a crucial motive of violence in this period: an entire family might be attacked in order to punish or demoralize just one of its members. But maintaining the belligerence of the guerrillas was also the way in which the *comandantes* of both the ERP and the Montoneros tended—not always consciously—to hide from their members the true extent of their organizational crisis. The tenor of the clandestine guerrilla press remained triumphalist right through to the end. Internal documents of the Montoneros did give accurate information about the number of casualties.[42] However, demoralization was countered by claiming, falsely, that the vast majority of members seized by the security forces were holding out against their interrogators and by arguing that the sacrifices were not in vain; the organization, it was asserted, would reap huge moral and political prestige in return for its "sacrifices" on behalf of the people (whose resistance to military dictatorship the Montoneros, full of self-delusion, claimed to be leading by 1977).[43] The low levels of political sophistication and experience of most Montoneros, and their

40. Che Guevara, *Guerrilla Warfare* (Harmondsworth: Penguin, 1969), 14.
41. Juan Gasparini, *Montoneros: Final de cuentas* (Buenos Aires: Puntosur, 1988), 55.
42. Montoneros, "Informe del Consejo Nacional del Partido Montonero, Septiembre de 1977" (Cyclostyled document, n.d.) 17.
43. Gillespie, *Soldiers of Perón*, 258–59.

clandestine isolation from external realities, encouraged the leadership to present them with an inflated assessment of the organization's strength and influence; indeed, at this time the *comandantes* even went so far as to claim responsibility for the Cordobazo.[44]

Of course, there was some genuine reassurance to be derived from the size of the organization. By the end of 1975 the Montoneros had something like five thousand people under arms, and even though the casualty rate greatly accelerated the following year, it was conceivable that even a greatly depleted organization could stage a revival once the repression had eased. After all, there had been only about two hundred members at the end of the previous military regime,[45] yet the Montoneros had managed to outmobilize other Argentine political and social forces thereafter, and the Peronist Left had been given control of several ministries, universities, and provincial administrations in return for their contribution to the restoration of Peronism.

In addition to positive efforts to maintain morale, the Montonero leaders took steps to encourage discipline and punish infringements. To maintain morale and for purposes of self-legitimation, the Montoneros in 1975 began to award medals to their members for heroism (a move paralleled by the Argentine army's decision to issue medals itself for the first time in decades). The revival of morale was also one motive behind the order given by the Montonero leadership in 1978 for uniforms to be worn in the course of future operations.[46] On the other hand, the Montonero "Code of Revolutionary Justice" issued in 1975 stipulated severe penalties, including death, for a series of offenses including desertion, treachery, informing, insubordination, conspiracy (which also covered factional activity), fraud, abuse of authority, and covering up the nonfulfillment of orders;[47] and it is known that this sentence was passed and implemented on several occasions. Once a recruit had graduated from the periphery *(milicianos)* to the organization proper *(aspirantes, oficiales)*, there was no easy way out of the Montoneros. Members were expected to "resist until death" if cornered by the security forces or taken captive, and any failure to do so was punishable. Those who committed suicide when trapped, by taking their regulation-issue cyanide capsules, were sometimes posthumously awarded medals by the leadership. One member was promoted and decorated for helping his wounded girlfriend commit suicide.[48] But some of those who deserted, or

44. Montoneros, "Síntesis . . . 'El Miliciano Logístico,' " 5.
45. Gasparini, *Montoneros*, 91.
46. Ibid., 257–62.
47. Anzorena, *Tiempo de violencia*, 355.
48. Ibid., 356–57.

who gave away important information when tortured by their captors, were shot later by their own comrades. It may be the case that the harshness of internal discipline in the Montoneros was related to the organization's inadequate degree of compartmentalization. Juan Gasparini has argued that organizational deficiencies were behind the exorbitant demands the Montonero leadership made on their followers; in contrast, ETA's much tighter compartmentalization is said to account for its less demanding rules for captured members when tortured by their captors.[49] Certainly some arrests led to major human and infrastructural losses for the guerrillas in Argentina. However, the harsh regime of the Montoneros also derived from the organization's growing militarism. The ERP also became more militaristic, but its internal life differed from that of the Montoneros in this respect. No member of the ERP was shot for desertion or "treason," except Jesús Ranier, an alleged infiltrator accused of informing army intelligence about the ERP's intention to attack the Monte Chingolo garrison in late 1975.[50] The assault, aimed at capturing weapons while militarily occupying the southern zone of Buenos Aires, proved disastrous: about one hundred guerrillas were killed by the military, many allegedly after surrendering. The ERP never recovered from this massive loss.

ORGANIZATIONAL DYNAMICS

Following the Montoneros' announced resumption of their armed struggle in September 1974, it soon became evident that the nature of that armed struggle was changing. Militarism—the tendency to see the struggle predominantly in terms of war rather than political or social conflict—had always been present in the Montoneros, but it now became much more pronounced.

The new phase of violence was marked by a greater proportion of assassinations (the "punishment" of "traitors" to Peronism and the working class, and vengeance killings in response to guerrilla losses at the hands of the enemy); a less selective choice of targets; larger-scale, more sophisticated operations; an attempt to build a more formidable military structure; and more severe internal discipline. A parallel tendency saw

---

49. Gasparini, *Montoneros*, 150.
50. Julio Santucho, *Los últimos guevaristas: Surgimiento y eclipse del Ejército Revolucionario del Pueblo* (Buenos Aires: Puntosur, 1988), 204.

the growth of *aparatismo*, the tendency of the guerrilla apparatus to exert greater influence on guerrilla behavior as the apparatus became more extensive and sophisticated.

In 1973–74 the attitude of the ERP toward the new civilian regime was even more aggressive than that of the Montoneros. To some extent, each organization became caught up in a spiral of violence that was divorced from the early guerrilla ambition to build a people's army. Vengeance was a major motive behind this escalation: the Montoneros retaliated against Triple A attacks on their supporters; the ERP wanted revenge for the massacre of sixteen of its guerrillas who had been captured in Catamarca in 1974. The ERP announced that sixteen military officers would be killed in reprisal, and then proceeded to kill ten before calling off the campaign, having unintentionally slain their final victim's young daughter.

However, in regard to discipline, the ERP was less militaristic than the Montoneros, and it was certainly less *aparatista*. In principle, one might expect a left-wing guerrilla organization to be less militaristic than a nationalist one, given the authoritarian strain in Argentine nationalism and its frequent associations with the Argentine army, as opposed to the far stronger pacifist and democratic elements within the socialist tradition. However, the Cuban experience, together with the success of armed liberation struggles in China and Vietnam, had helped bring militarism to many parts of the Argentine Left as well, including the PRT-ERP. If the ERP was less *aparatista* than the Montoneros, this was arguably because the former had always envisaged revolutionary war as having both an urban and a rural dimension in Argentina. Having secured the financial wherewithal (over U.S. $30 million from kidnapping businessmen) and the required weaponry (through assaults on military bases) during 1973, the ERP launched a rural *foco* in the northern province of Tucumán in 1974 and placed most of their emphasis for the next two years on the rural *guerrita*. Although this rural insurgency soon collapsed when the army was given a free hand in the province in 1975, the ERP at least had shifted to a zone of combat where they could establish direct contact with the local population.

In contrast, through their pursuit of a much more exclusively urban approach, the Montoneros had a much greater preoccupation with organizational security, which tended to make the organization more defensive, introverted, authoritarian—and ultimately paranoid. One case that shows the mistrust harbored by leading Montoneros was that of Tulio Valenzuela in 1978. Head of the Rosario regional secretariat of the Montoneros, Valenzuela fell into the hands of the 2d Army Corps commanded by General Leopoldo Galtieri. The army subsequently kidnapped

Valenzuela's wife and young child in order to persuade him to accompany an assassination squad on a mission to Mexico, where the target was the exiled Montonero leadership. But once in Mexico, Valenzuela warned the guerrilla high command of the plot and thereby saved their lives. In spite of this action and his personal sacrifice—his wife and son inevitably "disappeared"—the Montonero leaders remained unconvinced of his loyalty. They therefore stripped him of his rank and sent him back into Argentina on what was virtually a suicide mission. Valenzuela was captured immediately and committed suicide.[51]

Militarism did not emanate solely from organizational dynamics. One source lay in the personalities of some of the people who founded or joined the organizations; another lay in the urban guerrilla strategy that demanded periodic escalation of the level of warfare, rather than a sustained low-level campaign designed simply to exhaust and demoralize the enemy; and third, there was what the Montoneros called the dialectic of confrontation: the tendency for violence to become increasingly reactive once the initial guerrilla threat had elicited a response from the state. However, militarism was also fueled by the development of the organization itself. Once the guerrillas had acquired the kinds of weapons that made them capable of assaulting a military garrison, the temptation to escalate the conflict in this manner became overwhelming, notwithstanding the risk that such actions would increase the social isolation of the guerrillas.[52]

Another way in which organizational dynamics influenced the course of violence was through mergers. Two Montonero incorporations were particularly significant in this respect: those that brought in the ENR and the FAR. As noted above, the former group had started out by assassinating two labor leaders. Publication by the Montoneros of a communiqué about one of these killings—in 1974, four years after the event—was a way of signaling that the punishment of union leaders opposed to the Peronist Left was now being placed openly on the Montonero agenda.[53] The Montoneros' policy toward union leaders, which seems to have been inherited directly from the ENR, was alternatively one of "crushing traitors" (four were killed) or—as in the case of Lorenzo Miguel, the so-called godfather of the union bureaucracy—of offering *not* to kill them if they conceded Montonero demands.

Meanwhile, through their fusion with the FAR in 1973, the Montoneros

51. Miguel Bonasso, *Recuerdo de la muerte* (Buenos Aires: Brugera, 1984), 185–99.

52. These tendencies were also present in other Latin American urban guerrilla experiences: see Richard Gillespie, "The Urban Guerrilla in Latin America," in *Terrorism, Ideology, and Revolution*, ed. Noel O'Sullivan (Brighton: Wheatsheaf, 1986).

53. *La Causa Peronista*, 27 August 1974.

became more committed to the cult of personality and technical perfection. The FAR's cult of strong leadership was reflected in the guerrilla joke that FAR members referred to their leader Olmedo as Dios.[54] The FAR had been a politically isolated tiny organization that had sought to make up for numerical weakness by means of technical proficiency. A group that entered it early on had in 1969 achieved the technical feat of *simultaneously* blowing up no fewer than fifteen Mimimax supermarkets in protest against a visit to Argentina by their owner, Nelson Rockefeller. When the FAR-Montonero merger took place, there were very detailed negotiations concerning the officer structure of the "Montonero army" that was to be built. The FAR provided the Montoneros with their *Manuel de táctica montonera*, a four hundred-page clandestine publication written by three FAR members of the armed forces. Its contents differed little from those of a conventional military manual. Among many pages devoted to the terminology of warfare, the importance of obeying orders, and so on, the only "unusual" features were chapters on the preparation of explosives and on self-defense.[55]

Although the smaller organization of the two, the FAR did much better than other groups that merged with the Montoneros in placing leading individuals in the top ranks. This may well have been related to the FAR cadres' technical expertise.

Montonero operations during 1975 certainly indicated improved technical proficiency, especially the damaging attack by Montonero frogmen on the navy's first modern missile-carrying frigate, and the remote-control destruction of a transport plane carrying forty-five antiguerrilla personnel in Tucumán, both during August 1975. At this time there were also operations that involved far more guerrillas than in the past. The city center of Córdoba was taken over twice by *milicianos* who blocked off approach roads with chains; and over one hundred—perhaps several hundred—Montoneros were involved in the most elaborate operation, in October 1975, which involved hijacking an airplane, taking over a provincial airport, attacking a major military garrison and capturing its cache of arms, and finally escaping by air. These large-scale operations were made possible not only by the mass recruitment success of the Montoneros in 1973–74 but also by their financial strength. During 1975 the

54. Information on the FAR comes from a former member of the organization and was given to me by Amanda Peralta in the interview referred to in note 31.

55. A much shorter Montonero training document, *Principios generales de la guerra* (N.p., n.d.), is also most revealing. It is based on three sources: the military texts of Perón (who merely reiterated the classical German works), Mao, and Liddell Hart. The only source material relating to revolutionary warfare was that of Mao, but he, of course, offered no wisdom regarding urban warfare.

Montoneros secured over U.S. $70 million in ransom money, chiefly from the kidnapping of the heads of a leading multinational company, Bunge y Born.[56]

The "political economy" of the guerrilla organization became more important thereafter. The Montonero leadership's control over a formidable, highly centralized apparatus, together with their own ruthlessness, helps to explain the relatively high degree of political control they exercised over their organization (when compared with many other Latin American guerrilla movements). Nonetheless, the use to which the money was put soon proved controversial. Operativo Camaleón, a plan to invest several million dollars on the eve of the 1976 military coup in houses and apartments for Montonero militants to live and meet in, supposedly more securely, provoked criticism from members who felt that the money was being used to strengthen the *aparato* instead of being invested in the mass struggle.[57] However, it was difficult for the dissidents to break away and establish an effective alternative. When a faction led by Rodolfo Galimberti left in 1979, they took almost $70,000 of the organization's funds with them. For this the Montoneros threatened Galimberti and his comrades with death, having accused them of desertion, insubordination, conspiracy, and fraud in a quasi-legal indictment that bore all the hallmarks of a state prosecution: even the accused's date of birth and identification number were given.[58]

Militarism and *aparatismo* proved politically counterproductive for the Montoneros because both tended to make guerrilla activities more remote from the concerns of ordinary citizens. Although the killings of federal police chiefs (the Montoneros assassinated three in two years) gave rise to relatively little public condemnation, the growing tendency of the ERP and Montoneros to regard all men in uniform (among others) as legitimate targets cannot have improved their public image.[59] The more militaristic approach was seen in the Montonero "police patrol" on the eve of the 1976 military coup—when guerrillas patrolled a street until they came across a policeman, whom they immediately shot—and in the huge size of bombs aimed at police targets during 1976, some of which claimed dozens of police lives. Certainly the police had been involved in regular death-squad activity since 1974, but clearly some

56. For more detail, see Gillespie, *Soldiers of Perón*, 174–205.
57. Peronismo en la Resistencia, *Reflexiones para la construcción de una alternativa peronista montonera auténtica* (N.p., 1979).
58. *Jotapé* (Buenos Aires), January–February 1989. Ironically, a decade later Galimberti obtained employment as the security chief at Bunge y Born, the multinational firm from which the Montoneros had extorted over $60 million in 1975.
59. Anzorena, *Tiempo de violencia*, 349–52.

police had been more involved than others. The central, though far from exclusive, emphasis of the Montoneros was still on attacking people who might loosely be regarded as "combatants" in the conflict, but within this context their violence was becoming less discriminate.

The Montoneros' militarism also proved counterproductive at the level of their psychological battle with the Argentine army. One cannot imagine the army being greatly alarmed by the Montonero letter sent to General Galtieri in 1978, in which the Argentine conflict was compared with the development of the Second World War and the Montonero "generals" threatened to launch a "Normandy landing" from exile.[60] On the other hand, Montoneros who were seized by military "task forces" during the "dirty war" often fell victim to their own militarism and as a result offered little resistance to their interrogators. Because they conceived of the struggle in military terms, they were forced to admit the reality of "defeat" when they had put to them details of their own army's losses and when the Montonero army's resources were compared with those of the Argentine army.[61] In such circumstances, the centralized nature of the guerrilla apparatus also proved a liability, for relatively few leaks of information were required to decimate it.

Finally, militarism proved corrupting of the Montonero leadership. The organization lost the spirit of fraternity of the early years, when all the members had shared the sacrifices and risks. Around 1976 the Montonero army issued orders that at all meetings its "soldiers" were to address one another, and particularly their superior officers, with the formal *usted* (you) instead of the familiar *vos*. The *comandantes* became more remote, elitist, and even narcissistic, posing in uniform for photographs of themselves presenting one another with medals and planning the grand strategy of their promised counteroffensive in front of huge maps of Argentina. They also became more cynical. The elimination of thousands of their own supporters, and of many thousands of others, were referred to by the leaders simply as "costs of war."

Thus, in several respects the leading Montoneros ended up resembling their adversaries. This provoked the following comment from a former FAP leader: "When one starts thinking like this, when you start wearing uniforms and adopt the ranks and organizational model of the enemy, you end up being the enemy. . . . The enemy has defeated you because he has managed to transform you into him."[62] A bizarre sequel, tending

60. Bonasso, *Recuerdo de la muerte*, 204–7.
61. Montoneros, "Memorandum 1: Explicitación política de la experiencia mantenida por militantes montoneros con la Marina de Guerra, en calidad de detenidos y bajo condiciones de secuestro" (Cyclostyled document, July 1979).
62. El Kadri and Rulli, *Diálogos en el exilio*, 45.

to support this judgment, was provided a decade later, in 1989, when leading Montonero survivors proposed to the former military chiefs who had been responsible for the destruction of their organization the celebration of a "Reconciliation Mass" at which the victims on both sides would be honored and the past symbolically buried.[63]

THE STATE RESPONSE

During the early years of the urban guerrilla activities, the state response was constrained by the fact that the military junta of 1966–73 had already met with political and economic failure. The armed forces were coming to recognize that the days of the regime were numbered, and General Lanusse (who headed the junta from 1971 to 1973) took the lead in seeking an orderly way of transferring power back to the political parties. There was some death-squad activity prior to 1973, but it was low-level and sporadic.[64] Unlike the later period, most of the people seized by the security forces did not "disappear." Although they might be tortured during initial interrogation sessions, detainees would be brought before a judge within a few days and subsequently would be treated according to the law. A special court staffed by nine judges was created to try cases involving subversion. Although it was used chiefly against the Left, this *camarón* at least preserved the appearance that "subversion" was being tackled by due process. However, this made the Trelew Massacre of August 1972 all the more shocking to public opinion.

Between 1973 and 1976, with Peronist administrations in office, both legal and illegal measures to counter "subversion" were increased. The ERP was banned in September 1973 following a major guerrilla attack on the army's medical headquarters in central Buenos Aires, and the following month the Montonero (albeit anonymous) killing of labor leader José Rucci provided the pretext for a purge of "terrorist and subversive Marxist groups" from the Peronist movement. A penal code reform introduced by Perón in January 1974 brought in much more severe punishments for guerrilla activities than had existed under the previous military regime; for example, arms possession could now receive a heavier sentence than murder.

Various legal measures that were adopted to deprive the guerrilla organizations of their publications and to undermine their presence and

---

63. Associated Press, New York, 7 September 1989.
64. Andrew Graham-Yooll, *Tiempo de violencia* (Buenos Aires: Granica, 1973), 125–60.

influence in certain universities, unions, and regional administrations were aimed also at frustrating other militant opponents of the government. The new Antisubversion Law introduced in September 1974 was designed primarily to counter guerrilla propaganda, but it also stipulated prison sentences of one to three years for leaders of strikes that were declared illegal. Under this law, journalists and editors were threatened with jail sentences of up to five years for reproducing information considered to be aimed at "altering or eliminating institutional order."[65] It was followed by a specific ban on even mentioning the guerrilla organizations by name. Thereafter, press reports of guerrilla incidents were dominated by references to "subversive delinquents," although a few newspapers tried to inform their readers by referring to the ODI, the "organization declared illegal" (that is, the ERP), and to the "Peronist guerrilla organization," or the "self-proscribed organization" (the Montoneros, regarded as having proscribed themselves by going underground again in September 1974).

Only when the Montoneros launched their big operations against the armed forces in 1975 did they finally lose their legal status—an event of purely symbolic importance, revealing the exhaustion of the Montoneros' credit within the official Peronist movement and the growth of military influence. Hitherto involved in counterinsurgency only in a support capacity, the army was sent into Tucumán with carte blanche to eradicate the ERP in February 1975, and in September it successfully pressured the government into outlawing the Montoneros. In October the armed forces secured for itself a role in a new Internal Security Council headed by the president, and the provincial police forces were placed under military control. In November the army, navy, police, and border guards undertook counterinsurgency operations throughout Argentina, the first of them in response to a bitter miners' strike at Sierra Grande. Finally, at the end of the year military pressure was again in evidence when the government banned the last legal Montonero front organization, the Authentic Party (PA), and its newspaper. Thus, the military became increasingly prominent in combating the guerrilla forces during the final thirteen months of Peronist government that preceded the coup of 24 March 1976.

The counterinsurgency measures of 1973–76 can be criticized on several grounds. First, they were never applied evenhandedly and thus lacked legitimacy. Far from representing a serious effort to put an end to political violence, the measures were little more than right-wing attacks on militant labor and the Left, and they affected the whole of the

65. *Buenos Aires Herald*, 27 September 1974.

Left and not only the proponents of violence. Second, the banning of various front organizations, such as the PA, destroyed any possibility of reintegrating elements of the guerrilla movement into conventional politics and thereby dividing the rebel organizations and weakening their capacity for violence. Third, the use of crude censorship helped undermine the democratic pretensions of the government while encouraging the guerrillas to resort to spectacular attacks that could not be hidden from the public eye. Fourth, many of the new laws whose draconian punishments alienated sectors of public opinion were in fact rarely applied to guerrilla detainees. Captured Peronist guerrillas mainly faced imprisonment without trial, and ERP contingents captured during combat appear to have been massacred on at least two occasions. Fifth, the governmental tactics resorted to by the Peronists played into the hands of the military, who were restored to prominence and flattered as if they did not themselves constitute a threat to democracy. And finally, the attempt at a legal response to insurgency was entirely vitiated by the government's coincident and extremely transparent sponsorship of illegal violence in the form of the Triple A death squad.

This originated in 1973, chiefly out of right-wing Peronist fears that the left wing, through its superior capacity to mobilize and organize people, would seize control of the Peronist movement and use it to gain power. The massive reception that was being organized to greet Perón upon his return from exile in June provided the occasion for the assembling of a loose right-wing federation of gunmen from the Social Welfare Ministry (headed by José López Rega), pro-Perón fascist organizations such as the Comando de Organización (C de O) and the Concentración Nacionalista Universitaria (CNU), and trade-union headquarters. Together with a motley collection of European fascist mercenaries, they unleashed the Ezeiza Massacre against unarmed columns organized by the Peronist Left, which was attempting to dominate the event. This was the birth of the Triple A, although the name was not used to claim responsibility for acts of violence until November and the Triple A's composition was to change somewhat following the incorporation of new Federal Police chiefs in 1974.

The violence at Ezeiza claimed many ordinary Peronists among the thirteen dead and four hundred wounded, since it was aimed at columns led by, but by no means exclusively composed of, the Peronist Youth. Subsequently, Triple A violence was more selective, but it was chiefly soft targets that were chosen: the death squad killed far more supporters of pro-Montonero youth groups and Peronist Left associates than it did guerrillas. Some of its victims were militants of the nonviolent Left. In all, the Triple A was responsible for two thousand deaths in thirty months, its activities facilitated by the involvement of the Federal Police and the complicity of the government and sectors of the military.[66]

One general observation concerning this and the preceding period is that civilian fascist groups generally were effective only when enjoying state support. During the 1960s several groups acted with impunity as "shock troops," attacking left-wing groups in the universities; and from late 1973, as the Peronist government moved steadily to the right, there was plenty of evidence of further state collaboration with violent right-wing groups. When the Córdoba police mutinied and overthrew the elected Peronist Left provincial governor Ricardo Obregón Cano in February 1974, they armed two hundred right-wing nationalists. And in February 1975 the C de O was allowed to take control of a primary school, where before long the children were being harangued by extremists and forced during physical education lessons to march in columns and make the Nazi salute.[67]

The main difference between Triple A violence and the "dirty war" was that in the latter simple assassination was no longer the aim. What was novel about the military's counterinsurgency effort was the use of about 340 secret detention camps, where detainees could be interrogated and tortured without legal constraints or time limits; the victims were only disposed of after every effort had been made to get them to denounce others.[68] Moreover, the vast majority of the victims of the military abduction squads simply "disappeared," many of them buried covertly in mass graves or dropped from aircraft into the River Plate. The post-1976 junta's primary motive for this procedure was to avoid the international opprobrium that open mass slaughter had brought to its Chilean counterpart in 1973, but the covert nature of the "dirty war" had the effect of feeding the culture of fear that now pervaded much of civil society. The *grupos de tarea* usually operated at night and behaved very much like an army of occupation, plundering the homes of their victims and destroying what they could not carry away.

It is no exaggeration to characterize these activities under the heading of state terrorism. Unlike the case of the Spanish Antiterrorist Liberation Groups (GAL), the victims were not in the main members of violent

66. González Janzen, *La Triple A*, and Horacio Verbitsky, *Ezeiza* (Buenos Aires: Editorial Contrapunto, 1985).

67. González Janzen, *La Triple A*, 112–13, and *La Opinión* (Buenos Aires), 12–14 October 1975.

68. Amnesty International, *Testimony on Secret Detention Camps in Argentina* (London, 1980); Alipio Paoletti, *Como los nazis, como en Vietnam: Los campos de concentración en la Argentina* (Buenos Aires: Contrapunto, 1987); CONADEP, *Nunca más;* and Eduardo Luis Duhalde, *El estado terrorista argentino* (Barcelona: Argos Vergara, 1983).

organizations. The military was responsible for at least fifteen thousand deaths, some three times the number involved in guerrilla organizations, even if one includes the least trained type of Montonero fighter, the *miliciano*. The "overkill" is partly explained by the junta's ruthlessness: its preparedness to torture relatives, friends, and acquaintances of guerrilla suspects in order to get at the guerrillas themselves. However, it could have adopted the model of repression used in Uruguay, where probably more people were tortured per capita than anywhere in Latin America but only about three hundred were killed. The Argentine junta, in contrast, killed thousands of innocent people.[69]

The other part of the explanation lies in the junta's very broad notion of subversion. General Videla was not simply trying to be provocative when he said that "a terrorist is not just someone with a gun or a bomb but also someone who spreads ideas that are contrary to Western and Christian civilization."[70] Psychologists and sociologists fell victim, often just because their professions were regarded as subversive. Of the nine thousand permanent disappearances reported on by the commission of investigation set up by the new Alfonsín government, some 30 percent were blue-collar workers, yet manual labor provided no more than about 10 percent of the urban guerrilla forces.[71] Militant workers were often referred to by the junta as "industrial guerrillas." So many ended up dead because the junta not only saw subversion in virtually all who disagreed with them but also regarded "subversives" as irredeemable.[72] The military chiefs were authoritarian personalities full of self-righteousness, and when the guerrillas began to target members of the armed forces, their response was one of fury.

Besides being indiscriminate, the violence used by the state was terrorist in the sense that it sowed widespread fear in society. This found reflection in the high degree of self-censorship accepted by the Argentine press during the "dirty war,"[73] the reluctance of the judiciary to act on human rights abuses, and the silence (when not the complicity) of the Roman Catholic church. Given the military regime's full involvement in the violence, it is accurate to speak of state terror and not simply state-sponsored terror.

69. CONADEP, *Nunca más*, 10.

70. *The Times* (London), 4 January 1978.

71. CONADEP, *Nunca más*, 480, and Peter Waldman, "Guerrilla Movements in Argentina, Guatemala, Nicaragua, and Uruguay," in *Political Violence and Terror*, ed. Peter Merkl (Berkeley and Los Angeles: University of California Press, 1986), 211.

72. David Pion-Berlin, "The National Security Doctrine, Military Threat Perception, and the 'Dirty War' in Argentina," *Comparative Political Studies* 21, no. 3 (1988): 398.

73. At least eighty-four journalists disappeared (CONADEP, *Nunca más*, 372–74).

It is significant that military repression continued at a high level for a good year after the guerrillas had lost their effective operational capacity. The ERP had been largely destroyed before the 1976 coup, and the Montoneros declined rapidly the following year, before abandoning their struggle in 1977 (although brief campaigns were launched from abroad in 1978 and 1979). Apart from the breadth of the military conception of subversion, organizational dynamics are relevant here. Having created an infrastructure of secret detention-and-torture centers and a circular routine of abduction-interrogation-intelligence-abduction, and having established an economy based on the "war booty" seized from victims (with shops established to sell the goods, and networks developing to farm out the babies born in captivity to mothers who were killed subsequently), the whole process acquired a dynamic of its own. Toward the end of 1977 it emerged that the most notorious detention center, the Navy Mechanics School (ESMA), finding that the "natural" supply of "subversives" was drying up, had been phoning factory managers to inquire whether they had any "troublemakers."

State terrorism in Argentina also had an international dimension. The junta cooperated on numerous occasions with the security forces of other Latin American military regimes. Earlier the Triple A (which ended up by being partly integrated into the military's "dirty war" infrastructure in 1976) had been responsible for the killing of Allende's commander in chief, General Carlos Prats, in Buenos Aires. In 1976 the foreign victims in Argentina included scores of Chilean exiles, a number of Uruguayan refugees (including senior politicians), and the former Bolivian president Juan Torres. Between 1977 and 1980 the junta's foreign allies repaid their debts by facilitating the abduction and assassination of more than a dozen refugees (mainly, but not exclusively, Montoneros) by Argentine military intelligence squads operating illegally in Peru, Uruguay, and Brazil. There were attempts to kill Montonero leaders in Mexico and Madrid. One woman was abducted in Lima, taken back to Argentina, then transported to Madrid, before being killed there, apparently with the intention of intimidating the large exile community residing in Spain.[74]

It may be argued that it is impossible to destroy an effective guerrilla movement without taking drastic measures against its periphery. However, the challenge was dealt with in Argentina in a way that went far beyond simply destroying the guerrilla organizations; it was the society that had engendered them that was attacked by the state.

74. Paoletti, *Como los nazis*, 434–38.

The military considered themselves victors once the "subversive delin-quents" had been destroyed, but in fact the "dirty war" proved politically costly to the armed forces. Since the junta only adopted the more coercive prescriptions of the National Security Doctrine and ignored its recommendation to improve general welfare, a regime that had been quietly welcomed by the middle class in 1976 soon found itself seriously lacking in political legitimacy.[75] For Argentina as a whole, the episode left many individuals and families nursing a sense of loss and often bitterness, especially since the Alfonsín government only put on trial a few of the most senior military officers. The other main legacy of the 1970s was uneasy civilian-military relations in the 1980s: a serious obsta-cle to democratic consolidation.

The form taken by the "closure" of political violence was less than satisfactory: no decisive institutional act or event brought it to a close; the violence simply subsided. Guerrilla violence gradually ended through military defeat, and in the late 1970s the regime eventually responded to international pressures to put an end to the "disappearances." President Carter's stance on human rights helped the cause of civilian opposition to the regime, not because of the direct impact of his economic sanctions, but because U.S. hostility undermined the self-confidence and rationale of military rulers who considered themselves to be fighting a war to defend "Western and Christian civilization." However, the preparedness to resort to violence when faced with rising civilian opposition was seen once more in 1982 in the invasion of the Falkland Islands. Defeat in the ensuing war with Britain sealed the fate of the regime, yet once more the military was able to depart from office with sufficient residual strength to prevent a radical purge by the succeeding civilian adminis-tration.

Some of the officers involved in the "dirty war" subsequently resur-faced in the course of three military revolts by *carapintadas* (soldiers operating unconstitutionally with their faces blacked) against the Al-fonsín government in 1987–88. They rebelled, not in an attempt to seize power, but rather to secure certain demands: an amnesty for the few officers punished for human rights offenses during the "dirty war," improved pay for the military, and the removal of their "constitutionalist" commander. Their actions, described by one newspaper as "a form of terrorism on a grand scale,"[76] had proved largely successful by the end of the decade.

75. Pion-Berlin, "National Security Doctrine," 1988.
76. *Financial Times* (London), 5 December 1988.

CONCLUSION

This case study has examined the relation between urban guerrilla warfare and terrorism, and the nature of state terrorism in Argentina. It has been seen that acts of terrorism may be carried out by urban guerrillas, although it may be difficult to establish a consensus concerning what constitutes a terrorist act. General definitions of terrorism (such as "political violence against civilians") provide some useful orientation but cannot be applied without regard to the context of violence, which crucially affects public perceptions of it. Argentina was a fairly violent country even before the 1970s, when the urban guerrilla movement was launched, and the problem of defining who the civilians were became particularly difficult. In many countries, individuals who surround themselves with bodyguards are regarded as exercising a legitimate right to self-defense; however, in the case of the Argentine trade-union bureaucracy, it is known that their bodyguards included quite a few individuals who were involved in offensive violence, some of them through the Triple A.

Notwithstanding their occasional use of terrorist tactics, those who waged the armed struggle in Argentina did not pursue a terrorist strategy. Although some of them eventually lost sight of the revolutionary ambitions of their *foquismo* and their violence became less discriminate in time, they did not use terror—coercion and intimidation of the rest of society—as a strategy to achieve their goals. It is important to remember that guerrilla warfare "comes from a different lineage to terrorism, since it derives more from conventional war."[77] Given this derivation, it is hardly surprising that as the assertive, semi-insurgent mass mood of the early 1970s weakened, and as the limitations of urban guerrilla warfare as a revolutionary strategy became apparent,[78] the Montoneros became more militaristic. This does not mean that urban guerrilla warfare cannot decline into terrorism; indeed, there was speculation in the Argentine press in late 1988, following a particularly violent bank raid, that so-called Montonero *gurkhas*, veterans from the 1970s, were planning a much more ruthless and indiscriminate campaign of violence for the future.[79]

It has also been suggested here that state terrorism left a more damaging legacy than did urban guerrilla warfare. The former was more

---

77. Paul Rich, "Long March to the Grey Zone," *Times Higher Education Supplement* (London), 21 April 1989, 15.
78. On the defects of the strategy, see Gillespie, "The Urban Guerrilla in Latin America."
79. "El fantasma de la guerrilla," *Somos* (Buenos Aires), 21 December 1988.

devastating because, unlike the guerrilla warfare, it operated with the full resources of the state behind it, and with impunity, at least while the military regime lasted. Although the guerrillas provided the military with a major pretext for their "dirty war," they were by no means the only cause of the military takeover of 1976. Hyperinflation, political corruption and incompetence, strong labor assertiveness, and the military's own ambitions also lay behind the violent change of regime. The "two demons" theory put forward by the Alfonsín government, according to which left-wing terrorism engendered state terrorism and the two together subverted liberal Argentina, is therefore somewhat simplistic.[80] The theory served as a convenient basis for moral condemnations of violence and as a political device to justify Alfonsín's very limited action against those responsible for the "dirty war," but it is of limited analytical value.

This is not to deny that very important relations existed between state and counterstate in the general escalation of the violence (as is underlined by the fact that there were some Montonero *autoatentados*, attacks on sympathetic Peronist Youth bases, designed to induce greater polarization).[81] Certain parallels at the level of the guerrilla and state terrorist economies have been pointed to, and the ever-growing militarism of the Montoneros (though not of all the urban guerrillas—contrast the FAP) has been emphasized. Some of these linkages help to explain the various cases of guerrilla collaboration with state terrorists or of guerrilla manipulation by state agencies and agents provocateurs; possible examples of such collaboration and manipulation are the ERP's assassination of Anastasio Somoza in Paraguay in 1980 and the La Tablada incident early in 1989, when a left-wing group took over a small military base on the outskirts of Buenos Aires in the belief that they would thereby frustrate a coup attempt.[82] Together with the examples of terrorists who joined the urban guerrilla movement and urban guerrillas who became *gurkhas*, the cases of collaboration and manipulation point to the existence in Argentina of a certain number of people for whom violent activity and militarism have been the main constants in their lives. However, these individuals seem to have constituted a tiny minority among the participants in the Argentine conflict; there were

80. "Demon Versus Demon," *Buenos Aires Herald*, 4 January 1989.

81. Gasparini, *Montoneros*, 85.

82. Patrick Wilmot, "Stroessner: Farewell to Illusions," *African Concord* (London), 18–24 February 1989, 30; Beatriz V. Goyoaga, "Former ERP Member Claims Army Incited Attack," *Buenos Aires Herald*, 3 February 1989, 3; and Juan Carlos Martínez Betelu, "Los militares argentinos utilizan la subversión," *El Independiente* (Madrid), 24 February 1989.

many more for whom political violence was embraced for much more instrumental reasons, even if their motives changed subsequently. Some of the urban guerrillas simply fought for the return of Perón and put aside their weapons when the general returned.

7

The Revolutionary Terrorism of Peru's Shining Path

David Scott Palmer

Shining Path (Sendero Luminoso, Sendero, or SL) is a political and ideological movement on the extreme Left in Peru that espouses its own interpretation of orthodox Maoism. It is not an organization based on a profound religious or ethnic cleavage in Peruvian society, even though it originated in a region heavily populated by Native American Indians.

This chapter was originally prepared in 1989 for the Terrorism in Context project sponsored by the Ford Foundation, and was substantially updated and revised in mid-1993 to take into account the many intervening developments in Peru. The author wishes to express particular appreciation for the support of the Ford Foundation and the gentle but firm leadership of Terrorism in Context project director, Martha Crenshaw. The author is also grateful for the assistance of Kara Bounds, José Gonzales, Cathy Harmon, and Ruby

dero does not see itself as a terrorist organization, but rather as a evolutionary movement fully engaged since 1980 in a people's war. Actions that others call terrorist Shining Path militants justify as a necessary part of a long-term struggle to take power in a country in which the elites have always violently exploited peasants and workers.

Thus, the analyst applies the label "terrorist" advisedly, fully aware that the term is specifically rejected by the leadership of the organization under study, that the government being attacked affixes the label to Sendero with the specific intention of thereby discrediting it, and that calling activities terrorist may have multiple political consequences. For the outside observer, however, there is no question but that many Sendero Luminoso actions since formally beginning the armed struggle in May 1980 merit the terrorist appellation, since they are consciously designed to intimidate, immobilize, and delegitimate established authority and those who support it.[1] This is as true at the local level, with the assassination of a justice of the peace, a native authority *(varayoh)*, or an elected mayor, as at the national level, with the murder of a navy admiral, a prominent journalist, or a congressman.

Part of central authority's dilemma is how best to respond to Shining Path (a.k.a. the Communist Party of Peru, or PCP, as it is called by its members). By labeling the movement terrorist and by emphasizing counterterrorism in its response, the government may well be playing into Sendero's hands. Its actions make the peasantry more fearful of authority; provoke local, national, and international revulsion against the government; and foster conditions that contribute to the generalization of violence in Peru by provoking others on the Left and the Right to carry out their own terrorist actions.[2] Analysts may be no less culpable than government, even if also quite unintentional.

For its part, Sendero terrorist actions are both selective and numerous, with a clear pattern of increasing frequency and growing geographical dispersal over time. From scores of incidents and dozens of deaths in the early 1980s, concentrated in the isolated and underserviced Ayacucho area, SL has been deemed responsible for thousands of incidents and

denDaas in the preparation of this chapter, as well as the critiques, commentary, and invaluable material of Gustavo Gorriti, Sandra Woy Hazleton, Cynthia McClintock, Richard Gillespie, and Gabriela Tarazona-Sevillano. Any errors of fact or interpretation are the author's alone. All translations from the Spanish original are the author's.

1. Martha Crenshaw, "The Subjective Reality of the Terrorist: Ideological and Psychological Factors in Terrorism," in *Current Perspectives on International Terrorism*, ed. Robert O. Slater and Michael Stohl (New York: St. Martin's Press, 1988), 12–46.

2. Manuel Jesús Granados, "El PCP Sendero Luminoso: Aproximaciones a su ideología," *Socialismo y participación* (Lima, Centro de Estudios para el Desarrollo y la Participación [CEDEP]) 37 (March 1987): 36–37.

hundreds of deaths in the late 1980s and early 1990s in almost every part of the country. Reliable sources attribute some 23,580 incidents and at least 23,610 killings, along with over 3,000 disappearances and $24 billion in direct and indirect property damage, to political violence in Peru from 1980 through 1992.[3] Until the dramatic capture of Sendero's head, Abimael Guzmán Reynoso, in September 1992, the organization had demonstrated a growing capacity over time to harass, to intimidate, and to immobilize. Even though the November 1989 municipal elections were successfully carried out in many parts of the country in spite of Sendero calls to boycott and threats to disrupt them, some four hundred of the almost eighteen hundred mayorships to be contested had no candidates willing to risk their lives to run, and about 120 candidates and mayors were killed.[4] The effects of Guzmán's capture on SL's operational capacity, at least in the short run, are suggested by the much lower levels of interference in the January 1993 municipal elections—about one hundred vacant mayorships and some twenty deaths among mayors and candidates.

Among the various terrorist organizations studied in this volume's chapters, Shining Path is far and away the most active and the most violent, and perhaps the most threatening to established authority. At a time when the capacity of Communist party ideology and discipline to capture the imagination and loyalty of citizens in many countries of the world has virtually collapsed, Sendero remains a dramatic exception. The explanation for this rests in large part on the circumstances of its founding and on its distinctive thirty-year trajectory.

The organization we now know as Shining Path began in a small provincial university in the early 1960s as one more group on the Marxist Left within a pluralistic Latin American academic context. In 1963 and 1964 there was no reason to believe it would ever be anything more than that. The activist young professor who led this particular "study group," Abimael Guzmán Reynoso, was one of several at the university at the time who covered the political spectrum from radical to government supporters to conservative. Like the others, the university group identified with Guzmán developed ties with national political movements in the 1960s and competed for influence in universities and unions around the country. Guzmán's organization was affiliated first with Castroite groups

3. Centro de Estudios y Promoción del Desarrollo (DESCO), *Violencia política en el Perú de hoy: Reporte especial* (Lima) 20 (December 1992): 14–15, and Comisión Especial sobre Violencia y Pacificación del Senado (as of mid-1992, Constitución and Sociedad), various publications. Comisión Especial figures on deaths and incidents are about 10 percent higher than those of DESCO. Property damage figures are those of the Comisión Especial.

4. DESCO, *Resumen Semanal* (Lima, DESCO) 547, 1 December 1989.

and then with the Maoist party breakaway after the 1963 Sino-Soviet split. This competition at the local and national level continued in the early 1970s, even after the formation of PCP-SL in 1970, when the final rupture with the Maoist Red Flag Party (Bandera Roja-BR) occurred. Sendero had some success with workers' and teachers' defense committees and in some universities, but most of all in the University of Huamanga in Ayacucho, where it had originated and which it controlled absolutely from 1968 to 1972 and was a major player through 1975.

The development of Shining Path into something other than one more radical, university-based political movement is the result of a combination of factors in the 1970s. One was the growing tumult in the University of Huamanga in the early 1970s while under Sendero control, which led to Sendero's marginalization and Guzmán's resignation from the university by the end of 1975. Others relate to SL being left largely on its own to concentrate on ideological formation through intensive study and on frequent travel by leaders to China (Guzmán is known to have made at least three extended visits before the end of the Cultural Revolution).[5] In addition, regular contacts with peasant communities in Ayacucho and neighboring Apurímac begun in the 1960s were expanded markedly in the 1970s. Former university students from the Indian communities (about 70 percent of Huamanga's student body came from Ayacucho) often served as the initial contact points. Many were primary school teachers who had been prepared between the mid-1960s and the mid-1970s in the training school of the university's education program when it was directed by Guzmán or controlled by Sendero militants. Greater exposure to rural Ayacucho and its Indian communities coincided with gradually worsening local conditions in the area and surely contributed to the militancy of the original Sendero leadership, in its entirety non-Ayacucho born and raised, Guzmán included.

The decision to prepare for the launching of the armed struggle was made in 1978, and after two years of intensive underground preparations, the first actions began on the eve of Peru's first national elections in seventeen years. Sendero's preparation period for embarking on its people's war coincided, paradoxically but significantly, with the opening up of the Peruvian political system after a twelve-year period of reformist, not repressive, military rule. This redemocratization was inclusive, not exclusive, with an emergent, large, and diverse Marxist and Christian Left (Izquierda Unida, IU) ready and able to take advantage of the opportunity, at least for a time.[6]

    5. Gustavo Gorriti, *Sendero: Historia de la guerra milenaria en el Perú*, vol. 1 (Lima: Editorial Apoyo, 1990).
    6. Jorge Nieto, *La izquierda y la democracia en el Perú, 1975–1980* (Lima: DESCO, 1980).

So, unlike most revolutionary movements—"Revolutions are not made, they come"—Sendero did not grow out of a national context of systemic and official repression or a systematic thwarting of opportunities for access to national politics.[7] Shining Path in a real sense made the revolution in Peru. Inappropriate government responses then contributed to creating the conditions that Sendero had already posited to justify its actions. The terrorism engendered by Guzmán's organization was one component of its deliberate action to force a repressive state response that would alienate the populace and make them more receptive to Sendero's message; it was not a reaction to standing state-terrorism practices. Given Shining Path's emphasis on defining the revolution on its own terms and proceeding in accordance with its own ideological interpretation, and given its ability to do so in Peru from 1980 on, it is important to analyze how the organization developed and why it has operated in such a distinctive fashion.

CONTEXT OF THE ORIGINS AND DEVELOPMENT OF SHINING PATH

To understand the larger context surrounding the origins and rise of Shining Path is to understand much of the organization's militancy and dynamism as well as its success.

Ayacucho's Isolation and Poverty

One key factor is the extreme isolation, remoteness, and poverty of Ayacucho, where Sendero began.[8] Almost 90 percent of the population of 500,000 was rural in 1961 and almost 70 percent in 1972. The capital of the department of Ayacucho, also named Ayacucho, had a glorious colonial history but experienced little change after independence. Even

7. Theda Skocpol, States and Social Revolutions (New York: Cambridge University Press, 1975), 17.
8. The following data are from Peru's 1961 and 1972 censuses and personal observations of the author, resident in Ayacucho in 1962–64 (full-time) and 1970–72 (part-time) and a regular visitor through the 1970s. For a fuller discussion of this and other information presented below, see David Scott Palmer, "Rebellion in Rural Peru: The Origins and Evolution of Sendero Luminoso," Comparative Politics, 18, no. 2 (1986): 127–46. But see also the important work of Carlos Iván Degregori, student and professor at the university, 1969–79, most particularly, Ayacucho, 1969–1979: El surgimiento de Sendero Luminoso (Lima: Instituto de Estudios Peruanos [IEP], 1990).

as of the early 1960s there were almost no paved streets, fewer than twenty-five thousand people, two buses and two or three score private cars, a small police detachment and no military, one radio station, a weekly four-page newspaper, no telephone, only evening electricity for most of the city, a short dirt runway fit for only the three scheduled DC-3 flights per week, and a single one-lane road connecting the region to the outside world and Lima, twenty-four hours away by car in good weather. The population of the department was overwhelmingly Quechua-speaking Indian, and four of its seven provinces were among the ten with the lowest per capita incomes in the country.[9] Only about 6 percent of the land was arable, water was in scarce supply, and few of the three-hundred-odd Indian communities and scores of small haciendas in the area produced more than subsistence-level agricultural goods most years. So Sendero got its start in one of the most isolated and poorest regions of Peru, where central government access had been historically intermittent, communications difficult or virtually impossible, poverty generalized, and Indians and Indian communities very predominant.

The University of Huamanga

The second factor is the dramatic effect on the region produced by the reopening of the University of San Cristóbal de Huamanga in 1959 (after having been closed in 1880 amid the general economic crisis in Peru produced by the War of the Pacific, 1879–83, with Chile). This was the first of a dozen new provincial universities that would be established in Peru in the 1960s as part of a larger plan to make public higher education accessible to a larger number of high school graduates. Huamanga, as the prototype and the only new public undergraduate institution established during Peru's last conservative civilian government (Manuel Prado Ugarteche, 1956–62), had several features that distinguished it from the more traditional universities.

Most significantly, the University of Huamanga was designed to serve as a catalyst for social and economic change in the region by offering to local youth an array of specializations most needed to address the problems of the Ayacucho area.[10] Instead of the traditional schools of law, medicine, and engineering, there were programs of education, applied anthropology, rural and agricultural engineering, and nursing. Instead of immediate specialization upon entering the university, stu-

9. Richard Webb, *Government Policy and the Distribution of Income in Peru, 1963–1973* (Cambridge: Harvard University Press, 1977).
    10. Fernando Romero Pintado, "New Design for an Old University: San Cristóbal de Huamanga," *Américas* (December 1961).

dents spent their first two years in "basic studies," a type of interdisciplinary liberal arts education, to broaden their knowledge of the world around them. In another major departure from previous higher education practice in Peru, the faculty was contracted on a full-time basis with salaries set high enough during the first few years to attract some of the country's best academics.

Furthermore, a specific mission of the university was to reach out to the wider community with an array of services in health, education, and local development. Substantial international economic and technical assistance contributed to experimental farms at Huallapampa and Alpachaca, integrated development projects in Indian communities around Pampa Cangallo, ceramic and weaving projects, and bilingual education. The Dutch and Danish governments were enlisted along with the Summer Institute of Linguistics, the Peace Corps, and the Fulbright Commission, among others. The result was a dramatic new pole of development stimulus in the region, centered around the activities of the university.

Although the institution's extension mission never changed, the orientation became more sectarian and less pluralistic in the course of the 1960s as more-radical elements gained control of the university and used their influence to ensure a Marxist orientation to most of the activities. The group that was to become known as Sendero Luminoso was instrumental in this process, beginning with the education program in 1963–64 and then more generally after gaining control of the university in the 1968 internal elections. So the distinctive contribution of Peru's first "new" university—active participation in various aspects of local development in one of the poorest regions of the country—was gradually infused with a radical, sectarian political content. Under the leadership of Professor Guzmán, first as education-program teacher, then as director of the teacher-training school, and finally as director of personnel of the university, the goal of forging an institution committed to the teaching and extension of Marxist principles in all of the university's activities was realized between the mid-1960s and the mid-1970s. With open enrollment, Huamanga expanded from about 550 students and 40 faculty in 1963 to almost 4,500 students and 200 faculty by 1972, even as it became less diverse and more committed politically.[11]

Development Programs of the 1960s

A third factor is the presence in the Ayacucho area of a substantial number of small-scale development programs in the context of the

11. Degregori, *Ayacucho, 1969–1979*, table 4, 253.

Alliance for Progress during the elected government of Fernando Belaúnde Terry (1963–68). His was an administration committed to rural
economic growth in response to the increasing mobilization of peasants
in some parts of Peru. Beginning with the land occupations in Cuzco's La
Convención valley in 1960, which were recognized de facto in 1962 by the
military junta (1962–63),[12] more and more peasant groups organized
locally to try to solve agricultural-production and land-scarcity problems.
Belaúnde's formal acceptance of the presidency on 28 July 1963 was
greeted with a simultaneous occupation of lands in several parts of the
country. This initiative required immediate attention to Peru's rural
problems by central government, producing an array of activities often
financed by international agencies. The brief outbreak of rural guerrilla
activity in the departments of Cuzco, Ayacucho, and Cerro de Pasco in
1965, though led by naïve urban-bred Castroite radicals and quickly put
down, lent new urgency to the developmentalist solutions then in vogue.
    The array of programs operating in Ayacucho during this period was
part of the larger national picture. They included potable water projects
in more than a score of district capitals (Peru's smallest unit of central
government authority), construction of small health clinics and primary
schools, and the expansion of the agricultural extension service, all with
Alliance for Progress funds. The Peace Corps worked in the area for
more than ten years, beginning in 1962, for various Peruvian government
agencies, most particularly in school lunch programs in every provincial
capital, in arts-and-crafts cooperatives in Huamanga and Huanta, and in
local community development activities throughout the region, primarily
in rural rather than urban areas. About two hundred volunteers spent
two years each in these and other activities over this period, with as
many as fifty scattered about the department of Ayacucho at one time at
the height of Peace Corps presence between 1965 and 1968. The Summer
Institute of Linguistics, a Protestant missionary organization long identified with Indian literacy programs, worked with the Ministry of Education to establish a string of thirty-four bilingual-education primary
schools throughout the province of Huamanga and to offer continuing
intensive training for their teachers in a modest but modern residential
complex just outside the city of Ayacucho. The Department Development
Corporation, a creation of the Prado administration, carried out its own
local activities; and the Popular Cooperation program of the Belaúnde
government brought scores of Peruvian university students into the area

    12. Wesley Craig, *From Hacienda to Community: An Analysis of Solidarity and
Social Change in Peru*, Cornell University Latin American Studies Program, no. 6 (Ithaca,
N.Y., September 1967).

during summer vacations to participate in a variety of self-help projects, mostly in remote Indian communities.

The central government in the 1960s spent about 3 percent of its revenues in Ayacucho, a sum proportionate to that department's share of the national population. Other governments and agencies had their own programs in the area during this period, primarily in agriculture. By the end of the 1960s road networks had been substantially expanded, a telephone system installed, the airport lengthened and paved, and a military garrison established. In addition, an important new highway that connected Ayacucho directly with the coast near Pisco was constructed with Japanese funds. Though also a dirt road, it cut the travel time to Lima in half.

These various activities combined to produce modest but discernible economic growth, increased access to education and health, and improved mobility for the substantial temporary migrations between urban and rural areas and for farm to market products. Major spontaneous migrations along with a concomitant expansion of agricultural and commercial activity occurred along the new road to the Apurímac River in the jungle. By national standards, poverty was still endemic in Ayacucho, but measurable progress had been achieved, much of it at the grass roots and much of it as the direct result of government or government-approved initiatives.

So the growing sectarianism of the University of Huamanga's extension activities in the late 1960s and early 1970s was counterbalanced for a time by this array of government programs, with generally positive consequences for the local, mostly peasant population. University students were active with their political agenda in some communities, while the government and its affiliates were involved with theirs in many others. By the early 1970s, however, the dynamic shifted markedly, largely due to inappropriate new government programs. The resulting decline in the well-being of many Ayacucho peasants made it even harder for them to cope after the earlier improvement in their situation, however modest. It set the stage for Sendero more easily to expand its access to and influence with a peasantry increasingly disquieted, disillusioned, and discontented.

Ideology

A fourth significant factor is the distinctive nature of the ideology and praxis of the Left in Peru generally, but particularly within the University of Huamanga. The original Communist Party of Peru, which dated from 1928, in the 1940s had experienced a Trotskyite breakaway faction that became involved in some peasant movements in the 1950s and early 1960s, particularly in the La Convención valley of Cuzco. But the fissures multiplied in the 1960s first with Castroites and then with Maoists forming their own parties and then redividing in various ways.[13]

These splits at the national level were also reflected within the student federation and the faculty at the University of Huamanga. But here there occurred over the course of the 1960s a growing predominance of more-radical groups, dramatized by the victory in the university elections of 1968 of what came to be Shining Path, then still affiliated with the national Maoist party, Red Flag. Radical study groups formed during this period to plumb the insights of the works of Mao and the Peruvian Marxist José Carlos Mariátegui, with special reference to their applicability to contemporary Peruvian rural reality. The perspective of these groups was sharpened by extended visits by a number of faculty to China during the Cultural Revolution there (1966–76), which had the effect of exposing them to the more extreme ideological positions of purges, permanent revolution, and revolutionary orthodoxy. The split with the Red Flag Party of Saturnino Paredes, formalized in 1970, drove the Ayacucho faction, now known as Shining Path, to greater isolation from the Maoist mainstream and to redoubled efforts to hew out a distinctive Marxist path to revolution. Control over the university's extension services permitted increased activity by Sendero militants in the countryside, which in turn gave them a sense of superiority over their erstwhile Lima-based colleagues.

They were advancing their Maoist vision of Marxism by action as well as by study instead of being satisfied by merely talking about it. The emerging conviction that they alone had discovered the keys to Marxist theory and practice by years of diligent study, conscientious application in the field, and the building of close ties between some Ayacucho peasants and the intellectual vanguard gradually produced a virtually unshakable faith in their uniqueness, even within the larger Marxist revolutionary community. They saw themselves, if you will, as the equivalent of the reborn Christian, the true carriers of the faith and, therefore, destined to eventual triumph no matter how daunting the odds.[14]

13. Lewis Taylor, *Maoism in the Andes: Sendero Luminoso and the Contemporary Guerrilla Movement in Peru*, Liverpool, England, Center for Latin American Studies, University of Liverpool, Working Paper 2, 1983, especially the chart of left political parties, 7. For the most recent left party listings and analysis, see Sandra Woy Hazleton, "Peru," *Yearbook on International Communist Affairs* (Stanford, Calif.: Hoover Institution Press, 1985–92).

14. Compare this account with that of Gordon H. McCormick, *The Shining Path and*

Leadership

The fifth key factor, leadership, contributed significantly to forging an organization that could attract subordinates and followers and galvanize them to action even at high personal cost. Both the increasing radicalism at the University of Huamanga in the 1960s and the rise of Sendero from the 1970s onward are closely related to the personal qualities and capacities of Professor Guzmán. From the time of his arrival in Ayacucho in 1962 as a junior professor of philosophy in the education program until his resignation and departure in 1975 after service first as director of the teacher-training school and then as director of personnel of the university, Guzmán was a radical activist. At the same time, he was considered an excellent, even charismatic teacher, as well as reserved, measured, and correct in his relation with faculty colleagues and students.[15]

He was believed to be identified with the Castroites during his first years at Huamanga; when a fellow faculty member would ask for a missing student, invariably one of the brightest in the class, classmates were known to sing a Cuban ballad and suggest that the professor speak to Guzmán. The conclusion drawn was that he was serving during this period as the conduit for resources from Cuba to support the Castroite faction in the University and as the facilitator for getting some students to Cuba for education and training. It is believed that this Cuban link was broken in 1965 over the issue of whether to launch guerrilla warfare at that time (Guzmán is thought to have been strenuously opposed and to have been vindicated when the ensuing rebellion was quickly crushed). Guzmán and his followers then solidified their identification with the Maoists and part of the Peruvian Beijing-oriented party until breaking away to establish their separate organization in 1970, which they called the Communist Party of Peru.

Guzmán's first major political success at the university was his behind-the-scenes maneuvering to get the Peace Corps removed from Huamanga.[16] Three volunteers had been invited in 1962 by then rector

---

Peruvian Terrorism (Santa Monica, Calif.: Rand Corporation, 1987), 16–17. See also Degregori, *Ayacucho, 1969–1979*, for additional background.

15. This was my experience as an academic colleague of Guzmán's at the university in 1962 and 1963. See also the comments of another contemporary, Dr. Luis Lumbreras, a distinguished anthropologist and archeologist who served as dean of social sciences at Huamanga from 1962 to 1965, interview in *Quehacer* (Lima, DESCO) 42 (August–September 1986): 34–43.

16. See David Scott Palmer, "Expulsion from a Peruvian University," in *Cultural Frontiers of the Peace Corps*, ed. Robert Textor (Cambridge: MIT Press, 1966), 243–70, for additional background and details. Gustavo Gorriti subsequently shared his own research with the author, which provided further insights.

Fernando Romero Pintado to teach English and social sciences (a fourth was added in 1963 in biology, and others were scheduled to begin teaching in 1964). An error in conduct in the classroom by one of the Peace Corps Volunteer (PCV) teachers was adroitly generalized to the entire PCV contingent and brought before the national student convention (by chance, in Ayacucho that year). There the threat of a national strike over the issue pressured the university council, originally supportive of the PCV teachers not involved in the initial incident, to terminate the volunteers' academic services. This event marked the first major step in the process of radicalization of the university and the first in which Guzmán was directly involved.

Professor Guzmán went on to hold key positions in the university. The directorship of the teacher-training school permitted the introduction of a more partisan political criterion and the use of his considerable academic and personal skills to attract and radicalize many enterprising students of humble origins. This relationship, in turn, gave access to many Ayacucho communities through the elementary school teachers, traditionally by intermediaries between the local scene and the world beyond and one of the few areas of central government services in Ayacucho that expanded in the 1970s.[17]

In fact, the origins of the radical teachers' union, the Sole Union of Peruvian Educational Workers (SUTEP), date from a student-parent massacre, mostly peasants, in Ayacucho's second city of Huanta in 1969, when they protested efforts by the central government to impose a fee on public school students who repeated failed courses. Many of the leaders of this protest were teachers or students trained under Guzmán in the university's education program.[18]

As director of personnel of the university from 1971 to 1974, Professor Guzmán controlled communications with faculty and students, scholarships and salary payments, extension services, the university press, and most day-to-day administrative matters within the institution. The patronage and influence involved with this position enhanced his already demonstrated ability to attract a substantial number of the most able students and faculty in the university and commit them to his radical course.

The first leadership group of Sendero was, without exception, from

17. Instituto Nacional de Estadística (INE), *Censos nacionales: VIII de población, III de vivienda, 12 de junio de 1981 Departamento de Ayacucho* (Lima: INE, 1983), 1: vii–xii.
18. Ricardo Melgar Bao, "Las guerrilleras de Sendero y la ilusión andina del poder" (Paper presented at the Twelfth International Congress of the Latin American Studies Association, Albuquerque, N.M., April 1985), 3–4. See also the detailed discussion in Degregori, *Ayacucho, 1969–1979*.

the university and from outside Ayacucho. This included Guzmán himself, born in Mollendo on the southern coast, educated in Arequipa, Peru's second city, and likely not to have known Ayacucho until he came there to take up his first teaching position.[19] Though already a Communist party member, part of his militancy and revolutionary conviction, like that of his closest circle, might have been derived from the impact of the poverty and isolation of Ayacucho, with which he had daily contact through his students, the extension programs to outlying communities, and the city itself. Another key element is the personal magnetism Guzmán projected, his dedication to the study of Marxist writings, and his ability to synthesize his insights in a pedagogical way that made everything seem so clear and correct. In a university in which the student body had grown enormously by the early 1970s and in which most of the outstanding Peruvian intellectuals originally attracted to Huamanga had departed, Guzmán's talents stood out even more.

Military Government Reforms of the 1970s

A sixth important factor drawn from the larger context that helps explain the rise of Shining Path in Peru is related to unintended consequences of some of the reformist policies of the long-term military government (1968–80). This regime broke with the incrementalist development pattern pursued by previous civilian administrations. The Peruvian armed forces represented the "new" professional military that had redefined national security in terms of national development in the 1950s and 1960s.[20] This perspective focused on the need to change the country in order to preserve it, and during the military *docenio* (twelve-year rule) Peru changed in a number of ways.[21] The government adopted an aggressive Third World stand. A number of large private corporations, both domestic and foreign-owned, were nationalized. The state expanded dramatically in size, from being one of the smallest in Latin America to one of the largest. The Marxist Left was legalized and legitimated, particularly labor unions, which proliferated at historically unprece-

19. For details of Guzmán's life, see Gustavo Gorriti, "Shining Path's Stalin and Trotsky," in *Shining Path of Peru*, ed. David Scott Palmer (New York: St. Martin's Press, 1992), 149–70; see also his *Sendero*, vol. 1.
20. Jorge Rodríguez Beruff, *Los militares y el poder* (Lima: Mosca Azul, 1983).
21. There are a large number of studies on this period. See, for example, Abraham F. Lowenthal, ed., *The Peruvian Experiment* (Princeton: Princeton University Press, 1975); Cynthia McClintock and Abraham F. Lowenthal, eds., *The Peruvian Experiment Revisited* (Princeton: Princeton University Press, 1983); and David Scott Palmer, "The Changing Political Economy of Peru Under Military and Civilian Rule," *Inter-American Economic Affairs* 37, no. 4 (Spring 1984): 37–62.

dented rates even as the government was attempting to construct a competing social-property structure combining workers and management in industry, mining, and agriculture. A major agrarian reform was undertaken, starting in 1969, that over the next ten years dramatically restructured Peruvian agriculture. Some 380,000 farm families gained access to new lands, mostly through the establishment of a variety of complex cooperative structures that often combined both Indian communities and former haciendas. Substantial foreign loans were contracted (a net increase of about $8 billion over the *docenio*), a large proportion from private banks, to help pay for these reforms.

However well intended and however significant their benefits for some sectors of Peru's population, the changes introduced by the military government also facilitated the rise of Sendero in a number of ways. Encouraging Marxist groups provided alternatives to Shining Path on the Left, on the one hand, which proved to be a major obstacle to the advancement of Sendero's guerrilla war.[22] But on the other hand, by letting the political dynamics within the universities largely take their own course in the 1970s, the military regime allowed the Sendero center at the University of Huamanga to become much stronger than it would have been had it been subject to closer review. The reformist phase of the military government, 1968–75, coincided with the period of Sendero control of the university and the concomitant expansion and deepening of radical study groups there.

In addition, the application of the agrarian reform in the Ayacucho area proved disastrous. This was mainly because this region had a much higher proportion of Indian communities to private haciendas than most other parts of the country, and the haciendas were both smaller and poorer for the most part.[23] As a result, the agrarian reform broke down the old system without providing an alternative that would generate new resources in its place. Historic animosities and tensions, previously moderated by the weight of the status quo and government mediation, increased, and most of the peasantry wound up worse off as a result.[24]

To make matters worse, the region was a lower priority for the

22. This is explicitly noted by Lewis Taylor, "Agrarian Unrest and Political Conflict in Puno, 1985–1987," *Bulletin of Latin American Research* 6, no. 2 (1987): 135–162. But see also Sandra Woy-Hazleton and William A. Hazelton, "Shining Path and the Marxist Left," in *Shining Path*, ed. Palmer, 207–24.

23. Antonio Díaz Martínez, *Ayacucho: Hambre y esperanza* (Ayacucho: Ediciones Waman Poma, 1969), ch. 1.

24. David Scott Palmer, *Revolution from Above: Military Government and Popular Participation in Peru, 1968–1972*, Cornell University Latin American Studies Program, no. 47 (Ithaca, N.Y., January 1993), 230–27, provides case studies in Ayacucho of the very negative results of the agrarian reform in the 1970–71 period. Table 12, 197, shows the high level of land conflicts unleashed by the agrarian reform.

military reformers and thus received fewer and less qualified government administrators as well as proportionally less economic assistance (government expenditures for Ayacucho declined from 3 percent of the total budget in the 1960s to less than 1 percent during the 1970s).[25] Furthermore, alternatives from the 1960s like the Peace Corps, foreign assistance, Popular Cooperation, and the Summer Institute of Linguistics were terminated or gradually squeezed out. The government institutions that replaced them in the area, like the National Social Mobilization Support System (SINAMOS), employed substantial numbers of university graduates for a time but did little to benefit peasants. And even this organization was eliminated by the end of the decade as a result of massive local protests.[26] The overall effect was a substantial decline in production and peasant well-being in the area even as alternative avenues of recourse were also being reduced. Shining Path's ongoing activities in the communities became more and more important, partly as a direct consequence of the application of central-government policies in the Ayacucho area.

Another consequence of military rule was the problem of debt repayment. Peru was the first Latin American country to experience the debt crisis, beginning in 1977, largely because of the overextension of government activities during the first years of the *docenio*, when the military regime tried to carry out too many reforms in too many areas too quickly. The constraints imposed on the country as a result have continued ever since the restoration of civilian rule in 1980, producing inflation, economic stagnation, and a substantial decline in the delivery of many government services. This has hit especially hard such peripheral areas as Ayacucho. Sendero, given its years of preparation and expanding presence in the area, was particularly well positioned to take advantage of the government's problems and the growing distress of the local population. Sendero Luminoso's historic decision to launch the people's war in early 1980 was, thus, far from fortuitous.[27]

THE ARMED STRUGGLE AND ITS CONSEQUENCES

The rise and expansion of political violence in Peru in the 1980s, which included terrorist actions both by the guerrillas and by the state, can be

25. Bao, "Las guerrillas de Sendero," 6.
26. Sandra Woy Hazleton, "Infrastructure of Participation in Peru: SINAMOS," in *Political Participation in Latin America*, vol. 1, *Citizen and State*, ed. John A. Booth and Mitchell A. Seligson (New York: Holmes and Meier, 1978), 189–208.
27. Taylor, *Maoism in the Andes*, 9–13.

understood only by examining the actions, the motivations, and the errors of Shining Path and the government alike.

Shining Path's Strategy

Various scholars and journalists have pursued Sendero's paper trail over the past twenty years, which reveals much of what Shining Path hopes to accomplish and how it will go about achieving its long-term objective of taking power in Peru. A 1974 Sendero document, "Development of the People's War," subsequently revised, lays out five phases that must be pursued:[28]

1. Development and infiltration
2. Building the party in rural areas through strikes, establishing people's self-defense groups, and organizing peasants and training cadres
   a. Centralization of the peasant movement
   b. Recovery of peasant lands
   c. Creation of party cells in each community
   d. Creation of peasant self-defense commands
   e. Creation of peasant cadre schools
   f. Strengthening the worker-peasant alliance
3. Undertaking the Prolonged People's War
   a. Guerrillas appear, with revolutionary action taken with popular support
   b. Support bases created and regional units organized
   c. Party remains in clandestinity
   d. Greater caution and secrecy to guard against increased activity by intelligence services
4. Creation of liberated zones and the appearance of a provisional revolutionary government
   a. Support bases expand, or two or more support bases join
   b. Provisional revolutionary government becomes the only political power in the zone
   c. Combat units are now regional units, not simply guerrillas
5. Prolonged People's War in which the war is total.

Although the timetable is flexible and phases may vary, depending on different local circumstances in different regions, these are the stages

28. As presented and analyzed by Raúl González, "Para entender Sendero Luminoso," *Quehacer* 42 (August–September 1986): 28–33.

Sendero anticipated well before actually undertaking the armed struggle. In this document there is explicit recognition, repeated in various forums since, that the proletarian leadership is the only guarantee of the revolution; but the revolution cannot be accomplished without seeking the support of the peasants, who are its main force. Furthermore, for success, the revolutionary provisional government, when established, must achieve an international audience and recognition.

The Sendero strategy is, at root, a prolonged war of attrition over an increasing expanse of the national territory, a war that is intended to force the government to increase its expenditures on military actions, thus making it less and less able to satisfy basic popular demands. In addition, militants work to create an increasingly chaotic situation in the cities that authorities will eventually not be able to control. Over time, the population, especially the third that lives in Lima, will lose its capacity to cope and will see in Sendero "the only authority capable of restoring order."[29] Military success is not Sendero's goal, according to some analysts. Rather, it is to paralyze the economy, destabilize the government, and force authorities into making unpopular decisions.[30]

However, the organization does pursue a long-term military strategy designed to take military advantage of the government's growing inability to manage the country. Following Mao, Sendero's prolonged people's war is to develop in three strategic phases in its relation to government forces: defense, equilibrium, and offense. Each is determined by the relative size and operational capacity of Sendero forces vis-à-vis those of the government. In the "strategic defensive" phase Sendero wages "guerrilla war" with small armed units; in the "strategic equilibrium" phase the armed struggle becomes a "war of movements" with much larger military forces, up to batallion size, capable of engaging government forces on equal terms.[31]

The Role of Terrorism

Given this strategic assessment, for Sendero the role of terrorism is central to attaining its objectives. "Shining Path is an insurrectional movement that uses terrorism within the more general framework of an

29. Henri Favre, in an interview with Raúl González in *Quehacer* 42 (August–September 1986): 22–23.

30. A view held specifically by Raúl González and Henri Favre, among others.

31. Carlos Iván Degregori, "Situación de Sendero Luminoso y de la estratégia antisubversiva después de la captura de Abimael Guzmán" (Draft paper presented at the Wilson Center Latin American Program Conference on Peru, Smithsonian Institution, Washington, D.C., 1–2 June 1993), 2.

armed people's struggle." Nevertheless, "no matter how extreme it may be, Shining Path violence is not gratuitous, uncontrolled, or indiscriminate."[32] Terrorism for Sendero has the specific objective of reducing the scope and capacity of government authority, thereby causing the center to lose legitimacy in the minds of the population. Selective killings of political authorities have been carried out since 1982; the first assassination of an elected major, Juan Inca Allccaco of the Popular Action Party (Acción Popular [AP]) of President Fernando Belaúnde Terry (1980–85), occurred in Huaya, Víctor Fajardo province, in the department of Ayacucho, on 13 July 1982.[33] Other local officials appointed by the government have also been the target of Sendero attacks, from district governors and lieutenant governors to justices of the peace to town councillors. Beginning in 1987, some public officials working in local development projects have also been killed, including a few of the estimated 550 foreign specialists once working in the countryside in technical assistance. A total of 261 political authorities were killed between 1982 and 1988, as well as ten foreigners, with another 122 government officials, elected and appointed, reported assassinated in the first six months of 1989.[34]

These actions have had the chilling effect on rural economic development programs Sendero has sought; most were withdrawn to the cities from mid-1989 through 1992. Assassination and intimidation of political officials also had a major impact at the local level. In early 1989 it was estimated that at least one-third of Peru's four-thousand odd honorific justice of the peace positions, long a mark of some status in the local community, remained unfilled at that time due to a lack of candidates.[35] In addition, over four hundred of the almost eighteen hundred elected mayorships in the country were believed to be vacant on the eve of Peru's November 1989 municipal elections due to the resignation or murder of incumbents.[36]

32. Henri Favre interview, *Quehacer* 21 (February–March 1983).

33. Piedad Pareja Pflücker and Eric Torres Montes, *Municipios y terrorismo* (Lima: Centro de Estudios Peruanos, 1989), appendix 2, 80.

34. See DESCO, *Violencia política en el Perú, 1980–1988*, vol. 1 (Lima: DESCO, 1989), table 7, 43, for fatalities through 1988, and DESCO, *Resumen Semanal*, selected numbers, for 1989 totals. The challenge of obtaining exact figures is illustrated by the contrasting totals compiled by Peru's Ministry of the Interior. Their statistics office reports 293 killings of political authorities between 1985 and 1989, including 116 for all of 1989 (Instituto Nacional de Estadística e Informática, *Indicadores sociales* (Lima: Dirección Nacional de Estadísticas Básicas, September 1990), bulletin 2, table 5.20, 86.

35. David Scott Palmer, "Peru's Persistent Problems," *Current History* 89, no. 543 (January 1990): 32.

36. Piedad Pareja Pflücker and Eric Torres Montes, *Municipio y terrorismo*, appen-

Regular sabotage of economic infrastructure and a few assassinations of foreign visitors over the past three years have produced similar consequences for the economy. Hundreds of millions of dollars of foreign exchange have been lost because mineral production has been prevented from reaching the coast for export or because tourist revenues have fallen. The Peruvian senate commission established to study the problem of terrorism and political violence, reconstituted in 1992 as Constitution and Society, estimated that over $10 billion in damage has occurred as a result of guerrilla actions since 1980, and some $14 billion in indirect losses through mid-1993. Although Sendero's campaign of political and economic terrorism seems far from provoking the collapse of the government, it has had a major negative impact on popular perceptions of security and well-being. A July 1989 survey, for example, showed that 56 percent of the population believed that Peru was on the brink of civil war, and 19 percent believed that a state of civil war already existed; furthermore, if Sendero called for an "armed strike," only 18 percent said that they would work normally.[37]

Shining Path's Organization

To work toward its objectives, Sendero has built a fairly elaborate political and military apparatus. The basic unit is the cell.[38] Each cell has five to nine members, including a leader, called the *responsable político*, as well as two explosives experts, a physical training instructor, and a person responsible for ideological training. Cells do not normally operate in their home regions, and members are not apprised of orders given to other cells, or of the identity of other members. Only one member, usually the *responsable político*, has direct communication with the next higher level of leadership. There is also a hierarchy of commitment and responsibility broken down into five distinct groups—premilitants, militants, military personnel, organizers, and leaders—of which the first three operate in separate cells. These cells are, in turn, coordinated by

dixes 4 and 5, 93–101. About sixty districts did not hold elections in 1986; thirty-nine mayors were killed from January 1987 through April 1989; and 174 resigned during that same period, most after receiving written death threats attributed to Sendero. About 175 more deaths and resignations occurred between May and November 1989.

37. An Apoyo survey published in *Perú económico* and reported in the Foreign Broadcast Information Service (FBIS), *Daily Report: Latin America*, 27 July 1989, 43–44.

38. The discussion following is drawn largely from James Anderson, *Sendero Luminoso: A New Revolutionary Model?* (London: Institute for the Study of Terrorism, 1987), esp. 31–32, and also from Gabriela Tarazona-Sevillano, *Sendero Luminoso and the Threat of Narcoterrorism*, Center for Strategic and International Studies (CSIS), Washington Papers 144 (New York: Praeger, 1990), 55–78.

the leader of the subsector who answers to a zonal director responsible to a regional committee. Planning and coordination between zones is carried out by a coordination committee, ultimately answerable, along with its regional counterpart, to the National Central Committee, the ruling body of Sendero (see Fig. 7.1).

The country is divided by the Shining Path leadership into six regional committees: Southern (Cuzco, Tacna, Puno), Eastern (Ucayali, Huánuco, San Martín), Northern (Ancash, Libertad), Central (Junín, Pasco), Primary (Ayacucho, Huancavelica, Apurímac), and Metropolitan (Lima, Callao—which in turn has six zones due to the concentration of population there). In the Metropolitan Region there are also four "special squads" with specific and distinct duties related to "annihilation," "assault," "containment," and "razing,"which carry out selected terrorist operations in a coordinated sequence.[39]

Much of the responsibility for the selection and implementation of specific operations rests with the regional committees and their commanders, giving the organization a substantial degree of local autonomy. This means that the dynamic of Sendero activities in one part of the country may in many cases bear little relation to that in another. It also gives to the movement a flexibility that rests with those who presumably know more about local situations than those at the top.[40] Nevertheless, initiatives coordinated from the Central Committee do occur frequently, as in attacks nationwide to commemorate some event (such as Guzmán's birthday on 3 December; the anniversary of the prison massacre in 1986, "Heroes' Day," 19 June; Independence Day on 28 July; or the date in 1980 marking the initiation of the "people's war," 17 May). Overall control remains firmly in the hands of the National Central Committee and, before he was captured, most particularly in those of Guzmán himself (whose nom de guerre was Comrade, then President Gonzalo). In addition, there are periodic party congresses (believed to have been held in 1979, 1982, 1985, and February 1988) to assess and critique the movement's progress.[41] A reconstituted Central Committee made up the remnants of the old (no more than three or four of the original nineteen) and filled out with regional and zonal leaders was set up in a December 1992 meeting of surviving directors and commanders.[42] However, given Guzmán's dominant role over the entire history of Sendero's existence, it is unlikely that the new Central Committee will be able to exert the

39. Tarazona-Sevillano, *Narcoterrorism*, 59–61.
40. Ibid., 58.
41. Ibid., 55.
42. Degregori, "Situación de Sendero Luminoso," 13.

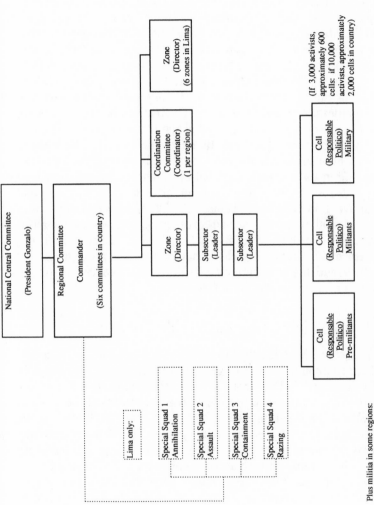

Plus militia in some regions:
Eastern [Huanuco], Primary [Ayacucho], and Southern [Puno]

Source: Adapted from Gabriela Tarazona-Sevillano. Sendero Luminoso and the Threat of Narcoterrorism. New York: Praeger, 1990, Fig. 3 and 4.

Fig. 7.1. Sendero Luminoso organization chart

same control as before September 1992. Regional committees will almost certainly be more autonomous as a result.

Although estimates vary widely, Sendero is believed to have grown from about 100 militants in 1980–81,[43] to 3,000 to 10,000 in 1987–88,[44] to 3,000 to 4,000 armed cadres, as many as 10,000 militants, and some 50,000 premilitants (sympathizers and occasional contributors or members of front organizations) by mid-1992.[45] Guerrilla casualties, mostly Sendero, have been high: the number of "presumed terrorists killed" through 1992 was 10,655 (see Tables 7.1 and 7.4). Among the casualties are many important Sendero figures, including entire cells, regional committee members, and members of the Central Committee. Even so, the number of reported incidents exceeded the thirteen-year average of 1,814 every year between 1985 and 1992 (see Table 7.2). The ratio of deaths per one hundred incidents also rose sharply during the four-year period beginning in 1989, even though both incidents and deaths declined by 30 percent through 1992, after both hit historic highs of 2,779 and 3,745, respectively, in 1990[46] (see Tables 7.1, 7.2, and 7.3 and appendix). Over 62 percent of all police and armed-forces political-violence casualties have occurred since 1989 (1,420 of 2,278) (see Tables 7.1 and 7.4). These gruesome data make abundantly clear that Sendero as an organization has clearly been capable of maintaining its destructive course in spite of increased pressure from government forces.

Explaining Shining Path's Growth

A number of factors, both internal to Sendero and outside the organization, may help to explain Sendero's growth. One is ideology, a complete system of values and beliefs from a basic Marxist conception of the class struggle (Marx), the dictatorship of the proletariat (Lenin), rural revolution (Mao), and nationalistic domestic Third World revolution (Mariátegui), with Guzmán as the living guide. The Sendero ideology provides a recognizable alternative value system in a group-solidarity setting that, when combined with actions, enhances one's self-worth.

It may be compared with a religious experience, an alternative to Catholic or Protestant activism, because of which the individual "con-

43. Sandra Woy Hazleton's estimate.
44. Sandra Woy Hazleton, "Peru," *Yearbook of International Communist Affairs, 1987* (Stanford: Hoover Institution Press, 1988), 115.
45. Interviews with foreign service officers of the U.S. embassy in Peru's political section, 29 June and 13–14 July 1992.
46. Some of these guerrilla-provoked incidents and deaths, up to 20 percent in some years, are attributable to organizations other than Shining Path.

Table 7.1. Deaths due to political violence, by year, 1980–1992

Victims	1980	1981	1982	1983	1984	1985	1986	1987	1988	Total
Police	0	6	31	52	56	45	100	139	137	566
Armed forces	0	0	1	9	26	31	29	53	143	292
Political authorities	0	0	11	27	35	19	43	40	86	261
Clergy	0	0	0	0	0	0	0	1	2	3
Foreigners	0	0	0	0	0	0	7	0	3	10
Civilians	2	5	41	655	1,750	712	461	562	734	4,887
Presumed subversives	9	71	109	1,226	1,721	630	781	341	404	5,292
Total	11	82	193	1,979	3,588	1,437	1,376	1,136	1,509	11,311

Victims	1989	1990	1991	1992	Total (1989–92)	Grand Total
Police	229	163	213	198	803	1,369
Armed forces	109	135	174	199	617	909
Civilians[a]	1,365	1,531	1,282	1,301	5,479	10,640
Presumed subversives	1,175	1,879	1,375	934	5,363	10,655
Total	2,877	3,745	3,044	2,633	12,299	23,610

SOURCE: DESCO, *Reporte especial* 20 (December 1992): table 1, 14.

[a] Civilian total 1989–92 includes political authorities, clergy, and foreigners.

Table 7.2. Incidents by year, 1980–1992, and by department, 1980–1987

Department	1980	1981	1982	1983	1984	1985	1986	1987	Total (1980–87)
Amazonas	0	6	2	2	1	0	2	0	13
Ancash	10	29	38	24	15	68	53	116	353
Apurimac	9	17	53	12	23	17	139	107	377
Arequipa	15	22	24	31	41	35	99	81	348
Ayacucho	48	150	323	460	655	362	354	404	2,756
Cajamarca	5	26	33	20	15	21	24	98	242
Cusco	8	75	29	32	30	68	69	47	358
Huancavelica	9	7	39	78	183	163	111	68	658
Huanuco	0	2	3	13	79	84	55	100	336
Ica	0	14	19	7	23	16	14	23	116
Junin	31	54	42	68	84	174	169	242	864
La Libertad	6	17	29	23	95	151	125	123	569
Lambayeque	12	15	25	15	21	68	66	42	264
Lima[a]	38	190	178	256	292	589	834	696	3,073
Loreto	6	11	3	3	1	18	0	11	53
Madre de Dios	0	0	1	0	1	0	0	0	2

Department	1980	1981	1982	1983	1984	1985	1986	1987	Total (1980–87)
Moquegua	1	14	2	0	1	0	1	2	21
Pasco	4	16	19	42	89	131	113	132	546
Piura	1	4	0	4	27	7	16	25	84
Puno	3	24	12	25	59	63	277	63	526
San Martín	0	0	0	4	11	8	23	5	111
Tacna	3	20	17	3	0	4	4	7	58
Tumbes	0	0	0	0	1	2	1	11	15
Ucayali	10	2	0	1	13	1	0	26	53
Total	219	715	891	1,123	1,760	2,050	2,549	2,489	11,796

	1988	1989	1990	1991	1992	Total (1988–92)
Total	2,792	2,113	2,779	2,144	1,956	11,784

Grand total for 1980–92 is 23,580.

SOURCES: 1980–87, DESCO, *Violencia política en el Perú*, vol. 1, table 2, 28; 1988–92, DESCO, *Reporte especial* 20 (December 1992): tables 1 and 2, 14.

[a]Lima incidents as a percentage of total: 1987 (the year before Guzmán's speech), 28 percent; 1988 (the year of Guzmán's speech), 28 percent; 1992 (the year of Guzmán's capture and after the urban campaign signaled in 1988 was well under way), 51 percent.

Table 7.3.   Total deaths per 100 incidents by year, 1980–1992

	No. per 100
1980	5
1981	11
1982	22
1983	176
1984	204
1985	70
1986	54
1987	46
1988	54
1989	136
1990	135
1991	142
1992	135
1980–92 average	92

SOURCE: Data in tables 7.1 and 7.2.

Table 7.4.   Police and armed forces deaths and presumed subversives deaths as a percentage of total deaths, 1980–1992.

	Police & Armed Forces (% of Total)	Presumed Subversives (% of Total)
1980	0	82
1981	7	87
1982	17	56
1983	3	62
1984	2	48
1985	5	44
1986	9	57
1987	17	30
1988	19	27
1989	12	41
1990	8	50
1991	13	45
1992	15	35
Average	10	51

1980–92 average: 61%.

SOURCE: Data in table 7.2.

vert" changes personal behavior and feels much better about himself or herself. It can also be an alternative to activity in a more moderate Marxist party or union, which Shining Path leaders view as a violation of radical orthodoxy because these parties or unions stoop to participating in what SL militants believe is a totally corrupt system. The myth of invincibility and of the inevitability of eventual triumph that SL training and flyers espouse appeals to an idealistic youth's inclination to self-sacrifice for the larger and longer cause. Purity is achieved and maintained by aloofness, discipline, intense training, spartan living, following the lead of the superior, and putting the movement ahead of self. Ideology is inculcated through the "popular schools" or through militant teachers trained at the University of Huamanga while the education program was under Sendero influence, teachers who are now working in other teacher-training programs or in public schools.

Another factor explaining Shining Path's continued destructive capacity is the array of popular fronts and organizations designed to support and publicize Sendero activities at the grass roots or to defend, protect, and help militants or family members. Sympathizers may become involved in one of several organizations: the Laborers and Workers Class Movement (MOTC), the Popular Peasants Movement (MCP), the Shanty Town Movement (MPJ), or the Women's Popular Movement (MFP), among others, all within the overarching People's Revolutionary Defense Movement (MDRP).[47] Perhaps the most important support organization is Popular Aid of Peru, which includes a number of groups—such as the Association of Democratic Lawyers and the Prisoners' Aid Committee—to provide medical and legal assistance, food, housing, transportation, and financial support.[48]

From among the most able of these activist Sendero sympathizers can come the replacements for the premilitant and militant cells of the party. A third important factor, then, is that a recruitment hierarchy begun with this group of legal (until 1988) organizations at the base has been capable so far of keeping a flow into the clandestine cell structure and so on up the ladder to the top. This is essential for Sendero, given the death or capture by authorities, through the first months of 1993, of at least fifteen of the nineteen members of the Central Committee and four of the five members of Sendero's politburo, as well as the capture—in the aftermath of the September 1992 Guzmán roundup—of about eighty

47. Tarazona-Sevillano, *Narcoterrorism*, 63; from documents seized in the apartment of Sendero leader Roger Valle Travesano in late 1987.

48. Ibid., 62–67. These groups have been illegal only since December 1988, when legislation was passed making support of terrorist organizations a crime.

leaders tied to Sendero's central command, between one hundred and two hundred zonal command leaders, and about one thousand members of the base forces (premilitants who are not party members).[49] Although the repeated prediction by President Fujimori that Sendero will be "wiped out" by the end of 1995 is widely viewed as a combination of hyperbole and wishful thinking, the organization's 1992 and early 1993 losses were heavy blows from which it will take some time to recover. Specialists, in fact, believe that Sendero will be unable to regain the macabre guerrilla stature or the momentum it had before the capture of Guzmán and a dozen key associates on 12 September 1992.[50]

In the past, however, similar major reverses for Sendero have produced only a relatively brief lull in guerrilla activities. One was the June 1986 uprising of Sendero prisoners in three Lima prisons, which resulted in 279 rebel casualties, one hundred of them after surrendering. Yet the last four months of 1986 witnessed some of the most violent Sendero attacks up to that point in their people's war. Another involved the aftermath of captures of important figures in 1988 and 1989. Osmán Morote Barrionuevo, believed to be a member of the National Central committee of Sendero and number two or three in the organization at the time, was captured in June 1988. During 1989 the third in command in Shining Path's Primary Region, David Orosco Tello, was reported killed in Apurímac as was Alfonso Manzoni Castilla, considered Sendero's number one military leader in the Northern Region. In addition, Samuel Vidal Espinoza, tenth in Shining Path's hierarchy, and eight members of Lima's Metropolitan Regional Committee were believed to have been captured in August and September.[51] Even so, Sendero came back with a vengeance in 1990, producing the most violent and most incident-filled year in the war's thirteen-year trajectory through 1992.

Given the past capacity of Shining Path's recruitment and advancement process to replace losses and come back stronger than before, the cadre and leadership deaths and captures of 1992 and early 1993 may also prove to be only temporary. The big difference this time is that the top leader was one of those captured, and most believe that his preeminent role since the founding of Sendero makes him truly irreplaceable.[52]

49. According to *Sí* (Lima weekly), 17 May 1993.

50. This was the conclusion of most of the attendees at the Seminario Internacional sobre Violencia Política en el Perú, Lima, 12–14 July 1993, sponsored by the Centro Peruano de Estudios Sociales (CEPES), the IEP, and the North-South Center of the University of Miami. However, *Perú Paz* (Lima: Constitución y Sociedad), reports that terrorist incidents in Peru over the first seven months of 1993 (January–July) totaled 890, a 15 percent increase over the same period in 1992 (775).

51. FBIS, *Daily Report: Latin America*, 12 June 1989, 40; 28 June 1989, 65; 4 August 1989, 3a; and 13 September 1989, 42.

52. See Gorriti, "Shining Path's Stalin and Trotsky."

A fourth factor helping to explain why Sendero was able to sustain its violent momentum through 1992, in spite of government pressure, is the large number of women involved at all levels of the organization, right up to the top positions in both the regional commands and the National Central Committee. Sendero's MFP was formed in 1975. During the early 1980s all the known secretaries of the Lima Metropolitan Committee were women, along with at least half of the leadership of the other regional committees.[53] Large numbers of women participate in Sendero's major military operations, and a woman is frequently charged with responsibility for delivering the fatal shot in the assassination-squad operations.[54] In 1987 alone, 491 women of the 790 captured were charged with "terrorist crimes."[55] It is speculated that women overcome the subordinate role and status historically ascribed to them in Peruvian society when they participate as equals in the Shining Path apparatus and lead many of its initiatives. Augusta la Torre of Ayacucho, the wife of Abimael Guzmán until her death in 1988, was a major force in Sendero and a member of its Central Committee.[56]

A fifth factor relates to the conscious effort by Sendero to recruit very young people for the organization. Militants in rural areas are often only fourteen or fifteen years old. The youth are perceived by the leadership as more idealistic and more easily formed. Without the outside commitments and experiences of their elders, they are also more easily and more completely committed to the Shining Path cause. Sendero thus secures strong and unquestioning supporters by attracting and educating them while their personal perceptions and values are still in flux. Older people are considered to be much harder to work with, less predictable in their commitment to the organization, and less trustworthy.[57] Today's fifteen-year-old militant, if he or she survives, will be tomorrow's twenty-two-year-old commander, organizer, or leader.

A sixth significant factor in Sendero's ability to maintain and even expand its activities, in spite of strong countermeasures by the military and police, has been leadership. In Guzmán, the Communist Party of Peru had from 1963 until 1992 a very special combination of intellectual and tactical ability. The image projected was that of an aloof but charismatic individual of remarkable powers of comprehension, interpretation,

53. Gabriela Tarazona-Sevillano, "Sendero Luminoso and the Threat of Narcoterrorism" (draft manuscript), 91G n. 10, and Anderson, *A New Revolutionary Model?* 32.
54. Tarazona-Sevillano, *Narcoterrorism*, 77.
55. José Gonzales, "Sendero de mujeres," *Sí*, 6 April 1987, 83.
56. Ibid., 85.
57. From an interview of Abimael Guzmán Reynoso by Luis Arce Borja and Janet Talavera Sánchez, in *El Diario* (Lima weekly), 24 July 1988, 36.

and capacity for prediction, totally sure of himself and of the rightness of the cause.[58] His analysis of Peru and the revolution is considered by his colleagues to be the equal of the great Marxist leaders, Marx, Lenin, and Mao, and thus worthy of elevation as "the fourth sword of Marxism."

Dramatic symbolic actions, such as simultaneously blacking out Lima and raising a huge hammer and sickle on a hill overlooking the city to commemorate President Gonzalo's birthday on 3 December, gave Sendero and its leader a larger-than-life appeal. Total withdrawal from public view for more than ten years, until a dramatic one-time interview in July 1988 with a sympathetic Lima weekly, El Diario, added to the mystery and the mystique.[59] What impressed many observers of Sendero's development in Peru was the total dedication of members to the leader. Also notable has been the apparent tactical flexibility of Shining Path, even with rigorous insistence on the consistent interpretation and application of orthodox ideological principles. This is usually attributed to the capacity of President Gonzalo and the quality of key lieutenants. That is why his capture on 12 September 1992, along with several of the key subordinates, was considered to be such a significant blow against Shining Path and the single most successful action carried out by the Peru government to date in its counterinsurgency struggle.

A seventh factor strengthening Shining Path's capacity to sustain and expand operations has been its access since the mid-1980s to a portion of the significant resources generated by coca and cocaine paste production and trafficking, largely in Peru's upper Huallaga valley. Though not conclusively proved, it is believed that Sendero garnered a minimum of $10 million a year (some estimates range as high as $100 million) between 1987 and 1992 from "taxes" on a large portion of the valley's 80,000 coca growers and from levies of up to $15,000 a flight on the mostly Colombian traffickers as they landed on the scores of clandestine runways in the valley to pick up their cargoes of cocaine paste. Many analysts have concluded that this income is used to pay salaries to Sendero militants, provide financial support to families of cadre killed in combat, and to pay for arrested comrades' jail maintenance and legal fees for court trials.[60]

Major external factors contributing to Sendero's ability to maintain its organizational capacity and militant activities include rapidly expanding university and secondary school education in Peru, combined with a

58. Even for those who claimed Guzmán was dead, a widespread view in the mid-1980s, the effect was the same.

59. Entitled, "La entrevista del siglo: El Presidente Gonzalo rompe el silencio," 2–48.

60. See David Scott Palmer, "Peru, the Drug Business, and Shining Path: Between Scylla and Charybdis?" Journal of Interamerican Studies and World Affairs 34, no. 3 (1992): 69–70, and sources cited there.

progressive erosion in economic opportunities.[61] In 1960 Peru had eight universities with 30,000 students. There were 10,000 unsuccessful candidates for entry that year. During the following decade an average of 6 percent of the government's budget went to university education. By 1970 there were twenty-nine universities, with 109,000 students and 41,000 unsuccessful candidates. As of 1980 the proportion of central-government budget devoted to university education had declined to 3.8 percent. In 1988 there were forty-seven universities in Peru, with an estimated total of 430,000 students and 260,000 unsuccessful candidates. By 1985 only 1.8 percent of government expenditures went to universities. Not only were some universities centers of radical activism and the objects of renewed attention by Sendero organizers in the late 1980s, they also found fertile recruiting grounds among those unable to enter. Furthermore, the quality of education offered in public universities deteriorated markedly, making graduates much less attractive to prospective employers.

In addition, overall employment opportunities for university graduates have been bleak largely because there has been net economic decline reported for Peru in fourteen of the eighteen years, 1975 through 1992 (after twenty-five years of virtually unbroken economic growth). The situation has worsened markedly since late 1987. Total economic activity was reduced by close to 50 percent between 1988 and 1992. Furthermore, inflation accelerated to historic highs—1,722 percent in 1988, 2,706 percent in 1989, and 7,650 percent in 1990—before being brought under control during the Fujimori government—139 percent in 1991 and 55 percent in 1992.[62] With economic problems continuing and university graduates increasing, the potential for mounting difficulties for Peru in the early 1990s at various levels was obvious. Economic opportunities in the formal economy were harder to come by (net economic growth was −1.3 percent in 1991 and −6.5 percent in 1992, and estimates of unemployment and underemployment combined increased from about 50 percent in the early 1980s to some 80 percent a decade later). Sectors of the population found their standards of living eroding (during the 1980s average real wages declined by about 35 percent). Many survived only by working in the informal economy, with low wages and no benefits, but also no taxes. Estimated to account for 40 percent of economic activity in Peru as of the mid-1980s, this sector is believed to have expanded

61. The following information is taken from Comisión Especial del Senado sobre las Causes de la Violencia y Alternativas de Pacificación en el Perú, *Violencia y pacificación* (Lima: DESCO and the Comisión Andina de Juristas, 1989), 200–201.
62. The 1988–92 inflation figures are those of Peru's INE.

considerably since as a survival mechanism for the fourteen million Peruvians (of a total population of twenty-two million) believed to live below a very conservatively drawn poverty line as of 1992.[63] Another option was the radical alternative offered by Sendero, which had a certain appeal—employment, restoration of self-respect, a coherent, fully defined belief system, and specific solutions to Peru's current problems.

Guzmán's 1988 Interview

The extended July 1988 interview of President Gonzalo, Guzmán's only public pronouncement until after his 1992 capture, when he was allowed to give a brief statement to reporters from a specially constructed "cage," sheds some light on the nature, conduct, and goals of the organization.[64] One major feature is the centrality of ideology as the guide to Sendero's Peruvian revolution. References are repeatedly made to the ideologies of "Marx-Lenin-Mao, principally Mao, Gonzalo thought."[65] Marx is heralded for his insights into the class struggle and scientific socialism; Lenin, for his contribution to understanding imperialism and the importance of revolutionary leadership; Mao, for emphasizing the role of the peasantry, the road to power from the countryside to the city, the length of the struggle, and the strategies for wearing down the enemy; and Gonzalo thought (with explicit acknowledgment of Mariátegui's contributions), for applying the general revolutionary principles to the specific circumstances of Peru. Although the general ideological tenets are fixed and immutable, as befits a "scientific" explanation of history, strategic flexibility in actions can be derived from the insights of Gonzalo thought for the revolution in Peru.

Sendero's commitment to ideology as a guide for action pervades the interview. Guzmán argues that the revolution could not succeed without it and that the failure to follow Marxist ideology faithfully explains why other parties in Peru as well as Marxist governments in other countries are hopelessly revisionist and doomed to failure (correctly anticipating the 1990 collapse in Eastern Europe and the Soviet Union). Adherence

63. Peru's informal economy is the subject of Hernando de Soto's pathbreaking work, *El otro sendero* (Lima: Instituto Libertad y Democracia, 1986). The estimate of the population below the poverty line was calculated by DESCO analysts after President Fujimori's August 1990 economic shock program and presented in September and October 1990 issues of one of that organization's publications, *Resumen Semanal*.

64. The following discussion and analysis are derived from the published text of the interview in *El Diario* cited above in notes 57 and 59.

65. A phrase noted repeatedly in the interview.

to ideology guides the party leadership in organizing the peasantry, in preparing the cadres, in pursuing specific actions against the government and in not pursuing others, and in preparing for the moment of urban insurrection. The guide of ideology, "principally Maoist," notes that a strong class alliance must be forged between the peasants and the working class for the revolution to succeed and that the revolution must be led by the working class.[66] Guzmán recognizes in the interview that the party does not yet have working-class militants in sufficient numbers to meet this requirement, suggesting that the party will begin to concentrate more in the cities.

Revisionism is viewed as the major problem both for international Communism and for the revolution in Peru because it denies the class struggle and the inevitable collapse of imperialism, as well as the key role of strong leadership by claiming "cult of personality." By being willing to participate in parlimentary politics and to accept nonviolent solutions, revisionists enable capitalism to be reestablished, and they divide the workers, their parties, and their organizations. "Revisionism is a cancer that must be totally removed in order to advance the revolution."[67]

Revisionism is also a problem for the party (PCP) and must be constantly recognized and extirpated because the struggle is lost the moment its leaders abandon their principles. The Peruvian Marxist revisionists have already done this, which the working class is beginning to recognize. "The rest [i.e., gaining their loyalty in the PCP] is a matter of time."[68] Because the party itself (the PCP) is a contradiction according to the law of contradiction, it is necessary to follow the dialectical struggle of two views within the organization itself, with the objective of ensuring that the "red line" always emerges triumphant. So constant purification within, through the mechanisms of plenary sessions and party congresses, is as necessary as maintaining the correct line without. Strong leadership is crucial to accomplishing these objectives, since "all revolutions generate leaders . . . and here we comply with the laws of revolutions. . . . The revisionist view goes against the dictatorship and the revolutionary process in general in order to behead it."[69]

66. Scholars have pointed out the capacity of Mao to build a multiclass alliance in China against the status quo and note that this has been a major difference between the revolution in Peru and that in China. See, for example, Colin J. Harding, "Antonio Díaz Martínez and the Ideology of Sendero Luminoso," *Bulletin of Latin American Research* 7, no. 1 (1987): 65–73. See also Deborah Poole and Gerardo Rénique, *Peru: Time of Fear* (New York: Monthly Review Press, 1992), esp. 46–56.

67. *El Diario* interview, 6. Similarities with anti-Communist pronouncements of the Augusto Pinochet military government in Chile (1973–90) are intriguing.

68. *El Diario* interview, 8.

69. Ibid., 11.

From various observations made by Guzmán in the 1988 interview it is clear that he did not see victory in the very near future. In part this is because of Sendero leadership's total commitment to ideology to provide the benchmarks that must be followed. It is also related to the recognition, as part of the ideological focus, of the special circumstances surrounding each individual revolution. Regarding the Peruvian case, Guzmán gave several reasons why the revolution will be a long and drawn out process.

1. The PCP had not yet built enough support among the proletariat: "It is one thing to be a vanguard; it is something else to be recognized as such by the workers themselves; and it will not happen overnight."[70] It was beginning to happen, Guzmán asserted, as the workers became disillusioned with the reformist parties, but there was still a great deal of work to do.

2. Popular committees "by the hundreds" and support bases were established in the countryside beginning in 1981–82 in the vacuum left by police withdrawals, and from them arose "the People's Republic of New Democracy (RPND) in formation" as well (because the military had not yet been defeated), but this had not yet occurred in the cities. There the People's Revolutionary Defense Movement (MRDP) was established, beginning in 1976, as part of the process of gaining more support for the revolution, but as yet there was no RPND.[71]

3. At some indeterminate point there will be an insurrection in the cities. It will be crucial for the PCP to capture and direct this once it has started, and to keep it from falling into the hands of the revisionists. Only then will the city, rather than the countryside, become the center of the armed struggle, and only at that point will combatants go from the countryside to the city to extend the popular war to the entire country.[72]

4. The armed struggle has three stages before victory can be achieved, and Peru's was still in the first, the "strategic defensive stage," with its guerrilla war, at the time of the interview. At some point, by expanding the popular war and getting the army to respond with its "genocidal counterinsurgency," the second stage, "strategic equilibrium," can begin (Sendero subsequently announced in May 1991, after intensive urban recruitment efforts, that this stage had begun). As the war becomes generalized and city insurrections occur, the shift is made to the "strategic offensive stage," revolution countrywide, and the establishment of the RPND.[73]

70. Ibid., 17.
71. Ibid., 16–17.
72. Ibid., 17.
73. Ibid., 20–21.

At no point in the interview was there any specific mention of the Indian or any placing of the armed struggle in ethnic terms. Peru was referred to as a country in which "peasants" dominated numerically, not Indians. The struggle was "in the countryside," not in Indian areas. The fight will go "from the countryside to the city," not from Indian to non-Indian. Class-based ideology dominated Sendero's analysis, strategy, and prescription, suggesting that the guerrilla struggle as perceived by the leadership was not oriented toward creating a new Indian state, restoring Indian values, tapping Indian messianism, or developing Indian systems of power. Guzmán's discussion was in classic Marxist class-based terms, and the projected etiology of revolution followed an exclusively class-based dynamic. The countryside is important to Sendero not because it is Indian but because it is heavily peasant and because Mao's strategy of revolution began in the countryside.

In the interview, Guzmán took particular offense to accusations that the movement was dogmatic and inflexible. His answer in part was that Gonzalo's thought integrates the specific aspects of the Peruvian case into more general Marxist ideology and gives the revolution its dynamism and flexibility. Different vanguard organizations are established in accordance with different local circumstances—from the PCP (see Fig. 7.1), to the Popular Revolutionary Army (ERP) to the RPND in formation, to the MRDP. Even the establishment of support bases in Sendero's area of greatest activity, Ayacucho, in 1981 and 1982, before the armed forces had entered the fight, illustrated to Guzmán the revolution's flexibility. He described this process as a response to an unanticipated power vacuum in the area that occurred after the police had withdrawn to the region's major population centers and before the army intervened. By the same token, the more-rapid-than-expected move to "strategic equilibrium" in 1991 occurred when Sendero leadership found that the inability of the government to respond in the cities was greater than anticipated. This explains the various announcements by Sendero spokespeople in 1991 and 1992 that generalized war and victory were imminent.

At a more general level, by following the principle of "strategic centralization and tactical decentralization,"[74] there follow necessarily different dynamics in different parts of the country. Organizationally, dividing the country into distinct regional commands reflected this principle. The expansion of Sendero presence in the coca-producing upper Huallaga valley from late 1987 onward was a dramatic case in point. Yet this flexible response occurred, Guzmán asserted, within an explicit common understanding of the more general ideological principles of the

74. Ibid., 27.

revolutionary process. This may explain why levels of incidents and deaths attributed to SL continued at high levels in the first months following Guzmán's capture, before dropping markedly in early 1993 (see Table 7.5).

Even the origin of the peoples' war responded to a specific diagnosis of the Peruvian case and the selection of the most auspicious moment for its launching. Guzmán noted that Sendero study of recent Peruvian history revealed that there had been a major political and economic crisis in the second half of every decade, with each succeeding crisis progressively more severe. The 1977–79 crisis was only the most recent at the time and was deemed the opportune moment to begin preparations for launching the armed struggle. In addition, the military regime of 1968–80, with its expansion of "bureaucratic capitalism," had ripened conditions for revolution (presumably by expanding government beyond its capacity to respond effectively, in spite of promises of substantial political, economic, and social change, which raised popular expectations only to have them frustrated).[75] Furthermore, it was concluded that "one

Table 7.5.   Incidents and deaths by month, April 1992–March 1993

	Incidents	Deaths
April	119	133
May	151	379
June	96	168
July	296	191
August	117	173
September	165	149
Six-month totals (to Guzmán capture)	924	1,193
October	119	175
November	272	254
December	167	89
January	154	157
February	72	153
March	78	79
Six-month totals (since Guzmán capture)	862	907
	(−9%)	(−24%)

SOURCE: DESCO, *Violencia política en el Perú de hoy: Reporte especial* 12–23 (April 1992–March 1993).

75. Various analyses of this process are available. See, for example, Palmer, *Revolution from Above*, 205–23, detailing the disaster of applying the agrarian reform to Ayacucho as early as 1972. A more recent review can be found in Colin Harding, "The Rise of Sendero Luminoso," in *Region and Class in Modern Peru*, ed. Rory Miller (Liverpool: University of Liverpool Press, 1987), 179–207.

and one-half to two years" after the elections and the transfer of power to civilians would be a good time to begin the peoples' war because the military would not want to engage Sendero due to their temporary exhaustion after twelve years in power, nor would the new civilian president want the military to act, "out of fear of another coup."[76]

In the interview, Guzmán also made specific note of the revolution's complete self-sufficiency, deriving what was needed from local sources. Food and sustenance came from the peasants who supported them, arms from the military and police by taking them, and dynamite from the mines and the road building crews. In this fashion the revolution did not become dependent on outside sources, with their own agendas and objectives, which might subvert the local dynamic of the revolutionary process. For the revolution to succeed, noted Guzmán, it must grow within a specific national environment in its own fashion, recognizing basic ideological principles but adapting them to local circumstances. "Only in this manner," Guzmán asserted, "can the revolution in Peru serve the cause of world revolution."[77]

The main focus of this twelve-hour interview was on the revolution and its origins, its foundations and its goals. There were also strong attacks on the Marxist "revisionists," "the principal enemy"; on the Peruvian state, "hopelessly corrupt"; and on the civilian parties, "sieves of contradictions," and "a pot full of blatherers." Guzmán commented later in the interview on the nature of the state, the New Democracy, that was to be created when the revolution was victorious. He did make note of the PCP's respect for religious beliefs, in the confidence that they would wither away as exploitation ended; of land to the tiller; the need to resolve the contradictions in the PCP; and the need to start building for socialism as soon as the revolution was victorious. The concern for purity, understood as correctly following Marxist principles, through application of the law of contradictions suggested that victory would mark a new wave of violence as merging contradictions were confronted and the correct line (the "red") emerged triumphant. However, the main purpose of the interview was not to sketch the future Sendero state but rather to analyze the dynamics of the revolution itself.[78]

76. *El Diario* interview, 18.

77. *El Diario* interview, 14. The phrase is also the title of one of Sendero's basic documents.

78. Many analysts of Sendero attribute this extraordinary, one-time interview in July 1988 to Guzmán's wish to redirect attention from the June capture in Lima of one of his organization's most important figures, Osmán Morote, and to buy time to redeploy all of Sendero's forces.

Shining Path in Action: Puno

Examples of Shining Path in action suggest some of the challenges faced in making the revolution work at the grass roots both in and beyond the original area in Ayacucho where Sendero had been active over a long period of time. Puno is one such place. Shining Path has had little success there in spite of several years of organizing efforts. Puno is a densely populated, largely agricultural highland department in southern Peru on the border with Bolivia. There are hundreds of Indian communities in the department, in predominantly Quechua- or Aymara-speaking provinces, along with former haciendas that were turned into production cooperatives during the military government's agrarian reform in the 1970s. However, this reform did not provide benefits to the residents of the communities, in spite of promises to do so and an inclusive new collective reorganization in which, theoretically, profits (but not land) were to be shared.

According to one informed account, Sendero began organizing in 1981 in two predominantly Quechua provinces of Puno, Azángaro and Melgar, with Quechua-speaking cadres from Ayacucho and Cuzco.[79] In spite of considerable peasant discontent over the failure of the agrarian reform of the 1970s to make good on its promises, Shining Path had difficulty in generating much support. This was in part because the Quechua areas of Puno were historically the most organized and the most militant and because other Marxist parties, especially Revolutionary Vanguard (VR) and various other factions that combined later into the Unified Mariátegu-ist Party (PUM), had been working there and had gained considerable support. In addition, the Catholic church in Puno was and is a major actor at the local level, especially with its initiative in the establishment of scores of community stores that provide necessities at reasonable prices. The left coalition, United Left (IU), won the first plurality in the 1983 municipal elections in the department of Puno, with 35 percent of valid votes and victories in four of nine provinces. In 1984, various left parties joined to form the PUM, which "dominated left politics in Puno"[80] and helped organize major land invasions in the area in December 1985.

Given this reality, Sendero operated in a less violent fashion in Puno than in Ayacucho in order to develop a political base; however, they did kill several mayors, beginning in 1985. Sendero also supported peasants in a number of land invasions but proved unable to protect them when

79. Lewis Taylor's "Agrarian Unrest and Political Conflict in Puno" is a detailed and lucid case study. The following discussion is drawn largely from this piece.
80. Ibid., 141.

government forces reacted. They entered a number of cooperatives and unexpropriated farms in 1986, destroying installations and distributing livestock to poorer peasants. Although these actions responded to peasant desires for access to land and reflected peasant hostility to the government cooperative program, Sendero's organizing capacity was much less than that of other parties on the Marxist Left, in part because it had been active in the region for a much shorter time.

As Sendero tried to expand its influence in Puno, a conflict is believed to have developed between the Central Committee and local organizers over how to proceed. The center pushed for violent actions against the "revisionists," while local leaders advocated a slower approach. "Patient political persuasion aside, the best way Sendero can win over [key individuals who command respect in the villages] is to promote indiscriminate state repression which would drive scores of experienced activists into clandestinity."[81] Ironically, some democratic parties in Puno provided Sendero with openings it might not otherwise have had. The centrist American Popular Revolutionary Alliance (APRA) won the 1986 municipal elections in the department with 53 percent of the valid vote, good for victories in seven of what were by then ten Puno provinces. This was largely on the coattails of APRA's 1985 national election success and the populist appeals in Puno by President Alan García through *ruminacuy*, or a mass gathering of the head of state with local leaders for an exchange of views and proposals to solve the area's problems.

However, APRA as a party in Puno was not historically strong or progressive and was quite opposed to peasant land invasions or other forms of activism. Key figures tended to be merchants or large landowners rather than peasants or workers. Repression and manipulation of the land issue by APRA against the Left and against the peasants gave Sendero opportunities to exploit the discontent. Even so, the non-Sendero Left continued its dominance of peasant revindication initiatives, including support for another wave of land invasions to accomplish what they could not get through the APRA-controlled government. In Puno, Sendero, because it has been unable to develop real bases of support among a peasantry that has other organized options available with a proven record, continues to be on the defensive. Terrorist tactics have proved counterproductive.

Shining Path in Action: Chuschi

The case of the district capital, peasant community, and market town of Chuschi, in an isolated corner of Cangallo province of the department of

81. Ibid., 145.

Ayacucho, some four hours by a rough dirt road from the department capital of the same name, illustrates yet another pattern of Sendero involvement and local population response.[82] It reflects the work of an anthropologist who has been visiting and studying the community since the late 1960s. Shining Path carried out the first action of its people's war there on 17 May 1980, followed by a concerted effort in the early 1980s to expand its influence in Chuschi and in other peasant communities along the Pampas River. SL actions that punished corrupt local officials or unfaithful husbands, tried and killed cattle thieves, and engaged in communal planting on the University of Huamanga's experimental farm of Alpachaca were greeted with considerable enthusiasm by most *comuneros*. During this period Sendero gained control of some nine communities in the Pampas River valley.

However, when Shining Path organizers abandoned community residents during a government military attack, after they had been made part of a Sendero people's army/militia (without guns), the guerrillas lost their momentum in the area. Subsequent efforts to organize communities forcibly into arrangements not related to their local production structure or activity cycle, to shut off market days (on which Chuschi had long depended), and to impose new planting procedures all failed. Support for Shining Path waned. As violence increased in the area, with the large-scale entrance of Peruvian military forces, most communities cast their lot with the government rather than with Sendero. Chuschi went so far as to request and receive in 1983 a permanent police garrison based in the community.

Shining Path failed in the Pampas River valley because it did not understand the complexities of the communities or their sense of time and space and because it tried to impose a set of procedures and controls that appeared to the *comuneros* simply to replicate the same structures of domination most were trying to escape. Sendero badly underestimated the peasants' awareness and sophistication. The peasants concluded that the government, not Shining Path, was in a better position to respond to their needs. The violence and disruption, though severe in many communities of the valley, provoked locally driven changes, such as more-educated and bilingual authorities, changes that could turn out to benefit the communities in future relations with the outside world. The rapid expansion of fundamentalist Protestant churches in the neighboring communities of Chuschi and Quispillacta may also have served to

82. This summary is drawn from Palmer, *Shining Path of Peru*, 5–6. It is based on the study in the same volume by Billy Jean Isbell, "Shining Path and Peasant Responses in Rural Ayacucho," 59–82.

draw significant portions of the communities' residents toward religious solutions to their problems other than the religion of violence of Shining Path.

Shining Path in Action: Andahuaylas

The case of Andahuaylas, a province in the rural, predominantly Quechua-speaking Indian department of Apurímac in the south-central highlands, is again quite different. As observed and analyzed by an American anthropologist in 1981–82 and 1985,[83] Sendero demonstrated its capacity to engage in guerrilla activities and to intimidate local populations but did not show it could organize rural areas into anything resembling a support base. This was the case even though this region did not have the high historic levels of military presence or long-standing mainstream Marxist organizations as did Puno. "In spite of its ability to attract sympathy and support among parts of the peasantry, it is highly unlikely that Sendero will be able to . . . control large areas of the Andes for long periods of time."[84]

In Andahuaylas, massive land invasions in 1974 by peasants organized by Revolutionary Vanguard (VR), led by Julio César Mezzich (who joined SL in the early 1980s), were met by military-government repression and the retaking of the lands to form government-run agricultural cooperatives. As in other parts of the Indian highlands, the cooperatives suffered from a lack of good administrative talent and funding from the center. Credit was given to some of the cooperatives and a small number of wealthier farmers rather than to the peasant communities. While the old haciendas disappeared, relatively few benefited; efforts at peaceful resolution from below by land invasions and occupations were repressed by the center in favor of their own solution.

Sendero succeeded in entering a number of villages and communities in Andahuaylas, in forcing a temporary withdrawal of police, and in killing a number of wealthier peasants and administrative officials. However, they did not establish any organization that could be sustained on a long-term basis. Shining Path cadres attacked cooperatives and other state enterprises, destroying their productive capacity and forcing government agents to withdraw. They also succeeded in getting residents of one community to organize to attack another, using to their advantage historic tensions and hostilities between the settlements of the area.

83. Ronald H. Berg, "Peasant Responses to Shining Path in Andahuaylas," in *Shining Path of Peru*, ed. Palmer, 83–104. The following discussion is drawn largely from this study.
84. Ibid., 103.

Government response tended to be repressive; "the police arrested and interrogated blindly, the numbers of 'disappeared' increased rapidly, and those whose relatives were taken away were left with great bitterness."[85]

Although Sendero may have failed to organize support bases in this part of the province, they did succeed by their terrorist tactics in both limiting the role of local representative government and in provoking a repressive central-government response that further antagonized and alienated the peasantry. This was the reaction Shining Path sought at that stage of their revolution. High levels of abstention, as well as blank and spoiled ballots (56 percent of registered voters, third highest in the country), in the 1986 municipal elections in Apurímac department, of which Andahuaylas is a province, suggested that Sendero's strategy was working.[86]

Shining Path's Impact on Voting: The 1986 Municipal Elections

A review of the levels of incidents and deaths in Peru's departments in 1986 in light of the 1986 municipal election results reveals a significant correlation between these incidents and the levels of abstention and void and blank ballots (.57, when the extreme cases of Tumbes [small percentage of voters], Madre de Dios [also small percentage of voters], and Lima [easier access to polls and more police protection] are removed).[87] This suggests that Sendero's strategy of intimidation by terrorist actions does have some effect on citizen voting. In departments where incidents and deaths are higher, more registered voters tend not to vote or, if they do, to deposit blank or spoiled ballots.

Five of the eight departments of Peru that had more than one hundred incidents and deaths attributable to political violence in 1986 also were among the eight highest in levels of void and blank ballots and not voting in the 1986 municipal elections (in order, Ayacucho, Huancavelica, Apurímac, La Libertad, and Pasco). Lima, Junín, and Puno were not. Lima was the lowest, explained perhaps by its large and relatively more sophisticated urban population, easier access to polling places, and relatively greater police protection, in spite of having the highest number

---

85. Ibid., 98.

86. Fernando Tuesta Soldevilla, *Perú político en cifras* (Lima: Fundación Friedrich Ebert, 1987), table 5.3, 193.

87. This figure was calculated using Spearman rank-order correlations, which were significant at the .05 level. Basic electoral data, standardized for population size (based on percentage of registered voters), is from Soldevilla, *Perú político en cifras*, table 5.2, 192, and DESCO, *Violencia política*, vol. 1, table 2, 28.

of incidents and deaths in 1986. Both Junín and Puno had fairly high levels of support for the IU in the 1986 municipal elections (seventh and tenth of twenty-three departments included), and Lima was among the highest in IU voting (second).

Sendero head Abimael Guzmán's observation that the "revisionists" (i.e., Marxist left parties participating in the political process) "are the revolution's greatest enemies" seems to be borne out by the information on voting support for the Left department by department for the country as a whole. There is a significant inverse correlation between the vote for IU in the 1986 municipal elections and political violence levels that year when the extreme cases of Apurímac (high incidence and high IU vote), Loreto (low incidence and low IU vote), and Puno (high incidence, high IU vote) are removed (.48).[88] For Peru as a whole, then, where the IU vote is stronger at the municipal level, Sendero tends to be weaker in terms of incidents and deaths. The Left's breakup in 1989, after IU had appeared just a few months earlier to be the leading challenger in the 1990 elections, both deprived Peru of an organized-political-party alternative to the failed policies of the García government and gave Shining Path new opportunities and openings at the local level, where IU had represented a major obstacle.[89]

Government Responses to Shining Path, 1980–1992

The government's response to the challenge of political violence and terrorism begun by Sendero but since undertaken by other groups as well has taken various forms since 1980. The larger political, social, and economic context for the government's antiguerrilla and antiterrorist actions includes the routinization of the electoral process at the national and local levels, until President Fujimori's surprise self-coup (*autogolpe*) on 5 April 1992, with voting for presidential and congressional candidates every five years since 1980 and municipal elections nationwide every three years. Suffrage is universal, and parties across the political spectrum from left to right have participated and won at one level or another. The center-right AP of Fernando Belaúnde Terry was the overall winner in both 1980 elections, the left coalition IU in 1983, the center-left APRA led by Alan García in 1985 and 1986, the coalition of right-leaning parties in the Democratic Front (FREDEMO) in 1989. The independent Alberto Fujimori won in 1990 (but without a congressional majority); a coalition

88. See note 87.
89. For additional discussion, see Sandra Woy-Hazleton and William A. Hazleton, "Shining Path and the Marxist Left," in *Shining Path of Peru*, ed. Palmer, 207–24.

favoring Fujimori achieved a majority in the special Constitutional Congress elections of November 1992; and a variety of independents not associated with Fujimori dominated the January 1993 municipal elections.

Both the Belaúnde and the García presidencies began auspiciously; economic growth characterized the first two years, followed by decline and crisis. Public support for the incumbent has followed the same pattern; the public turns to some other political alternative in each successive election. The Fujimori presidency followed a different course—drastic shock measures at the outset, which stemmed the economic hemorrhaging but did not generate net economic growth over the first half of his term. However, popular support remained quite high, and actually increased after the *autogolpe*. Political violence and terrorism have also tended to expand over time, adding to the suffering already experienced by the progressive erosion of economic opportunities. Migration to the cities and emigration to new countries were among the escapes sought by hundreds of thousands of citizens over the decade. Lima added well over a million migrants to its population in the 1980s; internal refugees totaled at least 200,000 by 1991; and emigration from Peru between 1985 and 1991 was estimated at over 400,000.[90]

The Belaúnde Administration

The elected civilian governments have responded to the guerrilla terrorist threat in different ways over these years. Initially the new elected government did not take the Sendero people's war very seriously. President Belaúnde (1980–85) was more concerned with getting democracy going again after the twelve-year military regime than he was with a small group active in an isolated rural area, whose members he repeatedly characterized as "bandits and cattle rustlers." In actual fact, from the first year of Sendero's declaration of the "people's war," incidents of political violence and terrorism occurred in a majority of departments of the country[91] (see Table 7.2). In addition, as early as

90. Robin Kirk, *The Decade of Chaqwa: Peru's Internal Refugees* (Washington, D.C.: U.S. Committee for Refugees, May 1991), 3, and Teófilo Altamirano, *Exodo: Peruanos en el exterior* (Lima: Pontificia Universidad Católica del Perú, Fondo Editorial, 1992), 73.

91. Since Shining Path often neither acknowledged nor took credit for specific actions, an indeterminate number were probably committed by others. In 1988 and 1989, the Rodrigo Franco Front (a counterterrorist action group believed to be sponsored by the then government party APRA) and the Tupac Amaru Revolutionary Movement (MRTA) claimed responsibility for about 20 percent of the incidents recorded. Sendero has claimed in internal documents a total number of actions about fifteen times greater than those reported in the newspapers and compiled by DESCO.

1981 there were more such incidents in Lima than in Ayacucho, although levels on a per capita basis were always much higher year after year in Ayacucho.

But President Belaúnde had other concerns. As part of the widespread popular enthusiasm for democratic rule, the new elected civilian government had the problem of dealing with pent-up political demands released after twelve years of military rule. These pressures militated for economic incentives to coax elites to return and invest, for renewed recourse to foreign loans for an array of new projects, and for shifting a number of programs and priorities of the former regime. The return to democracy, as Belaúnde viewed it, required that he respond to these expressed needs and demands, rather than thwart or repress them, in order to show how civilian rule was better than military government.

Sendero's call for revolution at this very moment did not fit the image of a civilian, democratic Peru. So it was ignored for as long as possible. When finally responded to, military force was the principal instrument used. Furthermore, the president repeatedly asserted that Shining Path had foreign support and advisors, even that it was directed from abroad. Such assertions, though not true, reinforced the perspective of a full-bodied democracy returning to Peru, with Sendero an isolated and insignificant entity.

Increasing numbers of incidents in Ayacucho in 1981, including the first killings of small landowners and prominent citizens, forced the Belaúnde government to declare a state of emergency in several provinces in Ayacucho in October. Some constitutional guarantees related to arrest, search, assembly, and freedom of movement were suspended so that authorities could deal with the problem, but civilians remained in charge. Units of specially trained police, the *sinchis*, rather than military forces, were sent in to clean things up. The *sinchis* only made matters worse by acts of indiscriminate violence, insensitivity to local needs, and regular late-night wanton behavior, making many Ayacuchans fear the *sinchis* more than Sendero. They were eventually withdrawn after strong local public protests, even though the smaller and more-isolated police stations in the Ayacucho hinterland were being subjected to increasing attacks.

For most of 1982 Sendero added to its arsenal by overrunning police posts, first the smallest and most isolated, then larger ones, killing one or two and taking uniforms, weapons, and munitions. The police responded by withdrawing to better-fortified larger stations in the largest population centers. For all intents and purposes, central-government authority gave up the Ayacucho countryside to Shining Path in 1981 and

1982.[92] Sendero used this unexpected opportunity to build support bases and the popular infrastructure it anticipated for its New Democracy.

In March 1982 Sendero conducted its first large-scale urban operation, in the city of Ayacucho; an estimated 150 armed cadres attacked the prison, killed the guards, and freed all the prisoners, including over fifty SL militants. It was a humiliating defeat for the government, all the more so because good intelligence was received that the attack was to occur and reinforcements of the Republican Guard (the police force with responsibility for Peru's prisons) had been sent up from Lima. The local commander did not take the intelligence seriously, so only four guards were on duty at the prison when the attack came. The reinforcements were asleep in the police barracks a dozen blocks away, where they were completely pinned down by a supplementary Sendero force. In a single night, Shining Path demonstrated to the region and the entire country its military and tactical capacity.[93]

In the aftermath, Sendero undertook a vigorous critique of all aspects of the operation, purged some elements, and reorganized its whole approach. All this happened when by any outside standard their attack had been extremely successful. As for the government, the offending commander was transferred to Lima, given a big farewell party by his Ayacucho colleagues, and eventually promoted.[94]

The central government was provoked to action by several blackouts of Lima (beginning in October and culminating with one in December scheduled to commemorate "Comrade Gonzalo's" birthday, in which a massive hammer and sickle glowed in the darkness on a hill overlooking the city). The blackouts were caused by destroying strategic transmission-line towers in the highlands (about 60 percent of Lima's power is generated by the Mantaro River tunnel turbines and transported via towers over the mountains to the coast). During the last week in December, five provinces in Ayacucho (soon expanded to seven to include one each in neighboring Huancavelica and Apurímac) were declared to be an emergency zone and were put under military control.

There followed over a year of forceful counterattacks on Sendero in this highland area, with multiple consequences. The guerrillas' organization in the region was very much disrupted, especially at the level of base communities. However, there were many examples of largely

92. See the detailed and gripping account of Sendero activity during this period in the Huancasancos-Lucanamarca area of Víctor Fajardo province in Raymond Bonner, "Peru's War," *New Yorker*, 4 January 1988, 31–58.

93. Gorriti, *Sendero*, vol. 1, ch. 14, 253–66.

94. For this case and many other insights about Shining Path, I am very much indebted to Gustavo Gorriti.

mestizo military abuses of the local, largely Indian population. Political-violence casualties skyrocketed in 1983 and 1984 (see Table 7.1). Sendero began to operate more extensively in other parts of the country and eventually modified its restricted exclusionary stand on membership to begin recruiting again in Lima universities and to work more actively with front groups and more publicly.

The government's response was mostly a military and a repressive one, illustrated by the ratio of thirty-nine civilian and presumed terrorist casualties in these two years for each military or police death (see Table 7.1). In spite of promises to combine military actions with economic aid, the government was not very forthcoming in practice. General Adrian Huamán, a Quechua-speaking Apurímac native who became chief of the Ayacucho area emergency zone in 1984, protested repeatedly that he was not able to win the war against the guerrillas there because the economic assistance he had been promised still had not arrived. After going public with his concerns, he was almost immediately removed from his post.

Sendero's efforts to expand into the upper Huallaga valley in 1984–85 were not very successful, unlike its attempt in the late 1980s. This was in part due to a successful military response that concentrated on the guerrilla problem and left the coca growers and drug traffickers alone. Shining Path got little support from the local population as a result; the Tupac Amaru Revolutionary Movement (MRTA), just starting out there, did not do much better. So the central government's efforts to deal with the growing guerrilla/terrorist problems were successful in some areas.

The García Administration

The Alan García Pérez administration (1985–90) at first took a different approach to the problem of political violence. Young, dynamic, and enthusiastic, García led his revitalized party, APRA, to its first ever presidential victory after it had rediscovered its nationalistic reformist roots in the early 1980s. Asserting the distinctive contribution that he planned to make during his term regarding the problem of terrorism and political violence, García emphasized respect for human rights by the military and police forces, an anticorruption campaign, a peace commission open to dialogue and the search for conflict resolution, administrative and fiscal decentralization, economic aid, and agricultural development by improved prices and increased farm credit. The "Andean Trapezoid," or highland region encompassing Peru's poorest and most-Indian provinces, was singled out for special attention. The APRA administration started with high hopes and took a number of concrete steps to accomplish its objective of ending political violence in Peru. In 1985 and 1986 there were measurable advances on the three major fronts of military and police purification, organized initiatives for peace, and economic progress. Hundreds of military and police officers and enlisted personnel considered to have possibly been corrupted by the drug-trafficking problem, affected by Sendero ideology, or involved in human rights violations were removed from their posts, transferred, or retired. The Peace Commission was established and began to explore alternatives for ending the violence. Several hundred million dollars were made available to fund the agricultural development plans and the reconstruction of damaged rural infrastructure, with almost immediate results as measured by improved agricultural production and farm income.

Sendero responded in 1985 with a sharp increase in incidents in departments outside its original base in Ayacucho, Huancavelica, and Apurímac, particularly in Lima, Junín, Pasco, Ancash, and Lambayeque (see Table 7.2), and with the assassination of a few APRA and government officials. The meeting in Lima in June 1986 of the Socialist International was to have been the launching pad for President García's bid to become a major Third World spokesperson. These aspirations were dealt a severe blow when Sendero launched a number of attacks, including an abortive assassination attempt on García himself, as the conference was taking place. The youthful president's fate was sealed, however, at least within the Socialist International arena, when Shining Path prisoners revolted in three Lima prisons and were brutally repressed. García and his cabinet apparently gave the military orders to do what they had to do to quell the revolt.[95]

The prison revolt and government response in mid-1986 marked the beginning of a second phase in the García administration with regard to antiguerrilla policy—repression and recentralization. A major bureaucratic struggle played itself out over the consolidation of eight different intelligence services of different military and civilian government agencies. A perceived gap between information gathered on terrorist activities by the agencies and its use was held responsible for often preventing an effective response. The agencies were eventually joined in the National Agency Against Terrorism (DINCOTE). A similar struggle over merging the three traditional military branches of army, navy, and air force finally produced the Ministry of Defense. One fear expressed by the services was that consolidation at the cabinet level would give the military less influence over policy issues. In practice, such fears did not

95. Sandra Woy Hazleton, "Peru," *Yearbook of International Communist Affairs, 1986* (Stanford: Hoover Institution Press, 1987), 134.

materialize. However, it cannot be determined with precision how many of the occasions marking government success against Sendero can be attributed to either the unification of intelligence services or the establishment of a single military ministry. Nevertheless, the government has appeared to have greater success against Sendero since these changes than before—the painstaking police intelligence work leading to the capture of Guzmán and some three hundred mid- and upper-level SL cadres in late 1992, as well as the virtual dismembering of MRTA, dramatically demonstrates increased central-government counterinsurgency capacity.

There is also ample evidence of growing frustration among the authorities with the intractability of the insurgency, and of a substantial increase in human rights violations believed to have been committed by government personnel during the latter half of García's term (see Table 7.6). Deaths of police and military personnel also increased substantially in 1987 and 1988 in a context of growing casualties of political violence. Incidents declined, but deaths rose dramatically in 1989, particularly in the category of "presumed terrorists." Fewer prisoners were taken, and reports of disappearances and other human rights violations increased more than tenfold between the first two and the last two years of the

Table 7.6. Reports of disappearances, by year

	State Dept.	Public Ministry
1980	0	—
1981	0	9
1982	1	9
1983	160	766
1984	661 (includes 1983)	951
1985	180 (through August)	529
1986	175 (through October)	385
1987	200	115
1988	280	
1989	404	
1990	302	
1991	279	
1992	145	

SOURCES: Department of State, *Country Reports on Human Rights Practices*, annual; Ministerio Público, as compiled in INE, *Indicadores sociales*, table 5.28, 96.

NOTE: Peru's Ministry reported a total of "close to" five thousand cases of disappearances 1983–90, whereas the State Department total is less than half that figure through 1992. This suggests both the difficulty of getting very accurate figures and the different criteria used to determine the disappeared. The State Department reports only "new" cases brought forward in a given year; Public Ministry figures are less precise, at least before 1987.

García administration.[96] Agricultural credits and other forms of rural assistance had to be cut sharply in 1988–89 due to the government's escalating economic travails; at the same time, the number of provinces declared to be in the emergency zones increased from thirty-five to eighty-one (see Table 7.7). This implied a de facto expansion of military control over a significant proportion of Peru's population, complete with curfews and the curtailing of normal activities.

This occurred in the larger context of an insurgent movement that appeared to be growing, with more operations being carried out and its influence being expanded more openly and on its own terms to new areas. Confidence in the government began to erode as economic difficulties mounted. One of the most dramatic successes of Shining Path during this period was its expansion once again into the upper Huallaga valley. This began in late 1987 with clashes with the MRTA, temporarily driven out of most of the valley in 1988. Shining Path consolidated its position during that year, forcing the government out in many places and, starting in November and December 1988, inviting journalists to witness the degree of operating control and apparent support of the local popula-

Table 7.7.   Provinces declared in states of emergency by year

	No. of Provinces
1980	0
1981	5
1982	14
1983	24 plus entire country 5/30–9/9
1984	26 plus entire country from 3/20–9/3 and 11/27–30
1985	20
1986	24
1987	36
1988	44
1989	71
1990	90
1991	50 plus parts of 11 others
1992	62

SOURCES: 1980–84, from Piedad Pareja Pflücker and Eric Torres Montes, *Municipios y terrorismo* (Lima: Centro de Estudios Peruanos, 1989), appendix 6, 102–5; 1985–91, from Department of State, *Country Reports on Human Rights Practices*, annual report submitted to Congress and published each February in Washington, D.C., by the U.S. Government Printing Office. 1992 estimated from population data in 1992 Department of State annual report.

96. Amnesty International, *Peru: Human Rights in a State of Emergency* (New York: Amnesty International, August 1989), 4–5.

tion. In March 1989, Sendero demonstrated its capacity when an estimated two hundred heavily armed militia besieged and captured the
police garrison at Uchiza. The police force was humiliated, the army did
not respond to relieve their besieged comrades-in-arms, and the minister
of the interior resigned in disgrace. This represented yet another cruel
blow to the García government.[97]

Beginning in late June and July, however, the army began to respond
energetically to the challenge, intercepting and decimating several SL
columns (and some MRTA forces, also) and restoring central government
control over most of the upper Huallaga valley by late October and
early November. To affirm government control, the Peruvian military
commander in the area, General Alberto Arciniega, held a massive
demonstration in the Uchiza town square to drive home the point that
the government could win. In his speech, General Arciniega observed
that the government would protect the economic interests of the peasants and that eradication of coca would not be continued.[98]

The increasing levels of political violence in 1989 were revealed in the
dramatic rise in the number of presumed terrorists killed to levels
more than three times those of 1988. García started his administration
emphasizing pacification, peace, and economic progress as the best strategies for dealing with political violence, but finished with the same
military approach his predecessor had pursued. The big difference was
that García could point to some tangible successes against the terrorists,
from capturing important figures and entire regional committees to the
dislocation of Sendero from the upper Huallaga valley, at least temporarily. Even so, Sendero made a concerted effort to disrupt the 1989
municipal elections as part of its larger campaign progressively to cut
the periphery off from the center. It successfully prevented elections in
about 25 percent of the country's municipalities by a campaign of incumbent and candidate intimidation and assassination. And in 1990 both
incidents and deaths due to political violence reached new highs. It was
still obvious, then, that political violence and terrorism in Peru was far
from over ten years after it began.

The Fujimori Administration

The 1990 election of political newcomer Alberto Fujimori reflected widespread popular disillusionment with politics as usual and the bankruptcy

97. *Caretas* (Lima), 17 April 1989, 10–15.
98. For a fuller account, see José E. Gonzales, "Guerrillas and Coca in the Upper
Huallaga Valley," in *Shining Path of Peru*, ed. Palmer, esp. 112–18.

of the traditional parties.[99] While the new government focused on resolving Peru's worst economic crisis since its total prostration in the 1880s after the War of the Pacific, Sendero advanced, notably with its urban strategy of softening up Lima shanty towns; increasing its influence in the universities, especially San Marcos and La Cantuta, the teacher-training college; and recruiting in the face of sharply deteriorating economic circumstances. Shining Path spokespersons even began to speak of the possibility of all-out victory in the 1990s. While the government did succeed in stabilizing the domestic economy by 1991 and in advancing toward reinsertion into the international economy as of early 1992, economic growth remained elusive. After Fujimori's nemesis, Alan García, wriggled out of government attempts to neutralize his political debt by bringing him to trial for corruption in early 1992 and was beginning a campaign to oppose government policies after being re-elected APRA party chief, the president startled almost everyone by "temporarily" suspending congress and the judiciary on 5 April 1992.[100]

Popular support for Fujimori surged—to over 80 percent in some polls—but other developments were largely negative. Most governments suspended their economic assistance programs. The World Bank, the International Monetary Fund (IMF), and the Inter-American Development Bank (IADB) postponed their $2–$3 billion reinsertion package. The combination doomed any possibility of regenerating the Peruvian economy in 1992, and for part of 1993 as well. Political parties lost their link between the grass roots and central government through Congress, leaving the guerrillas with new opportunities at Peru's social and economic periphery. Sendero advanced rapidly into the breach with increased recruitment and attacks, culminating in a July 1992 urban offensive. This left a number of buildings destroyed or damaged, twenty-five dead and 250 injured, and a new image of invincibility for SL after a

99. For an account of the first years of the Fujimori government, see the annual surveys in the February or March issues of *Current History*, by David Werlich in 1991 and 1992 and by Cynthia McClintock in 1993.

100. Another explanation is suggested in military documents leaked to the Lima weekly *Oiga*, which put forth a plan by which the armed forces would carry out a coup to implement drastic measures to wrest control of the country from Sendero's advance and the "traitor" García's debacle if President-elect Fujimori did not agree to their terms. The clear implication was that Fujimori went along with the plan, thus explaining his about-face with the economic shock program, his immediate retirement of several top military officers, and the *autogolpe*. What is not explained as well by this scenario is the progressive undermining of military professionalism and institutional standards, or the important role of Vladimiro Montesinos, a cashiered army captain and alleged CIA contact and drug-trafficking conduit, as Fujimori's chief military advisor ("Historia de un traición," *Oiga*, 12 July 1993, 22–35).

series of bombings in hitherto safe sections of Lima, such as Miraflores and elementary schools for military officers' children.

The dramatic 12 September capture in Lima of SL founder and chief strategist Abimael Guzmán Reynoso gave the government a badly needed psychological boost. Within weeks, some three hundred other important SL figures had been rounded up, tried, and sentenced under much stricter guidelines implemented after the 5 April *autogolpe*. Much of the leadership of MRTA was also captured. At long last, the government appeared to be gaining the upper hand. Deaths and incidents of political violence declined markedly in the early months of 1993 (see Table 7.5), as did the efficiency in implementation of many of the guerrilla operations that were carried out. Given SL's remarkable resiliency since the beginning of the people's war in 1980, President Fujimori's repeated assertions that terrorism will be over by 1995 seem exceedingly optimistic. However, there was no question, as of mid-1993, that the momentum of the conflict had clearly shifted in the government's favor. Restoring democratic forms with 1992 congressional constitutional-convention elections and January 1992 municipal elections and the substantial normalization of international economic relations also added considerably to the Peruvian government's cause. However, there continues to be widespread concern over President Fujimori's authoritarian tendencies, his efforts to deinstitutionalize and informalize the political process, and military unrest.

CONCLUSIONS

Political violence and terrorism in Peru, measured by the number of incidents and deaths, peaked in 1990. In qualitative terms, however, the impact of the continuing violence increased up until Guzmán's capture, due to more-selective targets and sharper focus on Lima, where psychological effect was greatest. Year in and year out, the government frequently appeared to play into the hands of Sendero's strategy. First it gave the guerrilla cadres time and space to grow. Then it applied military force in an often indiscriminate manner, thus alienating local, usually peasant populations. When the government finally began to get things right on counterinsurgency policy in 1985 and 1986, the momentum could not be sustained, due to disastrous macroeconomic policies that impoverished millions with runaway inflation. Government human rights violations multiplied as well. The drastic economic measures required to undo the damage at the macro level further increased human misery at the micro level, besides virtually guaranteeing two or three years more without economic growth. The *autogolpe*, as well, played into the guerrillas' hands by putting aside democratic processes and cutting off normalization of international economic relations, further delaying real economic growth.

Sendero took full advantage of the opportunities presented it. They expanded the organization and recruitment, especially in Lima. They increasingly invoked citywide armed strikes in urban centers around the country. They continued to damage the country's infrastructure as well as, and sometimes simultaneously, set off car bombs for maximum psychological effect. And their agenda of highly selective assassinations and intimidation, in Lima shanty towns especially but also in other sensitive locations around the country, moved inexorably forward.

The result of government errors, on the one hand, and Sendero's adroitness, on the other, was, not surprisingly, an erosion over time of government capacity and legitimacy, particularly in those provinces and urban slum areas where the Shining Path converts had been most active. As the central government became more and more bogged down by severe economic constraints, more and more opportunities opened up for Sendero to advance, even though the guerrillas themselves lacked the installed capacity to take full advantage of them. Government authorities were further hampered by continuing the long-standing practice of focusing attention on the provinces, which frequently resulted in inappropriate or even counterproductive policy formulation and implementation. Bureaucratic rivalries among different government agencies and political parties that put narrow partisanship and short-term gain above the country's interests complicated the process still further. Therefore, widespread decline in the Peruvian public's confidence in the ability of central government to respond to their needs and demands is not surprising. In addition, the cleavage between national society as represented by the central government, on the one hand, and the Indian culture of the central and southern Andean highlands (and increasingly of Lima shanty towns), on the other, remains sharply defined. Efforts by the center to bridge the gap have been ineffective at best, counterproductive and racist more typically.

Democracy should have been a major bulwark against the advance of Shining Path in Peru, but as it was practiced in the 1980s, it contributed significantly to the generalization of violence and to its own erosion. Citizens, increasingly unable to count on democratic governance at the center to help them meet even their most basic needs of security and sustenance, turned more and more to their own devices. The informalization of politics through grassroots neighborhood or community groups organized to provide food and security took the place of formal programs and institutions that no longer functioned or that never reached those who most needed them. Just as the informal economy grew to meet the necessity of scratching out a living somehow as the formal economy lost its capacity to do so, so too did the informal polity grow to meet other but equally basic needs.

Given this lugubrious context, what is most surprising is that Sendero did not advance even further with its revolutionary project. One major reason is that the organization is to a significant degree a prisoner of its own ideology. Shining Path has repeatedly encountered some acceptance when it has first moved into a community or a neighborhood, but has lost its effort to win over people, by insisting on imposing an ideologically correct model on them that bears little relation to their needs and even less respect for their customs or traditions. Terror and intimidation then become the chief mechanisms to retain influence and control. These rarely are the bases for generating genuine support, and Sendero lacks the cadres for maintaining its grip through these insidious devices.

Another significant factor holding Shining Path back has been the presence of a wide variety of local organizations that do respond or appear to be more likely to respond to people's needs. Some of these are long-standing—Catholic church programs, local units of political parties or labor unions, neighborhood associations, traditional Indian community structures, or urban extensions of community-based mutual-aid groups. Others—the array of informal local organizations like soup kitchens, mothers' clubs, neighborhood defense committees or the rural peasant equivalents, the *rondas campesinas*, or evangelical Protestant churches—are more recent, often emerging to meet specific local needs. Although Sendero has been able to penetrate some of these groups and turn them to their own purposes, more often than not they are driven off or reported to the authorities.

A third main factor limiting the Shining Path is the dependence on a single leader. The cult of personality assiduously developed by Guzmán to enhance the possibility of a correct revolutionary victory became an albatross around the neck of the organization when he was captured after twenty-five years of total control. It is simply impossible to replace him. Even though the organization has become institutionalized, given the length of time it has been in existence and will almost certainly continue, it is quite likely to take a different course. Regional committees may now predominate, or a more moderate leadership may emerge, or Sendero may break up into warring factions based on differences in strategy, ideology, or personality. To regain anything resembling the momentum it had before Guzmán's capture, SL needs both time to reorganize and an opponent—the government—that returns to its blundering ways.

Given the government's very mixed record since Sendero emerged, this is not at all out of the question. In mid-1993 there were some disquieting signs. The general who directed the painstaking intelligence work of the police force's office against terrorism (DINCOTE), which led to the capture of Guzmán, other top SL personnel, and many of Sendero's computer records, was removed from his post by President Fujimori. Elements of the military were restless over the president's involvement in promotions and armed-forces policies, which some saw as undermining the professionalism and institutional integrity built up over thirty to forty years. A coup plan was disrupted in November 1992 and its alleged leaders jailed, and reports of improper conduct and human rights abuses by military personnel beholden to President Fujimori regularly surfaced in the Peruvian press.

While opinion polls still showed Fujimori with high ratings (around 60 percent in June 1993), signs of disquiet over continuing recession, particularly in the provinces, were on the increase. The 31 October 1993 national referendum on Peru's new constitution confirmed such disquiet. While the constitution was approved, by a vote of 54 percent to 46 percent, in fourteen predominantly rural and agricultural departments the "no" vote won a majority. The national economy was in the process of turning around by late 1993, given the normalization of Peru's international economic relations earlier in the year, but it was not clear whether the multitude of microeconomic projects designed to reach Peruvian society's grass roots quickly would actually do so. Many believe that the government has only until mid-1994 at most to take advantage of the space opened up by Sendero's retrenchment and demonstrably improve the well-being of Peru's long-suffering poor. Otherwise, a revitalized SL would be likely to step into the breach, stronger than ever. Early signs that this might be beginning to happen could be found in a 15 percent increase in terrorist incidents during the first seven months of 1993 compared to the same period in 1992.

Another set of issues relates to whether the "directed democracy" that emerged after the April 1992 *autogolpe* can effectively meet Peru's political needs, since Shining Path and the political parties have been shown to be unsatisfactory alternatives, the former due to its glorification of political violence and terror, the latter due to their dismal track record in the 1980s. President Fujimori holds his "directed democracy" project up as the only viable solution. But the new Constitutional congress cum legislature elected in November 1992 with a majority of Fujimori supporters was slow, weak, and vacillating, threatening the sitting president's plan for reelection in 1995 under the new constitution. The municipalities, once seen by Fujimori as a new nonparty base of support, seemed to have different ideas. Although independents won many key mayorships, including an unusual reelection of Lima's popular Ricardo Belmont, in January 1993, they were, by and large, not Fujimori supporters. Perhaps as a result, the president then appeared to pull back from a plan that would have used the municipal governments as a key channel to deliver the resources so badly needed at the grass roots. The ongoing informalization of politics that Fujimori's policies further encouraged may very well not provide the platform with which the president can consolidate his directed democracy after all. A new anti-Fujimori political alternative, the Democratic Forum, began to emerge in mid 1993, but it was too early to tell whether this would come to represent a viable option. In a climate of such political uncertainties and some indications of public disillusionment with the political machinations of the center, clearly demonstrated in the October 1993 constitutional referendum, Sendero could become the beneficiary.

Among the larger issues raised by the Shining Path movement in Peru is the distinction between a guerrilla organization with terrorism as a major instrument, like Sendero, and a purely terrorist organization for which the act is a goal in itself. Shining Path's ability to sustain itself over the years suggests the greater staying power and efficacy of an ideologically driven movement with terrorism as a strategy for advancing the revolution.

The combination in Sendero of an emphasis on ideological purity and a praxis that is often (though certainly not always) pragmatic is also instructive. Cadres are shaped by both ideological instruction and preparation in specific specialties that are applied regularly in practice and then critiqued. The constant experience and organizational pruning strengthens cadres and develops leadership. The discipline shown by Sendero elements in prison suggests the effect of ideological and practical training. In their strategy for taking power, leaders announce individual rights to private property and respect for religious beliefs to expand their support base. Although it is doubtful that Sendero can win, the organization seems capable of sowing selective death and destruction for some time to come. Since 1980, terrorism has become institutionalized in Peru, some without question state-sponsored, but mostly guerrilla-provoked. The consequences in human and material terms have been devastating for society and the country at all levels. Sendero may not win, but through its systematic, selective, and methodical terrorism, Peru is certainly the loser.

APPENDIX:

Political Violence in Peru—Analysis of Data, 1980–1992

The patterns of political violence in Peru since 1980 are complex. Furthermore, one always needs to interpret aggregate data with care. The information itself is subject to errors in gathering, and some of the categories, especially "civilians" and "presumed subversives," are themselves subject to mistakes based on the criteria used by the individuals who originally collected or reported the information. In addition, total numbers of incidents and deaths also vary, depending on the organization that collected them. The principal entities that have attempted to gather a complete set of data on political violence for the entire period 1980–92 are DESCO, the Ministry of Defense, and the Special Senate Commission on Political Violence and Pacification (Bernales Commission), now known as Constitution and Society. Human rights information has been gathered by the National Coordinator for Human Rights and by various outside agencies, including Amnesty International, Americas Watch, and the U.S. Department of State. By using one source for political violence data, in this case DESCO, one can assume that whatever errors might creep in are consistent over time and that methods of collection are similar as well. This makes it possible to analyze the data, over time and within categories, with greater confidence than if they came from multiple sources.

There are, then, some observations that can be made about patterns and trends in political violence in Peru from 1980 through 1992. These include the following:

1. Both incidents and deaths have tended to increase over time. The total number of incidents has exceeded the thirteen-year average (1,814 per year) every year since 1985. Deaths also exceeded the average (1,813 per year) over each of the last four years (1989–92), as well as in 1983 and 1984, when the government initiated its first substantial military response to the Shining Path threat.

2. Although the average numbers of incidents and deaths over thirteen years are almost identical, the death to incident ratio has varied considerably, peaking in 1983 and 1984 (at 176 and 204 deaths per 100 incidents) after being very low between 1980 and 1982. Although there was a substantial ebb from 1985 through 1988 (46 to 70 deaths per 100 incidents), the ratio jumped significantly in 1989 and remained consis-

tently high through 1992 (135 to 142 deaths per 100 incidents). This most recent pattern suggests the increasingly violent nature of the conflict since 1989, even though total deaths per year due to political violence have declined substantially—by 30 percent since the peak year of 1990 (3,745 deaths). Incidents have declined by a similar proportion between 1990 and 1992 (2,779 to 1,956, or 30 percent as well).

3. Deaths of military and police personnel have increased almost every year since Shining Path declared its "people's war" in May 1980, with only slight decreases in 1985 and 1990. The year 1992 was the most violent to date, with 397 military and police deaths recorded. Over the course of the conflict, a total of 2,278 armed-forces and police personnel have been killed by guerrillas (909 military and 1,369 police). Increasing armed-forces fatalities amid declining political-violence deaths suggests that Shining Path may have become more selective over time in choosing its victims—military and police, local political authorities, development workers in certain locations, and local peasant militias. In another example, 86 political authorities were killed in all of Peru in 1988; 115 were killed in Lima alone in 1992.

4. Deaths of presumed subversives have been substantially higher year in and year out than those of the Peruvian government forces, for a total over thirteen years of 10,655. Total civilian deaths (which include political authorities, about 10 percent of the civilian total for years in which data is available from DESCO figures) over the same time period are almost the same, 10,640. Since the armed forces became formally involved in 1983, the number of "presumed subversives" deaths as a percentage of total deaths from political violence has ranged between 62 percent (1983, or 1,226) and 27 percent (1988, or 404), with a substantial decline recorded between 1990 (1,879 or 50 percent) and 1992 (934 or 35 percent). The decline in 1987 and 1988 may be related in part to tighter conduct standards imposed by President García and also to the armed forces' own internal decisions to reduce their military engagements of the guerrillas. The more recent decline in "presumed subversives" deaths likely has a different explanation—including closer scrutiny by human rights organizations; tighter internal monitoring in the ultimately successful 1991 quest for U.S. military aid and during aid implementation between October 1991 and April 1992; and, perhaps most important, improved military and police intelligence gathering, which shifted Peruvian government counterinsurgency strategy toward tracking down and capturing key guerrilla figures rather than military confrontation and engagement.

5. The geographical shift in the proportion of incidents and selective assassinations by the guerrillas from the provinces to Lima over the

period 1987 (the year before Guzmán's *El Diario* interview presaging a more urban-oriented strategy by Shining Path) through 1992 is quite marked. While 1992 total incidents were 21 percent less than 1987 (1,956 and 2,489, respectively), those recorded in Lima increased from 28 percent of the total to 51 percent. Concerning the killing of local political authorities, 115 assassinations occurred in Lima's outlying poor districts in 1992; 40 occurred in the entire country in 1987 (and 86 in 1988).

6. Early comparisons of incidents and deaths in the months immediately before Guzmán's capture in September 1992 with those just following indicate that the Shining Path organization has been adversely affected to a significant degree. In the six months April–September 1992, 944 incidents and 1,193 deaths were attributed to political violence; this compares with 862 and 907, respectively, from October 1992 through March 1993, a decline of 9 percent in total incidents and 24 percent in the number of deaths. Although this may only point up a temporary setback, most analysts concur that Guzmán's capture, along with that of key computer files on Shining Path's organization and personnel and some three hundred other upper-echelon militants, has severely damaged the guerrilla institution. Other indications supporting this view are the increased number of poorly executed Shining Path attacks and the explicit recognition in internal documents of the return to a "strategic defensive" posture vis-à-vis the government, after having achieved, by their definition, a "strategic equilibrium" in 1991, with every expectation of moving to the "strategic offensive" in late 1992 or early 1993.

Part III

Identity, Culture, and Territorial Claims

8

The Culture of Paramilitarism in Ireland

Charles Townshend

I weary, weary
Of the long sorrow—And yet I have my joy:
My sons were faithful, and they fought.
        —Padraig Pearse, "The Mother"

This is not meant to be a purely historical study, much less a short history of the Irish question. Nevertheless, it is the work of a historian, and its working premise is the explanatory value of thick description. It invokes the hope that what is good history can also be, as Gabriel Almond said of a related study, "better theory."[1] It aims to arrive at a characterization of terrorism shaped by the perceptions of participants in the Irish conflict. It rests, however, on the assumption that the

1. Foreword to Tom Bowden, *The Breakdown of Public Security: The Case of Ireland, 1916–1921, and Palestine, 1936–1939* (Beverly Hills: Sage Publications, 1977), x–xi. For my usage of *culture*, see Alan MacFarlane, *The Culture of Capitalism* (Oxford: Blackwell, 1987), xv–xvi.

existence of conflict is self-evident and that political violence—both violence consciously directed to political ends and violence perceived as having political significance—has been a recurrent element in Irish public life.[2]

That is not to say that Irish politics have been dominated, distorted, or even routinely influenced by violence. Though such implications have been quite common,[3] it would be easy to produce copious evidence of the "normality" of Irish public life throughout most of the period of the Union and from a point quite soon after the apparent catastrophe of the civil war in 1922–23. It is even possible, though it is less easy, to contend that life in the six counties of Northern Ireland has been largely "normal" through the quarter century of the present troubles.[4] Such an argument can be pressed a certain distance. It is a necessary corrective to the portrayal of the situation as a social dissolution of Lebanese proportions and points to the constraints that have thus far stayed the slide into outright civil war.

Still, it is misleading to deny altogether the public perception of the troubles as a "crisis" or even "catastrophe."[5] It is plainly the case that Northern Ireland is not a "normal" political society. Political violence, whether measured crudely by fatalities or by some larger calculus of intimidation, has been commonly foregrounded in both inside and outside views of Northern Ireland. Its modes have been plausibly traced back into the nineteenth century and earlier. Its impact on socialization and political culture has been a matter of widespread concern, not to say alarm. Assumptions about the legitimacy of violence, not so much within as alongside the political process, have repeatedly manifested themselves. The dysfunctionality of violence has been less easy to demon-

2. This is part of the argument in Charles Townshend, *Political Violence in Ireland: Government and Resistance Since 1848* (Oxford: Clarendon Press, 1983). See also Peter Alter, "Traditions of Violence in the Irish National Movement," in *Social Protest, Violence, and Terror in Nineteenth- and Twentieth-Century Europe*, ed. Wolfgang J. Mommsen and Gerhard Hirschfeld (London: St. Martin's Press, 1982), 137–54.

3. For example: "On an overview of Irish history, it is hardly too much to say that violence, or incipient violence, was the normal condition in which society existed" (Patrick O'Farrell, *England and Ireland Since 1800* [London: Oxford University Press, 1975], 161).

4. John Darby, *Intimidation and the Control of Conflict in Northern Ireland* (Syracuse, N.Y.: Syracuse University Press, 1986).

5. Instances of the former usage would be too numerous to mention, though not all are very careful about the precise meaning of the (basically medical) analogy. Cornelius O'Leary launched the contemporary scholarly usage with his article "The Northern Ireland Crisis and Its Observers," *Political Quarterly* 42 (1971): 255–68, and his book (with Ian Budge) *Belfast: Approach to Crisis: A Study of Belfast Politics, 1613–1970* (London: Macmillan, 1973). Tom Nairn, *The Break-up of Britain: Crisis and Neo-Nationalism* (London: NLB, 1977), uses the notion of "legitimacy crisis" developed by Habermas.

strate in Ireland than ordinary notions of modernity would suggest. The main aim of this chapter is to give an account of how and why political violence has worked.

SEMANTICS

Any selection of data is made by definition of terms. Political terminology, particularly in the region of notions like disaffection, revolt, rebellion, and civil war, is often contentious because it is apt to involve matters of life and death. As far as contention is concerned, the notion of terrorism has possibly established a class of its own, though any attempt to measure political violence more generally encounters related problems of categorization. When does an "affray" become a "riot," or "resistance" become "insurrection"? There can be no single answer to such questions; the answers are provisional social constructs, shaped by the tolerances of differing cultures. Of course, analysts can, like legislators, impose exact definitions (the precise head count of an affray is laid down in English law, as is the difference between "actual" and "grievous" bodily harm), but these arbitrary fixed points only serve to indicate the dizzying instability of conventional usage or the easygoing public tolerance of synonymity. Eugene V. Walter showed how Max Weber's attempt to clarify his analysis of violence by distinguishing *Gewalt* from *Gewaltsamkeit* had been missed by his translators, and most likely by his German readers too, since the discriminations required are abstract rather than real.[6]

Violence means the rupture of norms. It cannot be delimited only in abstract terms or limited to actual physical harm. People use a wide repertoire of language, gesture, and action to intimidate others and secure their acquiescence. The ultimate reference of intimidation is physical harm, so threats, whether verbal or nonverbal, must be regarded as violence. Essentially, violence is a reciprocal construction: the intended victim's perception is integral to the would-be perpetrator's act. Nowhere is this reciprocity more crucial than in the almost wholly subjective form of political violence commonly labeled terrorism.

A pivotal term of measurement in the assessment of political violence is *intensity*, not just because General Frank Kitson and a later school of

6. Eugene V. Walter, *Terror and Resistance: A Study of Political Violence* (New York: Oxford University Press, 1969), 49–51. See also George A. Kelly, "Conceptual Sources of the Terror," *Eighteenth-Century Studies* 14 (1980): 18–36.

American military theorists have incorporated it in their reformulations of what used (tautologically) to be called guerrilla warfare. (In fact, *guerrilla* itself contains the same problem: On what dimensions are small wars small, and how far does diminution go?) For Montesquieu, *terreur* was the effect of a high intensity of *crainte*.[7] Intensity indicates measurement in degree, amount, frequency, and so on, and also extremity of emotional response. Each of these parameters is obviously different. In terms of degree, the most intense form of violence is homicide, but a conflict that produces one homicide is likely to produce dozens of less complete forms of hurt. Can 10 deaths and 100 maimings across 1,000 square miles over 10 months be measured as less intense than 100 deaths over the same area and period? Both may be "low intensity" by the scale of Clausewitzian battle, where the same totals of "casualties" are routinely created in 10 minutes within 1,000 square meters. But setting the threshold between "normal" and "low" is a matter of cultural bargaining.

Kitson's program of low-intensity operations was intended, among other things, to convince regular soldiers that although counterinsurgency operations bore little resemblance to their conventional image of "war," they formed a recognizable—and creditable—military task.[8] Intensity here relates principally to physical concentration of force, since Kitson's argument was that a high intensity of consistent mental effort was required to conduct such operations successfully. On these lines it might be suggested that the extended nervous strain engendered by some "low-intensity" conflicts exceeds the stress of conventional war, in which sporadic bursts of violence are separated by prolonged periods of inactivity.

All this is merely to register that in using—unavoidably—notions such as uprising, rebellion, insurgency, or war (whether internal, civil, protracted, small, people's, or guerrilla), we are invoking social perceptions. One of the clearest categorical frameworks for political violence was set up by Gerhard Botz to classify events in Austria between 1918 and 1934.

His two parameters provide a means of incorporating three measures of intensity, but that is a simple matter alongside the ambiguities that saturate the categories of "unrests" and "clashes," or the untransferable specificity of *Feme* execution. In spite of these, his description of the

    7. George A. Kelly, *Mortal Politics in Eighteenth-Century France* (Waterloo, Ont.: University of Waterloo Press, 1986), 294.
    8. Frank Kitson, *Low-Intensity Operations: Subversion, Insurgency, Peacekeeping* (London: Faber and Faber, 1971).

Table 8.1.   Forms of political violence

Participants Duration	Few (up to 5) Short	Many (6–500) Medium	Very many (more than 500) Long
Organization: Organized	Assassination *Feme*-murder Bomb-terror	Clash	Coup d'état Putsch
Structured	Assault Clash	Clash	Putschist action Insurrection
Amorphous	Insults Political brawls	Lynchings	Riot Unrests

SOURCE: Gerhard Botz, "Political Violence in the First Austrian Republic," in *Social Protest, Violence, and Terror in Nineteenth- and Twentieth-Century Europe*, ed. Wolfgang J. Mommsen and Gerhard Hirschfeld (New York: St. Martin's Press, 1982), 310.

Austrian struggle as "latent civil war" may help to illuminate the nature of other internal struggles, including that in Ireland. The three levels of organization may be simultaneously present in any internal conflict, but it is important to recognize that sustained targeted violence requires an organizational structure. Whether the analyst labels a nineteenth-century rural secret society amorphous or structured may be, in the strict sense, an academic matter; the main point is that discriminations can and should be made even where evidence is, in the nature of things, ambiguous. It would be useful to add to the vertical classification a fourth measure qualifying structure, that of strategy. The intention behind a violent act is crucial to its nature. A lynching, for instance, may be part of a directed social struggle or it may be an isolated response to a transient local crisis.

Civil war is a notion that should not be diluted or prostituted. It bears an awe-inspiring image of social breakdown, and one may (mercifully) never know whether the latent form contains the possibility or merely the fear of this ultimate catastrophe. But because it is more exact than "crisis" or the still less specific "troubles," it brings into focus those anxieties that feed and are fed by the erosion of stability and public security. The reason for preferring the description "latent civil war" is the range of manifestations of conflict, from individual intimidation to riot, ambush and mass strike, that have recurred in Ireland. The place of terrorism in this gamut of violence is salient but, like everything else in this sphere, is riven with ambiguity. The usage of the term is, again, socially conditioned, hence the clichéd status of the maxim, one person's terrorist is another's freedom fighter, which nonetheless conveys the inescapable relativism of the issue. The official (or state) definition of terrorism always boils down to "illegal force," since the state claims the monopoly of legitimate coercion. Legitimacy, naturally, falls to public judgment. The official definition is correct as long as it is accepted by the public as a whole; but since in reality the public is plural, the definition must vie with others, more than one of which may be accepted by a "significant public."

The analyst must conclude that acts and individuals viewed as terrorist differ from place to place and from time to time. Some operational definition is still obligatory, and I am working with this one: "the deliberate induction of fear in the belief that fear itself is sufficient to produce political results." Fear is induced by violence, and more fear is usually created when force is used against defenseless people; then a few acts of violence may spread fear far and wide, so that there may be no correlation between the intensity of violence and the intensity of terror. Coercion is a complex process, and the process—above all a matter of social interpretation—is a principal concern here.[9]

On the day this chapter was drafted, two items were front-page news in Britain. A car bomb outside a police post in Warrenpoint, County Down, killed a young woman and wounded twenty people. At the same time, a series of killings by a Mexican cult that dismembered its victims, opened their skulls, and cooked and ate their brains was described. A more terrifying outbreak of violence than this latter would be hard to imagine, yet there was no suggestion that the members of the cult should be viewed as terrorists. Those who placed the bomb in Warrenpoint, on the other hand, were. The reason is that their action formed part of a pattern whose public intent was understood. Its provenance could be confidently charted. It brought to at least twenty-nine the total of "civilians" killed in attacks by the Provisional Irish Republican Army (PIRA) since the massacre of Protestants in a Remembrance Day parade at Enniskillen, County Fermanagh, on 8 November 1987 (a pattern of events that had included a public announcement that one of the PIRA units responsible for the original massacre, the Donegal-Fermanagh Brigade, had been disbanded). Shock and revulsion were reported among the nationalist community. (The woman killed was a Catholic.) An unprecedented rift appeared to be opening up in the republican politico-military strategy; the Sinn Fein leader Gerry Adams publicly recognized the damaging effect of indiscriminate killing.

9. Eugene V. Walter, "Violence and the Process of Terror," *American Sociological Review* 29 (1964): 248–57. See also H. D. Lasswell, "Terrorism and the Political Process," *Terrorism* 1 (1978): 255–63. For a version of the definitional problem, see Timo Airaksinen, "An Analysis of Coercion," *Journal of Peace Research* 25 (1988): 213–27.

Responsible commentators, however, pointed out that the IRA had survived similar or bigger mistakes in the past. After the Enniskillen slaughter one journalist was told by an IRA spokesman that "the outer reaches" (of the republican support base) were "just totally devastated," but their central base could "take a hell of a lot of jolting and crisis."[10] With due allowance for hyperbole, even "total devastation" has proved transient, noiselessly repaired by the deep and steady force of republican sentiment, historically armored against the shock of failure.

PERIODICITY

It is this proofing process that requires historical explanation. To provide anything like a satisfactory historical account would require at least a large book, but here it is important to indicate the variety and periodicity of social movements in Ireland that have accepted the utility of violence. The present PIRA is the lineal descendant of the Irish Republican Brotherhood, first established in the mid-1850s. It is thus an exceptionally durable organization in its own right, but it arguably has also incorporated a larger tradition of social resistance stretching back in coherent form to the mid-eighteenth century.[11]

On the antirepublican side, the continuity of the roots of the Ulster Defence Association and other loyalist organizations is more tenuous: even the celebrated (and exaggerated) Orange Order, established in the 1790s, was—at any rate officially—wound up for a generation in the mid-nineteenth century. But the loyalist incorporation of history has been, if anything, more vivid and concrete than that of the nationalists.[12] For contemporary Protestants the symbolic weight of the Ulster Covenant and the Ulster Volunteer Force of 1912 is vast and seems to have been transmitted effectively through superficially different organizations like the "B" Special Constabulary and the Ulster Defense Regiment. The point of all this is that whether or not a simple, direct transmission of

10. David McKittrick, "IRA's Toll of Civilian Deaths Grows Despite Public Stance," *The Independent*, 13 April 1989.

11. Charles Townshend, "The Process of Terror in Irish Politics," in *Terrorism, Ideology, and Revolution*, ed. Noel O'Sullivan (Brighton: Wheatsheaf, 1986).

12. Frank Wright, "Protestant Ideology and Politics in Ulster," *European Journal of Sociology* 14 (1973); A.T.Q. Stewart, *The Narrow Ground: Aspects of Ulster, 1609–1969* (London: Faber and Faber, 1977); David W. Miller, *Queen's Rebels: Ulster Loyalism in Historical Perspective* (Dublin: Gill and Macmillan, 1978); and Terence Brown, *The Whole Protestant Community: The Making of a Historical Myth*, Field Day Pamphlet no. 7 (Derry, 1985).

organizational culture can be demonstrated, Irish political positions are complex historical formations containing accretions of attitudes and symbols over two centuries or more.[13]

By the end of the eighteenth century, three tiers of organizations had come into existence: at the local, rural level, a skein of associations (or secret societies) practicing nocturnal intimidation; at the central level, a conspiratorial revolutionary separatist club planning to end British rule by insurrection; and somewhere between these, a loose set of reactive groupings dedicated to upholding the "constitution" (the Williamite settlement following the 1688 revolution) and the Protestant Ascendancy. The expression of this last interest was already complicated by its ostensible need to maintain the British connection, coupled with its inability to define the content of its Britishness as either political or religious. Its position had initially been constructed to defend a common Protestant view of internal and international politics, but was eventually to prove detachable from the political culture of the parent state.

The same broad pattern of organization persisted through the mid-nineteenth century, and the interpermeability of local and central modes became more evident. It is notoriously difficult to interpret the agendas of rural secret societies, and extension of the term whiteboyism—derived from the simple bed-linen disguises rigged up for nocturnal terrorist outings—to blanket the multiplicity of tiny oath-bound groups over the course of a century remains contentious.[14] Yet the persistent cross-echoes in the content of their oaths, their repertoire of violent acts and threatening notices, their social profile and that of their victims, argue a cohesion of sorts. Rural unrest remains, in the words of the outstanding modern authority on nineteenth-century Irish society, a profoundly mysterious phenomenon;[15] but its ambiguity contributed to its resilience. Again, it is contentious to suggest that underlying these diverse, short-range accumulations of resistance, there was a wider alienation of a whole ethnic community.[16] That argument, in its simplest form, was a gloss placed by nationalist polemicists on a resistless mass of phenomena. Still, the findings of recent scholars, who detect more evidence of inter- or intrafamilial conflict than of communal assertion as the motor of everyday violence in the Irish countryside, are not necessarily incompati-

13. Oliver MacDonagh, "Time's Revenges and Revenge's Time: A View of Anglo-Irish Relations," *Anglo-Irish Studies* 4 (1979).

14. Michael Beames, *Peasants and Power: The Whiteboy Movements and Their Control in Pre-Famine Ireland* (Sussex: Harvester Press, 1983).

15. K. Theodore Hoppen, *Elections, Politics, and Society in Ireland, 1832–1885* (Oxford: Clarendon Press, 1984), 398.

16. David FitzPatrick, "Agin the State," *Times Literary Supplement*, 20 July 1984, 815.

ble with arguments for the existence, however rudimentary, of an "unwritten law" invoking, at some level, an alternative political authority.[17]

The central point here is not whether the existence of an informal or subliminal counterstate (the "alternative government" that stalked the official reports) can be demonstrated. Rather, the point is to stress the low working legitimacy of the British state apparatus in Ireland and the high friction encountered—for whatever reason—in the quotidian administration of the law, even in the theoretically nonpolitical sphere of landlord-tenant relations.[18] The classification of land-related crime by the Royal Irish Constabulary (RIC) as agrarian recognized the special public status of the "land question."[19] Routine law enforcement was problematic in nineteenth-century Ireland, and not only when—as happened several times—substantial areas passed wholly under the control of "banditti," Rockites (small bands linked merely by their use of a common mythical chief, Captain Rock), or Ribbonmen (nominally political adherents of the mainstream nationalist movement). The British authorities were perennially conscious of their incapacity to duplicate in Ireland the infrastructure of gentry administration that was the bedrock of English public order.[20] In 1847 the prime minister, Lord John Russell, lamented that just twenty "gentlemen like those we have in Hampshire and Sussex" would suffice to pacify the Irish countryside.[21]

To say that the British state had low legitimacy is not to say that it had none, or that its opponents all had more. But its local opponents did have better prospects of acquiring legitimacy than did violent opponents of the state in England. As long as they operated within traditional constraints, agrarian terrorists were remarkably successful.[22] Their violence was decoded by its audience with little difficulty; it was usually intended to secure reduction of rents in bad years or to prevent new

17. David FitzPatrick, "Class, Family, and Rural Unrest in Nineteenth-Century Ireland," in *Ireland: Land, Politics, and People*, ed. P. J. Drudy (Cambridge: Cambridge University Press, 1982), 68–69. See also Joseph Lee, "The Ribbonmen," in *Secret Societies in Ireland*, ed. T. D. Williams (Dublin: Gill and Macmillan, 1973), 26–35, and Samuel Clark, *Social Origins of the Irish Land War* (Princeton: Princeton University Press, 1979), 65–104.

18. E. D. Steele, *Irish Land and British Politics: Tenant-Right and Nationality, 1865–1870* (Cambridge: Cambridge University Press, 1974), 3–42.

19. Townshend, *Political Violence*, 6–9.

20. Oliver MacDonagh, *Ireland: The Union and Its Aftermath* (London: George Allen and Unwin, 1977), 35–36.

21. Russell to Clarendon, 3 December 1847, Bodleian Library, Clarendon MSS Box 43.

22. Lee, "The Ribbonmen"; George Cornewall Lewis, *On Local Disturbances in Ireland, and on the Irish Church Question* (London: B. Fellowes, 1836); and Hoppen, *Elections, Politics, and Society*, 341–435.

tenants from taking over land from which families had been evicted. Like the police, the people generally recognized that public dimension of intimidatory violence. (Indeed, they may have exaggerated it to rationalize their inability to stand up against it; this was the burden of the oft-repeated charge that the Irish lacked "civic courage").[23] The effectiveness of rural terrorism was due, in the words of its pioneering investigator in the 1830s, to the perception of any "criminal" involved as being "as it were an executioner, who carries into effect the verdict of an uncertain and nonapparent tribunal."[24]

Such an alternative judicial power was probably easier to imagine in a period when the memory of the German *Femgericht* was still quite vivid, and the term remained a fairly common literary device.[25] It may, as Cornewall Lewis speculated, have accounted for the special cruelty of secret-society violence, giving "their opinion the weight of the law of the State by arming it with sanctions as painful as those employed by the criminal law" (though not, of course, exact equivalents: cruel as it then was, the English law did not need to throw people naked into thorn pits or lacerate their flesh with wool cards).[26] The political significance of the rural terror was not straightforward, but neither was it a mere figment of the official or revolutionary imagination. Identification with the "croppies" (Catholic insurgents of 1798) was a leitmotiv in vernacular intimidation; the promise to "wade knee deep in Orange blood" was a recurrent rhetorical flourish in secret-society oaths; and the startling millenarian impulse of Pastorini's prophecy that the Protestants would be destroyed in 1825 has recently been demonstrated.[27] It has also been plausibly contended, against those who saw Ribbonism as politically irrelevant, that the associations contained an "unofficial political network" (E. J. Hobsbawm's phrase) with a special vision of society.[28]

23. Lord Derby to Lord Eglinton, 3 December 1858: ". . . the intense moral cowardice which is characteristic of Irishmen" (Scottish Record Office, Eglinton MSS 5344). Forster to Lord Ripon, 17 July 1881: "The greatest of all Irish evils is the cowardice . . . of the moderate men" (quoted in T. Wemyss Reid, *The Life of the Rt. Hon. W. E. Forster* [London: Chapman and Hall, 1888], 2:330). Horace Plunkett, *Ireland in the New Century* (London: J. Murray, 1904), 79: ". . . the moral timidity in glaring contrast to the physical courage."

24. Lewis, *On Local Disturbances*, 77.

25. A. M. Sullivan, *New Ireland* (London: Cameron and Ferguson, 1877), 1:33–45, 69.

26. Lewis, *On Local Disturbances*, 77.

27. James S. Donnelly, Jr., "Pastorini and Captain Rock: Millenarianism and Sectarianism in the Rockite Movement of 1821–24," in *Irish Peasants: Violence and Political Unrest, 1780–1914*, ed. Samuel Clark and James S. Donnelly, Jr. (Madison: University of Wisconsin Press, 1983), 102–39.

28. Tom Garvin, "Defenders, Ribbonmen, and Others: Underground Political Networks in Pre-famine Ireland," in *Nationalism and Popular Protest in Ireland*, ed. C.H.E. Philpin

The difficulty for historical analysis is to trace and test the links between this informal terrorist polity and the central conspiratorial revolutionary organization of the later nineteenth century, the Irish Republican Brotherhood (IRB). On one level there was a wide gulf between them. The IRB leadership rejected terrorism per se and espoused open insurrection, the honorable fight in which Ireland's soul would be saved as its independence was won. It condemned agrarian violence not least for its sordid, material motives.[29] But it seems unlikely that the attitudes of the IRB Supreme Council purists were widely reproduced in the rural communities themselves, where Fenians, as members of the IRB were colloquially known, had more-constructive relations with Ribbon societies and followers of the parliamentary strategy.[30] The outstanding example of cross-fertilization was the founding of the Land League by the old Fenian Michael Davitt in 1878, initiating the mobilization of the peasantry for the intensification of the land struggle known as the land war. The controlling idea of Fenianism was physical force, the straightforward repudiation of Daniel O'Connell's belief in moral force as an agent of change, in favor of the conviction that Britain's grip on Ireland would never be broken except by armed force. Its founders, James Stephens and John O'Mahony, drew this conviction directly from the Young Ireland group that had split from O'Connell's nonviolent Repeal Association in the 1840s, drawing above all on the grim doctrine of John Mitchel: his "cult of violence, his disdain for democratic politics, and his glorification of hatred."[31]

What an acute historian of modern Ireland calls Mitchel's "career of frenetic Carlylean attitudinizing" was to be of real and deadly weight for his mental heirs.[32] Violent rhetoric might serve as a palliative for frustrated activists but could dictate the terms of future action. Stephens engraved his own dogma in a famous passage: "I was as sure as of my own existence that if another decade was allowed to pass without an endeavour of some kind to shake off an unjust yoke, the Irish people would sink into a lethargy from which it would be impossible for any

(Cambridge: Cambridge University Press, 1987), 219–44; see also M. R. Beames, "The Ribbon Societies: Lower-class Nationalism in Pre-Famine Ireland," in ibid., 245–63.

29. This attitude ran from Charles J. Kickham (see R. V. Comerford, *Charles J. Kickham: A Study in Irish Nationalism and Literature* [Dublin: Wolfhound Press, 1979], 146) to Austin Stack (see J. A. Gaughan, *Austin Stack: Portrait of a Separatist* [Dublin: Kingdom Books, 1977], 259–60).

30. R. V. Comerford, *The Fenians in Context: Irish Politics and Society, 1848–82* (Dublin: Wolfhound Press, 1985).

31. Ibid., 37.

32. R. F. Foster, *Modern Ireland, 1600–1972* (London: Allen Lane, 1988), 316.

patriot to arouse them."[33] The powerful fusion of one-step millenarian hopes with the call to repeated assertions of the national claim was here fixed for good.

The Fenian organization attempted its insurrection in 1866–67, and failed.[34] In September and December 1867 it attempted to release Fenian prisoners in Manchester and Clerkenwell, with scarcely greater success. In these desperate attempts, however, it discovered a far more potent application of violence than the insurrectionism of its theorists. The armed attack on a police van in Manchester in which a policeman was killed led to a dubious court case that produced the Manchester Martyrs, initiating a process that was to be repeated many times over the next 120 years.[35] The explosion that was intended to blow down the wall of Clerkenwell prison but that instead killed several inhabitants from the surrounding tenements became, unintentionally, an effective act of urban terrorism: its impact on British public opinion was electrifying.[36] Yet in spite of this, the high-minded IRB chiefs never accepted the legitimacy of indiscriminate killing or even of targeted assassination in the Russian manner. Once their attempts at open rebellion had failed, they entered a period of stultifying inactivity extending over thirty years from the early 1870s.

The IRB was paralyzed by its recognition of the futility of armed action without mass support (as specified in its 1873 constitution)[37] and by its inability to find an alternative means of mobilizing the people, apart from the Mazzinian-Blanquist insurrection to which it was dedicated. At the same time, its unilateral declaration of war against England served to legitimate and inspire the actions of others who were prepared to adopt means like "propaganda by deed." At least three independent groups waged this war in the 1870s and 1880s: Jeremiah O'Donovan

33. James Stephens, "Reminiscences," *Weekly Freeman,* quoted in Robert Kee, *The Green Flag: A History of Irish Nationalism* (London: Weidenfeld and Nicolson, 1972), 306.
34. It is surprising, in view of its seminal importance, that there is no full study of the 1867 insurrection. Before Comerford, *Fenians in Context,* the only substantial work on the movement was Leon O'Broin, *Fenian Fever: An Anglo-American Dilemma* (New York: New York University Press, 1971), and idem, *Revolutionary Underground: The Story of the Irish Republican Brotherhood, 1858–1924* (Dublin: Roman and Littlefield, 1976), supplemented by T. W. Moody, ed., *The Fenian Movement,* Thomas Davis Lecture Series (Dublin, 1968).
35. *The Irishman,* 27 November 1877, referred to the anniversary of the executions as the "feast of the uncanonized" and added a semisecular prayer: "In nomine Patris et Filii / Et Spiritus Sancti—swearing me / To watch and wait, and foster my hate / To walk in the red paths of the Three."
36. Townshend, *Political Violence,* 37.
37. T. W. Moody and Leon O'Broin, eds., "The IRB Supreme Council, 1868–78: Select Documents," *Irish Historical Studies* 19 (1975).

Rossa's Skirmishers, the Irish-American Clan na Gael, which set itself to exploit the destructive power of Nobel's new explosive,[38] and most briefly but most spectacularly the Irish National Invincibles. These last, for all their shadowy evanescence, were unquestionably a terrorist group. Their single accomplished operation, the assassination of the two leading members of the Irish Executive in 1882, was only explicable as part of a project of paralyzing British rule in Ireland.[39]

A series of political, legal, and operational adaptations enabled the British state to ride out the episodic challenge of Irish terror in the 1880s.[40] The next revival of the physical-force doctrine only occurred during the great systemic crisis of the early twentieth century, when violence was unhinging many of the fixed points of "liberal England." The threat of political violence was first focused to great effect by Unionist opponents of Home Rule. The formation of the Ulster Volunteer Force (UVF) precipitated that of the nationalist Irish Volunteers, which at last provided the IRB with the means of achieving mass participation. These paramilitary militias at first seemed designed to threaten old-style insurrection, but the period from the start of Bulmer Hobson's reorganization of the IRB in 1906, and especially from the publication of his pamphlet *Defensive Warfare* in 1909,[41] to the establishment of the Irish Free State in 1922 was marked above all by the emergence of guerrilla methods. The 1916 rising in Dublin was an aberration from this development, and there were few aberrations in the direction of pure terrorism. What the Irish Volunteers, renamed the IRA in 1919, were able to do was to fuse the national revolution with the tradition of local violence that had remained quite vigorous despite the general settlement of the land war in the 1900s.[42]

Hence, the enforcement terror initiated in 1919 rapidly achieved a weight of credibility that insurgent movements in other contexts have

38. K.R.M. Short, *The Dynamite War: Irish-American Bombers in Victorian Britain* (Dublin: Gill and Macmillan, 1979).

39. Tom Corfe, *The Phoenix Park Murders: Conflict, Compromise, and Tragedy in Ireland, 1878–1882* (London: Hodder and Stoughton, 1968), is the best account; the insider's (embellished) version is P.J.P. Tynan, *The Irish National Invincibles and Their Times* (London: Chatham, 1894).

40. Townshend, *Political Violence*, 105–80. Bernard Porter, *Origins of the Vigilant State* (London: Weidenfeld and Nicolson, 1987), describes the emergence of the secret police.

41. Bulmer Hobson, *Defensive Warfare: A Handbook for Irish Nationalists* (Belfast: Sinn Fein, 1909).

42. Paul Bew, "Sinn Fein, Agrarian Radicalism, and the War of Independence, 1919–1921," in *The Revolution in Ireland, 1879–1923*, ed. D. G. Boyce (London: Macmillan, 1988), 217–34.

striven for in vain.[43] For instance, the high degree of social cohesion displayed in the 1918 boycott of the RIC was not the product of skillful decision making or even fortunate timing. The boycott emerged naturally out of the experience of rural communities in the land struggle, so naturally, indeed, that it looked even more inevitable than it was. The "four glorious years" of 1918–21 stand out as the climax of the nationalist myth of the "risen people," a myth whose power has fueled republican intransigence ever since. Defeat in the civil war was accommodated by a cerebral sleight of hand that one penetrating historian has called the "triumph of failure."[44] Through almost fifty years of impotence after 1923, it sustained the IRA's claim to continue the armed struggle until the absolute unitary independence declared by the first Dail Eireann in January 1919 was achieved. The rigidity of the republican position has not been absolute. The authority of the second Dail was eventually abandoned; the last twenty years of armed action have produced several major shifts of direction; and it is unlikely that many contemporary *Oglaich* (IRA volunteers) see themselves, or are seen by the nationalist public, as simply taking up where Liam Lynch quit. (Lynch was the last antitreaty Republican commander in the field at the end of the Irish civil war, which was never ended by any formal agreement or treaty but only by a "simple quit" on the part of the Irregulars, as the Free State called them, maintaining their right to restart hostilities in the future.) But it remains impossible to grasp the nature of the present armed resistance without recognizing the imprint that history lays on it.

CONTEXT

Cultural history in Ireland is still in its infancy. Pioneering essays like F.S.L. Lyons's *Culture and Anarchy* and Oliver MacDonagh's *States of Mind,* luminous as they are, cast most of their light in the sphere of writers and rulers.[45] Intermittently pyrotechnical displays like Tom Garvin's *Nationalist Revolutionaries in Ireland* and Jeffrey Prager's

43. Charles Townshend, "The Process of Terror," 43.
44. Ruth Dudley Edwards, *Patrick Pearse: The Triumph of Failure* (London: Victor Gollancz, 1977). See also note 80 below.
45. F.S.L. Lyons, *Culture and Anarchy in Ireland, 1890–1939* (Oxford: Clarendon Press, 1979), and Oliver MacDonagh, *States of Mind: A Study of Anglo-Irish Conflict, 1780–1980* (London: George Allen and Unwin, 1983). Lyons recognized the need to "seek our evidence of diversity in all the manifold circumstances of Irish life from the furniture of men's kitchens to the furniture of their minds" (4).

Building Democracy in Ireland formulate larger structural perspectives but also remain impressionistic in their grasp of mass opinion.[46] The most successful and straightforward cultural studies have so far been the work of anthropologists and geographers.[47] However rash it might be to accept Prager's antinomy of "Irish Enlightenment" and "Gaelic-Romantic" cultures as it stands, some working models at that level of generality are needed. The problem is not so much with Prager's definition of these traditions or with their utility in articulating the process of state building in Ireland. It is rather the paucity of concrete evidence of their public relevance or their capacity to mobilize people in the conflicts that actually occurred.

Prager in fact set himself a daunting task at the start of his study, following Keith Michael Baker's identification of "common discourse" as the mark of "community." The interaction involved in the framing of claims is constrained within that discourse, which in turn sustains, extends, and on occasion transforms. Political authority is in this view a matter of linguistic authority, both in the sense that public functions are defined and allocated within the framework of a given political discourse and in the sense that their exercise takes the form of maintaining that discourse by upholding authoritative definitions of (and within) it.[48]

Prager adds that "through this realm of discourse, the formulation of collective goals or purposes, although historically conditioned, is constantly subject to redefinition and respecification through both debate and social contest. . . . The challenge is to describe the cultural universe of Irish men and women that illuminates and explains their responses to a shifting political reality."[49] This is indeed a crucial challenge that remains unmet. If the Irish Enlightenment and Gaelic-Romantic cultural traditions "served to orient the population" or, as he puts it earlier, "actively vied with each other for the hearts and minds of the people,"

---

46. Tom Garvin, *Nationalist Revolutionaries in Ireland, 1858–1928* (Oxford: Clarendon Press, 1987), and Jeffrey Prager, *Building Democracy in Ireland: Political Order and Cultural Integration in a Newly Independent Nation* (Cambridge: Cambridge University Press, 1986).

47. E.g., Rosemary Harris, *Prejudice and Tolerance in Ulster: A Study of Neighbours and "Strangers" in a Border Community* (Manchester: Manchester University Press, 1972); M. W. Heslinga, *The Irish Border as a Cultural Divide: A Contribution to the Study of Regionalism in the British Isles* (Assen: Van Gorcum, 1971); Michael Hechter, *Internal Colonialism: The Celtic Fringe in British National Development, 1536–1966* (Berkeley and Los Angeles: University of California Press, 1975); and F. W. Boal and J.N.H. Douglas, eds., *Integration and Division: Geographical Perspectives on the Northern Ireland Problem* (London: Academic Press, 1982).

48. Prager, *Building Democracy in Ireland*, 23.

49. Ibid., 35.

the people have to be the principal locus of analysis. Prager's Gaelic-Romantic tradition is an essentially racial community ("brethren connected by a common ancient ancestry"), Irishness defined as the antithesis of Saxondom: "rural, agricultural and Catholic."[50] Why did ordinary people accept this as an apt description of themselves?

The most striking feature of the nationalist self-image composed in the nineteenth century was its dependence on religious identity. As late as the 1840s this was still a matter of misunderstanding between O'Connell and the Protestant Young Irelander Thomas Davis.[51] The Fenians had a reputation for being anticlerical and fell under the ban of the Catholic hierarchy; at grass roots, though, Fenianism was routinely, uncontentiously Catholic. As political Protestantism (or unionism) organized against Home Rule in the 1880s, the Catholic complexion of the national movement became more pronounced,[52] and the Irish version of "integral nationalism" (which, like Maurras's French version, took Catholicism to be the living sign of a pre-Christian race) reached full expression in the pungent journalism of D. P. Moran. Moran's dictum "The foundation of Ireland is the Gael and the Gael must be the element that absorbs" has been often and rightly quoted: it probably had a bigger moral impact on unionists than on nationalists.

The implicit racism of Moran's prejudices has until recently been rather ignored.[53] It should not now be exaggerated, but we do need an explanation for what Moran saw as the commonsense point that "when we look out on Ireland we see that those who believe or may be immediately induced to believe in Ireland as a nation are, as a matter of fact, Catholics. . . . the Irish nation is *de facto* a Catholic nation."[54] The provision of such an explanation is well beyond the scope of this chapter. The salience of religious motifs in the transmission of political violence is, however, inescapable. Martyrdom is a notion that has been so devalued in modern political propaganda that there must now be some difficulty in gauging its force in a culture that does not automatically adjust it to hyperbole. Moreover, the twentieth-century republican movement

50. Ibid., 45, 44.
51. T. W. Moody, "Thomas Davis and the Irish Nation," *Hermathena* 102 (1966): 5–31.
52. Marianne Elliott, *Watchmen in Sion: The Protestant Idea of Liberty*, Field Day Pamphlet no. 8 (Derry, 1985).
53. Alf MacLochlainn, "Gael and Peasant: A Case of Mistaken Identity," in *Views of the Irish Peasantry, 1800–1916*, ed. D. J. Casey and R. E. Rhodes (Hamden, Conn.: Archon Books, 1977).
54. *The Leader*, 27 April 1901. D. G. Boyce, *Nationalism in Ireland* (Baltimore: Johns Hopkins University Press, 1982), 243, comments that "any racial undertones were ones that he recognized, not ones that he invented."

found a way of heightening the significance already attached to certain kinds of death.

On 25 July 1917 the RIC arrested Thomas Ashe, the most successful surviving commander of the 1916 rebellion, for sedition. He immediately began a hunger strike, which ended with his death after force-feeding in Mountjoy Gaol two months later. Ashe's death, and those of succeeding republican hunger strikers, was technically suicide, and it had a great impact on Catholic sensibility. In such a context, suicide may indeed be an act of spiritual terrorism. In any case, his death marked the physical-force movement indelibly. It led to the first Fenian funeral at which a Catholic bishop officiated; and at Ashe's graveside in Glasnevin his successor Michael Collins provided an oration that was as threatening as it was brief: "Nothing additional remains to be said. The volley which we have just heard is the only speech which it is proper to make above the grave of a dead Fenian."[55]

Part of the impact of this oration derived from its contrast with the more florid performance delivered at O'Donovan Rossa's funeral by Patrick Pearse in 1915, whose peroration—"The fools! the fools! the fools! they have left us our Fenian dead, and while Ireland holds these graves, Ireland unfree shall never be at peace"—nonetheless furnished an equally potent manifesto. It would be incautious to say that all republicans followed the idiosyncratic syncretism that Pearse elaborated, expressed most fiercely in his poem "Mionn," where a litany of Irish heroes—Hugh and Owen Roe O'Neill, Patrick Sarsfield, Lord Edward FitzGerald, Wolfe Tone, and Robert Emmet—is bound together with the famine corpses, the tears of exiles, God, Christ, Mary, Saint Patrick, and Colmcille into an oath to "free our race from bondage, / Or . . . fall fighting hand to hand / Amen."[56] But his vision of an apostolic succession heightened the historical sense inherent in nationalism, providing a framework in which the new generation of martyrs—beginning with himself—would acquire enhanced meaning. The succession was in time to incorporate Terence MacSwiney and Bobby Sands.[57]

Living through the barren years after 1923 was often associated by republicans with "keeping the faith."[58] Pearse concluded his poem "The Rebel" with an insurgent prayer: "Do / not remember my failures /

55. Sean O'Luing, *I Die in a Good Cause: A Study of Thomas Ashe, Idealist and Revolutionary* (Tralee: Anvil Books, 1970), and Piaras Beaslai, *Michael Collins and the Making of a New Ireland* (London: G. G. Harrap, 1926), 1:166.

56. *An Barr Buadh*, 16 March 1912.

57. *The Irish Freedom Movement Handbook: The Irish War* (London: Junius, 1983), 53–54.

58. Townshend, *Political Violence*, 374–81.

But remember this my faith." Endurance, sustained by the recurrent metaphor of the "phoenix flame," became the test of conviction. But what may be seen as the sacral culture of physical force was always ballasted by the secular culture of communal resistance stemming from the land struggle. Control of the land is still a life-and-death issue in the marches of Fermanagh, and the transference of rural modes of conflict into the rapidly urbanizing Northeast during the nineteenth century permanently shaped the nature of conflict there.[59] Belfast became what a modern geographer calls "the urban encapsulation of a national conflict."[60] Communal clashes, only falling short of civil war in duration rather than intensity, erupted repeatedly between the 1860s and 1920s. The trigger for this collective violence was usually symbolic: the erection of a statue of O'Connell, or a parade commemorating the relief of Derry. Such parades were (and are) the most striking form that the transmission of political culture can take, asserting the Protestant ascendancy on the basis of Catholic disloyalty.[61] They were a form of communal intimidation that remained socially functional whether or not they provoked a violent response. They expressed the solidarity of Protestants in defense of "freedom, religion, and laws" (or, more accurately, "religion, laws, and liberties") in a manner that was often characterized as tribal.[62]

By the early twentieth century, industrial conflict, far from eroding or superseding such traditional identities, had been incorporated into the vertical cleavage on the "constitutional issue." Indeed, the problems of employment in the industrial sector, though they provided occasional moments of apparent proletarian unity, triggered some of the most destructive communal terrorism of all.[63] "Defenderism" was not transported unchanged from the fields of eighteenth-century Armagh to the streets of Andersonstown in the early 1970s. But the public fears the Provisionals set themselves to answer were not new. Even the specifically "modern" grievances of the Catholic minority, discrimination, gerrymandering, and denial of civil rights, were the product of the old communal conflict that had been expressed in "partition."[64]

59. Stewart, *Narrow Ground*, 113 ff.
60. F. W. Boal, R. C. Murray, and M. A. Poole, "Belfast: The Urban Encapsulation of a National Conflict," in *Urban Ethnic Conflict: A Comparative Perspective*, ed. S. E. Clarke and J. L. Obler (Chapel Hill: Institute for Research in Social Science, University of North Carolina, 1976).
61. J. G. Simms, "Remembering 1690," *Studies* 251 (1974): 231–42.
62. For instance, Simms describes the erection of the statue of William III in College Green on 1 July 1701 as "the beginning of William III's transformation into a tribal deity" (ibid., 234).
63. Henry Patterson, *Class Conflict and Sectarianism: The Protestant Working Class and the Belfast Labour Movement, 1868–1920* (Belfast: Blackstaff Press, 1980).
64. J. Bowyer Bell, "The Escalation of Insurgency: The Experience of the Provisional

The most substantial analysis of the relations between the IRA and the community remains the study of a west Belfast borough called Anro by the pseudonymous Frank Burton, who saw the paramilitary organization as "a political isomorphism of the ideological meanings of Catholicism."[65] Since he wrote, the relations have, if anything, thickened, not only through the high-profile return to politics of Sinn Fein but also through the less newsworthy imbrication of paramilitary and economic activity (usually referred to when mentioned at all in the British press as "racketeering"). Structurally, if not ideologically, republican paramilitarism has established one more alternative state.[66]

Two further contextual elements of the present conflict need to be mentioned. The existence of an independent Irish state—albeit not recognized as such by republicans—since 1922 has provided a vital underpinning for the legitimacy of republicanism. Even in the quiet 1960s Richard Rose found that 60 percent of his Catholic respondents in Northern Ireland agreed that it had been right for the IRB to take up arms and fight for the republic fifty years before.[67] Of course, early assumptions (fed by the Dublin government's rhetoric, itself an uneasy recognition of the instability of the issue) that southern nationalists would play a direct role in the conflict have been replaced by a general realization of the republic's active disengagement and its consistent hostility to the IRA itself.[68] This has clearly been a major force in limiting the intensity of the conflict, though the (more or less involuntary) provision of sanctuary may have played a countervailing part in the persistence of paramilitary activity.

More directly engaged has been the self-conscious diaspora in Britain

---

Irish Republican Army, 1969–1971," *Review of Politics* 35 (1973): 389–411; Patrick Buckland, *The Factory of Grievances: Devolved Government in Northern Ireland, 1922–1939* (Dublin: Gill and Macmillan, 1979); and Charles Townshend, "Northern Ireland," in *Foreign Policy and Human Rights: Issues and Responses*, ed. R. J. Vincent (Cambridge: Cambridge University Press, 1986).

65. Frank Burton, *The Politics of Legitimacy: Struggles in a Belfast Community* (London: Routledge and Kegan Paul, 1978), 68. See also Edward Moxon-Browne, "The Water and the Fish: Public Opinion and the Provisional IRA in Northern Ireland," *Terrorism* 5 (1981): 41–72, and Tom Hadden, Paddy Hillyard, and Kevin Boyle, "Northern Ireland: The Communal Roots of Violence," *New Statesman* 54, no. 938 (1980).

66. James Adams, *The Financing of Terror* (London: Simon and Schuster, 1986).

67. Richard Rose, *Governing Without Consensus: An Irish Perspective* (Boston: Beacon Press, 1971), 483.

68. Ronan Fanning, " 'The Rule of Order': Eamon de Valera and the IRA, 1923–40," in *De Valera and His Times*, ed. J. P. O'Carroll and J. A. Murphy (Cork: Cork University Press, 1983), 160–71. See also Tom Garvin, "The North and the Rest: The Politics of the Republic of Ireland," in *Consensus in Ireland: Approaches and Recessions*, ed. Charles Townshend (Oxford: Clarendon Press, 1988), 95–109.

and America. The Irish-American segment has periodically intervened with efforts to aid the nationalist movement with men, money, and arms. Though such aid has at times taken spectacular forms, it is probably impossible to quantify either the material or the moral impact of this long-term intervention. Its erratic significance may be illustrated by the career of one individual, Sean MacStiofain, born in outer London as John Stephenson and first active with the IRA in a raid on Felsted school armory in 1953. MacStiofain was to be a prime mover among the dissident members of the IRA Army Council who established the Provisionals in 1969, and effectively led the organization until his arrest in November 1972 and eventually lost all control over it following the abandonment of his hunger strike at the Curragh in November 1973. He attributed his discovery of his Irish identity to a few words of his mother's, his "instinctive" mixing with Irish children at his Catholic school in Islington, and his adolescent exposure to "the vehement prejudices" of English workers, which led him to conclude that "there is an inherent anti-Irish feeling in most English people."[69]

MOBILIZATION

Republican

Mobilization for revolution has two elements that often prove to be as distinct in practice as they can be made in theory. The first is the organization of the revolutionaries; the second the mobilization of the people. Historically, the first has been more common than the second. Irish history contains plenty of examples of this discrepancy. Indeed, a mass rising of the kind expected by most nineteenth-century revolutionaries never happened, even in 1798. Nonetheless, 1798, like 1789 and Year II in France, became a potent myth that mobilized successive generations of revolutionaries. The Anglo-Irish war of 1918–21 fell well short of the ideal type, but through the brilliance of republican publicity, it generated a myth that was at least as potent. These are myths, I would suggest, in the strictly Sorelian sense that they simplify the world sufficiently to make action possible. A nationalist contemplating any actual "people" would be driven rapidly to loss of faith, if not suicidal despair. Simplification or idealization is the essence of the notion of the *Volksgeist* and the essential condition for nationalist activity. The myth

69. Sean MacStiofain, *Memoirs of a Revolutionary* (Edinburgh, n.d.), 16–20.

of the nation provides the reason for action; the myth of popular mobilization underwrites the feasibility of action. These myths are not wholly unchanging.

There is some reason to suppose that the Mazzinian vision of the people as, in characteristic predynamite metaphor, a kind of "powder keg" waiting to be ignited by the revolutionary spark was losing its potency in the later nineteenth century after repeated failures to materialize. It is well enough known that Engels finally declared that modern states were unlikely to be toppled by hastily raised mass levies at the barricades. From this standpoint both Lenin and Pearse (James Connolly too) were anachronisms. Their revolutionary voluntarism came at a time when things were changing, though the direction of change was still unclear. Anarchist terrorists had posited an alternative mechanism of revolutionary violence, propaganda by deed. But for most of them, like Malatesta, this was at root just another way of achieving the old ideal. Propaganda would arouse the people, who would ultimately triumph by sheer weight of numbers.

In Ireland, however, a quite novel mechanism for interlocking revolutionaries and people was emerging at this time—pragmatically rather than theoretically. Michael Collins's repudiation of traditional IRB insurrectionism in favor of guerrilla methods arose naturally out of Irish conditions.[70] The IRA established the viability of the numerical formula first laid down in print by T. E. Lawrence and later the staple of counterinsurgency manuals: "Rebellions can be made by two per cent active in a striking force and 98 per cent passively sympathetic."[71] The IRA did not dispense altogether with the old myth of the people. But the new relation provided a more sophisticated basis for the republican claim that they stood for the Irish popular will. The old Mitchelite elitism and cult of violence remained—indeed, contemporary critics of the IRA have harped on its militarist and dictatorial tendencies[72]—but the power of modern republicanism derived as much from the democratic credentials of the first Dail as from the inner meaning of the republic itself, which, as David Fitzpatrick has acutely observed, was a hollow vessel into

70. Charles Townshend, "The Irish Republican Army and the Development of Guerrilla Warfare, 1916–21," *English Historical Review* 94 (1979): 318–45.

71. T. E. Lawrence, "The Evolution of a Revolt," *Army Quarterly* 1 (1920), reprinted in M. Elliott-Batemen, John Ellis, and Tom Bowden, *Revolt to Revolution: Studies in the Nineteenth- and Twentieth-Century European Experience* (Manchester: Manchester University Press, 1974), 160.

72. This was the nub of Kevin O'Higgins's denunciations of irregularism, as it is of Conor Cruise O'Brien's equally pungent views of the Provisionals. See his *States of Ireland* (New York: Pantheon Books, 1972), 243 ff.

which each individual could pour his or her own dreams. The soft focus of the republican grail has always heightened its attractive power, though as a sequence of splits has shown, it is also fraught with potential for conflict within the movement. The most profound and enduring split was, of course, the "treaty split" and Civil War in 1922–23, but jarring conflicts also arose between de Valera's Fianna Fail and the IRA in the 1920s, and Peadar O'Donnell's Saor Eire and the IRA in the 1930s, foreshadowing the split between the official and provisional wings of the IRA during the 1970s and 1980s.

The republican movement has incorporated both progressive and traditionalist outlooks. As a consistent opponent of the British presence in Ireland, colonial or imperial, it has deployed plenty of progressive rhetoric. But internally, it has made little or no room for explicit socialists; rather, its Catholic nationalist mainstream has been doggedly conservative on social questions.[73] An extremely simple one-step model of liberation (Break the connection, Brits out) as a solvent for political, social, and economic problems has done service for a constructive ideology since United Irish times. Only recently has its naïveté begun to appear inadequate to some, though by no means all, republicans. As a result, Sinn Fein was impelled at one point to elaborate in unprecedented detail a specific constitutional policy project *(Eire Nua)* designed principally as a vehicle for containing Ulster identity within a national political framework.[74] Even so, the detail was sketchy, and the assumptions underpinning the viability of a federal constitution remain unconvincing to anyone who does not already accept the basic nationalist tenets. An important PIRA gunman who discovered Connolly while in jail (in the republic) and joined the Irish National Liberation Army (INLA) defined his object as the ending of "repression," a loose notion that might or might not go beyond a British withdrawal: "I genuinely wish there were another way of dealing with repression in Northern Ireland, but I believe there is no other way." "As I have often said to priests who condemn violence, if we can build a mass movement to end repression . . . then I would put down the gun in the morning. But don't forget, when the

73. Patrick Lynch, "The Social Revolution That Never Was," in *The Irish Struggle*, ed. T. D. Williams (London: Routledge and Kegan Paul, 1966), 41–54. See also Michael Laffan, " 'Labour Must Wait': Ireland's Conservative Revolution," in *Radicals, Rebels, and Establishments*, ed. P. J. Corish, Historical Studies no. 15 (Belfast, 1985), 203–22. The left-right distinction noted by some researchers in the psychology of terrorism (e.g., Martha Crenshaw, "The Psychology of Political Terrorism," in *Political Psychology*, ed. Margaret G. Hermann [San Francisco: Jossey-Bass, 1986]) is largely irrelevant in Ireland.

74. Sean Cronin, *Irish Nationalism: A History of Its Roots and Ideology* (Dublin: Academy Press, 1980), 209–13.

Northern Ireland people started a mass movement for reform, Paisley and Bunting came out with clubs to beat them off the streets for demanding one man one vote."[75]

The precipitant of the present conflict was not, however, traditional nationalism. Indeed, the civil rights movement in Northern Ireland could be seen, for a time, as symptomatic of the gradual abandonment by the "nationalist" minority of its refusal to recognize or participate in the Northern Ireland state's institutions.[76] People's Democracy (PD) was a new and radical-looking political organization, and on the nationalist/ Catholic side the situation in 1968–69 appeared more open-ended than ever before. The Protestant reaction was, however, enough to throw the clash back into a more obviously traditional configuration. The loyalist assault on PD was a straight reversion to 1920, with one crucial addition: the presence of television cameras. For this reason the blind eye that Britain had turned on Northern Ireland for fifty years was pulled open; British troops were sent in to restore public order; and at last the IRA's image of the six counties as a British colony was restored to reality.

The strength of the PIRA derives from its capacity to mobilize "the ideological meanings of Catholicism." At street level this means a fairly explosive mix of political nationalism and communal sectarianism—a direct echo of "defenderism." Powerful (if jaundiced) testimony to the nature of this mix is provided by the PIRA leader Jim Sullivan, who held that the Provisionals "unfortunately went for quantity instead of quality with the result that without any shadow of doubt they finished up with a bunch of young lads who were in it just to fight Prods" (Protestants).[77] The immediacy of this motivation is a matter of daily experience and report. "We're chasing those black [Protestant] bastards who shot our people out," said one of Patrick Bishop and Eamon Mallie's respondents who until the night of 15 August 1969 had no connection with a republican organization and had a Protestant grandfather and a cousin in the Royal Ulster Constabulary (RUC).[78] The socialization of such "sixty-niners" in the Catholic—especially Christian Brothers—school system of west Belfast or Derry provided a ready-made view of the other community (which the Protestants in their turn cultivated with equal assiduity).[79]

75. Ken Heskin, "The Terrorists' Terrorist: Vincent Browne's Interview with Dominic McGlinchey," in *Ireland's Terrorist Dilemma*, ed. Yonah Alexander and Alan O'Day (Dordrecht: M. Nijhoff, 1986), 100–102.

76. John Darby, *Conflict in Northern Ireland: The Development of a Polarised Community* (Dublin: Gill and Macmillan, 1976), 149.

77. Patrick Bishop and Eamon Mallie, *The Provisional IRA* (London: Heinemann, 1987), 121.

78. Ibid., 116–17.

79. John Darby et al., *Education and Community in Northern Ireland: Schools Apart?* (Coleraine: New University of Ulster, 1977), and Dominic Murray, "Schools and Conflict,"

The PIRA's operational repertoire shows, in its breadth, the gamut of functions the organization serves. Measurement of this range can be made by classifying both methods and targets. Lethal violence is only the most spectacular means of inducing fear, and in Northern Ireland it has formed the tip of an iceberg of less visible coercive intimidation. Less absolute forms of physical harm—from beatings, croppings, and tarrings to woundings (notably "kneecappings") by gunshot or electric drill—have been routine modes of maintaining the integrity and prestige of the organization. Such routine operations, besides reinforcing the ascendancy of the PIRA over its rivals both nationalist and loyalist, have served to demarcate (or to confirm the demarcation of) territory and have provided a rudimentary structure of public order.

At the start of the conflict in the early 1970s demarcation of territory reached an intensity amounting to virtual secession, but since the "no-go" areas were reentered by a large-scale military operation (Motorman) in July 1972, the appearance of alternative government has been lower in profile.[80] Still, the normalization of enforcement terror has been evident in everyday social and economic life and in the significant semantic shift to the new usage of the term *paramilitaries* in place of the value-laden terms *(rebels, gunmen, terrorists)* originally available. This has provided a vital escape route for civilians caught in a destructive moral and literal crossfire, while it has inevitably bolstered the plausibility of the organizations' claim to be waging war.

That claim is of course much more plausible, even to outsiders, in the case of the IRA and the smaller socialist Irish National Liberation Army group than in the case of the loyalist "paramilitaries," if only because the former can aim their most newsworthy lethal attacks at uniformed servants of the Crown and so appear to strike directly at the British state. Over its long war, the PIRA has wrung reluctant recognition (whether admiration, acquiescence, or the fierce hatred expressed in the English tabloid press) of its continuing capacity to hit hard targets. This sort of recognition is all but impossible to measure, but the impression made by relatively infrequent successes against hard military and police targets seems to erase the detestation provoked by indiscriminate killings.

Discussion of what is a "legitimate target" in such a conflict is the core

---

in *Northern Ireland: The Background to the Conflict*, ed. John Darby (Belfast: Appletree Press, 1983), 136–50.

80. In assessing Motorman's impact, however, Bishop and Mallie remark that "there was no immediate lowering of morale. Republicanism is steeped in failure" (*Provisional IRA*, 181–82). See also Desmond Hamill, *Pig in the Middle: The Army in Northern Ireland, 1969–1984* (London: Methuen, 1985), 112 ff.

of the whole issue. Communities that feel threatened or embattled may well accept the need to "fight Prods" by means ranging from burning out houses to random gunning of pubs frequented by the other side. Such collective terrorism is calculated to reinforce the physical segregation that originally shaped the urban conflict, which has become sharper under the pressure of years of violence but which itself forms a major mode of controlling the incidence of violence.[81] After the 1989 Warrenpoint explosion of a van bomb near a hardware store, David McKittrick of the *Independent* pointed to the steady expansion of the PIRA's list of legitimate targets, which now include judges and magistrates, senior civil servants, unionist politicians and loyalist "paramilitants," prison officers, businesspeople, and workers who deal with the security forces, in addition to traditional "civilian" victims like "spies and informers."[82]

Public reading of the legitimacy of an attack is a sensitive political indicator. Attempts to kill senior politicians or other representative figures can hardly be surprising—in fact their relative infrequency may be more surprising—but they may be viewed as evidence not only of murderousness but also of contempt for democracy. Responses to such attacks largely reflect and confirm the existing polarization of public opinion, raising the question whether terrorism or paramilitarism has a significant capacity to achieve positive, as distinct from negative, objectives.[83]

A striking example of a paramilitary organization's failure to read public opinion is provided by Eamonn McCann in his penetrating account of nationalism in Derry. After the shooting of thirteen civilians by the First Parachute Regiment on Bloody Sunday in 1972, the official IRA believed that a major series of revenge attacks was justified and issued orders "to kill every British soldier we could." The policy misfired; the shooting of Ranger Best, the "son of solid and inoffensive parents who lived in a council house in Creggan . . . outraged that very feeling of communal solidarity which the last three years had created and which

81. However, statistics on people returning to areas from which they have been driven might prove surprising.

82. *The Independent*, 13 April 1989. McKittrick offered no measure of the extent to which Provisional ideas of legitimacy were accepted by any significant public.

83. Perhaps the only exception that may prove to have significance is the British "Troops Out" movement, which has taken various forms. The journal currently bearing the title *Troops Out* ("produced by a collective drawn from branches of the Troops Out Movement in London") is a frankly republican production (the cover of its March 1989 issue commemorating the Gilbraltar killings carried a large picture of Mairead Farrell with the legend "Remember Mairead Farrell Killed by the SAS March 6 1988") without general circulation. The "Time to Go" group has secured peak-hour airtime on BBC2 and later time on Channel 4.

was absolutely essential to the maintenance of Free Derry."[84] The setback was a serious one for the PIRA, and the heady days of the "no-go" areas as liberated zones were numbered. But the sensitivity of the PIRA to public feeling has not markedly changed, and it is to a large extent the public rather than the paramilitaries who ultimately give way. No misconceived or botched operation has yet proved catastrophic for any republican group.

Loyalist

The unionist mobilization into violence at many points prefigured that of the nationalists. It would be hard to say which of the two is likely to prove the more irreducible. Currently, the prestige of loyalist paramilitary organizations (Ulster Defence Association, Ulster Freedom Fighters, Ulster Volunteer Force) is not high, but the Protestant community has its own myths of popular mobilization, which parallel those of the nationalists. The Williamite war has been constructed into a composite symbol of resistance (the siege of Londonderry) and triumph (the battle of the Boyne). Of even greater resonance and relevance is the anti–Home Rule movement, symbolized by the Ulster Covenant, the original UVF, and the granite figure of Sir Edward Carson. The experience of the provincial strike in 1974 is perhaps more problematic and speaks of the almost unprecedented fragmentation of what was once called the unionist monolith.[85]

Yet despite pervasive and novel uncertainty about the proper mode of action in the present crisis, there is little sign that fundamental unionist attitudes have become less monolithic in their simplicity. The general notion of a Protestant "way of life" retains wide currency, and though the visual symbol of King Billy on his white horse may be less in evidence, the old slogans—We will not have Home Rule; No surrender; Not an inch; and, more disreputably, No popery—remain powerfully expressive definitions of the ground on which loyalists are prepared to fight, or at least to threaten to fight by organizing in military fashion. The best observer study of Protestant activism accepted the view that modern paramilitary groups can be seen as products of traditional Northern Ireland society, not subverters of the old order but extreme versions of it. Those who formed and joined them were used to uniforms,

84. Eamonn McCann, *War and an Irish Town* (London: Pluto Press, 1974), 167.
85. David McKittrick, "The Class Structure of Unionism," *Crane Bag* 4 (1980): 28–33. Although Robert Fisk was probably correct to give his book *Point of No Return* (London: Times Books, 1975) the subtitle *The Strike Which Broke the British in Ulster*, over fifteen years in the direction of breakage seems less conclusive than the subtitle would suggest.

punitive discipline, parades, and a system in which one gave and received orders. But they were unfamiliar with democratic organizations and unused to making their own decisions.[86]

According to this reading, the Protestant working-class rank and file were integrated into unionist organizations by their simple one-issue platforms, which rendered internal democracy superfluous, if not actually subversive. Class tensions that certainly existed within the "monolith" only became overt when the gentry leadership showed signs of deviating from the strict path of defending the Protestant constitution. The paranoid nature of loyalism, with its deliberate cultivation of the "siege mentality," has meant that such deviation by the "fur coat brigade" is commonly feared, and the response to this—for instance, the UVF's reaction to the (principally rhetorical) concessions to Catholics initiated by Terence O'Neill after 1966—has been violence against Catholics.

There have been a number of attempts to demonstrate that the components of Protestant identity meet the criteria of nationality and that Ulster unionists are thus a nation.[87] None of these demonstrations has been wholly successful, though since in practice the ultimate proof of nationhood is the capacity to vindicate it by force of arms, there is a degree of circularity in all such analysis.[88] Plainly, Ulster Protestants have come close to such self-assertion on several occasions over the last century but have never taken this collective responsibility. At present the principal barrier is lack of confidence in any specific outcome; exponents of United Kingdom integration (the original antidevolution position of 1886), Northern Ireland devolution à la Stormont (with or without power sharing), and Ulster independence vie for support. It is possible that in the future terrorist violence will be used in a bid for control by one of these persuasions, but so far Protestant paramilitarism has been limited to the traditional single-issue politics of communal ascendancy. In spite of the Reverend Ian Paisley's efforts on more than one occasion to re-create a representative militia like the original UVF, street activists have remained marginal (as the label Ultras indicates).[89] Nonethe-

---

86. Sarah Nelson, *Ulster's Uncertain Defenders: Protestant Political, Paramilitary, and Community Groups and the Northern Ireland Conflict* (Belfast: Appletree Press, 1984), 43.

87. In fact, the New Ulster Political Research Group—which, like its parent body, the Ulster Defence Association, once advocated a unilateral declaration of Ulster independence—has, in the wake of the Anglo-Irish Agreement, embraced consociation, rather than exclusive nationality, as the basis for Ulster politics (*Common Sense* [Belfast, 1987]).

88. Edward Moxon-Browne, *Nation, Class, and Creed in Northern Ireland* (Aldershot: Gower Books, 1983), 1–17. Cf. the objections to independence in Kevin Boyle and Tom Hadden, *Ireland: A Positive Proposal* (Harmondsworth: Penguin, 1985), 32–33.

89. The launching of the Third Force in the late 1970s was unsuccessful; the most recent creation, Ulster Resistance, has so far, since 1986, failed to become a mass movement.

less, in 1986–88 their activities began to run at a higher level than over the previous twenty years, rising from two killings in 1985 to sixteen in 1986, fourteen in 1987, and eighteen in 1988. After that a rash of allegations of collusion between loyalist paramilitary groups and the security forces, murky deals with the South African secret service, and a rising sequence of blatantly sectarian killings screwed up the pitch of civil conflict. The conscious embattlement of the Protestant community was producing consistent internal migration to more homogeneous ethnic areas.[90]

EFFICACY: STATIC MOMENTUM

The question that is probably most often posed about the Irish conflict is not How did it arise? but Why does it go on? The durability of the IRA, the uncanny resilience of the loyalist worldview, and the sheer insolubility of the "problem" (as a distinguished political scientist recognized)[91] have repeatedly impressed themselves on observers. Nobody put the outsider's bafflement, frustration, and contempt better than Winston Churchill, introducing the Irish Free State Bill in the House of Commons on 16 February 1922:

> The differences had been narrowed down, not merely to the counties of Fermanagh and Tyrone, but to parishes and groups inside the areas of Fermanagh and Tyrone, and yet, even when the differences had been so narrowed down, the problem appeared to be as insuperable as ever, and neither side would agree to reach any conclusion. Then came the Great War. . . . Every institution, almost, in the world was strained. . . . The mode and thought of men, the whole outlook on affairs, the grouping of parties, all have encountered violent and tremendous changes in the deluge of the world, but as the deluge subsides and the waters fall we see the

There are useful accounts of loyalist paramilitarism in Arthur Aughey and Colin McIlheney, "The Ulster Defence Association: Paramilitaries and Politics," *Conflict Quarterly* 2 (1981): 32–45, and "Law Before Violence? The Protestant Paramilitaries in Ulster Politics," *Eire-Ireland* 19 (1984): 55–74.

90. "Arms Shipment Put Loyalist Paramilitaries in Big League of Terrorism," *The Independent*, 24 April 1989.

91. Richard Rose, *Northern Ireland: A Time of Choice* (London: Faber and Faber, 1976), 139. See also John Whyte, "Interpretations of the Northern Ireland Problem," in *Consensus in Ireland*, 43.

dreary steeples of Fermanagh and Tyrone emerging once again. The integrity of their quarrel is one of the few institutions that have been unaltered in the cataclysm which has swept the world.[92]

But as a number of recent writers have warned, we must beware of assuming that history in Ulster has come to a halt, as though fixed in some monstrous time warp. The fact that the lineaments of the conflict have altered surprisingly little over a century does not mean that they will never change. The persistence of latent civil war calls for continuing explanation.

The conclusion indicated by this historical analysis is that political violence persists because it is effective. Its efficacy is the primary condition of its adoption, readoption, legitimation, and containment. This is not to deny that at certain periods or levels of conflict there can emerge what has been called a subculture of violence, in which for organizational or psychological reasons violence becomes self-validating, or autotelic. Walter put the distinction with typical lucidity: "As long as terror is directed to an end beyond itself, namely control, it has a limit and remains a process. . . . Under certain conditions, terror becomes unlimited and therefore no longer a process but an end in itself."[93] It is plainly more feasible for the historian to analyze objective processes than subjective psychological states, and that is the final aim of this paper. But analysis must start from recognition that the two are connected and that in internal war or guerrilla insurgency the psychological element is more salient than it is in regular or conventional war. Insofar as strictly objective measurement of regular military action is possible (and Tolstoy, of course, held that it is not at all), measurement of insurgent and anti-insurgent activities is much more subjective. Public perceptions form the lines of maneuver and the *places fortes* of a guerrilla campaign.[94]

So the crucial question about the process of terror is not How much damage was caused? but What message did the damage convey? The message may or may not approximate the one intended by the terrorists. A longish list of possible messages could be drawn up without much difficulty: it would include We are strong enough to do this; We mean

92. Winston S. Churchill, *The World Crisis: The Aftermath* (London: T. Butterworth, 1929), 319.

93. Walter, *Terror and Resistance*, 14.

94. Michael Elliott-Bateman, "The Battlefronts of People's War," in Elliott-Bateman, Tom Bowden, and John Ellis, *The Fourth Dimension of Warfare*, vol. 2, *Revolt to Revolution* (Manchester: Manchester University Press, 1974), 313–61, and Charles Town-shend, *Britain's Civil Wars: Counterinsurgency in the Twentieth Century* (London: Faber and Faber, 1986), 33–36.

business; Our opponents cannot protect you; and so on. In the case of the IRA it is evident that all these kinds of statements made by acts of violence were grasped at quite an early stage, certainly by 1921.[95] Despite many vicissitudes in the intervening years, the IRA has never lost sight of this deliberate application of harm as communication. Most important, such messages were on the whole clearly understood by their principal audience, the Catholic community in the six counties.

By contrast, these acts have communicated radically different messages to their secondary audiences, the British public and the northern unionists. McCann recorded that local attitudes toward the systematic bombing of Derry city center by the IRA under Martin McGuinness were "fairly equivocal": The nationalist community saw the force of the PIRA view that the main victims were the workers who lost their jobs, and the fact that the campaign drove the Protestants still further to the right "was to be regretted." But "as against that, every bomb planted was a minor victory in the endless battle of wits against the security forces. . . . Every blast was a dramatic demonstration of the fact that we, who had been scorned for so long, could now strike out in an unmistakable fashion and make the establishment scream."[96]

The theoretical capacity of terror to fracture the state as the symbol of public order and clamorously to break the monopoly of legitimate coercive power (which organized criminals also break, but quietly) has been effective only within ethnic limits. Outside them the paradoxical outcome has been, if anything, reinforcement of the attitudes and policies the IRA needed to undermine. This has been as clear at the practical, administrative level—where the suspension of the devolved Northern Ireland legislature and its replacement by direct British rule in 1972 looked at first like a republican success but has come in time to be a larger obstacle to their aims—as at the attitudinal level, where an ingrained British reaction has been the refusal to "give way to force" whatever its cause.

Thus, the control exerted by republican coercion has fallen short of its final objectives but has proved ample to guarantee the endurance of the IRA. Since its rapid enlargement with "sixty-niners," the organization has nurtured its social roots. The kind of infrastructural imbrication portrayed in a sequence of literary and dramatic works over the last decade, such as Aisling Donelan's radio play *Flying High*, has given

95. Chief of staff, IRA, to OC Fingal Brigade, 6 April 1921; GHQ IRA, Training Memorandum no. 2, 23 April 1921. Both in University College Dublin Archive, Mulcahy MSS P7 A/II/17.

96. McCann, *War and an Irish Town*, 106.

contemporary paramilitarism a more substantial handle on reality than any preceding revolutionary movement. The result is an ill-defined and unstable hybridization of political and military campaigning signaled in a bunch of neologisms—*paramilitary, paramilitant, parapolitical.*

Paramilitarism is admittedly not a wholly satisfactory analytical term, arising as it has from the need to avoid partisan labeling of activists as terrorists, rebels, guerrillas, and so on. (Indeed, *activism* may well be a better term for the hybrid form, but it is already far too widely used for more harmless activities. Loyalist activism follows a specific Ulster custom of "public banding," which may be seen as a species of vigilantism.) The adjective *paramilitary* has been used historically to describe organizations markedly different from those in Ireland today, notably the German *Wehrverbande* that form the subject of James Diehl's *Paramilitary Politics* and the original UVF and Irish Volunteers of the pre-1914 period. In noun form, however, recent usage of *paramilitarism*, through its very looseness, signals the odd collection of functions exercised by contemporary organizations. Though terrorism (according to my earlier definition) has formed a salient component of paramilitarism, it has not been an independent one. Certainly, in the case of the PIRA, repeated strategic shifts testify to a long-term subordination of particular media (terror among them) to the basic message (independence). To the extent that PIRA was "terrorist" in the early 1970s, measured by the frequency of indiscriminate slaughter, it was even then articulating a widely understood political view. By the 1980s it had shifted to more carefully targeted violence and was experimenting with conventional political activity, but without any loss of uncompromising rigidity or ruthlessness. Its members would probably still prefer to describe themselves as rebels or guerrilla fighters, but the dynamic connotations of rebellion or insurgency are missing from the PIRA's campaign. Despite episodic successes and setbacks, the republic is going nowhere, yet it keeps on going. The notion of paramilitarism contains its paradoxical form of static momentum. The element of militarism in paramilitarism is problematic. Militarism is itself an imprecise notion, in which adherence to military values (discipline, loyalty, probity) is commonly yoked with more extreme social Darwinian ideas about the value of war. To be politically significant, militarism must incorporate not only the urge to behave like a soldier (the sense attributed to the Montoneros by Richard Gillespie in Chapter 6 of this volume) but also the belief that military values and methods should be projected into the political sphere or, indeed, should replace "politics" as understood—or caricatured—by soldiers. Diehl quotes a striking example of the *Freikorps* political outlook, which may stand for others: "We must enter politics and try to create a generation of leaders who unite the courage to act, the character, firmness, energy and composure of the soldier with the spirit, flair, cleverness, and snake-like cunning of the politician."[97] Few politicians are flattered by this description of their qualities or drawn to the political structure of "national dictatorship" that militarism would create.

Accusations of militarism have been leveled at the IRA since the early 1920s, as have charges of fascistic addiction to action for its own sake.[98] The political value of adoption of the title *army* by the Irish Volunteers in 1919 has been widely attested, though it sits oddly with the native antimilitarism of the English and the long-standing Irish hostility to the British army as the instrument and symbol of imperial power. In fact, the relations between the "army" and the Dail ministry continued to be awkward.[99] It is clear enough that the adoption of quasi-regular military organization (from companies through battalions to brigades and even divisions) served the IRA's self-image as much as its public image.[100] The projection of this "secret army" structure into the urban battleground of the 1970s was perhaps even dysfunctional, as Bishop and Mallie argue: the old pseudo-regular model called for "phantom columns" with "inaccurate and padded membership lists."[101] The public might take a dim view of the result, as did the Falls Road businessman who told them, "When you heard who the new officer commanding the Provisionals in our district was you had to laugh. Many of them were the scum of the area. They had the political awareness of Glasgow Celtic football fans."[102]

Since then the military structure of the organization has become more sophisticated, but the limited political vision of a substantial segment of both the PIRA and its loyalist counterparts is one reason why, for all its relentless grimness, the conflict has not spiraled out of control and unraveled the society of the North. Civil war has remained latent rather than actual because the most assiduous practitioners of violence have kept their eyes fixed on the street corner rather than the offices of

97. James M. Diehl, *Paramilitary Politics in Weimar Germany* (Bloomington: Indiana University Press, 1977), 94. See also Peter H. Merkl, *Political Violence Under the Swastika* (Princeton: Princeton University Press, 1975), part 4.

98. A noteworthy early example can be found in F. X. Martin, ed., "Eoin MacNeill on the 1916 Rising," *Irish Historical Studies* 12 (1961): 234–40. The full-blown Free Stater assault opened with P. S. O'Hegarty, *The Victory of Sinn Fein: How It Won It, and How It Used It* (Dublin: Talbot Press, 1924).

99. Kevin B. Nowlan, "Dail Eireann and the Army: Unity and Division," in *The Irish Struggle*, 67–78. See also David Fitzpatrick, *Politics and Irish Life, 1913–1921: Provincial Experience of War and Revolution* (Dublin: Gill and Macmillan, 1977), 210–11.

100. Townshend, "Irish Republican Army," 335–36.

101. Bishop and Mallie, *Provisional IRA*, 108.

102. Ibid., 121.

government. The street grid itself has been a creator and a limiter of violence.[103] Any complacent notion that the level of violence has become "acceptable" to either the authorities or the communities is soon ruptured by periodic outrages, but sheer force of habit has made many of the trappings of guerrilla terrorism practically invisible. It is possible that basic assumptions about the nature of normality have altered over the twenty years of irregular warfare; certainly nobody in Britain in 1969 would have believed it possible for troops to maintain public order for more than a few months at most. Force of circumstance may be driving the six counties to a form of political life that is permanent and yet in no sense a solution.

MIMESIS AND RECIPROCITY: STATE AND COUNTERSTATE

Efficacy may be the final guarantor of the persistence of paramilitarism, but it is not an independent variable. Like its obverse, legitimacy, it is a product of complex subjective and objective conditions, two aspects of which are indicated here. The first is the mimetic, recently trivialized as the "copycat" tendency. It is obvious that the heightened awareness created by political violence makes imitation likely in suitable circumstances. Things that work for others may work for you. The mimetic process is not simple or regular, but it is universal. Occasionally the results are unmediated, as when the Irish Volunteers were set up to parallel the UVF. More often, imitation is indirect and adaptive, as in the IRA's transmutation of the Boer guerrilla example (an experience that, by contrast, the British deliberately ignored as inapplicable in Europe). The astounding spread of irregular warfare throughout the world in the twentieth century has been facilitated, if not caused, by the proliferation of models—like those codified by Lawrence, Mao, and Guevara—whose attraction was compounded of efficacy and style: they have certainly had an aesthetic or moral as well as a utilitarian appeal. The "shadow of the gunman" in Ireland is the stuff of popular drama.

The second aspect is the interaction between resistance and government. The contention of my earlier work on political violence in Ireland is that this reciprocity persistently influenced the behavior of insurgent

103. F. W. Boal and J.N.H. Douglas, eds., *Integration and Division: Geographical Perspectives on the Northern Ireland Problem* (London: Academic Press, 1982), esp. R. Murray, "Political Violence in Northern Ireland, 1969–1977," 309–32.

groups, even those as loosely structured as the amorphous companies of Captain Moonlight or Captain Rock. It occasionally, but significantly, also led the state to imitate its opponents. The central thread in government policy in Ireland has long been identified as the oscillation between "coercion" and "conciliation." In fact much of what was called coercion was conceived as neutral law enforcement, but the secure establishment of these antithetical concepts in public discourse by, at the latest, the 1880s, shaped all subsequent perceptions. The British government would have found it very difficult to break out of this perceptual cage even if it had tried. In practice it seldom recognized the problem.

A brief analysis of three phases of British policy in Ireland may help to elucidate the extent to which its failures have been due to the general dilemma of "liberal democracy" in the face of political violence, as against the well-attested special ignorance and unconcern of British governments in relation to Ireland. The first is the land-war period of the 1880s; the second, the republican insurgency of 1916–21; and the third, the resumption of direct British rule in Northern Ireland since 1972.

To list the responses of governments to what they saw as terrorism in the 1880s would be to produce a catalogue of crimes and follies as chaotic as any historical story. The analyst's impulse to categorize and rank them needs to be controlled, but the distinction between Liberal and Conservative tendencies can be broadly followed. Both Gladstone's and Salisbury's adminstrations combined coercion and conciliation, though without accepting the popular view of their incompatibility. Both saw them as complementary aspects of the rule of law. The Liberals, who took office in 1880 just as the Land League was intensifying its campaign of rent assistance, put coercion first—in the shape of W. E. Forster's Protection of Person and Property Act of March 1881—but only after Forster's initial attempt to pass a Compensation for Disturbances Bill had failed in the House of Lords. Within the Liberal cabinet a rift soon emerged between those who believed that violence was caused by bad laws and those who attributed it to failure to enforce the law. Forster, chief among the latter, held that the agrarian "criminals" were a marginal collection of "old Fenians or old Ribbonmen or *mauvais sujets*" who would shrink into their holes if a few were arrested."[104] Forster got round the inconvenient fact that the rural community did not repudiate these bad lots by introducing detention without trial, thus overcoming the inability of the police to find witnesses to agrarian crimes.

But suspension of habeas corpus was politically costly, and Forster was eventually driven into resignation. For the rest of Gladstone's

104. Forster to Gladstone, 8 November 1880, in Reid, *Life of Forster*, 2:265.

second administration Irish policy was dominated by Earl Spencer, who was more attuned to Gladstone's own belief in the need for major reforms, leading to the 1881 Land Act and ultimately to the attempt to legislate Home Rule in 1886. Yet even these "anticoercionists" looked hawkish in Ireland. Gladstone's Leeds speech fulminating that "the resources of civilization against its enemies are not yet exhausted" left an enduring impression, and the radical Joseph Chamberlain likewise insisted that "liberty is a mere phantom unless every man is free to consult his interests under the protection of the law."[105] Law enforcement and the battle against dynamite terrorism were pursued by the Liberals through the drafting of soldiers as an auxiliary gendarmerie to assist the police, and enlargement of the secret police (the modern Special Branch has its roots in the early 1880s).[106] They appeared successful, but their methods were ominous. The home secretary observed that coercion, like caviar, was disagreeable at first but became increasingly palatable.

The Conservative disposition required less heroic experimentation in coercion but involved a significantly divergent form of conciliation. Ashbourne's Act of 1885 was the first installment of "constructive unionism," which rested on a massive scheme of land purchase whereby the Irish tenants became small landowners and thus—it was hoped—a conservative rather than revolutionary element. "Killing Home Rule with kindness" was a strategy that reached well beyond the 1880s, but it rested on a traditional reassertion of law and order by A. J. Balfour. Whereas the Liberals had treated the Land League MPs with kid gloves, Balfour got tough with the political leaders of the Plan of Campaign. Using the first permanent "coercion act"—the 1887 Criminal Law Amendment Act—and the robust dictum that "a crime does not become political because it is committed by a politician," he set the police to eliminate "incitement to violence." By this time the government's priority was not to reduce the level of violence but to counter the spread of communal ostracism, or "boycotting," which was the plan's principal weapon.[107] The authorities saw that though boycotting was nonviolent, it was not merely intimidatory but potentially lethal to its victims. They naturally believed that it was not spontaneous but was engineered by the terrorism of the agrarian secret societies under the aegis of the National Land League.

Though Balfour never decisively mastered the boycott, he established an awesome reputation. His countermeasures were consistent and bore

---

105. J. L. Hammond, *Gladstone and the Irish Nation* (London: Longmans, 1938), 251.
106. Porter, *Origins of the Vigilant State.*
107. Townshend, *Political Violence,* 198–206.

out Salisbury's levelheaded advice that "the only course is to go on 'pegging away' and by experience learn the precise limit of your powers."[108] Overall, however, and not least through his contemptuous assumption of the superiority of English standards of civilization, he confirmed the repressive image of British government in Ireland. His methods depended more on his charisma than on the construction of efficient machinery; the process of "tinkering with the police" went on through the 1880s as it had through earlier crises, only to be abandoned as soon as relative tranquillity was achieved.

The results of this neglect and underfunding of the police were to become crippling in the second, more obviously unsuccessful phase of British policy, after the republican rebellion in 1916. One major difference between these periods must be registered at the outset. Whereas Ireland had occupied the foreground of British politics in the 1880s, in 1916 it was even more marginal a distraction than usual. The 1880s had also seen outstanding political talents concentrated on Ireland; Balfour, above all, broke the rule that Ireland was the graveyard of ministerial reputations (a rule whose mythical nature well displayed negative British attitudes). In 1916 mediocrity was again the norm. Though Lloyd George flirted briefly with the Irish problem, he turned his attention to world affairs until late in 1920. Four years of drift set the seal on Britain's failure to make the union secure. In 1916 the incapacity of the police to prevent, or even to predict, the rebellion led to a panicky overreaction and drove Irish public opinion to the rebel side. Between 1917 and 1919 the weakness of the executive apparatus led the government into what the best historian of modern Ireland called the "almost inconceivable foolhardiness" of "pinpricking coercion."[109] At last, having thoroughly aggravated the situation, the government reinforced the ailing police with former soldiers, the notorious Black and Tans.

This was a desperate expedient whose only justification was the longstanding British dislike of military rule. Its dangers were perceived by many senior officials, who predicted the breakdown of police discipline, which finally, in late 1920 and early 1921, wrecked Britain's liberal self-image. Cabinet discussions on the issue of emergency powers were certainly shaped by awareness of the threat to liberal democratic norms posed by the need to control political violence. When the Restoration of Order in Ireland Act (ROIA) was drafted in July 1920, several ministers

108. Salisbury to Balfour, October 1887, Balfour MSS, British Library Add. MS. 49688 fol. 153.
109. F.S.L. Lyons, *Ireland Since the Famine* (London: Weidenfeld and Nicolson, 1971), 386.

felt that "it was a decision of the gravest moment to utilize machinery intended for time of war in time of peace, and considerable anxiety was expressed at thus handing over the whole administration of the law to soldiers."[110] In fact, no such handing-over occurred. Aversion to martial law pushed the government into what was surely a worse alternative, covert counterterrorism. The most noticeable impact of ROIA was to drive many IRA men into hiding, where they set up the first full-time guerrilla units. These "flying columns" soon inflicted a new degree of damage on police and military patrols and provoked a new level of police violence in reprisal. Attempts by the army to control such violence were quietly blocked by senior ministers who believed that the violence could break the IRA's grip on the supposed "moderate majority" of mainstream Irish nationalism. Here was an unmistakable mimetic reaction. As a jaundiced unionist historian (Sir James O'Connor) put it, "The English rapparee was to beat the Irish rapparee." The worst thing was that counterterrorism seemed almost to work: the people were cowed, and the security forces got more information about the rebels. But the underlying logic was flawed. The government had no evidence for its hope that a moderate majority remained to be prized apart from the IRA extremists. Official illegality in fact had the opposite result.[111]

The constructive thread in British policy was throughout a feeble counterweight to perceived repression. Not until December 1920 was a major constitutional reform enacted, and that was from the nationalist standpoint a degradation of the Home Rule plans that had failed before 1914. In between, "conciliation" took the form only of occasional gestures—such as the release of prisoners on Hamar Greenwood's accession to office as chief secretary in April 1920—that were not supported by anything more than pious rhetoric. It was left to the military commander in Ireland to urge that economic reconstruction might be a better way of winning the support of Irish opinion.[112] The government preferred to deal in constitutional abstractions and political solutions.

In this, and in its resolute determination to brand its violent opponents as unrepresentative extremists—until the stupendous moment at which it brought Michael Collins into the comity of statesmen—the British government's policy at this time prefigured its later response to violence in Northern Ireland. In the period since the resumption of direct administration in 1972, governments have boxed the political compass from

110. Cabinet Conference, 26 July 1920, PRO CAB 23 22, C.51(20) App.IV.

111. Charles Townshend, *The British Campaign in Ireland, 1919–1921* (Oxford: Oxford University Press, 1975), 106 ff.

112. E.g., General Macready to Sir John Anderson, 28 May 1920, Anderson MSS, PRO CO 904 188/2.

negotiation with the IRA through a revolutionary substitution of power sharing for the British dogma of majority power, via the notion of full "integration" round to the renewed acceptance of an all-Ireland framework. Whatever else they may be accused of, they can hardly be accused of a lack of inventiveness. Probably the charge that sticks is lack of realism, though it is one that sticks to many others beside the government. Self-deception, unfortunately, is a more serious problem for governments than for less responsible bodies. There has been no sign that, except transiently and aberrantly, senior ministers have treated republican activism as anything but a criminal conspiracy. Repudiation of the IRA as a terrorist organization is a perfectly reasonable—indeed more or less unavoidable—attitude for a liberal democratic government to take. Some obvious conclusions that would have to be drawn from the fact that the IRA is both untouchable and immovable have not, however, been drawn.

The familiar combination of mediocrity and unconcern marked the Heath administration's first attempt to apply British political reasonableness to Northern Ireland. Reginald Maudling's unguarded reaction to his first experience of the province—"Bring me a large scotch . . . what a bloody awful place"—should no doubt have been consigned to the dustheap of historical trivia, but it never was. It perfectly expressed the generally assumed relation between the two countries. All the careful work of William Whitelaw, all the pieties of Merlyn Rees, all the businesslike optimism of James Prior, could never change that assumption. By resurrecting the chief secretaryship and endowing it with even greater powers, Britain had been driven to do what Lloyd George had made every effort not to do: impose Crown Colony government on Ireland. It was indeed a grim dilemma, which Lloyd George himself had set up. The only two forms of government that were workable, the Stormont system and direct British rule, were both unacceptable; and the only acceptable forms were unworkable.

The outcome has been nearly twenty years of political paralysis in which adminstrative policy has been determined by the civil service in the Northern Ireland Office and the security of the state has rested directly on the army. As an alternative to internment without trial, the judicial system itself has been redefined to obviate the need for witnesses or juries.[113] The army has looked in vain for clear definition of the order it has been committed to restore and for formal powers to impose it. In this the present situation precisely parallels that of 1920–21, except that

---

113. The most coherent critique of this process is Kevin Boyle, Tom Hadden, and Paddy Hillyard, *Law and State: The Case of Northern Ireland* (London: Robertson, 1975).

it has gone on for ten times as long. Instead of recruiting Black and Tans, the government has preserved the primacy of the police (and thus the civil power) through "Ulsterization," enhancing the size and power of the almost wholly Protestant RUC and Ulster Defence Regiment. The conduct of these forces—beyond British scrutiny, as the Stalker affair demonstrated—is still the salient grievance of the Catholic minority in Northern Ireland; and any hope that the 1985 Anglo-Irish Agreement would lead to reform has so far been disappointed.[114]

In the circumstances the army's achievement has been remarkable: it has for long periods reduced violence to the mysterious "acceptable level"—which has gradually become equivalent to the unavoidable level—and it has avoided becoming politicized. (One may suspect, however, that the reason for this is the same reason Irish policy has been a "bipartisan question" in the British parliament: the parties do not wish to have to formulate a policy, and the army does not wish to rule.) Despite some alarm on the Left about the "Kitson experiment," it seems likely that the increasing involvement of secret forces implementing unavowed security policies in Northern Ireland is a sign of aimlessness rather than conspiracy. This is not to underestimate the extent of the demoralization of British political culture that the protracted distortion of traditional standards is producing and that may in the end be the most enduring legacy of paramilitarism.

CONCLUSIONS

The argument advanced here is that the contentious history of the six-county area of Northern Ireland has produced a protracted blurring of the conventional boundary between politics and violence, or peace and war. Provisional Sinn Fein's open attempt to exploit this categorical ambiguity with "a ballot paper in one hand and an Armalite in the other" is only the most recent version of a strategy that has repeatedly emerged in the past. The notion of "latent civil war" has been taken to indicate the fundamental political antagonism that in part legitimates the threat and use of violence. The contested nature of the state makes war a possibility, though the complexity of the political constellation exerts limiting pressures. The PIRA, in particular, is engaged in three analyti-

---

114. Deputy Chief Constable John Stalker's official inquiry into the "shoot to kill" allegations has been suppressed in the interests of "national security," but it has been effectively published by himself in *Stalker Affair* (London: Penguin, 1988).

cally distinct armed struggles: first, an attenuated projection of the civil war of 1922–23, in which the old IRA fought against the Dublin government to preserve the integrity of the republic; second, a communal battle to assert the identity of the nationalist minority in the North in the face of Protestant dominance; and third, a projection of the Anglo-Irish war of 1916–21, a war of national liberation against the colonial power of Britain. But though these wars may be analytically separable, they are necessarily fought simultaneously. In a war without fronts, the activists cannot control the effects of their acts, each of which will be interpreted differently by its different antagonists and may produce contradictory results.

The complexity of political contention in Northern Ireland has led to the notion that the problem is insolubility itself. This may well be so; at least, any possible modus vivendi will have to break new ground in departing from conventional ideas of "solution." The Anglo-Irish Agreement of 1985 has been welcomed by many commentators for its undogmatic, not to say ambiguous, nature.[115] Unfortunately, there is no reason to suppose that it can produce, any more than did previous constitutional schemes, a means of turning the political alienation of the minority community into participation without *pari passu* turning the participation of the majority into alienation. As long as the British government remains unable to cope with salient minority grievances, above all in the sphere of law and public security, the state will continue to be perceived as partisan and illegitimate.

The illegitimacy of the state plainly contributes to the legitimacy of violent opposition. More particularly, it creates a public tolerance of forms of violence that are widely perceived as terrorism. The executive power of the paramilitary organizations rests on fear, in a more unmediated way than does the power of established states. The consensual assumption that naked force is an illegitimate form of authority seems to be as widely held in Northern Ireland as anywhere else; what is different there is that a significant public recognizes the political validity of an organization that claims to be at war against the established state. As Eamonn McCann put it, the IRA "claimed recognition as the sole inheritors of the republican tradition, a status which, once asserted, cannot by its nature be subjected to democratic contestation. . . . Theirs was a philosophy which presented the people . . . with no problems. One might disagree with it, and many did, but it was not in our tradition to

115. There is a set of radical critiques in Paul Teague, ed., *Beyond the Rhetoric: Politics, the Economy, and Social Policy in Northern Ireland* (London: Lawrence and Wishart, 1987).

disrespect it."[116] The only available and plausible contestant with the IRA for the allegiance of the minority is the nationalist parliamentary Social Democratic and Labour Party (SDLP). This is a formidable modern political organization that has consistently denounced violence and espoused the positive notion of consociation. There can be little doubt that if the British government were to make to the SDLP the kind of concessions that it made in 1921 to the Irish Free State, the eventual triumph of the democratic movement over the IRA would be as certain as it was then. To do so, however, it would have to reverse the assumptions on which it originally refused to permit Northern Ireland to be incorporated in the Free State: the right of loyalists to define their own political identity. So far there is no sign, even in the most optimistic nationalist interpretation of the Anglo-Irish Agreement, that this is a possibility.

116. McCann, *War and an Irish Town*, 111–12.

9

Political Violence and Terrorism in India: The Crisis of Identity

Paul Wallace

Terrorism is a reality in India and in the neighboring countries of Sri Lanka, Bangladesh, and Pakistan. Ethnic, religious, and linguistic factors provide the fuel that in the 1980s exploded into movements of political violence directed against the state and, in turn, involved repressive measures that often were seen as state terrorism. In its contemporary form, political violence raises new issues of public policy for the state and necessitates a reexamination of societal and economic processes.

Major questions involve the nature of the state response and its own role as a causal agent. Excessive reliance on force and draconian measures can alter the state itself toward increasingly authoritarian modes. At the other end of the society-state spectrum, particular social elements encourage the votaries of political violence through passive as well as active support. Political violence married to terrorism does not allow for "innocent" bystanders.

Perspective is vital in the examination of these complex phenomena. India no longer is the "soft state" described by Gunnar Myrdal in 1968,[1] if it ever was. A more appropriate categorization is that of a "rising middle power."[2] It has survived the passing of its founding fathers, its "tall leaders," and has not been balkanized as suggested in a landmark 1960 analysis.[3] India and the adjoining countries have survived the "dangerous decades," constructing in the process notable degrees of self-identity as national entities and impressive state institutions. Movements involving political violence, therefore, are less likely to pose an insurrectionary challenge to the unity of the state than to serve as a vehicle for extremists expressing particular demands and frustrations.

Bangladesh's emergence from Pakistan as an independent state in 1971 is a notable exception to this generalization, and it appeared that Sri Lanka in the 1980s might succumb to militant movements. Ethnic violence approaching civil war in the small island state of Sri Lanka presented a major threat to national unity. Through 1992 more than twenty-five thousand people died in the continuing ten-year-old Tamil insurrection in the North, and another twelve to sixty thousand died between 1988 and 1991 in crushing left-wing Sinhalese rebels in the remainder of the island.[4]

Terrorist movements, on the one hand, are assisted by the diversity of peoples, languages, and religious practices that overlap national boundaries in the vast South Asian subcontinent of over one billion people. On the other hand, the diversity and consequent crosscutting identities also provide a buffer against insurrection.

Even within India's major problem state, Punjab, there is a bustling sense of normalcy despite a decade of escalating violence in which over fifteen thousand terrorist-related deaths have occurred between 1985

1. Gunnar Myrdal, *Asian Drama: An Inquiry into the Poverty of Nations*, (New York: Pantheon, 1968), 66 and ch. 18, sec. 14, "The Paramount Dilemma of the 'Soft State,' " 895–900.

2. John W. Mellor, *India: A Rising Middle Power* (Boulder, Colo.: Westview Press, 1979).

3. Selig S. Harrison, *India: The Most Dangerous Decades* (Princeton: Princeton University Press, 1960). Its cover jacket starkly asks the pessimistic question, "Can the Nation Hold Together?" Harrison, in the 1950s, sees striking similarities between India and the pre–World War I Austro-Hungarian Empire. Regionalism and caste lobbies, along with the passing of India's nationalist "tall leaders," in his view, open the prospect for the balkanization of India. In particular, see chs. 3 and 4, and pp. 319–23.

4. Reuters, *India West*, 12 June 1992, 43; 24 July 1992, 39; and 8 January 1993, 35.

and 1991,[5] with more than one thousand killed every year since 1987 (see Table 9.1). Nevertheless, Sikh "militants," as they term themselves, proclaiming the goal of an independent Khalistan, have failed to generate sustained hostility between the majority Sikh and minority Hindu communities so as to drive the Hindus from Punjab and, in a counterreaction, force Sikhs in other states to seek refuge in Punjab. Communalism—the term for religious conflict in South Asia—does rise at times; suspicions and apprehension flare; but ordinary interactions continue in both rural and urban areas.

Terrorism in Punjab, in contrast to that in Northern Ireland and Lebanon, is not reflected in a siege state with the major contestants essentially walled off from each other in ghettolike enclaves. In Punjab, "the real weapon of the terrorist is unpredictability."[6] "Soft targets," such as migrant laborers and defenseless villagers—and in 1992 the

Table 9.1.   Violence in Punjab, 1981–1993

	Civilians and Police Killed	Police Killed	Extremists Killed	Total Killed	Extremists Arrested
1981	13	[2]	14	27	84
1982	13	[2]	7	20	178
1983	75	[20]	13	88	296
1984	359	[20]	77	436	1,630
1985	63	[8]	2	65	491
1986	520	[42]	78	598	1,581
1987	910	[95]	328	1,238	3,750
1988	1,949	[110]	373	2,322	3,882
1989	1,168	[201]	703	1,871	2,466
1990	2,467	[506]	1,320	3,787	1,759
1991	2,591	[497]	2,177	4,768	1,977
1992	1,518	[252]	2,111	3,629	1,502
1993[a]	38	[21]	472	510	454
Totals	11,684	1,776	7,675	19,359	20,050

SOURCES: Data compiled from: Government of India, Ministry of Home Affairs, National Integration Council, Meeting 31 December 1991. Annexure 1, *Profile of Violence in Punjab*, 11. Office of the Director-General of Police, Punjab as cited in K.P.S. Gill, "The Dangers Within: Internal Security Threats," in Bharat Karnad (ed.), *Future Imperilled: India's Security in the 1990s and Beyond* (New Delhi: Viking Penguin Books, 1994), 118, 120.

[a]1993 data from January 1 to September 10 only.

5. Editorial, *Times of India*, 29 May 1992, 12.
6. M. J. Akbar, *Riot After Riot: Reports on Caste and Communal Riots in India* (New Delhi: Penguin, 1988), 115.

families of police, Sikh and Hindu alike—fall to the automatic firepower of the terrorists, as do targeted military, political, and government personnel.

Normalcy and terrorism, consequently, coexist in Punjab and the adjoining states and national capital. A decade of daily killings by militants and of militants, in the form of "encounters," has established a macabre norm and numbed the populace into resignation as the figures have been reported almost routinely along with the other news of the day. Government actions, emphasizing a law-and-order approach, appear most often to be more concerned with managing the problem than resolving it.

Even Julio Francis Ribiero, India's supercop with a reputation as "a one-man army,"[7] had become pessimistic by 1987. Political violence in Punjab proved more implacable than earlier troubles in Gujarat and Delhi. He could only offer the discouraging prospect of an impasse in which the police and paramilitary forces could control terrorism "to a manageable extent as had been done in Ireland." Eliminating terrorism, Ribiero concluded, was not possible, since "it was in the heart and mind of those perpetrating it in the cause of misplaced sentiments of philosophy."[8] The *Economist* stressed the self-perpetuating nature of Punjab extremism: "Terrorism has ceased to be a means to an end, and become an end in itself."[9]

Containing terrorism has prevented it from developing into a more widespread insurrectionary movement and has enabled a version of normal life to exist, including continued high levels of agricultural output. But Ribiero's "bullet for a bullet" policy and periodic government efforts to address more deep-rooted problems have been unsuccessful this past decade in preventing daily terrorism in Punjab. Violence, rather than politics, has become the norm for both the government and the extremists. As one analyst concluded in 1987, "Both state and individual [i.e., the militant group] terrorism consider use of violence as [a] substitute for political action or mass mobilization. . . . terrorism has become integral to the political and social life of Punjab."[10] Another observer summed up the prevailing pattern as a "fight between just the police and militants."[11]

Thus, it is clear that the use of force to maintain law and order is

7. *Statesman* (New Delhi), 22 July 1986, 1.
8. *Times of India*, 10 January 1987.
9. *The Economist* (London), 11 March 1989, 58.
10. Pramod Kumar, "Punjab Crisis: A Political Diagnosis," *Mainstream*, 14 November 1987, 17.
11. Surinder Awasthi, *Times of India*, 26 May 1992, 11.

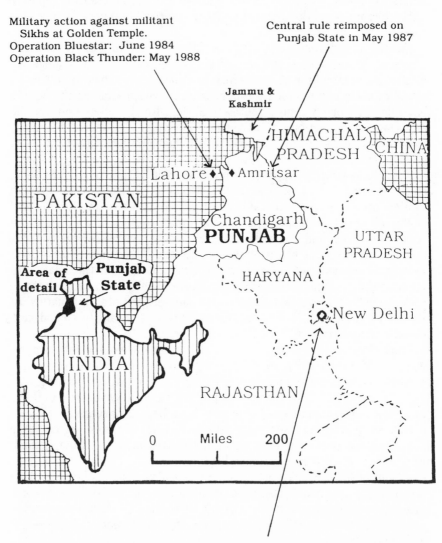

Military action against militant Sikhs at Golden Temple. Operation Bluestar: June 1984 Operation Black Thunder: May 1988

Central rule reimposed on Punjab State in May 1987

Jammu & Kashmir

HIMACHAL PRADESH   CHINA

Lahore♦   ♦Amritsar

PAKISTAN

Chandigarh

PUNJAB

UTTAR PRADESH

Area of detail   Punjab State

HARYANA

New Delhi

INDIA

RAJASTHAN

0   Miles   200

Prime Minister Indira Gandhi assassinated by Sikh members of her body guard, 31 October, 1984. Organized mobs kill thousands of Sikhs in Delhi riots.

Adapted from Richard P. Cronin, India's Punjab Crisis: Issues, Prospects, and Implications (Washington, D.C.: Library of Congress, Congressional Research Service Report for Congress 87-850 F. 6, October, 1987), vi.

Fig. 9.1. India's troubled Punjab state

necessary but not sufficient.[12] Restarting a meaningful political process is essential to break what can be termed the stalemate of violence. Election campaigning in 1991 for the national and state legislatures did bring forth moderate politicians who had been, as several individuals remarked to me, hiding in their bunkers.[13] Many militant groups also contested, highlighting the differences in their ranks. A window of opportunity had opened. But for complicated, narrow partisan reasons, elections were postponed at the last minute and not held until February 1992. At that point, most moderate Sikhs as well as virtually all militants boycotted the elections, resulting in an abysmally low turnout of 21.6 percent. Rural Sikhs appeared to be more united—and intimidated—in opposition to the system than before the elections.[14] New political opportunities will have to be consciously created if the cycle of violence is to be reversed.

SIKH MILITANCY AND IDENTITY

Of Punjab's population of twenty million, a moderate number of militants violently oppose the state.[15] There are about two to three hundred "hard-core terrorists," who comprise the leadership of about 150 groups ranging in size from ten to four hundred. The total number of active militants engaged in political violence is probably around four thousand, plus supporting elements.[16]

12. As with most generalizations, dissenting views remain. Five months after becoming Congress (I) chief minister of the state, Beant Singh emphasized that "Punjab was more of a law and order problem rather than a political one" (Dinesh Kumar, *Times of India*, 1 August 1992, 9).
13. Interviews in Punjab during the tenth general elections, June 1991.
14. For a description and analysis of the 1991 and 1992 elections, see Paul Wallace, "India's 1991 Elections: Regional Factors in Haryana and Punjab," in Harold Gould and Sumit Ganguly, eds., *India Votes: Alliance Politics and Minority Governments in the Ninth and Tenth General Elections* (Boulder, Colo.: Westview Press, 1993), 403–28, and Gurharpal Singh, "The Punjab Elections 1992: Breakthrough or Breakdown?" *Asian Survey* 32, no. 11 (1992): 988–99.
15. The 1991 census figure is 20,190,795 (Amulya Ratna Nanda [census commissioner], *Census of India 1991, Provisional Population Totals* [Paper-1 of 1991] [New Delhi: Samrat Press, March 1991], 3).
16. These are educated estimates for 1992 based on a variety of published sources and interviews. The official numbers appear to remain relatively constant over time, ranging between 300 and 2,000 despite the state figures on killings (see Table 9.1) and captures. Kanwar Pal Singh, director general of Punjab Police, stated on 21 and 29 January 1989 that "nearly 300 hard-core terrorists" belonging to the major groups "were still at large" (*The Tribune* [Chandigarh], 31 March 1989, 1). The deputy inspector general of Police (Jalandhar range) stated to newsmen on 8 April 1988 that there might be some 2,000-odd terrorists operating in Punjab (*Times of India*, 10 April 1988, 1). At about the same time, *India*

These figures can vary considerably, depending on the success of government operations and the recruitment ability of the militants at any point in time. Thus, in October 1992, the director general of Punjab police, K.P.S. Gill, boasted of the success of the police during the previous six months. He told reporters that less than one hundred "militant outfits" survived from the former total of 240, and recruitment had stopped due to the lack of support from the villagers.[17] These boasts have to be taken in the context of managing rather than resolving the basic problems, a context in which the violence thus continues.

What is more important to the Punjab problem than the number of Sikh terrorists is the religious identity of Sikhs and their ethnic identity as Punjabis. It is puzzling to most non-Sikhs that Sikh religious and ethnic identities should be a contentious issue. It is even more surprising to most of India that separatism and terrorism emerged in the 1980s from a community that appeared to be eminently successful and prosperous.

As early as the 1920s, Sikh religious identity became institutionalized in a self-governing temple-management system. The successful struggle for control of their own temples, it must be emphasized, used Gandhian methods that were militant but nonviolent despite opposition that at times used violence.[18] Sikhs, who constituted the Punjab's core of the Indian nationalist movement for independence, strongly opposed the partition of India and the creation of Pakistan in 1947. Economically, the essentially agrarian Sikhs were recognized as early as the nineteenth century as India's best farmers. They overcame the ravages of partition to again make Punjab India's granary and, since the late 1960s, a worldwide example of the "green revolution" in agriculture. Per capita

---

Today reported that "armed militants" were estimated at between 2,000 and 3,000 (30 April 1988, 35–36). Union home minister Buta Singh, replying to a question in Parliament regarding a report that more than 10,000 Sikh terrorists were trained in Pakistan in guerrilla warfare during the Zia regime, dismissed it as "highly exaggerated." He said it was not possible to estimate the numbers (*Times of India*, 17 March 1989, 7). A government estimate early in 1992 provided a total of 1,236 for the category of "hard-core terrorists" and an increase in the scope of violence; i.e., 50 percent of the violence in 1989 occurred in 13 of the 217 police stations in the state. By February 1992, 60 percent of the violence had expanded to 47 police stations. The use of automatic weapons and bombs had similarly increased (*Times of India*, 9 February 1992, 15). An official estimate of 1,600 armed militants in Punjab in mid-1992 did not explain why this figure was so high despite claims of 1,000 militants killed and 600 arrested during the previous six months (Reuters, *India West*, 10 July 1992, 9).

17. *Times of India*, 13 October 1992, 1.

18. Paul Wallace, "Religious and Secular Politics in Punjab: The Sikh Dilemma in Competing Political Systems," in *Political Dynamics and Crisis in Punjab*, ed. Paul Wallace and Surendra Chopra (Amritsar: Guru Nanak Dev University, 1988), 1–44.

income is the highest in India, and rural income from agriculture in Punjab is almost three times that of the national average.[19] Politically, Sikhs secured the redrafting of Punjab's boundaries in 1966 through a nonviolent movement, raising the proportion of their population in the smaller state from less than 40 percent to 60 percent. There were no significant transfers of population as in the partition of 1947 or in the emergence of successor states within the former Yugoslavia in 1992. Every head of the elected Punjab governments since 1966 has been a Sikh. They play an extraordinary role in the military, police, and transport, in addition to agriculture. They are increasingly successful in the professions and are entering commerce in ever larger numbers. Notable progress is seen in education, health, and particular areas of entrepreneurship. Sikhs clearly constitute one of India's fastest developing and leading communities.

Economically, socially, numerically, and politically they have been successful in Punjab and increasingly throughout India. Yet discrimination against Sikhs is the most consistent charge of the terrorists and nonviolent militants in Punjab. Rapid social change and continuing modernization have not reduced the anxieties of a minority religious community. To the contrary, at least among a significant percentage of the Sikh population, these fears of discrimination have deepened. A key mobilizing tenet for major movements in the past as well as in the present has been that the Sikh *panth* (religion) is in danger.

This apparent paradox between objective success and feelings of discrimination can at least partly be explained by the Sikhs' relation to the larger India and by their own internal dynamics. Economically, their success, though notable, is limited by central-government policies in areas such as agricultural pricing, free movement of food grains, industrialization policies, and redistribution of their resources to other states. Socially, Sikhs are divided by caste, status, and various attitudes toward the practices of their religion. Numerically, they are a majority in the state of Punjab, but not overwhelmingly so, and constitute only 1.9 percent of India's population. Politically, social factors, factionalism, and competing political parties split the community.[20]

19. Punjab from 1976–77 to 1978–79 had an average per capita rural income from agriculture of Rs 1,627; the all-India average was Rs 638 (Economic Intelligence Service, *Basic Statistics Relating to the Indian Economy*, vol. 2, *States* [Bombay: Center for Monitoring the Indian Economy, 1983], 8.4). The time period selected is just before the advent of terrorism. Detailed economic data is provided in Paul Wallace, "Religious and Ethnic Politics: Political Mobilization in Punjab," in *Dominance and State Power in Modern India: Decline of a Social Order*, ed. Francine Frankel and M.S.A. Rao (New Delhi: Oxford University Press, 1990), 2:465–75.

20. A more detailed analysis of these differences is presented in the following sections of this chapter and in Paul Wallace, "Sikh Minority Attitudes in India's Federal System,"

Terrorism is designed to exploit Sikh fears so as to manipulate them toward the ultimate, through vague, goal of Khalistan, an independent Sikh-controlled state. If that somewhat utopian notion proves unattainable, many, and perhaps most, of the terrorists are prepared to fall back on alternatives, which range from bargaining for positions of personal power within the existing quasi-federal system, purportedly with enhanced state autonomy, to continuing profitable illegal activities such as extortion and smuggling gold, drugs, and weapons.

The initial spark for contemporary terrorism in Punjab was provided by the charismatic Sant Jarnail Singh Bhindranwale, who rose from obscurity in 1978 as head of a religious seminary to become, in journalistic parlance, the Ayatollah Khomeini of Punjab. Admittedly, violence has a long history in Punjab, and militancy has been part of the Sikh political tradition. Nonetheless, since the British conquest of Punjab in 1849, militancy had generally been channeled into nonviolent movements.

Bhindranwale's appeal drew on the theme of discrimination against Sikhs and on exhortations to violence, as illustrated by the following quotations from his tape recorded speeches:

> Sikhs are living like slaves in independent India. Today every Sikh considers himself a second rate citizen. . . . How can Sikhs tolerate this?[21]

> I cannot really understand how it is that, in the presence of Sikhs, Hindus are able to insult the (scriptures). I don't know how were these Sikhs born to mothers and why they were not born to animals, to cats and bitches. . . . Whosoever insults the Guru Granth Sahib [Sikh holy book] he should be killed then and there.[22]

Discrimination and violence refer back to identity as a community and the shared sense of threat. Bhindranwale reified these themes in his conceptualization of a true, orthodox Sikh based on his interpretation of the tenth and last Guru, Gobind Singh. In powerful language, he mined deep-rooted Sikh images: "I'll tell you how we are slaves! We have a minority complex. But don't consider yourself a minority. . . . Our father

---

in *Sikh History and Religion in the Twentieth Century*, ed. Joseph T. O'Connell, Milton Israel, and William G. Oxtoby (Toronto: University of Toronto, Center for South Asian Studies, 1988), 256–73.

21. Quoted in Mark Juergensmeyer, "The Logic of Religious Violence: The Case of Punjab," *Contributions to Indian Sociology* 22, no. 1 (1988): 70.

22. Quoted in Joyce Pettigrew, "In Search of a New Kingdom of Lahore," *Pacific Affairs* 60, no. 1 (1987): 16.

[Guru Gobind Singh] says, 'When I make my single Sikh fight against 125,000 enemies only then do I deserve to be called Gobind.' "[23]

Bhindranwale did not fear for the safety of individual Sikhs, nor did he appear to be overly concerned about economic matters. To the contrary, economic success and modernization threatened the community by encouraging backsliding from Sikh norms as he defined them. Aggressive self-assertion, violence as needed, and perhaps even the goal of a Khalistan were needed to counter the forces that were diluting the religious community.

Religious and secular threats were a crucial part of Bhindranwale's framework. Sikhism had emerged as a new religion in the fifteenth century, at least partly out of and in reaction to Hinduism, and today even moderate, antiterrorist Sikhs fear reabsorption into Hinduism.[24] Secular forces in the form of modernization and a secular state struck a chord in parts of the Sikh population as threatening the religious community. As Mark Juergensmeyer points out, some Sikhs saw these two threats as combining "forces in the 1980s as the Hindu right exercised increasing political power and Mrs. Gandhi's Congress Party allegedly pandered to its interests."[25]

Religious revivalism and fundamentalism,[26] therefore, were employed dynamically and violently by Bhindranwale to preserve and advance his vision of the community. Revivalism—or, more appropriately, revitalization—necessitates selecting particular elements to be emphasized from the corpus of a tradition. Sikhism, as all religious faiths, encompasses a broad range of principles and practices extending from the pietistic syncretism of its founder, Guru Nanak (1469–1538), to the militancy of its tenth and a final prophet, the warrior-leader Guru Gobind Singh.

THE ORIGINS OF MILITANCY IN SIKH TRADITION: THE *KHALSA*

Militancy became clearly and ritualistically established by Guru Gobind Singh, Bhindranwale's model, in order to preserve the threatened Sikh

23. Ibid., 15.

24. Khushwant Singh, *The Sikhs* (London: George Allen and Unwin, 1953), 184. See also idem, *History of the Sikhs*, vol. 2, *1839–1964* (Princeton: Princeton University Press, 1966), 19–22. Khushwant Singh is a leading Sikh novelist, historian, journalist, and sometime politician who consistently and fearlessly has opposed terrorism and militant Sikhism.

25. Juergensmeyer, "Logic of Religious Violence," 67.

26. For a clear exposition of these terms and their application to South Asia, see Robert Eric Frykenberg, "Fundamentalism and Revivalism in South Asia," in *Fundamentalism, Revivalists, and Violence in South Asia*, ed. James Warner Bjorkman (Riverdale, Md.: Riverdale, 1988), 20–39.

community against the hostility of the Muslim Mughal rulers and the local Hindu hill rajas. In 1699, Guru Gobind Singh gathered Sikhs together at his ancestral hill settlement for renewal and revitalization. *Amritdhari* (baptism in which *amrit*, a nectar composed of sweets, is consumed) joined all of his followers together in a militant rebirth to fight for the new *khalsa*, the community of the pure or, functionally, as a noted historian describes it, "an order, as a society possessing a religious foundation and a military discipline."[27]

The *khalsa* constituted a brotherhood irrespective of caste. All men were commanded to take the name Singh (lion), one common among the Rajput warrior caste in India, and to follow a set of commandments that set them apart from other religions.

Physically, males became distinguished from other peasants in Punjab, and therefore less likely to hide from their Muslim rulers, by the commandment not to cut their hair *(kesh)*. That was the first and most noticeable *k*. The other four symbols starting with *k* that a *khalsa* Sikh had to wear were *kirpan*, a sword; *kara*, a steel bracelet for brotherhood; *kangha*, a comb; and *kach*, knee-length shorts then worn by soldiers. Special rules of conduct forbade smoking, chewing tobacco, drinking alcohol, or eating meat from animals not killed with one blow. Subsequently, Guru Gobind Singh attempted to resolve the politically vexing problem of succession by pronouncing that with his death the Guruship would no longer reside in a person but in the community of followers and in the sacred book, the *Guru Granth Sahib*.[28]

Khalsa Sikhism thus became established as the mainstream element of the community. The founder, Guru Gobind Singh, is still portrayed astride his white horse, carrying the two swords representing spiritual and temporal power, *miri* and *piri*. He accentuated and formalized trends long present in an embattled Sikhism. Guru Hargobind (1606–45), the sixth leader, wore both swords and constructed the Akal Takht (the Throne of the Immortal), representing temporal authority, directly across from the spiritual center, the Harmandir Sahib, the two symbolically most important buildings in the Golden Temple complex and Sikhism.[29] As in Islam, which constituted the majority religion in Punjab

27. W. H. McLeod, *The Evolution of the Sikh Community* (Delhi: Oxford University Press, 1975), 4.

28. Ibid., 13–16, and Khushwant Singh, *History of the Sikhs*, vol. 1, *1469–1839* (Princeton: Princeton University Press, 1963), 767–85.

29. Harjinder Singh Dilgeer, *The Akal Takht* (Jullundur: Punjabi Book Company, 1980), 18–19, and G. S. Nayyar, *Sikh Polity and Political Institutions* (New Delhi: Oriental Publishers, 1979), 58–72. The Harmandir Sahib, which is located in a large tank or pool, often is referred to as the Golden Temple, as is the entire complex. The domes of the two major buildings are each covered with gold.

during the preindependence period, religion and politics among the Sikhs became commingled and at times inseparable.

Sant Jarnail Singh Bhindranwale dramatically reemphasized the *khalsa* model of Sikhism—spiritual and sacral—in a personal and unyielding manner as he entered the public arena in 1978. He combined the almost monkish and ascetic elements of his seminary, the Damdami Taksal, with the warrior element of the Nihang Sikhs, a fanatical sectlike warrior component of the Sikh military during the nineteenth century.[30] Ethnic revivalism in this mode is more than simply "the golden past" becoming "the new social hammer."[31] It attempts to provide a millenarian model emphasizing the purity and sanctity of the ethnic community while warning that the *panth*, the community and religion, is in danger.[32]

Thus, Bhindranwale attempted to become a modern Guru Gobind Singh, reformulating Sikhism to confront contemporary social, economic, and political problems. Violence became a core element of the movement, symbolized by the bandoliers over clothing, the hit squads engaged in assassination, and the promise of an eternal reward for the martyr *(shaheed)* who gives his or her life for the *khalsa*. At the height of his power in 1984, Bhindranwale ruled like a reborn Guru, delivering spiritual commands, issuing temporal orders, and pronouncing judicial judgments from his fortified abode in the Sikh version of the Vatican, the Golden Temple complex in the city of Amritsar.

Ruling from the Golden Temple in 1984, however, did not necessarily translate into unifying all or most Sikhs. Contemporary militants emphasize, as did Bhindranwale, their version of a fundamentalist *khalsa* model that all Sikhs must follow. Reality is otherwise. Efforts or movements to establish conformity to a particular model are almost three centuries old but have always confronted the anvil of an essentially pragmatic, hardworking, largely peasant culture difficult to mold in a uniform pattern. Differences among Sikhs in this context are many.

Mainstream Sikhism is symbolized by *khalsa* Sikhs who wear long hair *(kesh)*. These *keshdhari* Sikhs venerate the nine Gurus who preceded Guru Gobind Singh as carriers of a revealed religion but vary in the

30. Singh, *History of the Sikhs*, 1:207n. Nihangs continue to use the exaggerated language of the early warriors, as when boasting that a Sikh is equal to an army of 125,000 men *(sava lakh)* or when defecating that he is going to "conquer the fort of Chittor" (ibid., 218n). For a personal account of the tenuous life of wandering contemporary Nihangs, see Sarah Lloyd, *An Indian Attachment* (New York: Quill, William Morrow, 1984).

31. Chand Joshi, *Bhindranwale: Myth and Reality* (New Delhi: Vikas 1984), 6.

32. I acknowledge Harjot Singh Oberoi for his use of "the millenarian model" in relation to Bhindranwale as well as an earlier "messianic leader," Ram Singh of the Namdhari movement of the 1860s ("Two Poles of Akali Politics," *Sikh Review* 31 (1983): 46–48).

degree to which they observe the large corpus of traditions with their equally large variety of practices or condone the violence of the contemporary movement. Trimming beards, drinking alcohol, and engaging in other forbidden practices has not been unusual in the past. Bhindranwale criticized these Sikhs as straying from the true path or falling prey to modernization.

There also are minority Sikh groups that style themselves as followers of Guru Nanak, the revered founder of Sikhism. They refuse to accept *khalsa* initiation and rituals, and many wear their hair short. There are other Sikhs with social practices almost indistinguishable from those of Hinduism, groups that profess a living Guru, such as the Nirankaris with which Bhindranwale engaged in violent clashes in 1978, and even those who participate in contemporary interfaith religious movements such as the Radhasoamis.[33] These are not mutually exclusive categories or practices and are sometimes found within the same social groups, families, or even individuals.

Factionalism is another prominent trait of Sikh political culture. An old Punjabi proverb expresses this facet of Sikh history and contemporary politics succinctly: "The greater threat to a leader comes from his followers." Guru Gobind Singh reacted, as did Bhindranwale, to his fragmented context directly and militantly, as indicated by a couplet attributed to him: *"Koi kissi ko raaj na day hai. Jo lay hai nij bal say lay hai.* (Nobody will give you power. You have to wrest it by force.)"[34]

Thus, the millenarian vision propounded by Bhindranwale is a militant version of the fundamentals of the true faith, seeking to unify its followers and protect them from the discrimination and evil influences of outside forces. Politically, a revitalized ethnic identity forged in the *khalsa* model has increasingly emphasized the necessity of Khalistan, an independent state for Sikhs. It is an important symbol of the contemporary extremist movement, although Bhindranwale did not unequivocally press the demand. Clearly, it adds a political and geographical dimension to Sikh ethnicity.

Nonetheless, the Khalistan conceptualization remains vague and poses the potential problem of Sikhs ruling as a numerical minority. At one extreme it calls for an independent state that would encompass large parts of India extending down to the Indian Ocean. An intermediate version would include Maha, or greater Punjab, including the adjoining predominantly Hindu state of Haryana, at least one district of Rajasthan

33. Mark Juergensmeyer, "Patterns of Pluralism: Sikh Relations with Radhasoami," in *Sikh History*, ed. O'Connell, Israel, and Oxtoby, 53–69.
34. Cited in *India Today*, 30 April 1988, 41.

State with a large number of Sikh farmers, and Delhi as the capital. Either of these versions would result in a substantial Hindu majority. Although *Khalistan* has become a code term separating militants from moderates, there is a compromise version that thus far has not received serious attention. It is the conceptualization of a Sikh *quam*, or nation, within a more federalized, decentralized India. Thus far, the central government has reacted to any rendering of the term *nation* as tantamount to secession and has balked at any significant reduction of central-government power. And some Sikh extremists, although they oppose political violence, also reject possible compromise positions. They adamantly advocate either an independent nation or a reformulated Punjab with only token powers conceded to the center.

Militants hark back to what is commonly termed the Sikh kingdom of Maharajah Ranjit Singh (1780–1839; maharajah from 1801). He brought order out of the turbulent, almost chaotic, conditions of eighteenth-century Punjab by consolidating the independent Sikh confederacies *(misls)* in central, Manjha, Punjab. His new state expanded rapidly from the areas adjoining Afghanistan in the West to the central plains (Sutlej River) in the East, and from Kashmir in the North to what is approximately the southeasternly running Sutlej River. Even the Sikh chiefs in eastern Punjab (cis-Sutlej, or Malwa area) acknowledged his suzerainty from 1806 until the signing of the Treaty of Lahore in 1909, when British pressure forced Ranjit Singh to withdraw from the domain that directly bordered British control. As one scholar concluded, "A real political cleavage was created for the first time between the Manjha and the Malwa sections of the Sikhs," one of the bases of contemporary Sikh factionalism.[35] Nonetheless, Maharajah Ranjit Singh, with his capital in Lahore, reigned in a vast area encompassing the Punjab and North-West Frontier Province areas of contemporary Pakistan, Jammu and Kashmir, and core areas of the central plains of present-day Punjab, India. Military conquest came largely through his Sikh chiefs and troops. Extremists in the 1980s can cite the Sikh kingdom under Ranjit Singh as the embodiment of the popular Sikh slogan scrawled on walls in Punjab and Delhi, Raj karega khalsa (The khalsa shall rule). Even the moderate Khushwant Singh writes that Ranjit Singh derived his title from that "mystic entity, the *Panth Khalsaji*," and that "he was impelled by the weight of tradition that . . . it was the destiny of the Sikhs to rule."[36]

Models, however, are seldom unambiguous. Sikhs were the third

35. Gulshan Lall Chopra, *The Panjab as a Sovereign State (1799–1839)* (Ph.D. thesis, London University [Hoshiarpur: Vishveshvaranand Vedic Research Institute, 1960]), 41.

36. Singh, *History of the Sikhs*, 1:201–2.

largest religious community after Muslims and Hindus in the new kingdom. Kushwant Singh concludes that Maharajah Ranjit Singh "convinced the people" that he was not establishing a Sikh kingdom "but a Punjabi state in which Muslims, Hindus, and Sikhs would be equal before the law and have the same rights and duties." He carefully respected and patronized other religious faiths, even allowing his Muslim and Hindu wives to retain their respective faiths. Equally, if not more, important, his court "reflected the secular pattern of his state." He had a Hindu Dogra prime minister, a Muslim foreign minister, and a Hindu Brahmin finance minister. Important military commanders also were drawn from different faiths.[37]

SIKH IDENTITY AND INSTITUTIONALIZATION

Maharajah Ranjit Singh's powerful kingdom fell to the British in 1849, a decade after his death. A new imperial framework provided an overlay to the social order, reinforcing particular features as well as providing a window of change into the larger world. Sikh identity continued to be molded in two very different institutional contexts. One was the world of the army; the other, the new organizations that sprouted at least partly in response to British rule.

Sikhs quickly became an important component of the Indian army. Recruiting handbooks associated Sikh military loyalty and bravery with religious identity, specifically the "rituals and symbols associated with the *khalsa*."[38] Baptism, unshorn hair, *gurdwaras* (Sikh temples), and adherence to religious holidays maintained and reinforced the *khalsa* version of Sikhism.[39]

Ethnic identity, however, remained questionable in the world outside of the military and British officialdom. Sikhs responded to the concerns

37. Ibid., 203 and 294–95.

38. N. Gerald Barrier, "The Sikhs and Punjab Politics, 1882–1922," in *Political Dynamics*, ed. Wallace and Chopra, 507. Barrier cites A. H. Bingley, *Sikhs: A Handbook for Indian Army* (Government of India, 1918) and editorials in Khalsa Akbar, 14 February and 29 July 1898.

39. British identification with the *khalsa* version of Sikhism went to the extreme of counting only "nonsmoking *keshdaris*" in the 1881 census. This policy contrasted sharply with the first British census of 1855, in which Sikhs were not enumerated separately (J. S. Grewal, "Legacies of the Sikh Past for the Twentieth Century," in *Sikh History*, ed. O'Connell, Israel, and Oxtoby, 25).

of their community, including a concern for their own identity, by forming modern organizations in the new pattern then springing up throughout India. The process is comparable to and part of what is usually termed the Indian renaissance and revivalism of the nineteenth and twentieth centuries, in which religious communities engaged in reexamination, reform, and reaffirmation of their identities.[40] Competition ensued in Punjab between the major religious groups—Muslims, Hindus, Sikhs, and Christians—to increase or maintain their adherents and for state resources.

Singh Sabhas—new Sikh organizations—became the major organizational expression of the social elites drawn from the old aristocracy as well as the new professions. The first of these organizations was formed in 1873, and by 1900 there were 116 Singh Sabhas inculcating the *khalsa* subtradition, so that a "single Sikh identity began to crystallize in the first decade of this century."[41] They insisted that Sikhs be distinguished from Hindus "as a separate community" and engaged in educational and social reform, including the founding of *khalsa* schools, and in other measures to restore Sikhism to "its pristine purity."[42]

A communal tract of the period captures the essence of Sikh revivalism in its title *Hum Hindu Nahin*, which translates, "We are not Hindus."[43] In 1902 a coordinating body for the Singh Sabhas, the Chief Khalsa Diwan, assumed leadership, providing a political dimension to the social and religious emphases of the Singh Sabhas.[44]

Militancy returned to Sikh politics as ethnic mobilization swept past the narrow social bases of the Singh Sabhas in the form of a dynamic mass movement developed to bring Sikh temples under the control of *khalsa* Sikhs. The *gurdwara* reform movement began as early as 1895 as a product of the cultural nationalism engendered by the Sikh reformers.[45] Simply stated, Sikhs wanted to manage their own temples, which they asserted were controlled by priests who were more Hindu than Sikh,

40. For the clearest and most carefully researched monograph using the concepts of revivalism and renaissance for India, see David Kopf, *British Orientalism and the Bengal Renaissance* (Berkeley and Los Angeles: University of California Press, 1969).

41. Harit S. Oberoi, "From Ritual to Counter-Ritual: Rethinking the Hindu-Sikh Question, 1884–1915," in *Sikh History*, ed. O'Connell, Israel, and Oxtoby, 149.

42. *Allen's Indian Mail*, 11 March 1889; quoted in *History of the Khalsa College Amritsar* (Amritsar: Khalsa College, 1949), 2.

43. Kenneth W. Jones, "*Ham Hindu Nahin:* Arya Sikh Relations, 1877–1905," *Journal of Asian Studies* 32, no. 3 (1973): 457–75.

44. Surjit Singh Narang, "Chief *Khalsa* Diwan: An Analytical Study of Its Perceptions," in *Political Dynamics*, ed. Wallace and Chopra, 70.

45. Teja Singh, *The Gurdwara Reform Movement and the Sikh Awakening* (Jullundur: Desh Sewak Book Agency, 1922), 87.

who misappropriated funds, and who engaged in immoral practices. The more moderate Chief Khalsa Diwan circulated a pamphlet on the subject in 1915, but subsequently "the matter was dropped as impracticable."[46]

A series of events continued to radicalize Sikh consciousness. These include the Gurdwara Rikab Ganj incident in New Delhi in 1914 involving the destruction of a wall of the temple. In 1914 Indian immigrants, primarily Sikhs, aboard the ship Komagata Maru were refused admittance to Canada and were returned to India, creating another situation threatening to the British. The newly formed Ghadr (revolutionary) party, basically Sikh, used the incident as a symbol of the discrimination against Sikhs and Indians. According to the then lieutenant governor of Punjab, revolutionary uprisings in which four hundred people were jailed and 2,500 restricted to their villages were attempted in Punjab.[47]

Sikh mobilization also received impetus from the nearly one hundred thousand Sikhs from Punjab and Delhi who served in the Indian army during World War I. They constituted 26 percent of the Punjab contingent, a portion considerably greater than their 12 percent population figure.[48] Expectations of political reform were dashed by repressive government measures following the war. In particular, the Jallianwala Bagh massacre in Amritsar in 1919 resulted in 379 killed and over two thousand wounded, about a third of whom were Sikhs.[49]

These various currents fed into the mass movement that became institutionalized in the *gurdwara* reform movement after World War I and is viewed by some contemporary scholars as the basis for Sikh separatism. An estimate of the mobilization during the agitational period from 1921 to 1925 can be derived from the following figures: 30,000 Sikhs were arrested, 400 were killed, 2,000 were wounded, and Rs 1.5 million were assessed in fines.[50]

Two dominant and interrelated institutions of Sikh politics emerged

46. Teja Singh, *Essays in Sikhism* (Lahore: Sikh University Press, 1944), 183.

47. Sir Michael O'Dwyer, *India As I Knew It, 1885–1925* (London: Constable and Company, 1925), 197. An excellent scholarly presentation is by Harish Puri, *Ghadr Movement: Ideology, Organization, and Strategy* (Amritsar: Guru Nanak Dev University, 1983). For the major work on the Hindu academician who founded the party in California in 1913, see Emily C. Brown, *Har Dayal: Hindu Revolutionary and Rationalist* (Tucson: University of Arizona Press, 1975).

48. Government of Punjab, *The Punjab and the War*, comp. M. S. Leigh (Lahore: Superintendent, Government Printing, 1922), 44. For a fine collection of scholarly articles, see Dewitt C. Ellinwood, Jr., ed., *India and World War One* (Delhi: Manohar, 1978).

49. Singh, *The Sikhs*, 106, and idem, *History of the Sikhs*, 2:162–64.

50. "The Sikh Movement," based on the papers of Sardar Gurbachan Singh, ed., *Akal Nirmal Gazette* (Tarn Taran), in H. N. Mitra and N. N. Mitra, *Indian Quarterly Register* 1 (1925): 90.

from the movement: a Sikh subpolitical system in the form of an elected temple-management committee (the Shiromani Gurdwara Prabandhak Committee, or SGPC) and a Sikh political party (Akali Dal) that dominated it. The Akal Takht in the Golden Temple complex was the birthplace of the SGPC in 1920. An assembly of Sikhs elected 175 members to manage Sikh shrines.[51] More-radical elements composed the "semi-military corps of volunteers known as the Akali Dal (army of immortals),"[52] which mobilized and trained the largely rural forces for the takeover of the temples. In contrast to the other, more-elitist parties in Punjab, including the Congress party, the Akali Dal emphasized mass mobilization and militant tactics with the clear goal of bringing all Sikh temples under the authority of the SGPC.

Five years of struggle ensued with the British government, which followed a narrow, legalistic, law-and-order approach until 1925, when a compromise favorable to the reformers resulted. The struggle and victory established the SGPC as central to Sikh politics and ethnicity. In conceptual terms, the SGPC can be described as a political system for Sikh affairs.[53] Its management of the Sikh temples has provided it with a large income (see Table 9.2), patronage through appointments, and a communications system through the temples that reaches every village and urban area with Sikhs. It has external relations, both direct and

Table 9.2.   SGPC budgets, 1964–1988

Year	Rupees	$ Equivalent[a]
1964	6,306,000	1,340,000
1970	20,000,000	2,600,000
1977	30,000,000	4,000,000
1980	60,000,000	8,000,000
1988	130,000,000	9,600,000

SOURCES: Interview with Arjan Singh Budhiraja, secretary of the Akali Dal (Sant group), SGPC headquarters, Amritsar, 24 April 1964; *The Tribune*, 27 November 1970; *The Hindu*, 11 July 1977; *The Tribune*, 20 November 1980; and *The Hindu*, 4 April 1988.

[a]The dollar equivalents were calculated on the basis of the rates of exchange prevailing during the period.

51. A general assembly of Sikhs met at the Akal Takht, elected a committee of 175 members, and named it the SGPC on 15 November 1920. It was formally inaugurated, again at the Akal Takht, on 12 December. Mohinder Singh, *The Akali Movement* (Delhi: Macmillan, 1978), 88.

52. Singh, *History of the Sikhs*, 2:198.

53. For a more detailed description and analysis, see Wallace, "Religious and Secular Politics."

indirect, with the Punjab government, under whose laws it operates, and with Sikh and other groupings whose activities relate to SGPC concerns. The internal dynamics of the system have revolved around the relations between the contending political parties and groups. This latter aspect is perhaps best symbolized by the Teja Singh Samundri Assembly Hall in the SGPC headquarters in Amritsar, which contains opposing rows of benches, based on the British House of Commons model, for accommodating the ruling and opposing parties. Individual Sikh leaders and their contending groups contest for supremacy locally and then within the SGPC. Akali Dal dominance in this "Religious Parliament of the Sikhs,"[54] and thus in Sikh politics, continued from the initial period until challenged by Sant Bhindranwale and the extremists in 1984.

Khalsa Sikhs clearly dominated the major Sikh institutions of Punjab as a consequence of the *gurdwara* reform movement, even though non-*khalsa* Sikhs could and did vote in the elections held every five years.[55] Whether this key development in the building of Sikh identity is the forerunner of the Khalistan movement and terrorism approximately sixty years later is a politically volatile question requiring that one distinguish between religious separatism, relevant primarily to cultural identity, and political separatism. Revisionist scholarship is beginning to rethink the *gurdwara* reform movement linking religious and political separatism in a manner that I conclude is unwarranted.

One carefully researched study of the *gurdwara* reform period by Rajiv Kapur, a Hindu scholar, concludes that by 1920 "the evolution of Sikh communal consciousness had led to political organization" that "bred militancy and saw the emergence of a *khalsa* nationalism." The case study provided in Kapur's book reveals how the revitalized Sikh identity and its new institutions were employed; but not in the form of "Akali fanaticism," as Kapur asserts. It is true that the Akalis employed militant tactics. Nonetheless, they basically followed a Gandhian strategy of noncooperation and nonviolence, at times coordinated with the Congress nationalist movement, as the author himself documents.[56]

Moreover, the durability and the militancy of the movement are at least partly attributable to the severity and the insensitivity of the government. As the author admits, negotiations between the Sikh re-

54. Harish K. Puri, "Akali Politics: Emerging Compulsions," in *Political Dynamics*, ed. Wallace and Chopra, 301.
55. For a study of the 1979 SGPC elections, see Surindar S. Suri and Narinder Dogra, "A Study of SGPC Elections, March 1979," in *Political Dynamics*, ed. Wallace and Chopra, 123–34.
56. Rajiv A. Kapur, *Sikh Separatism: The Politics of Faith* (London: Allen and Unwin, 1986), 92, 105, 123.

formers and the government were suspended in 1922 at least partly because of "official repression."[57] It took three additional years of massive agitations led by the Akali Dal before a compromise could be effected that in its major features conceded the SGPC/Akali demands. The level of Sikh politicalization, consequently, is at least partly attributable to the government.

Kapur is correct in stating that the Sikh Gurdwaras Act of 1925 "provided an institutional structure for Sikh communal separatism."[58] It is equally notable that this did not translate into political separatism even when Sikhs were uprooted from western Punjab during partition in 1947. To the contrary, Sikh ethnic demands in regard to their temples and community were processed—mediated—through the political system successfully. The SGPC and its dominant political party, the Akali Dal, became an institutionalized part of the larger Punjab political system and the nationalist movement of succeeding decades.

Religio-political separation did not overtake Punjab until the 1946 elections, and it was not the Sikhs but the Muslims who provided the driving force. Until then, the intracommunal ruling Unionist Party, although Muslim dominated, successfully resisted the pressures of the Muslim League, with its goal of an independent Pakistan, until the 1946 elections. The Muslim League went from 22 to 75 seats in the 175-seat Punjab Legislative Assembly, while the Unionist Party fell from 120 to 20, only 13 of which were held by Muslims.[59] Akalis, in fact, joined in a coalition with the Unionist and Congress parties to form a ministry in an attempt to retain a united Punjab, and this attempt "outraged and affronted" the Muslim community.[60] Political separation occurred a year later, with the larger Muslim-majority part of Punjab becoming part of the new country of Pakistan.

SIKHS AND OTHER COMMUNITIES

Punjab emerged in 1947 as a state in which adherents of the Sikh religion remained a decided minority despite the geographical changes; almost all of the Muslims migrated to Pakistan or to other parts of India. One

57. Ibid., 49.
58. Ibid., 7.
59. *The Hindu*, 25 February 1946.
60. Penderel Moon (a former deputy commissioner and secretary to the governor of Punjab), *Divide and Quit* (Berkeley and Los Angeles: University of California Press, 1962), 70.

hundred years had passed since Sikhs were the central element in the large area ruled by Maharajah Ranjit Singh. British conquest and annexation in 1849 provided a new reality. Numbers became increasingly important as each religious community competed in the spheres of government service and education and in elections based on separate communal electorates.

Recruitment to government service clearly illustrates the competition and the political problem. A government publication in 1945 spelled out the *principle* of communal recruitment as offering "to every community a chance, proportionate to its population in the province, to enter Government service." All thirty-seven departments of the government practiced communal recruitment by 1945.[61] Political *reality* differed markedly from the principle, since a formula acceptable to the competitors could not easily be devised.

As Table 9.3 indicates, there were significant changes in the formula over time. But the formula did not adhere strictly to population percentages. Sikhs, for example, constituted about 14 percent of the population, but were allocated 20 percent in the formula. Punjab's leading Muslim politician, Fazl-i-Husain, stated the problem frankly and polemically in a 1936 pamphlet entitled *Punjab Politics*. Muslims, he wrote, seek "to obtain their rights on a population basis," Hindus "want to retain their present position of advantage," and the Sikhs desire "some loot or other in every affray that may be on."[62]

Table 9.3. Formulas for communal recruitment to government services, 1925–1945

	1925	1932	1941	1945
Muslims	40%	50%	50%	50%
Hindus	40%	33%[a]	30%[a]	25%
Sikhs	20%	17%	20%	20%
Others	—	—	—	5% (2.5% Scheduled Castes and 2.5% other communities)

SOURCE: Compiled from Government of Punjab, *Pamphlet Showing the Systems Adopted by Departments of the Punjab Government to Ensure Equitable Recruitment of All Communities into Government Service* (Lahore: Superintendent, Government Printing, 1945), v.

[a]Including others.

61. Government of Punjab, *Pamphlet Showing the Systems Adopted by Departments of the Punjab Government to Ensure Equitable Recruitment of All Communities into Government Service* (Lahore: Superintendent, Government Printing, 1945), v and 1–54.

62. Quoted in Azim Husain, *Fazl-i-Husain: A Political Biography* (Bombay: Longmans, Green, 1946), 304n.

It is true that competition existed among all three major communities, as well as with the small but important Christian community, before independence. Nonetheless, the history of the region tended toward Hindu-Sikh alliances against the Muslims. The Pakistan movement reinforced this political tendency. It threatened to and eventually split Sikh population centers and separated them as well from their richest agricultural lands and some of their most important religious shrines. During the violence attending partition, Sikhs again became "the sword arm of the Hindus," as they had been during the Mughal period.

Partition, however, changed the communal calculus and political context (see Table 9.4). Muslims migrated from Indian Punjab, while Hindus and Sikhs left the new Pakistani Punjab. Hindus constituted a large 64 percent majority statewide, but with politically significant regional demographic differences. Hindu concentrations were most pronounced in the southeast plains and northeast hill areas of postpartition Punjab, whereas Sikhs constituted a majority in the central plains. Geographic concentration encouraged the Sikhs to mount political movements for further alterations in the state's political arrangements, since Sikhs were still a minority, with 33 percent of the state's population. Identity issues related to language and script and, subsequently, a Sikh-majority state were central. Efforts toward resolution of these issues, ranging from conventional political maneuvering to mass movements, became a regular feature of Punjab politics.

Less than a year after independence and the reconstitution of the

Table 9.4. Religious composition of the three Punjabs

	Pre-independence 1931	Before Punjabi Suba 1961	After Punjabi Suba 1971	1981
Muslims	52.4%	1.94% (393,314)	.84% (114,447)	1.0% (168,094)
Hindus	30.2%	63.57% (12.9m)	37.54% (5.58m)	36.9% (6.20m)
Sikhs	14.3%	33.33% (6.8m)	60.22% (8.16m)	60.75% (10.19m)
Total population	24,969,408	20,30,812	13,551,060	16,788,915

SOURCES: Government of India, *Census of India, 1931*, vol. 17, *Punjab*, part 2, *Tables*, by Khan Ahmad Hasan Khan (Lahore: Civil and Military Gazette Press, 1933), 277–79. Idem, *Census of India, 1961, Paper No. 1 of 1963, Religion* (New Delhi: Manager of Publications, 1963), ii–v. Idem, *Census of India, 1971*, series 1, part 2-c (i), "Social and Cultural Tables" (Delhi: Controller of Publications, 1977), 92–95. Government of Punjab, *Statistical Abstract of Punjab, 1983* (Chandigarh: Economic Adviser to Government, 1984), 38. Government of India, *Census of India, 1981, Paper No. 4 of 1984* (Delhi: Controller of Publications, 1984), 494–517.

state, the Akali Dal publicly proclaimed a set of demands in Amritsar that included granting its "backward tribes" the same preferential treatment as Hindu scheduled castes (which was granted), recognition of the Punjabi language and Gurmukhi script for official and educational purposes, and the demarcation of Punjab into a "Punjabi-speaking province on a linguistic and cultural basis."[63] A compromise concluded the following year, in October 1949, proposed that the regional languages be made official at the district level and that Punjabi, as the second language, be taught as a compulsory subject. It satisfied neither the Akalis nor the major Hindu revivalist organization, the Arya Samaj.[64]

A more extremist position then came forth from Master Tara Singh, premier Akali leader since the SGPC movement. He called for a Sikh-majority state at a conference in Amritsar on 22 October 1949. An editorial in the region's most important newspaper, the *Tribune*, emphasized that this was the first time that a demand had been made that Punjab "should be so divided as to ensure a majority for the Sikhs."[65] Opposing these essentially political demands were not only Hindus but what were called nationalist Sikhs, an important component of the Congress Party, and other Sikhs who did not want Punjab further reduced in size.

Akali Dal disappointment with the recommendations of the All-India States Reorganization Commission sparked the Akalis to new efforts on behalf of a Sikh-majority state. Massive agitations for a Punjabi Suba (state) mobilized approximately ten thousand Sikhs offering themselves for arrest in 1955.[66] The States Reorganization Commission emphasized the danger to Hindu-Sikh relations in the "agitation in favour of the proposed Punjabi-speaking State . . . a regrettable consequence of which has been the inflammation of communal passions in this region." One specific example it cited was the "repudiation by large sections of the Hindu community of the Punjabi language as their mother tongue" in the census.[67] Hindu political parties and organizations vociferously opposed the Akali Dal demands and made their own.

63. *The Tribune*, 10 May 1949. Unsuccessful Akali demands were made even earlier, in March, following its coalition with and entry into the Congress Party (ibid., 19 March 1948).

64. *The Tribune*, 3 October 1949, and Ghanshyam Singh Gupta, *The Case of the Arya Samaj Regarding Language Problem in Punjab* (Delhi: Sarvadeshik Arya Pratinidhi Sabha, 1957), 5–15.

65. *The Tribune*, 24 October 1949.

66. Akali sources claimed that twelve thousand were arrested (*Times of India*, 13 July 1955, as cited in Baldev Raj Nayar, *Minority Politics in the Punjab* [Princeton: Princeton University Press, 1966], 244).

67. Government of India, *Report of the States Reorganization Commission* (New Delhi: Manager of Publications, 1955), 141.

In this politically and communally volatile context, Pratap Singh Kairon became the first Sikh chief minister of Punjab, taking charge of the ruling Congress Party in January 1956.[68] His ascriptive assets included being a Jat, the premier agricultural caste for Hindus as well as Sikhs, and being from Amritsar. He also had a growing reputation as a decisive, strong, and politically skillful nationalist-oriented leader, which reputation brought him consistent support from the Union government. He quickly reached a compromise—similar to the 1949 proposals—with the Akali Dal in regard to territorial differences. Regional committees were established in Punjab for the "Punjabi" and the "Hindi" regions, and the capital, Chandigarh, was not included in either.[69]

Hindu organizations reacted with a "Save Hindi Movement" led by the Jan Sangh and the Arya Samaj, with support from the more orthodox Sanatan Dharm. It lasted from June to December 1957, mobilizing thirty thousand volunteers and resulting in the arrest of about eight thousand participants.[70] Chief Minister Kairon skillfully controlled and disassembled the movement. But in 1960–61 he again had to confront a Punjabi Suba movement.

A watershed in Punjab politics was the 1960 movement, during which the Akalis changed the basis of their leadership as well as their tactics. Accommodation and communal harmony became the major themes, overcoming the irredentist conflictual model. Master Tara Singh represented the irredentist position. During the movement he accelerated his rhetoric, describing it as *dharma yudh*, a religious war, and he continued to define Punjabi Suba in Sikh communal terms. Akali sources claimed that over fifty-seven thousand were jailed during the movement, although the government figures are a more modest, but still impressive, twenty-three thousand.[71] Master Tara Singh's lack of success in achieving Punjabi Suba, as well as the growing importance of rural leaders within the Akali Dal, led to the ascendancy of a new leadership led by Sant Fateh Singh. Although a Sant, a religious leader, he placed more emphasis on language than religion,[72] thereby tactically shifting the major issue to a

68. *The Tribune*, 15 and 22 January 1956.
69. Government of India, Ministry of Home Affairs, *The Punjab Regional Committees Order*, 1957, S.R.O. 3524 (New Delhi, 4 November 1957). For a succinct, excellent analysis, see Joan V. Bondurant, *Regionalism Versus Provincialism: A Study in Problems of Indian National Unity* (Berkeley: University of California, Indian Press Digest Monograph no. 4, 1958), 116–24.
70. Nayar, *Minority Politics*, 308.
71. Singh, *History of the Sikhs*, 2:299.
72. *Indian Express*, 12 January 1961, 1.

criterion that the government had recognized as legitimate since 1953 in the ongoing process of states reorganization.[73]

Sant Fateh Singh represented more-moderate elements that placed emphasis on a Punjabi-speaking state *along with* Hindu-Sikh harmony rather than conflict. He also represented younger elements and rural Jats, in contrast to Master Tara Singh, the longtime leader who was from a merchant caste. A common characterization in Punjab was that the *jathedars*, rural Jat-led Sikhs, took over from the *bhapas*, more urban and merchant-led Sikhs. The rural-based Sant group manifested a more moderate approach compared to that of the more extremist, urban-based Master group. On one level Sant Fateh Singh's empirically developed model distinguished between ethnicity based on Punjabi elements—the most important of which were language and territory—and religion. It thus was inclusive of Hindus and other Punjabi speakers. On another level, it encountered resistance, particularly from Hindus in the central plains who saw the model as a thinly veiled attempt to secure a Sikh-majority state.

Sant's group established its dominance within the Akali Dal and the SGPC, while the previous dominant group split to become a dissident, but minor, Master (Tara Singh) Akali Dal. The Sant group's primacy in Sikh politics, and a series of propitious events, enabled it to achieve a limited version of Punjabi Suba, a Sikh-majority state, in 1966. These events included the dismissal of Chief Minister Kairon for corruption,[74] the weakening of the Punjab Congress Party, a war with Pakistan, and the rise of Sant Fateh Singh's credibility with the Union government due to his and the Sikh contribution to the war.

Sikhs for the first time became a majority in Punjab, with 60 percent of the population, although the state's boundaries had been reduced essentially to the central plains. Southeast Punjab became the new state of Haryana, and hill areas in the north were joined to Himachal Pradesh. Hindus were reduced to a minority of 37.6 percent in the truncated Punjab. Nonetheless, the same two major political parties, the Congress and Akali Dal, contested for dominance, while the same secondary political parties, the Jan Sangh and the two Communist parties, the CPI and the CPI-M (Communist Party of India-Marxist), continued to play a minor role.

Elections in the newly reconstituted Sikh-majority Punjab in 1967

73. For a detailed discussion and analysis, see Paul Brass, *Language, Religion, and Politics in North India* (London: Cambridge University Press, 1974), ch. 6.

74. For the findings of the Das Commission, see Government of India, Ministry of Home Affairs, *Report of the Commission of Inquiry* (Delhi: Manager of Publications, 1964).

failed to produce an Akali Dal majority. Congress remained the single largest party, with forty-eight seats and 37 percent of the votes; the Akali Dal won twenty-six seats and 25 percent of the votes. Moreover, the Akali total included two seats won by the dissident Master group. Achievement of Punjabi Suba maintained Akali dominance with the SGPC system, but Akali lacked sufficient support to gain a majority in the statewide secular system.

Two major factors relegated the Akalis to a minority position in a Sikh-majority state. First, in Punjab the Sikhs are the rural majority in all but one district, Hoshiarpur, whereas the Hindus dominate all urban areas (see Table 9.5). Even in Amritsar, the site of the Golden Temple and center of contemporary terrorism, Hindus constitute 55 percent of the urban population. By contrast, its Sikh rural majority of 91.4 percent is the highest in Punjab. Patiala, a major green-revolution district in the Malwa area, has a Hindu urban majority of 64 percent and a Sikh rural majority of 65 percent. Akalis, therefore, as a Sikh political party, were essentially limited to rural Punjab.

The second factor is that *Sikhs are socially and politically heterogeneous* rather than homogeneous. Dominant land-owning Jat Sikhs normally cannot depend on political support from non-Jat Sikh agricultural laborers and service providers. Lower-status castes such as the Mazhabi,[75] Rai, Cheemba, Ramgarhia, and Lohar Sikhs are more likely to support the Congress or Communist parties. Sikh merchant castes such as the Khatris and Aroras have their own affiliations, including those with dissident Akali Dals.

Jats, who compose at least one-half of the Sikh population in Punjab and are the dominant element in the Akali Dal,[76] also are subject to personal and group factionalism. Consequently, the Congress Party always has had a Jat element, as represented by Chief Ministers Pratap Singh Kairon in the pre–Punjabi Suba period and Darbara Singh in the succeeding period. Moreover, key elements of the two Communist parties also consist of Jats. Akali dominance in the Sikh SGPC system

75. The Federation of Mazhabi Sikhs offered to join the Arya Samaj and Jan Sangh in an agitation against the formation of Punjabi Suba in March 1966. A spokesman asserted that "the Sikh Scheduled Castes had been reduced to a position of mere serfs by the Sikh landlords who would literally crush the Mazhabi Sikhs if Punjabi Suba was formed" (*The Tribune*, 16 March 1966).

76. Census figures for caste groups other than the scheduled castes have not been enumerated since the 1931 census. Amrik Singh, Center for Policy Research in New Delhi and former vice chancellor of Punjabi University, Patiala, asserts that "Jats constitute approximately two-thirds of the total Sikh population" ("Sikhs at the Turn of the New Century," in *Sikh History*, ed. O'Connell, Israel, and Oxtoby, 426–27). Robin Jeffrey estimates the Jat percentage as between 50–60%. *What's Happening to India*, op. cit., 48.

Table 9.5.   Punjab districts, rural-urban percentage by community, 1981

District		Hindus	Sikhs
Amritsar:	Total	22.5	75.6
Rural		6.5	91.4
Urban		54.9	43.6
Patiala:	Total	42.3	56.0
Rural		33.3	64.7
Urban		63.6	35.1
Gurdaspur:	Total	48.1	44.6
Rural		40.2	51.4
Urban		76.7	20.1
Firozpur:	Total	44.3	54.3
Rural		34.7	64.2
Urban		76.9	20.6
Ludhiana:	Total	32.3	66.5
Rural		10.9	88.3
Urban		61.7	36.5
Jalandhar:	Total	55.9	42.9
Rural		45.4	53.5
Urban		75.1	23.3
Kapurthala:	Total	38.8	60.2
Rural		27.5	71.5
Urban		65.2	33.7
Hoshiarpur:	Total	59.4	39.2
Rural		56.7	41.9
Urban		75.3	22.9
Rupnagar:	Total	41.8	56.6
Rural		36.6	62.0
Urban		60.8	36.9
Sangrur:	Total	23.7	69.6
Rural		15.9	80.1
Urban		50.0	34.0
Bhatinda:	Total	23.0	76.3
Rural		11.6	87.7
Urban		61.8	37.3
Faridkot:	Total	20.6	78.7
Rural		9.0	90.4
Urban		57.5	41.6

SOURCE: Computed from data in Government of Punjab, *Statistical Abstract of Punjab 1987* (Chandigarh: The Economic Adviser to Government, 1988), 64–65.

enabled them to mount massive campaigns on Sikh issues but did not translate into majorities in the state legislative assembly.

An even more constricted political base confronted the Jan Sangh, the mirror image of the Akalis. Its Hindu urban base, shared with the Congress Party, enabled it to compete effectively only in the relatively few towns and cities in the largely rural state. The two communal parties—the Akali Dal and Jan Sangh—were bitterly opposed to each other on rural-urban issues and communal issues such as language. Clearly, the Congress Party benefited as a secular, intercommunal party, surmounting the rural-urban differences; and with support from the national party, Congress ruled government. These basic political facts became even more apparent with the results of the 1967 elections.

Akali tactics until the advent of Punjabi Suba in 1966 were not solely movement oriented. Accommodation within the Congress Party occurred twice, in 1948–51 and 1956–60. One scholar has labeled this an Akali infiltration strategy,[77] but it did provide alliance experience in an intercommunal coalition. Political skills developed within the SGPC, and assembly political systems also were important assets to the Akali Dal. Consequently, Akali frustration with the results of the 1967 elections did not have to be channeled into another mass movement for Sikh demands. An accommodationist option became available as the Congress Party struggled over leadership problems that delayed it from turning its leading position in the assembly into a majority.

Sant Fateh Singh's dominant Akali Dal and the Jan Sangh accomplished the unprecedented feat of allying in an anti-Congress United Front Ministry. It lasted only eight months, and then defections and political instability led inexorably to president's rule in August 1968.[78] Nevertheless, the alliance continued, enabling it to return to power in February 1969. It also resulted in the Akali Dal winning 43 of the 104 assembly seats, making it for the first time the single largest party in the assembly.[79] Defections to the Akali Dal subsequently provided it with a majority, rendering the alliance, in its view, unnecessary. Ending the alliance proved disastrous in the 1972 elections: the Congress Party returned to power with sixty-five seats and 42.8 percent of the vote, and the Akali Dal won twenty-four seats and 27.6 percent of the vote.[80]

77. Nayar, *Minority Politics*, 124–29.

78. *The Tribune*, 24 August 1968.

79. *The Tribune*, 12 February 1969. A lucid, firsthand discussion of the political dynamics of the period is provided by D. C. Pavate, *My Days as Governor* (Delhi: Vikas, 1974).

80. *The Tribune*, 15 March 1972. It also should be noted that a Congress "wave" occurred throughout the country as a consequence of India's defeat of Pakistan and the emergence of Bangladesh in 1971.

A reinvigorated alliance emerged in 1977, following the twenty-month national emergency orchestrated by Prime Minister Indira Gandhi. Akalis resisted Congress "feelers" that shortly after the onset of the emergency encouraged them to condemn it in extreme terms as an "onslaught on the civil liberties, freedom of press and freedom of speech, a rape on democracy and a great step towards dictatorship."[81] A nonviolent "Save Democracy Morcha [movement]," launched within a month of the emergency's proclamation, continued until its end. It is estimated that forty thousand Akalis were arrested or detained, including its president and eighteen Akali members of the assembly.[82] A common bond of resistance to the emergency and, in many cases, shared confinement added another element to Akali–Jan Sangh (reformulated as part of the new Janata Party) relations.

The CPI-M joined them in 1977, and together they won all thirteen parliamentary seats from Punjab in March and an impressive majority in the assembly in June. Akalis won enough seats, 58 out of the 117, to form a government on their own but chose to maintain the alliance.[83] Meaningful accommodation between the rural-oriented Akali Dal and the Hindu and urban-based Janata Party was impressive for the two-year period following June 1977. Potentially explosive issues that divided the two parties both internally and in regard to each other were handled with moderation and skill.

For example, Akali leaders who later became extremists, SGPC President Gurcharan Singh Tohra and Akali President Jagdev Singh Talwandi, agreed with the position of a religious leader who undertook a fast unto death on behalf of incorporating Chandigarh and Punjabi areas of Haryana into Punjab. Nonetheless, they opposed disturbing Hindu-Sikh harmony, affirming that all issues would be solved through "peaceful negotiations."[84]

Punjab's ruling alliance resulted from internal political dynamics. It also reflected developments in New Delhi, where the loosely allied elements of the ruling Janata Party included the Akali cabinet minister Surjit Singh Barnala as well as a minister of state. In July 1979, the national Janata Party collapsed, at least partly over charges of Hindu communalism against the Jan Sangh elements within it. Akali president Talwandi and his group used these charges in Punjab to end the twenty-

---

81. Amarjit Singh Narang, *The Spokesman* 27, no. 19 (1978): 6–7.
82. Ibid. *The Economic and Political Weekly* 12, no. 13 (1977): 532, emphasized the "sustained agitation" throughout the state and the appearance in Amritsar of an Akali jatha "almost every day to flout the orders" of the government.
83. *Economic and Political Weekly* 12, no. 25 (1977): 1000–1001.
84. *The Spokesman* 27, no. 28 (1978): 1.

six-month coalition despite the efforts of the Akali chief minister, Prakash Singh Badal, to maintain it.

Effectively, the Akalis split into "two warring factions" that sabotaged each other in the subsequent 1980 parliamentary and state assembly elections, which were swept by the Congress Party.[85] Predictably, agitations and, subsequently, violence replaced electoral politics as the primary methods of the major actors contending in and responsible for Punjab. Moderates began to lose control and subsequently had to become more militant themselves in order to compete for Sikh support.

MILITANCY, TERRORISM, AND DEINSTITUTIONALIZATION

What became known as the Punjab problem, beginning with the advent of terrorism in 1981, can be conceptualized as political deinstitutionalization and the breaking down of a structural formula[86] between elites that had slowly and steadily developed at least since the 1920s. Deinstitutionalization took the form of the weakening or destruction of existing structures of authority—including political parties, the state parliamentary system, the bureaucracy, and the police—and in the domain of Sikh politics centered in the SGPC temple-management system. The major political parties, the Congress (I) (I for Indira Gandhi), the Akali Dal, and the Bharatiya Janata Party (BJP), formerly the Jan Sangh), became less important as the fulcrum of politics shifted increasingly to the revivalist, extremist, and terrorist movement symbolized by the charismatic Sant Jarnail Singh Bhindranwale.

According to a variety of published accounts,[87] Bhindranwale received

85. *The Tribune*, 11 January 1980. For a detailed analysis, see Paul Wallace, "Plebiscitary Politics in India's 1980 Parliamentary Elections: Punjab and Haryana," *Asian Survey* 20, no. 6 (1980): 617–33.

86. Cynthia Enloe uses this concept in *Ethnic Conflict and Political Development* (Boston: Little, Brown, 1973), 263. Consociationalism is a similar concept. See Arend Lijphart, *The Politics of Accommodation: Pluralism and Democracy in the Netherlands* (Berkeley and Los Angeles: University of California Press, 1968), and Hans Daalder, "The Consociational Theme," *World Politics* 24, no. 4 (1974): 604–21.

87. For example, see the following: Robin Jeffrey, *What's Happening to India?* (London: Macmillan, 1986), 135–36; Amrik Singh, "An Approach to the Problem," in *Punjab in Indian Politics: Issues and Trends*, ed. Amrik Singh (Delhi: Jawahar Nagar, Ajanta Publications, 1985), 1, 11; A. S. Narang, *Storm over the Sutlej: The Akali Politics* (Delhi: Gitanjali Publishing House, 1983), 229; and Lloyd I. Rudolph, "India and the Punjab: A Fragile Peace," in *Asian Issues 1985* (New York: The Asia Society and University Press of America, 1986), 37. Additional documentation follows.

assistance from the Congress (I) to destabilize the Akali Dal. In the words of a carefully researched article from the *Times of India*, Bhindranwale "was originally a product, nurtured and marketed by the Center to cut into the Akali Dal's spheres of influence." Lelyveld of the *New York Times* credits Sanjay Gandhi with recruiting Bhindranwale "after his mother's fall from power in 1977." Bhindranwale began his rise to public prominence on 13 April 1978, in a violent encounter with the Nirankaris, a nonmainstream community of Sikhs who believe in a living guru. Eighteen Sikhs were killed in what one scholar has described as a "provocative stage management."[88]

In 1979 Bhindranwale competed against the Akali candidates in the SGPC elections but won only four seats.[89] Giani Zail Singh, successively Punjab Congress chief minister, union home minister, and president of India, and Sanjay Gandhi are credited as the major architects of the party's Bhindranwale strategy. "Little did they realize," according to national columnist Kuldip Nayar, "that they were creating a Frankenstein" whom they could not control after resuming power in 1980.[90]

Key developments occurred in 1981–82 that set the stage for the ensuing tragedy. Ganga Singh Dhillon, a Sikh businessman from the United States, publicly raised the demand for Khalistan at an educational conference held in Chandigarh in March 1981 that was sponsored by the conservative Chief Khalsa Diwan.[91] Until this time, support for the extremist concept of a completely autonomous or independent state remained largely outside India, promoted by Jagjit Singh Chauhan, the former Punjab minister residing in England. As the self-appointed president, he issued nonaccreditable Khalistan passports, sought membership in the United Nations, and raised funds and secured support primarily from overseas Sikhs. A week after the conference, extremist Dal Khalsa and Nihang Singhs, both fringe groups, raised Khalistan banners during the Holi festival at Anandpur Sahib, the birthplace of *khalsa* Sikhism.[92]

Moderate Sikh leaders, such as Akali Dal president Sant Harcharan Singh Longowal and the former chief minister Prekash Singh Badal

88. Ayesha Kagal, "Armed Coup in Golden Temple," *Times of India, Sunday Review,* 19 December 1982, I, VI; Joseph Lelyveld, *New York Times Magazine,* 2 December 1984, 43; Harish K. Puri, "Religion and Politics in Punjab," in *Religion, State, and Politics in India,* ed. Moin Shakir (Delhi: Ajanta Publications, 1989), 338.
89. Suri and Dogra, "A Study of SGPC Elections," 136.
90. Kuldip Nayar and Khushwant Singh, *Tragedy of Punjab: Operation Bluestar and After* (New Delhi: Vision Books, 1984), 31.
91. *The Tribune* and *Indian Express,* 18 and 19 March 1981.
92. *National Herald,* 22 March 1981, 6.

reacted strongly and politically. They denounced the Khalistan demands as instruments "raised at the instigation of Congress (I) leaders" and the Chief Khalsa Diwan as "a pro-Government and pro-Congress (I) stage."[93] Rejecting the notion of a separate Sikh state continued the moderate pattern set by Sant Fateh Singh during the Punjabi Suba movement. A fear existed that, as Master Tara Singh publicly expressed it in the 1960s, Punjabi Suba would be but a stepping stone to a separate Sikh state. Sant Fateh Singh replied, "I think this demand will end for good. It was a useless demand and has practically fizzled out. . . . The Punjabi Suba is our last demand."[94]

Moderate Akalis tended toward the same views fifteen years later. But Sant Longowal's dominant Akali Dal faced increasing competition as its dominance in the Sikh political system weakened. Rebel Akali leader Jagdev Singh Talwandi pursued a more communal militant strategy after losing the presidency of the dominant Akali Dal and forming a dissident Akali Dal in 1980. He reached back in a calculated manner to resurrect the 1973 Anandpur Sahib Resolution. Passed by the Akali Dal following its defeat in the 1972 elections, the resolution emphasized an autonomous and expanded Punjab. It failed to catch fire and seemingly died during the national emergency called by Prime Minister Indira Gandhi in 1975 and the ensuing Akali control of the state government from 1977 to 1980.

Talwandi began his movement in April 1982. Longowal and the dominant Akali Dal also began a movement in April, but it focused on a more secular issue; they sought to stop work *(nahar roko)* on the Yamuna-Sutlej canal so as to retain a maximum amount of water for Punjab. Sant Bhindranwale, leading a major revivalist movement by this point, followed in July with a separate movement for the release from jail of All India Sikh Students Federation (AISSF) leader Amrik Singh.

Competition for Sikh support temporarily abated as the three movements allied on 4 August 1982 behind the Anandpur Sahib Resolution and Longowal as the overall "dictator." Longowal's Akali Dal seemingly reasserted its earlier dominance, but in undertaking responsibility for the more extreme demands, Longowal needed meaningful concessions from New Delhi in order to be seen as effective. If concessions were not forthcoming, and they were not, Longowal risked losing support to the more militant groups. One immediate cost to the moderates was that the alliance "successfully alienated opposition parties with whom they could share a political future."[95] An eminent moderate Sikh accused the Longo-

93. *The Tribune*, 14 April 1981, 3.
94. Quoted in P. C. Joshi, "Triumph of a Just Cause," in *Punjabi Suba: A Symposium* (Delhi: National Book Club, [1966]), 120.
95. Ayesha Kagal, *Times of India*, 19 December 1982, 6.

wal Akali Dal of attempting to "destabilize the Congress government through agitation."[96]

Opportunities and risks were involved for all three major political forces. Militant tactics, however nonviolent, promoted a more favorable context for the continuing extremist and violent movement led by Bhindranwale. On the other hand, Longowal's Akali Dal hoped to regain control of the expanded Sikh political forces sufficient to return to a more conventional political process.

Negotiations between the Akali Dal and New Delhi, beginning in October 1981 and continuing periodically until mid 1984, focused on various versions of what collectively are termed the Anandpur Sahib Resolution.[97] The changing nature of the Sikh demands underlined their fundamental political nature, although protracted central-government intransigence encouraged extremism.[98] It is doubtful that the original 1973 version ever received serious consideration in regard to the center-state provisions. Its version of state autonomy would have restricted central authority to defense, foreign relations, currency, and general communications for all states.

New Delhi could not treat this seriously. It could, however, consider a reformulated version passed by the Akali conference held at Ludhiana on 28–29 October 1978. Limiting the center to only four spheres of control had been replaced by an endorsement of "the principle of State autonomy in keeping with the concept of Federalism." The most specific part of the resolution on this subject was the statement that "it has become imperative that the Indian constitutional infrastructure should be given a real federal shape by redefining the central and state relations and rights."[99] In this form, the Akali Dal formulation was in the mainstream of continuing efforts by various states and groups to redress the imbalance of a purportedly federal system that tilted precariously toward overcentralization.[100]

96. Khushwant Singh, "The Genesis of the Hindu-Sikh Divide," in The Punjab Story, ed. Amarjit Kaur et al. (New Delhi: Roli Books International, 1984), 18–19.

97. The different versions of the Anandpur Sahib Resolution and subsequent Sikh demands are contained in Government of India, White Paper on the Punjab Agitation (New Delhi, 10 July 1984), 5–22, 61–90.

98. For example, an agreement would be reached between the negotiating parties, and then a different version would be placed before Parliament. In the words of a noted scholar, "Indira Gandhi had changed her mind" (J. S. Grewal, The New Cambridge History of India: The Sikhs of the Punjab [Cambridge University Press, 1990], 222).

99. Ibid., 72–73.

100. For a review of the major political and constitutional problems, see Paul Wallace, "Center-State Relations in India: The Federal Dilemma," in India 2000: The Next Fifteen Years, ed. James Roach (Riverdale, Md.: Riverdale, 1986), 146–65.

Prime Minister Indira Gandhi and the central government took a hard line. They chose to emphasize the more extreme elements of the Sikh demands and treated them essentially as tantamount to secession. Thus, New Delhi put moderate Sikhs at a competitive disadvantage in the increasingly militant and violent political arena.

Sant Bhindranwale gradually wrested effective control of the Golden Temple premises from the Akali Dal. The two political forces contested for dominance to the extent that in April and May 1984, as intimidation and killings continued in Punjab, each side charged the other with assassinations. The number of violent incidents increased monthly. In October 1983 the number rose to thirty-six; the previous month it had been nine. In May 1984 there were over fifty violent incidents. These included setting fire to railway stations, bank robberies, attacks on the police, bombings and other indiscriminate shootings, and the killing of Hindu passengers forcibly taken from buses.[101]

Longowal's core political base began to flow away; about a third of his SGPC members and district Akali presidents reportedly defected to Bhindranwale.[102] In this context of increasing discord between the major Sikh factions and of heightened levels of violence, the central government abruptly switched tactics from negotiations to military force.

OPERATION BLUESTAR AND ITS AFTERMATH

Operation Bluestar in June 1984 attempted to resolve the Punjab terrorist problem with massive military operations against the Golden Temple complex, the combing of other *gurdwaras* in Punjab, and military occupation of the state. Approximately seventy thousand troops from the Indian army and paramilitary forces sealed off the city of Amritsar and the state of Punjab. About one thousand people were killed in two days of fighting around the Golden Temple, including almost one hundred soldiers and about four hundred pilgrims.[103] One report states that fifty-five women and fifteen children were among the people killed.[104]

101. Grewal, *Cambridge History*, 223.

102. *India Today*, 15 May 1984, 30–31, and Gurmit Singh, *History of Sikh Struggles*, vol. 2 (New Delhi: Atlantic Publishers and Distributors, 1991), 99.

103. *India Today*, 30 June 1984, 8–21; Mary Ann Weaver, "Visit to Sikhdom's Damaged Symbol," *Christian Science Monitor*, 20 June 1984, 7; *New York Times*, 9 June and 29 July 1984; Government of India, *White Paper*.

104. *India Today*, 15 August 1984, 33.

The three major leaders of the terrorist movement died within the heavily fortified Golden Temple complex. Bhindranwale had provided the charismatic leadership. Amrik Singh had secured youthful recruits through his leadership of the AISSF and had had a particularly close relationship with Bhindranwale.[105] Former major general Shahbeg Singh, a hero of the Bangladesh liberation war of 1971, had supervised military training and fortifications. Charges of corruption had led to his dismissal from the army just before his expected retirement, and he then joined Bhindranwale.

These three individuals had directed the growing terrorist movement in Punjab during the preceding three years. A convenient inaugural date for the terrorist campaign is September 1981, when octogenarian Lala Jagat Narain, a Hindu and the largest publisher of vernacular newspapers in Punjab, became the first prominent victim of a hit squad. Narain had a reputation as a Hindu communalist among most Sikhs.[106] He also had been a prominent Indian nationalist and a minister in the postindependence Punjab government. His son, Mahesh Chandra, assumed control of the newspapers but also fell to an assassin's bullets shortly before the assault on the Golden Temple.

Violence progressively increased, beginning with the launching in August 1982 of the Akali-led combined movement on behalf of the Anandpur Sahib Resolution. From that point to Operation Bluestar in June 1984 over 350 people were killed by terrorists or by the police in what they termed encounters.[107]

From the government's perspective, attempts at negotiation had not been productive, and terrorism had increased to the point that repressive measures were necessary. Law and order and the unity and integrity of India became the paramount responsibilities of the government. Most Sikhs, and many non-Sikh journalists and intellectuals, believe that the Congress government did not bargain in good faith, undermined possible agreements, and encouraged Bhindranwale in order to exacerbate differences within the Akali Dal and further divide the Sikh community.

National elections, held in December 1984, also are cited as a major reason for the government not resolving the Punjab problem. The ruling Congress Party, it is charged, played what was popularly labeled the Hindu card, designed to promote the party as a defender of Hindu interests and Indian national unity against minority threats. National

105. Joshi, *Bhindranwale*, 5–7.
106. Puri, "Religion and Politics in Punjab," 311.
107. Congressional Research Service, 5, as cited in Richard P. Cronin, *India's Punjab Crisis: Issues, Prospects, and Implications* (Washington, D.C.: Library of Congress, Congressional Research Service Report for Congress 87-850 F, 6 October 1987), 51n.

columnist Pran Chopra wrote in 1983, "There is bound to be a Hindu backlash as Hindus have herded under the Congress (I) umbrella, since Mrs. Gandhi has so well cast herself now in the image of a Hindu goddess. Herding them [Hindus] in is one part of Mrs. Gandhi's motives, as it was in [Muslim-majority Kashmir] too; another part is to use 'insecurity' on the border for beating her drum of 'India in danger.' "[108]

After Operation Bluestar, ethnic identities inevitably sharpened as Sikhs reacted to destruction of their holy center. Khushwant Singh reveals the emotional impact of Operation Bluestar on even moderate Sikhs in an interview with a New Delhi journal: "I said for once that I was not living in a secular India but in a Hindu India. Because, for once I discovered from the reactions, that the entire reaction—the adverse reaction—was almost entirely Sikh, that the favorable reaction was almost entirely Hindu. . . . And this is what I feared that this kind of army action would result in—a total polarisation of views between the Sikh and the Hindu and that has taken place."[109] Kuldip Nayar, a respected Punjab Hindu journalist, registered a similar reaction. In his book coauthored with Khushwant Singh, he states dramatically that "Punjab's tragedy is that there are no Punjabis any more in Punjab— only Sikhs and Hindus."[110]

Extremism and terrorism continued despite the loss of the militants' top leaders and despite the military presence in Punjab. The situation only worsened with the assassination of Prime Minister Indira Gandhi by two of her Sikh bodyguards on 31 October 1984. Large-scale violence against Sikhs followed almost immediately, providing a major communal aftershock to the Operation Bluestar earthquake. Sikhs and civil rights organizations charged that Congress politicians, and the cooperation of the police, exercised a major role in the killing of over two thousand Sikhs and the burning of their property.[111] A commission reported that

108. Pran Chopra, "Where Has All the Song and Dance Gone?" *Illustrated Weekly of India*, 11 December 1983, 11. See also D. L. Sheth, "Wooing the Hindu Voter," *Indian Express Magazine*, 9 December 1984, 1. A contrary view is set forth in *Sunday*, 6–19 January 1985, 26–27.

109. Khushwant Singh, *Choice*, September 1984, 8.

110. Nayar and Singh, *Tragedy of Punjab*, 7.

111. The official Figure of 2,717 killed consisted almost entirely of Sikhs, some of whom were deliberately burned to death. "Unofficial figures are considerably higher" (Mark Tully and Zareer Masani, *From Raj to Rajiv: Forty Years of Indian Independence* (New Delhi: Universal Book Stall, 1988), 136–37). See also *Who Are the Guilty? Report of a Joint Inquiry into the Causes and Impact of the Riots in Delhi from 31 October to 10 November 1984* (Delhi: Govinda Kothari, president of the People's Union for Civil Liberties, November 1984); and Amiya Rao, Aurobindo Ghose, and N. D. Pancholi, *Report to the Nation: Truth About Delhi Violence*, foreward by Justice V. M. Tarkunde (Delhi: Citizens for Democracy, January 1985), 1–54.

some three-quarters of the approximately 405 Sikh temples in Delhi were the objects of a "systematic attack."[112] About fifty thousand Sikhs fled to Punjab from other parts of India,[113] and refugee camps for approximately two thousand Sikhs were set up in Delhi for those whose homes were destroyed or who felt unsafe.[114]

Sikh insecurity increased further as a consequence of the national election campaign held in December 1984. Prime Minister Rajiv Gandhi consistently emphasized the theme of the unity and integrity of India, code for the Sikh secessionist threat in Punjab. In this litany the Congress Party served as the sole protector of the state, and even national opposition parties were accused by Rajiv and other Congress leaders of having been sympathetic to secessionist Sikh demands. Visual dimensions of the alleged Sikh threat were suggested dramatically in an omnipresent election poster of the slain Mrs. Gandhi delivering a speech in which she states, "Whenever I will die, every drop of my blood will make India strong, and will keep alive a united India."[115]

A MISSED POLITICAL WINDOW OF OPPORTUNITY: THE PUNJAB ACCORD

Congress swept the national elections with 401 of the 508 seats in the Lok Sabha, a four-fifths majority. Its success reflected a sympathy wave rising from the assassination of Indira Gandhi and sustained by the "unity and integrity of India" theme. However, reconciliation rather than repression followed. Quickly and surprisingly, the young prime minister applied "a healing touch," as it became popularly labeled, to a series of concerns. In a nationwide address immediately following the elections, he declared solving the Punjab problem his number one priority. Even former prime minister Charan Singh, a vitriolic critic, stated in an interview that "they have begun well with humility."[116] Independent analyst Bhabani Sen Gupta represented the prevailing view in comment-

112. Report of the Citizen's Commission, headed by Justice S. M. Sikri, former chief justice of India, 1985, 35 ff., as cited in Patwant Singh, "The Sikhs and the Challenge of the Eighties," in *Sikh History*, ed. O'Connell, Israel, and Oxtoby, 419.
113. *Times of India*, 23 December 1984, 2.
114. *Indian Express*, 11 January 1985, 7.
115. Personal observation in India during the elections.
116. He did qualify the praise by adding that the fear remained that Rajiv "may follow in the footsteps of his mother, who followed a megalomaniacal policy based on elitist philosophies" (*India Today*, 31 January 1985, 21).

ing that "Rajiv Gandhi has suddenly changed the political climate of India from one of confrontation to conciliation."[117]
The government took several initiatives in the following two months. Major Akali leaders, including Sant Longowal, were released from internment. The prime minister, while touring Punjab, announced an economic development package including the first major heavy industrial plant for the state.[118] A commission of inquiry was appointed to investigate the allegations of organized violence against Sikhs following Mrs. Gandhi's assassination. The government lifted a yearlong ban against the AISSF and stated that more of the approximately twelve hundred jailed Sikhs would be released.[119] A continuing "secret" dialogue, leaked and reported regularly in the press, ensued with various Sikh groups.

Prime Minister Rajiv Gandhi culminated this political approach by reaching an agreement with Sant Longowal, which received a cheering ovation when read out to members of both houses of Parliament on 24 July 1985.[120] Key elements of the Punjab Accord included:

- Referral of the Anandpur Sahib Resolution to a commission on center-state relations appointed in March 1983.
- Transfer of Chandigarh, the capitol shared by Punjab and Haryana, to Punjab.
- "Rehabilitation" of Sikhs who deserted the army following Operation Bluestar.
- Compensation to innocent persons killed during the Punjab agitation.
- Extension of the judicial inquiry into the Delhi riots to include Bokaro and Kanpur.
- Consideration of an All India Sikh Temples Act.
- Referral of Punjab and Haryana's river waters dispute to a tribunal for adjudication.
- Promotion of the Punjabi language by the central government.

Rajiv revised the meaning of his election slogan to hail the accord as a "new phase of working together to build . . . unity and integrity." Longowal, in turn, declared that "the period of confrontation is over. The *morcha* stands automatically withdrawn."[121]

Yet terrorism did not cease during this period of continuing political initiatives and negotiation. To the contrary, a new tactic involving bombs

117. Bhabani Sen Gupta, "The New Politics," *India Today*, 31 January 1985, 59.
118. *New York Times*, 17 March 1985.
119. *India Today*, 30 April 1985, 8, and *New York Times*, 12 April 1985, 3.
120. *Times of India*, 25 July 1985, 1.
121. *Times of India*, 25 July 1985, 1, 12.

within booby-trapped transistor radio cases, placed primarily in bus and train stations, heightened public fears. Nineteen bomb blasts took place in Delhi alone on 10 and 11 May 1985. Haryana, Rajasthan, and Uttar Pradesh were also affected.[122] In addition to terrorists, sympathetic groups and even important Sikh leaders usually considered to be moderates, such as Prakash Singh Badal, opposed the accord, as did the neighboring states of Haryana and Rajasthan, which objected to provisions contrary to their interests.[123] In retrospect, it is clear that general Sikh support flowed toward the accord during this period, as subsequently registered by the high turnout for moderate candidates in the September 1985 state elections. Until the elections, the direction of Sikh support remained questionable.

Rajiv Gandhi could reach this compromise, first, because, unlike Indira Gandhi, he learned an important lesson in dealing with terrorism: Political initiatives have to be pursued consistently and with integrity regardless of the political violence that may be continuing. Earlier, during the long and unsuccessful negotiations between Sikh leaders and Prime Minister Indira Gandhi, terrorist actions upset the negotiations when agreement appeared near or, according to some reports, had been reached. According to another view, government used terrorism as an excuse to break off negotiations. Whatever the truth, terrorism provided a rationale for the government to put less emphasis on the political dimension of the situation.

Second, the Rajiv government seriously considered the Anandpur Sahib Resolution. This varying basket of political issues had been labeled secessionist, resulting in the Operation Bluestar military response in June 1984. Thirteen months later, a new prime minister concluded it was not secessionist but negotiable. Perhaps he had learned that negotiating stances engender the essence of politics, which is compromise; thus, emphasizing the positive elements is more productive than employing a worst-case scenario.

Conciliation continued with the announcement that state elections would be held in September 1985 to restore a political order that had been suspended under president's rule—that is, governance by the center—since October 1983. Terrorist high drama continued in Punjab with Longowal's assassination on 24 August. But even this shocking event only marginally delayed the elections as the center relentlessly

122. "The Return of Terrorism," *India Today*, 31 May 1985, 8–19.

123. Two days after the signing of the accord, a faction of the AISSF shouted slogans such as Longowal is a "traitor to the *panth*," in front of the Akali Dal (L) office at the Golden Temple complex and nearly came to blows with the Akali youth wing (*Times of India*, 26 and 28 July 1985).

pursued the reestablishment of the political process. Elections were held in September. A sympathy wave for Longowal's Akali Dal propelled it into power with, for the first time, an absolute majority, 73 of the 117 seats. An unusually high voter turnout of 67.58 percent—despite extremist calls for a boycott—further legitimated the moderate position.[124]

Prime Minister Rajiv Gandhi clearly assisted the Akali Dal, even though his Congress (I) party contested the election strongly and independently. National columnist Janardan Thakur, traveling through the state during the elections, remarked that he did not see one poster of Indira Gandhi, although the walls were "plastered with confusing, 'fifty-fifty posters' of Rajiv and Longowal." People, he concluded, could easily get the impression "that they were fighting on the same side as in a way they indeed were." Veteran British election specialist David Butler flew from England because this was the only election he had known "where the ruling party [was] so eager to lose."[125]

Nonetheless, moderate Akali Dal dominance proved to be short-lived. Two problems emerged: nonimplementation of major elements of the Punjab Accord and renewed terrorism and revivalism.

The government failed to effect the transfer of the capital, Chandigarh, to Punjab, as the accord required. The two concerned states could not agree on a compromise, and New Delhi could not exert pressure, due to perceived political costs. Comparable political calculations stymied other important parts of the accord. Veteran BBC correspondent Mark Tully and his colleague Zareer Masani concluded that Rajiv Gandhi "backed down on the sensible accord" when "his party told him it was damaging its electoral prospects in the crucial Hindi-speaking states of northern India."[126]

Failure to implement the accord encouraged the extremists, led by Bhindranwale's revivalist Damdami Taksal seminary and the AISSF, to retake control of the Golden Temple complex on 26 January 1986. No one leader had succeeded Bhindranwale. To the contrary, leadership struggles within and between groups ensued in both the militant and moderate parts of the political spectrum. As the often progovernment *Times of India* editorialized, "The inevitable failure of the Union government to implement the basically flawed Punjab accord has been overtaken by a renewed struggle for leadership of the Sikh community."[127]

124. For complete results and analysis of the elections, see Paul Wallace, "The Sikhs as a 'Minority' in a Sikh Majority State in India," *Asian Survey* 16, no. 3 (1986): 372–75.

125. Janardan Thakur, "Behind the Akali Victory," *Times of India Sunday Review*, 13 October 1985, I; Butler quoted in *India Today*, 15 October 1985, 25.

126. Tully and Masani, *From Raj to Rajiv*, 142.

127. *Times of India*, 28 January 1986, 8.

Another military action ensued on 1 May 1986, but the extremists fled the Golden Temple complex in advance. This action, labeled Operation Search, nonetheless had a clear political result. It almost immediately split the Akali Dal moderates in the state assembly. Twenty-seven legislators formed a splinter party and joined the extremists in condemning as a betrayal the center's treatment of the accord.[128] Chief Minister Surjit Singh Barnala's Akali Dal remained the single largest party, with forty-six seats, but had to rely on Congress support to remain in power.[129]

Barnala became increasingly isolated when the five high priests of the Sikhs' major temples, heretofore nonpolitical, "excommunicated" him and declared the formation of a new Unified Akali Dal.[130] Fighting back, Barnala repudiated the allegations,[131] disciplined dissident party leaders, and held mass rallies in various parts of the state.[132] Support, however, ebbed as the middle ground continued to erode. He lost three additional Akali legislators,[133] making his party even more dependent on Congress support; at the same time, he criticized the Congress government in New Delhi for not implementing the Punjab Accord.[134] Once again, central-government actions—or nonactions—were eroding moderate Sikh support and assisting the extremists.

Prime Minister Rajiv Gandhi in 1987 also had to confront a weakened political position. Election reverses, charges of corruption, internal Congress Party problems, and major trouble spots elsewhere in India and in South Asia provided a context markedly different from that of the honeymoon year of 1985. Implementing the accord, moreover, could damage Congress electoral prospects in state elections due in the adjoining, Hindu-majority Haryana state. Therefore, instead of new initiatives in Punjab designed to buttress the political process and rebuild the institutional complex, he suspended the assembly and returned the state to president's rule on 11 May 1987.[135]

128. *Indian Express*, 25 July 1986, 7.
129. *Times of India*, 3–5 May 1986.
130. *The Hindu*, 12 February 1987.
131. *Times of India*, 13 February 1987.
132. Agricultural Minister Harbhajan Singh Sandhu pledged his loyalty to the new Unified Akali Dal on 14 February and resigned as head of the Amritsar District Akali Dal before being expelled by Barnala (*Times of India*, 16 February 1987).
133. *Times of India*, 15 February 1987.
134. *Times of India*, 9 March 1987.
135. *Times of India*, 12 May 1987. If appealing to the Haryana electorate on the basis of not compromising in Punjab was part of the strategy, it backfired calamitously, since the alliance led by Lok Dal routed the ruling Congress (I) by winning four-fifths of the assembly seats in June (*India Today*, 15 July 1987).

Thus, in Punjab the political approach remained in the background as the state focused almost exclusively on a law-and-order approach. On 11 February 1988 the entire state was designated a "notified area" under section 5 of the Terrorists and Disruptive Activities (Prevention) Act (TADA) of 1987. An official spokesman explained that at least 254 people had been killed since 1 January, "including senior leaders and activists of the Congress, CPI, BJP and police personnel."[136] This was followed by dissolution of the suspended assembly and, in March 1988, by the Fifty-ninth Constitutional Amendment, which empowered the government to declare a state of emergency in Punjab, thereby suspending fundamental rights, and to extend president's rule by a period of three years.[137]

The long period of president's rule continued until state elections were finally held in February 1992. Congress (I) returned to power, but only as a consequence of a Sikh boycott that resulted in a 21.6 percent voter turnout that contrasted sharply with voter turnout over 60 percent in the six previous elections. A massive military presence continued. Government intransigence and the fragmentation of political forces in the state during the 1980s resulted in political deinstitutionalization.

DEINSTITUTIONALIZATION AND THE MILITANTS

Punjab's impasse has involved not only the moderate political forces and center-state relations. It has also fragmented the militants who operated outside the more conventional party politics, as well as the "moderate militants" who attempted to straddle the line between the militants and the moderates. Sant Bhindranwale's death in Operation Bluestar in June 1984 created a martyr but did not lead to an individual or institutionalized successor.

Satyapal Dang, a major leader of Punjab's Communist Party of India and one of the few consistent activists against terrorism, points out that the Khalistanis were divided into three broad groups even before Operation Bluestar, which removed the "common umbrella" of Bhindranwale's religious seminary, the Damdami Taksal, and the AISSF. One broad group, or trend, he calls "victims of fundamentalism . . . religious fanatics." A second is composed of unemployed and disillusioned youth. The third, which he says is the largest, consists of "the anti-social

136. *Times of India*, 12 February 1988, 1.
137. *The Hindu*, 1, 7, 8, and 9 March 1988.

and criminal elements." After Bhindranwale's death, they lacked "a unifying force."[138]

Following Bhindranwale's death, his father, Baba Joginder Singh, served in a titular position as head of a United Akali Dal. But India's dynastic principle does not seem to work in reverse. The father did not effectively succeed the son. Radical Sikh leaders did proliferate from the Damdami Taksal, Bhindranwale's seminary, from the AISSF, from shadowy terrorist groups, and from other sources. Major splits opened within and between each of the groups, including the AISSF. Another religious figure temporarily emerged into political prominence, thrown up by the militants as a unifier, but he withdrew in frustration, stating that the "sword is not the answer . . . you can rule the bodies of the people with Sten guns but not their minds."[139]

The four major groups and their subgroups maintain a high level of violence. They comprise the Babbar Khalsa, the most zealously religious, with a specialty in bombs; the Bhindranwale Tiger Force (BTF); the Khalistan Liberation Force (KLF); and the Khalistan Commando Force (KCF). In early 1992 the KCF reputedly had sixty-three subgroups, or bands, operating under its banner; the BTF had thirty; the Babbar Khalsa, twenty-seven; and the KLF, twenty-five. Another twenty-two groups reportedly operated independently, for a total of 167 terrorist groups.[140] Major leaders, usually with titles like Lieutenant General, are killed, and entire subgroups are eliminated, by police and paramilitary forces and as a consequence of intergroup conflict. Nonetheless, the four major groupings and the structure continue.

Other somewhat amorphous groups have included the Dal Khalsa, which is credited by the United States with hijacking an Indian plane to Pakistan in 1981.[141] A Punjabi sense of humor is suggested by the name of a new group identified in March 1988, the Khalistan Black Cats Commando Force.[142] It obviously takes its name from the government's most elite paramilitary unit, the Black Cat Commandos of the National Security Guard, which spearheaded Operation Black Thunder in May 1988.

138. Satyapal Dang, *Genesis of Terrorism: An Analytical Study of Punjab Terrorists* (New Delhi: Patriot Publishers, March 1988), 146.
139. *India Today*, 15 August 1987. Darshan Singh Ragi had gained prominence as a singer of religious hymns. A general Sikh meeting at the Golden Temple empowered him as acting head of the Akal Takht, the temporal center of the Golden Temple, in an effort to evolve a common political approach.
140. *Times of India*, 9 February 1992, 15.
141. *Times of India*, 23 August 1988, 17.
142. *Times of India*, 17 March 1988, 17.

In theory, the Panthic Committee, an underground umbrella group formed by insurgents in 1986, served as a self-constituted policy body for the extremists. Its spokesmen inside the Golden Temple complex issued statements for the committee; in April 1988 they reiterated its determination to "fight to the finish" for the goal of Khalistan and denied that the militants had anything to do with the killings of innocent people.[143] Its five members, first publicly identified on 23 September 1987, were all wanted men carrying rewards.[144]

Gurbachan Singh Manochahal, head of the BTF, was considered the "mastermind" of the committee.[145] It is difficult, however, to determine the nature and extent of the committee's jurisdiction, since each of the many groups and subgroups related to it, appear to operate autonomously, spontaneously, and somewhat paranoically. For example, in a resolution in August 1988 praising President Zia ul-Haq of Pakistan following his death in an airplane crash, the Panthic Committee included a "strange instruction" to Manjit Singh, interned president of the AISSF. It ordered Manjit to sever his alleged connections with "government agents."[146]

Manochahal himself came under attack in May 1989. A statement delivered to newspapers and news agencies in Amritsar on 1 May announced that Manochahal and Wassan Singh were removed from the committee because they were responsible for incidents of looting, snatchings, extortions, killing of innocent people, and misappropriation of funds.[147] The names of replacement members were furnished in the statement.

Organizational efforts by the Panthic Committee also include the formation of an international body, the Council of Khalistan, in 1987 "to direct political, economic and social affairs of the Sikh community" and to assume responsibility for the "foreign policy of Khalistan." Included are notable Khalistan supporters from overseas as well as from within

143. *Times of India*, 5 April 1988, 1.
144. The Panthic Committee consisted of Baba Gurbachan Singh Manochahal, Bhai Gurdev Singh Usmanwali, Bahi Wassan Singh Jafarwal, Bhai Dalvinder Singh (alias Bhai Shagbeg Singh), and Bhai Dalbir Singh (alias Bhai Udhey Singh) (*Times of India*, 24 September 1987, 1).
145. Rahul V. Nayer, "Will Rode Be Another Raagi? Militants in No Mood to Compromise," *India West*, 22 April 1988, 21.
146. *Times of India*, 24 August 1988, 8.
147. Bhai Jasbir Singh Chaharu in London and Bhai Sukhwinder Singh Ladoo of Patiala were the new members. They joined Bhai Tajinder Babbar, Bhai Dalvinder Singh, and Bhai Sukhwinder Singh Goga (Press Trust of India [PTI] [Amritsar], "India West," 12 May 1989, 12).

India.[148] It is difficult to evaluate the impact of the council inside Punjab. Statements are issued to both the extremists and the Indian government. The council, for example, according to Indian press reports, issued a warning to unnamed Sikh groups on 31 March 1988, threatening "stern action" if they continued killing Sikh families, women, and children, and urging Sikh head priests to "expose" these elements.[149] In April it published an open letter to the Indian government, demanding that it withdraw its paramilitary forces from the "Sikh homeland."[150] It probably has a more important role as a symbol of external support, through its allied organizations that provide funds and lobby foreign governments.

There are few reported efforts at forming coalitions by the activist groups. One such effort did occur on 3 May 1988. Four of the leading organizations—the KCF, the KLF, the Babbar Khalsa, and the AISSF—established, with the approval of the head priest of the Akal Takht, a five-member committee to maintain the sanctity of the Golden Temple and to stop its "misuse." Misuse included openly displaying weapons in the complex, firing inside it except when security forces do, torture or beating, and writing threatening letters from the complex to extort money. Two other major groups, the BTF and the Jhamke group of the KCF, however, issued statements the same day, refusing to recognize the committee or its code. "Lieutenant General" Kharaj Singh Thande of the BTF used one of the strongest pejoratives in accusing some members of the committee of being "government agents."[151]

Factionalism also is rampant in the powerful AISSF, although Gurmit Singh has the ascriptive qualifications for leadership, since he is related to Bhindranwale and was "trained and nurtured" by him and Amrik Singh, the AISSF leader slain in Operation Bluestar.[152] The AISSF, however, has long been split into at least two major parts, with Gurmit heading one and Manjit Singh the other. Manjit's faction reportedly is the "front organization for the outlawed KLF," and the International Sikh Youth Federation (ISYF) is affiliated with it.[153] Gurmit's faction has

148. The Council of Khalistan members consisted of the following: Dr. Gurmit Singh Aulakh (U.S.), president of the council, Dr. Arjinder Singh Sekhon (U.S.), Mr. Tejinder Singh Babbar (Canada), Mr. Tejpal Singh Dhami (Canada), Mr. Harinder Singh, Mr. Shamsher Singh of Akal Federation, Mr. Satnam Singh of Akal Khalsa, Mr. Gurnam Singh Bandala, Mr. Wadhwa Singh Babbar, Mr. Resham Singh Malmohri, and Mrs. Sakatar Singh of AISSF (*Sikh Herald* 2, nos. 1–4 [1987]: 1).

149. United News of India (UNI) and PTI reports from Amritsar in the *Hindu* and the *Times of India*, 1 April 1988, 1.

150. *India West*, 13 May 1988, 25.

151. *Times of India*, 4 May 1988, 1, and *India West*, 13 May 1988, 37.

152. *Times of India*, 11 June 1988, 8.

153. *India Today*, 30 September 1987, 43; and 15 November 1987, 44.

been strongly attacked by KCF and BTF leaders as "government agents."[154]

As is to be expected in such a volatile situation, a wide variety of leaders and subchiefs continue to emerge and carve out their territories. They include Avtar Singh Brahma, leader of the KLF—who, before his death, daringly "scamper[ed] through the verdant fields of Punjab's border districts on horseback"[155]—as well as Manochahal, several self-constituted "generals," and an even larger number of "lieutenant generals." Less flamboyant but more religiously revivalist and zealous is the Babbar Khalsa, which was headed by Sukhdev Singh Babbar until his violent death on 9 August 1992.[156] Ribiero, then head of Punjab's police and paramilitary forces, identified the Babbar Khalsa as "the most ruthless" of the four main terrorist groups and "the only group with a fierce religious orientation."[157]

It can be hypothesized that power within the terrorist-extremist spectrum will shift more to the better-educated, politically skillful individuals who place less emphasis on spectacular terrorist acts and more on applying calculated pressure, including violence, on the state. Many extremists feel that government repression of terrorism in Punjab and competition among militant groups have reduced the prospects for an independent Khalistan. More than a decade of violence has not resulted in an independent Sikh state in "liberated areas" or in Hindus leaving the state so as appreciably to change the approximately 60:40 Sikh-Hindu population proportions.

Thus, the goal of some terrorists, including important newly developing leaders, is to "emerge as key factors in any future 'settlement.' "[158] While interviewing in Amritsar in May 1991, I was told by several informants that many militants are riding openly in cars, wearing expensive clothes, and sending their children to elite schools. Some were also engaged in the election campaign then under way but postponed at the last minute. Politics can be an alternative route to prestige, power, and resources. The dangers involved in government repression as well as militant factionalism provide powerful inducements to seek a safer life-

154. *Indian Express*, 21 July 1988.
155. Chandan Mitra, "Anatomy of the Terrorist Challenge in Punjab," *India Perspectives*, July 1988, 22.
156. The Babbar Khalsa denied the police version of Sukhdev Singh Babbar's killing in an encounter, asserting that he consumed poison after his arrest (*Times of India*, 17 August 1992, 7).
157. *New York Times*, 6 October 1987, 5.
158. Chandan Mitra, "A New Star on Terrorist Firmament," *Times of India*, 14 September 1988, 1.

style. These same factors, however, can result in charges of betrayal and death.[159]

Regionalism, class, religious fervor, and personalism operate as factors within and between the various groups. For example, some of the better-educated young leaders from affluent families, such as Charanjit Singh Channi, oppose the "Bhindranwale strategy of creating mayhem" in the western Manjha region so as to force Hindus to migrate from this border area, leaving a de facto Khalistan. Channi, with his base in Ludhiana (central Doaba region), and his associates have moved into the eastern Malwa region but lack influence in Manjha, which encompasses Amritsar and the prime areas of terrorist activity.[160]

OPERATION BLACK THUNDER, TERRORIST SETBACK, AND CONTINUED IMPASSE

Political violence designed to secure Khalistan received a severe setback in Operation Black Thunder, conducted by well-trained military units from 9 to 18 May 1988. Terrorists and other militants were cleared from the Golden Temple complex in a surgical operation led by the Black Cat Commandos of the National Security Guards and involving three thousand paramilitary personnel. In contrast to previous actions, the operation took place under full public scrutiny, using a minimum of force. No tanks rolled over the *parikrama*, the walkway surrounding the water. Nor were the extremists forewarned, so that they could escape. Military forces effectively used snipers and applied continual pressure, including a blockade. About thirty militants were killed, and two hundred surrendered on the final day. Reporters toured the captured positions, noting the results of the fighting and personal effects; in one case, "between guns and knives" lay an English copy of Mark Twain's *Tom Sawyer*, "with some passages underlined."[161]

159. Dinesh Kumar, reporting in Punjab, emphasized the private rethinking of militant leaders with whom he spoke. He described an "ardent follower of Bhindranwale" who fought against the army during Operation Bluestar in 1984. "In a pensive mood, he had spoken frankly about the futility of terrorism and the militants' demand for Khalistan—all off the record. A few days later he was killed by a rival militant group" (*Times of India*, as carried in *India West*, 17 January 1992, 17).

160. Ibid.

161. *New York Times*, 23 May 1988, 4. Another source, perhaps distinguishing between militants in general and terrorist militants, states that "at least 156 terrorists" surrendered in two batches, 15 and 18 May (Mitra, "Anatomy of the Terrorist Challenge in Punjab," 18–19).

Over a hundred journalists and television personnel provided live coverage. Their highly public presence probably contributed to the restrained use of force and certainly enhanced the government's credibility, especially in its efforts to "preserve the sanctity of the temple." Moreover, most Sikhs were sensitive both to the military restraint and to evidence, which quickly mounted, of temple desecration by the militants, including torture and murder.[162]

Terrorist leadership and ranks obviously were damaged, but not destroyed. The Panthic Committee lost its two leading spokesmen. Jagir Singh died in the temple complex, and Bhai Nirvair Singh surrendered.[163] "Lieutenant General" Kharaj Singh Thande (alias Phalwan) of the BTF committed suicide by taking cyanide pills. Major leaders of the KCF surrendered, including "Lieutenant General" Malkiat Singh Ajnala, "Lieutenant General" Bhag Singh, Nishan Singh, and Chanchal Singh.[164]

Nevertheless, the KCF remained "almost intact," led by "General" Labh Singh, "Lieutenant General" Sukdev Singh Jhamke, and Channi.[165] Security forces killed Labh Singh on 12 July 1988. On his person was an unsigned eight-page report analyzing reactions to Operation Black Thunder. It stated that the lack of Sikh protest against the operation indicated that "they have been alienated by the extortion of money, indiscriminate killings and other anti-social activities." Referring to factional fighting among militants, the document called for an end to "vengeance killings."[166]

Intramilitant conflict is one explanation for the somewhat ironic situation wherein significantly more Sikhs than Hindus were killed by Sikh militants usually from 1987 through 1991.[167] Table 9.6 lists the number of killings by religious community. The percentage of Sikhs killed increased at a steady rate from 54 percent (478) in 1987 to 71 percent (1,847) in 1991. Another explanation is that the state of heightened suspicion in which militants operated resulted in the frequent killing of suspected informants. Most important, the militants operated primarily in a rural environment in which the predominant population was Sikh.

162. Excellent analytical and visual coverage can be found in *India Today*, 31 May 1988, 5 (editorial entitled "Challenge of Openness") and 36–43. See also the editorial in the *Indian Express*, 20 May 1988.

163. *New York Times*, 16 May 1988, 3, and *Times of India*, 18 May 1988, 1.

164. *Times of India*, 19 May 1988, 15.

165. *Times of India*, 20 May 1988, 1.

166. *Times of India*, 15 July 1988, 1, and *India West*, 22 July 1988, 8.

167. In an unusual public appeal, the AISSF-Manjit group issued a press statement in May 1992 calling on militant groups to stop killing Sikhs for at least one month. It stated that "the cause of such a large number of militants being killed was the inter–militant group rivalries" (*Indian Express*, 16 May 1992).

Table 9.6.   Hindus and Muslims killed by militants in Punjab, 1981–1991

	No. of Hindus	% of Hindus	No. of Sikhs	% of Sikhs
1981	10	77	3	23
1982	8	62	5	38
1983	35	47	40	53
1984	237	66	122	34
1985	45	73	17	27
1986	324	63	193	37
1987	425	47	478	53
1988	858	45	1,044	55
1989	442	38	734	62
1990	743	30	1,694	70
1991	744	29	1,847	71
Totals:	3,871		6,177	

SOURCE: Data reported in the *Times of India*, 9 February, 1992, 15, from the Government of India, Ministry of Home Affairs.

Modern weapons play an increasingly important role in enabling the terrorists to engage in large-scale violence whatever the fluctuating level of their support. Increased firepower is probably the major reason for the escalation in the number of killings since 1987. In 1988 government authorities expressed their concern about the terrorists' acquisition of a large number of Chinese-built AK-47 assault rifles, which were used extensively by the Afghan mujahideen groups and flowed across the permeable border from Pakistan.[168] They first made their appearance in Punjab in December 1987 and were followed by antitank rockets and other missiles. American-made Stinger antiaircraft missiles were reported in February 1988,[169] but if they exist, they remain dormant.

The escalation of weaponry continued, including rocket launchers, grenades, various types of bombs, plastic explosives, and mines. Improved versions of many of the weapons continue to be reported. Confessions stemming from Operation Black Thunder reveal the high cost of items: Rs 25,000 for an AK-47, Rs 45,000 for a rocket launcher, and Rs 3,500 for one explosive charge.[170] The variety of means for providing funds ranges from criminal activities to the solicitation of highly motivated supporters among the Sikh diaspora overseas. The criminal activities include bank robberies, extortion, ransom, and smuggling; the long-

168. *Times of India*, 2 April 1988, 1.
169. *The Economist*, 7 May 1988, 27.
170. *Times of India*, 19 May 1988, 15.

established smuggling routes now include a lucrative trade in drugs and weapons.[171] Extortion alone is estimated to have totaled over $3 million (100 crores) between 1987 and 1992, turning "several terrorists into minimagnates." In 1992 the death of the Babbar Khalsa chief, Sukhdev Singh, led to the revelation of a luxury lifestyle in Patiala, including a palatial "White House."[172] Pakistan, which assists the militants in many ways, presumably also provides funding.

Ranged against the violent Khalistani groups are a vast array of government paramilitary organizations headed by the Central Reserve Police Force (CRPF) and the Border Security Force (BSF). A list of the other paramilitary groups that have been used includes the Assam Rifles, the Indo-Tibetan Rifles, the Railway Protection Forces, and of course, the Punjab police. A force of seventy thousand police and paramilitary were employed against the militants in mid-1988.[173] Twelve new BSF battalions were raised in 1989–90, the CRPF has been expanding rapidly, and the Indo-Tibetan Border Police raised six new battalions in 1991 for bank security in Punjab.

Expenditures for central police forces more than doubled from 1986–87 through 1991–92.[174] In April 1992 the Punjab state government revealed that it planned to recruit fifteen thousand additional state police during the year to bring its total to seventy thousand men and officers. This figure does not include the Home Guards and Special Police officers, which add another forty thousand.[175]

Regular army units are in addition to the police and paramilitary forces. They normally are stationed in large numbers in the cantonments, or barracks, in this key border state. Over one hundred thousand troops were designated to provide security for elections originally scheduled for June 1991 and subsequently held in February 1992. They continued to assist in providing security and with police search operations long after

171. A Canadian parliamentary delegation of three MPs investigated conditions pertaining to Sikhs in Punjab in January 1992. "Concern was expressed about alleged involvement of Canadian Sikhs in financing Sikh terrorist groups and about the alleged financing, training and provision of arms by the Pakistan government in both the Kashmir and the Punjab" (*Report: The Canadian Parliamentary Delegation Visit to India, January 15–22, 1992*, Barbara Greene section, 2). Greene concluded that "there is a huge criminal element operating in both Pakistan and India" and that "it is easy for criminal elements to obtain weapons in the region" (ibid., 9).

172. Kanwar Sandhu, "The Wages of Terrorism," *India Today*, 31 October 1992, 34–36.

173. *India West*, 13 May 1988, 39, and *Times of India*, 22 May 1988, 1.

174. Budget information and succinct descriptions of the central police and paramilitary groups are contained in the *Sunday Mail*, 28 July 1991.

175. *Indian Express*, 20 April 1992, 3.

the elections.[176] Civic action programs reminiscent of U.S. efforts to win the "minds and hearts" of villagers in Vietnam also are undertaken by the regular army. The *Times of India* described some of these actions in an article with the headline "Army Wins Hearts in Punjab." These civic action programs have provided schools, teachers, bridges, footpaths, bus service, agriculture programs, sanitation, and even sports equipment and coaches.[177] Regular police, its reputation tarnished by charges of atrocities, followed the army's lead in 1992 with their own civic programs and medical camps.[178]

Building a fence and placing concertina wire coils along the seventy-five-mile land border between Punjab India and Pakistan was announced in April 1988, and a border district in Rajasthan was subsequently added to the project.[179] Sealing off the border areas remains a herculean task despite the fence, continual technological and human improvement in the BSF, and the assistance of the regular army.[180]

It is probably impossible to fence or effectively patrol the Ravi and Sutlej rivers so as completely to seal off these major parts of the border area. Kashmir, Rajasthan, and even Gujarat provide further routes well known to smugglers. Thus, in 1991 the smuggling traffic in gold and narcotics compared with that in 1990 appeared to have been significantly diverted from the Punjab border to Kashmir. Nonetheless, sizable amounts of both still filtered through Punjab (see Table 9.7). By 1992 it appeared that Gujarat had become a major entry point for smuggling weapons from Pakistan.[181]

176. Prabhjot Singh, Reuters, "Bid to Wipe Out Militant Leadership in Punjab," *India West*, 10 July 1992, 9.

177. *Times of India*, 28 February 1992, 7. A Reuters report also emphasized the civic accomplishments of the military, particularly along the border areas, including the stringing of power lines, curbing petty crime, and holding medical clinics (*India West*, 28 February 1992, 12).

178. Kanwar Sandhu, "Punjab: A Golden Opportunity," *India Today*, 30 November 1992, 38. An excellent article by Chandan Mitra contrasts the largely positive response to the army with that to the police. He points out that the army largely confines "its role to patrolling and cordoning" instead of directly fighting the militants, and its medical camps are particularly effective in "terrorist-infested villages" from which most doctors have fled. Moreover, the "polite firmness of the army is in stark contrast to the boorish . . . behavior of the police" (*Hindustan Times*, 26 May 1992, 1).

179. *India West*, 29 April 1988, 1, and *The Statesman*, 18 March 1989, 8.

180. Amit Baruah, "Army Leaving Punjab Quietly," *The Hindu*, 13 May 1992. Baruah notes that the large number of army troops originally brought into Punjab for the elections is now being reduced in a "gradual, quiet" manner. One area of deployment involved sealing the border with Pakistan.

181. Ashraf Sayed, "Gujarat Found to Be Main Entry Point for Pak Arms," *India West*, 2 October 1992, 4.

Table 9.7. Gold and narcotics smuggling, Punjab and Kashmir, 1990–1991 (in millions of rupees)

	1990		1991	
	Gold	Narcotics	Gold	Narcotics
Punjab	241.8	63.1	154	1.2
Kashmir	11.4	.48	100.2	.9

SOURCE: Rahul Kumar, "Smuggling of Gold Declines in Punjab," *Economic Times*, 25 June 1992. NOTE: Narcotic seizures in Punjab, however, rose during the period January–April 1992 to Rs 4.2 million.

The costs of these security arrangements are described as "staggering." One estimate is that Punjab's annual security budget has ballooned from Rs 150 million in 1985 to Rs 3 billion in 1992. These figures do not take inflation into account, nor do they include the central government's financial participation. Nonetheless, the increase is astronomical in Indian terms, and Punjab, with debts totaling over Rs 60 billion, is becoming "one of India's most indebted states."[182]

Political cooperation between India and Pakistan becomes essential in this context. An opening appeared after President Zia ul-Haq's death in an airplane crash in August 1988 and the elections that followed in November. Prime Minister Benazir Bhutto, who assumed office in December, appeared to have reversed Zia's policy of assistance to Sikh terrorists. Arms dealers in Darra Adam Khel, a tribal area in Pakistan near Afghanistan, openly compared the two Pakistan leaders. President Zia "was God's gift to us," stated one arms merchant. Another explained that "we always had guns here. But cannons, gas masks, rockets, all that came from Zia. God bless him." By contrast, the summary comment about Prime Minister Bhutto was that "she has destroyed our business." More specifically, the traders compared 1988, when "each new batch of Sikhs was buying better, bigger, more expensive weapons," with the situation in mid-1989, when fewer Sikhs "buy so little" and "want to travel light now."[183]

The change in policy, if it did occur, was short-lived. Kashmir became another center of political violence after December 1989, involving Pakistan even more directly than it had been in Punjab. Training camps sprang up, and the supply of weapons from the Pakistan part of Kashmir accelerated, and the flow of weapons also increased from the areas bordering Gujarat state from 1989 through 1992.[184]

182. Chandran Mitra, *Hindustan Times*, 4 June 1992.
183. Shekhar Gupta, "Darra Adam Kehl: Arms for the Asking," *India Today*, 31 July 1989, 42–47.
184. Sayed, "Gujarat," 4.

An impasse exists in Punjab because the groups espousing violence as a means of securing an independent Khalistan have been contained by government forces. Even the government, however, admits that its most successful military action, Operation Black Thunder in May 1988, had a limited result. "The initial gains of the 'Black Thunder' were somewhat neutralized with the militant organizations re-grouping," states a Punjab government report in December 1988. "External patronage" from "across the Border" as well as "conflicts within the militant camp" are blamed for the continued high level of violence.[185]

The report describes new and renewed efforts to cope with the law-and-order situation, to provide relief and rehabilitation to the victims of violence and to migrants, and to address many underlying problems and needs, such as industrial development, creation of more job opportunities, "eradication of corruption," rural development, and power and irrigation. These are important but often-played themes.

In 1992 the government again claimed, in the words of several commentators, to have "turned the tide" against the terrorists.[186] Major leaders were targeted and killed; the militants were on the defensive; and peasants in villages formerly under the militants' sway reportedly have become disillusioned with their killings, rapes, and criminal activities generally.[187] Moreover, elements of a political process were restarted after the June 1991 cancellation of elections and the nonparticipatory elections of February 1992. In contrast to the abysmally low 21 percent turnout for the general elections in February, municipal elections in ninety-five cities and towns in September drew almost 70 percent of the electorate. Also in contrast to the February elections, militants did not intimidate, and major parties did not boycott.[188]

As in 1985 after the Punjab Accord or in 1988 after Operation Black Thunder, possibilities for conflict resolution were present in Punjab. Nonetheless, even the progovernment *Times of India* cautioned in an editorial on the 1992 municipal elections that "while security action can curb the terrorists temporarily, only the democratic process can destroy the roots of terrorism." It added that "this is the lesson which the political establishment failed to learn in 1985" and questioned whether

185. Government of Punjab, Public Relations Department, "Background Note: An Over View on Law and Order Situation in Punjab in 1988 " (Cyclostyled report, 28 December 1988), 3.

186. Khushwant Singh, "Turn of Tide Against Terrorists in Punjab," *Times of India,* 29 October 1992, 6, and Kanwar Sandhu, *India Today,* 30 November 1992, 38.

187. See note 186 and Dinesh Kumar, "Punjab Ultras Losing Sympathy," *Times of India,* 26 August 1992, 13.

188. *Times of India,* 7 and 8 September 1992, 1, 17.

the "same mistake will not be repeated."[189] Moreover, somewhat balancing the terrorism of the militants is the terrorism of the police. Punjabis, particularly in rural areas, face "terrorist outlaws" and are subject to "the methodical brutality of their protectors—the police—who often choose to enforce the law by breaking it."[190]

CONCLUSION

Punjab's problem after a decade of violence remains the search for a political solution in the context of an enhanced Sikh identity. Political violence and terrorism by Sikh militants and counterterrorism by the state do not lead to resolution but have become central to the problem. There is no simple solution as was promised in 1985 with the Rajiv Gandhi–Sant Longowal Punjab Accord. Failure by the national government to implement that promising window of opportunity led to further deinstitutionalization of government, political parties, and even the militants engaged in violence. Therefore, a political solution will not be the product of one act but will result from the patient rebuilding of a political process.

Reestablishing a political process will determine the extent to which a Sikh identity becomes more irredentist or more accommodative. This *khalsa* Punjabi identity was born under Guru Gobind Singh in 1699, revived in the Singh Sabha and *gurdwara* reform movements, and revitalized by Sant Jarnail Singh Bhindranwale. Political violence, terrorism, fuels the separatist path. Punjab's lengthy history also provides solid evidence that the *khalsa* Sikh identity can be part of a Punjabi identity that includes non-Sikhs and a federal India. Compromises that are central to a political process will permit the development of conceptions of identity that are not mutually exclusive.

Accommodation is a process of mutual adjustment. Hindus and Sikhs share many cultural characteristics in Punjab, including language. Religious separatism, even accompanied by religious revivalism, does not necessarily mean political separatism. Hindus who insist the Sikhs are part of Hinduism or treat all or most Sikhs as terrorists incite them to anger. As long as religious insecurity is present, Sikhs can be mobilized

189. *Times of India*, 8 September 1992, 16. Kanwar Sandhu also questioned whether the government had "the statesmanship and political vision to seize this crucial opportunity" (*India Today*, 30 November 1992, 38).

190. Kanwar Sandhu, "Punjab Police, Official Excesses," *India Today*, 15 October 1992, 28–31.

through the slogan, the *panth* (religion) is in danger. Leaders have the choice of cooperating as Punjabis and Indians or of deconstructing larger identities in favor of mutually exclusive categories.

Political opportunism and internal rivalries sharpen the emphasis on militant politics, particularly when religious symbolism and revivalism are used to mobilize followers. Nonetheless, it is important to reemphasize that nonviolence accompanied Sikh militant politics until the 1980s. In the preindependence period, the temple reform movement led by the Akali Dal political party further delineated Sikh identity through a mass movement and enhanced effective Sikh participation in both Punjab and nationalist politics.

Similarly, the Punjabi Suba movement, which succeeded in creating a Sikh majority state in 1966, used militant but nonviolent tactics. Moreover, rural moderates who emphasized Sikh-Hindu accommodation replaced the more extremist and Sikh exclusivist Master Tara Singh urban-based leadership during the movement. Coalitions between formerly antagonistic Sikh and Hindu parties competed effectively against the Congress Party, which also included both Sikhs and Hindus. Political leadership drew different religious communities, as well as rural and urban forces, together, instead of separating them.

Sikh religious revivalism became violent only after 1978 with the emergence of Sant Jarnail Singh Bhindranwale as a fundamentalist opposed to the moderate, mainstream Sikh leadership. Congress Party leaders used him during this period in efforts to disrupt the ruling Akali Dal party. After returning to power in 1980, the Congress governments at the state and national levels continued to be tolerant and even protective of Bhindranwale and his increasingly violent followers until the movement seemed to threaten the state.

An alternative authority system, loosely directed by Bhindranwale from the Golden Temple in Amritsar, increasingly replaced the normal institutions of politics and governance, which New Delhi itself had undermined. Negotiations with more-moderate, mainstream Sikh leaders were not pursued consistently by New Delhi, and new outbreaks of violence were allowed to abort what appeared to be successful agreements. A central principle emerging from this situation is that the negotiating parties, rather than outside forces engaged in violence, must control the agenda. Political violence can indicate weakness as well as strength.

When the central government finally moved, it abandoned the political path for a heavy-handed military action. Operation Blue Star in June 1984 succeeded in killing Bhindranwale and his top lieutenants, but it did not deal with the political problems. Even moderate Sikhs were incensed by the nature of the action in the Golden Temple complex and the seeming threat to Sikh dignity and security. Nor did terrorism diminish. To the contrary, Bhindranwale's charismatic leadership was replaced by a hydra-headed movement without a center. Motives shifted from religious revivalism to religious zeal to purely exploitative purposes, including criminality. Terrorism escalated in a context where restraining moral influences were replaced by competitive groups fighting for leadership, territory, and resources.

Windows of opportunity for reestablishing a workable political process in Punjab have opened periodically, but the opportunities have been squandered. Prime Minister Rajiv Gandhi's 1985 initiatives resulted in an overwhelming electoral mandate in Punjab for moderate governance. But the central government failed to follow through in implementing the compromise it had negotiated, probably because of short-range political considerations. At other important points the central government failed to support the Sikh moderates, thereby leaving the Sikh-dominated rural Punjab to the militants.

Elections scheduled for June 1991 were postponed at the last minute at the request of the Congress Party, even though the militants were divided and the Sikh moderates were participating. Narrow partisan interests took precedence over the opportunity to restart the political process. Moderates as well as militants boycotted the subsequent elections in February 1992 because the government continued to follow a policy of repression rather than negotiation.

Political problems, including political violence, thus come back full circle to politics. India remains a democracy, however imperfect, which is the most helpful dimension of this long-term problem. Open discussion with a full range of opinions continuously takes place, and dissemination through the media and public groups is excellent. Moreover, there is a depth of political development in Punjab and India that has not yet been completely squandered. Democratic political leadership, which contributed so significantly to deconstructing Punjab, can play the opposite role.

V. P. Singh, who replaced Rajiv Gandhi as prime minister in 1989, took meaningful symbolic actions, almost immediately after being sworn in, by going to pray at the Golden Temple in Amritsar. He emphasized that a "healing touch cannot be brought about at the point of bayonets, but with love, faith and the people's cooperation." In contrast to the massive security that accompanied Rajiv Gandhi as prime minister, V. P. Singh rode in an open jeep and received a "massive, spontaneous response" to his conciliatory gestures.[191]

191. *New York Times*, 8 December 1989, 3.

But, V. P. Singh's minority government, as well as the short-lived successor administration of Chandra Shekhar, proved to be too weak and too occupied with issues of political survival to move beyond symbolic measures. Narasimha Rao's Congress Party, which came into power in June 1991, has generally taken a hard line on Punjab as well as Kashmir, although the prime minister has a reputation for consensus politics.

Possibilities for consensus politics continue to exist in Punjab. Militant excesses in the form of rape, extortion, and the like have lessened militant legitimacy. Moderate political forces can reenter the political process when realistic opportunities exist, such as in municipal elections in 1992 and village elections in January 1993. They must, however, provide results that matter to their constituents—in particular, protection of civil liberties. Political leadership has to relearn to work together in a political process.

GLOSSARY

Akal Takht: See Golden Temple complex.

AISSF: All India Sikh Students Federation, a militant Sikh student organization. Splits into factions.

Akali Dal: Major political party of the Sikhs.

amritdhari: Baptism in which amrit, a nectar composed of sweets, is consumed.

Bhindranwale, Sant Jarnail Singh: Sikh priest and principal leader of the militant Sikhs from 1980 until his death in the Golden Temple complex during the 1984 Operation Bluestar.

Golden Temple complex: Sikh religious center, located in Amritsar. Its two major buildings are the Golden Temple (Harmandir Sahib, "Temple of God"), the spiritual symbol, and the Akal Takht ("Throne of the Immortal"), the temporal symbol.

gurdwara: Literally, the "door of the Guru." A Sikh temple.

Guru: A religious teacher. In Sikhism, the founder and subsequent nine successors.

Guru Gobind Singh: Tenth and last Sikh Guru. Reformulated Sikhism in 1699.

Guru Granth Sahib: Holy book of the Sikhs compiled from the writings and sayings of the ten Gurus.

Harmandir Sahib: See Golden Temple complex.

khalsa: The Sikh brotherhood or community reformulated by Guru Gobind Singh in 1699.

Khalistan: "Land of the pure." Name of the sovereign state demanded by Sikh militants.

morcha: A nonviolent movement.

Operation Black Thunder: A surgical paramilitary operation against Sikh militants in the Golden Temple complex in May 1988. In contrast to Operation Bluestar, casualties were few, and the militants were humiliated.

Operation Bluestar: A large-scale military assault in June 1984 on Sikh militants who had fortified the Golden Temple complex. Hundreds were killed, and widespread Sikh alienation resulted.

panth: Religion.

Punjab Accord: A July 1985 agreement between the center and the states of Punjab and Haryana regarding Sikh and Punjab grievances. It remained largely unimplemented. Also known as the Rajiv-Longowal Accord after the former prime minister Rajiv Gandhi and Sikh leader Sant Harchand Singh Longowal.

Sant: Title given to a holy man or religious leader.

SGPC: Shiromani Gudwara Prabandhak Committee, an elected Sikh temple management committee that is vitally important to Sikh politics, resources, and communications.

10

Political Violence in a Democratic State: Basque Terrorism in Spain

Goldie Shabad and Francisco José Llera Ramo

We had fed the heart on fantasie
The heart's grown brutal from the fare;
More substance in our enmities
Than in our love . . .
  —W. B. Yeats, "Meditations in Time of Civil War"

Spain differs from all other Western democracies, not only in the strength of its peripheral nationalisms but also in the level of violence associated with center-periphery conflicts. Among Western countries, only in Northern Ireland have deaths due to terrorist acts associated with ethnic conflicts surpassed those in Spain. Euzkadi ta Askatasuna (Basque Homeland and Freedom, or ETA) has not been the only terrorist organization in Spain. Other Basque radical separatist organizations, as well as right-wing counter-ETA terrorist groups, have been responsible for over one hundred deaths in the last decade and a half. ETA, however, has been the primary terrorist actor between 1968 and 1992. It has also been the main object of police repression during those twenty-four years, with more than 100 ETA militants killed, more than 20,000 arrested, and more than 600 imprisoned in Spain and 700 in France in 1992 alone. ETA was founded in 1959 by a coalition of radical youth groups, one of which had split from the historic Basque Nationalist Party. Its primary aims from the beginning have been Basque independence and recuperation of Basque culture and language. These objectives continue to be at the center of ETA's ideological program, the five-point KAS Alternative, which it set forth in the mid-1970s as the minimum conditions to be met by the Spanish state in exchange for ETA's abandonment of political violence. Most of the five points are radical nationalist demands. The first of these is reform of the 1978 Spanish constitution to accept the right of self-determination; a second is the assertion of the territorial integrity of all Basque provinces in Spain, which means the revision of the 1979 Basque Autonomy Statute to allow for the incorporation of Navarra into the Basque Autonomous Community; a third is the demand for the institutional predominance of Euskera (the Basque language); the fourth point calls for the unconditional amnesty for all political prisoners and the withdrawal of all Spanish police and armed forces from Basque soil. The last refers to the conditions of labor and expresses solidarity with the working class. Apart from this, no other mention is made of leftist ideological principles.

ETA's strategy of armed struggle was adopted in 1962, but in the 1960s and early 1970s ETA engaged in only sporadic acts of violence against the authoritarian and ultra-Spanish nationalist Francoist regime. The most dramatic and consequential of these was the assassination in 1973 of Prime Minister Carrero Blanco, heir apparent of Franco, an event that helped to bring about the demise of the authoritarian regime. After Franco's death in 1975, ETA violence increased dramatically, particularly during the transition to democracy and the granting of regional autonomy to the three Basque provinces (Alava, Guipúzcoa, and Vizcaya) in 1979–80 (see Fig. 10.1). Of the more than six hundred deaths attributable to ETA between 1968 and 1991, about 93 percent occurred after Franco's death; about 27 percent took place in 1979 and 1980 alone, during which time the Basque Autonomy Statute was being negotiated and elections to the first Basque regional government were being held. Thus, despite the rebirth of democracy in Spain and the achievement of autonomy for the Basque region, ETA continued to act as though "nothing had changed."

But things had changed. Civil liberties were restored, political competition became legitimate, autonomous trade unions were permitted, and open expression of ethnic nationalist sentiments—even of demands for territorial independence of ethnically distinct regional populations—was

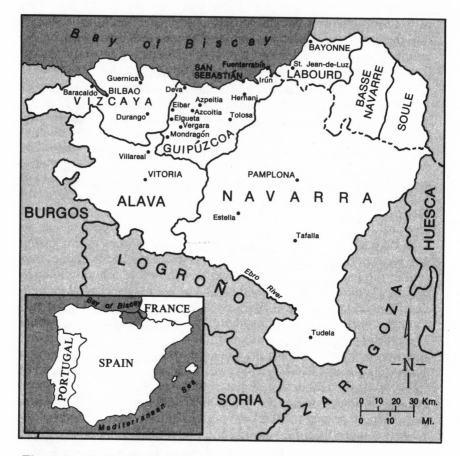

Fig. 10.1.   The Basque region

allowed. Why then did ETA violence not only persist but escalate after the restoration of democracy? Was this part of its original plan? Did political and social circumstances in the Basque Country make possible a continuation of ETA's activities? Or "are members of terrorist organizations, once assembled, like the sorcerer's apprentice who, unwilling to be dismissed when the job is done, continues the violence?"[1]

The endurance of ETA in the context of the rebirth of Spanish democracy and the granting of autonomy to the Basque Country presents an interesting puzzle. Why did the armed struggle go on, and what were

1. Peter Merkl, "Approaches to the Study of Political Violence," in *Political Violence and Terror: Motifs and Motivations,* ed. Peter Merkl (Berkeley and Los Angeles: University of California Press, 1986), 3.

the effects of ETA violence on the new democracy and on Basque society and politics? We address these two questions by analyzing (1) the sources of ETA violence at different points in time; (2) changes in the nature, structure, and strategies of ETA as a separatist terrorist organization; and (3) the various effects of ETA in the context of Spanish democracy and Basque autonomy.

First, however, we should specify the geopolitical limits of our research. According to Basque nationalists, Euskadi—the Basque Country, or the Basque nation—is composed of seven territories or provinces: four in Spain and three in France. Thus conceived, Euskadi has about 2,900,000 inhabitants living in an area of 20,644 square kilometers. But this notion of the Basque Country, which originated in the late nineteenth century, conflicts with a more complex reality (see Fig. 10.1). On the administrative level, the three French provinces (8.2 percent of the whole Basque population and 14.3 percent of its territory) are little districts of the larger so-called Pyrenees Atlantiques region. The four Spanish provinces are presently divided into two autonomous, or self-governing, regions, each having different social structures, institutions, and party systems: on the one hand, there is the unprovincial autonomous community of Navarra with 17.6 percent of the Basque population and 50.5 percent of the territory; and on the other, there are the three provinces of Alava, Guipúzcoa, and Vizcaya, which make up the autonomous community of the Basque Country, or Euskadi. Neither Navarra nor Euskadi, it is important to note, is ethnically homogeneous. In the latter, about thirty percent of the population were born outside of the region and an additional 11 percent are first-generation Basques. The frame of reference for our analysis is the Basque Autonomous Community, in which Basque nationalist parties are dominant and ETA has drawn most of its militants, focused most of its violent activities, and received its greatest popular support.

SOURCES OF ETA VIOLENCE

No one can say for certain why separatist political violence occurs in one setting and not in another. Why, for example, in the Basque Country and not in Catalonia? Why in Northern Ireland and not in Scotland? The decision by individuals to engage in violence or to join a terrorist organization is a contingent one. Moreover, it is difficult in complex settings to isolate cause from effect. Once violence does take place, the effects of such violence may themselves become causes of violence at a

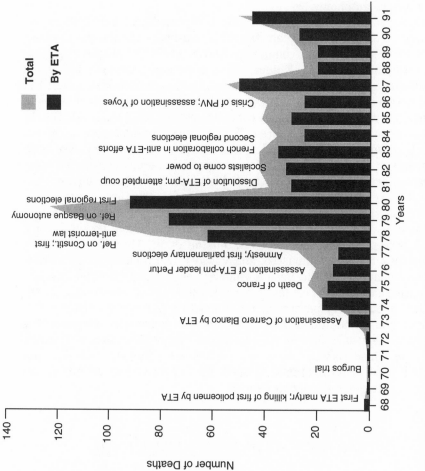

Fig. 10.2. Number of deaths in terrorist actions in Spain, 1968–1991

later time. Yet it is possible to explain why such individual choices are more apt to be made in certain societies than in others, and why violence, should it occur, is more likely to be viewed sympathetically than negatively by politically significant segments of the population. Explanations of Basque nationalism and of ETA violence, in particular, focus on the interaction of several distinct, but related, characteristics of the Basque Country and of its relation to the Spanish state.[2] These range from structural characteristics, to the cognitive, evaluative, and affective orientations of different groups involved in a center-periphery conflict, to the ideological views and personal motivations of those who choose to engage in violence rather than pursue more "normal" political activities.

No effort is made here to present a comprehensive and detailed analysis of the causes of ETA violence. Instead, after briefly discussing the socioeconomic underpinnings of Basque nationalism, we focus primarily on what we consider to be the most direct, general explanatory factor: the political and cultural context of ETA violence during both the Franco and post-Franco eras.

The Socioeconomic Context of Basque Nationalism

Basque nationalism, as an ideology and movement, emerged in the 1890s largely as a result of various social developments associated with rapid industrialization. During the course of its economic transformation, traditional Basque society, founded on small-scale agriculture and commerce, was changed to a society based on mining, heavy industry, shipbuilding, and banking. Between 1842 and 1868, industrialization was first localized in the provinces of Vizcaya and Guipúzcoa[3] where the resultant dramatic

2. The literature on Basque nationalism is extensive. Excellent studies include Javier Corcuera, *Orígenes, ideología y organización del nacionalismo vasco* (Madrid: Siglo XXI, 1979); Antonio Elorza, *Ideologías del nacionalismo vasco* (Madrid: Guardarrama, 1978); Eugenio Ibarzabal, *Cincuenta años de nacionalismo vasco (1928–1978)* (San Sebastián: Ediciones Vascas, 1978); Juan J. Linz, "Early State Building and Late Peripheral Nationalisms Against the State: The Case of Spain," in *Building States and Nations*, ed. S. N. Eisenstadt and Stein Rokkan (Beverly Hills: Sage Publications, 1973), 32–116; Stanley Payne, *Basque Nationalism* (Reno: University of Nevada Press, 1975); and Alfonso Pérez-Agote, *La reproducción del nacionalismo: El caso vasco* (Madrid: CIS, 1984). For studies of ETA, see Robert P. Clark, *The Basque Insurgents: ETA, 1952–1980* (Madison: University of Wisconsin Press, 1984); José M. Garmendía, *Historia de ETA*, 2 vols. (San Sebastián: Haranburu, 1979); Gurutz Jáuregui, *Ideología y estrategia política de ETA (1963–1987)* (Madrid: Siglo XXI, 1981); John Sullivan, *ETA and Basque Nationalism* (London: Routledge and Kegan Paul, 1988); and Joseba Zulaika, *Basque Violence: Metaphor and Sacrament* (Reno: University of Nevada Press, 1988).

3. Manuel González Portilla, *La formación de la sociedad capitalista en el País Vasco, 1876–1913*, 2 vols. (San Sebastián: Haranburu, 1981).

growth in population size and urbanization provided favorable conditions for the later rise of Basque nationalism. Two other developments associated with industrialization were also of great importance for Basque ethnic mobilization. Industrialization created a different system of social stratification in which a new class of Basque industrialists and financiers became dominant and were soon incorporated into the Spanish oligarchy. Efforts by this group to integrate the Basque provinces economically and politically with Spain provoked intense hostility from the traditional petite bourgeoisie.[4] In addition to the emergence of a new financial and industrial oligarchy, a working class also developed, as thousands of farmers from impoverished areas of Spain moved to urban areas in the Basque Country. With the rise of this new immigrant working class, Spanish trade unions and anticlerical leftist parties became major social and political protagonists in the Basque Country. These changes in class formation and their political expression posed serious threats to the socioeconomic and political status of the traditional urban middle class and to the hegemony of Catholic and rural Basque culture. It was among these segments of society that Basque nationalism developed and flourished.

Another period of rapid social and economic transformation occurred during the so-called economic boom between 1960 and 1975.[5] The population of Euskadi increased by 44 percent, and this time all three provinces experienced growth. Once again, immigration from other parts of Spain was an important factor contributing to population growth (40 percent in the 1950s and 48 percent in the 1960s). By 1975 only 51 percent of those living in the three provinces were natives born of Basque parentage; 8 percent were of mixed parentage; 11 percent were first-generation Basques; and 30 percent had been born in other parts of Spain. Sixty percent and 40 percent of residents of urban and metropolitan areas, respectively, had some Basque ancestry; this compares with 85 percent of the rural population.[6]

As a result of this "second" industrial revolution, the active population in Euskadi increased by 25.2 percent between 1960 and 1975; the increase in Spain as a whole was only 9 percent. The sectoral distribution of this expanding work force once again radically altered Basque society and had important implications for Basque nationalism in the late Franco

---

4. Corcuera, *Origenes*.

5. Milagros García Crespo, Roberto Velasco, and Arantza Mendizábel, "La economía vasca durante el franquismo," in *La gran enciclopedia vasca* (Bilbao: 1981).

6. Luis C. Nuñez, *La sociedad vasca actual* (San Sebastián: Txertoa, 1977).

period and the transition to democracy. The native Basque population became increasingly middle-class and urban, and in time the political and social influence of this nationalist bourgeoisie supplanted that of the Basque, but Spanish-oriented, oligarchy. The nationalist movement itself became increasingly interclassist.

The immigrant proletariat remained a distinct, but increasingly substantial, segment of Basque society.[7] Rather than undermine ethnic solidarity, these major social and economic changes helped to promote it. They did so not only through the creation of modern infrastructures for ethnic mobilization but also by the very threat they posed to the declining, but increasingly idealized, traditional Basque culture.[8] Indeed, during the 1950s and 1960s it was primarily traditional institutions, like the church and family, that sustained ethnic solidarity.[9]

The transition to democracy coincided with an economic crisis in Spain. Because the Basque Country was a region of early industrialization and heavy industry, this economic crisis was felt most acutely in Euskadi. Policies of industrial restructuring, combined with ETA actions against Basque industrialists (in the form of assassinations, kidnappings, and the imposition of a system of "revolutionary taxation"), resulted in high levels of unemployment, particularly among the young (see Table 10.1). This provided additional fertile ground for complaints about economic exploitation of the Basque Country by Madrid, as well as for recruitment of new ETA members.

Table 10.1. Unemployment rates in Basque provinces by age, 1988 (in percentages)

Age (yrs.)	Alava	Guipúzcoa	Vizcaya	Euskadi
16–24	37.4	43.2	50.5	46.5
25–34	18.8	20.0	27.4	24.0

SOURCE: Instituto Vasco de Estadística (Basque Institute of Statistics), *Encuesta de Población Activa* (Study of the active population).

7. For discussion of these changes, see Francisco J. Llera, "Procesos estructurales de sociedad vasca," in *Estructuras sociales y cuestión nacional en España*, ed. Francesc Hernández and Francesc Mercadé (Barcelona: Ariel, 1986), 58–185.

8. Estimates of the Euskera-speaking population in the Basque region vary, but most agree that by 1970 about 20 percent of the Basque population were Euskera speakers, down from about 40 percent in the 1930s. The proportion of the population who speak Euskera has grown somewhat since the establishment of regional autonomy. According to census data, in 1986 about 25 percent were Euskera speakers.

9. Jesus Arpal, *La sociedad tradicional en el País Vasco* (San Sebastián: Haranburu, 1979), and Zulaika, *Basque Violence*.

The Political Context

The political relation between the Spanish state and the Basque provinces has historically been a conflictual one. Although Spain was an "early" state, "the political, social and cultural integration of its territorial components—nation building—was not fully accomplished."[10] Several provinces (including those of the Basque Country and Catalonia) had for lengthy periods of time enjoyed considerable political autonomy from Madrid. This in turn allowed regional minority cultures and languages (like Euskera and Catalan) to persist despite efforts by the center to promote a single Spanish (or Castilian) language and national identity.

To preserve their traditional culture and historic political rights (the *fueros*), Basques figured prominently in the two nineteenth-century Carlist struggles against liberal and centralist governments in Madrid. The Carlists were defeated, and seven hundred years after they were first established, the Basques lost their *fueros* in 1876. The Basques' struggle against centralism and their ultimate defeat coincided with the dramatic changes associated with industrialization. Thus, in the late nineteenth century numerous segments of Basque society perceived threats to their collective identity coming both from Madrid and from new groups within the Basque Country itself. It was at this time that Basque nationalism as an ideology and a movement arose.

The Partido Nacionalista Vasco (PNV) was founded in 1892 by Sabino Arana, and it participated in elections for the first time in 1895. Initially, Basque nationalism, as formulated by Sabino Arana, was extremely ethnocentric. It revolved around the reconstruction of a collective identity based on the Basque language, racial distinctiveness, ultra-Catholicism, and a xenophobic rejection of everything Spanish (including the Castilian-speaking immigrants in the Basque Country).[11] The political objectives of Basque nationalism, however, were less clear. After Arana's death in 1903, three different political models crystallized within the nationalist camp: the "possibilism" of those who believed that the Spanish state would reestablish Basque provincial government under the *fueros*; the "regionalism" (autonomy) of the *euskalherriakos*; and the separatism of the *aberrianos* (patriots).[12] All three models coexisted uneasily within the PNV, and conflicts among their proponents were a source of numerous schisms and the founding of smaller nationalist parties. Such differences over long-term objectives, as well as over how to achieve them,

10. Linz, "Early State Building," 33.
11. Juan Aranzadi, *Milenarismo vasco* (Madrid: Taurus, 1981), and Corcuera, *Orígenes*.
12. Antonio Elorza, "La herencia sabiniana hasta 1936," in *Nacionalismo y socialismo en Euskadi*, ed. Colectivo (Bilbao: IPES, 1984), 117.

have persisted to this day both within the PNV and between it and other nationalist groups.

Just as the civil war was about to erupt, the Second Republic granted political autonomy to the Basque provinces. Basque nationalists, despite their religious and conservative views, allied themselves with the Republican forces against Franco. Once again they were on the losing side. Franco branded Vizcaya and Guipúzcoa "traitorous provinces"[13] and, in the process of creating a highly centralized regime, abrogated the last vestiges of their autonomy, the *conciertos económicos*.[14]

In order to eradicate Basque distinctiveness once and for all and to create "a single personality, Spanish,"[15] the Francoist regime engaged in physical and symbolic repression of any outward manifestation of Basque cultural and political identity. As a result, Basques, and particularly nationalists, came to view their territory as suffering "military occupation" by an illegitimate Spanish state. Thus, the duality of "us" (Basques) versus "them" (Spain) became even further entrenched as a part of Basque political and cultural reality.[16]

The fact that intensely felt ethnic sentiments and political interests could not be expressed through legitimate channels led to growing frustration among younger Basques. This frustration was fueled by the passivity of both the PNV government in exile and of older nationalists in Spain. Younger Basque nationalists, such as those who founded or later joined ETA, sought new, more radical ways both to oppose the Francoist regime and to express their ethnic identity. Occupation and war, together with defense of Euskera, became the central pillars of the post–civil war nationalist discourse among younger Basques.

Direct experience of repression and violence did not subside in the Basque Country even as the Francoist regime during its last decade became less harsh and effective in its attempts to exercise control over society (see tables 10.2 and 10.3). Between 1956 and 1975, the Franco regime declared twelve states of exception. Five of these affected all of Spain, including the Basque Country. One was declared in Asturias only. The remainder were singularly directed toward the Basque provinces of

13. Alava sided with Franco during the civil war.
14. These were tax administration procedures that were established for Navarra and the three Basque provinces following the First Carlist War. They allowed Euskadi both to assess and to collect all tax revenues, including those which were to be remitted to the central government.
15. Quoted in Robert P. Clark, "Language and Politics in Spain's Basque Provinces," *Western European Politics* 4 (January 1981): 93.
16. Gregorio Moran, *Los Españoles que dejaron de serlo* (Barcelona: Planeta, 1982); Jáuregui, *Ideología*; and Pérez-Agote, *La reproducción del nacionalismo*, 16.

Table 10.2. People detained by police in Euskadi, 1968–1987

Year	Detained	Year	Detained
1968	434	1978	287
1969	?	1979	561
1970	831	1980	2,140
1971	?	1981	1,300
1972	616	1982	1,261
1973	572	1983	1,157
1974	1,116	1984	1,879
1975	4,625	1985	1,118
1976	?	1986	990
1977	Amnesty	1987	601

SOURCE: *Egin* (1988): 163.

Guipúzcoa or Vizcaya or both (as well as Asturias in one instance). "An estimated 8,500 Basques were directly affected during these states of exception either through arrest, imprisonment, and torture or by fleeing into exile to avoid the police or vigilante groups."[17] Given that the Basque population was small, the likelihood was great, even if one had not had direct experience with the violence of Spanish security forces, that one knew of a friend or family member who had had such experience. "Most people in the Basque Country saw the violence of [both branches of ETA] as much less of a threat than the behavior of the security forces, who in 1974–75 alone killed 22 people. . . . Such incidents provoked demonstrations and renewed brutality by the police when dispersing them. They also inspired a steady flow of recruits to ETA."[18]

As Tables 10.2 and 10.3 show, the pattern of ETA and counter-ETA violence, of mass demonstrations and indiscriminate repression of Basque protesters, did not subside even after Franco's death in 1975 and during the transition to democracy.[19] This pattern of ongoing violent confrontation had a number of effects that help to account for the persistence of ETA. It confirmed to many ETA activists the effectiveness of its strategy of action-repression-action. It lent credibility among many nationalists to ETA's view that even with the demise of the Francoist regime and uncertain progress toward regional autonomy, "nothing had changed"—at least for the Basque Country. And it ensured ETA's continued ability to draw new recruits to its ranks.

Once the transition to democracy was initiated, Basque nationalist

17. Clark, *The Basque Insurgents*, 241.
18. Sullivan, *ETA and Basque Nationalism*, 161.
19. Ibid., 197, 206–7, and 231.

Table 10.3.   People killed by police, died in jail, or executed, 1968–1988

	Basques or in the B.C.		Rest of Spain	Event
	Of ETA	Other	Rest of Spain	Event
1968	1	—	?	ETA's first martyr
1969	2	3	?	First assassination by ETA
1970	—	3	?	Burgos trial
1971	—	—	?	
1972	4	—	?	
1973	4	—	?	Assassination of Carrero Blanco
1974	4	—	?	
1975	8	12	14	Death of Franco
1976	3	13	16	
1977	4	8	27	Amnesty / first election
1978	12	4	20	Ref. on constitution
1979	6	10	35	Ref. on autonomy
1980	9	—	25	First regional election
1981	6	—	9	Dissolution of ETA-pm
1982	5	2	—	PSOE in power
1983	—	—	—	
1984	11	—	—	
1985	2	—	—	
1986	6	—	—	Crisis of PNV
1987	1	—	—	
1988	3	—	—	

SOURCES: Andrés Casinello, "ETA y el problema vasco," in *Terrorismo internacional*, ed. Salustiano del Campo (Madrid: Instituto de Cuestiones Internacionales, 1984), 265–308; Miguel Castells, *Radiografía de un modelo represivo* (San Sebastián: Ediciones Vascas, 1982), 38; *Eqin* (1977–88); José L. Pinuel, *El terrorismo en la transición española* (Madrid: Fundamentos, 1986); and Spanish Ministry of Interior, reports on the results of antiterrorist activities of security forces.

unity weakened as a proliferating number of groups vied for electoral support and sought legitimacy as the singular and most effective representative of the Basque people. This provided opportunities for competitive outbidding and for the branding of some groups by others as traitors to the nationalist cause. In the context of ongoing violence, such rivalries within the nationalist camp also encouraged a further radicalization of the political climate in Euskadi and a far higher level of mass mobilization than elsewhere in Spain. At the same time, "years of political indoctrination within the strictly . . . dual scheme of antagonism to Madrid could not be easily shed when a more elaborate context, with different options on the Basque side, emerged."[20] Thus, despite increased pluralism,

20. Zulaika, *Basque Violence*, 186.

whenever difficulties were encountered in the process of autonomy, all nationalist groups continued to perceive the Basque Country as the victim and Madrid as the oppressor. These tendencies, too, provided fertile ground for ETA's persistence after Franco's death.

Finally, one must take into account as an explanation of its persistence after Franco ETA's own conception of the political struggle in which it was engaged. As early as 1964 ETA made an explicit distinction between its own objectives and those of the broader anti-Francoist movement of which it was an important part: "The anti-Franquistas struggle against Franco as though Spanish oppression of the Basque Country did not exist. We struggle against Spanish oppression as though Franco did not exist."[21] Moreover, if ETA violence had proved to be effective in helping to bring about democratization and had been viewed as a legitimate strategy by others, why then would violence not be an equally effective and justifiable way to achieve independence?

The Cultural Context: A Culture of Violence

Post-civil war generations of Basques grew up in a climate of physical and symbolic violence and repression, in which all things Basque were labeled by the authorities as "traitorous" and as falling within the realm of social transgression. This climate was reinforced by the transmission from older to younger generations of historical memories of earlier periods of violence against the Basque Country, as had taken place during the Carlist and civil wars. The choice made by a segment of the Basque community to engage in violence against the violence of the "occupying forces" of the Spanish state—a choice understood, if not wholly supported, by others—contributed further to the rise of a "culture of violence" in Euskadi.[22] This culture of violence, we argue, is the most direct explanation of ETA terrorism and its endurance.

The importance of collective memory of oppression, especially if it is sustained by direct experience over successive generations, cannot be underestimated. Such memory

21. Luciano Rincón, *ETA (1974–1984)* (Barcelonia: Plaza y Janés, 1985), 186. Translated by Goldie Shabad, as are all subsequent translations, unless otherwise noted.

22. The term "culture of violence" as used here refers solely to political violence. It by no means suggests either that criminal violence was and is more widespread in the Basque Country than elsewhere in Spain or that criminality is viewed with greater tolerance by Basques than others. See Francisco J. Llera, "Violencia y sobrevaloración de la lengua: Conflicto simbolico en el País Vasco," in *Comportamiento electoral y nacionalismo en Cataluña, Galicia y País Vasco*, ed. José Pérez Vilariño (Santiago: Universidad de Santiago, 1987), 157–86.

creates a shared understanding from which oppressors . . . are forever excluded. It transforms experiences into traditions, as the sons learn to see themselves in the fathers, to discover the earlier in the later, as the many stories of the many generations are made into the single story of the struggle to survive, and are sanctified. . . . Because it abolishes time and dissolves place, collective memory is an instrument of continuity. . . . In the memory of oppression, oppression outlives itself. The scar does the work of the wound.[23]

This collective memory of oppression, reinforced by daily experience of attacks upon Basque language and identity, consolidated the idea central to early Basque nationalism of two fundamentally conflicting social, political, and symbolic realities: that of the ethnic "we" of the Basque Country and of the patriot versus that of the Spanish "they" of Madrid and of the traitor to the patriotic cause.

Furthermore, by placing all expressions of Basque identity into the category of social transgression, the Francoist regime helped to make the formerly impermissible—including violence—permissible. More important, it made the resort to violence, in the minds of many Basques, a morally justifiable response: "If the situation is to be defined in terms of violence, there is already an ever present institutional violence; any response to it, even pacificism, is violence. Violence, therefore, is the basic agent of social change; and whoever refused to participate in it lacks personal commitment."[24]

The idea of a collective identity based on these dualities was supported and reproduced throughout the Franco period by a dense network of interpersonal relations (especially the *cuadrilla*) and informal organizations (dance groups, mountaineering clubs, cooking and eating circles, and so forth) at the local level.[25] These came to constitute a virtual underground society, sustained by its own norms, myths, and symbols, that was distinct from and opposed to the "legitimate," public domain imposed on the Basque Country by the violence of the Spanish state.

Within this underground society, violence as a response to oppression by the Spanish state was legitimated and made sacral by religious symbolism and by the active support of the lower clergy. As has been noted in many studies of ETA, in the late 1950s and early 1960s many

23. *New Republic*, 5 June 1989, 20.
24. Zulaika, *Basque Violence*, 55.
25. Ander Gurrutxaga, *El código nacionalista vasco durante el Franquismo* (Barcelona: Anthropos, 1985), 311.

Catholic groups and ETA in rural or semiurban communities were indistinguishable as organizations, and many small religious groups were subsequently transformed into ETA cells.[26] Many ETA activists of the 1950s and 1960s made explicit connections between their resistance to institutional repression and Christian models of sacrifice and martyrdom; to be an *etarra* was to lead an exemplary life.[27] As the anthropologist Joseba Zulaika states in his study of Basque violence in the village of Itziar, "In situations in which the very survival of the historical and cultural frames of reference are at stake (and this is how most Basques perceive their fate), the defense of that identity may present itself as the ultimate sacrament."[28] Thus, traditional religious ideas of morality and salvation were transferred to the secular domain of the nationalist cause, including the path of violence, and in the process armed struggle itself became sanctified and ritualized.[29]

With the sacralization of armed struggle on behalf of Basque identity, violence was no longer viewed simply as a political strategy or as just one part of the larger conflict between "us" and "them." Rather, by the end of the Franco period and particularly for generations socialized in the 1960s and 1970s, violence had become a central reference point of Basque social and political reality, one that was made dramatically manifest by direct experience with actual incidents of violence.

The symbolic universe that had developed during the Francoist period, in which all things Basque were overdramatized and political violence was turned into messianic struggle,[30] could not be so easily transformed and "rationalized" once the Francoist regime came to an end and democracy was restored. Such a symbolic universe and its particular forms of ritual political behavior were highly resistant to adaptation to changes of the political environment. "After having experienced for twenty-five years a political education in which ritual performance and martyrdom were essential for patriotic self-defense, a change in attitudes is tantamount to an epistemological change affecting the very premises on which political order and personal identity are founded."[31]

This was all the more true for ETA activists. For them, the adoption

26. Ibid., 284 and Clark, *The Basque Insurgents*.
27. Zulaika, *Basque Violence*, 55 and 66.
28. Ibid., 286.
29. Gilbert Durand, "Structure réligieuse de la transgression," in *Violence et Transgression*, ed. Michel Maffesoli and André Bruston (Paris: Anthropos, 1979), 23–24.
30. Andrés Ortiz Oses and F. K. Mayr, *El inconsciente colectivo vasco* (San Sebastián: Txertoa, 1982); Jon Juaristi, *El linaje de Aitor: La invención de la tradición vasca* (Madrid: Taurus, 1987); and Aranzadi, *Milenarismo vasco*.
31. Zulaika, *Basque Violence*, 339.

of a flexible and more moderate stance would have been equivalent to "concession and defeat" and would have "trivialized the torture and death endured by the martyrs to ETA's cause."[32] The private, but politicized, underground society, which had developed in response to repression and which sustained and reproduced a reformulated Basque collective identity and symbolic universe, also could not be so easily dismantled or rationalized to fit the new public realm of pluralist democracy.

Thus, the culture of violence and its social underpinnings persisted well after their raison d'être had disappeared, and continued to serve as a context in which ETA could draw new recruits and mobilize public support.

ETA AS AN ORGANIZATION

Post–civil war generations of Basques inherited a dual legacy of nationalism and violence from their elders. This legacy was in time internalized and reformulated in direct response to physical and symbolic repression by the Francoist dictatorship. Moreover, because of the regime's high degree of centralism, ultra-Spanish nationalism, and suppression of any overt manifestation of Basque identity, for many younger Basques the Spanish state itself became synonymous with authoritarianism.[33]

In this context of suppressed nationalism and of physical and symbolic violence, a student organization (Eusko Ikasle Alkartasuna, or Basque Student Solidarity) was founded in the late 1940s at the Catholic University of Deusto in Bilbao. Its purpose was to promote Basque identity and, in particular, the Basque language, Euskera.[34] Student activists were arrested by the Spanish police in 1950, but two years later a new group, Ekin, was formed. Two other groups of young people joined this new organization in 1953 and 1954. The first was a segment of Herri Gaztedi (Catholic Country Youth) located in the high valleys of Guipúzcoa.[35] The second was a radicalized segment of Euzko Gaztedi del Interior (EGI, the youth section of the Basque Nationalist Party), which had

32. Ibid., 349.
33. Francisco J. Llera, "Legitimation Crisis and Atrophy of the Nation-State in Spain: The Basque Case" (paper presented at the Eleventh World Congress of Sociology, New Delhi, 1986).
34. Ibarzabal, *Cincuenta años*, 359.
35. Pablo Iztueta, *Sociología del fenómeno contestatario del clero vasco: 1940–1975* (San Sebastián: Elka, 1981), 265.

become frustrated with the conservatism and passivity of older generations of nationalists.

ETA was founded in 1959 by a coalition of these radical youth groups. From its inception, ETA asserted claims for the independence and reunification of the seven Basque provinces, the defense of Basque identity and language, the struggle against police repression and military occupation of the Basque Country by the Spanish state, and solidarity with workers' demands.[36]

These principles have remained constant throughout ETA's history. Despite recurrent internal conflicts over the primacy of the nationalist or the class struggle and a socioeconomic program couched in vague leftist rhetoric, ETA has been first and foremost a separatist organization. What has changed over time, depending on constraints imposed by police action, the political environment, outcomes of internal disputes, and the ideas of persons occupying leadership positions, have been its ideological emphases, strategies, organizational structure, membership characteristics, and targets of violence. These changes, in turn, have led to further internal divisions and outright schisms. Thus, the history of ETA has been one of crises, schisms, and change.

A Brief History of ETA

Due to the need to establish a solid basis for the break with and radical criticism of traditional and moderate Basque nationalism, represented by the PNV, and to position itself at the forefront of the Basque nationalist struggle, ETA's most active period of theoretical and political discourse occurred between 1959 and its first assembly in 1962.[37] The first assembly's principles defined the organization as a "Basque revolutionary movement of national liberation," thus signaling the adoption of a strategy designed to provoke a climate of insurgency against the regime. At the same time, ETA's socioeconomic program was ambiguous and interclassist and was expressed in populist and antioligarchic rhetoric. This vague opening to leftist ideologies was to create a major source of ongoing division within ETA over its ideological self-definition as an ethnonationalist versus leftist movement.

After these initial efforts to articulate a program and strategy, more-concrete guidelines came from outside the organization with the publication in 1963 of *Vasconia* by Frederico Krutwig. In addition to arguing for independence as the prime objective, Krutwig stressed an extreme

36. Garmendía, *Historia de ETA*.
37. *Documentos "Y,"* 18 vols. (San Sebastián: Hordago, 1979).

version of the ethnolinguistic definition of Basque identity, gave new meaning to Sabino Arana's idea of "occupation" by identifying it with colonialism, and outlined a revolutionary strategy modeled on Third World struggles for decolonialization.[38] Krutwig's application of the model of colonialism to the Basque Country, in particular, served to legitimate ETA's subsequent leap from nonviolent resistance to the Francoist regime to revolutionary warfare against the Spanish state. In 1963 ETA held its second assembly, during which the notion of colonialism and certain Marxist tenets were incorporated into ETA ideology.[39]

In 1963 ETA made its first contacts with the Spanish Communist party and suffered the consequences of police repression in the aftermath of a series of workers' strikes. Due in part to these events, ETA's third assembly held in 1964 resulted in a qualitative change in its ideological formulations, a change that was to have significant political consequences. It was at this assembly that ETA approved "Insurrection in Euskadi," a document written in exile in France for the political education of its militants.[40] It was at this meeting, too, that the strategy of armed struggle began to take on sacral overtones and to be sublimated into the idea of messianic liberation led by a vanguard of the enlightened.[41] The example set by the burgeoning workers' movement, the influx of militant workers to ETA, and the patchwork of different ideological tendencies in the organization led to the fourth assembly in 1964.

The assembly's "Letter to the Intellectuals"[42] was ETA's first attempt to organize a leftist nationalist movement and to define a strategy based on the principle of action-repression-action, aimed at capitalizing on increasing popular and labor mobilization against the regime. Efforts by the PNV shortly thereafter to mobilize support in Guernica to celebrate Aberri Eguna (Homeland Day) provoked ETA to make its own appeal to the Basque people for the creation of a Basque Nationalist Front.[43] In its call for unity, ETA combined the two basic principles of its ideological and strategic program, namely, the struggles for national and social liberation.

With ETA's growth after 1964, three distinct, but often overlapping, tendencies emerged within the organization.[44] The first, promoted by the founders of ETA in exile in France, stressed ethnolinguistic principles

38. F. Sarrailh de Ihartza (Federico Krutwig), *Vasconia* (Buenos Aires: Norbait, 1963).
39. *Documentos "Y"* 2:433.
40. Ibid. 3:21, 127. Jáuregui, *Ideología*, 225–37.
41. Aranzadi, *Milenarismo vasco*, 400.
42. *Documentos "Y"* 3:507.
43. Ibid., 199.
44. Federico Krutwig, *Vasconia y la nueva Europa* (Baiona: Elkar, 1978), 58.

428 Identity, Culture, and Territorial Claims

and was virulently anti-Spanish. The second had as its model anticolonial struggles and emphasized the importance of guerrilla warfare. The third was proworker in its ideological thrust. French actions against the first group and police repression in Spain against the second resulted in the dominance of the third faction in 1965 and 1966. This group replaced the strategy of national liberation with that of "class struggle," to be based on Marxist-Leninist principles and collaboration with the burgeoning workers' movement (including "Spanish forces" both in Euskadi and Spain as a whole). However, a fragile coalition of the first two tendencies decided to convene the fifth assembly in late 1966[45] to denounce this new strategy, which they viewed as a betrayal of ETA as a nationalist movement and the result of "Spanish" infiltration of the organization.[46] In response, the proworker faction declared that the fifth assembly was fraudulent and withdrew from it. Members of this faction were then expelled from the organization in early 1967.[47]

Among the new leadership, younger, "anticolonialist" elements, who considered themselves Marxists, were in a majority. As a consequence, many of the founders of ETA, alleging continued "Spanish" influence among the newly dominant group, left the organization following the second part of the fifth assembly held in March 1967.[48] Thus, 1967 marked a period of generational succession within ETA, the ideological implications of which were contradictory emphases on Marxist class struggle and national liberation, combined with a strategy of insurrection modeled after Third World anti-imperialist guerrilla warfare.[49] This was also the period when the principle of action-repression-action began to be put into effect. ETA militants increased in number, as did the frequency of successful violent actions.[50] In 1968 the first ETA militant was killed, and in response, ETA assassinated its first policeman. Both events aroused considerable popular support for ETA in the Basque Country.

As a consequence of increasing terrorist actions and growing worker militance, the regime declared four states of exception between 1967 and 1969, which were felt particularly harshly in the Basque Country. Due to successful police action against ETA, most of the top leaders were imprisoned, and ETA faced the prospect of imminent breakup. ETA had

45. *Documentos "Y"* 5:173.
46. *Branka* (San Sebastián: Ediciones Vascas, 1979).
47. Jáuregui, *Ideología*, 311–58.
48. Patxo Unzueta, *Los nietos de la IRA: Nacionalismo y violencia en el País Vasco* (Madrid: El País/Aguilar, 1988), 102.
49. K. de Zunbeltz [J. L. Zalbide], *Hacia una estrategia revolucionaria vasca* (Ciboure: Hordago, 1975).
50. Federico de Arteaga, *ETA y el proceso de Burgos* (Madrid: Aguado, 1971), 345–50.

to restructure its leadership and reconsider its strategy. The dispersion in exile or imprisonment of ETA leaders resulted in the emergence of a new set of leaders from ETA's workers' front in Bilbao, as well as in the reappearance of disparate tendencies within the organization. ETA's new leaders proposed that a new workers' party be formed and that mass action, mobilized by a broad interclassist national front, take priority over armed struggle. Meanwhile, many exiled ETA activists formed "Red Cells" to study Marxism and to formulate a strategy for combining nationalism and socialism that would be less reliant on Basque nationalism's traditional basis of support among the petite bourgeoisie. Another group of so-called *milis*, supporters of colonialist theses, advocated the pursuit of the armed struggle to the extreme. And a fourth group of proviolence activists did not accept the new leadership at all.

Outside the organization per se was a fifth tendency, that of the ethnolinguists and founders of ETA, now involved in the journal *Branka* and in the Association for Refugee Aid led by another exiled ETA founder, Telesforo de Monzón. With their radical ethnolinguistic nationalism, these outside groups played an important role in supporting, both theoretically and politically, the "militarists" within ETA.

The sixth assembly was convened in 1970 to resolve these differences.[51] Instead, it resulted in even sharper divisions, and ultimately ETA split apart once again. Those who had been active in the Red Cells and who supported the creation of a revolutionary workers' party resigned from ETA and formed a separate organization. Those who advocated armed struggle on behalf of radical nationalism refused to give their support to the decisions made by the sixth assembly and sharply criticized the leadership for having abandoned nationalism and for having come under the influence of Spanish Communist groups. Those who supported ETA's leadership took on the name ETA-VI, to distinguish themselves from their radical nationalist critics who dubbed themselves ETA-V.

In December 1970, shortly after these splits occurred, the Burgos trial was held, involving sixteen ETA militants.[52] The trial was one of the most significant events in ETA's history. For the first time, massive demonstrations, strikes, and occupations of churches in Euskadi took place in support of ETA's demands and its prisoners.[53] Indeed, by the

---

51. Garmendía, *Historia de ETA* 2:98.

52. The Burgos trial resulted in the commutation of six death penalties and a total of five hundred years of imprisonment for those convicted. For accounts and analyses of the trial, see Gisèle Halimi, *Le procès de Burgos* (Paris: Gallimard, 1971); Lurra, *Burgos: Juicio a un pueblo* (San Sebastián: Hordago, 1978); and Kepa Solaberri, *El proceso de Euskadi en Burgos* (Paris: Ruedo Iberico, 1971).

53. Sullivan, *ETA and Basque Nationalism*, 92–94.

early 1970s ETA came to be at the forefront of the resistance movement against the authoritarian regime. Not only did many political groups in the opposition applaud, at least implicitly, ETA's strategy of armed struggle, but several also supported certain of its political objectives. Even historic parties with strong centralist traditions, like the Socialist and Communist parties, included in their manifestos and programs the right to self-determination of culturally distinct regions and the incorporation of Navarra into the Basque Country.

ETA-VI, in particular, viewed the outpouring of public support during the Burgos trial as a vindication of its strategy of forming a mass movement based on the combined goals of national and social liberation. And for a short period of time it was more successful than its rival in drawing new members. After the Burgos trial, however, police repression against ETA intensified, and many of ETA-VI's leaders went into exile, making it difficult for the leadership to remain in close touch with activists in Spain. Moreover, its de-emphasis of armed struggle and vacillation on crucial questions, such as the status of Euskera and Basque independence, also began to hinder the recruitment of new militants to ETA-VI. By 1972, a majority faction within ETA-VI decided to abandon the organization and to unite with the Trotskyite Liga Communista Revolucionaria, a group active throughout Spain.

Although ETA-V was in the early 1970s far weaker than ETA-VI, the radical nationalism of the former, coupled with its emphasis on armed struggle, was "to prove, in the long run, more in tune with ETA's traditional social base than was ETA-VI's Marxism."[54] Moreover, compared with its rival, ETA-V was perceived by other Basque nationalist groups as being a much more acceptable member of a populist "national front." The number of ETA-V activists grew considerably with the incorporation in 1972 of many radicalized members of the PNV's youth group, EGI. As ETA-V became stronger, it decided to hold an assembly in September 1973 to endorse its leadership and the decision to reorganize into four fronts, among which the military front would be dominant. It was the leaders of the military front who, without consulting others, decided on the assassination, rather than the kidnapping, of Prime Minister Carrero Blanco.

The successful assassination of the prime minister in December 1973 showed the regime to be vulnerable to attack and helped to precipitate the demise of Francoism. It also provoked a new crisis within ETA-V (henceforth ETA). The disaffected within the subordinated workers' front broke from the organization in May 1974 and founded the first

54. Ibid., 129.

radical *abertzale* (patriotic) party, the Langille Abertzale Iraultzalean Alderdia (Patriotic Revolutionary Workers Party, or LAIA). ETA itself then divided into two factions: the first consisted of the leaders in France, who defended the priority and autonomy of armed struggle; and the second, of activists in Spain, who wished to combine military and political strategies in the context of high levels of mass mobilization. In late 1974 a definitive split occurred between these two factions. In its "manifesto," ETA-militar (ETA-m) appealed to mass organizations to form a "popular front for independence" in order to prepare for the final stage of the struggle against the dictatorship. But at the same time, it stressed the primacy and autonomy of the militarist leadership of the movement.[55] ETA-politico militar (ETA-pm) opted for a unified leadership combining political and military struggle against the regime. Despite these differences, both organizations had the same political objectives (independence, monolingualism for the Basque Country, and socialism) and the same basic strategy of popular revolution.

The end of the Franco regime in 1975 and the onset of democratization caught ETA without having resolved its internal conflicts over the relation between political and armed struggle and the organizational and functional role of the militarist branch of the organization. The battle between the militarist (ETA-m) and politico-militarist (ETA-pm) wings intensified. Among a growing number of ETA-pm leaders and militants, the use of violence was viewed primarily as a means to achieve certain goals—the release of ETA prisoners, for example. Now that the political environment had begun to change, other means to achieve these goals could complement, if not replace altogether, armed struggle. ETA-pm sought to participate in the political process, to enter into negotiations with the Spanish state, and, at the same time, to escalate its use of violence in order to bargain from a position of strength. For ETA-m leaders and their supporters, however, terrorism had by this time acquired a logic of its own and had assumed a more expressive than instrumental role. Hence, acts of violence were to continue irrespective of changes in the political environment, which in any case were thought to be illusory. The military faction rejected the process of political reform because it expected that reform would fail, thus making way for a prerevolutionary climate and *ruptura*.

ETA-pm decided at its seventh assembly to foster political organizations in order to create a leftist mass party to compete in the newly emergent pluralistic environment. This conformed to ETA-pm's thesis of "splitting," which argued for the dependence of the military leadership

55. Garmendía, *Historia de ETA* 2:181.

on the legal, political leadership and for the possible dissolution of the military branch in the long run. Already in 1974, ETA-pm had created a new nationalist trade union, Langille Abertzalean Batzordea (Patriotic Workers Council, or LAB), and in 1976 it founded a new *abertzale* Marxist-Leninist party, Euskal Iraultzale Alderdia (Basque Revolutionary Party, or EIA).

This party was but one of several radical nationalist groups formed at this time. In 1974 a split of the Basque movement ENBATA (The Wind) in France gave rise to a new party, Herriko Alderdi Sozialista (Popular Socialist Party, or HAS), which converged in 1975 with Euskal Alderdi Sozialista (the Basque Socialist Party, or EAS) to form a new revolutionary *abertzale* socialist organization. Eusko Herriko Alderdi Sozialista (Basque Popular Socialist Party, or EHAS), led by Santi Brouard.[56] Another group, Herriko Alderdi Sozialista Iraultzalea (Popular Revolutionary Socialist Party), arose out of this split as well, but aligned itself with ETA-m and later became the core of the antisystem coalition Herri Batasuna. Several of the founders of ETA, now associated with the journal *Branka*, together with a splinter group of the historic nationalist trade union Eusko Langileen Alkartasuna-Solidaridad de Trabajadores Vascas (Basque Workers Solidarity, or ELA-STV), created a new social democratic patriotic party, Euskal Sozialista Biltzarrea (Basque Socialist Assembly, or ESB), in 1976. Euskadiko Sozialista Elkartze Indarra (Socialist Unification of Euskadi, or ESEI), another moderate socialist party of young professionals, was founded in the same year.

Amid this growing political fragmentation within the nationalist camp, the desire to restore some semblance of unity, the need for continued popular mobilization, and the struggle over ETA's legacy gave rise in 1975 to Koordinadora Abertzale Sozialista (Socialist Patriotic Coordinator, or KAS). KAS was established for the purpose of creating a united patriotic socialist coalition,[57] and was composed of both ETAs, LAIA, LAB, Langille Abertzale Komiteak (Patriotic Workers Committee, or LAK), HAS, EAS, and Eusko Langileen Indarra (Force of the Basque Workers, or ELI). At the end of 1976, KAS approved the so-called KAS Alternative, whose origin was ETA-pm's manifesto of eight points for the Aberri Eguna of 1975. The alternative program, composed primarily of radical nationalist demands, was later set forth by ETA-m as its primary condition for entering into negotiations with the Spanish state.

Both ETA-m and ETA-pm rejected the Reform Law of 1976 and the

---

56. Santi Brouard was later assassinated in 1984 by the anti-ETA terrorist group GAL (Grupos Anti-terroristas de Liberación).

57. Naxto Arregi, *Memorias del KAS, 1975–1978* (San Sebastián: Haranburu, 1981), 49.

1978 Spanish constitution and continued to engage in violence. But by 1979–80, during the time of the establishment of the Basque Autonomous Community, ETA-pm had come to accept the primacy of political action and the leadership role of Euskadiko Ezkerra (EE), a coalition comprised of EIA and factions of the Basque Communist party, HASI, Acción Nacional Vasca (Basque National Action, or ANV), and ESEI. In 1981, shortly after the attempted coup d'état by a segment of the military, ETA-pm was dissolved, and those members who wished to continue the armed struggle joined ETA-m. Since that time, EE evolved into a Basque socialist party, participated actively in the institutionalization of Basque governmental bodies, and in January 1993 merged with the Basque branch of the Socialist party. It also served in the early 1980s as a mediator between former members of ETA-pm and the Spanish government in implementing the policy of social reinsertion, whereby persons not guilty of violent acts could be reintegrated into society without penalty.

The disbanding of ETA-pm in 1981 left ETA-m as the primary terrorist actor and resulted in a sharp reduction of violent actions. ETA-m and its affiliated political group, Herri Batasuna (a coalition formed in 1978 consisting of HASI, other mass organizations of KAS, and parts of LAIA, ESB, and ANV), continued to perceive the new Spanish democracy as Francoism in disguise and, despite Basque autonomy, to hold fast to the view of an ongoing war between the Spanish state and the Basque Country. Conceiving of itself as an authentic "people's army," ETA's strategy has been to bring about an "armistice," through negotiations, in which the Spanish government would accept the political conditions set forth by the KAS Alternative. In the interim, ETA's objectives have been to delegitimize existing political institutions established by both the Spanish constitution and the Basque Autonomy Statute and to gain legitimacy for itself as the true and only representative of the Basque people. To achieve these objectives, ETA has sought, through its network of organizations of the Basque Movement of National Liberation (MVLN), constantly to mobilize its supporters and public opinion. But as recent internal ETA documents reveal, violence is to accompany mass mobilizations until ETA's ultimate objectives are achieved (see Fig. 10.3).[58]

Since 1981 ETA-m has evolved into a secret army composed of small cells of three- to five-member commandos with direct connections to the military leadership in France. The military leadership is at the apex of an extensive and complex social movement (MVLN) that divides the

58. KAS, "Political Negotiations" (1988, photocopy).

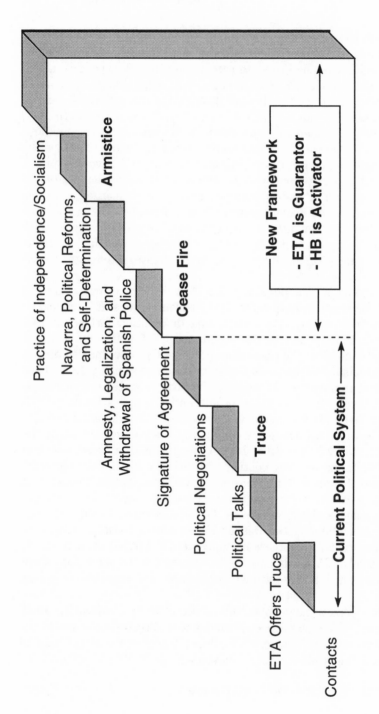

New Framework
- ETA is Guarantor
- HB is Activator

Practice of Independence/Socialism

Navarra, Political Reforms, and Self-Determination

Armistice

Amnesty, Legalization, and Withdrawal of Spanish Police

Cease Fire

Signature of Agreement

Political Negotiations

Truce

Political Talks

ETA Offers Truce

Current Political System

Contacts

Source: Internal document of Herri Batasuna, 1988

Fig. 10.3. The negotiating strategy of ETA for the 1990s

tasks of political mobilization among "legal" organizations. KAS is at the second echelon in the line of command, in which the main political party (HASI), the trade union (LAB), the youth organization (JARRAI), prisoners' support groups (proamnesty committees), and popular committees (ASK) come together. All of these, moreover, are part of Herri Batasuna, which competes in elections but which does not participate in representative institutions above the local level. Finally, at the periphery of ETA is a network of specialized organizations having to do with religious matters, education, the promotion of the Basque language, mass media, ecology, women, drugs, students, children, international solidarity, and prisoners and refugees.

As internal documents of KAS meetings reveal, ETA's leadership is directly involved in important decisions taken by the organizations associated with it. HASI has had three leadership successions since its founding in 1977, and ETA intervention was always decisive. A historical member of ETA's executive committee was the second candidate on Herri Batasuna's list for the first European Community elections in Spain, and a significant number of the coalition's candidates for local or regional bodies have been imprisoned *etarras*. Since the military leadership of ETA believes that a war is being fought between the Basque people and the Spanish state, it brooks no criticism of its decisions and strategies. A psychological climate of fear and threat surrounds those who dissent, particularly in moments of crisis. The assassinations of Pertur, leader of ETA-pm, in 1976 and of Yoyes, who accepted the government's offer of social reinsertion, in 1986 underscore the credibility of threats against "betrayals" or criticism from within. Expulsions, dismissals from leadership positions, and silence have been the penalties for dissent by lesser figures within ETA and its affiliated associations.

Despite these efforts by ETA's military leadership to stifle debate and dissent, the adoption by the Spanish government in 1984 of the policy of social reinsertion and the hope among some ETA members that talks between the leadership and the Spanish government would lead to an end to the armed struggle gave rise in the 1980s to new conflicts within the organization. The main division has been between the most radicalized and violent members (active leaders and prisoners in France and prisoners in Spain accused of killings) and those who have grown weary of the struggle and have the possibility of returning to a normal life in Euskadi (the deported, refugees, and prisoners untainted by violent acts). Moreover, the imprisonment or exile from France of many top leaders and the ensuing problems of communication with rank-and-file members and affiliated groups have undermined the cohesion among organizations of KAS, particularly between those which demand more political autonomy for their actions (HASI and a part of Herri Batasuna) and those which advocate strict commitment to ETA's leadership (proamnesty committees, most of Herri Batasuna, JARRAI, and LAB). ETA's three-decade-long history has been marked by conflict, crisis, and change (see Fig. 10.4). Most of its assemblies have been contested, protracted, or duplicated by a disaffected or expelled segment of the organization. None of ETA's leaders has enjoyed legitimacy for any extended period of time, and if not because of imprisonment or exile, succession to top positions has tended to occur by way of a coup d'état.

Throughout its history, the sources of ETA's factionalism and instability have been intense conflicts over four main issues: the priority to be given to national versus social liberation; the emphasis to be placed on mass political activity and, after Franco's death, on participation in democratic institutions versus armed struggle, and how best to reconcile these two strategies; the relation between the political and military branches of the organization and the degree of autonomy to be permitted to the latter; and, finally, the desirability of links with "Spanish" political forces. Divisions over these issues have never clearly demarcated one group from another. Rather, depending on time and circumstances, views on these issues have overlapped in different ways and have thus resulted in unstable and temporary coalitions among ETA factions. But differences over ideology and strategy have not been the sole sources of internal conflict and instability. Power struggles among leaders have played their part as well, and divisions among the rank and file have often been determined less by differences over ideology and strategy than by friendship patterns and personal ties to one or another leader.

The assumption by ETA of leftist ideologies and discourse at different moments in its history was primarily the result of changing contextual circumstances and was used as a means to incorporate new social sectors and issues into the nationalist movement.[59] The accretion of such ambiguous leftist discourse gave ETA an increasingly populist image. But at every critical moment for the organization, the old guard of radical nationalists eventually triumphed and guaranteed that orthodoxy would prevail. Language and Spanish occupation of the Basque Country remained the prime elements of ETA's symbolic capital, the main sources of the legitimacy accorded its violent struggle and of the effectiveness of its mobilization efforts.

With the growing "militarization" of ETA in the 1980s and its reduction to a more hard-core violent nucleus, internal conflicts have tended to

---

59. Luigi Bruni, *Historia política de una lucha armada* (Bilbao: Txalaparta, 1987), and Pedro Ibarra, *La evolución estrategia de ETA (1963–1987)* (Donostia: Kriselu, 1987).

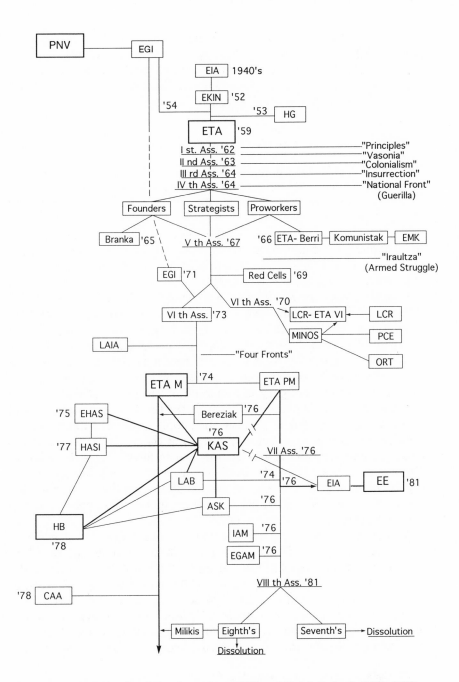

Fig. 10.4. Organizational development of ETA and Patriotic Left, 1952–1982

focus on how to respond to actions taken by the Spanish state and other political forces in the Basque Country. As its numbers have dwindled and its ability to broaden its base of support has declined, internal debate over goals and strategies has lessened considerably. Its primary aim has become the very survival of the organization itself.

Leaders and Members

As Robert Clark has pointed out, it is difficult to characterize ETA membership because there are several categories, levels, and functions of ETA activists, as well as "moments" in the gradual incorporation of *etarras* into the organization.[60]

The *liberados*, or *ilegales*, are the leaders and are characterized by their highest decision-making status, their full-time involvement in the organization, and their commitment to the use of violence. Leaders, moreover, are well known to the police. The second rank is composed of the *legales*, who are not known to the police, who lead a normal life and are employed outside the organization, and who have a variable commitment to ETA. Depending on their function, the *legales* are grouped into three different categories. The first are the *enlaces* (or links), who engage in communication activities; the second are the *buzones*, who serve as drop points for material for and from the organization; and the third category is composed of the *informativos*, who are responsible for intelligence gathering. In the third tier are supporters of ETA, whose function is to prepare and supply logistical support for the activities of the other groups by providing them with transportation, food, clothing, documentation, shelter, and so forth. These three layers also represent successive phases of recruitment and commitment to the organization; individuals may move up after they have completed a period of probation in local cells and have gained the approval of top people responsible for recruitment.

It is obviously not easy to determine the exact size of a clandestine organization such as ETA. Gathering data from different sources, Clark estimated that membership has ranged from a low of 6 to 70 during the first years of ETA's history, to between 200 and 600 during the 1960s, to between 100 and 400 in the 1970s, to about 500 in 1981.[61] More recent calculations by the Spanish police indicated the existence of twenty operative commandos in 1984 with around ninety activists. Nine commandos were *ilegales* (four in Guipúzcoa, two in Vizcaya, and one each in

60. Clark, *The Basque Insurgents*, 142.
61. Ibid., 220–22.

Alava, Navarra, and Madrid). The other eleven were *legales*. Spanish police calculated that by the end of 1988 the overall number had declined to fewer than fifty active members.

Fragmentary information from police records or from indirect and secondary sources also provides some data about the social characteristics of ETA members and the changes that have taken place in this regard during the last decade. All sources point to the Basque origin of more than 80 percent of ETA members during the 1960s and 1970s. The percentage born of immigrant parents increased slightly in the 1980s. But there was a significant difference between the ethnic origins of historic *liberados* in jail during 1980–81 and of those arrested during the same years (73 percent versus 56 percent of Basque parentage), thus suggesting a significant increase (from 15 percent to 23 percent) of *etarras* coming from an immigrant background.[62] Moreover, data from police records show that the most violent terrorists between 1983 and 1988 were immigrants who had joined ETA after 1982: Juan Toledo, 29 years of age, accused of 17 killings; Antonio Troitino, 31, accused of 32 assassinations; Domingo Troitino, 33, of 24; and Ramón Caride, aged 44, accused of 27 deaths. These figures indicate that the above individuals were in charge or were members of commandos responsible for more than 70 percent of all ETA killings between 1983 and 1988.[63]

The socioeconomic characteristics of ETA members have also changed somewhat over time. In the 1960s and 1970s, 90 percent of *etarras* were men; in the 1980s, however, male numbers declined to about 80 percent.[64] In the 1960s, 44 percent of *etarras* were drawn from the working class, 40 percent from the middle class, and 14 percent from the farm population.[65] But many of these had experienced some degree of upward mobility: 47 percent were students, 18 percent were members of the working and middle class, and 16 percent could be categorized as belonging to the upper class. During the 1970s the proportions of ETA members from the lower (34.3 percent) and middle (45.6 percent) classes increased, while those who had upper-class origins declined, as did those who were students (11.4 percent).[66] The unemployed (8.6 percent) appeared among

62. Spanish Ministry of the Interior, report on the results of antiterrorist activities of security forces, 1982.
63. *Tiempo*, 5 May 1989.
64. See the diary of Maria Dolores González Kataraïn, " 'Yoyes,' . . . the First Woman Leader of ETA in the 1970s," in *Yoyes: Desde su ventana*, ed. Elixabete Garmendía, Gloria González Catarain, Ana González Catarain, July Garmendía, and Juanjo Dorronsoro (Iruña: Garrasi, 1987).
65. Unzueta, *Los nietos de la IRA*, 181.
66. Clark, *The Basque Insurgents*, 145.

ETA's ranks for the first time. Data for the 1980s show a similar social profile: 2 percent were from the upper class, 42.8 percent from the middle class, and 33 percent from the working class; 15.8 percent were students; and 6.4 percent were unemployed.[67]

In all three decades of ETA's history, those from urban areas constituted about 70 percent of its membership. However, comparison of the geographical origins of ETA members in the 1980s[68] with those in the 1960s[69] reveals some changes. ETA activists from Bilbao and its surrounding area decreased from 38 to 26 percent. During the same period those from the San Sebastian area increased from 16 to 20 percent, as did the numbers drawn from Vitoria in Alava (from 2 to 5 percent) and from Pamplona in Navarra (from 0 to 7 percent). The proportion of etarras from rural and semiurban areas of Guipúzcoa and Vizcaya remained steady at 19 percent and 15 percent, respectively, while those from comparable areas in Alava increased by 5 percent and in Navarra by 3 percent.

Data about ETA prisoners and about militants arrested by the police show a slight decline in the mean age of recruitment of ETA members from 27.8 years of age in 1980–81, to 26.5 in 1985–87, to 26.2 in 1988. (This, in turn, suggests an aging of those who are still active in the organization.) The age distribution of those joining ETA, as revealed by recent police files, shows that between 1985 and 1987, 12.7 percent of ETA members were 20 years of age or younger; 31.5 percent were between 25 and 29 years of age; 10.2 percent were between 30 and 35; and 11.3 percent were 36 years of age and older. Comparable figures for 1988 were 21 percent (20 years of age and younger), 22.8 percent (25–29), 8.7 percent (30–35), and 15.6 percent (36 years and older).

In sum, a few changes can be noted, particularly in the 1980s, in the socioeconomic characteristics of ETA members. There were more etarras of mixed Basque or immigrant backgrounds, more who were unemployed, and more women, indicating a change in the circumstances and motivations leading to involvement in ETA. Moreover, more etarras in the 1980s than in the previous two decades joined at an earlier age and were drawn from traditionally weaker strongholds of Basque nationalism, such as Alava and Navarra. Nonetheless, the overwhelming proportion of ETA members continued to be Basque males in their twenties and thirties from urban areas of Vizcaya and Guipúzcoa.

67. Spanish Ministry of the Interior, reports on antiterrorist activities, 1982 and 1988.
68. Ibid., 1989.
69. Unzueta, Los nietos del la IRA, 177.

Kinds and Targets of Violence

During the more than thirty years of its existence, ETA has been responsible for more than five hundred assassinations, more than one thousand injuries, sixty kidnappings, innumerable bombings, armed assaults, and robberies, and an extended regime of "revolutionary taxation." Table 10.4 shows the annual distribution of mortalities attributed to ETA, as well as to others. ETA has been responsible for more that 70 percent of all people killed in terrorist actions in Spain during the last twenty years. As Table 10.5 shows, the majority of its victims have been police and military officers, a clear reflection of ETA's objective of making manifest the Spanish occupation of the Basque Country and the war of the Basque people against the Spanish state.

Table 10.4. People killed in terrorist actions, 1968–1991

	By ETA	By Extreme Right	By GAL	By Other*	Total
1968	2	—	—	—	2
1969	1	—	—	—	1
1970	—	—	—	—	—
1971	—	—	—	1	1
1972	1	—	—	1	2
1973	7	—	—	1	8
1974	19	—	—	—	19
1975	16	—	—	10	26
1976	15	3	—	3	21
1977	12	6	—	10	28
1978	64	8	—	13	85
1979	78	22	—	11	111
1980	93	29	—	2	124
1981	30	4	—	4	38
1982	31	1	—	12	44
1983	34	—	2	8	44
1984	24	—	9	—	33
1985	31	—	11	1	43
1986	24	—	2	15	41
1987	49	—	1	8	58
1988	19	—	—	15	24
1989	19	1	—	5	25
1990	25	—	—	5	30
1991	45	—	—	7	52
Total	639	74	25	132	860

SOURCE: See table 10.3.

*Including activists dead in terrorist or police actions.

Table 10.5.   Classification of ETA's mortal victims, 1968–1991 (in percentages)

	Percent
Police	45.1
Military officers	13.0
Citizens	34.9
ETA members	3.9
Local politicians	2.0
Industrialists	1.0
National politicians	0.1

SOURCE: Spanish Ministry of the Interior, reports on antiterrorist activities.

A second type of ETA violence has been kidnapping. Sixty have occurred since 1970 (Table 10.6). Most of these were perpetrated against Basque industrialists in order to raise funds for ETA's activities, as well as to influence public opinion. Six of those kidnapped were eventually killed (one military officer, the chief engineer of a Basque nuclear plant under construction, a member of a well-known Basque family, and three

Table 10.6   Kidnappings by ETA, 1970–1991

	No. of Kidnappings
1970	1
1971	—
1972	1 (assassinated)
1973	1
1974	4 (2 assassinated)
1975	—
1976	—
1977	1 (assassinated)
1978	4
1979	13
1980	10
1981	6 (1 assassinated)
1982	6
1983	6 (1 assassinated)
1984	—
1985	3
1986	2
1987	1
1988	1
1989	1
1990	—
1991	—

SOURCE: Contemporary press reports.

other industrialists), eight were injured, and four were rescued by the police. Kidnappings have also served as a way to coerce thousands of other Basque industrialists and professionals into paying a sizable annual "revolutionary tax" to the organization.

Basque industrialists were also the target of nearly five hundred attacks (bombings, sabotage, robberies, and armed assaults) between 1972 and 1983.[70] The second prime targets of attack have been banks, firms in crisis or in the midst of strikes, and, since France's decision in the late 1980s to cooperate with Spanish anti-ETA efforts, French firms.

In recent years there has been a qualitative change in the kind of violence practiced by ETA. Violent actions have been more indiscriminate and fatal, more frequently directed against collective targets (e.g., supermarkets, police headquarters), more often staged in the largest Spanish cities (Madrid, Barcelona, Zaragoza), and more sophisticated in the use of weapons. One can only speculate, but such changes tending toward more extreme, albeit less frequent, violent activities may have been the result of a loss of support for ETA among the Basque public in the late 1980s and hence the result of the erosion of the ties between ETA and the community it purports to represent.[71]

The International Dimension

The international dimension of ETA violence has been apparent in three areas: first, the role played by France as a refuge and center of operations for ETA members since the early 1960s; second, international connections between terrorist and revolutionary groups in Europe and Third World countries to obtain arms, training, and support; and third, as has been described earlier, the borrowing of foreign models to define strategy and to achieve legitimacy, thereby "internationalizing" the Basque struggle.

The Basque Country has an extended border with France that is difficult to control. Moreover, Basques live on both sides of the border, and French Basques have a long tradition of solidarity with, and giving refuge to, exiles from Spain, particularly after the civil war. The so-called French sanctuary was an important resource for ETA for a number of reasons. For much of the time, ETA's leadership was in exile in France; French sanctuary helped to legitimate the Basque struggle against the Franco regime; and it provided the opportunity for ideological education for some of ETA's leaders.

70. *Deia*, 6 June 1983.
71. Remarks made by Michel Wieviorka at the Conference on Terrorism in Context, 8–10 June 1989, Wesleyan University, Middletown, Conn.

The French government arrested several ETA activists, including members of the executive committee, for the first time in 1964 and began its policy of banishment from the Basque provinces in France. However, by that time most Basque refugees had achieved residence status and were protected in their activities. After the assassination of Carrero Blanco in 1973, the French government slowly began to change its policy toward ETA. In 1974 it banned all separatist organizations; in 1976 it made more difficult the achievement of resident status; and in 1977 it initiated a policy of preventive detention. A major contributor to the change in French policy was the increase in violence in France on the part of Iparretarrak, the most active of French Basque groups. At the same time, right-wing counterterrorist organizations (GAL, the Apostolic Anticommunist Alliance [AAA], and so forth) began their operations in the Basque French provinces. They were responsible for more than sixty violent actions between 1975 and 1982, in which nearly one hundred people were killed, most of them ETA members.

The increase in violence on French soil, the approval of the Spanish constitution in 1978 and the Basque Autonomy Statute in 1979, and the entry of Spain into the Common Market and NATO all led to the French government's adoption in the 1980s of a much harsher anti-ETA policy. As a result, most members of ETA's executive committee have either been jailed or deported by the French government, and between 1986 and 1988, French authorities turned over two hundred captured *etarras* to the Spanish government. This radical departure in French policy has severely constrained ETA's ability to carry out frequent actions and has exacerbated internal organizational problems of coordination and communication.

As for ETA's connections to other terrorist organizations, some members have been given training in Third World socialist countries, such as Yemen, Algeria, Libya, and Cuba. Available data suggest that ETA's arms come from the Middle East, and some of its funds have been provided by the Libyan government. Purchase of weapons, mostly from Communist Czechoslovakia and the former Soviet Union, was coordinated with other European terrorist groups. Since the 1970s, the closest and most continuous links with foreign terrorist organizations have been with the IRA.

The international dimension of ETA violence has also been reflected in its various efforts to ally itself ideologically with and to model its strategy on Third World anticolonial insurgent movements. As it turned out, these foreign models were largely inapplicable to Basque society. ETA was never able to create a broad-based insurrection movement or to engage in full-scale guerrilla warfare. Nonetheless, the adoption of anticolonial models of armed struggle in the early 1960s had significant repercussions for ETA and for Basque nationalism and society. It was a significant ideological factor contributing to ETA's decision to engage in violent activities and therefore served as a major source of internal conflict and schisms.

AFTER FRANCO: THE PERSISTENCE OF ETA VIOLENCE AND ITS EFFECTS

The effects of ETA and its violent activities during the latter part of the Franco era are easily discernible. ETA's assassination of Franco's heir apparent, Carrero Blanco, in 1973 showed the regime to be vulnerable and contributed to the demise of authoritarian rule. More important, ETA was instrumental in fomenting and mobilizing demands for regional autonomy, as well as the desire for outright independence among a significant minority of Basques. ETA also helped to perpetuate the "culture of violence" that would later serve as an obstacle to democratic consolidation in the Basque Country. ETA thereby ensured that the "Basque question" and that of center-periphery relations more generally would be at the forefront of the political agenda once the Spanish transition to democracy had begun.

The persistence of ETA and its dramatic escalation of violence during the transition and the period of negotiations over the Basque Autonomy Statute and elections to the Basque regional government (1977–80) had equally significant effects on Spanish democracy and, in particular, on Basque politics, society, and economy. Although the causal role of terrorism is "difficult to distinguish from those of other phenomena," because "its effects are diffused and modified over time,"[72] one can say with certainty that ETA violence and the counterviolence of state authorities in the first years of democratic rebirth posed one of the most serious challenges to the new regime. Spanish democracy has withstood that challenge and is widely regarded as having achieved consolidation. Although a great deal of ambiguity continues to surround the degree of support given by the state to right-wing anti-ETA terrorist groups, such as GAL, and much criticism has been leveled against the government for the alleged torture of ETA prisoners by the police, the new regime did

72. Martha Crenshaw, "Introduction: Reflections on the Effects of Terrorism," in *Terrorism, Legitimacy and Power*, ed. Martha Crenshaw (Middletown, Conn.: Wesleyan University Press, 1983), 6.

not succumb to state-sponsored terrorism in order to combat ETA. Nonetheless, by raising serious doubts about the legitimacy of the new regime among both Basques and ultra-Spanish nationalist groups (particularly within the military), ETA violence jeopardized the transition to democracy and slowed considerably the process of democratic consolidation in the Basque Country.

The purposes of ETA violence after Franco's death remained, in a very general sense, the same as before. While Franco was alive, ETA sought to delegitimize the Francoist regime, to expand and mobilize the Basque nationalist community, and to show both the repressiveness of the Spanish state and the ineffectiveness of such repression in the face of growing violent and nonviolent opposition to the regime. Despite redemocratization and the granting of autonomy to Euskadi, the fundamental aims of ETA's violence continued to be mobilization of the Basque public behind its goal of national liberation and the delegitimation of now democratic (including newly established Basque) political institutions. In short, ETA continued to engage in violence as part of its larger political struggle against the state in order to persuade the public to see the world in its own terms and to thereby gain the public's allegiance.[73]

ETA sought to achieve its goals by affecting—in different and often contradictory ways—the attitudes and behavior of a multiple set of target groups or audiences. Apart from seeking to instill fear in the classes of individuals who were the principal victims of ETA violence, its symbolic or psychological effects were directed toward the manipulation of the attitudes and behavior of six principal audiences: the Spanish government, from which it sought both to wring concessions and to provoke a repressive response against Euskadi; the military, in whose eyes it wanted to make the democratic regime look weak and ineffective; Spanish public opinion, which ETA sought to polarize; the Basque public and particularly the nationalist community, whose support ETA wanted to mobilize; Basque governmental institutions and political parties, which ETA wanted to portray as betrayers of the nationalist cause and from which at the same time it wanted to gain support; and, finally, ETA supporters and activists (including those in rival groups claiming ETA's legacy), among whom it wanted to maintain solidarity and commitment to the struggle and to infuse with a sense of self-esteem and power. To borrow Ian Lustick's terminology, ETA violence was at one and the same time both solipsistic and other-directed.[74]

73. Alex Schmid, "Goals and Objectives of International Terrorism," in *Current Perspectives on International Terrorism*, ed. Robert O. Slater and Michael Stohl (London: Macmillan, 1988), 48, and Martha Crenshaw, "The Subjective Reality of the Terrorist," in ibid., 12.

74. See Chapter 12 in this volume.

To what extent, then, did the persistence and, indeed, escalation of ETA violence in the aftermath of Franco's death achieve their intended effects? What impact did these "audiences," in turn, have on the course of ETA violence? Explanations of the effects of ETA violence after the demise of the Francoist regime lie in a complex and dynamic interplay among four major factors, which together define the opportunity structure in which ETA operated:[75] ETA's embeddedness in an open, pluralistic political environment, in which numerous nationalist groups competed for support and legitimacy and in which more moderate Basque forces gained dominance; the degree of weakness or instability of the dominant political coalition at a given moment; the degree of popular support for ETA; and the effectiveness of the government's response to violence. The ways in which these four factors interacted differed over time.

The Effects of ETA Violence During the Transition Period: 1975–1981

This period was one of remarkable institutional change in Spain. A reform law was enacted in 1976 that, among other things, permitted the formation of political parties. In 1977 elections for the constituent Cortes were held, and in 1978 a new constitution was ratified. This constitution explicitly acknowledged the multinational and multilingual character of Spanish society and established the principle of regional autonomy on which the transformation of the highly centralized state would be based. In the autumn of 1979 Euskadi (and Catalonia) regained autonomy, which they had lost as a result of Franco's victory in the civil war, and elections for the Basque parliament were held in March 1980. In that same year, the Spanish government restored to the Basque provinces of Guipúzcoa and Vizcaya the *conciertos económicos* (the system of tax privileges) that had been abrogated by Franco in 1937. The transition came to an end in the aftermath of an aborted coup d'état on 28 February 1981 by segments of the military who were provoked to act, in large part, by escalating ETA violence and the concessions made by the central government to demands for regional autonomy.

As significant and fast paced as these changes were, the transition period from beginning to end was marked by great uncertainty over its

75. The concept "political opportunity structure" has been used by others to account for the emergence of different varieties of collective action. It is also helpful, we would argue, in explaining outcomes of collective action, including political violence. See Sidney Tarrow, *Struggle, Politics, and Reform: Collective Action, Social Movements, and Cycles of Protest* (Occasional Paper no. 21, Cornell University, Center for International Studies, 1989), 32–39.

eventual outcome and how different segments of Spanish society might respond to each turn of events. Moreover, the "dominant coalitions" resulting from the 1977 and 1979 parliamentary elections were minority UCD (center-right) governments, which were dependent on other political parties not only for legislative support but, more importantly, for broad-based acceptance of the constitution and of the restructuring of the centralized state toward *un estado de las autonomías* (a state of the autonomies). Many factors contributed to the uncertain and precarious nature of the transition. Not least of these was the level of polarization of opinion and intensification of demands for autonomy in Euskadi and Catalonia, set amid ongoing mass mobilizations and increasing ETA violence and counterviolence by the state.

In 1977 opinion in Spain as a whole was rather divided with regard to the question of the structure of the state: 46 percent stated a preference for the status quo, a highly centralized state; 45 percent favored either a limited or an extensive degree of regional autonomy; only 3 percent agreed to the notion of independence for certain regional populations.[76] By spring 1979, after two years of heated political debate, considerable media attention paid to the issue, and increasing ETA violence, Spanish public opinion had grown more favorably disposed toward autonomy (56 percent) and far less inclined toward centralism (30 percent).[77]

Not surprisingly, public opinion in the Basque Country with regard to the structure of the state showed a strikingly different pattern. In 1977, 45 percent of Basques favored limited autonomy, another 18 percent preferred more extensive regional self-government, and 16 percent declared themselves for independence. Preference for a highly centralized state was a distinctly minority view.[78] Two years later, shortly after the ratification of the constitution, one out of every five Basques favored independence, and those preferring autonomy had declined to a bare majority of 54 percent. Thus, whereas in Spain as a whole preferences for a limited degree of autonomy became more widespread during the transition, in Euskadi opinion became more polarized and extreme.[79]

76. Juan J. Linz, Manuel Gómez-Reino, Francisco Andrés Orizo, and Darío Vila, *Informe sociológico sobre el cambio político en España, 1975–1981* (Madrid: Fundación FOESSA, 1981), 24.

77. The 1979 data reported here come from a spring postelection survey of 5,439 Spaniards that was part of a collaborative research project by Richard Gunther, Giacomo Sani, and Goldie Shabad. Respondents in Euskadi were oversampled to allow for detailed analyses of regional attitudes and behavior.

78. Juan J. Linz, *Conflicto en Euskadi* (Madrid: Espasa-Calpe, 1986), 101; see also Francisco J. Llera, "Continuidad y cambio en la política vasca: Notas sobre identidades sociales y cultura política" (Paper presented at the 1989 Annual Meeting of the Asociación Española de Ciencia Política, Gerona, 16–18 March 1989).

79. The continued support for nationalist goals notwithstanding, increased separatist

Basque opinions toward ETA also stood in sharp contrast to views held by the Spanish population as a whole (see Table 10.7). Less than 20 percent of Basque respondents in 1978 and 1979 surveys, for example, described ETA terrorists as "crazy" or as "common criminals." And only one out of three regarded them as "manipulated by others." Instead, almost half of Basques saw *etarras* either as "patriots" or "idealists." The Spanish public held a far less benign view of ETA terrorists. (It should be noted, however, that at least in 1978 a near majority took what might be regarded as a rather neutral stance by depicting them as "manipulated by others.") As can be seen in Table 10.8, Basques were also far more inclined than was the Spanish public in 1979 to lay responsibility for violence on the government (whether of then prime minister Adolfo Súarez or Franco). In accord with such differences in their images of terrorists and in their perceptions of those culpable for violence, Basques were also more likely in 1979 than were Spaniards as a whole to opt for negotiations as the preferred means of ending violence (see Table 10.9).

Clearly, no consensus existed among Basques during the transition period over either the issue of autonomy or the question of political violence. Indeed, with regard to the former, Basque public opinion was by 1979 quite polarized. Still, despite increasing violence or perhaps because of it, support for nationalist goals was high and had in a short

Table 10.7.   Images of ETA terrorists (in percentages)

	Euskadi Respondents			Spain Respondents		
	1978[a]	1979[b]	1982[b]	1978[a]	1979[b]	1982[b]
Terrorists are						
Patriots	13	15	16	4	6	2
Idealists	35	32	38	17	17	11
Manipulated by others	34	38	32	47	46	31
Crazy	11	9	29	18	17	32
Common criminals	7	10	29	21	30	58

[a]SOURCE: Juan J. Linz, *Conflicto en Euskadi* (Madrid: Espasa Calpe, 1986), 627–28.

[b]SOURCES: Gunther, Sani, and Shabad, 1979 survey: Gunther, Linz, Montero, Puhle, Sani, and Shabad, 1982 survey.

NOTE: Percentages do not add up to 100 because respondents were allowed to give multiple answers.

terrorist violence in Euskadi is in conformity with similar trends elsewhere, as reported in Christopher Hewitt, "Terrorism and Public Opinion: A Five-Country Study" (Paper presented at the 1989 Annual Meeting of the American Political Science Association, Atlanta, Ga., 31 August–3 September 1989).

Table 10.8.   Who is responsible for political violence? (1979, in percentages)

	Euskadi Respondents	Spain Respondents
Regional groups	11	16
Extreme leftist groups	37	41
Extreme rightist groups	46	44
Government	49	28
Police	29	3
Students, youth	8	7
Franco regime	50	29

SOURCE: Gunther, Sani, and Shabad, 1979 survey.

NOTE: Percentages do not add up to 100 because respondents were allowed to give multiple answers.

Table 10.9.   What should be done to eliminate violence? (1979, in percentages)

	Euskadi Respondents	Spain Respondents
Accept terrorist demands	3	2
Negotiate with ETA	43	20
Maintain order, within the law	37	48
War on terrorism	3	15
Military rule	1	5
NA	13	10
N	929	5,439

SOURCE: Gunther, Sani, and Shabad, 1979 survey.

NOTE: Percentages do not add up to 100 because respondents were allowed to give multiple answers.

period of time moved in a more radical direction. Moreover, a significant segment of the Basque public, including those who supported more-moderate stances and parties, saw ETA in a positive light, responded to ETA's view that a war was being waged against the Basque people, and shared ETA's strategy of entering into negotiations with the Spanish state. The patterns of opinion were quite different in Spain as a whole. But perhaps most noteworthy about Spanish public opinion during this period was the apparent failure of ETA violence to move it either in the direction of conciliation or in the direction of repression. Either shift would have fit with ETA's strategy. Instead, a near majority of Spaniards opted for "maintaining order, within the law," as the best way to deal with political violence. This choice boded well for an ultimately successful transition.

Basque public opinion was reflected in the outcomes of the 1977 and 1979 parliamentary elections and was mirrored (and shaped) by the views and behavior of Basque nationalist elites.[80] In the 1977 parliamentary election, the Partido Nacionalista Vasco (PNV) obtained a plurality of the votes cast in the Basque provinces of Alava, Guipúzcoa, and Vizcaya; and it, together with Euskadiko Ezkerra (EE), then associated with ETA-pm, received a total of 34 percent. Basque nationalist parties became increasingly dominant between the 1977 and 1979 general elections; their proportion of the vote grew from 34 percent to 51 percent. Although the PNV garnered a majority of votes going to nationalist parties and a plurality of the total votes cast in Euskadi in both 1977 and 1979, support for the more extreme nationalist groups increased substantially during this period. In particular, Herri Batasuna, which for the first time fielded candidates, obtained 15 percent of the vote. This trend was even more apparent in the outcome of the first election in 1980 to the Basque parliament.[81]

Thus, neither in the two Spanish general elections held during the transition nor in the 1980 parliamentary election in Euskadi did a single Basque party emerge with a hegemonic position within the Basque nationalist camp, let alone with a credible claim to be the singular representative of the Basque people. Hence, in Euskadi, not only did Basque nationalist parties compete with Spanish political forces (particularly the Spanish Socialist party), but increasingly, Basque nationalist parties vied among themselves for popular support. Basque nationalism is unique in this regard. In other Western democracies in which micronationalist movements exist, indeed in Catalonia as well, only one major party has emerged to represent the interests of the ethnic minority or regional group.

The existence of multiple contenders (including ETA) for the support of the Basque nationalist community established complex relations among them, ones that were characterized by both intense conflict and dependence. During the transition, this was manifest in the rhetoric and behavior of the historic PNV, the most moderate of Basque nationalist groups. Although the PNV did not obtain a majority of the total votes cast in Euskadi in the 1977 and 1979 general elections, its plurality position meant that it would be the main representative of Basque nationalism during the constituent process and in negotiations over the autonomy statute. In both instances, PNV representatives took extremely divisive stands and behaved in ways threatening to a success-

80. Richard Gunther, Giacomo Sani, and Goldie Shabad, *Spain After Franco: The Making of a Competitive Party System* (Berkeley and Los Angeles: University of California Press, 1986), 351–66.

81. For a discussion of these trends, see Francisco J. Llera, *Postfranquismo y fuerzas políticas en Euskadi* (Bilbao: Universidad del País Vasco, 1985).

452   Identity, Culture, and Territorial Claims

ful outcome. During the constituent process, for example, the PNV justified its demands for home rule on the basis of the *fueros*. According to Basque nationalists, these rights could not be granted (and hence could not be constrained) by any Spanish constitution, since they had historic precedence over the constituent process itself. In opposition to the way in which the draft constitution recognized the *fueros*, the PNV walked out of the Cortes during the vote on the constitution and recommended to its supporters that they actively abstain from the 1978 constitutional referendum.

Both EE and Herri Batasuna advocated outright rejection of the constitution. Consequently, only 45.5 percent of Basques voted in the constitutional referendum (which compares with a level of turnout of 67.7 percent throughout Spain). Only 31.3 percent of eligible Basque voters, in contrast to 59.4 percent of eligible Spanish voters, endorsed the constitution, and 23.8 percent voted no. Much was and continues to be made by ETA and Herri Batasuna of the illegitimacy of the constitution in light of the failure of the Basque people to give it their approval during the referendum.

The stridency of PNV rhetoric and its rancorous behavior during this decisive phase of the transition were due, in part, to its adherence to traditional elements of PNV ideology. But they were also attributable to the PNV's vulnerability to challenge by more radical or separatist forces, both parliamentary and extraparliamentary. For fear of losing credibility and support, the PNV could not appear to be too moderate or too conciliatory toward the "agents of the Spanish state." The PNV had little recourse, when confronted by pressure from the more extremist elements, other than to adapt its style of discourse and behavior.

Thus, already at this crucial point in the transition, one can see the effects of ETA violence, of sympathy for ETA among a sizable minority of Basques, of the strong presence of Herri Batasuna as an antisystem political rival, on the most moderate Basque nationalist group.[82] A dynamic of competitive "outbidding" was established between the PNV and the more extreme groups, which, in turn, militated against the adoption of pragmatic stances toward center-periphery issues and exacerbated polarization of public opinion in the Basque Country. It also intensified feelings of hostility and distrust between Basques and non-Basques, between Basques and the central government, and between Basque parties and Spanish parties of the Left and Center-Right, thus

82. See Leonard Weinberg and William Lee Eubank, "Political Parties and the Formation of Terrorist Groups," *Terrorism and Political Violence* 2, no. 2 (1990): 125–44.

making conflicts over center-periphery relations more difficult to resolve.[83]

Apart from the dynamic of competitive outbidding, ETA violence and
Herri Batasuna's presence reinforced and brought to the surface once
again the PNV's longstanding ambivalence regarding the Basque Country's relation to the Spanish state. One PNV elite interviewed in 1978
frankly stated that the party's long-range goal was "to reunify the
Basque provinces so that we can join our brothers in France."[84] A
member of the Euskadi Buru Batzar (the top organ of the PNV) affirmed
this point in another interview: "The Basque nation consists of four
Spanish provinces and three French provinces. We are very much aware,
however, of the slight possibility of uniting this territory in the short
term. Nevertheless, we are in the long run still in favor of this unification." Nonetheless, he went on to say, "we are not *independentistas.*"

The PNV's ambivalence was also reflected in its stance toward ETA.
A party official, when asked about terrorism in an interview in Guipúzcoa
in 1979, angrily replied, "I remember perfectly French patriots who
fought against Petain. . . . Then, they were called terrorists. Well, the
Vichy government spoke of terrorists. Today they are patriots. . . .
Everything is very relative. They speak of the terrorism of ETA, but I
would never speak of ETA terrorism." Another said in a 1978 interview,
"We must bear in mind that ETA was born out of the violence of the
Franco regime, but this very clearly is not a sufficient excuse for their
present acts." Nevertheless, "as long as the Spanish state does not
take effective and clear steps designed toward reversing discrimination
against Basque culture, it will be very difficult for us to explain to ETA
why they should lay down their guns."

The combination of ETA violence and the PNV's ambivalence with
regard to both its ultimate objectives and ETA had a number of consequences. First, the central government was forced to grant greater
concessions to Basque nationalists than Spanish political elites had initially been willing to make. To have done otherwise would have threatened the legitimacy and future stability of the new democracy.[85] Thus,

83. Goldie Shabad, "After Autonomy: The Dynamics of Regionalism in Spain" in *The
Politics of Democratic Spain*, ed. Stanley G. Payne (Chicago: Chicago Council on Foreign
Relations, 1986), 111–180; Goldie Shabad, "Creating the State of the Autonomies," in
Electoral Change and Democratic Stability in Spain, ed. Richard Gunther and Goldie
Shabad (in progress); and Goldie Shabad, "Still the Exception: Democratization and Ethnic
Nationalism in the Basque Country," in ibid.

84. As part of two larger research projects in which Shabad was coprincipal investigator, 203 interviews with national- and provincial-level party elites were conducted in 1978,
1979, 1981, and 1983. This statement was translated by Richard Gunther.

85. Shabad, "Creating the State of the Autonomies."

the PNV's politics, coupled with ETA violence, achieved, at least for the PNV, a great deal of what it wanted with regard to Basque autonomy. Second, even after the approval of the Basque Autonomy Statute in autumn 1979 and the establishment of a PNV-led Basque government in 1980, the PNV continued to complain either that the autonomy statute was inadequate or that Madrid was being extremely recalcitrant in transferring decision-making powers to Basque authorities. These complaints served not only to undermine further the legitimacy of the Spanish state in the eyes of the Basque public but also to weaken the legitimacy of the newly established institutions of the Basque Autonomous Community. And finally, such complaints by the PNV about the persistence of a "centralist" mentality among Spanish political elites lent credence to ETA's claim that even with regional autonomy, "nothing had changed," and provided justification, however implicit, for ETA's continued use of violence.

In sum, the various effects described above bear out the argument made by Peter Merkl about the multiple opportunities for both conflict and tacit collusion between moderate and extremist nationalist groups, particularly in the context of a relatively weak political coalition in the center and intense and polarized public opinion in the periphery:

We can easily imagine a game of pretense, for example, in which the moderates and extremists appear to be in pitched competition for popular support when, in fact, there may be collusion underneath. The two can use one another to expand their appeal to the public. The moderates, moreover, can use their illegal accomplices as a battering ram to make their own demands seem more reasonable, while the extremists use the refusal to grant the moderates' demands as the perfect excuse for extreme actions. . . . The moderates can maintain and conserve advances and concessions won for the nation by the extremists because the moderates are already playing a legitimate and recognized role.[86]

Two further effects of ETA violence (and counter-ETA violence by the state) during the transition should be noted. ETA violence created a climate of fear in the Basque Country that led, in turn, to a "spiral of silence," especially among supporters of Spanish political parties.[87] In response to a 1979 survey question that asked about the level of fear of active political involvement in their community, Spanish Socialist and

86. Merkl, "Political Violence," 29–30.
87. Linz, Conflicto en Euskadi, 16–17, and Cambio 16, 11 May 1987.

center-right party voters were far more likely than Basque nationalist party supporters to say that there was "some" or "a great deal" of fear. As a consequence, would-be supporters of the Socialist party, the center-right UCD, and the right-wing Popular Alliance were more likely than other party sympathizers to abstain during the 1977 and 1979 elections, thus contributing to the electoral successes of Basque nationalist parties.

ETA violence did not, however, promote passivity on the part of some elements of the Spanish military. Since military and police officers were the principal targets of ETA assassinations, concessions by the government to Basque nationalist demands heightened perceptions in some quarters that the Spanish government was weak in its dealings with "separatists." For many of the "ultraloyalist" elements of the military, democracy had come to mean the dismemberment of Spain itself. As the Francoist newspaper *El Alcázar* (read by many army officers) ominously announced on the eve of Basque and Catalan autonomy referenda in autumn 1979, "Today it is decided whether Spain should exist or commit suicide."[88] Neither enamored with the new democracy nor willing to accept what in their eyes would soon become an *España rota* (broken Spain), some segments of the military staged an unsuccessful coup on 23 February 1981.

In sum, the dynamics of the transition in the Basque Country were characterized, in large part, by a "dialectic of rocks, clubs and tear gas,"[89] of ETA violence and counter-ETA violence, and of mutual recriminations among political groups. Although regional autonomy was achieved, the manner in which it was obtained exacted a considerable toll on the new Spanish democracy and especially on the Basque Country itself. "By their counterexample, the Basque provinces prove that the process of transformation that occurred in Spain was not inevitable."[90]

After Autonomy: PNV Dominance in Basque Politics

In the period between 1981 and 1985, during which time the PNV controlled Basque autonomous institutions and a majority Socialist government came to power in Madrid, the level of ETA violence declined dramatically. To a certain extent, this drop in violent actions was due to the dissolution of ETA-pm in early 1981. But the fact that the democratic regime had survived the coup, that dominant, single-party governments

88. *New York Times*, 26 October 1979.

89. Richard Gunther, *Politics and Culture in Spain* (Ann Arbor: Center for Political Studies, Institute for Social Research, University of Michigan, 1988), 36.

90. Edward Malefakis, "Spain and Its Francoist Heritage," in *From Dictatorship to Democracy*, ed. John H. Herz (Westport, Conn.: Greenwood Press, 1982), 224.

were in place in both Madrid and Vitoria, and that institutionalization of Basque regional bodies had begun all provided a less favorable political environment for continued high levels of ETA(-m) violence. Nonetheless, terrorist activities persisted at a level well above that of the late Franco period and continued to have a negative impact on Basque society and on the democratic regime. However, the effects of political violence in this period were somewhat different from that during the transition, particularly with regard to public opinion.

By 1982, according to survey data,[91] the Spanish public had become far more unfavorable in its perceptions of ETA militants (see Table 10.7). Moreover, 74 percent of all Spaniards in the 1982 survey, many more than the 62 percent in 1979, placed themselves at the most negative position on an eleven-point "feeling thermometer" measuring the degree of sympathy or hostility toward ETA; only 3 percent in 1982 were either neutral or positive. The pattern of preferences regarding the structure of the state, however, remained virtually identical to that of 1979. Growing abhorrence of ETA violence in the aftermath of the attempted coup was not translated into a desire to return to the centralized state of the Franco regime.

Basque public opinion, once again, exhibited markedly different patterns, although in certain instances a convergence of views can be discerned. Basque attitudes toward autonomy versus independence remained remarkably stable and polarized in the years immediately following the granting of autonomy. Approximately one out of every four Basques favored independence, and support for autonomy increased by only 3 percent. At the same time, like all Spaniards, the Basque public also grew more hostile toward ETA between 1979 and 1982. Those placing themselves on the negative side of the feeling thermometer measuring sympathy or hostility toward ETA rose from 53 percent to 82 percent (see Fig. 10.5). The mean self-placement of PNV and EE voters (but not of Herri Batasuna supporters) also became more negative. Moreover, as the data in Table 10.7 show, about three times as many Basques in 1982 than in 1979 were inclined to label *etarras* as "crazy" or as "common criminals." A similar shift took place in the images of ETA terrorists held by PNV and EE sympathizers. What is equally apparent from these various data, however, is the persistence of strongly pro-ETA views held by a sizable number of Basques (reflected in the stability

91. The 1982 data come from an autumn postelection survey of 5,463 Spaniards that was part of a collaborative research project by Richard Gunther, Juan Linz, José Ramón Montero, Hans-Jürgen Puhle, Giacomo Sani, and Goldie Shabad. Respondents in Euskadi were oversampled to allow for detailed data analysis.

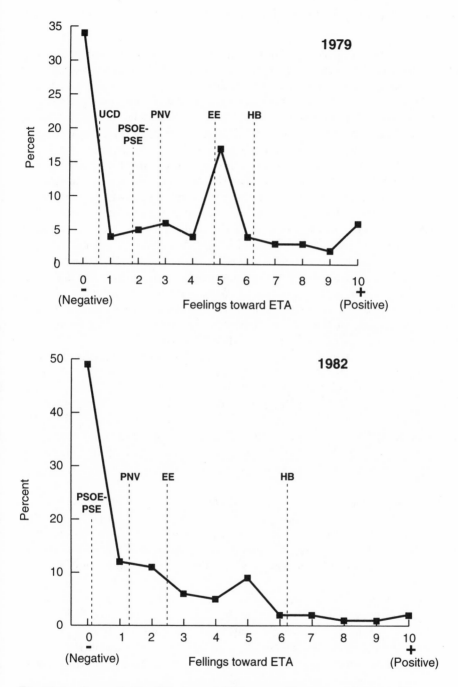

Fig. 10.5. Sympathy/hostility toward ETA among Basques, and mean self-placement of partisan groups on feeling thermometer, 1979 and 1982

of electoral support for Herri Batasuna), as well as the continuing feelings of ambivalence or sympathy toward ETA among a significant minority of moderate Basque nationalists.

A survey conducted in 1985 showed that the Basque public continued to be conflicted in its opinions. On the one hand, 76 percent of all respondents said that the immediate abandonment of the armed struggle by ETA would be a positive step toward improving the situation in Euskadi. In response to another question, only 16 percent believed that ETA should continue to exist. On the other hand, only 40 percent of those interviewed rejected outright the five-point KAS Alternative of ETA and Herri Batasuna as a basis for negotiations with the Spanish state; only 36 percent favored French collaboration with the Spanish government to combat ETA; and 63 percent favored negotiations between the central government and ETA.[92] Thus, although the percentage of the Basque population expressing unequivocal support for ETA was by this time a small minority, it was, nonetheless, sufficient for the "terrorists to feel themselves supported in their actions. This is what is so serious and at the root of the whole problem of violence, that there are still to be found nuclei that defended its existence."[93]

Although during this period PNV and EE leaders repeatedly made public announcements against the use of violence, more often than not their actions and their public statements showed the effects of the ongoing scenario of overt conflict and tacit collusion. This was reflected in moderate nationalist party leaders' continuing ambivalence about the relation of the Basque Country to Spain, the legitimacy of the constitution, and ETA. Complaints about the inadequacies of the autonomy statute and about the pace of transfers of authority from Madrid persisted.

A high-ranking PNV leader, when asked in a 1983 interview whether the full realization of the autonomy statute would satisfy nationalist aspirations, replied, "I believe so. . . . If we enter into the realm of feelings, I would say that my people are *independentistas*, and the thesis of my party is to form a Basque state. Well, this happens many times. I also have the desire to be rich instead of living on a salary. . . . so I think people here are very, very realistic. . . . I don't have the temptation to form a Basque state." He went on to remark, however, that "if I were to say today that I am Spanish, that I renounce Basque independence, I would immediately be kicked out of my party." An internal PNV document made clear that there had been no renunciation of the goal of

92. *Cambio* 16, 8 July 1985, 27.
93. Ibid., 28.

independence and that should the defense of (Basque) national identity require it, the PNV would not vacillate in assuming its responsibility for achieving it.[94] In 1985 Jesus Intxausti, former president of the PNV, proclaimed, "I want independence as much as Herri Batasuna does."[95] Whether or not this was the true goal of the PNV, statements such as these served a purpose. As a Basque Socialist party leader commented about the *victimismo* of the PNV government in a 1983 interview, "The PNV always ups the ante for electoral purposes. Despite what happens, it always claims to be under the heel of Madrid, the one that is oppressed."

Little change was also exhibited in the PNV's ambivalence toward ETA and in its reluctance to condemn ETA violence publicly, despite growing hostility among Basques as a whole. Time and time again between 1981 and 1985 the PNV-led Basque government strongly criticized the various efforts of the central government to combat ETA. The PNV government responded negatively, for example, to extraditions by foreign governments of suspected ETA members. Garaikoetxea, then head of the Basque regional government, criticized the use of such a strategy and asserted that the Spanish government had fallen into the temptation to "go to the extreme" in its struggle against ETA. The PNV government during this time also showed great reluctance to cooperate fully with the central government's use of police measures to combat ETA. As PNV senator Joseba Eloségui said during a conference on political violence and terrorism held in autumn 1984, "The fathers of ETA members belong to the PNV, and they propose that the *peneuvista* father denounce his *etarra* son to the Guardia Civil. . . . Before doing that, we are obligated . . . to resort to political measures."[96] Apart from the psychological truth revealed by this statement, ETA still remained useful to the PNV as a means to wrest further concessions from the central government or to quicken the pace of transfers of decision-making authority.

Not surprisingly, Socialist leaders, both in Euskadi and in Madrid, responded harshly to PNV criticisms of the central government's antiterrorist actions. One Basque Socialist leader accused Garaikoetxea of a lack of loyalty to the constitution.[97] Damboranea, another prominent Basque Socialist leader who had been extremely outspoken in his opposition to Basque nationalism, said that the ambiguous posture of the PNV

94. *El País*, 11 February 1985, 15.
95. *Cambio* 16, 15 April 1985, 23.
96. *Cambio* 16, 5 November 1984, 23.
97. *El País*, 23 July 1984, 1.

is "one of the major difficulties in the pacification of Euskadi." He added that the PNV's attitude is an "inadmissible gesture of disloyalty against Spanish democracy. . . . The PNV fears the end of ETA and is disposed to make it more difficult to bring it about."[98]

Damboranea nicely summed up the complex interaction between the PNV and ETA. The PNV "cannot dare to condemn the convent [ETA] because they are orthodox; it cannot renounce *posibilismo* because that is its salvation. As a consequence, its ambiguity persists: ambiguity in its behavior, ambiguity in its words, and in its strategy. . . . It wants at one and the same time to be with the constitution and with ETA."[99]

The continued strength of Herri Batasuna—now even more antisystem than before[100]—ongoing ETA violence, vituperative relations between the PNV and the Socialist party, and escalating tensions between the Basque government and Madrid all poisoned the political climate in Euskadi and gave rise to disturbing tendencies during this period. One rarely, if ever, for example, heard the word *Spain* spoken by a Basque nationalist. The rejection of the idea of Spain was reflected in the so-called war of the flags that broke out in the summer of 1983 and again in 1984. The *guerra de las banderas* was precipitated in some instances by the refusal of Basque nationalist–controlled local governments to fly the Spanish flag alongside the *ikurriña* (the Basque emblem) and, in other cases, by the seizing and removal of the Spanish flag by Herri Batasuna sympathizers. The rationale for such behavior was provided by a leader of Herri Batasuna in a 1983 interview: "The Spanish flag is the same as under Franco. It is a symbol of torturers, of those who have repressed us all our lives. It shows us that nothing has changed. But now they ask us to love it, respect it." Tensions produced by the war of the flags were not confined to Euskadi. An editorial in *Diario 16*, a Madrid daily, warned, "Don't we realize that the 'military malaise' could be back with us in a few months if things in the Basque Country keep going on like this."[101] Indeed, it was during this period that many presumed ETA members were themselves assassinated, both in Spain and France, in what came to be called the dirty war (*la guerra sucia*). Although little is known about Grupos Anti-terroristas de Liberación (GAL), those who were primarily responsible for such acts, it is widely believed that members of Spanish security forces were involved.

In sum, the continued polarization of Basque society and ambivalence

98. Ibid., 2, 21.
99. Ricardo García Damboranea, *La encrucijada vasca* (Barcelona: Argos Vergara, 1985), 105.
100. Shabad, "After Autonomy," 145–46.
101. *New York Times*, 22 August 1983.

of moderate Basque nationalists, in the context of a deteriorating economy, were in large measure both the consequences of ongoing ETA violence and the sources of its endurance. In the words of a former Socialist minister of the interior, "Something paradoxical has occurred in the Basque Country. In these moments, it is the corner of Spain that is most remote from democratic principles practiced in Europe. Today, all of Spain looks like Europe, except the Basque Country. It is the corner in which intolerance, fanaticism, and violence are most entrenched. . . . They are the ones who today represent the old Spaniard, the Spaniard that we wish no longer existed—the intolerant Spaniard, fanatic."[102]

This period began to come to a close in late 1984 and early 1985. After the victory of the PNV in the February 1984 regional elections, in which its electoral support increased by 4 percent over that received in 1980, the party was rent by severe internal conflicts. These led in December 1984 to the resignation of Garaikoetxea as head of government and to his replacement by José Antonio Ardanza. In exchange for Socialist assurances to support certain PNV legislative initiatives in the regional parliament, the PNV and the PSOE pledged their "willingness to uphold the constitution, the statute of autonomy, and other related laws, as well as decisions handed down by the courts."[103] In addition, both parties agreed to cooperate in the struggle against terrorism. The pact thus obligated the Basque government to support more openly and unambiguously than heretofore Spanish constitutional arrangements and to oppose more vigorously separatist violence. The pact signaled a turning point in the dynamic of confrontation between the PNV and Basque Socialists and between the Basque and central governments. It also made possible the swifter resolution of conflicts over remaining transfers of authority to Euskadi.

In March 1985 the Basque government for the first time explicitly and publicly condemned ETA. This was precipitated by the assassination of the chief of the Autonomous Basque Police (Ertzantza). This first violent attack by ETA against institutions and persons of the Basque government was widely supposed to have been its response to involvement by the Ertzantza in antiterrorist efforts. In an unanimous motion, the Basque parliament demanded that the terrorists put down their arms and asked the Basque people to make no concessions to those who kill or who are their accomplices.

102. *El País*, 8 August 1983, 15.
103. *El País*, 21 January 1985, 12. For an analysis of the significance of these events, see Francisco J. Llera, "Euskadi '86: La encrucijada de la transición," *Cuadernos de Alzate* 4 (1986): 52–63, and idem, "Crisis en Euskadi en los procesos electorales de 1986," *Revista de Derecho Político* 25 (1987): 35–74.

The End of ETA?

Between the early and late 1980s, Basque public opinion became more negative toward ETA and separatist violence. A survey conducted in 1987 found that the number of Basques holding positive images of *etarras* had declined since the early 1980s, especially among supporters of the PNV and EE as well as of the Socialist party. Moreover, 80 percent of respondents either agreed or strongly agreed with the statement that "violence is no longer necessary to achieve political objectives." Still, almost one out of four respondents in that same survey viewed *etarras* as "patriots" or "idealists," and another 34 percent were unwilling to state their opinion. A Basque government study, conducted in November 1987 by Juan Linz and Francisco J. Llera, found that a slight majority of all Basque respondents (but a far more substantial majority of nationalists) agreed with the inclusion of the various points of the KAS Alternative in negotiations between the Spanish government and ETA.[104] Only a small minority expressed disapproval. For example, 63 percent of all respondents agreed that a referendum on self-determination should be a point of discussion between the two sides. Hence, despite the discernible decline in pro-ETA sentiments, a politically significant minority of Basques in the late 1980s appeared still to be indeterminate in their opinions and open, therefore, to influence either by ETA or by prosystem forces.

Nonetheless, from 1985 on ETA found itself operating in a markedly different, less hospitable political environment. The leadership of the PNV and EE (the latter by this time far more moderate in its nationalism than before) became increasingly explicit and vehement in their condemnation of ETA violence. Moreover, tensions within the PNV led to a schism in 1986 and culminated in the formation of a new political party, Eusko Alkartasuna (EA), headed by Garaikoetxea. The Basque nationalist camp became even more fragmented than before, since four parties now competed for popular support. As a consequence, the PNV did not win a legislative majority in the November 1986 regional elections, and after a protracted period of negotiations, a governmental coalition was formed by the PNV and Basque Socialists. Hence, opportunities for the PNV to engage in openly ambivalent and conflictual behavior became more constrained. Furthermore, with the increased fragmentation of the Basque nationalist community, the PNV, EE, and EA became more preoccupied with interparty rivalries and protecting their own positions than with their implicit or explicit relation to ETA.

104. Francisco J. Llera, "Continuidad y cambio en la política vasca," table 8.

The uncertainty and potential instability surrounding both the periods of internal PNV conflicts and the formation of the PNV-Socialist governing coalition were marked by increases in ETA violence, particularly in 1987. However, the rise in the number of deaths caused by ETA during 1985 and again in 1987 was less the result of more frequent actions than of a few "spectacular" incidents of indiscriminate violence in which numerous civilians were killed. Overall, the organization's ability to inflict sustained and high levels of damage and to affect the behavior of moderate Basque nationalists had deteriorated.

In addition, the multipronged strategy of the Socialist government in Madrid to combat ETA violence proved increasingly successful. Police actions met with greater results, and cooperation by the French government led to the capture, imprisonment, or deportation of a significant number of ETA leaders. The policy of "social reinsertion," which allows individual ETA militants who repudiate armed struggle to be reinserted into Basque society, also served to reduce the ranks of ETA members to its more hard-core elements. As has already been noted, the possibility of social reinsertion also opened serious divisions within ETA and the MLVN over what response should be taken toward this policy. The reaction of the most militarist elements was clearly demonstrated in the 1986 ETA assassination of a former ETA leader, Yoyes. But this action resulted in even further dissension between hard- and soft-line ETA activists and sympathizers. Finally, the decision to allow the Autonomous Basque Police to collaborate with state security forces in antiterrorist activities also brought about a more favorable political climate in Euskadi in which to combat ETA.

As a consequence of these positive developments, the central government began openly to pursue another of its strategies for bringing an end to ETA violence. Madrid acknowledged publicly for the first time in August 1987 that it was engaging in negotiations, or "talks" (as it prefers to call them), with ETA. As a government spokesman said, "There have been, there are, and there will be dialogues with ETA."[105] In response to the government's reversal of its long-held public opposition to such talks, ETA quickly published its own communiqué in which it rejected the government's demand for a cessation of violent activities as a precondition for discussion, and instead declared that a truce could only occur at the end of negotiations, which were to be based on the KAS Alternative and conducted with the "real powers" (*poderes fácticos*) of the state, namely, the military and the oligarchy.

Nonetheless, a number of significant events transpired in quick succes-

105. *Cambio* 16, 9 November 1987, 36.

sion in late 1987 and early 1988 that gave reason for optimism that ETA violence might soon come to an end. On 10 November 1987 all political parties represented in the Cortes (including the PNV and EE) signed the Pacto de Estado against terrorism, thereby providing the government with a consensus for its differentiated policies toward ETA. The response of ETA to the signing of this agreement was a violent action the following day in Zaragoza in which eleven persons, including some children, were killed. Talks with the exiled leader of ETA were immediately halted. In mid-December of that year, however, the government declared that it would resume discussions if a truce with ETA were declared. An even more significant turning point was reached in Basque politics on 12 January 1988. After difficult negotiations, all parties in Euskadi, with the exception of Herri Batasuna, signed an historic agreement of their own against violence and for the "pacification and normalization" of the Basque Country. Shortly thereafter, ETA offered a truce if the government would resume talks. Moreover, ETA dropped its insistence that only its own five-point KAS Alternative serve as a basis of discussion, and it agreed, for the first time, to allow the participation of political-party representatives in talks. In mid-February 1988, by which time ETA actions had ceased for almost three months, the government said it was disposed to reinitiate contacts with exiled ETA leaders.

These events led the Basque public to be more optimistic than before about the possibility of a cessation of violence. According to a February 1988 survey conducted by Spain's Center of Sociological Investigations, two-thirds of all respondents in Euskadi believed that ETA's situation had deteriorated in the past few years. Fifty-six percent claimed that it was "very" or "somewhat likely" that negotiations would bring an end to ETA terrorism. (In Spain as a whole, however, only 29 percent were similarly confident.) Moreover, when asked about ETA's motivations for offering a truce, 40 percent agreed with the statement that its offer was "sincere and showed ETA's willingness to negotiate." In contrast, smaller percentages expressed a cynical view: only 18 percent agreed with the notion that "ETA doesn't really want peace, and its offer of a truce is a manipulation of public opinion"; 21 percent concurred with the statement that ETA only wanted "to gain time in order to reorganize itself." The kidnapping by ETA of a Basque industrialist in late February 1988, however, once again brought an abrupt halt to the resumption of talks and undermined expectations for an end to violence in the near future. It took over a year (March 1989) for discussions between the government and ETA to resume, but these too ended in failure. Increasing frustration with ongoing, albeit diminished, ETA violence and dashed hopes that this time the "talks of Algiers" might bear fruit had a clear and decisive impact on Basque public opinion. Massive anti-ETA demonstrations, involving hundreds of thousands of people and supporters of all political parties (other than Herri Batasuna), were held in Euskadi in March 1989. For the first time, these demonstrations overshadowed the ever-present "antirepression" pro-ETA disturbances.

ETA's behavior in the late 1980s was reflective of its changed circumstances. On the one hand, the willingness of ETA to cast aside its conditions regarding talks with the Spanish state indicated that the organization's leadership had come to realize that ETA's position had deteriorated in terms of its ability to recruit new members, to carry out sustained effective actions, and to enlarge, let alone maintain, its degree of popular support. Thus, it was best to "negotiate" while ETA could still do some damage and extract some concessions from the state. But along with this changed stance toward talks, what the simultaneous acts of violence and abrupt withdrawal from negotiations also suggested was that ETA had become increasingly divided between hard-line and moderate elements. It was with the latter that the government pursued its discussions.

What might such talks accomplish were they to take place? Most likely, ETA would be reduced to its most violent core, a group of militants concerned primarily with the very survival of the organization. And although electoral support for Herri Batasuna might not decline substantially, ETA sympathizers in Euskadi would most likely be reduced to a politically insignificant minority. ETA violence would not cease were these developments to occur; however, its impact on democratic consolidation and especially on Basque society and politics would be far less grave.

CONCLUSIONS

There is no single explanation of ETA violence and its persistence after the rebirth of Spanish democracy. As we have argued, various characteristics of Basque society, but especially the "culture of violence" that developed during the Francoist years, facilitated the decision made by certain individuals to engage in terrorist activities on behalf of the Basque nationalist cause. These characteristics, like historical memories of repression, the perceived severity of the threat to Basque culture and language, the idealization of traditional Basque society, and the culture of violence legitimated by religious symbolism and sustained by local-level social structures, also help to explain why separatist violence was more probable in Euskadi than in Catalonia.[106]

Once ETA was formed and the choice was made in the early 1960s to pursue the armed struggle, both the internal dynamics characteristic of clandestine organizations and a supportive "underground society" at the local level helped to perpetuate ETA violence after Franco's death. The uncertainty of the outcome of the transition, the continued exercise of violence by state authorities in Euskadi during the years immediately following Franco's death, the polarization and radicalism of Basque public opinion, and the relations among Basque nationalist groups account for ETA's endurance as well. Finally, one cannot dismiss as an explanation ETA's own proclaimed objective, which was not the end of authoritarian rule but independence for Euskadi.

All this is not to say that ETA violence was inevitable or that it remains so. The audiences to whom violence is directed have an impact on terrorist organizations. Their responses—particularly those of the government, the "public" that the organization purports to represent, and rank-and-file members—constitute part of the changing context in which terrorists operate. Effective responses by the government (whether in terms of political or police measures), declining popular support for political violence, and disunity within ETA and its affiliated organizations—all of which occurred in the Basque Country in the late 1980s—make it difficult to continue to engage in terrorism. Although hard-core militants may remain active, their number and overall impact are likely to diminish.

What can be concluded about the effects of ETA violence? Two primary goals of terrorist organizations, whether they be ideologically left or right, religious or nationalist, are to undermine the legitimacy and the stability of the existing regime. How effective such organizations are in achieving these goals depends on a number of factors. One of these is the nature of the regime itself, although the impact of regime type is itself conditioned by other variables. Authoritarian regimes, such as Francoist

106. It should be noted that we have not argued here that the extent of Francoist repression in the early years of the dictatorship, as indicated by number of violent deaths or political prisoners or even degree of economic exploitation, was greater in the Basque Country (or Catalonia) than elsewhere in Spain. For an argument that this was in fact not the case, see Andrés de Blas Guerrero, "El problema nacional-regional español en la transición," in *La transición democrática española*, ed. José Felix Tezanos, Ramón Cotarelo, and Andrés de Blas (Madrid: Editorial Sistema, 1989), 607 n. 8. This point is, of course, the subject of much debate and polemics. Our argument here is simply that the subjective response to repression was different in the Basque Country than elsewhere and that it was this subjective response that led to a favorable climate for the emergence and persistence of ETA.

Spain, are by their very nature far less inhibited by legal and normative constraints from countering the violence directed against them. Moreover, clandestine organizations have fewer opportunities, particularly in more repressive periods, to get their message across to their intended targets and to acquire essential resources such as militants, weapons, funds, safe houses, and so on. But at the same time, grievances provoked by repression of class interests or of religious and ethnic sentiments may foster growing and increasingly radical popular discontent with existing rule. This, in turn, provides a favorable climate for oppositional violence.

Democratic regimes, on the other hand, have a greater ability to lay claims to legitimacy and loyalty. They provide opportunities for voicing demands and expressing dissent through peaceful means. But should political violence occur, democratic governments, unlike authoritarian regimes, are faced with an unenviable choice. They may choose to act within the boundaries set by the constitution—and risk failure and being made to appear ineffective in the eyes of the public and the military—or they may resort to extralegal means to combat threats to the regime; this would not only undermine democratic rule itself but also provoke that segment of society in whose name the terrorist organization acts. Either extreme—failure of democratic means, or state violence—may achieve the terrorist organization's goals of delegitimation and instability.

The choices made by democratic governments for countering political violence are conditioned by a number of factors. One, of course, is the particular mix of values of governing elites themselves, their assessments of the circumstances they face and of the likely outcomes of differing strategies, and their perceptions of the pressures placed on them from rival political elites. These normative, cognitive, and affective orientations may, in turn, be influenced by other variables, such as the actual scope and frequency of violence wreaked by antisystem forces and the patterns of opinion of various segments of the population.

Another factor, which we have emphasized here and which differentiates democratic from authoritarian regimes and hence their possible responses to political violence, is the embeddedness of terrorist organizations in a pluralistic political environment. The interaction between the terrorist group and more moderate "alegal" or prosystem political forces that also represent the relevant social group may have an effect on public opinion, the severity of political violence, and ultimately the decisions made by governing elites on how to combat terrorism. We have argued here that it is too simplistic to view the interaction between these two kinds of groups as one of rivalry alone. Although it is true that the existence of legal channels for the expression of group interests may undercut frustration and support for organizations like ETA, the presence of extremist groups willing to use violence may be implicitly encouraged and overtly manipulated by more moderate forces to strengthen their bargaining position vis-à-vis the state. The relation between the two, therefore, is apt to be one of conflict *and* collusion, and both types of interaction potentially serve the interests and objectives of each group.

Thus, there is a complex array of factors that determine the effectiveness of oppositional violence at any given time and under a particular type of political rule. It is difficult to say, based on the Spanish case alone, whether terrorism is more effective under authoritarian or democratic rule. The Francoist regime did not end because of ETA, nor did democracy fail to consolidate because of ETA violence. At the same time, ETA violence did hasten the demise of Francoism, if only through its assassination of the dictator's heir apparent, Carrero Blanco. And it did jeopardize the transition to democracy by reinforcing or provoking hostility to the evolving rules of the game in two different quarters. Basque nationalists refused to endorse the constitution and only gave it "backward" and ambiguous legitimacy through subsequent support of the autonomy statute. And a segment of the military came very close to toppling democratic rule in its February 1981 coup attempt. Although ETA activities did not lead to the destruction of democracy, they did help to change the rules of the game in another way. As Basque nationalist leaders have argued, without the constant pressure exerted by ETA violence, political elites in Madrid may not have felt as impelled to grant concessions to demands for Basque autonomy and for a fundamental restructuring of the centralized state. Ironically, without such concessions, democratic consolidation may not have been possible.

To say that ETA did not prevent democratic consolidation is not to conclude that ETA had no serious negative consequences. But these were primarily confined to the Basque Country. The persistence of ETA after Franco's death helped to sustain a culture of violence and, in so doing, placed major obstacles to the evolution of more rational and secular patterns of social and political interaction. It polarized and radicalized public opinion in Euskadi and called into question the legitimacy of the new regime. And it significantly affected the behavior of other, more moderate nationalist groups, thus making the resolution of center-periphery conflicts more difficult to achieve.[107]

Given these negative effects, it is fortuitous that separatist violence

107. Goldie Shabad, "Still the Exception? Democratization and Ethnic Nationalism in the Basque Country," in *Electoral Change*, ed. Gunther and Shabad.

did not occur in other ethnically distinct regions of Spain, such as Catalonia and Galicia. Had it spread to other areas and not been confined primarily to the Basque Country, Spanish democracy might have been stillborn.

Part IV

Nationalism and State Formation

11

The Effectiveness of Terrorism in the Algerian War

Martha Crenshaw

Contemporary American audiences probably best recall the Algerian war in images from the 1966 film *The Battle of Algiers*, a compelling and enduringly popular contribution to revolutionary mythology, not least because the leader of the terrorist underground in Algiers plays himself.[1] Even in France, written analysis of the war mirrors a general interest in the events of 1956 and 1957. Reports of terrorism dominated press headlines in France during the entire course of the war, from 1954 to 1962, but of the few analytical studies that have appeared since the

---

1. See Piernico Solinar, ed., *Gillo Pontecorvo's "The Battle of Algiers"* (New York: Scribner's, 1973), 164. Pontecorvo explained that the idea for the film came from Yacef Saadi.

war, fewer still extend their examination of history beyond descriptive accounts of the Battle of Algiers.[2]

This neglect is unfortunate, since terrorism during the Algerian war extended far beyond the confines of the Battle of Algiers. Furthermore, the relevance of the Algerian case to the present is indisputable. The revolutionary-nationalist terrorism of the Front de Libération Nationale (FLN), which formed part of a broad political and military struggle for independence from French rule, is widely supposed to have succeeded in attracting international attention to the cause of Algerian national self-determination, mobilizing the Algerian population against French rule (in part by provoking indiscriminate repression against civilians), spreading insecurity among European settlers in Algeria, and making the war unpopular in France. The FLN became a powerful model for later national liberation organizations, such as the Palestine Liberation Organization. It inspired groups as diverse and distant as the Front de Libération du Québec in Canada and the Argentine "urban guerrilla" movement, as well as Palestinian nationalists.

But similarly motivated revolutionaries and nationalists were not the only imitators of the FLN. In 1960 the French government's decision to open negotiations with the FLN to decide Algeria's fate provoked a right-wing backlash from the French military and the European settler community in Algeria, contributing to the genesis of the Organisation de l'Armé Secrète (OAS), a prototypical counterrevolutionary terrorist organization that was explicitly modeled on the FLN, or rather the OAS image of the FLN.

Furthermore, French policy in Algeria anticipated many aspects of the contemporary response to terrorism—the temptation to ascribe it to foreign intervention rather than indigenous discontent, discriminatory labeling of violence according to political interest, and elaboration of military doctrines to guide and justify the response. Among the French public, especially intellectuals, the conflict generated anxiety over the effects of terrorism and of the response to terrorism on democracy and on the relations between civil and military authority.

The complexities of terrorism in the Algerian war raise many more

2. René Gallissot, "La guerre d'Algérie: La fin des secrets et le secret d'une guerre doublement nationale," *Le mouvement social* 138 (January–March 1987): 78. In Martha Crenshaw Hutchinson, *Revolutionary Terrorism: The FLN in Algeria, 1954–1962* (Stanford, Calif.: Hoover Institution Press, 1978), I argue that terrorism served multiple functions for the FLN. One should also note the sections on Algeria, both FLN and OAS, in Roland Gaucher, *Les terroristes: De la Russie tsariste à l'O.A.S.* (Paris: Albin Michel, 1965).

important questions than this analysis can answer. They concern the nature of revolutionary and counterrevolutionary terrorism in a war of national liberation, the reasons for its use in different forms and on behalf of different interests, and its consequences for the conduct of a colonial war, for French democracy and stability, and for the future government of Algeria. In this chapter I choose to explore the problem of the outcomes of terrorism, especially in terms of its effectiveness in producing important political change.[3] Would the outcome of the Algerian war have been the same in the absence of terrorism? Here the distinction between effectiveness and success is relevant. To be effective, terrorism need merely produce a decided or decisive effect, which may not reflect the original intent of the actor. Thus, explaining effectiveness requires knowledge of outcomes but not necessarily of intentions. However, to claim that terrorism is successful implies that it is effectual, in the sense of producing the effects its users sought and anticipated. Its consequences must be those envisaged by the decision makers in question. Making an argument that terrorism is successful thus presumes that terrorism is instrumental and that the strategy behind it can be discovered. Terrorism can be effective without being successful, since it can produce decisive results that are nevertheless counterproductive; but if it is without any important consequences, it has clearly failed.

It is thus logical to ask what factors determine both effectiveness and success. Such an inquiry requires not only describing political results and linking them to terrorism but also identifying the barriers that lie between the intentions behind and the results of political action. These are difficult tasks. Not only are the intentions of political actors hard to know under the best of "normal" circumstances, but governments and oppositions may initiate terrorism or counterterrorism as considered responses to the actions of an adversary only to discover they cannot control the process they have set in motion. What begins as strategy can end in the pursuit of vengeance for its own sake. Explaining terrorism in Algeria requires understanding the concept of *engrenage*,[4] through which

3. The subject of the outcomes of violence has been neglected in the general literature. See Ted Robert Gurr, "Theories of Political Violence and Revolution in the Third World," in *Conflict Resolution in Africa*, ed. Francis M. Deng and I. William Zartman (Washington, D.C.: Brookings Institution, 1991), 186–87; see also Martha Crenshaw, "Current Research on Terrorism: The Academic Perspective," *Studies in Conflict and Terrorism* 15, no. 1 (January–March 1992): 1–11.

4. The concept of *engrenage* is central to understanding the use of terrorism in the Algerian war. It implies a process that once begun is both involuntary and mechanistic. Literally, it refers to the engaging of gears or cogs in a wheel. Practically, it means a tit-for-tat cycle of violence and retaliation.

terrorism acquired an independent dynamic by becoming an end in itself rather than a means to political ends. This self-indulgent violence tended to escape the control of the actors who initiated it, because of the nature of terrorism and because of the specific historical context.

The first section of this chapter situates terrorism in the structure of in the Algerian conflict, which was at its most basic a war to expel a foreign colonial occupier. Yet terrorism was not simply a reflection of interests in implementing or preventing self-determination but part of a complex series of struggles for power within both nationalist and colonialist camps. What was at stake was not just independence or colonialism but who was to govern on either side. I next compare the origins and consequences of the two terrorisms of the FLN and OAS. I am not so much concerned with terrorism from above—that designed to control the behavior of constituent populations, forestall resistance, or create a rival political authority—as with terrorism against those in power. My main subject is terrorism that claims victims from the adversary's civilian population in order to influence the attitudes of that audience as well as those of one's own constituency.

TERRORISM IN THE ALGERIAN CONTEXT

The pattern of conflict in which terrorism is embedded conditions the motivations of actors and the consequences of their actions, particularly the perceptions of audiences, and it shapes the conceptions of terrorism held by the parties involved and even by detached observers. Although the Algerian war appears to be a simple case of a nationalist challenge to colonialism, each side actually was divided within itself over questions of legitimacy, and those divisions stimulated violence. The primary axis of the war was the conflict of interest between the French—driven in part by a "colonial consensus" that linked the possession of colonies, especially Algeria, to the identity and prestige of the French nation[5]—and a nationalist movement determined to throw off a repressive colonial regime. Yet serious internal conflicts figured within the Algerian war.

5. See Tony Smith, *The French Stake in Algeria, 1954–1962* (Ithaca, N.Y.: Cornell University Press, 1978). See also Raoul Girardet, *L'idée coloniale en France de 1871 à 1962* (Paris: La Table Ronde, 1972).

Neither side was united. To some observers, the war was accompanied by two civil wars and was thus *doublement nationale*.[6]

Although the FLN emerged to dominate the nationalist movement in Algeria, during the early years of the war the FLN had a strong rival in the Mouvement National Algérien (MNA), against which the FLN fought a bitter war of assassinations and recriminations. Intranationalist violence characterized the early consolidation of the FLN's position in Algeria and even more so the mobilization of the Algerian emigrant population in France. The MNA did not lose influence until 1958, four years after the war started. As late as 1960 de Gaulle threatened to negotiate with them if the FLN would not see reason. Furthermore, this internal Algerian struggle led not only to clashes between armed militants of the two movements but also to a battle between them to gain the support of the uncommitted population. The FLN also sought to destroy any competitors who might constitute a moderate "third force" that would be more acceptable to the French as a negotiating partner. In contrast to the PLO, the FLN permitted no competition and no alliances. From the beginning, the FLN was committed to becoming the only legitimate body with whom the French could deal and the only possible government in a future independent Algeria.

On the French side, lines were drawn between metropole and settlers, civil and military authorities, and proponents and opponents of Algérie française. The war even produced major constitutional change, in the transition from the Fourth to the Fifth Republic. Initially the Fourth Republic faced nearly irresistible pressures from the settler population to maintain French Algeria; this population's relatively large presence (almost a million Europeans out of a total Algerian population of ten million in 1954), emotional attachment to the Algerian homeland, and resistance to democratic reforms shaped the policies made in Paris and their implementation in Algeria. But the commitment to keeping Algeria was not exclusively a preoccupation of *colons* or *pieds-noirs* in Algeria.[7] Until late in the war, the idea of relinquishing Algeria (which in formal

6. Gallissot, "La guerre." The interpretation of the war as an intersection of multiple conflicts served as the theme of a colloquium held in Paris in December 1988 under the auspices of the Institut d'Histoire du Temps Présent and the Centre National de Recherches Scientifiques. The proceedings are published in Jean-Pierre Rioux, ed., *La guerre d'Algérie et les français* (Paris: Fayard, 1990).

7. The settlers of Algeria, most of whom were from Mediterranean rather than exclusively French backgrounds, were divided between rich landowners, *colons*, and the majority working classes, or *pieds-noirs*. According to a recent estimate, of the settler population 400,000 were descendants of the original French settlers of the nineteenth century, 400,000 were of various Mediterranean origins, and 150,000 were Jews. See Evelyne Lever, "L'OAS et les pieds-noirs," *L'histoire* 43 (March 1982): 11.

terms was not a colony but an administrative region of France) was anathema in France itself. As the war progressed, however, the consensus over colonial policy eroded, and the metropolitan supporters of Algérie française eventually found themselves a beleaguered, though strident, minority. Terrorism contributed to dissolving the conception of Algeria as an integral part of the French identity.

To further complicate the picture, the specter of military intervention loomed over French politics from 1957 until 1962. De Gaulle's unusual assumption of power in May 1958, following a protracted and frustrating governmental crisis in Paris, responded to an appeal from military commanders in Algiers. General Jacques Massu, who had come to head the Algiers region because the civilian authorities could not halt terrorism, called in a public speech for de Gaulle's return to office to fill the power vacuum left by the indecisive Fourth Republic executive. In 1961, after the installation of the Fifth Republic, four of France's most prestigious generals conspired to mount a coup d'état when they realized that de Gaulle meant to negotiate with the FLN. The significance of OAS terrorism against the Fifth Republic in 1961 and 1962 was heightened by the fact that it was an expression not just of settler dissatisfaction but of military revolt against republican institutions. Thus, the French government, like the FLN, sought both to determine the future of Algeria and to establish or maintain a particular political legitimacy.

The motivations behind the formation of a nationalist organization driven to seek separation through armed struggle (in contrast to citizenship and equality within some "integrated" French system) were deeply rooted in Algerian history. The initiation of conflict was gradual, not abrupt, despite French perceptions of its unexpectedness. It began as a political process in the years after the First World War. The beginning of the war is recognized as 1 November 1954, the *Toussaint*, or All Saints' Day, the date on which the newly formed FLN, through its leaders in the Comité Révolutionnaire d'Unité et d'Action, symbolically threw down the gauntlet by organizing a series of small-scale bombings, raids, and shootings directed against French security forces throughout Algeria. However shocked the French may have been, and this shock seems to be more retrospective than contemporaneous, the outbreak did not mark a sudden transition from passive acceptance of French rule to open rebellion. The FLN did not spring up over the night of the *Toussaint*. In 1950 the Mouvement pour le Triomphe des Libertés Démocratiques (a nationalist organization established in 1946 and the precursor of the MNA) had established an underground Organisation Spéciale (OS) to prepare an armed insurrection. Although short-lived (its members were quickly arrested by the French), it became a model for the FLN in terms of organization, membership, and strategy. Many early FLN militants gained experience in the OS (or, like Ben Bella, in the French military during World War II).

Yet the origins of the events of 1954 can be traced further back in history, directly to 1945, when Muslim riots in the area of Sétif caused approximately a hundred European casualties. The French authorities answered with bombardments of Algerian villages, mass arrests, and summary executions. European settlers formed vigilante squads to comb the countryside. Estimates of Algerian deaths range from a hardly modest figure of fifteen thousand to a high of forty-five thousand. The terrible memory of Sétif was a compelling motive for violent nationalism in the 1950s. It found an echo in similar circumstances at Philippeville in 1955, when Europeans were attacked by Algerian mobs. These deep historical grievances provided each side with justification for seeking revenge.

These necessarily brief references to the past suggest that the issue of responsibility for terrorism is related to the conditions that create and sustain community and identity as well as political legitimacy. Whereas the French conceived of themselves as the defenders of an essential outpost of Western civilization reacting to an unexpected outburst of violence that could only be comprehended as primitive or subversive, Algerian nationalists regarded French oppression and coercion, demonstrated so conclusively at Sétif, as a catalyst—even perhaps an opportunity—for building an Algerian identity through counterviolence. French rule had relied almost exclusively on force since the conquest of Algeria in 1830. Measures that would have provided the vast majority of Algeria's inhabitants (to most of whom even citizenship was denied) with anything approaching a state of equality, freedom, or prosperity—hence any stake in French Algeria—were vigorously suppressed by the powerful settler lobby that largely controlled Algerian policy formulated by the national assembly in Paris. A divided and ambivalent French authority in World War II and subsequent defeat of the French military in Indochina in 1954, only months before the onset of revolution in Algeria, promoted the hopes of Algerian nationalists but stiffened French resolve not to lose another battle or abandon another territory, especially after Tunisia and Morocco received their independence in 1956. Each side saw itself as the defender of fundamental values and as the victim of the unprovoked and unjustifiable violence of the other. Moderates such as Albert Camus and other liberals and intellectuals who proposed a civil truce in 1956 did exist on each side to urge the consideration of alternatives to violence, but extremists dominated decision making in both camps until the Gaullist takeover in 1958. Terrorism was a factor in both polarization and intensification of communal loyalties.

When de Gaulle came to power in May 1958, he struggled to assert control over French policy and to formulate his own conception of both French and Algerian futures. To make this conception work, he had to rein in the French military, who by 1958 virtually ruled Algeria and whose loyalty to the civilian government in Paris was tenuous. Both the necessity of combating the rebellion, manifested in rural insurgency and in urban terrorism that took its most spectacular form in the 1956–57 Battle of Algiers, and the weakness of the central institutions of the Fourth Republic had resulted in the abdication of civilian authority in Algeria. De Gaulle's conviction that the only possible solution was an independent Algeria appears to have emerged fitfully, even grudgingly, as the alternatives he offered—a referendum on autonomy, the offer of a cease-fire in the form of a *paix des braves*, economic reform through the Constantine Plan, and even an incontestable military victory through the Challe Plan in 1959–60—failed to end the conflict on French terms. Undoubtedly he also began to see Algeria as an obstacle to his grander ambitions for France on the international scene. Despite the last-ditch efforts of the OAS, FLN obstinacy and its capacity to continue a low-level war of attrition paid off in the settlement finally reached at Evian in 1962, following two years of talks. The French accepted not only full independence and recognition of the FLN but also conceded the two FLN demands that had prolonged both the negotiations and the terrorism that accompanied them—the rights of the future European minority in Algeria and the control of oil in the Sahara.

In such protracted and intense conflicts, the general level of violence is so high that terrorism does not stand out in the relief that it does in conflicts of lesser magnitude. The distinctions between terrorism and other styles of political violence can easily be blurred. Leaders of the FLN were indignant that bombs they delivered by hand to cafés and restaurants were condemned as "blind terrorism," whereas French bombs dropped from the air were not, despite their disproportionate destructiveness and indiscriminacy with regard to combatants and noncombatants. That the term was used as a political label is both undeniable and unsurprising. Nevertheless, members of the conflict did not hesitate on occasion to refer to themselves as terrorists.[8]

Political bias in identifying terrorism often obscures a deeper theoreti-

8. See the biography by Khalfa Mameri, *Abane Ramdane: Héros de la guerre d'Algérie* (Paris: L'Harmattan, 1988), 147. He characterizes a militant in Algiers whose fear of the French had made him excessively cautious as a "terrorized terrorist."

cal problem: Is the violence of the rebel comparable to the violence of the state? Is it possible to speak of both actions in the same terms or to judge their effectiveness by the same standards? Conventionally governments are thought to be both legitimate authorities and possessors of superior power, and their challengers are both illegitimate and weak. Yet the legitimacy of the French state in Algeria was weak not only in the eyes of the Muslims who constituted the vast majority; even the loyalty of the European settlers was conditional, because it was contingent on the willingness of the metropolitan government to uphold their dominant position. French sovereignty over Algeria was recognized internationally, although in practice the mountainous interior was not secure even in 1954. And as the revolution progressed, the principle of colonialism lost legitimacy in world politics. Views of the rights of colonizers underwent a transformation as international values changed. National self-determination became the prevailing moral standard after the 1960s. The legal distinction between Algeria as a department of France and Algeria as a colony appeared increasingly arbitrary.

Even if the French government could not command unqualified loyalty from its Algerian constituents, minority or majority, or sympathy from its Western allies, it did possess superior coercive power. This does not mean, however, that in general any structure of oppression based on the application of force should be labeled terrorism. The term has to be limited to the systematic resort to exemplary violence or the threat of violence against a small number of victims in order to change the attitudes of much larger popular audiences.[9] Thus, only specific government practices can qualify as terrorism. In this sense, the use of torture or the resort to the guillotine, a particularly dreadful form of execution, may be considered terrorism when they are intended to create fear in the population and to discourage potential resistance, rather than simply to acquire information or to punish. Similarly, if terrorism is defined as violence that society regards as unacceptable, whether according to the rules of war or the standards of peace, then violence that is unusually cruel or arbitrary in the view of the targeted audience, and that the perpetrator knows to be such, can reasonably be considered terrorism.

The usage of the term *counterterrorism* is even more perplexing. It is used to describe both a government's use of terrorism to oppose terrorism from a challenger and any official response, legal or otherwise, to terrorism. I use it here to refer to reactive terrorism by those in power. This approach draws a distinction between a policy of counterterrorism

9. See ch. 1, "The Concept of Revolutionary Terrorism," in Hutchinson, *Revolutionary Terrorism*, 18–39.

and what Eugene V. Walter has termed a regime of terror, which implies that the foundations of government are built on creating a state of emotional terror in its citizens.[10] Democracies, for example, might practice counterterrorism in specific instances, although their authority is not comprehensively based on stifling potential resistance from society through intimidation. These instances seem often to occur in foreign or "occupied" territory, where the military is in charge and procedures for democratic accountability are weak.

A much broader conception of terrorism is found in Pierre Vidal-Naquet's classification of four different processes of terrorism in Algeria.[11] He argues that judicial, or legal, terrorism, which applied repressive laws and sentenced rebels to the guillotine, extremist terrorism from the European civilian population, military terrorism from the paratroopers who ruled Algiers in 1957, and nationalist terrorism, principally FLN bombs, all interacted to bring about an irreversible separation of European and Muslim communities, although this may not have been their intent. Since French rule in Algeria was founded on the principle of a coercive response to Muslim self-assertion, one cannot evaluate the intentions behind nationalist terrorism without interpreting it in terms of multiple sources of terrorism. The point is not that the FLN had no choice but terrorism, or that nationalist violence was never brutal or cruel or arbitrary, but that pervasive and forceful repression of opposition constrained choices and incited terrorism out of vengeance as much as calculation. Yet it is equally important to recognize that the magnitude of force the French could bring to bear far exceeded nationalist capabilities and that the French response to Muslim violence (for example, at Sétif in 1945 or Philippeville in 1955) was immensely disproportionate. Disregard for the standards of proportionality and discrimination in response, which are critical to Western conceptions of just war, undermined French legitimacy at home and prestige abroad.

Terrorism is usually defined as instrumental and purposive violence, part of a strategic plan. It is not, however, entirely so. In Algeria, violence was often calculated for effect, but these calculations could be motivated by the desire for revenge as much as the desire to produce a change in the behavior of the adversary. Terrorism can become an end in itself. Cruel cycles of retaliatory violence, among Algerians and between Europeans and Algerians, proved impossible to bring to a halt. The FLN

10. See Eugene V. Walter *Terror and Resistance: A Study of Political Violence* (New York: Oxford University Press, 1969).

11. See his preface to the book by Jean-Luc Einaudi, *Pour l'exemple: L'affaire Fernand Iveton* (Paris: L'Harmattan, 1986), 10–11. Iveton was a European Communist who was executed for attempting to bomb the Algiers gasworks.

bombings that initiated the Battle of Algiers in 1956, for example, were responses to French executions of FLN prisoners and to civilian extremist violence, particularly the bombing of a house in the Algiers Casbah. The value of terrorism as vengeance lies in its ability to satisfy an enraged, frustrated, and often humiliated constituency in the immediate and short term. It is a means of controlling one's constituency more than influencing the adversary, but its effectiveness surely depends on the visible pain it inflicts.

It is equally difficult to draw the line between what is terrorism and what is not when analyzing violence among Algerians, which reflected antagonism between FLN and MNA, Arabs and Kabyles, among factions, tribes, and clans, and social classes. Most significant was the violence in both France and Algeria between FLN and MNA, still a little-known aspect of the war. This violence is sometimes described as terrorism, sometimes as a civil war or a war within a war, sometimes as gangsterism or banditism or criminality, but most often as a *règlement de comptes*, or settling of scores. According to Mohammed Harbi, political rivalries often degenerated into uncontrollable personal or tribal vendettas.[12] Each side blamed the other for not stopping the killings, kidnappings, and armed attacks, which left 4,000 dead and 9,000 wounded among the emigrants in France (who at the time numbered 500,000) after violence escalated in January 1956. Historian Charles-Robert Ageron estimates 10,000 Algerian deaths due to the FLN or MNA in Algeria and France combined.[13] This figure should be compared to the fewer than 3,000 French civilians killed in Algeria itself.[14] Whatever terminology proves convenient or acceptable for analytical purposes, in popular language the practice of lobbing grenades or bombs into the social establishments frequented by one's enemies has come to be called an attack *à l'algérienne*.[15]

The FLN's efforts to dominate the resistance also included measures to control both metropolitan and Algerian Muslim populations by enforc-

12. Mohammed Harbi, *Le F.L.N. mirage et réalité: Des origines à la prise du pouvoir (1945–1962)* (Paris: Editions Jeune Afrique, 1980), ch. 11, "Guerre dans la guerre: Le F.L.N. contre le M.N.A. (1954–1962)," 143–62.
13. Charles-Robert Ageron, "Les français devant la guerre civile algérienne de 1955–1962," in *La guerre*, ed. Rioux, 55.
14. According to Guy Pervillé, 2,788 French civilians in Algeria were killed in incidents of terrorism, 7,541 were wounded, and 875 disappeared before the Evian Accords in March 1962. See his "Combien de morts pendant la guerre d'Algérie?" *L'histoire* 53 (February 1983): 89.
15. See Charles Villeneuve and Jean-Pierre Péret, *Histoire secrète du terrorisme* (Paris: Plon, 1987), 60. They refer to the attack on the Drugstore–Saint Germain in Paris in 1974, which was mounted by the infamous Carlos.

ing bans on smoking and drinking (in part a boycott of French products but also an expression of Islamic puritanism) and punishing the disobedient as "traitors." Such boycotts also served to separate the Muslim population from the French government. In 1957 this policy led to the massacre of the inhabitants of a small hamlet who had transferred their allegiance to the French (in part because of the taxes and punishments such as physical mutilations that the FLN imposed). The "Melouza affair" (known by the name of the nearest town) caused consternation in France, where the Communist party accepted the FLN claim that French troops had perpetrated the atrocity. Such violence by the FLN against Muslim populations which was extensive, could be interpreted as a form of terrorism from above, or a regime of terror. At the end of the war, French authorities estimated 16,378 Muslim civilian deaths, but this figure is probably an underestimate, and it does not, in any case, include the Muslims who fought for France during the war and who were killed after independence (the estimates range from a minimum of 30,000 to a maximum of 150,000).[16]

Regardless of terminology, intra-Algerian struggles in France and in Algeria proved detrimental to the FLN cause. Blind attacks on Europeans in Algiers, shootings in Paris, massacres of peasants—all combined to create an image of the FLN as fundamentally antidemocratic.[17] Even the Communist party understood that violence among Algerians played into the hands of the supporters of Algérie française. French labor unions were indignant that the victims of violence were workers. However, the FLN consistently rejected interference—perhaps because the leadership was unable to prevent vendettas—and killings among Algerians continued unabated. Ageron notes that the FLN more than once expressed surprise that the French public did not react with more sympathy to their appeals for solidarity against police repression and against the OAS in France. They concluded too quickly, he explains, that the answer lay in racism or indifference, and forgot the fear, anger, insecurity, and disgust caused by intra-Algerian terrorism, which strengthened an image of the FLN as not only undemocratic but unrepresentative of Algerians. Racist stereotypes were only reinforced. Ageron agrees that it was legitimate to denounce the "crimes" of the OAS but reminds his readers that the OAS used Algerian terrorism as both model and justification.[18]

---

16. Pervillé, "Combien de morts," 92. Of the 210,000 *harkis* only 60,000 were relocated to France. The fate of the rest is unknown.

17. See Ageron, "Les français," and Benjamin Stora, "La gauche et les minorités anticoloniales françaises devant les divisions du nationalisme algérien (1954–1958)," in *La guerre*, ed. Rioux, 63–78.

18. Ageron, "Les français," 62.

FLN TERRORISM AGAINST THE FRENCH

Terrorism against European civilians—bombings, shootings, and selective assassinations of notable political figures—figured prominently in the war, especially in Algeria, but in metropolitan France as well. The FLN generally acknowledged that this activity was terrorism, although of course justifiable. It was intended to compel the French government to accede to demands as well as to reinforce the authority of the FLN within the nationalist movement and its legitimacy in the eyes of audiences in Algeria, France, and the world. In France, violence against the French and their property was meant to "bring the war home."

The Battle of Algiers

The Battle of Algiers represents a classic case of urban terrorism. It was a contest between the FLN's underground network, the Zone Autonome d'Alger (ZAA), under the leadership of Yacef Saadi, and the French paratrooper units under General Massu, who took charge of the Algiers region in January 1957. The battle opened in September 1956 with FLN bombings of popular gathering spots for European youth. It ended in the fall of 1957, when the leadership of the ZAA was crushed through arrests and killings.[19]

The decision to organize attacks on Europeans in Algiers was collective and high-level, the work of the FLN's top leadership, the Comité de Coordination et d'Exécution (CCE), an executive body established as a result of the Congress of Soummam, a meeting in Algeria's Soummam Valley held in the summer of 1956 to assess the course of the revolution. A complex set of factors impelled the leadership to move in the direction of urban terrorism.

A key motive was vengeance, driven by the FLN leadership's perception that the popular demand for anti-French action had to be satisfied if the FLN was to maintain its credibility. Two events exacerbated Muslim anger. In June 1956 Robert Lacoste, the resident minister of Algiers, decided to begin guillotining condemned FLN prisoners. In August a group of European extremists bombed a house on the rue de Thèbes in the Casbah of Algiers, causing nearly a hundred casualties. Although an investigation immediately identified the right-wing "ultra" group

---

19. Two basic accounts of the events from different viewpoints are General Jacques Massu, *La vraie bataille d'Alger* (Paris: Plon, 1971), and Mohamed Lebjaoui, *Bataille d'Alger ou bataille d'Algérie?* (Paris: Gallimard, 1972). Memoirs also include Yacef Saadi, *Souvenirs de la bataille d'Alger* (Paris: Julliard, 1962), and Zohra Drif, *La mort de mes frères* (Paris: Maspéro, 1960).

responsible, no charges were brought, probably because of police complicity.[20] This combination of repressiveness and vigilantism also deepened the disillusionment of many nationalists who had earlier hoped that French liberals might be influential in shaping policy on Algeria and who had trusted the Socialist party's 1956 campaign promise to seek peace in Algeria. Prime Minister Guy Mollet's capitulation to extremist sentiment in his nomination of Lacoste as resident minister, his request for special powers to suppress the rebellion, and the failure of liberal efforts to institute a civil truce left moderate nationalists dismayed and discouraged. One Algerian writer argues that the prospect of "blind and collective terrorism" against Europeans was never even mentioned before the June executions, although *groupes de choc*, the "shock troops" of the ZAA, were already in place in Algiers.[21] The FLN's top leadership was at the Soummam conference during the month of August when the rue de Thèbes bombing occurred, so their reaction was delayed.

The political situation of the CCE also compelled them to act in the fall of 1956. One of the leadership's central aims was to gain the support of the Algerian population and to engage the masses in the struggle. The CCE had deliberately chosen Algiers as its headquarters and constituted the city as an autonomous zone, independent of Algeria's regional-zone structure of *wilayas*. Failing to defend or avenge the population of Algiers would have undercut the legitimacy of the newly installed leadership and would have weakened their ability to influence Algeria's urban populations. Terrorism, then, was not an alternative to mass struggle but a way of mobilizing and controlling collective action.

Furthermore, two of the resolutions agreed to at the Soummam conference were now being put to the test. The leaders assembled there, who themselves represented the interior *wilayas*, agreed that in the conduct of the war, leaders and militants within the country should take precedence over leaders who initially were established in Cairo. Terrorism in Algiers would prove that the revolt could be directed from within the country and that resistance need not depend on the exiled leadership. The leaders also thought of urban terrorism as a fundamentally political strategy. Thus it was seen as a practical demonstration of

20. See Bernard Droz and Evelyne Lever, *Histoire de la guerre d'Algérie, 1954–1962* (Paris: Editions du Seuil, 1982), 97. The same group was later responsible for a bazooka attack on General Raoul Salan in January 1957 (see ibid., 98–99). At the time, he was considered insufficiently sympathetic to the cause of French Algeria.

21. Mameri, *Abane Ramdane*, 240 and 243. In general, see his ch. 19, "Alger la rouge, capitale de la révolution," 235–51. Lebjaoui (in *Bataille d'Alger*, 18–19) also calls the September bombings a reply to European terrorism.

the supremacy of politics over military strategy, which was a second premise agreed to at Soummam.

Two members of the CCE appear to have been the key figures in these decisions. One was Larbi Ben M'Hidi, one of the original leaders of the 1954 uprising. The other was Ramdane Abane, who quickly rose to prominence within the FLN after his release from prison in 1955. Ben M'Hidi apparently felt that only urban terrorism could win popular support in Algeria and recognition abroad.[22] As early as the spring of 1955, Abane developed firm convictions about the direction of the war. He apparently wanted to base the struggle on mass participation and to unite all Algerians, regardless of past affiliations, social class, or ethnic background. He also had a sophisticated conception of what a revolutionary war should be: not a military contest but a symbolic, or psychological, conflict. Tactics that could seize the popular imagination were thus essential. Algiers, as the most powerful symbol of French colonialism, was a natural site. Abane also placed a premium on efficient organization, an essential precondition for urban terrorism, and he had already begun creating an underground structure in Algiers. By September 1956 five thousand militants organized in the ZAA, under Ben M'Hidi's operational authority, had seized control of the Casbah from the criminal elements who pervaded Muslim society, and established a secure network of underground cells.[23] The possession of this capability was critical to the initiation of terrorism in the fall of 1956, and it indicates that the events that apparently precipitated terrorism as a response to French repression—the executions and the bombing in the Casbah—determined the timing of the opening of the Battle of Algiers but not necessarily the FLN's judgment that urban terrorism against European civilians would be a useful strategy.

Moreover, it seems clear that Abane deliberately sought to "accelerate repression," that is, to provoke French counterterrorism.[24] His view was that separating the Algerian people from the colonial system required a sharp and brutal break. The possibility of compromise had to be banished. He argued that the provocation of French repression was a necessary evil, justifiable because it would force the population into the arms of the FLN. Yet it is also claimed that Abane did not necessarily

22. See Yves Courrière, *La guerre d'Algérie*, vol. 2, *Le temps des léopards* (Paris: Fayard, 1969), 394–95. Courrière's four-volume history of the war is still regarded as comprehensive and reliable, although journalistic. Based on extensive interviews with participants, it is frequently cited by Algerian sources. Other observers, however, find Courrière too sympathetic to the FLN.

23. Droz and Lever, *Histoire de la guerre*, 128.

24. Mameri, *Ramdane Abane*, 132–38.

consider attacks on European civilians essential to a strategy of moving the war to the cities. The executions and the rue de Thèbes bomb forced his hand.[25] Possibly Abane also promoted a radical line in order to maintain his authority within the FLN, since his accession to power was recent and he was not well liked, because he was dictatorial and autocratic.[26]

The idea of moving the struggle to the capital was also a result of the FLN's evaluation of the progress of the war, which in 1954 and 1955 consisted largely of poorly coordinated and hence inconsequential rural guerrilla warfare that the French could easily dismiss as traditional banditry.[27] The burden of the struggle was thus borne by the peasant population and the Armée de Libération Nationale (ALN) in the countryside. Urban terrorism could create a diversion to relieve military pressure on the rural ALN units.[28] This line of reasoning might imply that urban terrorism resulted from the failure of rural guerrilla warfare. However, instead of being pessimistic about the course of the war, the FLN leadership at this time was apparently unduly optimistic. Abane and Ben M'Hidi are said to have thought that victory was close and that terrorism could rouse the Algiers population to an open revolt that would be the final step to independence. Under revolutionary conditions, then, terrorism would serve to mobilize popular mass action as much as to intimidate the French. It would be the final push.

Thus, the general strike that the FLN called for January 1957, to coincide with a meeting of the U.N. General Assembly, may have been the result of overconfidence.[29] It was also part of a concerted campaign to attract international attention. FLN leaders generally agreed that only urban terrorism could put Algerian independence on the international agenda. The FLN was determined to see the General Assembly debate the question in 1957, since the Bandung conference of 1955 had given significant impetus to the forces of anticolonialism. International attention would also reinforce the dominance of the interior leadership.

25. Ibid., 243. Droz and Lever (*Histoire de la guerre*, 128) say that the decision was made at the Soummam congress but also that the rue de Thèbes bombing removed Abane's last scruples.

26. Harbi, *Le F.L.N.*, 197.

27. Attacks on individuals, which the French refer to as *attentats*, in cities were common throughout the war, however. What distinguished the campaign in Algiers was its indiscriminateness and its intensity, as well as its location.

28. This is suggested by a number of courses, including Harbi, *Le F.L.N.*, esp. ch. 13, "L'échec d'Abbane (1956–1957)," 195–205. See also his important edited collection of documents, *Les archives de la révolution algérienne* (Paris: Editions Jeune Afrique, 1981).

29. See Harbi, *Le F.L.N.*, 197. See also Slimane Chikh, *L'Algérie en armes ou le temps des certitudes* (Paris: Economica, 1981), 101.

According to Slimane Chikh, "In intensifying the struggle in the interior of the country and in carrying agitation to the capital, the CCE intended to show the Algerian public and international opinion that the principal resource of the struggle for national liberation was in the interior."[30] The FLN organization in the metropole, the Fédération de France du F.L.N., supported the decision to call a general strike. They felt that France was on the verge of financial ruin and that public opinion in Algiers and in France could be turned against the war. In their view, the duration of the war was likely to be short, and terrorism could hasten its end.[31]

Clearly the FLN expected to provoke a reaction from the French government. However, it is doubtful that they foresaw the intensity and scope of the repression that actually resulted. In the short term, repression was so comprehensive and devastating that the principles that supported terrorism were contradicted. In hindsight, anyone could have foreseen that the European population of Algiers would not tolerate FLN terrorism. The police forces seemed incapable of bringing it to a halt, since the FLN underground organization was well entrenched. Nor could the police control the European reaction. The December 1956 funeral of an important leader of the settler community assassinated by an FLN team precipitated mob attacks on Muslims. An uncontrollable cycle of retaliation and provocation quickly developed, in part because of popular pressures but also because of the decentralization of the FLN underground. From the FLN perspective, operational autonomy at the lower levels of the organization was necessary for both security and efficiency. Although the CCE had given the original order to attack European targets, a committee could not direct day-to-day operations. In fact, the French military captured and killed Ben M'Hidi in February. Shortly thereafter the CCE fled Algiers for Tunisia, abandoning the principle of the primacy of the interior. The conflict developed into a "battle" between the ZAA and the paratroopers who were brought in to stop terrorism, each force enjoying considerable autonomy from higher political authority.

The FLN's January call for a general strike came when European panic was at a height because of terrorism. In desperation, Lacoste called on General Massu, commander of the Tenth Paratroop Division, to assume responsibility for maintaining order in Algiers. Police inability to

30. Chikh, *L'Algérie en armes*, 102. Translated by the author, as are all subsequent translations, unless otherwise noted.
31. Harbi, *Le F.L.N.*, 197. See also Ali Haroun, *La 7e Wilaya: La guerre du FLN en France, 1954–1962* (Paris: Seuil, 1986).

stop terrorism resulted not just from the intractability of the problem but from the settlers' rejection of reinforcements from metropolitan France and their preference for paratroopers.[32] In turn, the paratroopers welcomed Lacoste's invitation. The military doctrine of *guerre révolutionnaire*, elaborated as a result of counterinsurgency experiences in Indochina and now applied to Algeria, conveniently justified political intervention.[33] The doctrine recommended pacification of populations (often through resettlement) and psychological action, both fundamentally political tasks. As a result, the army became the government in many areas of Algeria. The lines between civil and military authority were erased.

Initially the military responded to terrorism by instituting a rigid control of the Muslim population of Algiers. Paratrooper units sealed off Muslim quarters of the city and systematically interrogated and registered or arrested their inhabitants. No Muslim could enter the European sections of Algiers without passing through checkpoints manned by the military. (The FLN circumvented this tactic by selecting Algerian women who could pass as Europeans to carry bombs into downtown Algiers.) Colonel Yves Godard, who later became a leader of the OAS, designated himself chief of police. Seizing the records of the police intelligence division (Renseignements Généraux), the paratroopers arrested fifteen hundred suspects on the first day of Godard's appointment (8 January 1957). Only fifty of these suspects were subsequently turned over to the police to be charged with crimes.[34]

The military also relied on the acquisition of information through torture. Although torture was common in Algeria from the beginning of the rebellion, the method assumed a critical importance in the French response to urban terrorism. There can be no doubt that the highest levels of government consented to the practice. The paratrooper units made no attempt to conceal their reliance on torture, although some (very few) officers disapproved. General Massu himself excused the use of torture and admitted that it was institutionalized and systematic.[35] Colonel Roger Trinquier, Massu's assistant and one of the principal exponents of the *guerre révolutionnaire* doctrine, similarly argued that

32. Jacques Delarue, "La police en paravent et au rempart," in *La guerre*, ed. Rioux, 257–68.

33. See Claude d'Abzac-Epezy, "La société militaire, de l'ingérence à l'ignorance," in *La guerre*, ed. Rioux, 248. On French counterinsurgency doctrine, see the excellent analysis by Peter Paret, *French Revolutionary Warfare from Indochina to Algeria* (London: Pall Mall Press, 1964).

34. Delarue, "La police," 260.

35. Massu, *La vraie bataille*, 166–70.

torture was a reality that rebels should anticipate. It was unexceptional, simply one of the risks of war.[36]

Repression may have been effective in the short run and in the local setting, since the FLN networks were completely destroyed and the city of Algiers secured for Europeans, but the long-run political implications were costly for the French. In June 1957 the paratroopers arrested a professor at the University of Algiers, Maurice Audin. He subsequently disappeared, a victim of the summary executions that often followed the torture of suspects. His case was taken up by the university community and widely publicized in France. Another intellectual, Henri Alleg, then published an account of his arrest and torture at the hands of the paratroopers.[37] These two cases, as well as open criticism of torture from within the military,[38] provoked public outcry in France, primarily on the Left and from intellectuals. Prime Minister Guy Mollet appointed a special commission to investigate these charges, with minimum effect, but the government also reacted with more defensiveness than liberality by censoring the press. The effect of these revelations on French public opinion was not dramatic, and most French continued to resist the idea of withdrawal from Algeria. Yet recognition of the use of torture contributed to the growing unpopularity of the war. Discomfort over the methods used to combat terrorism now supplemented dislike for conscription and distress over the cost of the war.[39]

Although Albert Camus was not typical of French intellectuals, because of his personal ties to Algeria, still his reaction to FLN terrorism illustrates the painful dilemma that trapped many liberals. Since the 1930s Camus had criticized French policies in Algeria and defended Algerian dissidents. However, in 1957 his remark that he would defend his mother before he would defend justice, made when he was in Stockholm to accept the Nobel Prize for Literature, created a scandal. As noted in a recent study of French intellectuals and the Algerian war, his situation demonstrates a general problem for intellectuals who are engaged in politics, not in choosing sides in the conflict but in approving

36. See Roger Trinquier, *Guerre, subversion, révolution* (Paris: Robert Laffont, 1968), 70. This was also the attitude Raymond Aron voiced in an interview I held with him in Paris in 1970.

37. Henri Alleg, *La question* (Paris: Minuit, 1958). The book was published in February and seized by the government in March, but seventy thousand copies had already been sold. The government's action provoked an open protest by four of France's leading authors—Mauriac, Martin du Gard, Malraux, and Sartre (Droz and Lever, *Histoire de la guerre*, 161).

38. General Jacques Pâris de la Bollardière later wrote his account of the affair in *Bataille d'Alger, bataille de l'homme* (Paris: Desclée de Brouwer, 1972).

39. Droz and Lever, *Histoire de la guerre*, 148.

all the actions of the chosen side. Aversion to terrorism and to violence against civilians often makes political engagement problematic.[40] Camus had been a patron of the failed movement for a "civil truce" in Algiers in 1956, which had earned him the admiration of many Muslims but death threats from the European community, and since then had refused to comment on the war. He had, however, explained his position privately: "If a terrorist throws a grenade in the market at Belcourt, where my mother shops, and kills her, I would be responsible if, in defending justice, I have also defended terrorism. I love justice, but I also love my mother."[41] In his comments at Stockholm, he had explained that his silence over the past year and eight months was due to the fear that any declaration he made could only be divisive and aggravate the terror, in light of the hatred that had grown on both sides. He noted pointedly that he had always condemned terror and that now he must condemn terrorism as well.[42]

As a reflection of FLN strategy, the Battle of Algiers spelled "a crushing defeat," according to Mohammed Harbi.[43] The now-discredited CCE went into exile, an event that decisively influenced the future of the FLN because the leadership was now exiled from Algerian territory for the duration of the war. The principle of the primacy of the interior leadership had to be dropped ignominiously. The ZAA effectively ceased to exist as its cadres were arrested or killed. The urban population was left without leaders or structure, creating a vacuum that persists today. Harbi even blames Abane's eventual death on the departure from Algiers.[44] After the CCE transferred its headquarters to Tunis, bitter recriminations broke out among the leadership. Abane, who might have found allies had the CCE remained in Algiers, was politically isolated and vulnerable. His rivals for power within the FLN assassinated him in Morocco in 1957.

A further consequence of the ZAA's defeat was a phenomenon known as the *bleuite*. The *guerre révolutionnaire* doctrine stressed psychological warfare, including "intoxification." Accordingly French military intelligence seized the opportunity furnished by the defeat of the ZAA to

40. Jean-Pierre Rioux and Jean-François Sirinelli, eds., *La guerre d'Algérie et les intellectuels français* (Paris: Editions Complexes, 1991), 13. See also David L. Schalk, *War and the Ivory Tower: Algeria and Vietnam* (New York: Oxford University Press, 1991).
41. Albert Camus, *Essais* (Paris: Bibliothèque de la Pléiade, 1965), 1843. This is quoted by Roger Quilliot in his commentary on the collected essays.
42. Ibid., 1881–83, containing the Stockholm declaration and a letter of clarification to *Le Monde*.
43. Harbi, *Le F.L.N.*, 199.
44. Ibid., 205. This is a seldom-discussed episode.

mount a counterintelligence operation to convince the leaders of the rural *wilayas* that the students and intellectuals fleeing from the city to the countryside were actually French agents (who were called *bleus de chauffe* because of the blue work clothes they were assigned to wear). The *wilaya* leaders reacted with widespread torture and a bloody purge of "traitors," leaving in the immediate aftermath an estimated two thousand Algerians dead.[45]

There was no mass insurrection as a result of urban terrorism, but Pierre Montagnon concludes that nationalism took a decisive hold in the Algiers Muslim population as a result of French repression. Because the French authorities suspected all Muslims of being terrorists and persecuted them simply for their identity, the consciousness of separation grew.[46] The FLN defeat, in his view, was more apparent than real. Abane's goal of provocation succeeded over the long term. In December 1960, when de Gaulle visited Algiers, thousands of Muslims took to the streets to call openly for independence. By dividing Muslims from Europeans, terrorism and the response to terrorism revealed the flaws in the conception of "integration" between Algeria and metropolitan France. The French government would not have applied the same methods to a domestic terrorist group, such as Corsicans or Bretons, nor were they applied to the OAS. The empire came to be seen as something that was not noble or civilizing but brutal and dirty.

René Gallissot suggests that the significance of the Battle of Algiers lay in two consequences for the Algerian future. First, the shift of the war to the countryside negated the concept of an urban struggle led by cadres with political experience, as Abane had prescribed in the Soummam program. This reversal did not mean that the war was transformed into a peasant revolution, as Frantz Fanon and the future leaders of Algeria liked to claim, but it relegated militants who were urban, modern, and francophone to secondary status. Second, the displacement of the CCE to Tunis not only stifled the idea of the primacy of the interior forces but brought to power a military leadership with few political skills. The FLN as a political entity never really came into existence.[47]

The authority of the French government and its commitment to

45. Droz and Lever, *Histoire de la guerre*, 209. For a horrifying account of the effects of the *bleuite* on the morale and fighting capabilities of the ALN, see Mohammed Benyahia, *La conjuration au pouvoir: Récit d'un maquisard de l'A.L.N.* (Paris: Arcantère, 1988). Certainly the system that was instituted in these areas could be called a regime of terror.
46. Pierre Montagnon, *La guerre d'Algérie: Genèse et engrenage d'une tragédie* (Paris: Editions Pygmalion/Gérard Watelet, 1984), 213.
47. Gallisot, "La guerre," 95–96. See also William B. Quandt, *Revolution and Political Leadership: Algeria, 1954–1962* (Cambridge: MIT Press, 1969), 129–32.

democracy were damaged as well. The Fourth Republic relinquished its political authority to the military not only in Algiers but throughout Algeria, where military units were relegated the tasks of day-to-day governing. The military had grown suspicious of politicians after the defeat in Indochina. Now mistrust hardened into contempt for the indecisiveness of the leaders of the Fourth Republic. The extreme means used in Algeria could only be justified in terms of an absolutely worthy end, the maintenance of French Algeria, an integral part of the national territory. Criticism of torture, which was regarded as essential to the defeat of terrorism, only made the military more defensive and more committed to eventual victory. Furthermore, the paratroopers emerged from the Battle of Algiers as triumphant heroes to the Europeans. As some factions of the military, particularly the elite paratrooper units, transferred their allegiance from the institutions of the republic to the cause of French Algeria, an environment conducive to the emergence of the OAS was created. So, too, were the conditions for the collapse of the Fourth Republic, which fell in 1958.

Terrorism in France: The Second Front

The FLN's metropolitan branch, the Fédération de France du F.L.N. (FFFLN), managed operations in France. For the first four years of the war, the FFFLN concentrated on trying to wrest control of the Algerian workers in France (an important source of funds) away from the MNA, which was the traditional representative of Algerian nationalism. Yet the CCE also intended to carry the war to France in the sense of making it painful for the French population, using the same methods of urban terrorism they considered appropriate for Algiers. Their purpose was to divert the attention of the French security forces from Algeria and also to make the war unpopular with the civilian population of the metropole. In January 1957 an emissary from Algeria arrived in Paris with the mission of organizing retaliatory strikes to exact revenge for French violence in Algeria. Only his arrest a month later kept him from organizing attacks on targets such as the metro. He was quickly replaced, and the FFFLN began the process of creating an efficient *organisation spéciale*. Its first action, in May 1957, was the assassination of a prominent pro-French Algerian leader who was visiting French officials in Paris.[48]

De Gaulle's return to power in 1958 provoked both the formation of a

---

48. See Mohammed Lebjaoui, *Vérités sur la révolution algérienne* (Paris: Gallimard, 1970), 77. See also Haroun, *La 7e Wilaya*, ch. 5, "Le second front," 85–111.

provisional Algerian government (the Gouvernement Provisoire de la République Algérienne, or GPRA) and a renewed determination to carry the struggle to France. What the FLN hoped to achieve, other than to bring the war home to France, was apparently a repressive reaction that would expose the latent racism behind French policy. Yet even the directions issued by the CCE reflected the intraelite conflict between extremists and moderates. The CCE announced that although the FLN intended to avoid civilian casualties, it disengaged itself in advance from responsibility for them. Simultaneously, this announcement urged the French population to take a stand to bring the war to an end through a negotiated solution.[49]

Strategic calculations about the utility of terrorism were based on FLN assumptions about the role of metropolitan public opinion. According to Mohammed Harbi, until 1956 the FLN leadership was relatively optimistic about the possibilities of French support for a negotiated solution, but the passage of the special powers law in March 1956, under a Socialist government, destroyed this hope. It also reinforced the power of extremists within the FLN who saw no possibility other than armed struggle and whose nationalism bordered on xenophobia. According to Harbi, the FFFLN was more sensitive than the central leadership to the contradictions inherent in a strategy that pretended to persuade by the use of force, so that its leaders defied repeated orders from the CCE. As a result, the central FLN leadership purged opponents of terrorism from the ranks of the FFFLN. Harbi claims that after May 1958 elites who had no interest in French support or in coexistence with the Europeans of Algeria controlled FLN policy. From then on, plans for assassinations of French politicians and armed attacks on French territory went unchallenged. Ferhat Abbas, as the new president of the GPRA, told a newspaper interviewer in October that the FFFLN was behind attacks on civilians and that the CCE had tried to restrain them.[50] Yet Ali Haroun, who was an FFFLN leader, argues that the FFFLN leadership was constantly concerned with separating the French people from their political leaders, that they always wanted to make an ally out of the French populations, and that they never even tried to launch a campaign of "blind terrorism," although it would have been ridiculously easy.

49. *El Moudjahid*, no. 29, 17 September 1958, 9. See also *Le Monde*, 28 August 1958, 3. For a discussion of the ambiguities in the FLN's public position, see Hutchinson, *Revolutionary Terrorism*, 93–99.

50. Front de Libération Nationale, Fédération de France, *Documents à l'addresse du peuple français*, no. 1, January 1959, 8 and 10–11, and *Le Monde*, 15 October 1958, 2. Ali Haroun, however, disputes Abbas's contention; he says there was no restraining order from above and no conflict between the GPRA and the FFFLN (*La 7e Wilaya*, 109–10).

Arguments from lower-level militants that terrorism should be adopted to avenge police repression were always rejected.[51]

The first wave of anti-European terrorism in France immediately preceded the French constitutional referendum of September 1958, which the FLN hoped to derail. In August and September terrorism caused twenty-two French deaths.[52] The FLN attacked police stations— including the Paris *préfecture*, where three policemen were killed— munitions factories, and oil refineries (oil was apparently targeted as a symbol of French colonial exploitation). Particularly alarming to public opinion was a huge explosion and fire at Mourepiane, near Marseille. On 15 September the FLN attempted to assassinate Minister of Information and former governor general of Algeria Jacques Soustelle. They unsuccessfully tried to bomb the Eiffel Tower, although this was later explained as an attempt to destroy a radio transmitter operated by the French intelligence services. Ali Haroun claims that although the attempt on the Eiffel Tower aroused a wave of indignation and accusations that the FLN was directed by a bunch of terrorists, the bomb would not have damaged the tower itself.[53]

Despite Haroun's denials, tension between the central leadership and the FFFLN seems to have grown. In August 1959 a confidential report to the GPRA advocated terrorism in France as an urgent priority. The report claimed that the August 1958 offensive made the French feel the danger of war and constituted a "victory" for the FLN. The FLN's ability to act in a hostile environment impressed both the French people and their military leaders and won respect and recognition. Already the lapse in violence had diminished the positive effects of the August bombings.[54]

After de Gaulle announced a policy of self-determination for Algeria in September 1959, the FLN softened its views somewhat, but some elements of the leadership still held the French public responsible for the crimes of the army in Algeria. In an interesting analogy, the FLN

51. Haroun, *La 7e Wilaya*, 106–9.

52. Courrière, *La guerre d'Algérie*, vol. 3, *L'heure des colonels*, 407, and Haroun, *La 7e Wilaya*, 92–97 and 111. According to press accounts, there were sixty-seven French deaths in the four years between 1956 and 1960, most bystanders in clashes between Algerians or between Algerians and the police. Twenty police were killed in the same period. See *Le Monde*, 24–25 January 1960, 5.

53. Haroun, *La 7e Wilaya*, 103.

54. See Ahmed Boumendjel, "Le gouvernement provisoire de la république algérienne face à la France," in *Les archives*, ed. Harbi, 250–53 and 256. It is worth noting that the report uses the term *terrorism* specifically. Boumendjel, whose brother was a victim of the Battle of Algiers, later represented the FLN in negotiations with the French government at Melun. See Montagnon, *La guerre d'Algérie*, 319.

accused the French of being as guilty as the Germans were for the atrocities of the Second World War.[55] When talks opened between the GPRA and the French in Melun in June 1960, the GPRA issued orders to cease all armed action in France. The FFFLN complained that such a halt would certainly have a favorable effect on French public opinion but not on morale within the organization. They had been planning another August 1958 as a response to French repression and now had to demobilize and call it off. In November 1960 the police killed one of the FFFLN's leaders, leading to the discussion of the possibility of "collective reprisals" such as bombs in the metro, but Haroun asserts that "reason triumphed": "Blind terrorism is neither morally acceptable nor politically profitable."[56]

Although the FFFLN described the terrorism of the summer of 1958 as successful and claimed to wish to repeat it, terrorism in France did not have a decisive impact on French policy or on the fortunes of the FLN, other than to increase the incidence of police persecution and mistreatment of Algerian workers.[57] The leaders of the FFFLN's *organisation spéciale* had to flee the country after the "offensive" in 1958, and the French installed Muslim auxiliary forces (the *harkis*) in Paris, who then became the most frequent targets of FFFLN violence. Terrorism may have contributed to the coercive reaction to Algerian proindependence demonstrations in 1961 and the tolerance some police showed for the OAS. Haroun himself complains that the FFFLN's actions were misunderstood. The press portrayed them as gratuitous terrorism, which aroused xenophobia among the French public, when in reality their attacks were carefully planned, each decision to "execute" someone, especially a European civilian, scrupulously reviewed, with no intention of alienating the French public.[58]

Terrorism and Negotiations

As the possibility of a negotiated compromise became a reality, terrorism continued. It served to pressure the French to recognize the legitimacy of the FLN (and thus to reject alternatives) and to agree to specific FLN demands. De Gaulle's projected compromise solutions, such as elections without prior recognition of the FLN, were dangerous because they were attractive to some sectors of Muslim opinion. At least one interior

55. Mohammed Harbi, "Le FLN et l'opinion française," in *La guerre*, ed. Rioux, 45–52.

56. Haroun, *La 7e Wilaya*, 406 and 429.

57. Montagnon's history of the war, for example, does not mention metropolitan terrorism. Droz and Lever mention it only briefly, without discussing its consequences.

58. Haroun, *La 7e Wilaya*, 425–26.

wilaya leader went over to the French. Consequently terrorism in Algeria accompanied terrorism in the metropole in the summer of 1958, although the CCE encountered opposition to this decision, especially from the Tunisians and the Moroccans on whose goodwill the FLN's ability to position ALN units on the frontiers depended. Nasser, on the other hand, supported the extremists.[59] The FLN found itself in a position of extreme military weakness after the successes of a massive French military offensive known as the Challe Plan, in 1959 and 1960. General Challe was appointed commander in chief to replace General Salan in the fall of 1958. Under his direction, the French reinforced the Morice Line on the Tunisian frontier to interdict supplies and reinforcements for the ALN and began a series of sweeps from west to east. The military estimated 26,000 "rebels" killed and 10,800 captured.[60] ALN units in the rural interior were badly fragmented, and the French strategy of *quadrillage*, based on leaving substantial units in place to protect the population and guard communications after ALN forces were wiped out, paralyzed the FLN's political and administrative apparatus.

Only terrorism remained if the FLN wanted to influence French decisions.[61] Each political overture from de Gaulle elicited attacks on French civilians. For example, in September 1959 de Gaulle invited the FLN to participate in elections but refused to recognize the GPRA as the sole legitimate representative of the Algerian people. The FLN then bombed department stores in Algeria. In August 1960, after the Melun talks in June failed to achieve a resolution, uniformed ALN forces fired on a European crowd at a beach near Algiers, killing twelve civilians. A bus exploded in Algiers in September. Such attacks continued sporadically through 1960 and 1961.[62]

Divisions and frustration within the nationalist camp may have accounted for some of these incidents. The internal *wilayas* were increasingly isolated from the central leadership after 1959. The ALN units on the front line understandably resented the comforts enjoyed by the provisional government and ALN formations stationed across the border. This argument is not, however, completely compatible with evidence that the interior leaders were eager for a settlement and an end to the fighting that terrorism could be expected to prolong. Perhaps terrorism was related to the struggle between extremists and moderates within the GPRA, since terrorism could have been meant to hold the GPRA to

59. Droz and Lever, *Histoire de la guerre*, 211–12.
60. Montagnon, *La guerre d'Algérie*, 296.
61. See Droz and Lever, *Histoire de la guerre*, 267–69.
62. See Hutchinson, *Revolutionary Terrorism*, 69–70. One finds little discussion of these events in either French or Algerian sources.

an intransigent line. Or it could have been meant to pressure the French or the GPRA into the concessions that would bring the war to an end. In the end, the French won the Algerian war (which still is not officially designated as a war) militarily. The ALN was decisively defeated. But military victory did not end the threat of terrorism, which served as a constant reminder that the pacification of Algeria would never be complete and that holding on would be costly. In creating insecurity among the European population, terrorism pressured the French government to come to terms. The tragic and ironic counterpoint was that it simultaneously fueled European extremism, which made it harder for the government to grant the FLN's demands.

OAS TERRORISM

Established in 1960, the OAS moved to action in January 1961 with the assassination of a liberal European lawyer in Algiers. The organization represented an alliance of military leaders—such as Generals Raoul Salan and Edmond Jouhaud and Colonel Yves Godard, one of the heroes of the Battle of Algiers—and a disparate and unruly group of civilian extremists. Factionalism was rampant despite the outer trappings of military discipline and the deliberate imitation of FLN organization and tactics, particularly the cellular underground structure of the Algiers zone. Each leader brought his own personal entourage into the OAS, which seriously hampered operational coordination. The only efficient sections of the OAS were the assassination squads, known as Delta Commandos, under the command of a former paratrooper, Roger Degueldre. They numbered under a hundred former military and European activists. The total number of active OAS members in Algeria was probably around a thousand, but the *pied-noir* population provided enthusiastic auxiliary support. The operational command structure was split between Madrid, Algiers, and Paris. The metropolitan organization, OAS-métro, resisted directions from the putative OAS world headquarters in Madrid. Algiers and Oran were empires to themselves. Despite the carefully cultivated image of calculated violence (*L'OAS frappe ou il veut*), the reality was otherwise.

The origins of the OAS lie in the convergence of a number of factors. One was a political culture of violent extremism and intrigue among the European settlers of Algeria that nurtured paramilitary formations. To this set of attitudes was added an often virulent racism. The *pieds-noirs* of Algeria admitted no compromise with Algerian aspirations. With few exceptions, their conception of political relations between Algerians and Europeans was based on the belief that force was required to maintain the dominance of the minority over the majority. The prospect of majority rule, an independent Algeria governed by Muslims, invoked only despair. A recent analysis has pointed out that "for the 900,000 Europeans of Algeria the defense of French Algeria was not a political choice but a vital reflex, the defense of an identity."[63] Because the issue was what was to be lost, not what was to be gained, the extreme Right had always found a more sympathetic hearing in Algeria than in France, where the partisans of Algérie française initially came from diverse political currents, including supporters of reforms and of negotiations with the FLN. Yet it is also fair to say that there was little in the FLN attitude after 1959 that could bring comfort to settlers. In the negotiations between the French government and the GPRA, extremists within the FLN displayed little faith in the future of coexistence, and radicals had replaced moderates in the leadership by the summer of 1961. Terrorism against Europeans during the negotiations spread fear and exasperation through a European community whose anxiety was intensified by the suspicion that the government in Paris planned to abandon them.

The military wing of the OAS drew its strength from the elite paratrooper units, although the top leadership included Generals Raoul Salan, the former commander in chief in Algeria and hero of Indochina, and Edmond Jouhaud, who was raised near Oran. The Tenth Paratrooper Division, the victors of the Battle of Algiers who had since become "an army within an army,"[64] supplied many of the colonels who became active in the OAS. Colonel Godard, who is described by General Jouhaud as the real driving force behind the OAS, had acted as chief of police in Algiers.[65] Colonel Lacheroy was an author of the doctrine of *guerre révolutionnaire*, a strong influence on the development of OAS strategy. The *guerre révolutionnaire* doctrine and experience combating the FLN taught the OAS the simple lesson that terrorism was effective. The myth of the efficacy of terrorism was a reaction to the failure to win the "hearts and minds" of the Algerian people as well as a lesson badly learned. The failure to win Algerian loyalty had to be explained by some means other than the power of nationalism or the inappropriateness of French methods.[66] Muslims were thought of as either intimidated by the FLN or

---

63. Serge Berstein, "La peau de chagrin de l'Algérie française," in *La guerre*, ed. Rioux, 209.

64. Droz and Lever, *Histoire de la guerre*, 291.

65. Edmond Jouhaud, *O mon pays perdu: De Bou Sfer à Tulle* (Paris: Fayard, 1969), 213.

66. The concept of efficacy implies that some inherent quality in terrorism confers the power to achieve a desired effect.

sensitive only to force, an analysis that proceeded logically to the remedy of applying superior force, or counterterrorism. It was also intolerable to think of throwing away the military victory that the Challe Plan of 1959–60 had produced. Some officers were also consumed by bitterness at having been betrayed by the man they had brought to power in May 1958 in confident, though vain, hopes of preserving French Algeria. It is also indisputable that some military were genuinely committed to the Muslims whom they had recruited to the French cause (200,000 Muslims were serving in the French army in 1960).

Thus, by 1960 two groups were poised to oppose the move toward independence. As de Gaulle's intentions slowly clarified, the proponents of Algérie française absorbed the realization that they had been mistaken, if not deceived. Their first impulse was to foment a popular insurrection in Algiers, and failing that a coup d'état, but as it happened, neither tactic succeeded in moving the army to the side of French Algeria. The first disappointment came with the Barricades Affair of January 1960, when civilian extremists, responding to FLN terrorism and what was perceived as government "softness" toward it, attempted to engineer an urban uprising in Algiers. Although de Gaulle had to promise not to negotiate with the GPRA and to establish special courts for FLN terrorists, the revolt was crushed, and those military officers who had shown too much sympathy for it were transferred or removed from active service. Significantly, the regular army did not join the rebels, although paratroop units refused to fire on the insurgents (whose leader, Pierre Lagaillarde, had attired himself illegally in the famous paratrooper camouflage uniform). The government outlawed activist organizations and forced the most extreme of the extremists underground.

The second disillusionment for Algérie française supporters was the failure of an April 1961 putsch led by the impressive foursome of Generals Salan, Challe, Jouhaud, and Zeller. Not only did the *coup manqué* demonstrate unequivocally that the conscript army would not follow its former commanders into revolt, but it constricted the choices open to its instigators. The officers who had supported the putsch had nowhere to go but underground or jail. The militants who chose to go underground had nothing more to lose and were the most hardened and determined. The moderate conspirators had dropped out, leaving only those willing to risk everything. Furthermore, proindependence riots accompanying de Gaulle's visit to Algeria in December 1960 revealed for the first time the extent of popular support for the FLN. Clashes between the European and Algerian communities during the riots had left over a hundred Muslims dead. Any reconciliation was becoming increasingly unlikely.

It is difficult to say that OAS expectations of what terrorism could accomplish were ever realistic.[67] OAS intentions were ambiguous from the start. The organization was badly divided over goals as well as strategy and tactics. The self-proclaimed headquarters in Madrid insisted that the center of activity should be Paris, whereas OAS leaders in Algiers naturally considered Algeria the central theater. OAS networks in both Oran and Constantine proceeded with more autonomy than consistency or efficiency. In all settings, OAS unity was more symbolic than real. Shadowy factions, some criminal, hid behind the facade of the OAS imprimatur. The strategic plans elaborated by the OAS were most often fantastical. A former OAS commando leader is reported to have said, "To talk of strategy is absurd. That's a big word. There was no strategy as such." He continued, "When I look at what the Palestinians have done and how effective they have been, I have regrets. I realize that we were really amateurs."[68]

It seems that initially the OAS sought to create the conditions for a mass insurrection of the European population. Terrorism was to be a catalyst for collective action, just as the FLN intended it to be in 1956. Beyond that, possible goals included the overthrow of the metropolitan government and installation of a rightist regime, secession from France, or partition. In order to mobilize Europeans, the OAS organized warning campaigns of *plasticages*, or plastic bombings, as well as propaganda campaigns featuring pirate radio broadcasts. The targets of terrorism included European liberals, "traitors," and Algerians identified as FLN supporters. OAS leaders intended such "conditioning" to demoralize the government, spread insecurity, and incite the European population to resistance. However, as insurrection appeared increasingly unlikely, the OAS settled into a war of attrition. Terrorism grew less selective and more vindictive. The OAS warned ominously that each time a supporter of French Algeria was killed by the FLN, an Algerian or a supporter of independence would be killed in retaliation.[69]

On 1 June 1961 the OAS assassinated the newly appointed commissioner of police, but the summer passed uneventfully, perhaps because OAS leaders drew hope from the impasse in which French and FLN

67. On the OAS in general, see Morland, Barangé, and Martinez (pseuds.), *Histoire de l'organisation de l'armée secrète* (Paris: Julliard, 1964), or, in English, Paul Henissart, *Wolves in the City* (London: Rupert Hart-Davis, 1971). *OAS parle* (Paris: Julliard, 1964) is a collection of OAS documents. See also Alexander Harrison, *Challenging De Gaulle: The O.A.S. and the Counterrevolution in Algeria, 1954–1962* (New York: Praeger, 1989).

68. Harrison, *Challenging De Gaulle*, 152–53.

69. See the testimony of Jean Morin, former delegate general, at General Salan's trial, in *Procès du général Raoul Salan* (Paris: Nouvelles Editions Latines, 1962), 112–14.

negotiators found themselves at Evian and again at Lugrin. In the fall of 1961, however, when the army in Algeria announced official support for police efforts to suppress the OAS, the OAS responded with a sharp escalation of terrorism. The French government countered by dispatching special undercover police units from the metropole (the *barbouzes*), who engaged in practices that resembled gang warfare as much as police operations (kidnappings, for example). By November the OAS was able to manage roughly three hundred *plasticages* per month. In December, in an effort to separate government and society, the OAS began to assassinate government employees, including not only civilian bureaucrats but police and military personnel. Between 1 May 1961 and 31 January 1962 the OAS was reported to have killed 47 Europeans and 222 Muslims in a total of 5,000 attacks.[70]

In March 1962 the French government and the GPRA concluded the Evian accords, granting Algerians the right to decide their future. A cease-fire was signed. Acutely conscious of the pressure of time, the OAS was desperate, first, to prevent the signing of the agreement and, when that proved impossible, to block its implementation. OAS orders now called for systematic attacks on the security forces and indiscriminate attacks on Muslims, including mortar rounds fired into the Algiers Casbah. Their purpose was apparently to provoke Muslim attacks on Europeans, which would in turn provoke counterattacks, although they tended to portray themselves as merely defending helpless Europeans from the FLN. They reasoned that if civil war broke out, the army would be forced to intervene. However, a reconstituted ZAA succeeded in restraining the Muslim population while mounting selective retaliatory attacks against Europeans. This provoked more OAS terrorism. Typical of the OAS was the labeling of educators and liberals as FLN sympathizers. In March, four days before the Evian accords were signed, a Delta Commando raided an educational center for Muslims and "executed" six teachers, both European and Muslim, including the well-known Kabyle writer Mouloud Feraoun. The OAS also tried a last time to provoke a popular insurrection, but their efforts to mobilize the inhabitants of the Bab el Oued section of Algiers led only to bloody and futile clashes between civilians and troops. The rupture between settlers and the regular army was now complete.

In March and April the top military leaders of the OAS—Salan, Jouhaud, and Degueldre—were arrested, leaving civilian activists nominally in command. When a referendum approved the Evian accords as well as the institution of a provisional executive to oversee the transfer

70. *Le Monde*, 15 February 1962.

of power, the OAS turned to indiscriminate and destructive terrorism intended to return Algeria to the state in which the French had found it in 1830. Despite pleas from Salan and Jouhaud in their prison cells to halt terrorism, the "scorched earth" policy continued until an accord was signed directly between the FLN and the OAS in June. In one week in May the OAS reportedly killed 230 Muslims. The week before, a car bomb at the Algiers docks left 62 Muslims dead. The OAS burned the library of the University of Algiers. At Salan's trial in May the Algiers police reported a total of 239 Europeans and 1,383 Muslims killed by the OAS. At the same time, the OAS perversely turned to attacks on departing *pieds-noirs* who were now abandoning Algeria in vast numbers—100,000 left in May.[71] This massive exodus left the OAS isolated and bereft of purpose, and the organization quickly disintegrated.

The opponents of terrorism within the OAS at this stage argued not so much that it was futile or unjustifiable as that it antagonized anti-FLN Muslims with whom a tactical agreement might be struck. Critics pointed out that the public found the motives behind such indiscriminateness incomprehensible and that the image they created was that of *règlements de comptes* rather than a political strategy. But the OAS leaders were too desperate and too isolated to heed orders to bring terrorism under control.[72]

In Paris the OAS-métro organization resisted the centralizing tendencies of both Madrid and Algiers headquarters. Recognizing quite sensibly that the appeal of Algérie française was now limited in France, the metropolitan organization adopted anti-Communism as a substitute and initially drew substantial support from the far Right, including a number of former militants from the Poujadist movement. The OAS appeared fascist and corporatist, posing as an opponent of both capitalism and Marxism. Far from being a clandestine underground, the OAS in France openly solicited adherents. Some deputies in the National Assembly endorsed its activities and voted accordingly. Public rallies were held in its defense. In 1961 the OAS indulged primarily in property bombings and extortions, their targets liberal politicians and intellectuals, Communists, journalists who reported unflatteringly on their activities, and businesspeople who refused to pay. However, ineptitude and carelessness tended to tarnish its credibility. In its early days the OAS was typically treated as a somewhat sinister nuisance, not a security threat.

71. On this period, see Fernand Carréras, *L'accord F.L.N.-O.A.S., des négotiations secrètes au cessez-le-feu* (Paris: R. Laffont, 1967). See also Courrière, *La guerre d'Algérie*, vol. 4, *Le temps du désespoir*, 620–24.

72. On opposition within the OAS to continued terrorism in 1962, see Gaucher, *Les terroristes*, 336–38.

The public and the government only began to take the OAS seriously as a result of another feature of OAS metropolitan strategy: the attempt to assassinate de Gaulle. In September 1961 the OAS tried to blow up de Gaulle's car at Pont-sur-Seine. Apparently, OAS leaders thought that a power vacuum in Paris might increase the influence of the Right and sabotage French-GPRA negotiations. Yet the assassination attempts against de Gaulle continued long after such a purpose could have been accomplished.[73] Ultimately vindictiveness rather than political aspirations lay behind the campaign to assassinate de Gaulle.

After the revelation of a serious threat to de Gaulle's life, the French government began to combat the OAS with new vigor. *Le Monde* reported that 225 members of the OAS were arrested within a week of the Pont-sur-Seine bombing.[74] De Gaulle was determined to bring the military back into line, he lacked any sympathy or patience for the *pieds-noirs*, and he was armed with the extensive executive powers conferred upon the office of the president by the constitution of the Fifth Republic. Even so, he could not depend on loyal implementation of anti-OAS measures.

In Algeria the security forces refused to intervene on the side of the Europeans, but they were still unenthusiastic about pursuing the OAS. Claude d'Abzac-Epezy notes that the distinction between the legal and the illegal army was not always clear. Active or passive complicity was not uncommon, in part because "those who chose legality did not do so without remorse or without sometimes a secret admiration for those who had chosen adventure."[75] As a consequence of both police and military unwillingness to take a stand, the OAS became the only law in Algeria. Oran, in particular, was completely under OAS control by 1962. The minister of the interior had already, in May, charged a member of the cabinet with coordinating anti-OAS efforts. After his narrow escape at Pont-sur-Seine in September, de Gaulle's decision to go outside normal channels and deploy special police forces to track down the OAS leadership was apparently based on several factors: the assassination of the police commissioner of Algiers only a week after he had taken office, the conviction that some unknown number of police either provided

73. Jacques Delarue, a police commissioner active in the anti-OAS struggle, has published his recollections of this period in *L'OAS contre de Gaulle* (Paris: Fayard, 1981). He explains that his purpose is to counter the stream of publications by former "stars" of the OAS, who brag about trying to assassinate de Gaulle. As yet, government archives have not been opened.

74. *Le Monde*, 15 September 1961, 1.

75. D'Abzac-Epezy, "La société militaire," 9. See also the special issue of *La nef*, nos. 12–13 (July–September 1961).

intelligence to the OAS or were waiting to choose sides, and the assumption that even if the Algiers police did act against the OAS, the local force was too well known to the OAS to permit them to track down Salan and Jouhaud.[76]

In metropolitan France the government's response to the OAS was slow in shaping. Only in December and later did the government outlaw the OAS, issue orders for the arrest of Salan and other key leaders, or bring to trial any of those responsible for *plasticages*.[77] The police were often halfhearted in their pursuit of the OAS. In contrast, they were quick to suppress a Muslim demonstration against a curfew order in October 1961. These attitudes were probably affected by earlier FFFLN terrorism. In January 1962, however, the OAS conveniently furnished another provocation by bombing the Quai d'Orsay. Shortly thereafter press reports announced to some alarm that the OAS had organized cells in high schools and colleges. The escalation in OAS violence in January coincided with the arrival in France of an envoy from Salan with instructions to organize more-serious operations and to put an end to the uncoordinated and often pointless *plasticages* that made the OAS not only unpopular but ridiculous. Thefts of arms, explosives, and uniforms multiplied, giving the impression that the OAS was becoming dangerously ambitious. The number of OAS attacks increased, especially against Communists, and OAS operations began to cause casualties.[78] On 7 February ten *plasticages* occurred in one day: one government minister, two journalists, two professors, one senator, and two police officers.[79] The turning point for the OAS in the metropole was probably the next day, with the "Métro Charonne" affair. Nine people were killed when the police tried to break up an anti-OAS demonstration. When hundreds of thousands of Parisians attended the funerals of the victims, it could no longer be said that opposition to the OAS came only from the Left. Nevertheless, the OAS continued desperately to try to provoke a civil war in France as well as in Algeria, according to Salan's instructions, which apparently reached the metropole on 20 March.[80] One such effort was a car bomb exploded in front of the building in which a peace movement was holding a meeting. None of these exercises, however, was successful. The overwhelming ratification of the Evian accords in an April referendum showed that the OAS had failed to sway French public opinion.

76. See Delarue, *L'OAS contre de Gaulle*, 12–13.
77. *L'année politique* (1961): 163.
78. *L'année politique* (1962): 4–5.
79. *Le Monde*, 9 February 1962.
80. Delarue, *L'OAS contre de Gaulle*, 123.

In April and May and on into the summer in Paris came the trials of OAS leaders. In 1961 de Gaulle for the first time invoked the emergency-powers clause of the constitution to ensure that military rebels were tried by a military court from which there was no appeal. This initiative involved him in a conflict with the council of state, which found the transfer of cases unconstitutional. The military tribunal first condemned General Jouhaud to death, without attenuating circumstances. (De Gaulle later pardoned him.) In May, however, the tribunal handed down a life sentence for Salan due to extenuating circumstances. De Gaulle promptly abolished the high military tribunal and established a special state security court.[81] Most OAS militants received prison sentences, but several were executed, including Degueldre, head of the Delta Commandos. All OAS officers still in prison, including Salan, were amnestied during the electoral campaign of 1968 in an apparent attempt to secure right-wing support after the shock of the May student revolt.

OAS terrorism was the catalyst for other institutional changes in the French state. The assassination attempt at Petit Clamart in August 1962 prompted de Gaulle to call a referendum to require the direct election of the president of the republic.[82] The French public was deeply moved by de Gaulle's close call, which gave him the opportunity to implement a change he had favored since 1959. De Gaulle seemingly believed that his successor in the event of an assassination would need to rely on a wide base of popular support. Above all, he wanted to prevent a return to what he saw as the evils of a weak executive under the Fourth Republic.

A critical question is what effect OAS terrorism had on the future of the European population of Algeria. Could the European minority have stayed had the OAS not involved them in a frenzy of violence, especially in the summer of 1962? John Talbott thinks that OAS violence made it "well-nigh impossible" for the European to remain but that their chances were probably not good anyway.[83] Europeans would not have accepted integration into an Islamic Algerian nation, so the best they could have hoped for was the status of a protected foreign minority. No real union could have grown from the colonial situation. The ethnic identity of the Europeans of Algeria depended on their dominant position as colonizers. Yet most French accounts hold the OAS responsible for the panicked and unforeseen European exodus. René Gallissot asserts that the terrorism

81. This Cour de Sureté d'Etat was abolished by François Mitterand in 1981, when he also granted amnesty to a number of members of Action Directe. See Villeneuve and Péret, *Histoire secrète*, 33–34.

82. Didier Maus, "La guerre et les institutions de la république," in *La guerre*, ed. Rioux, 161–79.

83. John Talbott, *The War Without a Name* (New York: Knopf, 1980), 182.

of the OAS consummated the rupture between Europeans and Muslims that the war had widened. In his view the OAS reaction to the prospect of independence made it all the more urgent that de Gaulle negotiate a settlement with the FLN rather than wait for more favorable terms.[84] On the other hand, Tony Smith points out that had de Gaulle negotiated in earnest sooner than he did, since he gained no concessions by waiting, the OAS would not have had time to implant itself in the European population.[85] The kidnappings and disappearances of Europeans at the hands of Muslims and the seizures of European property might not have occurred if the OAS had not destroyed all semblance of order during the transition from French to FLN rule.[86] One observer concludes that OAS terrorism ended in "incoherence and exile" and an enhanced role for the FLN: "The OAS succeeded in diminishing considerably the means of action of the authorities, and the FLN appeared rapidly as the only possible partner of the government."[87] In addition to accelerating the European departure and making its conditions painful, the terrorism of the OAS also impeded the integration of *pieds-noirs* into French society. They were often blamed, whether fairly or not, for the atrocities of the OAS.[88]

All these findings emphasize the futility of OAS terrorism. Nevertheless, a series of recent interviews with repatriated *pieds-noirs* shows the OAS as admired still. According to this survey, former settlers continue to regard the OAS with some nostalgia as the authentic expression of what they recognize in themselves.[89] Furthermore, although the army lost credibility with the French public, the treatment of the military after the war encouraged in the army a "guilty sentimentality" or even admiration for those who had risked everything for their convictions. The army developed a "colonial cult," including a secret exaltation of the "heros" who chose faithfulness to their word and moral integrity, rather than security and legality. A strong anti-Gaullist strain was apparent in the high number of votes among the military for de Gaulle's opponent

84. Gallissot, "La guerre," 78, 92, 94, 97, and 104–7.

85. Smith, *The French Stake*, 182–83.

86. In 1964 the French government mentioned over one thousand Europeans kidnapped and killed between March and December 1962, but *pieds-noirs* claim over three thousand kidnappings. See Guy Pervillé, "Les accords d'Evian et les relations franco-algériennes," in *La guerre*, ed. Rioux, 484–93.

87. Jacques Suant, *L'affaire algérienne: Histoire d'une rupture* (Paris: Editions Publisud, 1987), 88.

88. Lever, "L'OAS et les pieds-noirs," 23.

89. Anne Roche, "La perte et la parole: Témoignages oraux de pieds-noirs," in *La guerre*, ed. Rioux, 533.

Tixier-Vignancourt, who had been Salan's lawyer, in the 1965 presidential elections.[90]

In the end, the OAS failed to achieve its objectives because they were unattainable. French Algeria could not survive without the support of the metropole. When French opinion shifted, so too did the fate of Algeria. The European settler population preferred life in France to staying on in an independent Algeria under Muslim rule. Had the alternative of repatriation not been available, they might have been willing, not necessarily to fight to the bitter end, but to accept the inevitable and compromise earlier with Muslim aspirations. The OAS also suffered from poor organization and direction and complete inability to anticipate the consequences of violent action. The expectation that the army would intervene in Algeria was illusory after the failed coup of 1961, thus practically from the beginning, despite the sympathies some officers may have held for the OAS.[91] The majority of the conscript army obeyed de Gaulle in 1961 and would obey him again. The idea that the OAS could provoke civil war in metropolitan France was a grandiose illusion, and their commitment to terrorism cost them the political support from the Right that they initially enjoyed. Furthermore, the military leaders of the OAS failed to understand the inapplicability of *guerre révolutionnaire* theories to the circumstances of a counterrevolutionary movement. The OAS consistently overestimated the power of terrorism to influence events in both Algeria and France. The myth of the efficacy of FLN terrorism was false.

CONCLUSIONS

Analysis of the Algerian case, including both FLN and OAS, suggests that terrorism is more likely to be effective than successful, because the political changes to which terrorism can plausibly be linked diverge from those its users seek. As a method of achieving radical political change, terrorism has no inherent efficacy. Indeed, from a strategic perspective it is often counterproductive. The effects of terrorism are multiple and

90. D'Abzac-Epezy, "La société militaire," 250.

91. Army units in Germany, many transferred from Algeria, seemed to have maintained closer contacts with the OAS than the troops in Algeria did. Salan is reported to have concluded in January 1962 that "the army, whose attitude will be determinant in one sense or another, will not play for us in Algeria. On the other hand, it can represent a capital factor in the metropole in light of the fact that favorable and sympathetic units are now stationed in France and Germany" (Delarue, *L'OAS contre de Gaulle*, 127).

offsetting; immediate and long-term consequences may cancel, reinforce, or balance each other. In the short run it may be easy to cause fear, anger, or enthusiasm, depending on the predispositions of specific audiences, but it is difficult to translate these emotional reactions into influence over political outcomes. As a mode of communication terrorist acts send out mixed signals. The strategy is thus difficult to control because its effects are hard to anticipate. It is also hard to control because it requires secrecy and operational autonomy, thus decentralized decision making, and because, especially under those circumstances, it frequently serves the ends of vengeance. My conclusions thus accord somewhat with those of Ian Lustick in the chapter that follows: instrumental violence, meant purely to influence the adversary's calculations rather than to promote solidarity within a constituent community, may be easier to bring to an end. Terrorism may thus be a serious impediment to conflict resolution.

In Algeria the general ends that terrorism was meant to serve were structured by the historical context. The conflicts that pitted both the FLN and the OAS against the French state were rooted in communal and ethnic divisions established under a colonial regime. The objective of revolutionary nationalism was to compel the French to abandon what was empirically, if not juridically, a colonial occupation that was already becoming costly and would soon become anachronistic in light of changes in the international system. FLN terrorism increased the cost of staying on. So, too, paradoxically, did the French response to terrorism, which discredited the military yet gave them the independent power to challenge the government's authority. Their defiance of de Gaulle strengthened his hand in the end. The OAS, while insisting that France pay the cost of upholding the colonial status quo indefinitely, actually increased that cost by fomenting disorder. For the French government, the logical solution to the challenge of the OAS was independence for Algeria, which of course solved the problem of the FLN as well.

Another obstacle to effectiveness is that the intentions behind terrorism may be inconsistent, contradictory, or unclear. Organizations planning terrorism, like all decision-making bodies, face value conflicts or suffer from lack of direction and of efficient management. Rational calculation of the relation between terrorism and collective purposes may be deficient. The strategic conceptions guiding OAS terrorism were notably confused. The FLN, though more unified than the OAS, was apparently divided over the benefits of using terrorism, because of conflicting values. For example, if the support of liberal French opinion was important, then terrorism against civilians, especially in metropolitan France, was unlikely to be helpful. On the other hand, if liberals were considered to have no influence or to be untrustworthy, then there was little to be lost by attacking civilian targets. Some FLN leaders thought the French might compromise, whereas others saw the conflict as zero-sum.

Belief in the inherent efficacy of terrorism as a catalyst for collective action can also be misleading. Terrorism is often called the weapon of the weak, a substitute for the ability to mobilize large numbers, but its use may actually reflect overconfidence about the readiness of a population to revolt. The FLN in 1956 and the OAS in 1961 and 1962 mistakenly believed that terrorism would precipitate popular insurrection. However, in both cases, revolutionary and counterrevolutionary, terrorism was insufficient, in part because it provoked government repression severe enough to discourage mass participation in resistance, as well as reprisals from the other side. In addition, it sometimes alienated or frightened the supporters it was meant to mobilize. It thus led to popular passivity, not activism.

Another common miscalculation is the expectation that terrorism will intimidate and demoralize the enemy's civilian population, thus inducing surrender to one's demands. This psychological assumption could be called the "strategic bombing fallacy," since it also misled decision makers in the Second World War and in Vietnam. FLN terrorism against Europeans and OAS terrorism against Algerians usually strengthened their respective determinations to resist. Fear did not lead to moderation and compromise. Generally fear was more likely to be supplanted by anger than by resignation. Had the power of the Europeans of Algeria not depended on the resources of the metropole, the war would probably have lasted much longer than it did because Europeans had come to see all Muslims as "terrorists." If we assume that the FLN intended to drive all European settlers out of Algeria and that coexistence was excluded from the beginning, then terrorism might be considered to have succeeded. But again, Algeria's Europeans had French citizenship and the right to return to the metropole, a right they would never have exercised had the French government been willing to stay on. But the political influence of the settler community in Paris decreased as the war progressed and as their particular interests became incompatible with the general interest of the state.

Even if intentions are formulated with some clarity, consistency, and attention to alternatives and their consequences, within the constraints imposed by the historical setting, aims may still be thwarted. One impediment to success is loss of control over implementation of the strategy. In particular, pressures to avenge victims of the violence of the enemy may overwhelm strategic calculations. The pursuit of vengeance is of course not entirely irrational from the organization's perspective. It is not necessarily unreasonable to try to satisfy the demands for revenge expressed by militants or constituents. The ability to satisfy this desire is in some ways a selective incentive. It promotes solidarity and cohesion and relieves frustration. An organization must often respond to government violence in order to maintain its legitimacy vis-à-vis its own supporters. But when vengeance becomes an end in itself, for the organization's cadres as much as for the people they represent, then it is likely to lose its instrumental character. This tension characterizes decision making in any violent conflict. It is especially acute for oppositions because they lack not only institutional means of control over the rank and file (in part because of the organizational structures dictated by security needs) but also strong claims to the loyalty of their constituents. The FLN was concerned about its status within the Algerian community until the very end of the war.

Inefficiency in practical implementation of a strategy is another source of discrepancy between intention and result. OAS ineptitude was legendary. Inefficiency as well as loss of control can create an appearance of randomness that makes it impossible for audiences to comprehend the reasons for terrorism. Even potential supporters may be alienated. Similarly, terrorism that shades off into *règlements de compte*, or personal account settling, seems petty and vindictive and is difficult to justify in terms of broad ideological frameworks.

A last factor preventing terrorism from attaining its objectives is the response of the adversary. There are limits to the ability of actors to predict the reactions of opponents. Terrorism may be intended to provoke repression that will polarize public opinion, but governments may respond with an unexpected power and determination that results in the destruction of the organization using terrorism, as happened during the Battle of Algiers. On the other hand, the OAS strategy of provoking a civil war that would compel military intervention failed not only because they could not mobilize the European settlers but also because de Gaulle succeeded in controlling the French military. OAS violence only made it more urgent to negotiate a settlement.

To look at the problem from another perspective, what are the conditions for success? Terrorism succeeded for the FLN initially as a way of putting the nationalist struggle on the national and international agendas, as a symbol of the intensity of resistance, and then as a tactic in a war of attrition, part of a protracted insurgency. Throughout the conflict it served as a constant reminder to the French government and the French public that security in Algeria was tenuous and that the two communities could never be united, even if a military victory was within French grasp. Gaining international and metropolitan recognition through urban terrorism meant that the nationalist movement could no longer be dismissed as a form of rural banditry, although the French persisted in seeing nationalism as Communist or Nasserite subversion rather than an indigenous phenomenon. But after the Battle of Algiers it took five more years of fighting to convince the French that their options had narrowed to a choice between indefinite military occupation, always challenged politically and militarily, and ending the colonial regime. Terrorism alone would not have brought about independence, and we can probably say that independence would have come without it, although it was integral to the struggle.

At the same time, it is undeniable that terrorism generated significant, though unexpected, political change. It is worth noting that unanticipated consequences are mixed; they are not always detrimental to the long-term objectives of the users of terrorism. The Battle of Algiers produced a defeat for the FLN that influenced the future course of the revolution and even of the development of the Algerian state, but the extreme French response radicalized the Algerian population and in France stimulated opposition to the war. It also set the stage for de Gaulle's return to power; whether another French government would have pursued the same policies is unknowable, but he is often given credit for settling the Algerian crisis. OAS terrorism then widened the gap between Europeans and Muslims, probably eliminating the possibility of more favorable treatment for the future European minority, and consolidated metropolitan opposition to the war. Terrorism on all sides thus contributed to the erosion of the political consensus that held Algeria essential to the identity of France.

12

Terrorism in the Arab-Israeli Conflict: Targets and Audiences

Ian S. Lustick

SOLIPSISTIC VERSUS OTHER-DIRECTED TERRORISM

We are all too familiar with use of the term *terrorism* to refer to threats or violence in suport of causes that the speaker or writer opposes. Today no epithet enjoys more universal acceptance than *terrorist*. Only the

An earlier and shorter version of this essay was published under the title "Changing Rationales for Political Violence in the Arab-Israeli Conflict," *Journal of Palestine Studies* 20, no. 1 (1990): 54–79. I would like to thank Martha Crenshaw, David Rapoport, Philip Mattar, Linda Butler, Ehud Sprinzak, John Talbott, and Ann M. Lesch for their comments on previous drafts.

very bold and the very precise are any longer willing to declare that *their* actions, or actions they support, are instances of terrorism.

Analysts of terrorism, however, are obliged to define the term so that it can be applied independent of their sympathy for or opposition to its referent. That requirement separates them immediately, and decisively, from political actors who use the term. But defining terrorism is notoriously difficult. This is partially because the taboo associated with the word itself is so powerful that different definitions unavoidably produce different political consequences. For example, if illegality is used as a criterion for the subset of violent or threatening behavior that is to be considered terrorism, analysis would thereby be slanted against opponents of states and would help camouflage state terrorism. If the innocence or noncombatant status of the specific targets of threats or violence are used as the main criteria for identifying terrorism, this will tend to cast states in the main terrorist role—states that, because they operate on a larger scale and employ armies and air forces that wreak "accidental" havoc as an inevitable corollary of their use, usually kill, injure, or terriorize many more "innocents" than even the most "successful" nonstate terrorists.

Another serious problem in defining terrorism in an analytically useful way is familiar to anyone who has ever tried to define power, that central concept in political science related to virtually all propositions about how "valued resources are authoritatively allocated." Such an all-encompassing concept resists definitions that distinguish it from causality itself. If the essence of terrorism is seen as an intent to manipulate the behavior of others by scaring them, there is little to distinguish it, in principle (and that is what counts, analytically), from deterrence. But if we are to include as terrorism the actions and threats (both explicit and implicit) of every police force, government, street gang, tax collector, district attorney, labor union, and so forth that uses deterrent techniques—that is, seeks to affect the calculations of adversaries or general publics by "setting an example" in specific instances or by conjuring images of unpleasant things that might happen if demands are not met—we risk losing our grasp of an empirical phenomenon discrete enough to warrant systematic consideration.

Considering terrorism in the context of Arab-Zionist or Arab-Israeli relations, my response to this predicament is to accept as instances of terrorism anything that at least one party to the conflict would label as such. In the polarized lexicon of Middle Eastern politics this pushes virtually all violence of Arabs against Jews or Jews against Arabs, except perhaps that contained in the heat of battle between contending military units, into the terrorist category.

By embracing an extensive, instead of intensive, definition of the concept, I escape the need to establish boundary conditions. Accordingly, classification of activities as terrorist or not ceases to be an issue. The price I pay for this analytic strategy is that I cannot pose questions about the "rationality" or effectiveness of terrorism. Nor can I produce general propositions about terrorist behavior, what terrorism is not, what it cannot do, or how it can be ended—questions that can only be asked and answered if an "objective" and intensive definition of terrorism as a particular kind of political behavior is advanced. The benefit of the approach is that it encourages attention to be shifted from these questions to others more likely to be answered convincingly.

In terms of Arab-Zionist or Arab-Israeli affairs (including, that is, both the pre-1948 and post-1948 periods), it permits attention to be focused on two types of violent or threatening behavior. The first I describe as "other-directed"—violence delivered against targets for the purpose of manipulating adversaries' behavior or changing their utility functions. The second I refer to as "solipsistic"—violence delivered against targets for the purpose of manipulating the behavior or changing the utility functions of the group with which the perpetrators identify. Without suggesting that these categories are either mutually exclusive or a closed set of all behaviors categorizable as terrorism (i.e., labeled by its victims as such), I do intend to demonstrate that change in the balance of political violence from solipsistic terrorism (directed toward the beliefs, intentions, and behavior of one's own group) to other-directed terrorism (directed at the beliefs, intentions, and behavior of adversaries) can serve as a vital marker of transformation in the meaning and potential for melioration of protracted conflicts. To accomplish this I trace the evolution of changing rationales for violence, first within the Zionist movement, the Yishuv (the Jewish community in Palestine), and the state of Israel, and then within the Arab world as it mobilized itself to oppose the Zionist enterprise. In this regard I of course pay special attention to changing rationales among the Palestinians for violence (or, more precisely, for behavior construed by their enemies as terrorism).

The first of two major claims I wish to advance is that in the development of both Zionism and Palestinian Arab nationalism the purpose of inflicting death and destruction on the enemy was seen quite prominently, though never exclusively, as serving the psychological needs of the group on whose behalf the violence was undertaken. In this sense both nationalist movements serve as exemplars of Frantz Fanon's theory of the psychological and political role of violence. According to his account of how historically oppressed peoples gain their liberation, perpetration of violent acts against others is a necessary "therapeutic" device. Only violence as an expression of freedom and power, showing death and the ability to kill as the great equalizer, can destroy the inferiority complex that is the colonizer's most dependable instrument of subjugation.[1] It is crucial to note that terrorist acts carried out in conformance with a normative application of Fanon's theory are not designed primarily to intimidate the adversary, elicit panic or concessions, or in any way affect the adversary's behavior. But such acts do have "wider targets." These are not the "oppressor" people or its government, but the "oppressed" and their self-styled representatives. It is their psyche, their sense of self-esteem, and their beliefs about what can and cannot be done, and at what cost, that are the targets. Fanonian terrorism is thus solipsistic.

The second claim I advance is that the historic transformation in the Arab-Israeli conflict that occurred after the 1967 war can be identified by tracing change in the modal rationale for political violence employed by each side against the other. My argument is that the hopes for peace that emerged in the 1970s, which came to fruition at the end of that decade between Israel and Egypt and which have a greater chance now than ever before of being realized between Israelis and Palestinians, have been associated with a fundamental shift from solipsistic rationales for political violence to other-directed violence. I contend that this shift, which ironically entails replacing "symbolic" violence with calculated efforts actually to hurt and terrorize adversaries, was a necessary step before opportunities for political compromise in this protracted dispute could even begin to be explored.

SOLIPSISTIC TERRORISM IN ZIONISM DURING THE EARLY YEARS OF THE STATE OF ISRAEL

The crucial role of this model of terrorism for understanding the dynamics of revolutionary nationalist movements is illustrated by Zionism's choice of Hayyim Nahman Bialik as the "national poet" of the Jewish people. One of Bialik's best known poems is entitled "The City of Slaughter." It is an evocative narrative of the Kishniev Pogrom, perpetrated against that Bessarabian city's Jewish population on 6 April 1903. Forty-five Jews were murdered in that pogrom and eighty-six wounded. "Russian eye-witnesses described people torn in two, babies' brains splattered, bellies split open, tongues cut out, women with breasts cut

1. Frantz Fanon, *The Wretched of the Earth* (New York: Grove Press, 1968), 94.

off, men castrated, blinded, hanged, hacked to death."[2] But the focus of Bialik's poem is not on the horrors of the event per se or on the innocence of the victims. Nor is the poem presented as an accusation against the Russian authorities, the church, or the police for encouraging, or at least failing to protect, the Jewish community. Nor does "The City of Slaughter" exhort Jews to leave Russia, join the Zionist movement, and build a new and better home in the land of Israel. Instead, the poem is a savage indictment of the cowardice of Jewish males, their complete lack of a sense of honor, their spinelessness in the face of bestial attacks on wives, children, mothers, and sisters, and their unwillingness even to contemplate self-defense.

> Note also do not fail to note,
> In that dark corner, and behind that cask
> Crouched husbands, bridegrooms, brothers, peering from
>   the cracks,
> Watching the sacred bodies struggling underneath
> The bestial breath,
> Stifled in filth, and swallowing their blood!
> Watching from the darkness and its mesh
> The lecherous rabble portioning for booty
> Their kindred and their flesh!
> Crushed in their shame, they saw it all:
> They did not stir nor move;
> They did not pluck their eyes out; they
> Beat not their brains against the wall!
> Perhaps, perhaps, each watcher had it in his heart to pray:
> *A miracle, O Lord, —and spare my skin this day!*[3]

Zionism's choice of Bialik as the national poet of the Jewish people is emblematic of a deep sense of shame at the behavior of Diaspora Jews in the face of recurrent anti-Semitism. Zionists emphasized the need to reject entirely not only the existential situation of Diaspora life—Jews living as a minority everywhere and a majority nowhere—but also the modal personality type that was seen as having been produced by centuries of obsequiousness.

The stereotype of the Diaspora Jew employed by Zionist writers, poets, and political leaders was of an overly clever, fawning intermediary

2. Howard Morley Sachar, *The Course of Modern Jewish History* (New York: Delta, 1958), 248.

3. Hayyim Nahman Bialik, *The City of Slaughter: The Selected Poems of Hayyim Nahman Bialik* (New York: Block Publishing, 1965), 118–19.

whose motto was to live another day by standing firm on no other principle. Saul Tschernichowsky's attack on this "Galut mentality" (the mentality of exile) in his poem "Before a Statue of Apollo," and his exaltation of the physical culture and strength associated with the Greeks, are unusually vivid but emotionally representative. Despising Diaspora Jews and the cult of weakness and death he says they represent, Tschernichowsky apostrophizes the god Apollo and issues a direct, purposeful, and blasphemous challenge to the very core of Jewish religious thinking:

> I come to you, before your statue kneeling,
> your image—symbol of life's brightness;
> I kneel, I bow to the good and the sublime,
> to that which is exalted throughout the world,
> to all things splendid throughout creation,
> and elevated among secret-mysteries of the Cosmos.
> I bow to life, to valour and to beauty,
> I bow to all precious things—robbed now
> by human corpses and the rotten seed of man,
> who rebel against the life bestowed by God, the Almighty—
> the God of mysterious wilderness,
> the God of men who conquered Canaan in a whirlwind—
> then bound Him with the straps of their phylacteries.[4]

Apart from the undeniable difficulty that any honest presentation of Zionist objectives would have created for examples to reach a modus vivendi with the Arabs of Palestine, there were powerful psychological, ideological, and cultural factors predisposing the overwhelming majority of Zionists against a posture of compromise or empathy when dealing with Arabs. Indeed, many early Zionist settlers in Palestine actually welcomed the hostility of local Arabs as an opportunity to express their "negation of the Galut." In this context, disputes and misunderstandings about pasturage or land rights that might well have been settled amicably often spiraled into reprisal, resentment, and hatred. In 1891 the noted "spiritual-cultural" Zionist Ahad Haam (Asher Ginsberg) wrote bitterly about the failure of Jewish colonists in Palestine to live up to the standards of justice and righteousness his particular brand of Zionist emphasized.

4. Eisig Silberschlag, ed., *Saul Tschernichowsky: Poet of Revolt* (Ithaca, N.Y.: Cornell University Press, 1968), 98.

And what are our brethren in Palestine doing? . . . They were slaves in the land of their exile and suddenly they find themselves in the midst of unlimited freedom, a wild kind of freedom which can only be found in a country like Turkey. This sudden change has produced in them a tendency to despotism, which always happens when "a slave becomes a king." They treat the Arabs with hostility and cruelty, trespassing on their territory unjustly, beating them shamefully without any valid reason and then boasting about it. No one is calling a halt to this contemptible and dangerous trend.[5]

Calling attention in 1907 to what he called "A Hidden Question," Israel Epstein, an early Zionist pioneer who helped found the first Hebrew schools in Palestine, criticized the absence of any discussion in Zionist circles about how to accommodate the Jewish presence in Palestine with the existence of the Arabs. The key psychological link between toughness toward Arabs and the pride Zionism sought thereby to foster among Jews is reflected in this early period in the way Epstein found it necessary to frame his call for compassion by reassuring his audience. "I am not suggesting for a moment," he wrote, "that we should humble ourselves and give in to the local inhabitants."[6]

The first Jewish self-defense group to form in modern Palestine, in 1907, was named after Bar-Giora, the last leader of the Jewish revolt against the Roman Empire. Its organizers, before coming to Palestine, had been active in self-defense groups formed in Jewish communities threatened with pogroms in Russia. In 1909 the Bar-Giora group expanded into Hashomer ("guard"). Hashomer's motto, chosen by Itzhak Ben-Zvi, a future president of Israel, was instructive of the spirit that infused the group: "Judea fell in blood and fire; in blood and fire shall Judea rise!" Adorned with Bedouin-style headdresses and mounted on horseback, Hashomer's carefully selected members served a crucial psychological and cultural role whose importance far exceeded whatever specific protection Hashomer could afford to isolated Jewish settlements. Indeed, those settlements were reluctant to hire Hashomer guards when Arab watchmen were available at more reasonable rates. Jewish plantation owners also criticized Hashomer for its aggressiveness in dealing with Arabs and its lack of restraint in using firearms.[7]

5. Quoted by Aharon Cohen, *Israel and the Arab World* (New York: Funk and Wagnalls, 1970), 60–61.

6. Yitshak Epstein, "A Hidden Question," *Hashiloah* (1907); quoted by Cohen, *Israel and the Arab World*, 67.

7. Gershon Shafir, *Land, Labor, and the Origins of the Israeli-Palestinian Conflict, 1882–1914* (Cambridge: Cambridge University Press, 1989), 138–42.

By the end of World War I, Hashomer, which never included more than one hundred men in its ranks at any given time, had disappeared. But the legend built on carefully constructed images of armed, proud, courageous Jews whose physical prowess could strike fear into Gentile (Arab) hearts served as inspiration for the Hagana. It helped prove to Zionists, both in Palestine and in the Diaspora, that the fundamental principles of the ideology on which the movement was based were valid, that the twisted Jewish personality of the Diaspora could be made straight under the "normal" conditions of a people living in its own land.

In the mid-1920s Yaacov Lamdan wrote the semiepic poem "Masada," evincing the same sense of shame and anger at what Diaspora Jews were perceived to be like that afflicted Bialik and Tschernichowsky. Lamdan evoked the heroic but doomed struggle of the last Zealot stronghold against the Romans, whose defenders took their own lives rather than submit to captivity, as emblematic of the entire Zionist enterprise. In this widely read and profoundly influential poem, Lamdan bemoans the cowardly, uninspiring human material available within the Jewish people. Hearkening to the call of Masada (i.e., the Land of Israel), he writes, are

> our brothers, they are coming to us. But oh woe, they are ped-dlers!
> They have heard that there is a crisis in Masada, that there is a battle, and they have come here as camp followers to store the spoil of battle. . . .
> And for money in deceitful scales, they sell everything . . . but if the battle should prove too tough, they would hasten to their boats, and sail to lands of safety.[8]

Lamdan calls instead for pioneers and warriors, trained "to bear the shield and draw the bow." But his choice of Masada as the symbol of the Zionist enterprise, and the resonance of this choice within the growing Yishuv, reveal expectations of ultimate defeat and destruction (since that is what happened to the historical Masada). Commenting on the choice of Masada as the title and focus of the poem, Leon Yudkin has remarked that "the picture we receive from the Masada struggle is of a people throwing its entire energy and resources into the battle, but which it is fated to lose. And this is the unspoken implication of the choice of the title. The people must fight, and fight to the last. But they will not win

8. Yaacov Lamdan, "Masada," trans. Leon I. Yudkin, in Leon I. Yudkin, *Isaac Lamdan: A Study in Twentieth-Century Hebrew Poetry* (Ithaca, N.Y.: Cornell University Press, 1971), 224.

out in the end."[9] Lamdan's point, therefore, is not so much that Jews do or should fight in order to elicit accommodative behavior from their enemies or even to achieve victory but that they fight, almost for its own sake, to "rise up and out to battle . . . in spite of everything, again to battle." The heavens are likened to a drum—"a silken, cheating drum"—pounded by "the hands of bitter-souled, pain-swollen fighters." The pioneers, says the poet, "smite foreheads on rocks, smiting until blood squirt out," fighting, not for victory, but simply to live up to the meaning of "Israel" (he who fights with God).[10]

In 1943, in the midst of the European Holocaust, David Ben-Gurion demonstrated how potent the Masada image was for Zionists by forcefully contrasting the disgrace of Jewish passivity in exile with the dignity of violent death in the Land of Israel.

> Comrades, we are gathered again in Masada, not that of the last ones but of the first ones in our generation. . . . These workers and guards left us the legacy of a new life and a new death. . . . For we had lived a life of exile in foreign lands, a life of dependence, shame, slavery, and disgrace; not only caused by others but also by ourselves, as a result of our acceptance of our weakness, of life in exile. . . . From now on, we shall guarantee a new death for ourselves, not a death of weakness, helplessness, and futile sacrifice. We shall die with arms in our hands.[11]

Thus, in a very real sense, the psychological target of Zionist violence was often the Jews. Jewish fights with or retaliation against Arab villages or bedouin tribes were motivated not only by considerations of self-defense but by the desire to set inspiring examples of physical prowess and heroism to Palestinian Jews and to prove to Diaspora Jews the validity of an important dimension of Zionist ideology. Even where this was not necessarily the motive behind particular actions, it often became the overriding theme in subsequent interpretations of it. In no case is this clearer than in the myth constructed around Josef Trumpeldor and the "defense of Tel-Hai."

Trumpeldor was an officer in the Russian army who came to Palestine and died in March 1920 in a clash with bedouin raiders at Tel-Hai, in the border area between Palestine and Lebanon. Despite the military

9. Yudkin, *Isaac Lamdan*, 71.
10. Lamdan, "Masada," 231, 220, and 232; Yudin, *Isaac Lamdan*, 214n.
11. Quoted by Yael Zerubavel, "The Social Construction of a Modern Myth: The Case of Tel Hai" (Paper presented at the Fourth Annual Conference of the Association for Israel Studies, New York, June 1988), 5.

irrelevance of the encounter, an elaborate mythology was created around his death, celebrating Trumpeldor as a heroic martyr whose last words were "Never mind, it is good to die for our country." In her analysis of the political function of the Trumpeldor myth for the Zionist movement, Yael Zerubavel comments that it "answered an immediate need to find actual expressions of the Jews' expected transformation from a submissive, helpless minority, subject to persecution by others, to proud, strong-willed, and defiant actors in control of their lives and land. . . . His fall during the defense of Tel Hai made him an ideal image of the new Jew and the new martyrdom that the Zionist revolution would create in the Land of Israel."[12] Zerubavel quotes numerous contemporary Zionist commentators, as well as Zionist children's literature (both pre- and post-1948), to show the rapidity and effectiveness with which Trumpeldor's death was mythologized.[13]

In 1921, the year following the Tel-Hai affair, the first serious Arab riots against Jews erupted. The resulting Jewish casualties led to the formation of the underground Haganah (Defense) army, which eventually became the mainstay of Israel's war of independence and the new state's own army, the Israel Defense Forces (Tzva Haganah l'Yisrael). The Haganah was organized and commanded by socialist Zionists. It was, in fact, the armed wing of the Histadrut, the Zionist trade union and cooperative organization in Palestine. Its official doctrine stressed *tohar haneshak* (purity of arms) and *havlagah* (self-restraint)—meaning that force was to be used only when, and to the extent necessary, for self-defense.

These were important norms not only within the Haganah but also later in the Israeli army. In the 1920s and 1930s a key component of the image of the Jewish fighter was as guardian of his family and his nation's future. Apart from the actual threat they posed to Jewish settlements, Arab marauders or pilferers also provided Haganah men with personal and sweet opportunities for displaying martial qualities of strength, endurance, and bravery. In this context it was convenient, even necessary, to view the Arabs, not as a rational enemy to be bargained with, violently or otherwise, but as an implacable, barbaric force to be withstood. In his 1936 poem "On Watch," Tschernichowsky celebrated the posture of "self-defense" in terms of the masculine Zionism that was his trademark.

This night too we'll do without sleep!
For an aged mother, a father grown old,

12. Ibid., 3–4. Zerubavel notes that many Israelis today believe Trumpeldor's last words were actually an earthy Russian curse.
13. Ibid., 5–6 and 11–16.

who sanctified God with all their might,
freed the son, and blessed the daughter
to righteous war with savage men,
with spoil-hungry, blood-thirsty desert men.

. . . .

This night too we'll do without sleep!
So the wife can slumber, fearless and deep;
her heart need not fear for her man in the field,
stubborn cactus to the grasp, he will not yield—
whatever his weapon—as guard he is keeping
for the children's home—and the children sleeping.[14]

But a controversy gradually developed within the Yishuv over whether violent measures had to be relegated *only* to defense when under attack. Such a doctrine meant that the use of violence was to be seen as a last resort, a tragically necessary part of a national struggle that would distinguish itself from others by the stringency of its moral standards. No reprisals, no preemptive attacks, and no ambushes would be allowed. "Purity of arms" and "self-restraint" also meant that other-directed terrorism, or violence against Arabs, designed to deter future attacks on Jewish settlements would be beyond the pale.

In the context of escalating Arab attacks in the 1930s, culminating in the Arab revolt of 1936–38, and set against the militant psychological stance that both the fundamentals of Zionist ideology and the concrete reality of life in Palestine encouraged, these norms, not surprisingly, were rejected by some Zionist groups and bent, broken, and virtually abandoned by the Haganah itself in the late 1940s. In 1929 the Haganah had come under the control of the overall Zionist organization in Palestine, the Jewish Agency. In 1931 divisions between socialist and nonsocialist Zionists led to a split in the Haganah and the formation of Haganah B, most of whose members maintained close links with Jabotinsky's right-wing revisionist Zionist movement. In 1936 Haganah B became the Irgun Zvai Le'umi (National Military Organization), known by its Hebrew acronym, I.Z.L. (Etzel) or simply as the Irgun. Etzel abandoned *havlaga*. It adopted an aggressive policy of severe reprisals against the Arab population and of violent resistance against the British. An even more extreme group, Lehi, broke from Etzel in 1939. Led by Avraham (Yair) Stern, Lehi (Freedom Fighters for Israel) refused to cooperate with the British in the anti-German war effort and undertook an assassi-

14. Translated in *Saul Tschernichowsky*, ed. Silberschlag, 171.

nation campaign against British soldiers, police, administrators, and diplomats.

Even within the Haganah itself the outbreak of the Arab revolt in 1936 generated strong pressures to abandon "self-restraint." Guerrilla bands were formed by Yitzhak Sadeh and later, with official British support, by Orde Wingate, a British officer with millenialist Christian beliefs and fervent Zionist sympathies. These units, known respectively as "the field companies" and "the special night squads," emphasized preemptive attack, aggressiveness, and, in the case of the night squads, brutality. Five years later their members served as the backbone of the Palmach, the elite "striking force" of the Haganah that bore the brunt of the fighting with the Arabs in 1948.

But despite erosion in the *havlaga* policy, the Hagana refused to endorse indiscriminate reprisals against Arabs. Implying that such actions were popular within the Yishuv as a whole, Edward Luttwak and Dan Horowitz have explained how "this allowed the I.Z.L., and later the Lehi to compete with the Haganah for the support of the more activist elements within the Yishuv."[15] In 1936 the Irgun began attacking Arabs unconnected with specific attacks on Jews; these attacks were a form of collective retribution for Arab attacks on Jews and were intended to intimidate the Arab population as a whole. By the fall of 1937 this developed into a large-scale campaign of anti-Arab terror, including machine-gun attacks on Arab trains, grenades thrown at buses, and milk-can bombs placed in Arab markets. In one three-week period in July 1938 Irgun attacks killed seventy-six Arabs.[16] On the eve of World War II the British crushed the Arab rebellion. By 1944 the focus of Irgun activity, now directed by (future prime minister of Israel) Menachem Begin, shifted to attacks on the British forces occupying Palestine and preventing Jewish refugees from reaching its shores.

Both the Irgun and Lehi were explicit in their use of violence against Arab or British targets in an other-directed terrorist mode, that is, as a way to affect the calculations and behavior of wider enemy populations by inflicting pain, suffering, and death on specific individuals or groups. But they were also clearer than the Haganah about solipsistic rationales for their violence, the extent to which their military posture and their actions were designed to send messages to *Jewish* audiences. In his statement of the raison d'être of the Irgun, Begin emphasized, against the background of the Holocaust, the intrinsic importance of violent

15. Edward Luttwak and Dan Horowitz, *The Israeli Army* (London: Allen Lane, 1975), 18.
16. J. Bowyer Bell, *Terror out of Zion* (New York: Avon, 1977), 49–54.

struggle to the crystallization and preservation of the Jewish nation. "When Descartes said: 'I think, therefore I am,' he uttered a very profound thought. But there are times in the history of peoples when thought alone does not prove their existence. A people may 'think' and yet its sons, with their thoughts and in spite of them, may be turned into a herd of slaves—or into soap. There are times when everything in you cries out: your very self-respect as a human being lies in your resistance to evil. *We fight, therefore we are!*"[17]

According to Begin, British rule of Palestine was based on perceptions of Jews as "timid supplicants," perceptions reinforced by the *havlaga* policy, which he characterized as a form of "psychological disarmament." One purpose of the "revolt" (within which he included the actions of both Lehi and the Irgun) was therefore to liberate Jews from a psychological constraint they had labored under for two thousand years of exile. Not to plead, he stressed, but to fight, this was what the "new generation," which had "turned its back on fear," would show that it had learned by living in its own land.[18] The most important word in the Revisionist lexicon—repeated over and over by both Jabotinsky and Begin—was *hadar* (honor). To gain *hadar* Jews needed a fighting army; they needed it, according to the Irgun, "like air to breathe." "An *Army*, fighting for the freedom of the Homeland and ready to defend it even at the price of life, is the one thing needed by the Hebrew people more than anything else. For without army there is no nation, no homeland, no *honor*."[19]

Changing the image of the Jew (or Hebrew, as Zionists sensitive to traditional connotations of the word *Jew* preferred to say), by forming an army and by fighting, was not only important for its effect on Arab and British perceptions; it was particularly important for changing Jewish images of themselves. This is evident in the symbol of the revisionist Zionist movement, an upraised rifle superimposed on a map of Palestine (including Transjordan). In the late 1940s a recruiting poster used by the Irgun in the United States featured a Jewish soldier charging forward with a submachine gun in his hand; it read (in part) as follows:

Lash for lash the Irgun strikes back—and the Hebrew is no longer the British whipping boy in Palestine.

17. Menachem Begin, *The Revolt* (1948; reprint, Los Angeles: Nash Publishing, 1972), 46 (emphasis in original).
18. Ibid., 40.
19. "Irgun Zvai Leumi: B'Eretz-Israel—Aims and Methods," in *Psychological Warfare and Propaganda: Irgun Documentation*, ed. Eli Tavin and Yonah Alexander (Wilmington, Del.: Scholarly Resources, 1982), 7 (emphasis in original).

The Hebrew fights today. He stands battling for a spot on earth to call a home.

The Hebrew fighter is fed up with promises and sympathy. He is through asking . . . the eloquence of his weapons tells the world that he intends to live.[20]

Another future prime minister of Israel, Yitzhak Shamir, was a leader of Lehi. In 1943, with the Holocaust in progress, Shamir publicly endorsed terrorism as an effective weapon against Israel's enemies, but *primarily* as a means of rallying the spirit and mobilizing the will of the Jewish people as a whole.

Neither Jewish ethics nor Jewish tradition can disqualify terrorism as a means of combat. We are very far from having any moral qualms as far as our national war goes. We have before us the command of the Torah, whose morality surpasses that of any other body of laws in the world: "Ye shall blot them out to the last man." We are particularly far from having any qualms with regard to the enemy, whose moral degradation is universally admitted here.

But first and foremost, terrorism is for us a part of the political battle being conducted under the present circumstances, and *it has a great part to play: speaking in a clear voice to the whole world, as well as to our wretched brethren outside this land, it proclaims our war against the occupier.*[21]

Although other-directed terrorism played an increasingly dominant role, it is important to understand the extent to which solipsistic rationales for terrorist activity against Arabs continued to be influential after Israel's establishment, especially in the design and implementation of

20. Reprinted in Samuel Katz, *Days of Fire: The Secret Story of the Making of Israel,* (Jerusalem: Steimatzky's Agency, 1968), 248–49. The poster was displayed in 1947.

21. Quoted in *Al-Hamishmar,* 24 December 1987, from an article in *Hehazit* (Summer 1943); translated in *Palestine Perspectives* 34 (March–April 1988): 15 (emphasis added). In his final campaign speech before the June 1992 elections, Shamir evidenced his continuing belief in the solipsistic importance of war and violent struggle as a crucial element in the health of the Jewish national movement. Speaking at a memorial to Lehi fighters of the prestate era, Shamir remembered the glory and heroism of his struggle and those of his comrades. "We still need this truth today," he concluded, "the truth of the power of war, or at least we need to accept that war is inescapable, because without this, the life of the individual has no purpose and the nation has no chance of survival" (*Yediot Acharonot,* 22 June 1992, reported by the Foreign Broadcast Information Service, *Daily Report: Near East and South Asia,* 23 June 1992, 34).

Israel's reprisal policy in the early 1950s. The 1948 war ended with armistice agreements signed between Israel and Jordan, Lebanon, Egypt, and Syria. The armistice lines served as borders, though the agreements did not endow them with the status of mutually recognized boundaries. The primary operational task of Israel's army between the end of the war in 1949 and the war with Egypt in October–November 1956 was to deal with border flare-ups and infiltration by Palestinian Arabs, including refugees bent on revenge or simply trying to return to their homes or harvest crops from their fields. Clashes over rights in the demilitarized zone near the Sea of Galilee took place between Israeli and Syrian forces. Although both Egypt and Jordan tried to prevent, or at least limit, incursions by Palestinians from the West Bank and Gaza Strip, by the mid-1950s some Egyptian support was being supplied to the fedayeen groups operating against Israel from Gaza.

In 1949, eighty thousand men were demobilized from the Israeli army. The creation of a substantial and effective military out of what was left was a slow and difficult process. The reprisal raids ordered in response to incursions by Arab infiltrators offered early evidence of the low quality of many soldiers and officers. In several of these early operations, units displayed both cowardice and ineptitude. In this context an elite unit was created to carry out reprisals, Unit 101, whose members were recruited from among outstanding soldiers demobilized in 1949.[22] Commanded by Ariel (Arik) Sharon, this unit was at first sent into action clandestinely.[23] Unit 101 was so successful that when Moshe Dayan became chief of staff in December 1953, the unit was merged with the paratroop battalion, and Sharon was appointed as commander. Its mission was not only to continue reprisal actions but to infuse the paratroops and, through them, the entire army with its elan and fighting effectiveness.[24] Between March and August 1954 the paratroop battalion successfully conducted nine large-scale raids on Arab villages in the West Bank and Jordan. "In Sharon's unit the General Staff had at last acquired a reliable military instrument which could be trusted to carry out its combat missions in full. *Equally important, it also had a body of men who could set standards for the rest of the Army. Just as the small Unit*

22. Luttwak and Horowitz, *The Israeli Army*, 108–10.

23. Unit 101's attacks were considered by the Ben-Gurion government to be the actions of civilians "in the border settlements who had lost their patience" (Ben-Gurion speech on Israel Radio, 19 October 1953, in response to the destruction of the West Bank village of Qibya; transcribed in *Davar*, 20 October 1953; translated in Livia Rokach, *Israel's Sacred Terrorism: A Study Based on Moshe Sharett's Personal Diary and Other Documents* (Belmont, Mass.: AUG, 1980), appendix 1.

24. Luttwak and Horowitz, *The Israeli Army*, 111–13.

101 had been used to reinvigorate the larger paratroop unit, Dayan hoped to use the new paratroop battalion as a morale-builder and tactical school for the mass of the infantry."[25] Thus, Israel's policy of reprisal, or retaliation, which led to hundreds of cross-border attacks and thousands of Arab casualties between 1949 and 1956, had as its "target" not only Arab governments and potential Arab intruders but also Israelis, both in and out of uniform.

Israel's most famous soldier in the 1950s was Meir Har-Tzion, recruited by Arik Sharon for Unit 101. Dayan called Har-Tzion "our greatest warrior since Bar Kokhba" and referred to him in an article on army spirit as "an amazing fighter and model combat leader" who was, among other things, "capable of enjoying the battle itself."[26] Har-Tzion's reputation for bravery preceded his entry into the army. He had repeatedly crossed into Jordanian and Syrian territory on personal exploratory hikes. Captured by the Syrians, he had survived beatings and captivity in Damascus. When his sister was killed by bedouin, Har-Tzion infiltrated into Jordan, captured five members of the tribe he suspected of responsibility, and knifed four of them to death before setting the fifth free to tell of what had happened. Displaying an "almost superhuman" courage, he became a legend in his own time, personifying "an Israeli version of the Indian Fighters in the American Wild West. Laconically killing Arab soldiers, peasants, and townspeople in a kind of fury without hatred, he remained cold-blooded and thoroughly efficient, simply doing a job and doing it well, twice or three times a week for months."[27]

Extracts from Har-Tzion's diary show how much direct personal satisfaction he and, one can presume, those who emulated him, took from implementing the "reprisal" policy. After describing in vivid detail the tension and violence of a 1954 raid on Hebron, in which every Arab man encountered was killed, he recounts his emotions returning to base.

We feel new energy now. A feeling of happiness overcomes us. We succeeded. We accomplished the action! Where are the doubts, the worries, the fatigue, the fear? A feeling of victory and power takes over. We are strong. Now we are not afraid of anything. . . .

The last meters. Here is the car visible in front of us. Arik [Sharon] welcomes us with a big smile and shakes our hand,

25. Ibid., 113 (emphasis added); see also Ze'ev Schiff, *A History of the Israeli Army* (New York: Macmillan, 1974), 80–82.

26. Shabtai Teveth, *Moshe Dayan: The Soldier, the Man, the Legend* (Boston: Houghton Mifflin, 1973), 210.

27. Amos Elon, *The Israelis: Founders and Sons* (New York: Bantam, 1972), 305.

excited. The time for retaliation had arrived. Retaliation for everything.

Similarly, after returning from a particularly bloody raid against the West Bank village of Nahalin, Har-Tzion remembers "gorging ourselves with the delicacies awaiting us" in the dining room of an Israeli settlement. "In the corner there is a group of senior army officers who came to closely watch the daring fighters. We lift our noses and look down at the world around us. Everything is as beautiful as a sweet dream which is all good. This is the joy of victory. The real joy."[28] The political and cultural salience of the legend of Har-Tzion for the next generation of Israelis is suggested by the publication of his diary in 1969, during the height of the War of Attrition and the struggle against PLO terrorism. In his "enthusiastic introduction" to the diary, Sharon described Har-Tzion as "the fighting symbol not only of the paratroopers, but of the entire Israel Defense Forces."[29]

Moshe Sharett served as Israel's prime minister from November 1953 to November 1955 and as foreign minister from 1948 to 1953 and from November 1955 to the middle of 1956. Sharett favored a much more carefully calibrated policy of retaliation than did Ben-Gurion, one sensitive to questions not only of scale but of timing and international public opinion. Contrary to Ben-Gurion and other Labor party militants, such as Chief of Staff Moshe Dayan, Defense Minister Pinchas Lavon, and Foreign Minister Golda Meir, Sharett also advocated Israeli openness toward tentative Arab peace overtures. In the course of explaining how his political opponents thwarted his policy preferences, Sharett's diary entries reveal a great deal about the nondeterrent motives surrounding the retaliation policy.

One of the most important of these was a perceived political need to satisfy the Israeli public's desire for revenge. Commenting on the arrest of Meir Har-Tzion and his companions in connection with the murder of four bedouin (described above), Sharett was upset at the public's sympathy with the perpetrators.

In the thirties we restrained the emotions of revenge and we educated the public to consider revenge as an absolutely negative impulse. Now, on the contrary, we justify the system of reprisal out of pragmatic considerations . . . without justifying the princi-

28. Meir Har-Tzion, *Diary* (Tel Aviv: Levin-Epstein, 1969), 171–72; quoted by Rokach, *Israel's Sacred Terrorism*, 64 and 65.
29. Elon, *The Israelis*, 307.

ple of pure revenge but without meaning to, we have eliminated the mental and moral brakes on this instinct and made it possible . . . to uphold revenge as a moral value. This notion is held by large parts of the public in general, the masses of youth in particular, but it has crystallized and reached *the value of a sacred principle* in (Sharon's) battalion which becomes the revenge instrument of the State.[30]

Public opinion was generally so belligerent that opportunities for partisan advancement were regularly available to "hawks" within the government. Confident of popular support in the event of public controversy, those in control of the army could and did engineer large-scale reprisal raids to derail peace initiatives or otherwise embarrass "doves" such as Sharett. Thus did Ben-Gurion authorize the Qibya raid shortly before leaving office, leaving it to Foreign Minister Sharett, who had opposed both the dimensions and timing of the attack, to explain it. In February 1955, with Ben-Gurion back in the government as defense minister, and Sharett as prime minister, American diplomacy had succeeded in bringing Nasser and Sharett close to a nonbelligerency agreement. Ben-Gurion proposed a small retaliation raid against an Egyptian position in the Gaza Strip. Sharett felt constrained to approve it in light of a recent act of Arab infiltration that had "shocked the public." Given the public mood, wrote Sharett in his diary, "a lack of reaction is unacceptable." Before the fact Sharett complained privately that Ben-Gurion, and not he, would get credit for the raid, but he was outraged when, instead of the ten Egyptian casualties that Ben-Gurion had estimated as the maximum, scores of Egyptians were killed and wounded, triggering a crisis in Egypt, bringing an end to American efforts toward an Israeli-Egyptian peace, and setting the stage for an Egyptian-Soviet alliance and the transfer of heavy Russian arms to Egypt. In November 1955 Ben-Gurion replaced Sharett as prime minister. In December, with Sharett, now foreign minister, in Washington negotiating for U.S. arms, Prime Minister Ben-Gurion suddenly (and without informing Sharett) ordered a large-scale reprisal raid against Syria. This directly undercut the foreign minister's prestige and his ability to build diplomatic bridges in the West.

Sharett soon left the government. Not long afterward the reprisal policy reached its climax in the October 1956 attack on Egypt, the logic and tactics of which resembled a retaliation raid on the largest possible

---

30. Quoted and translated by Rokach, *Israel's Sacred Terrorism*, 36, from Sharett's diary entry for 31 March 1955 (emphasis in original).

scale. Like the host of smaller raids that preceded it, the "Sinai Campaign" combined a desire to deter hostile Arab activity by promising disproportionate punishment for every wound inflicted on Israel (other-directed terrorism) with solipsistic rationales—motives pertaining not to the manipulation of Arab calculations or behavior but to Jewish/Israeli politics and psychology. Thus, according to Samuel Roberts, the Suez War stemmed from public pressures inside Israel for "the rigorous application of the policy of reprisals." After both Herut and the "activist"-oriented Ahdut ha-Avodah parties both made substantial gains in the 1955 elections, "the government, alarmed by the growing popularity of the militants, and fearful of a continuation of the trend, was prodded into adopting a harsher policy toward Egypt. . . . the pressure of public opinion played a significant role in leading the Israeli government to adopt the policy of preventive war in 1956."[31]

But there is evidence that this public mood was itself, at least partially, the result of a reprisal-and-propaganda campaign designed to maintain a high level of tension among Israelis and reinforce their distrust and even hatred of the Arabs. According to Yoram Peri's path-breaking analysis of civil-military relations in Israel, an important group of generals believed, after the 1948 war, "that Israel should initiate a second round of war. . . . The IDF's top echelons, led by the Chief of Staff, undisguisedly promoted this view. At the tactical level, it was evident in the activist climate prevalent in some army units, especially 101 Commando Unit headed by Major Arik Sharon. The generals openly encouraged an increase in retaliatory raids, both in quantity and scope, to force an escalation in tension."[32]

Supportive of Peri's analysis is a report of a May 1955 conversation between Chief of Staff Moshe Dayan and a group of top Israeli diplomats. In the midst of discussions about the possibility of an American-Israeli security pact to calm border tensions between Israel and Egypt, and Israel and Jordan, Dayan told his interlocutors that he was averse to such agreements—agreements that would spell the end of the reprisal policy. For Dayan, apparently, the most important purpose of the retaliation raids was their impact not on Arabs but on Israelis.

We do not need a security pact with the U.S. . . . [It] will only handcuff us and deny us a freedom of action, and this is what we

31. Samuel J. Roberts, *Survival or Hegemony? The Foundations of Israeli Foreign Policy* (Baltimore: Johns Hopkins University Press, 1973), 120–21.
32. Yoram Peri, *Between Battles and Ballots: Israeli Military in Politics* (Cambridge: Cambridge University Press, 1983), 237.

need in the coming years. *Reprisal actions which we couldn't carry out if we were tied to a security pact are our vital lymph.* First, they make it imperative for the Arab governments to take strong measures to protect the borders. *Second, and that's the main thing, they make it possible for us to maintain a high level of tension among our population and in the army. Without these actions we would have ceased to be a combative people and without the discipline of a combative people we are lost. . . . We have to cry out that the Negev is in danger, so that young men will go there.*[33]

SOLIPSISTIC TERRORISM, PALESTINIAN NATIONALISM, AND THE ASCENDANCY OF THE PLO

Arab poetry and literature pertaining to the Zionist presence in modern Palestine, and Palestinian poetry and literature, especially as it developed after 1948, emphasized themes of impotence, degradation, and humiliation. In fact, these ideas were present in the very earliest expressions of Palestinian Arab nationalism. In a "General Summons to Palestinians," issued in June 1914, by one of several newly founded societies committed to violent and nonviolent struggle against Zionism, the Arab people of Palestine were portrayed as having fallen in rank, from "masters, leaders, and scholars" to "the lowest and most despicable of people." "Our spirit has been blunted; our heart has died. Evil straits have taken possession of us in a way that disaster follows disaster. Happy is he who addresses an ear that hearkens. . . . Dangers have surrounded us already from every side, every direction, every corner: but does the wound of a dead man grieve him?"[34]

These motifs, describing a despised and lifeless people, that were so prominent in Zionist portrayals of the Jewish Diaspora, were increasingly accompanied by celebrations of Arab violence perpetrated against Jews. In this way anti-Jewish violence served Arabs and Palestinians, as

33. From Sharett's diary entry for 26 May 1955, quoted and translated by Rokach, *Israel's Sacred Terrorism*, 44 (emphasis added).
34. Neville J. Mandel, "Turks, Arabs, and Jewish Immigration into Palestine: 1882–1914" (Ph.D. diss., Oxford University, 1965), 480–81. Mandel's source for the text of the summons is a letter by A. Eisenberg to Gad Frumkin, dated 3 July 1914, cited by J. Rau, *The Attitude of the Yishuv to the Arabs: 1880–1914* (in Hebrew) (Jerusalem, 1964), 609.

anti-Arab violence served Zionist Jews, as a vehicle for raising national morale, proving the validity of important elements of the national ideology, and infusing the people in whose name the violence was perpetrated with enhanced self-esteem and renewed vitality. As in the Jewish-Zionist case, other motives were present as well, including the desire, by striking at some, to encourage others to emigrate from Palestine or discourage potential Jewish immigrants to stay away. But there can be little doubt that the primary audience for most organized Palestinian violence against Jews, at least until the early-1970s, was not Jews but Arabs, especially Palestinian Arabs.

According to Khalid Sulaiman, elegies written for Palestinian Arabs killed during the mandate period by either Jews or the British authorities do not mention the contribution their violent acts may have made to changing Zionist or British attitudes or to weakening the Jewish national home. Instead, the poems glorified the heroism of the slain while indicting the cowardice and moral degeneracy of the people as a whole, especially its leaders. Celebrating the "martyrdom" of two of the first leaders of organized violent resistance to the Zionist project, Shaikh Izz-id-Din al-Qassam and Shaikh Farhan al-Sal'di, the poet Mutlaq 'Abd al-Kahliq wrote:

> They, like lions springing out of the depths of the desert,
> sacrificed themselves for their country.
> They renounced pleasure in worldly things, not
> attracted by a cup of wine or a slim girl.
> Poor, they were; yet their concern was not to be rich,
> but to die honorably.[35]

'Abd al-Rahim Mahmud, who himself participated in the 1936 revolt and was later killed in 1947, also emphasized the demonstration of courage and a willingness for self-sacrifice, rather than any direct effect of his efforts on the Jews or the British, as of decisive importance. His actions, and the qualities they were seen to reflect, were evoked to shame his countrymen into action. The following passages are from two of his poems, "The Martyr" and "A Call for Jihad."

> In my hand I will bear my soul, ready to throw it into
> the abyss of death. A man should live with honor and
> dignity, otherwise he should die gloriously.

35. Khalid A. Sulaiman, *Palestine and Modern Arab Poetry* (London: Zed Books, 1984), 29–30.

The soul of the noble man has but two aims: either to
die or to attain glory. I swear I can see my
fate, but I quicken my steps towards it.
The only desire I have is to fall defending my usurped
rights, and my country.

To him who fears death I said: Are you afraid of
facing crises?
How can you stay still while your homeland cries for
help? Are you too cowardly to fight enemies? If so,
there is your mother's boudoir to break in.
For you, this meanness is fair enough.[36]

For both Palestinians and Zionists the figure most often cited as
emblematic of Palestinian violence before 1948 is Shaikh Izz id-Din al-
Qassam. Al-Qassam, along with several followers, was killed in a shoot-
out with British soldiers in 1936. In Zionist historiography, al-Qassam
was a "Muslim fundamentalist" and "terrorist" whose followers "murdered" innocent Jews and helped trigger what Zionist historians call the
"Arab riots" of 1936–38, a period during which, according to Ben-Gurion,
"Arab terror spread to all corners of the country."[37] In Palestinian
historiography, however, al-Qassam was among the first of the "fedayeen," the self-sacrificers, those whose willingness to lay down their
lives for Palestine enabled Palestinians to escape the humiliation of
Zionist success and kindle a healthy national consciousness.

Indeed, the role of Qassamite violence in the 1930s was much more to
inspire Palestinian Arabs (specifically Muslims) than to intimidate Jews.
Discovered and surrounded by the British while still in what al-Qassam
himself saw as a preliminary stage of his struggle, he is reported to have
ordered his men to "die as martyrs." "Al-Qassam's defiance and the
manner of his death," according to Abdullah Schleifer, "electrified the
Palestinian people." Schleifer acknowledges the primarily solipsistic motive behind the violence al-Qassam was preparing for when he died.
Despite the fact that the immediate objects of terrorist violence were to
be Jews or Britons, its primary target audience was to be Muslim Arab.
"Al-Qassam continuously returned to the theme that it is not a necessary

36. Ibid., 31–32.
37. Yehoshua Porath, *The Palestinian Arab National Movement, 1929–1939* (London:
Frank Cass, 1977), 132–39 and 183, and David Ben-Gurion, *Israel: A Personal History*
(Tel Aviv: Sabra Books, 1972), 48. For the Arab rebels as terrorists seeking to instill fear
in the Jewish community as a whole, see Yigal Lossin, *Pillar of Fire: The Rebirth of Israel*
(Jerusalem: Shikmona Publishing Company: 1983), 225–29.

condition that the Muslims be as strong in number and weaponry as their enemy when the fighting starts . . . even if he knows he is going to die . . . martyrdom inspires the other Muslims to continue the struggle and the martyr's death is kindling wood for *jihad* and Islam. . . . The *mujahid* must be the vanguard and light the way for those who will follow."[38]

The same interpretation of Qassamite violence is advanced by Ghassan Kanafani, who described his movement as a classic example of Che Guevara's *foco* theory of revolution. Guevara advocated dramatic displays of violence, not to destroy or intimidate the enemy, but to arouse the fighting spirit and solidarity of the "oppressed."[39] The death of al-Qassam and the militant activities of those of his followers who survived contributed powerfully to the eruption of the Arab revolt in the late 1930s. (Weakened by internecine strife, the revolt was crushed by British reinforcements on the eve of World War II.)

The full impact of Zionist success on Palestinian Arab consciousness and on the Arab world (including Arabic literature) was not felt until after the massive defeats inflicted by Israel on its neighbors in 1948 and in 1967. Although before 1948 Palestine had been the subject of some Arab poetry, in the wake of the 1948 defeat and the creation of the refugee problem (collectively referred to in the Arab world as al-Nakba, the "disaster" or "tragedy") a host of Arabic plays, stories, and novels pertaining to Palestine were published. Another literary outpouring on the subject was generated by the second major defeat, in 1967, known as *al-Naksa*, the "setback." In both waves of literary material the themes of an anguished, unbearable sense of despair and humiliation were dominant. This literature corresponded to the most influential analyses of their predicament published by Arabs, and it helped create the context, in the 1960s, for organized violent resistance by Palestinians— violence again motivated more by the message it would send to dispirited Arabs than by the extent to which it would damage or "terrorize" the Zionist enemy.

The two most influential analyses of the causes of the 1948 defeat were *The Meaning of the Disaster*, by Constantine Zurayk, a Lebanese Christian, and *The Lesson of Palestine*, by Musa Alami, a Palestinian Muslim. Both ascribed the crushing nature of the defeat to the backwardness and disunity of the Arab world, the ineptitude of its leadership, and the feeble spirit of the Arab masses. They described the extent of the

38. S. Abudullah Schleifer, "The Life and Thought of 'Izz-id-Din al-Qassam," *Islamic Quarterly* 5, no. 23 (1979): 69 and 72.

39. Ghassan Kanafani, *The 1936–39 Revolt in Palestine* (Committee for Democratic Palestine, n.d.); first published in *Shuun Filistiniya*, June 1972.

humiliation in excruciating detail, not in the least by comparing the Arabs, as fighters and as a national movement, unfavorably to the Jews.[40] Both Alami and Zuraky insisted that sweeping modernization of Arab life in social, economic, educational, military, and political spheres was the only way out of the Arab predicament. But the basis for all the institutional reforms and political realignments they saw as necessary was what Zurayk called "the first fundamental principle . . . to strengthen the sense of danger and sharpen the will to fight." "When this awareness grows strong, the will to struggle, which unfortunately is still weak among us, will grow with it. Our struggle in this battle was, in general, the struggle of an effete dilettante and not the struggle of one ready to die—as though only lip service and not actual obligations were involved."[41]

For Alami, as well, the crucial question was courage and self-sacrifice, qualities that, he noted scornfully, the contemporary Arab world lacked. The recovery of Palestine, he argued, was the only way for Arabs to regain their self-respect. And the only way to do that would be to emulate their ancestors who had destroyed the Crusader state in Palestine by displaying just these virtues. "Palestine and the self-respect of the Arabs must be recovered. Without Palestine there is no life for them. This our ancestors understood truly as of old. Their understanding was better than ours, when Europe attacked and took Palestine from them. They were willing to die for it and continued to struggle until they recovered it. Thus it is today."[42]

These political analyses, as shocking and bitter as they were, struck responsive chords among Arab intellectuals and closely corresponded to the themes dominating literary reactions to the Palestinian "catastrophe" as well. In the early 1950s the plight of the refugees was the focus of a great deal of literature—poems, plays, short stories, and novels. Themes of sadness, shame, impotence, and shock were predominant, along with heavily sentimentalized images of "the Return," expressions of bitter anger at the betrayal of Arab leaders, and calls for revenge.[43] This emphasis on the experience of humiliation and the imperative to revali-

40. Musa Alami, "The Lesson of Palestine," *Middle East Journal* 3 (October 1949): 397, and Constantine Zurayk, *The Meaning of the Disaster* (Beirut: Khayat's College Book Cooperative, 1956), 7–8, 25, 30–31, and 35–36. Zurayk was particularly emphatic in his unfavorable assessment of Arab versus Jewish nationalism.
41. Zurayk, *The Meaning of the Disaster*, 14 and 16.
42. Alami, "The Lesson of Palestine," 386.
43. Sulaiman, *Modern Arab Poetry*, 93–105, and Howard Douglas Rowland, "The Arab-Israeli Conflict as Represented in Arabic Fictional Literature" (Ph.D. diss., University of Michigan, 1971), 61–102 and 292–98.

538 Nationalism and State Formation

date Arab nationalism through the display of manly virtues (courage, discipline, and self-sacrifice) played a role in Arab violence against Israel identical to the role played by the ideological and psychological imperatives of Zionism in Jewish violence against Palestinians. In the Arab case, these political exhortations and literary tropes provided a paradigm for interpreting Palestinian violence against Israel—no matter how inconsequential in practical terms and no matter how "innocent" the specific victims—as an heroic and vital contribution to the national struggle, whether defined in Pan-Arab or Palestinian terms. This, in turn, encouraged the growth of fedayeen groups and created internal pressures, especially in Jordan and Egypt, to provide them with support.[44]

In the work of no other Palestinian author has the logic of movement from humiliation to violence and from violence to revitalization been more effectively or artfully expressed than in the fiction of Ghassan Kanafani. While serving as official spokesman of the Popular Front for the Liberation of Palestine, Kanafani, at age thirty-six, was killed by a car bomb planted by Israeli agents. His novella, *Men in the Sun*, was published in 1962 and is emblematic of his early work. Its themes are representative of much of the literature produced by post-1948 Palestinian writers. It is a story of three Palestinian refugees who try to smuggle themselves from Lebanon across the desert into the Gulf states to find higher-paying jobs. After their silent and meaningless deaths, suffocated within a tanker truck delayed at the border, the Palestinian driver bewails their fate. After discarding their bodies in a garbage dump, he robs them. The author's message: there is no life in exile, only humiliation and death.

Themes of lost dignity and the connection between manhood, self-respect, and violent struggle are repeated throughout the story. One of the three refugees thinks of his life in exile, "squatting like a dog in a miserable hut." Another is afflicted by knowledge of the "terrible truth, the truth which proclaimed his father had fled . . . fled . . . fled." The driver, who literally lost his manhood during the fighting in 1948, lives by the motto "Money comes first, then morals."[45] The one positive figure in the story is Ustaz Selim, whom one of the refugees remembers as the simple teacher in his villge whose commitment to violent resistance against the Jews distinguished him from all the others.

44. Avi Plascov, *The Palestinian Refugees in Jordan, 1948–1957* (London: Frank Cass, 1981), 87–90.

45. Ghassan Kanafani, *Men in the Sun* (Washington, D.C.: Three Continents Press, 1978), 13 and 28.

The mercy of God be upon you, Ustaz Selim, the mercy of God be upon you. God was certainly good to you when he made you die one night before the wretched village fell into the hands of the Jews. One night only. O God, is there any divine favour greater than that? It is true that the men were too busy to bury you and honor you in your death. But all the same you stayed there. You stayed there. You saved yourself humiliation and wretchedness, and you preserved your old age from shame.[46]

As Muhammad Siddiq has shown, in his study of Kanafani's work, the author's evolving political consciousness corresponded with broad trends among the Palestinian population, moving in the mid-1960s away from despair, alienation, and impotence toward commitments to self-reliance and armed struggle. Siddiq's analysis of Kanafani's early writings (1956–65) identifies a twin preoccupation with the humiliation of exile and the revitalizing role of violence.

When set in Palestine, the action in these stories invariably dramatizes the heroic sacrifice of individual fighters who fall as they make a last desperate stand. . . . When set outside of Palestine, the action of these stories invariably deals with the physical and psychological hardships the Palestine refugees experience . . . the Palestinian characters either retreat completely from involvement with external reality and perish under the weight of their personal sorrow, or they seek to overcome their hardships by concealing their true identity. In either case death, loss, and impotence often result.[47]

The point is that for Kanafani, as for most Palestinians of the time, violence inflicted on Jews was not valued for its effects on Jews individually or on Israel as a collectivity. Rather, it was valued for the signals it could send to Palestinians. In one Kanafani story written in 1965 the protagonists differ over whether violent struggle is appropriate or possible. The hero of the story concludes, in a flash of insight, that any practical questions about gaining the means to struggle or calculating its rationale are irrelevant. "You just cannot ask a fighter why he is fighting. It is as if you asked a man why he is a male."[48] Thus, Kanafani portrays violent struggle as an elemental aspect of being a man and, by extension,

46. Ibid., 11.
47. Muhammad Siddiq, *Man Is a Cause: Political Consciousness and the Fiction of Ghassan Kanafani* (Seattle: University of Washington Press, 1984), 86–87.
48. Ibid., 40, quoted from *Of Men and Rifles*.

as the chief vehicle for rebuilding Palestinian pride and national self-esteem.
Much, if not most, Arabic literature pertaining to the conflict with Israel has been written by non-Palestinian Arabs. Throughout the Arab world a tremendous outpouring of fiction and poetry on the subject was triggered by the shocking defeat of the Arab armies by Israel in 1967. Prevalent in this literature are the same themes I have indicated dominated Palestinian writing after 1948. In "Lament for the June Sun," written in 1968, the leading Iraqi poet, 'Abd al-Wahab al-Bayati, combined a sense of abject humiliation and loss of manhood with scathing criticism of Arab leaders and Arab society.

> In the cafés of the East we have been ground
> by the war of words,
> by wooden swords
> and by lies and quixotic knights.
> . . . .
> Engaged in vanities we killed each other.
> and here we are like crumbs.
> In the cafés of the East
> we [pass the time] in swatting flies,
> wearing the masks of the living.
> We are placed in the dunghill of history
> mere shadows of men.[49]

Commenting on the work of another outstanding Arab poet of the same generation, Nizar al-Qabbani, one Israeli scholar notes that after 1967 Qabbani's poetry "deals almost completely with the themes of the Palestinian problem . . . the bitter laments over the defeat, mixed with stupefaction. This feeling gradually gives way to anger against the leaders and the intellectuals who were responsible for the catastrophe, a call for revenge, support for al-Fath and the Arab terrorists who are regarded as the last hope for restoring the pride and glory of the Arabs."[50]

Qabbani's endorsement of the newly emergent Palestinian guerrilla organizations, led by Fatah (Fatah's first armed action took place on 1 January 1965), reflected a major shift in Arab prose and poetry away from sighing about the lost land and toward enthusiastic promotion of

49. Translated in Sulaiman, *Modern Arab Poetry*, 133.
50. Z. Gabay, "Nizar Qabbani, the Poet and His Poetry," *Middle Eastern Studies* 9 (May 1973): 218.

the image of Palestinian fighters as martyrs. What, asks Khalid Sulaiman, did the fedayeen represent for the poets he studied? The "Fida'i," writes Sulaiman, "represents the birth of a new Palestinian Arab who will no longer tolerate being helpless and crushed in refugee camps. . . . after the defeat in June 1967, the Fida'i is seen by the Arab poet as the only visible manifestation that the Arab nation is still alive, or has something to be proud of in its modern history, which has been dominated by shameful setbacks and defeats." Sulaiman quotes the poem "Fath" (1968), by Qabbani, as representative.

> After we died,
> after they prayed over our bodies
> and buried us,
> after our bones had calcified
> and we became worn out,
> after we suffered starvation and thirst
> the Fath came to us
> like a beautiful rose sprouting from a wound,
> like a spring irrigating salty deserts,
> And so we, all of a sudden, tore off our shrouds
> and rose from the dead.[51]

According to Howard Rowland's study of representations of the Arab-Israeli conflict in Arabic literature, the post-1967 period was dominated by the efforts of Arab writers to alleviate their own despondency over the defeat, and that of the Arab world as a whole, by glorifying the Palestinian guerrillas. They made, Rowland writes, "deliberate efforts . . . to aid in creating something which could be called the New Arab Man . . . depicting the Fedayeen as the ideal type of human being whom they feel all Arabs should emulate." As presented in post-1967 novels, plays, and short stories, this prototype is strikingly close to part of the ideal cultivated by early Zionists and represents a similar process of "reaction formation" against the dominant personality types perceived to have developed in "exile." "The New Arab Man—the guerrilla who will save his people's honor—is shown to be not only tough, courageous, and willing to sacrifice his life for his country. . . . The Fedayeen, in addition to this, are shown as being silent, practical, and realistic men who do their work without expecting either tangible rewards or a great martyr's

---

51. Sulaiman, *Modern Arab Poetry*, 140 and 141. See also Suhayl Idris, "A Salute to the Arab Fedayeen," first published in *Al-Adab*, February 1968; trans. Rowland, in "The Arab-Israeli Conflict," 322–23.

funeral." Drawing on the work of authors such as Yahya Yakhlaf, Layla
Usayran, Suhayl Idris, Hamid Yakuff, and Ghassan Kanafani, Rowland
points out how dramatically their fiction contrasts the "tough, taciturn,
and totally professional" fedayeen with the "humiliated, timorous refugee
living in a camp because he could not or would not fight for his country
in 1948."[52]

Consideration of the calculated purpose and actual role of "armed
struggle" for the Palestinian guerrilla organizations in the 1960s and
early 1970s shows how closely reality paralleled art in these respects.
However, early PLO doctrine ascribed at least a theoretically nonsolipsistic function to attacks on Israeli targets.

The founders of Fatah were inspired by the success of the Algerian
Revolution in eliminating the French presence through sustained and
violent struggle. But in Algeria the indigenous Muslims outnumbered
the European inhabitants (including half a million French soldiers) by
almost eight to one. In Palestine, Israeli Jews outnumbered Arabs two
to one and roughly equaled the total of Palestinians outside and inside
the country. In this context, and taking into account what was perceived
by Arabs as an extraordinarily high level of Israeli military proficiency,
no important guerrilla organization, including Fatah, ever claimed that
the violence of which Palestinians were capable could itself directly
destroy Israel or induce its capitulation to Palestinian demands.

Considering the establishment of the guerrilla organizations as relevant factors in the Middle East had been accomplished by the end of the
1960s, Hisham Sharabi suggested, in 1970, that serious thinking about
the strategic purpose of the armed struggle had only then become
relevant. Based on interviews conducted with Fatah and PFLP (Popular
Front for the Liberation of Palestine) leaders in Jordan in August 1969,
Sharabi reported that "protracted struggle" rather than a "decisive
military victory" was anticipated by "all resistance leaders." Although
this would result, in their view, "in the progressive wearing down of the
enemy," the crucial expectation was that Israel would react by wider and
increasingly ferocious retaliation against Arab targets. Sharabi reported
that the PFLP expected such spiraling violence to galvanize the Arab
masses into a long "people's war" that would "Vietnamize the Arab
situation," leading eventually to a military victory over Israel. Fatah, on
the other hand, contemplated at least the possibility that there could be
"a change of heart within Israel, among the rank and file of the Israeli
people, leading to . . . the rise of a new leadership with a new policy
based on peace and reconciliation."[53]

52. Rowland, "The Arab-Israeli Conflict," 329, 330, and 333.
53. Hisham Sharabi, 44–46.

In the case of the PFLP's strategy of "Vietnamization," the violence was other-directed, but it was not intended to affect Israeli intentions, policies, or behavior. Its purpose instead was to unleash a revolutionary transformation of the Arab world, giving rise to a mass people's war that would remove the Arab regimes and destroy (not change) Israel. Israelis, in other words, were to be the objects of violence but not the audience for it. In the case of Fatah, to the extent that Sharabi's account is accurate, violence against Israelis had at least a theoretical role as a mechanism for changing Israeli behavior by changing the incentive structure to which the Israeli people respond. Still, these links, even in Sharabi's analysis (which is slanted toward the interpretation of PLO thinking in as coherent and systematic a fashion as possible), are only implicit.

In fact, abstract discussions of the different forms a protracted people's war might take were largely irrelevant to the small scale of operations either the PFLP or Fatah were capable of sustaining. The more evident (nonsolipsistic) rationale for Fatah attacks before 1967 was the hope, not to soften Israeli policies, but to harden them—to goad Israel into large-scale retaliation policies. The increasing severity of these strikes would draw the Arab states into direct conflict with Israel, producing a cycle of war and Israeli expansion that would, it was theorized, lead to decisive battles between Israel and a united Arab world.[54] In the meantime, Israel's overextension would endow the Palestinian guerrillas with masses of new recruits and a larger array of vulnerable targets.[55] "The resistance leaders seem almost eager to see Israel expand, for the more Israel holds the more it has to defend, and the broader the target areas for the guerrillas. Moreover, people, when they begin to feel the harsh yoke of occupation, inescapably turn from observers into participants."[56]

In his analysis of PLO military thinking, William Quandt did attribute other-oriented terrorist objectives to Fatah, but only as a minor theme. Nor did he offer evidence of such thinking before the publication of an article, in 1971, by Nabil Sha'ath. Citing this article, Quandt explains that aside from "the mobilization of Palestinian sentiment on behalf of nationalist objectives," another, "more ambitious" objective was at times present, "that of bringing about changes within Israel that would make an eventual accommodation possible. Israelis, it was argued, could be forced to recognize the validity of Palestinian grievances. The burden of

54. See Schiff, *A History of the Israeli Army*, 166–67, and Edgar O'Ballance, *Arab Guerilla Power: 1967–1972* (Hamden, Conn.: Archon Books, 1974), 27.
55. Hisham Sharabi, *Palestine Guerrillas: Their Credibility and Effectiveness* (Washington, D.C.: Georgetown University Press, 1970), 50–51.
56. Ibid., 51.

continuing warfare, heavy defense spending, and costly casualties would also eventually serve to convince the Israelis to accept political arrangements in which Palestinian demands were granted."[57]

Despite evidence that some Fatah leaders viewed Israel itself as the target audience for their violence, the main purposes of their attacks, from the first Fatah raid against Israel on 1 January 1965 to at least the 1973 war, were solipsistic. According to Gérard Chaliand, the operations launched by the guerrillas were "intended to win popular support." By early 1969, he observed, the armed struggle had begun to bear fruit. His evidence is its effect on Arabs, not on Israelis. "Soon, the impression made by the resistance on Arab public opinion overtook the influence of Baathism and Nasserism and imposed itself upon the mass of Palestinians."[58] Violence against Jews, in other words, was fostered to persuade Arabs of Palestinian virtue, not to intimidate Israelis or contribute to a military victory over Israel.

Salah Khalaf (Abu Iyad) was one of the founders of Fatah whose association with Black September involved him in its most notorious terrorist activities. Before his assassination in the aftermath of the Gulf War, Khalaf was regarded as second after Arafat in the leadership of the PLO. In his autobiographical account, *My Home, My Land*, Khalaf cited Frantz Fanon as "one of my favorite authors," from whom he learned the lesson of how central was armed struggle for any nation desiring independence. Fatah, argued Khalaf, sought to apply Fanon's analysis to the Palestinians. In addition to the international attention it would gain for their cause, he emphasized what armed struggle would do *for* Palestinians, not *to* Israelis: "The founders of Fatah were well aware of Israel's military superiority . . . but still they set as their main objective the launching of the armed struggle. Not that we harbored any illusions regarding our ability to overcome the Zionist state. But we believed that it was the only way to impose the Palestinian cause on world opinion, and *especially the only way to rally our masses to the peoples' movement we were trying to create.*"[59]

In 1969 Arafat himself described the transformation of the Palestinians "from downcast refugees into aroused fighters" as "one of the greatest achievements of our revolution."[60]

---

57. William B. Quandt, *Palestinian Nationalism: Its Political and Military Dimensions* (Santa Monica, Calif.: Rand Corporation, November 1971), 78.

58. Gérard Chaliand, *The Palestinian Resistance Movement (in early 1969)* (Beirut: Fifth of June Society, n.d.), 19; originally published in *Le monde diplomatique* (March 1969).

59. Abu Iyad (with Eric Rouleau), *My Home, My Land: A Narrative of the Palestinian Struggle* (New York: Times Books, 1981), 34–35 (emphasis added).

60. Quandt, *Palestinian Nationalism*, 76n.

Evidence that Fatah's founders were correct in their assessment of the psychological importance of armed struggle for the masses of Palestinians was presented by Rosemary Sayigh in her study of Palestinian refugee responses to the emergence of the "Palestinian Resistance Movement" in the late 1960s and its eventual takeover of what she (and her interlocutors) termed the Revolution. "As an 18-year old schoolboy phrased it: 'The Revolution gave me the answer to who I am.' Instead of being part of a despised, marginal group of 'displaced persons' Palestinians now adopted en masse the role of vanguard of the Arab revolution. . . . This conscious adoption of a 'struggle-identity' encompassed Palestinians of all ages in the camps."[61]

Helena Cobban's 1984 study of the PLO reflects the consensus of relevant secondary literature on the purpose and effect of what she calls the rush into armed struggle. "The key political achievement of the armed national movement of the Palestinian exiles proved in the long run to be its role in defining a Palestinian renaissance around which the Palestinians remaining in Palestine could also organize."[62] According to Cobban, whatever rudimentary ideas Fatah's founders had about armed struggle's potential military contribution against Israel or about the importance of strong political organization were secondary to their desire to "galvanize" Arab societies and contribute to the "Palestinians' reassertion of their political identity. . . . In a certain sense, one was meant to marvel . . . not so much at how well they did it, but at the fact that they did it at all."[63]

Cobban stresses that in the wake of the 1967 war solipsistic motives for armed struggle displaced all others. This was the result of the shock of the defeat and the overwhelming response of Palestinians (and Arabs) to the image of violent struggle itself, regardless of the reality. Once launched, she contends, the armed struggle "took on a dynamic of its own," until

the "guerrilla idea" threatened to overwhelm all other thinking in the Palestinian sphere—despite the fact that the historic leaders

61. Rosemary Sayigh, *Palestinians: From Peasants to Revolutionaries* (London: Zed Press, 1979), 166.

62. Helena Cobban, *The Palestinian Liberation Organization: People, Power, and Politics* (Cambridge: Cambridge University Press, 1984), 256–57. For similar judgments about the primarily solipsistic rationale behind Palestinian violence against Israel in the mid to late 1960s, see Chaliand, *The Palestinian Resistance Movement*, 19; Abdallah Frangi, *The PLO and Palestine* (London: Zed Books, 1982), 102–8; Michael Hudson, "The Palestinian Arab Resistance Movement: Its Significance in the Middle East Crisis," *Middle East Journal* 23, no. 3 (1969): 307; and Yehoshaphat Harkabi, *Fedayeen Action and Arab Strategy*, Adelphi Papers no. 53 (London: ISS, December 1968), 12–15, 25, and 35–36.

63. Cobban, *The Palestinian Liberation Organization*, 253.

of Fateh still fully realized the limitations on its effectiveness at the purely military level. Since popular outrage at the Arabs' defeat of 1967 absolutely demanded that something—anything—be done to protest it, the Fateh leaders with their keen eyes for popular psychology could not stand aside, but instead developed their successive theories of trying to light the flame of struggle inside the newly occupied areas, and, when that failed, of at least showing that the Arabs could still stand and fight, which they did at Karameh.[64]

In many respects, what the death of Trumpeldor and his seven companions in the defense of Tel-Hai was to Zionism, Karameh was for the Palestinians. At this small Jordanian village in March 1968, Fatah fighters stood their ground against a large Israeli reprisal raid supported by tanks and thousands of soldiers. Although advised before the attack by the Jordanian high command to evacuate, and despite its contradiction of the classical theory of guerrilla warfare, Fatah ordered two hundred of its men to fight a pitched battle with the Israelis. The decision, according to Salah Khalaf, was based on the leadership's view that their primary "audience" was not Israeli but Arab. "Guerrillas by definition do not give battle to a regular army. Their effectiveness depends to a large extent on their mobility. However, political considerations inclined us to the opposite view. . . . the Palestinians, and more generally the Arabs, would never understand if once again we left the field open to the Israelis. Our duty was to set an example, to prove that the Arabs are capable of courage and dignity."[65] Despite Israel's seizure of Karameh, the death of five times as many Palestinian defenders as Israeli attackers, and the key role played by Jordanian armor and artillery, the fact that Palestinians had fought bravely, that some tanks had been abandoned by the Israeli army, and that twenty-three Israeli soldiers had been killed triggered an unprecedented outpouring of support for Fatah and its strategy of armed struggle above all else. The myth of Karameh (meaning "dignity" in Arabic) explains the meteoric rise of the PLO as a whole from semiobscurity to the central stage of Middle Eastern politics, the virtual takeover of the organization by Fatah, and a veritable flood of recruits into guerrilla training camps. Karameh was, in Chaliand's words, a highly successful act of "armed propaganda."[66] At the time of the battle of Karameh, Fatah commanded approximately two thousand

64. Ibid., 256.
65. Abu Iyad, *My Home, My Land*, 58.
66. Chaliand, *The Palestinian Resistance Movement*, 19.

men. Within three months it grew to fifteen thousand. Within the next two years total PLO strength rose to more than thirty thousand.[67]

CONCLUSION

The main purpose of this chapter has been to demonstrate how large a role solipsistic terrorism played in the development of Zionist and Palestinian consciousness and institutions. I have not claimed that other motives for violence were not also important, even, at times, more important. These included efforts to intimidate or destroy the enemy, attract world attention, or trigger larger conflicts (both regional and international).[68] Nor have I argued that solipsistic and other-directed rationales for political violence are mutually exclusive. Both are usually present, but in a changing balance. But without understanding the distinctiveness of solipsistic terrorism and its predominant role at key points in the movement of both peoples toward their national objectives, it is impossible to appreciate the importance of its relative decline as a factor, on both sides of the conflict, since the late 1960s and early 1970s.

In conclusion, I wish mainly to argue that for both Jews and Arabs other-directed rationales for violence (usually construed as terrorism by its victims) must take precedence over solipsistic motives if the two peoples are to move toward political compromise. I suggest that this has, in fact, occurred, and that decades of solipsistic terrorism may have contributed to the ability of each side to shift its attention from using violence to satisfy its own psychic and political requirements to using violence to manipulate the calculations and intentions of its adversary. The logic here is that the principle of settlement by bargained compromise, which since the middle of the 1992 has guided both the Israeli government and the PLO leadership, could not even be entertained until each antagonist had established its own political personality with enough coherence to treat it as the background to, and not the target of, attacks

67. Hudson, "The Palestinian Arab Resistance Movement," 300, and David Hirst, *The Gun and the Olive Branch* (New York: Harcourt Brace Jovanovich, 1977), 296. Concerning the importance for the image of heroic resistance at Karameh and its impact on the fortunes of Fatah, see O'Ballance, *Arab Guerilla Power*, 46–56; Sharabi, 25 and 29; and Cobban, *The Palestinian Liberation Organization*, 42–43.

68. Included within the category of other-directed terrorism meant to attract international attention or trigger conflicts would be the Munich Olympics operation and skyjackings carried out by Palestinian groups in the early 1970s and the Israeli-sponsored bombings against American installations in Egypt in the mid-1950s.

on its adversary. Only then did each take the other seriously enough, and respect the other enough, to seek the change in the other's behavior (i.e., to target each other's publics as audiences for the perpetration of violence).

Accordingly, despite escalation in the amount or viciousness of violence, dramatic changes in the meaning and purpose of that violence for its perpetrators can be seen to have signaled real progress toward a more peaceful future. With Israel's victory in the 1956 war and a second, even more astonishing demonstration of military superiority in 1967, Israelis became increasingly confident that Zionism had indeed created a "new Jew," willing and able to fight successfully for his rights. This provided Israeli society with the psychological resources necessary for many of its members to be prepared to take risks, to make concessions, for peace. However important it has remained, for internal political purposes, to retaliate harshly for deadly terrorist attacks against Israelis, and despite the prominence of revenge as a motive for many of these reprisal raids, solipsistic motives for violence against Arabs were increasingly displaced by other-directed rationales. Between 1967 and 1973 this was most saliently reflected in artillery barrages in the Jordan valley; air strikes, deep penetration raids, and commando incursions in Egypt; air strikes and punitive expeditions into Syria; and a host of attacks against targets in Lebanon. In addition to the actual destruction of military assets (and, in the case of the PLO, political infrastructures) these attacks were designed (wisely or unwisely) to affect the calculations of Jordanian, Egyptian, Syrian, and Lebanese governments about whether and to what extent they would use, condone, or allow violent activities against Israel. This was part of what Israelis called the War of Attrition, whose very name suggests how concretely they understood the fighting as other-directed terrorism—a struggle to terrorize or intimidate the Arabs more efficiently than they themselves were being terrorized.

Meanwhile, the Palestinians under occupation in the West Bank and Gaza Strip became more aware of both the strengths and weaknesses of Israel. This led to their advocacy of a Palestinian state in those territories, alongside of Israel, not instead of it. By 1973 this point of view had begun to exercise a significant influence on opinion within the PLO outside of Palestine. Combined with the self-confidence its solipsistic terrorism had helped build among Palestinians, this idea encouraged a Palestinian shift toward other-directed terrorism.[69] It is in this context

69. This was not reflected in an end to terrorist attacks. In fact, the most spectacular terrorist attacks on Israeli civilian targets took place between 1972 and 1978. But Fatah and the PLO as a whole, far from issuing the kind of exaggerated claims of destruction associated with its solipsistic attacks of the 1960s, either denied responsibility or asserted

that Nabil Sha'ath's 1971 article, referred to above, about the role of guerrilla violence in achieving productive political change within Israel can be understood. And thus does Rowland, in his study of representations of the Arab-Israeli conflict in Arabic literature, note that portrayals of violence against Israel inspired by "other-directed" rationales figured prominently, and for the first time, in the writings of Palestinians living in the territories occupied by Israel in 1967. "They become 'resistance fighters' just like those, for example, of Nazi occupied France, Norway, Yugoslavia or Russia during World War II. Their aim is to make Israeli occupation of their area so precarious and costly that the Israelis will be in a weak and defensive position and might prefer to withdraw from the West Bank (and possibly abandon the idea of maintaining the state of Israel in the Middle East)."[70]

Another turning point was the 1973 war, a conflict in which Arab military success against Israel on both the Syrian and the Egyptian fronts and the withdrawal of Israeli forces from at least symbolic amounts of territory in Golan and Sinai helped restore Arab self-confidence. Arab motives in this war were mixed: to attract the attention of the great powers to the urgency of resolving Arab claims against Israel, to convince Israel that the territorial status quo would be too expensive to maintain, and to provide the Arab states with the self-confidence and political flexibility associated with demonstrating courage and military prowess against Israel. Indeed, these were all crucial factors in setting the stage for the Egypt-Israel peace agreement and the de facto nonbelligerency that has been achieved between Israel and Jordan and even, it could be argued, between Israel and Syria.

A striking indication of how fundamentally the Israeli-Palestinian conflict has changed is the difference between the primarily other-directed terrorism that both sides used against one another during the *intifada*, which lasted in its most intense form from December 1987 to the summer of 1990, and the more prominent role of solipsistic terrorism, as I have described it, during most of their century-old struggle. For the young generation of Palestinians in the West Bank and Gaza Strip, throwing stones and Molotov cocktails at Israeli soldiers and settlers broke what they called the "barrier of fear." In this sense their violence was solipsistic and fits into the long pattern of Palestinian terrorism against Jews designed to build Palestinian national consciousness. In-

---

its objective was instrumentally other-directed (to trade hostages for prisoners or to disrupt negotiations that did not include Palestinian representatives), or was meant to keep international public opinion aware of the Palestinian issue.

70. Rowland, "The Arab-Israeli Conflict," 327.

deed, for many refugees, women, and others newly drawn into the political struggle by the *intifada*, its solipsistic aspect was its most salient dimension. But the discipline exhibited by the entire population in limiting the scale and nature of attacks against Israelis, and the careful guidance of its local leadership (the United National Command of the Intifada), were indicative of a decisive shift in the balance of motivation among West Bank and Gaza Arabs toward other-directed violence. An important purpose of the uprising for most Palestinians and its central purpose for the elites who have emerged out of it was to hurt Israelis— hurt Israeli soldiers, hurt Israeli settlers, hurt the Israeli economy, and hurt Israeli consciences. The immediate objects of the violence were, for example, settlers traveling in cars and buses, and soldiers and border police on patrol. But the target audiences for most of this activity were the Israeli government, Israeli public opinion, and also international, especially American, opinion. The objectives, very clearly and explicitly, were to intimidate, scare, "terrorize" the Israelis into ending the occupation by raising the felt costs of continuing it and to convince the outside world of the untenability of the status quo.

Disciplined implementation of this strategy reflected a systematically nonsolipsistic approach. Its effect on the Israeli body politic was complex, but no one disputes the fact that as a result of the *intifada* Israelis abandoned what opinion surveys had consistently shown to have been their most popular policy option toward the future of the territories— "maintenance of the status quo." Indeed, it is hard not to credit the efforts of the Palestinians of the territories with substantial achievements in the Palestinian struggle for national self-determination. The *intifada* was directly, if not wholly, responsible for a number of crucial developments that helped bring the peace process to the point of meaningful *nonviolent* bargaining over the terms of an interim accommodation. These include the PLO's formal acceptance of United Nations Security Council Resolution 242, its endorsement of a two-state solution, the American dialogue with the PLO, the energetic efforts of the Bush administration to orchestrate Arab-Israeli and especially Israeli-Palestinian peace talks, the unprecedently sustained U.S. pressure on the Shamir government over the loan guarantees, the rise to power in Israel of a Labor party government opposed to Israel's permanent rule of the territories and to expansive settlement efforts there, and, of course, Israel's breakthrough decision to recognize the PLO as the representative of the Palestinian people.

But for West Bank and Gaza Palestinians the cost of sustaining the *intifada* was tremendous—much higher, for example, in terms of casualties per capita, economic dislocation, and proportion of the population incarcerated, than the Irish struggle against the British in 1919–21. It is quite reasonable to assume the uprising could not have been mounted or carried through to the success it enjoyed had it not been for the high levels of national self-esteem that decades of solipsistic terrorism by Palestinians inside and outside the country helped to build. Certainly its disciplined implementation reflected a systematically nonsolipsistic approach and a national self-confidence strong enough to organize suffering as an act of courage, not of humiliation. It also entailed a very great degree of concern, analysis, and understanding of the other, the Israelis; mobilization around a political objective moderate enough for Israelis to contemplate as possibly preferable to the status quo; and images of Israelis realistic enough to make enforcement of politically expedient restraints possible. In sharp contrast to the exaggerated accounts of casualties inflicted on Israelis that were the norm in the press releases of Fatah and the PFLP in the late 1960s and early 1970s, the PLO and the uprising's leaders prided themselves on how few Israelis had been killed.

There is good reason to suppose that for Zionism, as for Palestinians, decades of solipsistic violence helped lay the psychological and political groundwork for equally stunning reversals. In the past, Jewish violence against Arabs was a source of pride and a proof of Zionist success in forging a new Jewish personality, but the dominant concern about such violence during the *intifada* was the extent to which it was inflicting psychological harm on Israeli soldiers, ruining the army's fighting spirit, brutalizing Israeli society as a whole, and destroying, in the process, key elements of what Zionism meant to accomplish. While Irgun commanders Meir Har-Zion and his superiors had often exaggerated their exploits in order to stoke the fires of nationalist self-confidence, Israeli army policy and practice duringthe *intifada* was to minimize the amount of violence it was inflicting on Arabs, even to the point of grossly misrepresenting the facts.[71]

Regardless of how far present Israeli proposals may be from what will be necessary to reach a negotiated settlement, and despite the brutality of the repressive measures used to subdue the uprising, Israeli policy was oriented toward affecting Palestinian calculations about what would be best for their political future. Instead of speaking only to themselves with their anti-Arab violence (solipsistic terrorism), seeking to destroy

71. See Middle East Watch, *The Israeli Army and the Intifada: Policies That Contribute to the Killings* (New York: Human Rights Watch, August 1990), and B'tselem, *Violations of Human Rights in the Occupied Territories, 1990/91* (Jerusalem: Israeli Information Center for Human Rights in the Occupied Territories, 1992).

(rather than change) Palestinian aspirations, or acting as if what Palestinians want and think is irrelevant for Israel's future, Jews are now engaged with Palestinians. Even if during the height of the *intifada* Israel terrorized by imprisonment, deportation, shooting, breaking bones, blowing up houses, and imposing curfews, the terrorism was in this instance other-directed; its perpetration and threats of escalation were primarily meant to affect Palestinians, not Jews.

The picture is grim but hopeful. It is of a continuing struggle for political control of Palestine/the Land of Israel between two peoples who believe they deserve as much of it as they can get. Each side has demands to make of the other. Each side has fresh and painful memories of the bloody results of the other side's violence. The point of this chapter, however, is that violence experienced as "terrorism" is not itself the problem. We may shrink from endorsing violence as a necessary part of solutions to political conflicts, yet we might acknowledge that it can make both perpetrators and victims more prepared for compromise and that the sheer amount of violence is not as relevant an indicator of how far from resolution a conflict might be than the rationales for it. After a century of violent contact, it appears that both Jews and Palestinian Arabs achieved enough coherence and confidence in their national identities, in part brought about by brutal acts of terrorism, to make their enemies the targets as well as the subjects of dramatic violence. That has meant, at least, that when Jews hurt Palestinians or Palestinians hurt Jews, they are primarily seeking something from each other, not something from themselves. It is fair to call such violence terrorism, but it is also communication. As such it opened up both the possibility of accommodation and the real hope of success.

13

Terrorism and Politics in Iran

Jerrold D. Green

It is not widely known that terrorism has a long history in the area that today composes Iran. Here of course I make reference to the sect of the Assassins. Founded by Hassan-i Sabbah, who was born in the city of Qom in the middle of the eleventh century, the Assassins were used by the "Old Man," as he became known, in an attempt both to create an

The author would like to thank R. K. Wild for his help in assembling information for this study as well as the following for sharing their impressions of recent events in Iran and, where appropriate, for their comments on this paper: Kemal Beyoghlow, Patrick Clawson, Martha Crenshaw, Steven Fairbanks, Ian Lustick, Tom Miller, Augustus Norton, Madelyne Patick, Barry Rubin, and Gary Sick. Naturally, the author alone remains responsible for the contents of this chapter, which was completed in August 1992.

empire and to propagate Ismaili Islam. Born a Twelver Shi'ite, Sabbah was gradually converted to Ismailism and eventually devoted his life to its expansion. Operating from his castle on a rocky mountain at Alamut, Sabbah dispatched missionaries to seek converts, and more-militant representatives to undermine and even kill those who opposed him. Ultimately, Sabbah became infamous for the latter, who constituted a cadre of well-trained and exceedingly devoted murderers whose expertise helped to add the word "assassin" to the English lexicon. Highly regarded and universally feared for their skillful ability to dispatch the Old Man's enemies, these precursors to modern terrorists were totally devoted to their master. Their willingness and even eagerness to die for him both terrified and impressed their enemies and competitors alike. The fact that the Assassins' compliance stemmed not solely from loyalty to Sabbah but also from more transcendental religious values made this devotion even more significant as well as terrifying.[1] For these men perceived themselves as working not merely for another man but for God.[2]

The above is mentioned because the rediscovery of the Assassins by observers of Middle East politics has not been inconsequential. For example, as a declassified U.S. government intelligence report notes in reference to the Assassins, "While there is no historical connection between this sect and current Iranian terrorist groups, the patterns of operation are essentially the same, and the cultural factors which aided the medieval sect continue to aid present groups."[3] No further information is provided to document what is meant by similar "cultural factors"

1. The "religious value" referred to here is a desire to die while doing the Old Man's bidding and thus to go directly to heaven, as he promised his disciples they would. Sabbah primarily recruited peasant boys whom he domiciled in a heavenly garden setting. Historians report that their every need was ministered to by beautiful young maidens and that the Old Man successfully tricked his followers into believing that they were actually living in paradise. To make them further malleable, they were plied with hashish. Admittedly, their view of religion was instrumental; they were eager to die so that they could go back to the beautiful garden and the pretty maidens, to heaven as it was described to them and as they had experienced it. Nonetheless, spirituality clearly played an important role in harnessing the efforts of the Old Man's disciples and in motivating them to do his bidding.

2. The discussion above is derived from Bernard Lewis, *The Assassins: A Radical Sect in Islam* (New York: Octagon Books, 1980). This book has become the standard work on the topic, and my brief discussion of Lewis's findings in no way does justice to his detailed and thorough scholarship.

3. This startling assertion is to be found in Air Force Office of Special Investigations, *Special Report: Terrorist Movements in Iran* (December 1975), 1. This report was obtained by Professor James Bill through the Freedom of Information Act, and I thank him for sharing it with me along with another report, published by the same office, entitled *Anti-American Terrorism in Iran* (December 1975).

or "patterns of operation." Still, on a superficial level the similarity between events in eleventh-century Persia and twentieth-century Iran are obvious and easy to grasp: two religious zealots, both with ties to the religious center of Qom, both with unquestioned commitment to their religious values, used violence to expand the sphere of their personal influence. Indeed, each devoted his life to the expansion of his respective religious community. Both were adherents to Islam, albeit of different sects, and each was willing to use violence in order to expand his circle of believers. Put somewhat differently, according to current folk wisdom, the situation in contemporary Iran, as ruled by Ayatollah Ruhollah Khomeini and his successors, is not that different from eleventh-century Persia during the time of Hassan-i Sabbah. Just as Sabbah's Assassins became synonymous with violence and lawlessness in the name of religion eight hundred years ago, so has Khomeini and those that have followed him in the modern Islamic Republic of Iran. Indeed, the conventional popular view of the Iranian Revolution is that it was a social upheaval dedicated to bringing Iran back to where it was in the past. Thus, it is assumed that Sabbah was a precursor to and a model for Khomeini and his followers. The difficulty with this analogy is that it does justice to neither the eleventh nor the twentieth centuries. Although lumping apparently telling similarities together, this perspective ignores profound and important differences. These differences are far more instructive than the apparent affinities that link the two. This issue is introduced at the outset of this chapter to highlight the problems and challenges inherent in the study of terrorism in contemporary Iran. Indeed, the topic is as politicized and shrouded by myth as are better-known issues such as the Arab-Israeli conflict or the Lebanese Civil War.

Many observers in government, the academy, and the media have already made up their minds about the role of terrorism in current Iranian politics. The Islamic Republic of Iran is regarded in Washington with skepticism, if not outright repugnance.[4] This is not difficult to understand. It is not by accident that the leaders of Iran are struggling to reverse their isolation. And this isolation is not only international but

4. I conducted both formal and informal interviews with a variety of United States government officials in Washington. My goal was twofold: first, to learn from experts on Iran in government how they interpreted recent events in Iran, and second, to learn how experts on terrorism perceived Iran's international role. I strived to determine how they regarded American policy toward terrorism in general and toward Iran in particular. It became abundantly clear that in government, as in the academy, there are experts on terrorism *and* there are regional experts. Occasionally one finds someone well versed in both areas, but this is rather rare. Thus, the fundamental conceptual problems inherent in the study of terrorism are not inconsequential.

556 Nationalism and State Formation

also domestic; many Iranians regard their own government as intractable
and harsh. As Amnesty International wrote in its *Iran Briefing* of 1987:

> Thousands of Iranians have been executed since 1979, many in
> secret. Anyone suspected of supporting the opposition has been at
> risk of arbitrary arrest and detention. Political detainees have
> been brutally tortured in prisons and detention centers through-
> out the country. Political trials are summary, with practically no
> defense rights at all. Courts impose amputations and flogging
> as punishments—punishments which contravene human rights
> standards by their cruelty and inhumanity.[5]

Thus, the Iranian government is feared not only in the international
community but also at home, where it has succeeded in alienating
thousands of its own people. The public persona of the Islamic Republic,
which reflects many of its abhorrent policies, makes Iran an exceedingly
difficult country to analyze in an objective and dispassionate fashion.
Iran has, in a limited sense, become an outcast in the international
community. These factors, when combined with the fact that Iran is
largely off-limits to political researchers, have led to ideological musings
in the place of the more detached and systematic types of political
investigation that are so desperately required.

In light of these factors, a study of terrorism in Iran must begin by
overcoming two obvious and disturbing clichés: The first is a widespread
and popular belief that Iran is a terrorist country and that it has always
been so; "assassination for the purposes of religious propagation was
virtually invented there." Second, the government of the Islamic republic
is cruel, harsh, and unyielding; it is capable of almost any barbarism
(N.B. the treatment of its own citizens); it is implacably opposed to the
West; and it will stop at nothing to accomplish its goals. Both of these
stereotypes contain elements of truth, particularly the second, although
each is fundamentally flawed. They are of little utility in helping us to
understand or analyze Iranian politics past, present, or future.

Despite a lingering sense in the West that terrorism in Iran is inevitable, the question is obviously much more complicated than people generally believe. For the purposes of this chapter it is assumed that in Iran
terrorism is not the product of inexorable primordial or cultural forces
and influences; *terrorism is a learned behavior.* Yet violence has histori-

5. See Amnesty International, *Iran Briefing* (London: Amnesty International Publica-
tions: London, 1987), 1. See also Amnesty International, *Iran: Violations of Human
Rights—Documents Sent by Amnesty International to the Government of the Islamic
Republic of Iran* (London: Amnesty International Publications: London, 1987).

cally been a central feature of Iranian political culture. The questions, therefore, are How is this behavior learned? Where does it come from? Why will a government resort to terrorism, and how does it persuade its citizens to undertake such activity? Throughout this chapter it is shown that during both the Pahlavi and Khomeini periods, terrorism of different sorts has existed in Iran. Yet it has been neither the sole, or even a primary, means of policy implementation for the government nor an oppositionist tool to challenge the state; rather, it has served as *one* means of political expression. Categorizing terrorism as a type of political character is in no way meant to condone it. For what is terrorism, after all, but a rejection of normal and accepted political practice? Yet ironically, those who employ terror often do so in the name of freedom and democracy. It should be noted, however, that terror is generally a means to an end, rather than an end unto itself. Iranian political elites and counterelites are nothing if not calculating and opportunistic, much like their counterparts in the West. For them, terrorism is one of several political options. The questions are Why is it selected? How is it used? and What is its purpose? Assuming that terrorism is merely one means to an end, this chapter will explore how it fits more broadly into Iranian political practice, when it is deployed, and when eschewed.

TERRORISM DURING THE EARLY YEARS OF THE PAHLAVI DYNASTY

Although political terrorism can be traced back through Persian history for hundreds of years, my concern in this chapter is with modern Iran. A recognizable historical epoch began with Reza Shah Pahlavi's ascent to the Peacock Throne in 1926, and thus my investigation begins with this period. During his reign Iran came to develop a distinct character that was to dominate the Pahlavi dynasty until the revolution of 1979. That is, the second shah, Mohammed Reza, was overthrown as a result of initiatives, policies, and directions initiated and undertaken by his father.

Reza Shah took control of the Iranian state with the goal of converting the country into a modern, Western-style, and westward-looking polity. His goals and tactics were heavily influenced by those of Kemal Ataturk in neighboring Turkey, and under Reza Shah's rule Iran gradually veered in directions that were not anticipated by many of its people and that were fundamentally unacceptable to many others. Although a fierce Persian nationalist, Reza Shah had little use for Islam, which he saw as a vestige of a bygone era that deprived the country of its rightful place as a regional power. Viewing the Islamic clerical establishment as backward looking, reactionary, unwilling to relinquish its vested power, and as a general impediment to the type of development that he desired for his country, Reza Shah devoted much of his time and power to combating it. Stories of his prohibiting traditional dress, having his soldiers rip the veils from observant women, or even riding his horse into a mosque have become enshrined in Iranian lore in a fashion that made the Pahlavis heros to a few and devils to many more.

Reza Shah's assault on Islam was far-reaching and exceedingly disruptive. One colorful, if not necessarily reliable, account squarely positions the roots of the Iranian revolution in this period and relates how Ayatollah Khomeini, then a young mullah, traveled through Iran in disguise and was forced to avoid urban centers so as to elude the shah's modernizing soldiers, who might have forced him to shave his beard and remove his mullah's turban.[6] It was here, the author opines, that Khomeini developed a deep and personal hatred for the Pahlavis. Although the veracity of this tale cannot be verified, it does reflect the degree to which Reza Shah disrupted traditional Persian/Iranian society. And in response to his efforts were sown the seeds of dissent that led to the Islamic revolution some fifty years later.

Iran quickly developed into a country dominated by Reza Shah. He had definite ideas about what Iran should look like and quickly strived to eliminate competition from all quarters. According to Ervand Abrahamian:

> Having undisputed political power, Reza Shah initiated a number of social reforms. . . . he implemented reforms that, however unsystematic, indicated that he was striving for an Iran which . . . would be free of clerical influence, foreign intrigue, nomadic uprisings and ethnic differences. . . . His long-range goal was to rebuild Iran in the image of the West—or, at any rate in his own image of the West. His means for attaining this final aim were secularism, anti-tribalism, nationalism, educational development, and state capitalism.[7]

Thus, Reza Shah effectively launched an attack on traditional Persian culture and its institutions. His goal was to convert Iran as it was into

6. This nondocumented but illustrative story appears in Amir Taheri, *The Spirit of Allah: Khomeini and the Islamic Revolution* (Bethesda, Md.: Adler and Adler, 1986), 78–80.

7. Ervand Abrahamian, *Iran Between Two Revolutions* (Princeton: Princeton University Press, 1982), 140.

Iran as he felt it should be. This goal necessitated a far deeper renovation and destruction than one would generally find in democratic societies, where advocates of one political party might be asked to vote for a competing party. For in Iran, Reza Shah sought much more fundamental changes while demanding that Iranians change themselves from who they were into who he felt they should be. And the changes he forced were geared to converting Iran from a heterogeneous society into a more manageable homogeneous one. It is difficult to appreciate how disruptive such efforts can be when people are compelled to change the way they talk, think, dress, relate to others, and so forth. It can safely be argued that Iran today is still struggling with and convulsed by many of the changes initiated by Reza Shah Pahlavi.

There was opposition to the shah's efforts from virtually every quarter. And the brutality and callousness that was employed to enforce Reza Shah's will often engendered equal brutality from those he was trying to suppress and promoted widespread animosity toward the emerging Iranian state. According to one scholar of the period:

> In his struggle to consolidate power and prepare the way for his new Pahlavi dynasty, Reza Khan authorized political assassination of some of his outspoken enemies, such as Mirzadeh Eshghi, the well-known liberal journalist and poet. His first chief of national police, Brigadier Muhammad Darghai, was nicknamed "Muhammad the Knife" because of his control of clandestine political assassinations of the new Shah's enemies.[8]

The shah's secret police ruthlessly and effectively controlled dissent, and the final years of his rule were not noted for significant terrorist activities. Yet in years to come the legacy of the Reza Shah period was one of conflict, terror, revolution, and more terror, with a dialectic emerging in which state violence and oppositional terror encouraged one another.

In 1941 Great Britain and the Soviet Union jointly brought the Reza Shah dictatorship to an end. And as the political and military currents of World War II swept Europe, Iran was not immune to these forces. Iran's intellectual and religious sectors were convulsed by conflicting intellectual currents, debates, doubts, and recriminations. Foreign military occupation as well as the absence of a genuine central government enhanced feelings of both Persian and Islamic nationalism among the country's dissatisfied politicized sectors. Each was dissatisfied for differ-

8. Sepehr Zabih, "Aspects of Terrorism in Iran," *Annals of the American Academy of Political and Social Science*, 463 (September 1982): 85.

ent reasons. For although both groups opposed foreign domination, the intellectuals were opposed to it for reasons of Persian nationalism, whereas the religious sector opposed domination of an Islamic country by nonbelievers. This group was even more critical of Britain than of the Soviets, since Britain's role and influence in Iran were of longer duration and greater significance to most Iranians. The burgeoning Left did particularly well because it was, at times, abetted by the Soviet occupiers; the religious community, on the other hand, was still fragmented.[9] It was during this period that the Tudeh Party reached the zenith of its influence and its ability to mobilize popular support. As Sepehr Zabih writes: "While the occupation lasted, the presence of foreign troops both aided and impeded large-scale acts of terrorism. . . . It encouraged terrorism because both powers, particularly the Soviet Union, gave free rein to political groups supporting their cause."[10] There is evidence to suggest that several of the Communist groups, including elements of the Tudeh, although hardly synonymous with terror in this period, relied on terrorist activities to advance their interests. The period of active Soviet involvement and influence in Iran was in effect the golden era for the Tudeh, which was able to enjoy unprecedented opportunities for political mobilization. Soviet attempts to infiltrate and subvert Azerbaijan and Kurdistan were particularly vigorous because these areas were closest to the Soviet border. As Zabih further writes: "The process of setting up Communist regimes (e.g. in northern Iran) involved a systematic and well-organized campaign of political assassination of Iranian politicians opposed to Soviet policies. Perhaps this was the first clear manifestation of transnational terrorism on a large and organized scale in this period."[11] Unsurprisingly, ethnicity triumphed over Iranian nationalism as border differences disappeared. Those Kurds and Azeris who shared a commitment to the Soviet Union actively worked to advance their causes irrespective of their citizenship. And although their efforts ultimately failed, there still exist today significant pockets of sympathy for the former Soviet Union both in Kurdistan and in Azerbaijan. Although pro-Moscow terrorism ultimately was unable to accomplish the goals of its

9. Far more has been written about the Left in this period than has been written about the religious sector. See, for example, Sepehr Zabih, *The Left in Contemporary Iran: Ideology, Organization, and the Soviet Connection* (Stanford, Calif.: Hoover Institution Press, 1986). See also the work by Ervand Abrahamian, including "The Strengths and Weaknesses of the Labor Movement in Iran, 1941–1953," in *Continuity and Change in Modern Iran*, ed. Michael Bonine and Nikki Keddie (Albany, N.Y.: SUNY Press, 1981), 181–202.

10. Zabih, "Terrorism in Iran," 86.

11. Ibid., 86.

architects, the terrorist activities of other groups were not so easily
thwarted.

During this period Islamic fundamentalism began to grow in influence
throughout the country. Most notable among fundamentalist groups,
from the perspective of terrorist activities, was the Fedayeen-i Islam,
which was founded in 1946 by a twenty-two-year-old theology student in
Tehran named Sayyid Navab Safavi.[12] This fundamentalist group embodied an ideology not uncommon to such Islamic groups. It called for a
return to rule by *shari'a* (Islamic law) and demanded a strict adherence
to Islamic principles, which were presented and interpreted in as narrow
and restrictive a form as possible. This group was small, and its members
were unsophisticated; its leader, Safavi, has been referred to as "a half-
educated fanatic." The first formal act of his group was the assassination
of Ahmad Kasravi.[13] In addition to being one of Iran's foremost thinkers,
Kasravi was often described as being an iconoclast.[14] According to one
historian of the period, Kasravi, "although not an atheist, . . . opposed
all existing religions."[15] Indeed, Kasravi went so far as to write that
"Shi'ism, in addition to being incompatible with wisdom and thus objectionable on this ground, is also a hindrance to [a meaningful] life."[16] This
conflict between those striving to impose Islamic rule in a strict and
doctrinaire fashion and those who preferred a more liberal and secular
political order has come to dominate Iranian politics in the fifty years
since the murder of Kasravi. And the Fedayeen-i Islam rapidly became
pawns in a high-stakes competition for power among a variety of contending groups. Their significance lies in the fact that as an avowedly terrorist
group their activities became part of the mainstream of Iranian political
life. That is, terrorism became a common and "normal" facet of political
expression in Iran.

Evidence of the tacit acceptance of political assassination in the Iranian
political context of the time lies in the fact that the assassins of Kasravi,
who had the temerity to shoot him in the chambers of a judge at the

12. Abrahamian, *Iran Between Two Revolutions*, 258.

13. Leonard Binder, *Iran: Political Development in a Changing Society* (Berkeley and
Los Angeles: University of California Press, 1964), 199.

14. See ibid., 81, where Binder describes Kasravi's "outrageous iconoclasm," and Abrahamian, *Iran Between Two Revolutions*, 258, who describes him as Iran's "most famous . . .
iconoclastic historian."

15. Azar Tabari, "The Role of the Clergy in Modern Iranian Politics," in *Religion and
Politics in Iran: Shi'ism from Quietism to Revolution*, ed. Nikki Keddie (New Haven:
Yale University Press, 1983), 60.

16. This is quoted by Farhad Kazemi, "The *Feda'iyan-e Islam*: Fanaticism, Politics, and
Terror," in *From Nationalism to Revolutionary Islam*, ed. Said Amir Arjomand (Albany,
N.Y.: SUNY Press, 1984), 160.

Ministry of Justice in Tehran, were ultimately acquitted. Members of the religious community used their influence to secure an acquittal, which was facilitated by the fact that the government was more fearful of the Tudeh Party and of Communist subversion that it was of the religious sector. Thus, it was felt that by "throwing" the wildly unpopular Ahmad Kasravi to the religious community, the clerics would then support the government and allow it to direct all of its resources against the Tudeh. In short, political assassination was tolerated in order to generate political support, and ideology was strengthened at the expense of the rule of law.

This period heightened the political involvement and influence of Ayatollah Sayyed Abol Qasem Kashani.[17] Kashani, for a period of approximately three years (1948–51), reportedly worked closely with the terrorist Fedayeen-i Islam, although direct ties have never been fully documented between the two. At the same time, he also formed his own group, named the Society of Muslim Warriors. His close association with the Fedayeen, it is hypothesized, contributed to the September 1946 Fedayeen assassination of Abdel Hussein Hazhir, minister of court and former prime minister.[18] These presumed close ties persisted until 1951, when Khalil Tahmasebi, a twenty-six-year-old carpenter and devoted Fedayeen member, assassinated Prime Minister General Ali Razmara at Tehran's central Shah Mosque on 7 March. Put on trial, Tahmasebi, according to one historian of this period, "owed his spectacular acquittal to the declarations of Kashani, who took responsibility for this execution, and congratulated its 'heroic' perpetrator."[19] Indeed, Kashani arranged for the release of the assassin in November 1952. Despite these events the differences between Kashani and the Fedayeen were profound, for the latter was dogmatic and promoted an austere form of fundamentalist Islam, whereas Kashani was best known for being a pragmatic and astute politician whose religious convictions never interfered with his personal political ambitions. For him the Fedayeen was merely a tool to be used and to be discarded when necessary. Although not a terrorist himself, Kashani was not above exploiting terrorists when it suited him.[20]

17. For an analysis of this complex individual's role in Iranian politics, see Yann Richard, "Ayatollah Kashani: Precursor of the Islamic Republic?" in *Revolutionary Islam*, ed. Arjomand, 101–24.

18. Shahrough Akhavi, *Religion and Politics in Contemporary Iran: Clergy-State Relations in the Pahlavi Period* (Albany, N.Y.: SUNY Press, 1980), 68–69.

19. Ibid., 110. Tahmasebi was subsequently tried and executed for his crime.

20. Abrahamian provides a social background analysis of Fedayeen members put on trial in the 1950s for their crimes, primarily assassinations. He notes that they were overwhelmingly young, lower-level bazaar employees, whereas Kashani was a seasoned and sophisticated politician. See Abrahamian, *Iran Between Two Revolutions*, 259.

The usefulness of the Fedayeen-i Islam to Kashani came to an end when the assassination of General Razamara on 30 April 1951 heralded the beginning of the Mossadeq era. As one observer of the period noted, it is "ironic" that the Fedayeen-i Islam would inaugurate an era of Iranian politics that was to become best known for its zealous commitment to Iranian nationalism rather than to Islam, in whose name the Fedayeen committed its crimes.[21] The meteoric rise to power of Dr. Mohammed Mossadeq was accompanied by demands by the Fedayeen that it be offered a share of power. Fedayeen leader Navab Safavi hoped to be appointed minister of religion in the new government. Yet Mossadeq, as well as Kashani himself, opposed sharing power with a terrorist organization and thus pushed the Fedayeen into its customary violent oppositional stance. For although the group shared Mossadeq's opposition to Britain's inordinate influence in Iran, the Fedayeen's Islamic frame of reference differed dramatically from Dr. Mossadeq's Persian nationalist perspective. Furthermore, since Kashani felt that the Fedayeen's usefulness to him had come to an end, he had no desire to elevate them to a position of influence at the apex of state power. Kashani preferred to use his influence with Dr. Mossadeq for other purposes. Unsurprisingly, as a consequence of the break, "the absolutism of the Fedayeen doctrine made the political Kashani a natural target";[22] and indeed, after his break with the Fedayeen, Ayatollah Kashani became a target of the unpredictable group's wrath.[23] The Fedayeen unleashed another spate of terrorist activities, beginning with an attempt on the life of one of Mossadeq's closest supporters, Dr. Hussein Fatemi, although the Fedayeen publicly acknowledged that Mossadeq himself had been their primary candidate for assassination. Having successfully assassinated Razamara, they made it quite clear that no one could elude them. According to one account, "Mossadeq took refuge in the parliament building barely a month after he was in office for fear of his life and the threat of retaliation by the *Fedayeen*."[24]

Recognizing that Mossadeq's political potential far outweighed that of the destructive and unsophisticated Fedayeen, Ayatollah Kashani threw his support behind the beleaguered prime minister; and the increasingly isolated Fedayeen, realizing that they could not kill everybody, temporarily ceased making threats against the lives of the regime's officials. As the turbulent events of the Mossadeq era continued to unfold,

21. For a brief description of this transition, see Richard W. Cottam, *Nationalism in Iran* (Pittsburgh, Pa.: University of Pittsburgh Press, 1964), 151–52.
22. Ibid., 152.
23. Ibid., 153.
24. Zabih, "Terrorism in Iran," 87.

terrorism as a means of political leverage became submerged in the general chaos that swept Iran. The Fedayeen continued to compete with others for political influence while still violently opposing Western influence in Iran. Yet their influence waned with their final act of terror in November 1955. Muzaffar Zu'l Qadr, a member of the group, attempted to assassinate Prime Minister Hussein Ala in Tehran's Shah Mosque just before Ala was to depart for Iraq to sign the Baghdad Pact. Iran's membership in the organization was perceived as yet another Islamic/Iranian capitulation to the West. The failed assassin was captured wearing a white shroud under his clothes inscribed with Qur'anic quotations. His actions prompted the government to round up the top leaders of the Fedayeen. Ayatollah Kashani was also arrested, although he was soon released. Navab Safavi and others were tried, and he, along with four associates, was executed in January 1956. A new era of conflict and terror began, and this terror has persisted as an inherent part of Iranian politics, albeit in changing forms, until this very day.

TERRORISM DURING THE MOHAMMED REZA SHAH PERIOD

The ideological and political character of terrorism during the reign of Mohammed Reza Shah Pahlavi was far different from that during the reign of Reza Shah. Several factors served to render the second shah highly sensitive to both real and imagined challenges to his power. For this reason his thirty-eight years in power were characterized by excessive personal insecurity and distrust that bordered on paranoia. Under the shah twenty-four different prime ministers served at the head of more than forty cabinets. There were two officially recognized attempts on the shah's life as well as others that were never publicly reported. The shah married three times but remained heavily influenced, some say virtually dominated, by his twin sister, Princess Ashraf.[25] In short, the period from 1941, when the Shah assumed power, to 1979, when he fled the country, were characterized by periodic turbulence and uncertainty.

The traumas of the shah's early years in power were to haunt him for life. He assumed the Peacock Throne after his father was forcibly removed by the British, who felt that Reza Shah was insufficiently anti-Nazi in the early days of World War II. The shah at times appeared to

25. See Jerrold D. Green, *Revolution in Iran: The Politics of Countermobilization* (New York: Praeger Press, 1982), 15–16.

be almost obsessed with the fact that he had been put in power by Britain and was virtually ruled by them from 1941 to 1946. The consequence of this was a love-hate relationship with the West that came to be a dominant feature of his rule.[26] In 1953 he was forced to flee the country by Dr. Mohammed Mossadeq and was only permitted to return after a coup sponsored by the CIA and Britain was staged in Tehran. The Mossadeq experience reaffirmed his dependence on the West and thus his inherent weakness. For although this dependence proved beneficial to the shah, it was not without cost, since he was extremely sensitive to the fact that he owed his throne to the British and to the Americans.

The Mossadeq experience made the shah keenly sensitive to challenges to his power, and the humiliation of having to flee the country significantly influenced the character of his rule until the Islamic revolution. In order to forestall subsequent such challenges and to insure independence from the West, the shah devoted considerable energy and resources to the creation of a security apparatus that could protect him and strengthen his hold over the country. In 1957 the shah founded his notorious secret police, SAVAK (Sazman-i Etila'at va Amniyat-i Keshvar [National Security and Information Organization]). Originally created with the help of the United States, Israel, and others, SAVAK succeeded in intimidating large sectors of Iranian society into submission. At its peak it was rumored that one in ten Iranians functioned as SAVAK informers. Although this proportion is probably inflated, the fact that this story was so often cited by ordinary Iranians highlights the fear with which this omnipresent and brutal force was regarded. SAVAK effectively minimized, although was never able totally to eliminate, open discussion about Iranian politics as well as criticisms of the shah and his rule.

The shah's insecurities grew, rather than diminished, over time. He created a complex collection of interlocking intelligence organizations that devoted much of their energy to overseeing the activities of one another. Insecurity and uncertainty were cornerstones not only of the shah's personality and rule but also of those who served him.[27] There is

26. The shah's complex feelings toward the West are best reflected in the several books that were published in his name. See, for example, Mohammed Reza Pahlavi, *The White Revolution* (Tehran: Kayhan Press, n.d.); *Mission for My Country* (London: Hutchinson, 1960); *Bi-su-yi Tammudun-i Buzurg* (Tehran: Sherkat-i Offset-i Sahami-ye Amm, 1978); *Réponse à l'histoire* (Paris: Editions Albin Michel, 1979); *Answer to History* (New York: Stein and Day, 1980). Although the final book appears to be a translation of the penultimate one, there are differences between the two.

27. For interesting analyses of the shah's personality, with particular attention to his well-known sense of insecurity, see the anecdotal and fascinating memoir of one of the shah's closest confidants and advisers, Asadollah Alam, *The Shah and I: The Confidential Diary of Iran's Royal Court, 1969–1977,* (New York: St. Martin's Press, 1992). For a more

566 Nationalism and State Formation

substantial evidence to suggest that the shah intentionally promoted these feelings so as to prevent any type of concerted collective action against him. For example, all military promotions over the rank of major were personally approved by the monarch, and senior military officers were forbidden to meet together without the shah's explicit permission. Military officers could not even travel abroad or marry non-Iranians without prior government approval.[28] The era of dictatorship that began in 1953 and continued until the revolution of 1978–79 fostered a spirit of alienation, discontent, and profound mistrust. The shah trusted virtually no one, and a corresponding degree of distrust and insecurity pervaded Iranian society.

In the absence of genuine loyalty or of more-conventional forms of affection or support for the monarch, or even for the institution of monarchy, the shah relied on material incentives and disincentives to perpetuate his power. The carrot and stick were favored instruments of sociopolitical control. As one description of the period notes:

> Under the dictatorial regime that developed after 1953 there were increasingly only two ways to deal with opposition, whether religious, nationalist, or Marxist. One was repression, including jailing, torture, and killing (the latter two especially in the 1970's). The other was co-optation of oppositionists. . . . The increase in good governmental jobs, salaries and perquisites as oil income grew made this an effective strategy for a time, but did not bring real loyalty to the Shah. Participation in decision making was not broadened and freedom of expression actually declined over time.[29]

The narrow range of options available to those Iranians eager to express their views on the political, economic, or social issues of the day effectively drove such people out of the system. That is, the shah foolishly precluded all popular input into the formation and implementation of government policies and thus forced oppositional groups to develop. Functioning as de facto antistate entities, such groups had no legal or officially sanctioned intrasystemic means of political expression. In short,

---

scientific view rooted in theories of social psychology, see the equally absorbing book by Marvin Zonis, *Majestic Failure: The Fall of the Shah* (Chicago: University of Chicago Press, 1991).

28. For an excellent portrait of this period, see Marvin Zonis, *The Political Elite of Iran* (Princeton: Princeton University Press, 1971).

29. Nikki Keddie, *Roots of Revolution: An Interpretive History of Modern Iran* (New Haven: Yale University Press, 1981), 144.

any individual or group that did not wholeheartedly agree with the shah and his government was regarded as a traitor or criminal. Certainly the overwhelming majority of groups that courageously persisted in attempts to express themselves chose to defy the shah in a nonviolent fashion. Others, however, turned to violence and terrorism as a means of resistance to the shah.

Throughout the 1960s Iranian politics took on a more violent character than before. Various demonstrations and marches, generally peaceful in nature, often evoked violent and brutal responses by the government, which was never reluctant to send in the military, which would employ any means necessary to break up illegal gathering. Thus, to a certain degree, violence was routinized as an integral part of Iranian politics. That is, if the government did not like what a group was doing, it would almost automatically resort to violence in order to terminate activities it deemed unacceptable. At the same time, the Iranian opposition was not immune to this changing feature of Iranian political culture. Because violence became a primary, common, and routine means of political expression for the government, segments of the opposition began to resort to violence with equal regularity. These segments did not comprise all or even large numbers of Iranians, because terrorism never became a universally accepted mode of oppositional political behavior in Iran. Still, the callousness of the shah's government as well as its total disregard for freedom and human dignity promoted a concomitant disregard for peaceful action by some of its opponents. Certain elements in Iranian society, out of sheer desperation, were willing to turn to terrorism because they felt that they had little to lose in their conflict with a government that was well known for its blatant lack of concern about the wishes of its people. The irony of the shah's rule was witnessed in his constant rhetorical reference to democracy and freedom that was inevitably accompanied by his practical and systematic denigration of them both.

Although the early 1960s were politically turbulent years for Iran, terrorism became a meaningful problem for the Iranian state only toward the end of the decade. During 1961–63 the military suppressed with little difficulty and unprecedented brutality several major demonstrations sponsored by the National Front in concert with various university groups. In these massive, bloody, and exaggerated government responses to what started out as peaceful demonstrations lie the roots of the terrorist activities that dominated the 1970s and culminated in the revolution of 1978–79. As one of the primary oppositional groups of the period wrote: "The bloody repression of 1963 was a major watershed in Iranian history. Until then, the opposition had tried to fight the regime with street protests, labour strikes and underground parties. The 1963 bloodbath, however, exposed the bankruptcy of these peaceful methods. After 1963, militants, irrespective of their ideology, had to ask themselves 'What is to be done?' The answer was clear: 'guerrilla warfare.' "[30] Despite the clear Leninist tone of the above, it reflects a sentiment common to many oppositional groups in Iran, non-Marxist and even Islamic, all of whom reached the same conclusion—peaceful protest would not lead to meaningful political reform. Indeed, throughout the decade there were many attempts, mostly unsuccessful, to initiate armed struggle against the regime. SAVAK successfully penetrated many of these organizations, both Islamic and Marxist, and the government was never seriously threatened by them.

In 1963 there were also demonstrations by the religious sector. These too were suppressed by the government with excessive and, ultimately, costly force. It was after one such demonstration that Ayatollah Khomeini was arrested. He subsequently was deported and began the circuitous exile through Turkey, Iraq, and France that culminated in his triumphant return to Iran in 1979. In January 1965 Prime Minister Hassan Mansur was assassinated by religious students thought to be affiliated with the semidormant Fedayeen-i Islam. Mansur was assassinated because of his well-known support for foreign oil concessions. Iranians were still critical of what was perceived to be yet another example of Iran's capitulation to foreign powers. Indeed, it is this subordination of Iran to the West, either perceived or imagined, that has remained a constant source of irritation and thus a rallying point for oppositional political activists throughout this century. This issue has plagued all regimes irrespective of ideology (e.g., monarchic, nationalist, Islamic) and remains an issue of great public concern and political sensitivity to this day. Thus, the Mansur assassination was hardly out of character with other oppositional activities, and it led to a concerted attack on the religious underground by SAVAK and the military. The security forces were for the most part successful, and terrorism by Islamic fundamentalist groups declined in this period. Yet violence by left-wing groups grew significantly as the 1960s gave way to the 1970s.

Most scholars of this period agree that the bloody violence of 1963 confirmed widespread beliefs that the shah was totally impervious to peaceful or gradual attempts to broaden the scope of acceptable political activity in Iran. Furthermore, oppositionists feared that if they were to

30. This statement comes from an article entitled "Armed Struggle" in *Mojahid* (1974), a publication of the Mojahedin. It is cited in Ervand Abrahamian's "The Guerrilla Movement in Iran: 1963–77," in *Iran: A Revolution in Turmoil*, ed. Haleh Afshar (London: Macmillan, 1985), 152.

engage in open and nonviolent protest, they would be brutally suppressed, as were the peaceful protesters of 1963. Therefore, violence appeared as the only effective avenue of political protest open to them.[31] And as a consequence of this, the 1970s unfolded as a decade of terror and counterterror.

On 8 February 1971 a group of armed young Iranians staged an attack on a gendarmerie station at Siakal in northern Iran near the Caspian Sea. The goal of the group was to release two of their colleagues who had been taken prisoner by the gendarmes for planning insurrection in the Caspian region. It was feared that the two would, under torture, reveal details of the broader scheme. Although they failed to release the prisoners, the young band made history; what became known as the Siakal incident led to a sustained period of terrorist activity against the Pahlavi monarchy, and this activity certainly contributed to the revolution of 1978–79.

Ervand Abrahamian provides the most thorough and comprehensive account of events during this period.[32] According to him, the shah's response to the events in Siakal was massive and immediate. He sent a large task force to track down and capture the perpetrators of the attack on the gendarmerie post. The security forces ultimately triumphed, although it was only after three weeks that they were able to report the capture of the eleven surviving attackers (two others died during the search operation). This series of events sent shock waves through opposition and government circles. It became clear that a small band of dedicated oppositionists could in fact disrupt the activities of the government while meaningfully challenging the shah's vaunted military machine.

The Siakal incident led to virtual open warfare between the shah and a variety of terrorist organizations.[33] Throughout the 1970s a plethora of such groups developed. Some only briefly appeared on the political scene and either disappeared as a result of the efforts of SAVAK or disintegrated due to internal differences among their members. Others,

31. Nikki Keddie also subscribes to this view; see *Roots of Revolution*, 236–37.

32. See Abrahamian, *Iran Between Two Revolutions*, and idem, "The Guerrilla Movement in Iran," 149–74. This latter piece was originally published under the same name in *MERIP Reports* 86 (March–April, 1980): 223–15. Other relevant work by Abrahamian includes *The Iranian Mojahedin* (New Haven: Yale University Press, 1989).

33. Use of the term *terrorist* presents definitional complications. For the Iranian government, members of these groups were considered to be "terrorists," whereas to opponents of the shah they were "freedom fighters" or, to use Abrahamian's word, "guerrillas." Given the analytical thrust of this paper, the actions of these groups are being considered under the rubric of terrorism, although this should be construed as a reflection of an analytical focus rather than an ideological preference on the part of the author.

however, grew and developed in a more systematic fashion. Among the two most influential were Sazman-i Cherik-ha-yi Fedd-i Khalq-i Iran (the Organization of the Guerrilla Freedom Fighters of the Iranian People) and the Sazman-i Mojahedin-i Khalq-i Iran (the Organization of the Freedom Fighters of the Iranian People). While the former came to be commonly known as the Marxist Fedayi, the latter became known as the Islamic Mojahedin. As is indicated above, a variety of other groups came and went or were less important than the two discussed here. Among the less important groups was the Tudeh Party, a traditional pro-Soviet Communist group, as well as innumerable smaller and less well known groups on both the Left and the Right.

Among the most notable features of both the above groups were the changing socioeconomic and generational attributes of their members. Historically, at least in the case of the original Fedayeen-i Islam group that was noted for its terrorist activities in the 1950s, the rank-and-file members were predominantly uneducated lower-echelon workers from the bazaar. However, the attributes of those willing to use violence against the state changed significantly. Analysis by Abrahamian of the social background of those killed in violent confrontations with the state, or killed after having been taken into custody by SAVAK, indicates that an overwhelming number of university students and graduates chose to become involved in violent antigovernment confrontations. At the same time, the majority of these intellectuals was less than thirty-five years of age. What is particularly noteworthy is that these educated and primarily young people were drawn not only to the left-wing Fedayeen but also to Islamic groups such as the Mojahedin. This trend is somewhat counterintuitive, for observers of social change traditionally have posited that increases in education promote concomitant decreases in religiosity. Yet Abrahamian has demonstrated that in Iran just the opposite appears to be the case.[34] Better-educated and more-sophisticated advocates of violent resistance to the shah also proved to be more resilient, imaginative, and difficult to suppress than had other such groups to date.

The number of fatalities throughout the period before the revolution was significant, reflecting the growing scope of terrorist activities. The Fedayi concentrated its efforts on such activities as holding up banks to obtain operating funds. At the same time, informers were executed, government officials and well-known supporters of the regime were

34. This not unlike the situation elsewhere in the Middle East, where Islamic groups successfully appeal to well-educated middle-class young people. For comparable findings, see Saad Eddin Ibrahim, "Anatomy of Egypt's Militant Islamic Groups: Methodological Note and Preliminary Findings," *International Journal of Middle East Studies* 12, no. 4 (1980): 423–53.

assassinated, and offices both of the government and of foreign powers perceived to be influential in Iran were attacked (e.g., banks and airline offices). The Mojahedin undertook similar activities. According to one analysis of the period, the Mojahedin targeted members of the military prosecutor's staff who oversaw the trials of arrested terrorists, American military advisers in Iran, and members of SAVAK, particularly its antiterrorism section.[35] Like the Fedayi, they too robbed banks, attacked foreign airline offices and oil companies, and assassinated government officials, informers, and official American personnel serving in Iran. Captured members of both groups were treated with incredible cruelty by SAVAK, and instances of torture, rape, summary execution, secret trials, and the like were the norm.[36] This helps to explain the almost total lack of restraint on the part of antistate activists during this period.

Although one group was Marxist and the other Islamic, the two shared certain broad similarities. The Mojahedin viewed itself as "progressive" and thus, unlike most Islamic groups, held a measure of respect and sympathy for Marxism. Indeed, almost immediately after the revolution, its religious credentials were challenged by Khomeini and his supporters, who represented a far more mainstream brand of Islam than did the Mojahedin then, or now, for that matter. Certainly the Mojahedin attempted to portray themselves in Islamic terms, but their avowed sympathy for Marxism helped their competitors within the religious community to portray them as less than genuinely Islamic. In Islamic terms it was not difficult to discredit the Mojahedin. Even the shah and his government referred to them as "Islamic Marxists," and their unusual religious character made them suspect to the average Iranian. The Mojahedin had its origins in the religious sector of the National Front Party rather than firmly within the religious community per se. In the years before the revolution they came under the influence of Dr. Ali Shariati, who was an opponent of the shah but who also was profoundly skeptical of the traditional Shiʿa clergy, which he viewed as threatening a dictatorship of another sort.

According to Abrahamian, the Mojahedin drew its members from the central provinces, whereas the Fedayi relied more on the northern cities. Mojahedin members were often the children of traditional bazaaris, clergymen, and others who had a core commitment to Islam. The Fedayi,

35. Zabih, *The Left in Contemporary Iran*, 86–87. Zabih's ideological orientation is diametrically opposed to that of Abrahamian, who is far more sympathetic to the Mojahedin than is Zabih. Thus, it is useful to read work by both scholars.

36. This was thoroughly documented by the International Commission of Jurists, Amnesty International, and even the United States government, all of which castigated the shah for his deplorable human rights record.

on the other hand, drew its membership from more secular strata of society as well as occasionally from non-Islamic minorities. Both groups were strongly opposed to what they perceived to be an excessive foreign and particularly American influence in Iran. Both felt that the shah was betraying Iran to foreign interests while exploiting the Iranian people.

The central leadership of the Mojahedin, primarily in the Tehran region, gradually grew closer to Marxism and away from Islam. Indeed, the son of Ayatollah Taleqani wrote a widely publicized letter to his father in which he asserted that only Marxism, not Islam, could liberate Iran. Not all Mojahedin members accepted this abandonment of Islam; thus, the organization was split into an Islamic group and a Marxist one. Each embarked on separate campaigns of terror, including bank robberies, bombings, attacks on foreign installations in Iran, the assassination of American military officers, strikes, and so forth. But by 1976 these two groups, as well as the Fedayi, had sustained devastating casualties. None of them had stimulated popular revolt against the shah's government, although collectively they had prompted from SAVAK a reign of terror against all opponents of the regime. Their reserves, both human and otherwise, were severely depleted by their all-out campaign against the regime, and although not defeated, they were weakened by their deadlock with the state.

Throughout this period Iran's human rights record deteriorated even more. Nonetheless, there was no viable opponent on the horizon able to wrest power from the shah. Throughout the latter part of the 1970s, opposition groups strengthened ties with Iranian student groups in Western Europe and the United States. These groups began their own well-publicized and highly effective protests and demonstrations against the government of the shah and its excesses. President Carter, despite his toast to the shah at Niavaran Palace on New Year's Eve 1977, where he referred to Iran as "an island of stability," also began to press the shah, later in the year, to improve Iran's human rights record. Various middle-class groups also began to attack the regime publicly and with great vigor and regularity. Assorted pamphlets, petitions, poetry readings, meetings, marches, and demonstrations were employed to highlight the shah's deficiencies. Somewhat to the chagrin of the more violent elements of the opposition who had been fighting the shah for years, the combined weight of these collective and peaceful efforts began to show. The shah, feeling the pressure, went on the offensive. Foolishly and inexplicably misreading the character of the urban middle-class secular intellectual movement that was peacefully criticizing him while pressing for reform, not for his removal from the throne, the shah impulsively attacked the far more dangerous and radical religious sector. In this period he made repeated reference to "Islamic Marxists," and his traditional resentment of the religious community dominated his actions. Yet why he chose not to respond to the genuine source of challenges to him remains unclear. It certainly represented a huge and ultimately critical error of judgment on the shah's part.

On 7 January 1978 a letter was published in the Tehran daily newspaper *Etela'at* that violently and crudely attacked the exiled religious leader Ayatollah Khomeini. The respected cleric was criticized for being a British agent and a pornographer and for a variety of other implausible and imagined sins. The response was instantaneous. Riots broke out in the religious city of Qom, south of Tehran, and significant numbers of protesters were killed or injured. This was the beginning of the Iranian revolution.

Among the revolution's most notable characteristics was the fact that it was almost entirely peaceful. Violence was employed primarily by the shah, although even he did not employ it as extensively as he could have. Despite sporadic antishah violence, the triumph of the Islamic religious sector led by Ayatollah Khomeini lay in its ability to mobilize millions of Iranians in *peaceful* opposition to the shah and his government. Short of killing millions of his citizens, the shah was virtually powerless to deter the huge numbers of people who opposed him. Basically, the entire country turned its back on the monarch and used work stoppages, strikes, religious processions, and demonstrations to express its collective will. Gun battles and assassinations were the shah's métier, and the opposition's conscious rejection of them cleverly worked to isolate the monarch while helping to mobilize most Iranians against him. The old Ayatollah deprived the shah of his most effective weapon, his virtual monopoly of the instruments of coercion. Furthermore, unlike the assorted violent oppositional groups, Khomeini was able to inspire millions of Iranians to oppose the shah. Neither the Fedayi nor the Mojahedin had been able to accomplish this. Khomeini's genuine Islamic beliefs and stature put him into much closer touch with the average Iranian than did the alien Marxism or incomprehensible demi-Islam inherent in the terrorist groups who ultimately hoped to challenge him as they had the shah. Although a detailed analysis of the Iranian revolution exceeds the scope of this chapter, it is important to emphasize that the revolution succeeded despite, not because of, the efforts of various groups committed to the use of violence.[37] Terrorism both preceded the revolution and

37. Among the many studies of the Iranian revolution and of the period immediately following it, see Abrahamian, *Iran Between Two Revolutions*; Akhavi, *Religion and Politics in Contemporary Iran*; Said Amir Arjomand, *The Turban for the Crown* (New York: Oxford University Press, 1989); Shaul Bakhash, *The Reign of the Ayatollahs: Iran and the Islamic Revolution* (New York: Basic Books, 1984); Michael M. J. Fischer, *Iran:*

followed it. Significantly, however, it was virtually nonexistent during the course of the upheaval itself, when the goal was expulsion of the shah. It is also important to note that although Khomeini and his supporters eschewed the use of violence, this aversion was tactical rather than ideological. Khomeini was never a Gandhi. He chose not to use violence, not because he had any sort of ideological opposition to it, but because he recognized early on that it would not work. After assuming power, Khomeini quite willingly turned to violence and was no less reluctant to use it than was his predecessor, the shah.

TERRORISM AND POLITICS IN THE ISLAMIC REPUBLIC OF IRAN

Although the revolution forwarded a new ruling elite as well as a radically different ideology, it is essential not to overlook the obvious: Iran remained Iran. Much changed, but much also stayed the same. For example, even the universally feared and despised SAVAK was not eliminated but merely had its name changed to SAVAMA (Sazman-e Amniyat va Etela'at-e Mellat-e Iran). In the postrevolutionary period, terrorism of two sorts rapidly became politically significant. The first mode of terrorism was that focused against the prevailing political order by dissident elements within Iranian society. For after the euphoria of the Khomeini ascent to power dissipated or, more precisely perhaps, happiness over the expulsion of the shah waned, many of the groups that supported Khomeini in the expectation of a share in the new political order came to oppose him just as they had the shah. Such groups came to the realization that Khomeini had exploited them, for despite encouraging them to help him oust the shah, the wily ayatollah had never intended to share power with them. Now that the monarchy had ended, Khomeini expected such groups to stand down in order to permit him to create the Islamic polity that he had always envisioned. In the excitement that swept Iran with the expulsion of the shah, many of the groups that supported Khomeini had done so out of anti-Pahlavi, rather than pro-Islamic, sentiment. Presumably sensitive to this, Khomeini had

From *Religious Dispute to Revolution* (Cambridge: Harvard University Press, 1980); Jerrold D. Green, *Revolution in Iran*; Dilip Hiro, *Iran Under the Ayatollahs* (London: Routledge and Kegan Paul, 1984); Eric Hooglund, *Land and Revolution in Iran, 1960–80* (Austin: University of Texas Press, 1982); Keddie, *Roots of Revolution*; Mohsen Milani, *The Making of Iran's Islamic Revolution: From Monarchy to Islamic Republic* (Boulder, Colo.: Westview Press, 1988).

intentionally obscured his political agenda so that anyone with an anti-shah grievance could comfortably support him. Oppositionists spent far more time in hating the shah than they did in evaluating Khomeini's capability to replace him or in considering the character of a Khomeini-dominated polity. Indeed, it is frequently forgotten that the ayatollah's ability to mobilize support was as much, if not more, the product of popular antishah sentiment than it was affection for Khomeini. Once the shah was gone, the ayatollah then concentrated on the creation of an Islamic society and polity—goals as unacceptable to many of his support-ers as had been the "designer Iran" favored by the shah. This led to terrorism of a sort that differed but little from that during the Pahlavi years.

Iranians who felt disenfranchised by or dissatisfied with the incipient Islamic political order attempted peacefully to modify it. Failing, some of them turned to terror just as they had during the reign of the shah. In this case, many of those who had been anti-Pahlavi terrorists soon became anti-Khomeini ones as well. They were particularly outraged that Khomeini had solicited their revolutionary support under false pretenses. They soon came to realize that the revolution they had supported had been stolen away from them. For although such groups never had a stake in Pahlavi Iran, as active participants in the revolution-ary struggle they felt that they had earned a stake in the new Iran. This, they thought, had been confirmed by the ayatollah himself. From the perspective of such opposition groups, the shah had brutalized them, but Khomeini had betrayed them.

The second mode of terrorism that flourished after the revolution was absent during the Pahlavi era: the systematic use of terror beyond Iran's national borders by the Iranian government. Although the shah relied on external terror to enforce his will, it was in a much more limited and discrete form than that which emerged after his overthrow. For example, in 1971 he reportedly ordered the execution in Iraq of former SAVAK chief General Teymour Bakhtiar, who had openly proposed to the CIA that it support him in an antishah coup.[38] The shah also had SAVAK agents in the United States and Europe spying on dissident Iranian students.[39] Reportedly, reprisals against the families of these students at

38. For details of the Bakhtiar assassination as well as the activities of SAVAK both at home and abroad, see William Shawcross, *The Shah's Last Ride: The Fate of an Ally* (New York: Simon and Schuster, 1988), 160–61, 198–203.

39. For a readable, though unreliable, account of SAVAK activities in the United States, see Mansur Rafizadeh, *Witness: From the Shah to the Secret Arms Deal: An Insider's Account of U.S. Involvement in Iran* (New York: William Morrow and Company, 1987). Rafizadeh was for many years the chief of SAVAK in the United States and has written a self-serving account of his experiences.

times occurred in Iran. Indeed, a primary role of SAVAK was to terrorize the Iranian population into submission to the shah. State-sponsored terrorism certainly characterized the Pahlavi era. During the current period of the Islamic republic however, terrorism is of a much different sort. This state-sponsored terror is much broader in scope. No longer focused in a limited fashion on dissident Iranians at home or abroad, terrorism has become a systematic and highly public mode of Iranian foreign policy. Under these circumstances the target is likely not to be Iranian, and rather than try to conceal acts of terror, the Iranian government parades them publicly and with great fanfare.

TERRORISM AND DOMESTIC POLITICS IN THE ISLAMIC REPUBLIC OF IRAN

Just as the shah's throne was never significantly in jeopardy because of terrorism, which he nonetheless found troublesome, terrorism in the early years of the Islamic republic proved to be disruptive but not a major threat to the existing political order. Indeed, although anti-Khomeini terror extracted a far higher toll in the Islamic republic than had anti-Pahlavi terror in the prerevolution period, terrorism was hardly a new feature of Iranian politics and has always been evident in this turbulent polity. Like the shah, Khomeini was more than able to weather the challenge because terrorist groups found it impossible to mobilize significant and sustained opposition to him. Thus, an analysis of domestic terrorism in the Islamic Republic of Iran is useful as a means to understand oppositional politics. Care should be taken, however, not to attribute excessive importance to such activities or to use them as a means to measure regime longevity or to evaluate its future prospects.

Almost immediately after attaining power in 1979 the Khomeini regime was the target of widespread, systematic, and highly publicized terrorist activities. A shadowy group named Forghan claimed responsibility for numerous assassinations and other disruptive activities. Army chief of staff Lieutenant General Qarani was assassinated in April; Ayatollah Mutahhari, chairman of the Revolutionary Council, was shot in Tehran in May; later that month Hojjat al-Islam Hashemi Rafsanjani was also shot, and Ayatollah Mufattah was killed, as was Ayatollah Qazi Tabatabai in Tabriz in November.[40] There were also attacks on foreign business-

---

40. These assassinations were widely reported in the Iranian press. Details of them were gleaned from a systematic reading of *Etela'at* for the latter portion of 1979.

men, mosques, journalists, and various supporters of the regime throughout 1979. The true character of the Forghan group was murky, although predictably it was accused, by the government, of being a CIA-backed group of renegade royalists, former SAVAK members, and so forth. Ultimately, it was revealed that the group was religious, ultraconservative, and fearful that the true Islamic character of the revolution was being betrayed.[41] By the end of 1979 the group was heard from only sporadically and ceased to be a meaningful factor in Iranian politics.[42]

Jockeying for power by numerous contending groups continued throughout the early years of the Islamic republic as Khomeini and his supporters tried to create a new political order while at the same time consolidating power. Iran quickly became politically polarized, with one pole represented by engineer Mehdi Bazargan, who could best be characterized as a liberal. Although committed to Islam, Bazargan was deeply devoted to a more secular form of government than that supported by most of Khomeini's religious followers, particularly those who were clerics. Although appointed prime minister by Khomeini, Bazargan found his efforts stymied by Khomeini's clerical followers, who did not trust him and felt that he was merely a holdover from the previous regime. This perspective was not accurate, despite the fact that Bazargan had received his "political education" during the Mossadeq era and that his values did differ significantly from those of Khomeini and his immediate supporters. Bazargan made little progress and as a reflection of his own frustration referred to himself as "a knife without a blade" in a widely publicized interview with Oriana Fallaci.[43] Under assault by both the Left and the Right, Bazargan was ultimately abandoned even by his own supporters, who realized that he would never be able to persuade Khomeini to create the type of government that they envisioned. The Left found Bazargan too pro-American, and he was politically excoriated for being photographed shaking hands with an American official at a meeting in Algiers. The religious Right was no more favorably disposed toward Bazargan and found it difficult to support a non-cleric as head of state. His tenure abruptly came to an end after the takeover of the American embassy by a group of militant "students" on 4 November 1979. Mehdi Bazargan proffered his resignation the follow-

41. Abrahamian, The Iranian Mojahedin, 51–52.
42. Etela'at on 30 March 1981 (9 Farvardin 1360) announced an attempt on the life of Ayatollah Rabbani Shirazi, who was a member of the Council of the Guardians of the Islamic Republic Constitution, by Forghan, but this and other reports were not substantiated and appeared very infrequently after 1979.
43. Oriana Fallaci, "Everybody Wants to be Boss," New York Times Magazine, 28 October 1979.

ing day. Although Khomeini was firmly in charge, Iran still needed a head of state.

In January 1980 Abolhassan Bani Sadr was elected president. He too had serious differences of opinion with Khomeini's clerical disciples, particularly with the Islamic Republican Party (IRP), which had been created by these supporters almost immediately after Khomeini's return from exile. Having the unabashed goal of turning Iran into a theocracy, the IRP viewed Bani Sadr as simply another Bazargan. The polarization that had accompanied Khomeini's rise to power in 1979 was further widened. And although Bani Sadr came to be associated with the Mojahedin at the end of his rule, in the early days he appeared to make a genuine effort to work with Khomeini despite being frustrated at every turn. For even though Khomeini was formally, verbally, and publicly opposed to a government of clerics, his actions belied this opposition and he systematically and regularly undercut Bani Sadr or allowed the IRP to do so. The IRP, on the other hand, noting that Khomeini had given it a virtual free hand, did everything in its power to oppose Bani Sadr, about whom it harbored profound reservations. It interpreted Khomeini's unwillingness to stop its actions as support for its oppositional activities. Bani Sadr, as president of the Islamic republic, was further marginalized by the ascent to power of Prime Minister Mohammed Ali Rajai, who, he later claimed, was foisted upon him by Khomeini. The two were never able to collaborate effectively, for whereas Bani Sadr represented the liberal, secular, Westernized tendencies in Iranian politics, Rajai stood for the more traditional, proclerical faction. Unfortunately for Bani Sadr, Rajai was far more in touch with the political realities and circles of power of the time than was Bani Sadr. In short, Khomeini created a type of government to which he actually seemed opposed. And in the case of Bani Sadr, it soon became clear that he lacked a mandate.[44] Thus, the already weak and marginal president became even more vulnerable.

The Mojahedin appeared to grow in influence during this period, successfully mobilizing huge demonstrations throughout Iran, and an increasingly isolated Bani Sadr found himself drifting in its direction. The Mojahedin were eager to find official legitimacy and support from the very heights of the regime and encouraged this drift as much as they could. In analyzing this movement, Abrahamian writes, "It was clear to Bani Sadr that he had only two choices. He could either submit to the IRP, become a ceremonial president, and in the process betray his

44. For additional information, see Abolhassan Bani Sadr, *My Turn to Speak: Iran, the Revolution, and Secret Deals with the U.S.* (New York: Brassey's, 1991).

democratic principles. Or he could continue voicing his opinions, risk alienating some of his turbaned allies, and join the *Mojahedin* in confronting the whole clerical establishment."[45] Rejai had the enthusiastic support of the IRP, but Bani Sadr stood the risk of total isolation.[46] The degree to which Bani Sadr had been rejected by Khomeini and those around him became abundantly clear in March 1981 when the hapless president ordered police to arrest those disrupting a speech he was delivering at Tehran University. The disrupters were found to be IRP members.

The schism between Bani Sadr and the IRP and Rejai rapidly became irreparable. Ostensibly to resolve the conflict, Khomeini appointed a three-man committee to seek reconciliation between the two factions. What it did was systematically rule against Bani Sadr while trying to curb his power and strip him of his remaining influence. As relations between the two sides further degenerated, Bani Sadr began openly to attack the government, the very government he ostensibly headed, as well as those forces in Iran that opposed him. Throughout the month of June the situation deteriorated to the point that Khomeini and Bani Sadr obliquely but publicly attacked each other. Khomeini offered Bani Sadr the chance to repent and to diassociate himself from the *monafeqin* (hypocrites), as the government referred to the Mojahedin. The more isolated Bani Sadr became, the closer he appeared to move to the Mojahedin, the only group he felt could effectively challenge the clerical establishment. On 19 June Bani Sadr called upon the Iranian people to rise up against the religious dictatorship. Massive demonstrations ensued, and on 21 June 1981 the Majlis voted to remove Bani Sadr from office. He went into hiding and on 29 July fled the country with Massoud Rajavi, the Mojahedin leader, and returned to France, where he had been in exile before the revolution.[47] Bani Sadr had his chance and lost it.

Bani Sadr's activities led to an eighteen-month period of terror and counterterror in Iran. The government began to round up those suspected of being opposed to the regime and announced the execution of over forty people in the week following Bani Sadr's removal from office and in the wake of the demonstrations of 21 June. On 28 June a sizable bomb exploded at the headquarters of the IRP, with more than seventy fatalities. Among those killed were Ayatollah Beheshti, chief justice of the Supreme Court, head of the IRP, and confidant of Ayatollah Kho-

45. Abrahamian, *The Iranian Mojahedin*, 65.

46. For a comparison of Bani Sadr and Rejai, see Milani, *The Making of Iran's Islamic Revolution*, 283–84.

47. For a detailed discussion of the rise and fall of Bani Sadr, see Bakhash, *The Reign of the Ayatollahs*, chs. 5 and 6.

meini, as well as twenty-six members of the Majlis, four members of the cabinet, seven assistant cabinet ministers, and numerous senior members of the party. The government moved quickly to fill the void, naming Mohammed Bahonar to replace Beheshti as head of the IRP, and Mussavi Ardebili to fill Beheshti's other position as president of the Supreme Court. In July presidential elections were held; Rajai was named president and Bahonar prime minister. Yet they, along with the head of the National Police, all perished in another explosion in August. The war of terror continued throughout this period. The head of Tehran's notorious Evin Prison was killed by the Mojahedin, as was the chief prosecutor, the governor of Gilan, the head of the Pasdaran (Revolutionary Guard) in Tabriz, and a variety of senior religious leaders throughout the country, including Ayatollah Dastegheyb in Shiraz.[48] According to some estimates, from one to two thousand government leaders and religious supporters of Khomeini died in this period.[49]

The government was not idle in the face of these severe attacks on its personnel and unleashed an attack of unprecedented severity on the Mojahedin as well as on other opposition groups. Thousands of regime opponents were rounded up, with those suspected of ties to the Mojahedin being particularly vulnerable. According to Abrahamian, in the weeks following the explosion at the IRP headquarters over a thousand people were executed, and an additional twelve hundred were killed in the wake of the Rejai and Bahonar assassinations. By November the number killed reached approximately twenty-seven hundred, the majority of whom were Mojahedin, although leftists, ethnic activists, and others were executed as well.[50] Finally, the secret headquarters of the Mojahedin were discovered in Tehran, and several of its top leaders were killed. Throughout this period thousands more were arrested and imprisoned. In short, the regime unleashed a "reign of terror" against its opponents, its brutality exceeding even that of the harsh Pahlavi re-

48. These disruptive acts are discussed in elaborate detail and with total subjectivity, accompanied by a chronology that enumerates terrorist acts against the state, in Islamic Propagation Organization of the Islamic Republic of Iran, *Felonies of the MKO Terrorists in Iran: A Study of the Use of Terrorism, Force, Threats, and Torture by the MKO Hypocrites to Demoralize and Subjugate Muslims: Members of the Party of God* (Tehran: Islamic Propagation Organization, 1983).

49. The higher number seems excessive, although precise statistics are currently unavailable. It was provided in an interesting book about day-to-day life in the Islamic republic. See John Simpson, *Inside Iran: Life Under Khomeini's Regime* (New York: St. Martin's Press, 1988), 200–201. The number one thousand was found in Zabih, "Terrorism in Iran," 93.

50. See Abrahamian, *The Iranian Mojahedin*, 68–69.

gime.[51] With the discovery of Mojahedin headquarters in Tehran and the arrest of some of its leaders in February 1982 and the flight out of Iran by the rest, the regime successfully broke the back of its terrorist opponents.[52] Although terrorism against the regime continues to this day, the Mojahedin has been forced to shift its activities to Iraq. This has further weakened them in the eyes of many Iranians who correctly saw them siding with Iraq against their own country during the Iran-Iraq War. In short, terrorism disrupted the regime, but given Khomeini's willingness to employ extraordinarily high levels of repression and to meet terror with counterterror, the government's political dominance was never truly threatened. For despite its brutality, bad governance, economic mismanagement, and disregard for human life, the regime of Ayatollah Khomeini still enjoyed core support until his death. As Richard Cottam notes:

> The most telling evidence of the size and importance of the core support group is evidenced by the crisis behavior of the regime. The regime easily survived assassinations and bombings carried out by the *Mojahedin* that decimated its top leadership. That type of resilience must reflect a popular support base from which new leaders can be drawn and which grants the regime unwavering support in moments of extreme duress.[53]

Although Cottam may appear to have exaggerated somewhat the regime's popularity, he is correct in noting the failure of terrorist groups to promote its overthrow. The Mojahedin waited for a popular uprising that never came. The group failed to appreciate that its ideology had little appeal to most Iranians and that Khomeini still enjoyed great popularity throughout much of Iran. Finally, it was unable or unwilling to recognize that terror in and of itself is simply destruction. That is, although assassinations, bombings, and all the rest served to highlight the vulnerability of the regime, terror alone offered no attractive alternative to the Iranian people, who were still willing to at least tolerate Khomeini until

51. For a chilling account of the Khomeini regime's brutality, including discussion and documentation of show trials, torture, amputation, and the large numbers of executions, even of minors, see the recent Amnesty International publications on Iran cited in note 5. Amnesty documents thousands of executions during the reign-of-terror period discussed here.

52. Among those killed was Mojahedin leader Musa Khaybani and his wife, as well as the wife of Mojahedin leader Massoud Rajavi, who was in exile in France at the time.

53. See Richard Cottam, "Inside Revolutionary Iran," *Middle East Journal* 43, no. 2 (1989): 175.

something better came along. Although the Mojahedin were more than effective terrorists, they proved to be totally inept political actors. They failed to forge meaningful alliances with other oppositional groups—as Khomeini himself had done during the revolution—while waiting for a popular uprising that never came. The Mojahedin demonstrated the historic inability of terrorism in Iran to stimulate significant political change or reform.

TERRORISM AND IRANIAN FOREIGN POLICY

Given the unique Islamic character of their revolution, many Iranians viewed it as more than a mere political upheaval. Rather, it was widely regarded as a long overdue response by oppressed Muslims to Western imperialism, in this case exercised through the shah, who was regarded as merely an agent of these oppressors, particularly the United States ("the Great Satan," in revolutionary parlance).[54] Given the manner in which the shah attained and maintained power, this perception is hardly far-fetched. And although many opposition movements challenged the shah, including a variety of terrorist groups, it is noteworthy that the one that was finally able to dislodge him was Islamic. The Iranian revolutionaries, who tend toward arrogance in analyzing their own revolution, have not forgotten that they succeeded in expelling the shah, the head of the sixth largest army in the world, after only one year of upheaval and without the use of force. Thus, it is no surprise that such Iranian Islamic revolutionaries turned their attention elsewhere in the hope of sharing their experience with others in the *umma* (Islamic world) who had fallen victim to the West and its insidious allies. Indeed, from

54. There are innumerable studies of Iranian-U.S. relations and of Iranian foreign relations somewhat more broadly defined, all of which reflect the widely variant ideological, analytical, and experiential orientations of their authors. Among the most useful are James Bill, *The Eagle and the Lion* (New Haven: Yale University Press, 1988); Richard Cottam, *Iran and the United States: A Cold War Case Study* (Pittsburgh, Pa.: University of Pittsburgh Press, 1988); Robert Huyser, *Mission to Iran* (New York: Harper and Row, 1986); Sir Anthony Parsons, *The Pride and the Fall* (London: Jonathan Cape, 1984); R. K. Ramazani, *Revolutionary Iran: Challenges and Response in the Middle East* (Baltimore: Johns Hopkins University Press, 1986); Barry Rubin, *Paved with Good Intentions* (New York: Oxford University Press, 1980); Gary Sick, *All Fall Down: America's Tragic Encounter with Iran* (Baltimore: Penguin, 1985); John Stempel, *Inside the Iranian Revolution* (Bloomington: Indiana University Press, 1981); William Sullivan, *Mission to Iran* (New York: W. W. Norton, 1981).

this perspective, what could be more ennobling than the liberation of one's coreligionists? One scholar of Islamic revivalism has paraphrased perceptions of the problem as follows: "Islam in the 20th century is facing a danger to its existence far beyond the scope of any that it has known in the past. This time the danger is internal; it comes from Muslim public figures . . . that allow themselves to be captivated by . . . Western ideas. . . . [The result] is a state of *jahiliyya* even worse than the one that preceded the appearance of the prophet Mohammed."[55] The solution to the problem is a return to a *shari'a* (Islamic law) and the reinvolvement of Muslims in political life, which they should never have abandoned in the first place. Corrupt political orders should be overthrown and replaced by genuine and militant Islamic ones.

It was such sentiments that came to dominate the worldview of many of the founders and leaders of the Islamic revolution in Iran. Intoxicated by their own victory, they felt it was their duty and obligation to share their triumph with other Muslims who were similarly oppressed. Thus, the export of the Islamic revolution became not simply a political goal but a holy mission. The revolutionary leadership in Tehran naïvely saw itself both as the salvation of Islam and as the leader of a new Islamic order. It gradually became evident, however, that few, if any, outside of Iran shared this grandiose vision. And the Iranian leadership that came to power after the revolution proved itself both divided and unworldly. The idealism of the revolutionaries was immediately corrupted by the sordid world of "real" politics.[56] Fissions within the ruling elite soon became evident as competing factions engaged in bitter conflicts with one another while vying for Ayatollah Khomeini's attention and support. Although a master politician himself, the ayatollah always managed to be perceived as someone above politics. Iran became a dictatorship without a dictator. For Khomeini, who had all of the authority of a dictator, refused to take the reins of power himself. Yet at the same time, he remained fundamentally unwilling to relinquish them to someone else. He did not want to rule but appeared reluctant to allow others do so in his stead. Thus, among his followers, the exigencies of day-to-day politics, both domestic and international, soon came to sully the idealistic and pristine Islamic values that were easily revered in the abstract but

55. Emmanuel Sivan, "Sunni Radicalism in the Middle East and the Iranian Revolution," *International Journal of Middle East Studies* 21, no. 1 (1989): 2. *Jahiliyya* refers to what is termed the age of ignorance, the period before the advent of Islam.

56. For a discussion of the relation between ideology and practical politics in the Middle East, see Jerrold D. Green, "Islam, Religiopolitics, and Social Change," *Comparative Studies in Society and History* 27, no. 2 (1985): 312–22, and idem, "Are Arab Politics Still Arab?" *World Politics* 38, no. 4 (1986): 611–25.

almost impossible to apply on a day-to-day basis. And despite the good intentions of those in Tehran, Muslims elsewhere did not necessarily care to be "saved" by what many viewed as the arrogant followers of "Imam" Khomeini. For example, a major stimulus to Iraq's initiation of war with Iran was Iran's use of terrorism to inspire a Shiʿa insurrection against the Saddam Hussein regime. This complicated rivalry between religious values and political power has dominated Iranian politics since the revolution.

The first and best-known act of international terror undertaken by the Islamic republic was the takeover of the American embassy in Tehran by a group of militants on 4 November 1979. Although this action took place in Iran, it clearly falls within the parameters of state-sponsored *international* terrorism because the embassy was legally U.S. territory. Interestingly, the Khomeini regime did not have forewarning of the takeover and took two days to determine how to respond to it. It was finally decided that the illegal action should be sanctioned, in large part to help force the resignation of Mehdi Bazargan and other liberal members of his government. This unambiguous abrogation of international law set the stage for further such actions by Iran. Political opposition to the United States in this period was certainly understandable, since the United States had foolishly decided to admit the shah for medical treatment in New York. Nonetheless, this hardly justified the takeover of a foreign embassy in Tehran. This takeover set Iran on a path of reckless and ill-conceived terrorist activity that ultimately proved far more costly than beneficial to the Islamic republic. And although they ultimately realized this, the Iranian leadership found it difficult to cease their acts of terror as well as to overcome the revulsion of an international community that labeled Iran a "terrorist state." This label has remained, for once a nation has strayed from acceptable political practice, it is difficult to modify international opinion of it. Yet lest we regard the United States as merely a naïve and supine victim of Iranian terrorist machinations, it should be mentioned that there are those who have accused American leaders of cold-blooded dealings with the hostage takers in Iran for pure domestic political gain in the United States. Here I refer to the much-debated and still-unproved theory of the "October surprise," discussion of which unfortunately exceeds the scope of this chapter.[57]

57. This theory was forwarded by Gary Sick in *October Surprise: America's Hostages in Iran and the Election of Ronald Reagan* (New York: Random House, 1991). According to Sick, supporters of Ronald Reagan, including George Bush and William Casey, engineered a delay in the release of the American hostages from the embassy in Tehran by the Iranians in order to weaken Jimmy Carter's bid for reelection. According to Sick, Iran received American arms transhipped through Israel in exchange for orchestrating this delay.

Throughout this period Iran devoted ever-increasing resources to exporting the Islamic revolution and to protecting its own gains at home. Embroiled in a painful war with Iraq that began in the autumn of 1980, Iran felt threatened by innumerable opponents who actively sought to subvert the revolution. According to one account: "The CIA spent $30 million in the mid 1980's funding anti-Khomeini groups. The Saudis poured $25 million into a failed coup attempt in 1982 . . . [and] between 1979 and 1982 Baghdad squandered $150 million to overthrow the Khomeini regime."[58] Thus, suspicions in Tehran about the isolation and vulnerability of the Islamic republic were well founded. What the Iranians failed to take into account, however, was their own responsibility in creating such widespread opposition to their government. Iranian bellicosity and subversion, such as their attempts to promote a coup in Bahrain in 1980, were well known in this period. Iran widely publicized a March 1982 seminar on Islamic government that was convened in Tehran. Here some 380 Islamic clerics from over seventy countries met to discuss how best to export Iranian-style Islamic revolution.[59] Subversion schools with pupils from all over the *umma* were constructed in Iran in order to instruct novice revolutionaries how best to overthrow uncooperative regimes.[60] Terrorist tactics were undoubtedly part of the curriculum, but the self-indulgent Iranians, acting in the name of Islam, considered themselves above laws that were written by and for anti-Islamic Westerners in the first place. Ever sensitive to threats to their own political order, the Iranians had no reluctance to subvert others. Ultimately failing to foment Shi'a uprisings in Bahrain and Iraq, where

---

Whether or not this particular incident actually happened, the willingness of the United States government to deal directly with terrorists, despite its stated aversion to such behavior, is best illustrated by the Irangate fiasco. For further discussion of the October surprise theory, as well as a report of a congressional investigation of it, see Neil A. Lewis, "Panel Rejects Theory Bush Met Iranians in Paris in '80," *New York Times*, 2 July 1992, A 10.

58. These figures appear in a book review by Dilip Hiro, "How We Sowed the Seeds of the Iran-Contra Affair," *Washington Post National Weekly Edition*, 22–28 May 1989, 36. The book under review is Amir Taheri, *Nest of Spies: America's Journey to Disaster in Iran* (New York: Pantheon Books, 1989). Hiro, a journalist who writes extensively on Iran, presents the figures but does not specify whether they are his or Taheri's. Taheri is generally an unreliable source. Nonetheless, in this instance it is clear that many interests sought to undermine the stability of the Islamic republic, and the figures presented are plausible.

59. For a discussion of this conference, see Robin Wright, *Sacred Rage: The Wrath of Militant Islam* (New York: Linden Press, Simon and Schuster, 1985), 26–29.

60. See Marvin Zonis and Daniel Brumberg, *Khomeini, the Islamic Republic of Iran, and the Arab World* (Cambridge: Center for Middle Eastern Studies, Harvard University, 1987), 31–36.

lation concentrations lived, the Iranians soon turned their
:o Lebanon, whose Shiʿa population was both needy and
aiready involved in armed conflict.

In Lebanon the Iranians found precisely what they had sought all
along. Sectors of the downtrodden Lebanese Shiʿa community reached
out to the Iranians and were grateful for their support. Inspired by the
Iranian revolution, some segments of this community were more than
willing to accept Iranian support in their conflict with other groups in
Lebanon as well as with the Israelis and at times the Syrians. According
to one source, Iran budgeted over $50 million per year for its activities
in Lebanon, which quickly became the centerpiece for Iran's export of
Islamic revolution.[61] And the Islamic Republic of Iran took its place
alongside other external actors, such as France, Israel, Syria, and the
United States, all of whom had tried to influence the course of events in
Lebanon. Tehran was no less mesmerized by the possibilities in Lebanon
than were any of the others, nor was Iran any more successful over the
long term.

On 4 July 1982 four Iranians in a car with diplomatic plates were taken
captive by the Israeli-backed Christian militia in south Lebanon. They
were never heard from again. Fifteen days later David Dodge, the acting
president of the American University in Beirut, was taken hostage.[62]
This dual set of kidnappings unleashed an era of unrestrained hostage
taking in Beirut, with Westerners, among them a number of Americans,
being the primary victims.[63] "Open season" was soon declared on both
official and nonofficial Americans in Beirut, although it should be remembered that the hostage-taking "game" was begun by Israel's Christian
surrogates and only reactively used by the Lebanese Shiʿa.

On 18 April 1983 a car bombing of the U.S. embassy in Beirut claimed
sixty-three fatalities, among them nine senior CIA officials, including the
head of the CIA's Middle East section, who happened to be visiting from
Washington. A little-known group called Islamic Jihad claimed credit for
the attack. On 23 October there was a car-bomb attack on an American
Marine encampment near the airport. Two hundred and forty-one Ameri-

61. See Ariel Merari and Yosefa (Daiksel) Braunstein, "Shiʿite Terrorism: Operational
Capabilities and the Suicide Factor," *TVI Journal* (1985): 8.

62. See Robin Wright, *In the Name of God: The Decade of Khomeini's Revolution* (New
York: Simon and Schuster, 1989), esp. ch. 4. The kidnapping of the Iranians is also
discussed by David C. Martin and John Walcott, *Best Laid Plans: The Inside Story of
America's War Against Terrorism* (New York: Harper and Row, 1988), 100–101. Martin
and Walcott identify one of the Iranians as Ahmad Motevasselian, commander of an Iranian
battalion of Revolutionary Guards stationed near Baalbek.

63. This was not a new tactic, since the Lebanese had been taking one another hostage
for years. Capturing foreigners proved a new refinement on an old mode of conflict.

can personnel were killed. Similar attacks occurred against Israeli and French targets. On 12 December 1983 six bombs exploded within ninety minutes of one another in different parts of Kuwait. The American and French embassies were targets, along with a power station, an oil facility, and other strategic targets. Seventeen young men, all members of a fundamentalist group named Al Dawa, were subsequently arrested and tried for these crimes. They were all convicted. Each was a Shiʿa; none was Iranian.

In February–March 1984 four American hostages were kidnapped in Beirut, among them William Buckley, the CIA chief of station. On 20 September another car bomb attack on the American embassy killed fourteen. On 14 June 1985 TWA flight 847 was hijacked. Thirty-nine Americans were held hostage in different parts of Beirut, and one American was brutally killed. The American hostages were released after Israel agreed to a release of prisoners taken in south Lebanon. Terrorist events throughout 1984–85 became almost daily occurrences. Planes were hijacked, individuals assassinated on several continents, and hostages taken in Beirut. In certain instances, such as the assassination of General Oveissi in Paris in February 1984, Iranian responsibility was obvious. Yet in most cases, despite sometimes overwhelming indications of Iranian complicity, evidence of Iranian support for terrorism was rarely clear and unambiguous enough to stand up in an American court of law. For example, the hijacking of an Air France plane to Tehran in August, a Saudi plane in November, and a Kuwait Air jet in December all appeared to be Iranian inspired. Yet the hijackers spoke Arabic, and in the Saudi and Kuwaiti cases the planes were even stormed by Iranian security forces.[64] Nonetheless, well-founded suspicions about Iranian support for the hijackers continue to persist. Gradually, although terrorism of this sort began to diminish, Beirut emerged as the primary arena of conflict.

By mid-1985 there were seven American hostages in Beirut, as well as four Frenchmen. The hostage takers were thought to be Islamic Jihad. To a large extent, the degree to which responsibility can be attributed to Iran for the taking and retention of foreign hostages in Lebanon would determine the degree to which Iran relied on terror as a foreign policy instrument. The Reagan administration "determined" that Iran was the dominant force in hostage-taking activities in Beirut and consequently found itself saddled with the Iran-Contra scandal. Others were not so

64. As Henry Precht writes in reference to the Air France hijacking: "The regime was swept by a bitter internal debate over how to react. The decision went against the hijackers." See his "Ayatollah Realpolitik," *Foreign Policy* 70 (Spring 1988): 112.

certain about Iranian dominance or even influence, however. Although it is absolutely clear that the hostage takers in Beirut were themselves Lebanese, it is unclear how much or what type of control or influence over them Iran could command. In the interplay of these perspectives involving terrorism and Iranian foreign policy lies confusion surrounding Iran's international role and uncertainty about whether it is a "terrorist state."

An official U.S. Department of State report noted that "Iran is currently one of the world's most active states supporting international terrorism and subversion against other countries."[65] Academic experts on the Middle East were somewhat less definitive. As Augustus R. Norton argued, "The evidence of Iranian complicity in terrorism mounts, although it remains unclear in many cases whether Iran has merely fostered the climate in which terrorism is readily rationalized, rather than playing a directive role."[66] As another scholar of the region noted, "Dominant opinion . . . has tended to exaggerate both the extent of Iran's influence over militant Muslims and the impact of the . . . Iranian revolution . . . on militant Islam as a whole."[67] Joseph Kostiner, an Israeli Middle East scholar, recognized the existence of Iranian-inspired terrorism, as did Norton, but he further asserted that "Iran had only limited influence and effectiveness in the Lebanese area."[68]

Even after the release of all American hostages in Beirut, Iran's role remains murky. For example, in a *Washington Post* article unambiguously entitled "The Iranian Hostage Connection: Tehran Held the Key to the Captives' Release from Lebanon," the conclusions as well as the proof are less than clear. Even U.S. government officials interviewed by the author are divided on the issue of Iranian influence. Although one official argues that Iran had "99.9 percent control," another notes that "Iran had a substantial amount of authority in almost all cases." Complete control, presumably in all cases, certainly differs from substantial authority in almost all cases. Yet a third official provides still another view; he notes that "Iran had 'about as much control as you do over

65. U.S. Department of State, Bureau of Public Affairs, *Iran's Use of International Terrorism*, Special Report 170, November 1987, 1.

66. Augustus R. Norton, "Terrorism in the Middle East," in *Terrorist Dynamics: A Geographic Perspective*, ed. Vittorfranco S. Pisano (Arlington, Va.: International Association of Chiefs of Police, 1988), 22.

67. Shireen Hunter, "Iran and the Spread of Revolutionary Islam," *Third World Quarterly* 10, no. 2 (1988): 730.

68. Joseph Kostiner, "War, Terror, Revolution: The Iran-Iraq Conflict," in *The Politics of Terrorism: Terror as a State and Revolutionary Strategy*, ed. Barry Rubin (Washington, D.C.: Johns Hopkins Foreign Policy Institute, SAIS, 1982), 126.

your 16-year-old son.'"[69] Thus, even U.S. officials are divided among themselves on this important issue.

Although it is generally agreed that Iran has been involved in terrorist activity, there is little justification for labeling Iran some sort of amorphous or generic "terrorist state." In the above sampling of government, journalistic, and academic opinion, it becomes evident that Iranian influence has limits. This is a more prudent and and analytically beneficial perspective, for even an estimate of the degree to which Iran relies on terrorism as an actual instrument of foreign policy would be more instructive than the simplistic assumption that terrorism is automatically Tehran's instrument of first resort in every case. Indeed, what we appear to know best about Iran is how little we actually know. And simple labels hinder rather than enhance analysis.

In its public utterings the Reagan administration appeared more than persuaded that Iran was a full-fledged terrorist state and that it was able to exercise almost total control over the hostages held in Beirut. The liberation of these hostages was elevated to the status of a primary American foreign-policy goal, leading to Irangate, which remains one of the most costly political blunders of the Reagan years. Through its exchange of weapons for hostages, the United States ironically increased the value of the hostages to those who took them. Although the tale of the Iran-Contra scandal falls well beyond the purview of this chapter, what is relevant is the conflict between those who felt Iran could free the hostages and those who felt it could not.[70] Obviously Robert McFarlane, Oliver North, and their Israeli counterparts, such as the late Amiram Nir, believed that Iran could, and thus visited Tehran in May of 1986 to press their case and arrange a deal. The talks in Tehran failed, and it gradually became clear that the Lebanese Islamic Jihad group had an agenda that at times differed significantly from that of its Iranian sponsors. Although the latter wanted weapons to use against Iraq, the former were more interested in strengthening their hand in Lebanon as well as in securing the release of the seventeen members of Al Dawa jailed in Kuwait. For among the prisoners in Kuwait was Mustafa

69. These quotes are from Don Oberdorfer, "The Iranian Hostage Connection: Tehran Held the Key to the Captives' Release from Lebanon," *Washington Post National Weekly Edition*, 27 January–2 February 1992, 6–7. For yet another view of this issue, see John K. Cooley, *Payback: America's Long War in the Middle East* (New York: Brassey's, 1991).

70. Among the many sources available for understanding Irangate, see Michael A. Ledeen, *Perilous Statecraft: An Insider's Account of the Iran-Contra Affair* (New York: Charles Scribner's Sons, 1988); R. W. Apple, *The Tower Commission Report: The Full Text of the President's Special Review Board* (New York: Times Books, 1987); National Security Archive, *The Chronology: The Documented Day-by-Day Account of the Secret Military Assistance to Iran and the Contras* (New York: Warner Books, 1987).

Youssef Badreddin, the brother-in-law and cousin of Imad Mughniyah, one of the heads of the Jihad group.[71] After arms were transferred to Iran, hostage Jenco was in fact released in July of 1986. But by September 1986 two more Americans were quickly taken hostage to compensate for Jenco. Robin Wright notes that in October of that year the Iranians informed the United States that they had "access" only to two hostages. Apparently the Lebanese held the others for reasons that did not directly affect Iran and that deprived it of any substantive influence.

The McFarlane visit to Tehran and the subsequent covert negotiations between Iran and the United States gradually became public knowledge in Iran. And despite the fact that Iran was dealing with both the United States and Israel in order to obtain badly needed weapons to use in the war with Iraq, there were ideologically committed Iranians who strongly opposed these dealings. It also may have been felt that the export of the Islamic revolution was at least as important as the war with Iraq. For in this period the Iranian government realized that perceptions of it as a terrorist state were impeding the war effort. An arms embargo, generalized isolation in the Middle East, and Iran's increasing unpopularity as a pariah state made its search for support against Iraq costly, frustrating, and unsuccessful. Realizing that ideological ambition must take a backseat to pragmatic politico-military concerns, Iran decided to improve its image. Toward this end it tried to curb extremist elements insensitive to these considerations.

In October 1986 Mehdi Hashemi, a leader of the Revolutionary Islamic World Movement and head of the Office for Global Revolution, as well as a protégé of the influential Ayatollah Montazeri, was arrested. Hashemi's background was controversial. Before the revolution he had been convicted of murdering Ayatollah Shamsabadi, then a rival of Montazeri. His death sentence was commuted under the shah to life imprisonment. After the revolution he was released, and his ties with Montazeri were strengthened due to his brother Hadi, who was married to the ayatollah's daughter and who eventually became Montazeri's spokesman. Hashemi was considered a radical, devoted to the export of the revolution at any cost. At his trial it was revealed that he had attempted to smuggle weapons into Saudi Arabia and had committed a number of other offenses. Hashemi's indictment was likely an indication that he had become a pawn in the conflict between Ayatollahs Rafsanjani and Montazeri, who

71. Although these hostages "disappeared" after the Iraqi invasion of Kuwait, it is widely believed that in the turmoil of the invasion they escaped from their prison or were released by the Iraqis and that they made their way to Iran or, in some cases, back to Lebanon.

were competing for influence. Hashemi was an exceedingly easy target, however, since he had committed a number of crimes. He was responsible for uncounted "antirevolutionary acts," which were presented in gory detail by prosecutor Hojjat al-Islam Ali Fallahian at his trial in Evin Prison.[72] The trial was widely publicized throughout Iran, and it is significant that almost immediately after the arrest of Hashemi, both his brother Hadi and Ayatollah Montazeri publicly distanced themselves from him.

In November of the same year, a small periodical in Beirut named *Al-Shira* published details of the McFarlane visit to Tehran and told of secret American arms transfers to Iran. The details of these activities were undoubtedly leaked to the magazine by supporters of Hashemi who hoped to help him by embarrassing and portraying his opponents as having engaged in treasonous dealings with the United States, Iran's nemesis. Although this did not help Hashemi, who was ultimately executed for his crimes, the story signaled the beginning of the Irangate scandal, which immediately rocked Washington. At the same time, it contributed to the eventual political demise of Ayatollah Montazeri, who was unable to distance himself sufficiently from Hashemi or to outwit Rafsanjani.

The Hashemi episode reflects a conscious decision on the part of Tehran to de-emphasize the terrorist component of its foreign-policy activities. Perhaps the reasons for this abandonment lay in Iran's inferior status vis-à-vis Iraq in the pursuit of the war and in a deteriorating economic situation at home. Iran may have rationally deployed terror and then chose, with equal rationality, to forgo it. The entire notion of a "terrorist state" implies the existence of a polity that irrationally opts for terror under any circumstances, no matter what the costs. Iran clearly does not fall within this category, for the Iranian leadership, despite its many flaws, seems to have experimented with terror and subsequently backed off from it when it became too costly or politically counterproductive. This is part and parcel of the conflict between ideology and pragmatism discussed earlier. The Hashemi affair highlights the triumph, perhaps only temporary, of the latter.

Iran's provocative behavior continued, although its tentative rejection of terrorism seemed to herald a modest reentry into the global system. By January 1987 there were twenty-two hostages from nine nations

---

72. Among the crimes of which Hashemi was convicted were kidnapping, establishment of private military organizations, theft o.˙ government weapons and property, treason, murder, and collaboration with SAVAK and the previous regime. A summary of the investigation of Hashemi was published in *Kayhan*, 13 August 1987 (26 Mordad 1336), 25–27, and *Etelaʿat*, 13–14 August 1987 (26–ε 7 Mordad), 29 and 32.

being held in Beirut, yet hostage-taking activity was no longer synonymous with Iran. And despite the fact that Tehran was still thought by some to exercise influence over the hostage takers, Iran was also regarded as a state trying to normalize its relations with the outside world. Even after Iranair Flight 655 was shot down by the United States on 4 July 1988, with 290 fatalities, Iran's response was muted despite convincing evidence that the United States may have provoked the incident.[73] It seemed that Iran had finally abandoned the use of terrorism. Yet complacency about Iran was soon to disappear.

On 14 February 1989, Ayatollah Khomeini issued a call for the death of Salman Rushdie, the author of the blasphemous and obscure *Satanic Verses*. This hugely disruptive event led to a break in diplomatic ties between Iran and Great Britain and a great deal of curiosity among Iran watchers and terrorism experts. Why would Khomeini risk all that he had so recently gained over something so trivial? Rushdie was a Muslim who wrote about Islam in an insulting fashion. Yet regrettably, Islam is defamed with great regularity in the West, even on occasion by Muslims themselves. Why had Khomeini chosen to speak out against this particular publication and with such harshness? In part, perhaps Khomeini placed spiritual considerations in front of pragmatic political ones. His call for assassination, a terrorist act by Western standards certainly, represented a reaffirmation by him of the values underlying the Islamic revolution in Iran. The publication of the novel highlighted a historical Western animosity to Islam, and as the head of what he perceived to be the only genuine Islamic state, Khomeini felt it was his obligation to speak out.[74] As if to humble analysts of Iranian politics, the ayatollah again demonstrated that predictions about Iran are risky propositions at best. He further demonstrated that he remained fundamentally uncomfortable with ideological concessions. Khomeini was never one to compromise. For him, the Islamic character of Iran had to be unambiguously reinforced on a regular basis.

Six weeks after the Rushdie affair began, Ayatollah Montazeri was

73. Although Iran accused the United States of acting belligerently, at the time of the attack Iran had such low international credibility that its accusations were largely ignored. Recent revelations in the United States, however, indicate that the attack may have occurred while the USS Vincennes was in Iranian territorial water and that the ship's commander intentionally provoked the incident. See Michael R. Gordon, "A Challenge to U.S. Version of Downing of Iran Airliner," *New York Times*, 2 July 1992, A 5.

74. For an interesting pair of analyses of the Khomeini attack on Rushdie, see Sharough Akhavi, "Behind Khomeini's Rushdie Edict: Politics? No, Religion," and Ahmad Ashraf, "Religion? No, Politics," *New York Times*, 25 March 1989, 13. Although Akhavi and Ashraf would like to argue different sides of the issue, they both appear to agree that for Khomeini, politics and religion were the same to begin with.

removed from power in a crude and humiliating way. And although for some time Iran appeared to have limited its involvement in Beirut and kept its distance from the hostage situation, fragmentary evidence indicates that Iran could have been shifting back toward the deployment of terrorism as an instrument of foreign policy. On 6 May 1989 Speaker Majlis Rafsanjani argued that the only way to end the Palestinian *intifada* on the West Bank was to kill Israelis and their supporters, particularly those of American, British, and French citizenship. This call was repealed four days later. There were persistent news reports that Iran was behind the bombing of Pan American Airways flight 103 over Scotland. It was rumored that Iran paid a Palestinian group to blow up the plane to avenge the American attack on Iranair flight 655. Iran never publicly claimed credit for the explosion, nor did the United States accuse Iran of being responsible for it, but obvious suspicions lingered.[75] However, the U.S. government ultimately concluded that Libya was behind the explosion and that Iran was no longer under suspicion. This led to outrage among many in the United States, including families of some of the victims, about an alleged whitewash of Iranian involvement as a payback for Iran's help in having the American hostages in Lebanon released.

Given Iran's record of terrorist acts, the Islamic republic will likely continue to be implicated in terrorist activities, sometimes justifiably and sometimes not, by an international community that is still uncertain how to deal with terrorism. Iran's dismal human rights record as well as its earlier support for terrorist acts allows a variety of parties in the West and in the Islamic world to point the finger at Tehran. As I have argued throughout this chapter, Iran's involvement in terrorism is rooted in a violent and unstable political history. This does not justify terrorism, but it does show that it is not merely a product of the Islamic revolution. Terror has been an intrinsic component of the historical pattern of Iranian political expression. However, the notion that Iran is some sort of crude "terrorist state" is analytically bankrupt. Iran appears to have selectively relied on terror as a means to export the Islamic revolution as well as to protect its gains at home. For the Iranian regime, terror is

75. According to the *New York Times*, the Iranian link was reported by the German magazine *Quick*. See the *New York Times*, 10 May 1989. Further details of the alleged Iranian involvement are presented in an article by Steven Emerson that documented meetings between Iranian Revolutionary Guards and Ahmed Jebril's Popular Front for the Liberation of Palestine—General Command. See Steven Emerson, "Closing in on the Pan Am Bombers," *U.S. News and World Report*, 22 May 1989, 23–24. See also Steven Emerson and Brian Duffy, *Pan Am 103: Inside the Lockerbie Investigation* (New York: Putnam, 1990).

a tool neither of first nor of last resort. Thus, the analyst of Iranian politics is confronted not by a terrorist state per se but by a state that is willing to use terror as it sees fit but that is also capable of eschewing it. It is the fashion in which terror is enmeshed in a broader set of political and military practices that makes its deployment both so hard to predict and so difficult to explain.

My goal has been neither to denigrate nor to ennoble Iran. Rather, I have tried to understand it, while recognizing that this troubled country is as preoccupied with seeking its own identity as we in the West are in trying to understand it. This crisis of identity was further complicated by the death of Ayatollah Khomeini in June 1989 and by the ensuing competition to fill the power vacuum that developed in the wake of his passing. If terror is perceived as an effective tool by aspirants to the ayatollah's power, it will most certainly be used. What is more than certain, however, is that the Iranian leadership, whatever its composition, will continue to struggle with the same types of issues that have dominated Iranian political life throughout most of this century.

Conclusion

14

Terrorism in the Context of Academic Research

Michel Wieviorka

For many years, terrorism was an "untouchable" issue, a topic that despite its practical impact was isolated from the field of scholarly research. Books and articles by self-appointed experts on this subject were far from brilliant. The best studies were usually written by journalists, not by social scientists. Most analyses were superficial and ideological. Today this formerly "untouchable" issue has become a worthy subject for inquiry, as evidenced by a major shift in the definition of terrorism.

Scholars used to feel uncomfortable with the notion of terrorism. They faced the problem not only of distinguishing terrorism from other forms of violence but also of setting clear theoretical bounds around their field of inquiry. Did Buonarotti or Babeuf, the Carbonari, or the Anarchists and Bolsheviks in Russia between 1905 and 1907 act like terrorists? How are terrorists different from guerrillas? Most conferences, books, and papers about this issue seemed to answer all such questions with a commonplace that now belongs to the prehistory of research on terrorism. Platitudinously, they concluded that no definition could be given of terrorism for the simple reason that one side's terrorist is the other's freedom fighter. This implied that the idea of terrorism was not a scientific category but a commonsense observation from the general public or, at best, from the persons actively involved in or directly concerned by the phenomenon. Therefore, the first obstacle to opening the field to research by social or political scientists, historians, or psychologists was getting around a popular, and generally confusing, definition of terrorism so as to reach a scientific one. Could the idea of terrorism be deconstructed and then reconstructed with a precise, practical meaning? This obstacle to research has been dealt with in two main ways.

First, the notion of terrorism can be seen as a social product: an image, psychological representation, or social conception. Accordingly, it is necessary to examine the processes whereby a society (or certain intellectual or political circles, for example) forms such an image. Studies are made of the social, cultural, political, economic, religious, and intellectual factors related to and the actors resorting to violence. It is assumed that these factors and actors create the conditions for applying the term "terrorist," regardless of the gravity of the violence or seriousness of the threat. The scholars who have adopted this viewpoint try to discover why policy makers or the mass media use "terrorism" instead of other words.

A second way of viewing this problem is to examine the actions or actors that are called terrorist (regardless of who calls them so), in the hope that as research proceeds, it will be possible to refine the description by adding other attributes. Thus, scholars analyze what violent actors say and do, the ways violence arises and escalates, or the processes that lead people to become involved. In my view, this exercise calls for the introduction of conceptual categories other than terrorism. The word does not disappear from the scholar's vocabulary, but its salience in the field of inquiry forces us to focus on defining it more precisely.

These two viewpoints are different but not necessarily incompatible. The effects of terrorism are "perverse" and unforeseeable because of the distance separating the social perception, image, or representation of the threat from its sociological reality. Both viewpoints are useful for studying terrorism, as well as other social or political issues (such as racism or delinquency). Although we agree that the commonsense notion of terrorism has to be deconstructed, we do not have to begin research by redefining it. Instead, its definition should be the outcome rather than the starting point of our analyses, the conclusion rather than a postulate.

There are at least two dimensions to terroristic activities: there is the fight against an enemy, but it is carried out in the name of a people, social class, nation, or religious community. Ethnocentric or ideological blinders should not keep us from seeing both aspects. In effect, terrorist actors do not just intend to threaten a certain category of people or menace the "other side." They also try to deliver a message to their own side, to potential allies, or to the governments that might support, even sponsor, their actions. In this respect, some situations are so complicated that it is useful to distinguish between primary and secondary audiences or to recognize an intricate set of interrelations among various actors with several targets and audiences. Furthermore, we should not forget that the rules of the game may change, old alliances fall apart, and new ones form. These two facets of terrorist operations—against enemies but also to win friends—should not be set at odds. It would be excessive to conclude that there are two distinct kinds of terrorism, for example, a "solipsistic" one (which Ian Lustick considers to be directed toward its own group's beliefs and practices) versus an other-directed one (which is directed at persons not belonging to the terrorists' reference group). A terrorist organization may be more or less solipsistic, more or less other-directed; but it is usually both at once, or at least over the long term.

Of special interest are extreme cases of "pure terrorism" in which ends and means are mixed up, violence has no limits, and the reference to a people, class, or nation is factitious. In such cases, one sees an intensification of the subjectivity of an actor who unrealistically identifies with abstractions such as the Proletariat, Revolution, Nation, or History. This subjectivity coincides with a "desubjectification" of the enemy, whom the terrorist treats as less than human. Evidence of this twofold process can be found in interviews with certain Italian terrorists. The actor defines his or her personal identity as the subject of history, but the enemy is an evil thing—a devil, savage, or beast. Both processes are at work to varying degrees within the terrorist personality. Before undergoing both hypersubjectivity (of one's self-identity) and infra- or metasubjectification (of the enemy), the actor may have experienced long years of struggle that started with "solipsistic" violence. Furthermore, even if one of these two processes seems to be primarily at work, we may be wearing ethnocentric blinders if we see only the violence directed against others, and we may be showing too much ideological comprehension if we talk only about the solipsistic aspect.

To study terrorism, it may be useful to make a clear analytical distinction between two different sorts of problems. On the one hand, terrorists, through their actions, involve other actors: the government, of course, but also political parties, churches, trade unions, intellectuals, social movements, and the mass media. These actions are part of a system of interactions, part of a game of political or military strategy. Actors react to one another's decisions, or even anticipate them. Thus, terrorism fits into a set of relations that should be subjected to a *synchronic*, or structural, analysis. On the other hand, terrorism follows a cycle of birth, growth, and decline. This life cycle may be simple or intricate, long or short. It may, though not necessarily, start with low-intensity violence that escalates beyond all limits. Thus, terrorism as a process of change should also be subjected to a *diachronic* analysis of how it has evolved in specific historical circumstances. I would like to emphasize several points relevant to this diachronic, or historical, analysis.

First, nearly all instances of terrorism are marked by both ruptures and continuities: continuities insofar as the ideology or religion that lends meaning to such actions usually has a tradition (Marxism-Leninism for far left terrorism, or Islamicism for certain radical Muslim groups); ruptures insofar as this ideology or religion as reinterpreted by terrorist actors is removed from normal or classical interpretations, which are rejected, transformed, or distorted according to specific political conditions.

A second point has to do with the patterns of growth and decline in terrorist organizations, specifically with the ways in which new activists are recruited and old militants leave or "exit." The people entering the organization may or may not come from diverse social origins, and their origins may affect the outcome of violence. Organizational doctrine may shift in order to attract recruits from new backgrounds, thus creating ideological "ruptures." An inability to recruit may be the most important cause of decline.

Third, we must dispute the widespread idea that the turning point in a terrorist's career is the first time he or she uses a gun or deposits a bomb. In fact, we now know that other moments are more important from the individual's viewpoint. As Donatella della Porta demonstrates in the Italian case, a decisive step occurs when the person accepts the commitment to become a professional or semiprofessional revolutionary or when she or he agrees to participate in underground operations that often lead to becoming a full-fledged terrorist. Thus, the group's decision to go underground is a key marker in the evolution of terrorism.

A fourth observation is that even though terrorism is a historical process for the group, movement, or organization practicing it, it may also be a major or minor phase in a broader historical process. In the case of the Armenian Secret Army for the Liberation of Armenia, terrorism seems to lie at the very center of the group's life history. However, for the Palestinian movement or the Algerian FLN, not all actions can be reduced to a question of terrorist violence, because terrorism was sometimes of secondary importance. Terrorism can be a substitute for war or revolution, but it can also be one phase, or theater, in a war or revolution. The fact that it is one part of a complex political or geopolitical process forces scholars to analyze terrorism in its context as Martha Crenshaw has explained in the first chapter in this volume.

These four remarks imply a fifth: the idea of process, of historical change or evolution, is different from and incompatible with the idea of cycles. True, in some cases we do observe a cyclical repetition of terroristic violence (for instance, within the model of action-repression-action, which predicts that each violent action will make the government increasingly reliant on force, which will in turn provoke even more violent and effective actions until the state caves in). However, we cannot adopt a cyclical theory based on a sort of mechanistic historical law when we cannot actually show that determinism is at work. The "success" or even the repetition of terrorism is not inevitable.

Most scholars, including those who have written for this book, distinguish two sorts of problems, or two kinds of terrorism. They compare "limited terrorism" to "terrorism without boundaries," or "terrorism" to "pure terrorism." Charles Townshend has done this by explaining that violence is less extreme when the terrorist actor focuses on the street corner rather than watching only the state. Some scholars differentiate between forms of violence that are effective and those that become "self-validating, or autotelic" (Charles Townshend), between terror "as a weapon" and "as an end per se" (Philip Pomper), or classically between instrumental and expressive terrorisms, or limited and unlimited terrorism.

These distinctions point to a serious problem. We cannot equate acts of violence performed by those who pursue a specific purpose and are able to abandon terrorism in a new political context with acts of violence by those who neither foresee nor expect an end to terrorism. Some groups are able to halt the use of terrorism when it no longer appears useful for their purposes; others seem to be satisfying an insatiable inner need. This distinction can be reformulated in more practical terms as the difference between terrorism as a *method of action* and terrorism as a *logic of action*.

As a method, terrorism is a common form of violence. It is a tool to be employed, a means of reaching a goal, for many different types of political actors. The actors' behavior can be deduced from their strategies; it can be reduced to calculations and tactics. In my opinion, terrorism is always a method, but under some circumstances, in some groups or movements, it is something else: the actor not only uses terror as a tool but accepts terror as an end in itself. The means become an end. In such cases of pure, extreme violence, terrorism is a logic of action that literally dictates the actor's attitudes and behaviors. He can no longer do otherwise.

Let me give a brief, simplified example. Regardless of what one thinks of Yasser Arafat, it is clear that on various occasions he has used terrorism as a method, but even though one suspects him of being a liar, it is also clear that since 1988 he can say that he has finished with terrorism and that he is turning to political and diplomatic activities. Although he has been responsible for some terrorism since the early 1970s, Arafat is not locked inside the logic of violence as such. In contrast, it is hard to imagine Abu Nidal existing without his terroristic operations. For him, terrorism seems to be a logic of action. He would not survive as a political actor were terrorism to be abandoned.

When the distinctions are reformulated in this way, we are led to question how some groups start by using limited violence as a tool but then become "pure" terrorists. In other words, how does the method become a logic of action? A simple answer is that this shift is generally the outcome of both an ideological process, whereby actors break with a doctrine, religion, or conception of history, and a social or political "distancing" phenomenon that occurs when actors lose contact with the class, nation, or community in whose name they claim to speak. The actor no longer represents a cause or reference group.

Even if the reference to a cause is fictitious, terrorist actors always act in the name of a people or for the sake of a historical project. As some cases analyzed in this book show, these actors must deal with more than one frame of reference. They act for the sake of two or three main causes and speak in the name of more than one reference group. Very commonly, the terrorist organization has to try to make its violence assume meanings related to the image of a divided community and also meanings associated with the unity of the same community. For example, an organization may have to speak in the name of a dominated or exploited social group (the working class, peasantry, or proletariat) and act for the sake of the whole community (nation, religion, or ethnic group). As Austrian Marxists realized at the beginning of this century, it is always difficult to represent both the whole community and one part of it against another. It is thus simpler to resort to terrorism when one has only one aim, to divide one's community from the larger community and to enhance its solidarity while driving the "enemy" community into hostility and violence.

It is noteworthy that violent actors themselves confront this incompatibility, although some appear oblivious to the dilemma. Orsini, for instance, spoke in the name of the Italian nation and also called for social change; he intended to kill Napoleon III for the sake of both Italy and a European revolution. The Russian populists acted on behalf of the peasantry but also in terms of a certain conception of national development. The Basques who belong to ETA are nationalists but also Marxist-Leninists who claim to be the vanguard not only of the working class but also of new social movements (such as the feminist and antinuclear movements). The Algerian FLN wanted both to separate Algeria from France and to win the support of metropolitan public opinion.

At this point, we can formulate a tentative hypothesis. Might not terrorism, especially pure terrorism, sometimes be the ideological outcome of the actor's need or will to combine, incorporate, and incarnate several contradictory meanings in a single struggle? The stronger the determination to express various meanings, and the stronger the incompatibility between these meanings, the more extreme violence will become. In other words, terrorism frequently mixes up so many different meanings, issues, and causes that the mixture is necessarily explosive. That is, terrorism that results from strategic contradictions is likely to be most dangerous.

In concluding this overview I would like to offer three observations concerning research on oppositional terrorism. First, we should bury a number of stereotypes. The more we know about terrorism, the less we should rely on commonplace assumptions. We are right, for example, to distinguish between anarchist and Marxist-Leninist terrorism, but such a difference cannot always be discerned in left-wing terrorist groups. Many organizations build on a Marxist-Leninist foundation but end with a thoroughly anarchistic or libertarian type of ideology. This happened in Italy and also in France with Direct Action. Another cliché sometimes taken to be a truism is that when terrorism ends, we should credit efficient counterterrorist operations. This premise is, of course, never absolutely false. Nevertheless, there are cases where the success of law-enforcement actions was founded on the failure of the terrorist ideology. For example, activists may feel that it is time to lay down their guns because violence has no meaning and leads to a dead end. This definitely happened in Italy, where far-left terrorism was waning (a phase during which violence did not decrease but to the contrary increased) while the Carabinieri led by Dalla Chiesa grew more and more effective. A third, much more platitudinous idea should also be laid to rest, namely, that terrorism can be explained in terms of a crisis. This easiest of explanations has usually been inspired by a functionalist quest to locate the causes of terrorism in the crisis of the state, political system, economy, culture, or society. The more we examine instances of terrorism, the less we can be satisfied with the notion of a crisis. Most authors here, while they do not deny the occasional importance of a crisis, push the analysis deeper. Yet another idea has been so hackneyed by journalists and public opinion that serious scholars, particularly social and political scientists, are wary of using it lest they revive skeletons that previous scholarship had relegated to the closet only with the greatest difficulty. According to this assumption, terrorism is a plot, a conspiracy of secret services, police, governments, terrorist states, or other centers of power who manipulate dim-witted actors. This book shows that manipulation does sometimes occur, police and terrorists do sometimes have dealings with each other, and psychological tactics are a tool of intelligence services. Azev's role in the Russian Socialist Revolutionary Party and the *bleuite* in the Algerian FLN are instances of this phenomenon. Although it is naïve to reduce terrorism to the manipulation of violent actors by foreign powers or secret services, it would also be shortsighted to refuse to investigate this sort of hypothesis when there is plausible evidence of external involvement in terrorism.

A second set of unsolved problems concerns the theoretical questions and debates raised by recent studies of terrorism, including those in this book. A central question is that of the appropriate levels of analysis— whether social, organizational, political, international, or individual— where determinants of causes and effects will be located. Distinguishing such levels implies that there may be a hierarchy among them. If there is, it has to be given a theoretical foundation. For example, a reason must be given for assigning causation at the level of the individual, not society. If variables are not ranked—and this is possible when terrorism is perceived as the result of a multitude of causes or factors—then our descriptive treatment of determinants must be as comprehensive as possible. I call this last perspective historical, in order to distinguish it from a sociological perspective that ranks levels of analysis. Whatever perspective is adopted, what is said about every level has to be connected. Is there, for instance, a connection between Nechaev's personality and the organization he created? How are personal or psychological problems related to political tensions or crises within a group? Is it contradictory to suggest that terrorism is the result of an organization's strategic choices and simultaneously to maintain that, at another level, a preexisting ideology or a surrounding political culture shapes the political life of the organization?

The problem of levels of analysis has further implications. Most scholars hesitate between two main poles of explanation: the state or government to which terrorists are opposed, and the social movement or community for whose sake they are supposedly acting. Both poles are productive of explanations, but if one reasons in terms of a hierarchy of levels, a choice has to be made. Is the reference to a nation, religious community, or social movement a more important explanatory variable than the nature of the state to be fought? Should analysis proceed from this reference and work its way up to the state, or should it proceed in the opposite direction? The answer is not obvious.

A third unanswered question concerns the history of terrorism. Is there a historical continuity in this phenomenon since the French Revolution and the secret societies of the nineteenth century? Two extreme points of view characterize answers to this question. The first insists on the unity of terrorism throughout the ages. The second considers each instance of terrorism unique, so absolutely different from others that it calls for detailed sociological, historical, and political analysis of the specific situation without any reference to previous experiences. This disparity of viewpoints is not specific to the study of terrorism. It crops up in most general debates between, for example, evolutionism and historicism in history, or universalism and relativism in anthropology. The debate is so far inconclusive.

To conclude, I would like to comment on what may be the principal problem for scholars researching terrorism, a problem they usually avoid discussing in public: the relation between the researcher and the subject of study. Until recently this problem was not salient because those who studied terrorism were less likely to be scholars than journalists, former military officers, witnesses, or other persons involved in terrorist experiences. As often as not they did not pretend to be objective. As sociological, political, psychological, and even historical research has developed, it has become necessary to locate reliable sources, to make contact with the actors, and—why not?—to define and control the conditions for a scientific study of terrorism and terrorists. The authors of these chapters have sometimes found new sources of information (literature, poetry, or court records, for example). Some of them know personally that terrorism is a research subject fraught with dangers on all sides. However, the problem I stress is not merely this physical danger. It concerns moral obligations. How should the scholar behave in the presence of actors belonging to a system of violence, whether they be terrorists, police, secret services, or the military? What is the appropriate attitude to take? What contradictions have to be tolerated in order to obtain access to sources and thus create the conditions for scholarly, knowledgeable inquiry? What professional standards should guide work on this controversial topic? Surprisingly, discussions about these questions occur among journalists more often than among social or political scientists. The time has come for us, too, to consider and define our own professional standards and our intellectual relation to this dangerous subject, terrorism.

Index